ACES HIGH

VOLUME 2

CHRISTOPHER SHORES

GRUB STREET · LONDON

Published by
Grub Street
The Basement
10 Chivalry Road
London SW11 1HT

British Library Cataloguing in Publication Data
Shores, Christopher, 1937-
  Aces high
  Vol. 2: A further tribute to the most notable fighter pilots of the
  British and Commonwealth Air Forces in WWII
  1. Fighter pilots – Great Britain 2. Fighter pilots –
  Commonwealth countries 3. World War, 1939-1945 – Aerial
  Operations, British
  I. Title
  940.5'44

ISBN 1-898697-00-0

Typeset by Pearl Graphics, Hemel Hempstead
Printed and bound in Great Britain by Biddles Ltd, Guildford and King's Lynn

Contents

Introduction and Acknowledgements

When we published the revised edition of *Aces High* in summer 1994, an *Authors' Special Note* was included, indicating our intention to follow the book with a slimmer addendum volume some 12 months later to incorporate additional photographs and any additions or corrections in regard to the published information which might have come to hand. In the light of this, readers with any such information or illustrations were encouraged to advise the publishers accordingly. The response has been overwhelming, and far from producing a slim addendum, now some four years later a much more substantial Volume II has been produced.

Even now, as the new manuscript goes to press, there remain some pilots regarding whom I would dearly have loved to be able to record more details. However, the list of my "mystery men", as I have termed them, has shrunk very considerably.

Some preamble is, as usual, necessary before launching into the body of the book. Sadly, my long time friend and colleague, Clive Williams, was not able to join me in the work for this volume, due to failing health which has greatly constrained his life in recent years. However, help from other sources has been splendid, and there are a number of people who I have singled out for particular thanks.

In the *Acknowledgements* section of the 1994 book it was most remiss of me to have overlooked the very considerable contribution of Michel Lavigne of Victoriaville, Quebec, Canada, who sent to me a host of photocopies of relevant logbooks, particularly of Canadian pilots — thank you, Michel, and my apologies for such an oversight. Since that time, the involvement of Bruce Burton has been pre-eminent. His skill in identifying the background, home town, etc of numerous pilots has been of tremendous help. Therese Angelo, Museum Research Officer at the Royal New Zealand Air Force Museum, filled in virtually all the remaining 'gaps' regarding New Zealanders, many of which 'gaps' had already been narrowed by my friend of many years, Paul Sortehaug of Dunedin. Indeed, Paul's own recently-published history of 486 Squadron, *The Wild Winds*, was also of great assistance.

Similar assistance regarding the Australian 'gaps' came from the Australian Department of Defence's Discharged Personnel Records Department, through the good offices of Mr D.Pullen. The Veterans Affairs Department and the Personnel Records Section of the National Archives of Canada both helped to the extent that they were able, given the limitations of Canada's restrictive Privacy Act. My thanks are due to them for their efforts; there are, however, a few 'gaps' remaining in regard to certain RCAF personnel. I am also extremely grateful to Sebastian Cox, Head of Air Historical Branch, Ministry of Defence, and to his colleague, Clive Richards, for their help and support in pointing me in the right direction to discover more details of my fellow-countrymen who served in the Royal Air Force.

Great assistance was also provided in regard to the Belgians by Guy Destrebeq of Brussels, and in regard to the French by Christian-Jacques Ehrengardt. Others who were particularly helpful with regard to the numbers of British pilots both with information and/or photographs, were Barry Marsden, who specialises in pilots with a Derbyshire background, I.Tavender, historian of those airmen awarded the Distinguished Flying Medal, Peter Sharpe, Wg Cdr D.R.Collier-Webb, RAF Retd, Wg Cdr A.Brookes, BA,MBA,FRSA, RAF (regarding 85 Squadron), Don Minterne (regarding 73 Squadron), Peter Hall (regarding 91 Squadron), Reg Wyness (regarding 111 Squadron and certain Czech pilots), Ian Piper (regarding 605 Squadron), Nicholas Thomas, Andrew Long, Roy Nesbit, and my friend John Young, Historian of the Battle of Britain Fighter Association, and himself an ex-Spitfire pilot who came close to qualifying for inclusion in *Aces High*.

Thomas F.Semenza of Connecticut, USA, checked all the aircraft serials in the individual pilots' claim lists, advising where there were obvious anomalies, discrepancies, or printing errors, the majority of which I have been able to resolve for this volume. Continued help was received from old friends Dilip Sarkar and Brian Cull; the latter's masterly *Ten Days in May* proved to be a piece of research that provided much more detail of those ill-recorded early engagements in France in May 1940. Similar help has been forthcoming from Russell Guest and Frank Olynyk, both of whom have undertaken further research on my behalf whilst staying at my home in London, and whilst in their native countries of Australia and the USA. John 'Jack' Foreman has also aided me in my researches, and I have obtained further considerable assistance from Michael Schoeman in South Africa.

Another new friend whose contribution has added immensely to the coverage that has now been possible in regard to the Polish pilots dealt with, is Wojtek Matusiak of Warsaw, who has contributed much both in terms of information and photographs for publication. In this he was greatly assisted by Robert Gretzyngier and Jozef Zielinski.

Finally, as always, my deepest gratitude goes to those pilots who provided details regarding themselves, and to the families of others who are sadly no longer with us. They are far too numerous to list here, and it would be invidious to name some at the risk of forgetting others. You know who you are, and the content of the book which follows speaks for itself in regard to the assistance you have all given me. My most grateful thanks to you all. There is just one who I must mention and express particular thanks to however; that is Jack Haddon, who in addition to assistance regarding his own activities, also provided me with a magnificent set of photographs illustrating a considerable number of the pilots included herein and in the previous volume, most of which have been incorporated in this volume.

In conclusion, apologies to those readers who have expected this book at an earlier date (including my long-suffering publisher, John Davies !). I regret that work on two previous books, coupled with a disastrous "crash" of my previous computer at a critical moment, the pressures of my "day job" as a director of DTZ Debenham Thorpe, and — perhaps above all — the slowing-down caused by the onset of more advanced years, have conspired to push back completion of the manuscript until now.

THE DOGS OF WAR

Rushing through the arcane halls,
Down the corridors of space,
Came with sudden fearsome horror,
Swift with flashing crooked crosses,
Thrusting forward massive bosses,
Came from out the sun the Hun,
Came in packs the dreaded Hun.

Swiftly fling the wings asunder,
Seeking for some cloud to hide in,
Twisting turning sunwards streaming
From red tracers fiery might,
Through the leaden cloying blindness,
Reaching, searching for God's light.

Chased we down the broken crosses
To the pit of black despair,
Yet still with unrelenting pace,
Fling they their steeds towards the sun,
Grotesquely dancing pirouettes
Until the race is run.

Through the cottonballs of hate,
Thunders Merlin through the gate,
Blast the crooked crosses there,
Blast them out of God's sweet air,
Chase them, blast them,'til they fall,
Spiralling down to Earth's grim pall.

Twisting turning, eyeballs screaming,
Through a hail of fire a beaming,
Fling the streaming wingtips high,
Searching for a secret haven,
In the high cathedral rafters
Of the unforgiving sky.

High in God's cold impartial bowl
Make one last shuddering turn, and find
Far down below the stage is still..
The curtain drawn..
The players gone..
No lines remain for them to say.
You flee for home.
All anger spent.

Bobby Bunting, Spitfire Pilot, 93 Squadron

Preamble

Before commencing with the main body of the book, a few words regarding the contents thereof. I have sought as scrupulously as possible to refrain from repeating information already published in *Aces High*, save where it is necessary in making corrections. Otherwise all the information is new to this title.

There are a number of new names, whose biographies are included for the first time. There is also, of course, a substantial body of additional information regarding many of those dealt with in the 1994 volume. This is so arranged that it may be read in conjunction with the previous biographical notes and claim lists.

The list of those claiming four victories has been modified — several of those pilots have now been "upgraded" to full coverage due to additional claims having been identified for them. There are also a number of new names included.

I fear that the proof reading of the list of V-1 "aces" in *Aces High* went sadly wrong somewhere along the line. This has been corrected and modified as necessary. More importantly however, there are a series of very brief biographical notes for all those included in this list who are not within the main body of the book, together with a listing of their claims, both against V-1s and aircraft. A chapter providing considerably more details on this particular subject has also been included.

Because fighter pilots attended or served with Operational Training Units (OTUs) in virtually all cases, there is a chapter detailing fighter OTUs and a number of the other specialist units in which many fighter pilots served, and which are frequently referred to in the biographies. There is also a short but detailed chapter relating to the allocation of RAF and RNZAF service numbers, which I believe will be very useful in indicating how these may add to knowledge of the pilots dealt with — or indeed, any other personnel of these air forces which the reader may subsequently wish to research.

The launch of *Aces High* in 1994 was accompanied by a fighter pilot symposium at the Royal Air Force Museum, Hendon, which was followed by a further unique event derived therefrom, some two years later. Details are provided in a closing chapter.

I have also provided some information regarding the activities of Commonwealth fighter pilots in Korea, and of the British Sea Harrier pilots in the Falklands. None became "aces" in the traditional sense, but the latter was the first major action in which pilots of the RAF and FAA played a significant part in aerial combat since 1945, and may well prove to have been the last.

Finally, several people have asked why no Bibliography was included in *Aces High*. Wherever a pilot has a biography or autobiography dealing with his life or wartime experiences, I have mentioned this within the individual notes on the man in question. Other books such as campaign and squadron histories have proved of great assistance, but the number involved is huge. I therefore decided that such a list, to be exhaustive, would be too long for inclusion, whilst not to be exhaustive would be incorrect and might well give offence to authors whose work was not listed. I therefore reiterate that I have referred to very many such works during my research, and have found most of them helpful to one degree or another.

CHAPTER ONE

The Squadrons and Other Units

165 'Times of Ceylon' Squadron
On page 44 of *Aces High* this unit is incorrectly identified as 164 Squadron. The notes relating to this latter unit appear directly above the subject unit.

OTHER UNITS

The Operational Training Units
Prior to the outbreak of war, pilots usually joined squadrons direct from Service Flying Training Units, where they had qualified as pilots, gaining their "Wings". It was with the squadron that they gained their specific training as fighter pilots, a procedure which gave no particular problems in the more relaxed atmosphere of peacetime.

As the RAF expanded, cadres were extracted from existing units to help form new squadrons, and the two Groups responsible for controlling fighters — Nos 11 and 12 — formed Pilot Pools to hold newly-trained pilots until they were allocated to specific units. Here they were provided with an introduction to modern service fighter aircraft. Soon more senior pilots, posted from staff or training duties to fighter units, were also attending these Pools for brief 'refresher' course on Spitfires, Hurricanes or Gladiators.

Once war had broken out, it quickly became clear that the opportunities to give any worthwhile training on the unit was likely rapidly to reduce, or indeed to disappear entirely. Therefore the Pools were formed into Operational Training Units, more formally to prepare the new or inexperienced for their early introduction to active service. Indeed, shortly after their formation, the withdrawal from France of some of the initial members of the AASF, who were already in need of a brief 'rest' from operations, allowed ex-members of 1 and 73 Squadrons to join the first two new OTUs to pass on the benefits of their actual experience to the neophytes. Thus was the pattern set for the next few years, which ensured that virtually every future fighter pilot passed through an OTU, whilst large numbers of 'tour-expired' veterans, or those recovering from wounds or injuries suffered on active service, were posted in for longer or shorter periods of instructing — or indeed, for conversion experience to other types of activity (i.e. conversion from day to night operations).

Initially, the first two such units were numbered consecutively, together with a number of Bomber Command training squadrons, which had similarly become OTUs. With a proliferation of such units throughout the RAF, numbers in the range 51-56 were allocated to UK-based fighter OTUs, the range 70-79 being allocated to OTUs to be formed in the Middle East. Rather than re-number the existing units at the start of the 50s series, an additional 5 was added to the front of the existing number allocated. New units were then numbered approximately in reverse order from the end of the range.

On 31 December 1940, 81 (Training) Group was set up within Fighter Command with headquarters at Sealand, to control all OTUs. A year later this Group moved to Avening, where it remained until April 1943, when the 12 OTUs it then controlled were passed to 9 Group for administration. A month later those units in the 41-43 range, which had been allocated to Army Co-operation Command, were transferred to Fighter Command on the disbandment of the former organisation and the formation of the new 2nd Tactical Air Force.

Thus, whilst on only rare occasions — mainly in 1940 — did such units actually become engaged in any form of aerial fighting, they did provide temporary homes for most of the pilots detailed in *Aces High*.

11 Group Pool/6 Operational Training Unit/56 Operational Training Unit/ 1 Combat Training Wing/1 Tactical Exercise Unit
Formed at Andover in January 1939, the unit moved to St Athan in July. It was renumbered 6 OTU on 10 March 1940, moving to Sutton Bridge, near Kings Lynn, Norfolk. Here it operated Miles Master advanced trainers, Hurricanes and Fairey Battles. On 1 November 1940 it became 56 OTU. The unit moved to Tealing in March 1942, where it remained until October 1943. A satellite airfield at Kinnell was also used, where during June 1943 556(T) Squadron, formed from within the OTU, undertook some convoy patrols over the Peterhead sector. The unit also formed 560 (OTU) Squadron

at Tealing during the late spring of 1943. Redesignation as 1 Combat Training Wing followed in October 1943, but on 1 January 1944 this became 1 Tactical Exercise Unit, involved in the training of fighter and fighter-bomber pilots. This unit was disbanded on 31 July 1944. However, in December 1944 56 OTU was reformed at Milfield, to train Typhoon and Tempest pilots. Final disbandment took place on 14 February 1946.

12 Group Pool/ 5 Operational Training Unit/55 Operational Training Unit/ 4 Tactical Exercise Unit

Formed in September 1939 at Aston Down with Gladiators and other aircraft, it became 5 OTU in March 1940, adding Hurricanes, Defiants and Blenheims to its inventory. On 1 November 1940 the unit became 55 OTU — the first to be renumbered in the new series. The Defiants and Blenheims were then handed to 54 OTU. With increasing numbers of Spitfires to hand,it moved to Usworth in Northumberland on 14 March 1941, using Ouston as a satellite airfield. A further move was later made to Annan, with Longtown and then Great Orton as satellites. In early 1944 the unit became a Day Pilot Holding Unit, but very shortly afterwards (on 26 January) it was redesignated 4 TEU, remaining at Annan. On 21 March 1944 it was renumbered 3 TEU, the former unit of this number having just been absorbed into 41 OTU. 'C' Squadron now formed 555 Squadron (which 55 OTU had been intended to create in an emergency), and this unit was despatched to Acklington for the defence of Tyneside during the Normandy invasion. In December 1944 the unit disbanded and 55 OTU returned to existence, training Typhoon ground-attack pilots. It was disbanded in June 1945.

7 Operational Training Unit/57 Operational Training Unit

Formed on 17 June 1940 at Hawarden, Cheshire, with Masters and Spitfires, the unit was renumbered 57 OTU on 1 November 1940. Many volunteers from other Commands attended the Unit during 1940, but the airspace in the area became very congested due to the presence close by of 5 SFTS at Sealand, and there were many accidents. Ultimately the unit moved to Eshott in November 1942, Boulmer being used as a satellite from March 1943. The unit was disbanded in June 1945.

58 Operational Training Unit/2 Combat Training Wing/2 Tactical Exercise Unit

Originally intended as a night fighter OTU, the unit formed in October 1940 at Grangemouth. In December however, it became the second Spitfire OTU, training activities actually commencing in January 1941. In October 1943 it was renumbered 2 Combat Training Wing, but within ten days this was changed to 2 Tactical Exercise Unit. The life of the unit with its new designation was short however, for it was disbanded on 25 June 1944. In March 1945 58 OTU was reformed by the renaming of the Day Fighter Wing of 41 OTU at Poulton (one of the ex-Army Co-operation Command units), equipped with Mustangs, moving to Hawarden, Cheshire. It was disbanded again on 20 July 1945.

59 Operational Training Unit

Formed at Turnhouse, Edinburgh, in December 1940, the unit moved its Hurricanes to Crosby-on-Eden in February 1941. In August 1942 a move to Milfield was made, where from March 1943 the unit specialised in training pilots for Typhoon squadrons. On 18 May 1943 the pilots of 31 Course formed 559 Squadron as a Typhoon conversion unit, moving to Brunton. 59 OTU was disbanded in January 1944 to form the nucleus of the new Fighter Leaders' School, but was reformed in February 1945 at Acklington as a half unit, again with Typhoons, operating for three months before once again being disbanded.

54 Operational Training Unit

Formed in December 1940 as a specified night fighter OTU, No 54 was initially based at Church Fenton with Blenheim Ifs and Defiants received from 55 OTU. It remained here until May 1942, when a move was made to Charter Hall, the unit's 'C' Squadron being based at Winfield. Beaufighters and Mosquitos steadily replaced the earlier types used. In November 1945 the unit moved to East Moor in the 12 Group area, and then in June 1946 to Leeming, where on 1 May 1947 it merged with 13 OTU to form 228 Operational Conversion Unit.

53 Operational Training Unit

Formed at Heston in February 1941, the unit's 'B' Flight moved to Llandow in Wales the following month, where it employed Rhoose as its satellite from April 1942 until May 1943. 'A' and 'C' Flights remained at Heston meanwhile, to form the nucleus of 61 OTU. In May 1943 53 OTU moved to Kirton-in-Lindsey, with Hibaldstow as its satellite. In May 1945 it was disbanded into 61 OTU. During its service, the OTU was involved mainly in the training of Spitfire pilots.

52 Operational Training Unit
Also formed in February 1941, but at Debden, the unit equipped initially with Masters and Hurricanes. In August 1941 it moved to Aston Down, where it specialised in the training of Spitfire pilots. It was disbanded on 10 August 1943, then forming 52 OTU (FLS). In October it was redesignated 52 OTU (Fighter Command School of Tactics), and in January 1944 moved to Milfield to be incorporated into the new Fighter Leaders' School.

60 Operational Training Unit
Formed at Leconfield in April 1941 from No 2 School of Army Co-operation at Andover, the unit initially trained Defiant crews for night operations. A move was made later to East Fortune, and in 1942 Beaufighters were received, but in November that year the unit transferred to Coastal Command to become 132 OTU. In May 1943 a new 60 OTU was formed at High Ercall from 2 Squadron of 51 OTU from Twinwood Common, to provide specialist training in Mosquito intruder operations. In October of that year the unit formed 60/63 OTU Combined Gunnery Squadron at Chedworth with elements of 63 OTU. On 15 September 1944 the unit moved to Finmere, the satellite airfield of 13 OTU, and here it was disbanded into that unit in April 1945, becoming part of this 2 Group intruder training unit.

61 Operational Training Unit
Formed at Heston in June 1941 as a Spitfire OTU from half of 53 OTU, No 61 moved to Rednal in April 1942. 53 OTU was incorporated into the unit in May 1945, while on 21 June it moved to Keevil and absorbed the Fighter-Reconnaissance Wing of 41 OTU. Finally, it became 203 Advanced Flying School on 1 July 1947.

51 Operational Training Unit
Formed at Debden in July 1941 as a night fighter OTU with Havocs and Blenheims, the unit subsequently moved to Cranfield. The Havocs were later replaced by Beauforts and Beaufighters, and a satellite was set up at Twinwood Farm in February 1942. In May 1943 the unit's 2 Squadron at this latter base became 60 OTU. 51 OTU was disbanded on 14 June 1945.

41 Operational Training Unit/2 Tactical Exercise Unit
The unit formed in September 1941 from No 1 School of Army co-operation at Old Sarum, flying Tomahawks and Lysanders. Mustang Is were added in April 1942, while Hurricanes took over from the Tomahawks. In November 1942 the unit moved to Hawarden, with various detachments around the country. Increasingly now it also trained Mustang fighter pilots. In February 1943 3 TEU was formed at Poulton with surplus fighter-reconnaissance pilots, but was absorbed into 41 OTU the following month. In February a new OTU was created at Poulton as 41 OTU Day Fighter Wing, as distinct from 41 OTU Fighter-Reconnaissance Wing at Hawarden. The former became 58 OTU on 12 March 1945.

63 Operational Training Unit
Formed quite late in the war, 63 OTU came into being at Honiley in July 1943 as a night fighter training unit in 9 Group. In October 1943 2 Squadron moved to Chedworth to become 60/63 OTU Combined Gunnery Squadron. 63 OTU disbanded on 21 March 1944.

132 (Coastal) Operational Training Unit
Formed in November 1942 at East Fortune with the aircraft and personnel of 60 OTU from Fighter Command, the unit trained long range fighter and strike pilots for Coastal Command duties, equipped with Blenheims, Beaufighters, and later, Mosquitos. On 11 February 1945 the Mosquitos were transferred to 8 OTU at Haverford West, although they returned in June 1945. The unit was disbanded in May 1946.

80 (French) Operational Training Unit
The unit formed at Morpeth, Northumberland, in April 1945 to train pilots for French Spitfire

squadrons in 2nd TAF. In July it moved to Ouston, where it was disbanded in March 1946.

OTHER UK-BASED UNITS

A number of other units were formed throughout the war which were to be staffed by fighter instructors, or were to employ such pilots, often on an operational or semi-operational basis, for development work on aircraft and tactics. Details of the more important of these unit are set out below:-

Air Fighting Development Unit
Formed in July 1940 from the Air Fighting Establishment at Northolt, the unit moved from 11 Group to 12 Group control at Duxford in December 1940. In emergency the unit was to form a 550 Squadron. In late 1942 the unit was reduced in size and in March 1943 moved to Wittering, where on 1 October 1944 it became the AFD Squadron of the Central Fighter Establishment.

Fighter Interception Unit/Fighter Interception Development Unit
The FIU has already been dealt with in *Aces High*. Formed in April 1940 at Tangmere, it moved to Shoreham in August and then to Ford in January 1941. It was redesignated FIDU at the end of August 1944, but a month later became the Night Fighter Development Wing of the new Central Fighter Establishment.

Fighter Experimental Flight
Formed on 1 October 1944 within the Night Fighter Development Wing of CFE from an embryo 'Ranger' Flight, the unit commenced intruder operations on 6 December 1944 from Wittering, using Coltishall as a forward base. It was disbanded in June 1945.

Fighter Leaders' School
Formed on 15 January 1943 at Chedworth as part of 52 OTU, the unit moved to Charmy Down during the following month. In August a move was made to Aston Down, where 52 OTU became 52 OTU (Fighter Leaders' School), renamed in October 52 OTU (Fighter Command School of Tactics). In January 1944 the unit moved to Milfield and was expanded into the Fighter Leaders' School. The initial staff included such pilots as Grp Capt J.Rankin, Wg Cdr F.Blackadder and Grp Capt Atcherley; 'A' Squadron included Wg Cdr S.B.Grant, Wg Cdr H.Godefroy, Sqn Ldr R.A.Buckham, Sqn Ldr G.C. Keefer and Flt Lt J.E.Sheppard; 'B' Squadron, Wg Cdr S.F.Skalski, Wg Cdr B.Drake, Sqn Ldr B.D.Russel and Sqn Ldr K.Lofts; 'C' Squadron, Lt Col K.Birksted, Wg Cdr R.M.Thomas, Maj W.Christie, Sqn Ldr G.Northcott and Capt B.Bjornstad. In December 1944 the school was absorbed into CFE at Wittering as part of its Day Fighter Wing.

Central Fighter Establishment
The nucleus of the new CFE formed at Tangmere in September 1944. In October it moved to Wittering, where in December it absorbed the Fighter Leaders' School, together with the various fighter development units. In January 1945 it returned to Tangmere, and in October moved to West Raynham, where it was to remain for many years.

Central Gunnery School
The CGS was set up at Warmwell in November 1939 to provide aerial gunnery training for the RAF as a whole. Initially most instruction was provided to gunners of bomber aircraft and Defiant turret fighters, and not until later in the war was a specialist fighter flight formed. The unit moved to Castle Kennedy in June 1941, Clevedon in December 1941 and to Sutton Bridge in April 1942. It was to the latter airfield that many notable fighter pilots were to come, both as instructors and as pupils to improve their gunnery skills. In February 1944 the school moved to Catfoss, and finally in November 1945 to Leconfield.

Bomber Support Development Unit
The unit formed in April 1944 from the Special Duties (Radar) Development Unit at Foulsham. Incorporated in 100 Group, the unit undertook much development of the role of the Mosquito night fighter in support of the bomber streams over Germany. In December 1944 a move was made to Swanton Morley, and here in July 1945 the unit was redesignated Radio Warfare Establishment.

The OTU Squadrons

With the setting up of the OTUs, provision was made that should invasion of the United Kingdom occur, each of the day fighter OTUs would become a fighter squadron, available for operations. Even after the threat of imminent invasion subsided, this facility was maintained in case of emergency. Indeed, as the OTUs became larger, they were instructed to be able to provide two squadrons each.

The Air Fighting Development Unit was similarly to be capable of providing such a unit. In practice, several of these units were formed at various times during 1942-44, some undertaking semi-operational duties in order to free first line units for priority tasks. These units were to be maintained as Advanced Training Squadrons run on operational lines at satellite airfields wherever possible. They were:-

Squadron	Unit	Comment
550	AFDU	Until late 1943, when an operational unit with this number was formed.
551	52 OTU	Also apparently 51 OTU.
552	52 OTU	Formed and flew some semi-operational patrols.
553	53 OTU	
554	53 OTU	
555	55 OTU	
556	56 OTU	
557	57 OTU	
558	58 OTU	Mobilised at Ayr in late 1942 for an exercise.
559	59 OTU	
560	56 OTU	
561	61 OTU	
562	51 OTU (?)	
563	58 OTU	
564	59 OTU	
565	61 OTU	
566	55 OTU (?)	

MIDDLE EAST UNITS

70 (Middle East) Operational Training Unit

Formed at Ismailia, Egypt, in late 1940 as a general OTU for the Middle East, the unit swiftly set up a fighter flight with Gladiators and Hurricanes. In June 1941 this element, together with the army co-operation flight, were detached to form 71 OTU.

71 (Middle East) Operational Training Unit

Formed in June 1941 from the fighter and army co-operation flights of 70 OTU, the unit moved to Gordon's Tree, Sudan, in September 1941 after Ismailia had been bombed several times. Here the army co-operation function was removed, forming its own 74 OTU. A further move was made to Carthago in May 1942, whilst a year later it returned to Ismailia, coming under 203 Group control in July 1943. It was disbanded on 11 June 1945.

73 (Middle East) Operational Training Unit

The unit was formed in November 1941 at Sheik Othman, Aden, equipped with Mohawks and Hurricanes, becoming the main fighter OTU for units of Western Desert Air Force. Following the Japanese entry into the war and the appearance of carriers of the Imperial Japanese Navy in the Indian Ocean, the unit formed a Mohawk Flight for the defence of Aden. In May 1942 this was re-equipped with Hurricanes and moved to Khormaksar in October. Immediately thereafter the OTU closed and was shipped to Egypt, where it reopened at the end of November at El Ballah. It moved to Abu Sueir in February 1943, involved in the training of fighter-bomber pilots, and in May came under the control of 203 Group. It was disbanded on 25 September 1945.

Air Fighting School (Middle East)/1 Middle East Training Squadron/1(Middle East) Central Gunnery School/ RAF (Middle East) Central Gunnery School

An air fighting school was formed at Edku, Egypt, in December 1941, moving to Bilbeis the following month for fighter pilot training. On 5 April 1942 it merged with 1 METS, which was just being formed at El Ballah, as was an Air Fighting Squadron, a Conversions Refresher Squadron, and an Instructors' Training Squadron, all under the control of 233 Wing. The enlarged unit was equipped in the main with Hurricanes, Tomahawks and Kittyhawks. On 1 March 1943 it was reformed as 1 (ME) Central Gunnery School, the Conversion and Refresher parts of the unit being detached to 75 (ME) OTU. In April 1943 the unit was renamed RAF(ME) CGS, the following month being transferred to 203 Group control. It remained in operation until December 1945, when it was disbanded.

FAR EAST UNITS

1 Operational Training Unit, India/ 151 (Fighter) Operational Training Unit
1 OTU, India, formed at Risalpur in June 1942, equipped with Mohawks, Buffalos and Hurricanes. At the end of July it was renamed 151 (Fighter) OTU, coming under the control of 223 Group to train fighter and ground-attack pilots. Control moved to 1 (Indian) Group in August 1945, and in March 1946 a move was made to Ambala, where the following month it was absorbed into the Advanced Flying School (India).

Air Firing Training Unit
This unit was set up at Amarda Road under the direction of Wg Cdr F.R.Carey in February 1943, to train RAF, IAF and USAAF fighter pilots in current fighter tactics and gunnery for application against Japanese aircraft. Its training proved very successful. It was disbanded in May 1945, its personnel and aircraft being transferred to the Tactical & Weapons Development Unit.

My thanks to Norman Franks for help with last-minute information:

DRAKE Billy

Corrections and additions to claim lists:

1940				
20 Apr			L1590 was P	
10 May			,,	
13 May			,,	
10 Oct	Bf 109E Probable	Hurricane I	N2462	213 Sqn
1941				
7 Jan	2	Ju 88s Damaged (not 1 and 1 shared)		
13 Dec			DD897	
1942				
6 Jun		The Bf 109 was confirmed by the Army		112 Sqn
12 Jun		Bf 109 on ground	Kittyhawk	,,
14 Jun		Bf 109 Damaged on ground	,,	,,
17 Jun	3	Bf 109s on ground	,,	,,
24 Jul		The claim was definitely for a Bf 110, not for a Bf 109		
,,		Bf 110 on ground	,,	,,
,,		Bf 109 on ground	,,	,,
1 Sep			EV165 (not EV365)	
13 Sep		Bf 109 Damaged also	,,	EV168 (not EV165)
26 Oct		Delete		
27 Oct		Probably an aircraft of 97ª Squadriglia, 9° Gruppo, 4° Stormo CT flown by Ten Anselmo Maggini, who was killed.		
30 Oct		He 111 on ground	,,	,,
,,		Bf 109 on ground	,,	LG21	,,
,,		Bf 109 Damaged on ground	,,	,,	,,
31 Oct	2	Ju 87s (not 1)		
2 Nov	2	Ju 52/3ms on ground	,,	LG21	,,
,,		Bf 109 on ground	,,	,,
11 Nov	2	Bf 109s on ground	,,	,,
,,		Bf 109 Damaged on ground	,,	,,
1943				
7 Jul		Probably an aircraft of 97ª Squadriglia, 9° Gruppo, 4° Stormo CT flown by Ten Flavio Fratini, who was killed. Drake's Spitfire V was JK228, and he was Wing Leader of the Krendi Wing, not the Hal Far Wing, as indicated in *Aces High*.		

REVISED TOTAL: 20 and 2 shared destroyed, 2 unconfirmed destroyed, 4 and 2 shared probables, 7 damaged, 13 destroyed on the ground, 4 damaged on the ground.

CHAPTER TWO

Service Numbers
(and a Reference to the Polish Air Force)

A brief description of the basis of service numbers was included in *Aces High* (page 89). Since publication of that book, a long and fruitful correspondence has taken place with Bruce Burton of Hove, Sussex, who has provided a wealth of information in regard to many of the pilots dealt with herein, arising from his research in depth of the *London Gazette*.

Additionally, he has instructed me in the intricacies of the allocation of Royal Air Force service numbers, as a result of which it has become clear that much can be deduced regarding a pilot simply from an understanding of the background to the service number(s) allocated to him. A detailed synopsis of that background is set out below, as a matter potentially of considerable interest to the enthusiast, and to those wishing to seek to identify the backgrounds of other RAF personnel.

Officers
Regular officer numbers commenced from 00001(in 1919), and reached 57600 by September 1945. Certain blocks of numbers were reserved for particular types of entrants, as is identified below.

Officers commissioned directly from civilian life into the Reserve of Air Force Officers received numbers in the 70000-70999 range. RAF Volunteer Reserve (RAFVR) officer numbers commenced at 72000 in 1937, reaching 89999 in January 1941. The block 60000-69999 (until then unallocated) was then introduced for RAFVR commissions, 69999 being reached by June 1941. Thereafter the number 100001 was allocated as the commencement of a new series which was to run on to reach 202000 by August 1945.

Officers both of the Auxillary Air Force and the Special Reserve (which was disbanded in 1936) received numbers in the 90000 series. Each Auxillary squadron was given a block number from which numbers were allocated to officers as they were commissioned into those units. It requires to be recalled that Auxillary officers were commissioned into squadrons, and not into the AAF as a whole, in the same way that Territorial Army officers were commissioned into specific regiments, and not into the TA as a whole. Indeed, until 1938 when an Auxillary officer transferred from one squadron to another, he relinquished his old number and received a new one from the squadron he was joining. Until 1941, Auxillary officers and men could only be posted away from their squadron to another unit with their permission, or at their request.

Foreign Nationals
Initially, Polish, Czech, Dutch and Belgian officers (and United States and other 'neutral' citizens) were commissioned into the RAFVR on arrival in the UK. When a number arrived together they tended to receive consecutive numbers, although no block seems to have been allocated specifically for them. For instance the numbers 83698-83707 all appear to have been allocated to Polish officers. Later, those nations which set up their own independent air forces within the UK (French, Poles and Norwegians, but not Czechs and Belgians), allocated their own specific numbering.

Allocation of Officers' Service Numbers
16000-16299	Cranwell graduates, 1923-1926
16300-21099	Uncertain
21100-21399	Accountant Branch, 1920-1939
22000-22199	General Duties Branch, 1925-1926 (apparently SSCs)
23000-23399	Chaplains, Medical and Dental Branches, 1920s-1939
24000-24299	General Duties Branch, SSCs, 1926-1927
25000-25199	Officers transferred from the Army to the General Duties Branch, and Naval officers seconded to the Fleet Air Arm, 1935-1938
26000-26299	Cranwell graduates, 1926-1930
27000-27199	General Duties Branch, SSCs, 1928

28100-28299	General Duties Branch, SSCs, 1929
29000-29299	General Duties Branch, SSCs, 1930-1931
31000-31599	Equipment Branch, 1933-1939
32000-32299	General Duties Branch, SSCs, 1931-1932
33000-33599	Cranwell graduates, 1932-1940
34000-34299	General Duties Branch, SSCs, 1933-1934
35000-35199	Commissioned Signals/Engineer/Armament/PT Officers (ex-Warrant Officers; Commissioned PT Officers transferred to the Admin & Special Duties Branch as Plt Offs and Flg Offs in 1939; the others joined the Technical Branch in April 1940)
36000-36299	Direct Entry Commissions, General Duties Branch, plus ex-NCO pilots, and transfers from the RCAF and RNZAF, 1934-1939
37000-42999	SSCs, including transfers from the Army, ex-RAAF cadets, RNZAF and RCAF, 1934-1939, and some transfers from the Army in March 1940

Uncertain block up to 57600 allocated to the RAF up to September 1945

60000-69999	RAFVR, January-June 1941
70000-70999	Reserve of Air Force Officers
72000-89999	RAFVR, 1937-January 1941
90000-90408	Auxillary Air Force, as follows:-
	500 Squadron 90000-90015
	501 Squadron 90016-90030
	502 Squadron 90031-90045
	503 Squadron 90046-90060
	504 Squadron 90061-90077
	600 Squadron 90080-90106
	601 Squadron 90125-90157
	602 Squadron 90158-90181
	603 Squadron 90182-90201
	604 Squadron 90206-90235
	605 Squadron 90241-90269
	607 Squadron 90274-90294
	608 Squadron 90296-90308
	609 Squadron 90318-90334
	610 Squadron 90335-90349
	611 Squadron 90352-90363
	612 Squadron 90370-90375
	614 Squadron 90383-90387
	615 Squadron 90397-90408
	616 Squadron (This unit inherited 503 Squadron's block when the latter was disbanded on 1 November 1938. 613 Squadron did not form until 1 March 1939, and appears not to have been allocated a block of numbers)
90400-91200	Allocated generally to the General Duties, Medical, Accountant and other Branches
100001-202000	RAFVR, June 1941-August 1945

After the outbreak of war in September 1939 further commissioning into the regular RAF was (with a few rare exceptions) confined to pre-war RAF NCOs and airmen. No further commissions were granted into the Auxillary Air Force or the Reserve of Air Force Officers. In consequence, AAF NCOs and airmen were commissioned into the RAFVR from September 1939, and from that date virtually all new entrants — commissioned and non-commissioned — were inducted into the RAFVR.

Allocation of Non-Commissioned Personnel Service Numbers
Because the number of non-commissioned personnel greatly exceeded the numbers of officers, the list of allocated numbers is much larger. It also includes a majority who did not become aircrew. It is nonetheless instructive in the circumstances of this book to detail the system, and it is presented here, together with a few typical examples of what can be learned from it.

1-175000	Ex RFC, transferred to RAF	April 1918

200001-260000	Ex RNAS, transferred to RAF	April 1918
260001-313000	RAF conscripts	June-December 1918
313001-316000	Ex RNAS, transferred to RAF	April 1918
316001-326000	Boy cadets	October-December 1918
326001-329000	Boy cadets	December 1918-March 1919
329001-335000	Aircrafthands	March-August 1919
335001-336000	Boy Entrants	August 1919-January 1921
336001-338000	Aircrafthands	August-September 1919
338001-338274	Transfers from Army and Navy	October 1938
338275-339299	Transfers from Army	November-December 1940
339300-339800	Transfers from Army (Middle East)	January 1942
339801-340000	Transfers from Newfoundland Army	July 1940
340001-360000	Aircrafthands	September 1919-June 1925
360001-360200	Aircrafthands (Maltese)	no date
360201-361200	Boy cadets (Canadian)	June 1918
361201-361600	Aircrafthands (Maltese)	May 1923
361601-370000	Boy Entrants	July 1922-January 1924
370001-370986	Aircrafthands	June-September 1925
370987-399999	Aircrafthands — not issued	
400000-410432	Transfers from Army and Navy	September 1918
410440-410999	Transfers from Royal Corps of Signals	October 1939
411000-412200	Transfers from Army (Middle East)	June 1936
411221-411230	Transfers from Navy (Middle East)	January 1933
411231-411250	Transfers of Yugoslavs from British Army	March 1944
411300-411749	Transfers from Army	March 1937
412000-412999	Transfers from Navy	March 1943
420000-495000	WAAFs	July 1940-April 1943
499000-499999	WAAFs for ROC duties	September 1943
500000-502000	Aircrafthands (Maltese)	no date
502001-504800	Transfers from Royal Corps of Signals	July 1940
504801-505000	Enlistments for intelligence duties	August 1939
505001-549999	Aircrafthands	June 1925-March 1938
550000-558000	Boy Entrants	October 1925-October 1939
558001-558503	Class 'E' Reserve (Meteorologists)	May 1927
559001-559292	Class 'E' Reserve (Imperial Airways)	June 1926
560001-579999	Aircraft Apprentices	January 1926-October 1939
580000-581786	Direct Entry Pilots & Observers	August 1935-October 1939
590001-594261	Apprentice Clerks	October 1925-October 1939
600000-605364	Special Reserve	August 1931-May 1936
605365-606000	Enlistments in Canada	May 1942-October 1943
606001-606200	British enlistments in NW Africa	December 1943
610000-654720	Aircrafthands	March 1938-October 1939
654721-654999	Czech enlistments in Canada	January 1942
655000-679889	Transfers from Army	January 1938
679900-679999	Transfers from Allied forces in UK	December 1944

The next series originally started for the pre-war reserves, also began logically. When the first conscripts entered under the Military Training Act in July 1939 however, previously unissued numbers began to be taken up, disrupting the logical sequence. Since they were conscripted into the RAFVR, the term 'Volunteer Reserve' became something of a misnomer from that point. It should be noted that not every number in a block was actually issued.

Further, while regular RAF NCOs retained their original service numbers, no matter how often they changed trades or duties, reservists did change numbers when transferring from one scheme to another. For instance, Class 'F' of the RAF Reserve of Pilots transferring to the RAFVR in 1937-38 relinquished numbers in the 700000 range for RAFVR numbers in the 740000-759999 block.

700000-700697	Class 'F' Reserve	September 1934-June 1936
700698-700800	British enlistments, Middle East	August 1941

700801-700850	Enlistments in Trinidad and Bermuda	September 1941-July 1942
700861-700999	Local enlistments, Middle East	November 1942
701000-702935	RAFVR conscripts	July-September 1939
703000-709999	Polish enlistments	March 1942
710000-710060	Class 'E' Reserve (direct entry)	January 1936
710061-711999	Enlistments in Rhodesia	June-November 1941
712000-712999	Enlistments in Middle East	November 1942
713000-717499	Enlistments in West Indies	December 1943-April 1944
718000-722999	Yugoslavs in North Africa and Italy	February-June 1944
723000-728499	Enlistments in West Indies	September-December 1944
729000-733999	Polish enlistments	May 1945
740000-759999	RAFVR pilots and aircrew	January 1937-September 1939
760000-762617	RAFVR Civilian Wireless Reserve	August 1939
769000-769399	Local enlistments, Middle East	August 1945
770000-771499	RAFVR Ground Section (ops Rooms)	October 1938-September 1939
771500-773999	Enlistments in India	November 1939
774000-776199	Local enlistments in Middle East	November 1939-June 1940
776200-776499	Southern Rhodesians in Middle East	June 1940
776500-776508	Local enlistments in Iraq	March 1941
776509-776599	Local enlistments in Middle East	January 1944
776600-777599	Maltese enlistments	February 1940-March 1941
777600-778999	Enlistments in Rhodesia	June 1940
779000-779499	Rhodesians in Iraq and Middle East	May-July 1940
780000-784999	Enlistments of Poles in UK	December 1939-August 1940
785000-786999	Enlistments in Far East	July 1940
787000-788999	Enlistments of Czechs in UK	July 1940-November 1941
791000-791094	French in Middle East and Aden	July 1940
791100-791200	Enlistments in Middle East	November 1940
791201-791900	Yugoslavs in Middle East	February 1944
792001-795000	Enlistments of Poles in UK	August 1940
795001-795750	Maltese enlistments	August 1942
796751-797750	Enlistments in Bahamas	January 1944
797751-787950	Belgians in South Africa	July 1943
797951-798449	Enlistments in Cyprus	August 1944
798450-798499	Enlistments in Rhodesia and Bechuanaland	January 1941
798500-799549	Enlistments in Newfoundland	August 1940

The 800000 series for the Auxillary Air Force began with great simplicity, with the second and third numbers being the same as the second and third numerals of the squadron number. Thus:-

800000-800999	600 Squadron
801000-801999	601 Squadron
802000-802999	602 Squadron
803000-803999	603 Squadron
804000-804999	604 Squadron
805000-805999	605 Squadron
807000-807999	607 Squadron
808000-808999	608 Squadron
809000-809999	609 Squadron
810000-810999	610 Squadron
811000-811999	611 Squadron

This sequence was disrupted in May 1936 when the Special Reserve Squadrons were transferred to the AuxAF, with the following numbers allocated:

812000-812999	500 Squadron
813000-813999	501 Squadron
814000-814999	502 Squadron

815000-815999   504 Squadron

Auxillary squadrons formed after May 1936 therefore received the following:-

816000-816999   612 Squadron
817000-817999   613 Squadron
818000-818999   614 Squadron
819000-819999   615 Squadron
820000-820999   616 Squadron

Thereafter:-

821000-879999   Balloon squadrons of the AuxAF
880000-897999   WAAF   March 1939

On the outbreak of war, NCO/airmen numbers were issued to the reception centres at Uxbridge, Cardington and Padgate, so that up to spring 1940 it is possible to tell at which centre an airman enlisted. With the setting up of many other reception centres it then became less easy:-

900000-934899	UK enlistments, Uxbridge	September 1939-June 1940
934900-934999	British residents in Malta	June 1940
935000-965999	UK enlistments, Cardington	September 1939-August 1940
966000-979000	UK enlistments, Padgate	September 1939-February 1940
979001-1149977	UK enlistments, Cardington and Padgate	February-August 1940
1149978-1150000	Dutch enlistments	March 1941
1150001-1299800	UK enlistments, various centres	April-May 1940
1299801-1300000	Belgian and Czech enlistments in UK	July 1940
1300001-1360800	UK enlistments, various centres	June 1940-February 1941
1361081-1361527	UK enlistments, Edinburgh	June-August 1940
1365001-1375000	UK enlistments, Edinburgh	August 1940
1375001-1424800	UK enlistments, Euston and Penarth	August 1940-March 1941
1424801-1425000	Belgian enlistments	January 1942
1425001-1649900	UK enlistments, various centres	April-October 1941
1649901-1650000	Dutch enlistments	April 1942
1650001-1692488	UK enlistments, various centres	from November 1941
1692489-1692500	Dutch enlistments	November 1941
1692501-1700000	UK enlistments, Padgate	June 1942
1700001-1800000	Deferred service	from September 1941
1800001-1814800	UK enlistments, Euston	December 1941
1814801-1815000	Belgian and Dutch enlistments	November 1942
1815001-1838234	UK enlistments, various centres	July 1942-November 1943
1845001-1845166	UK enlistments, Penarth	October 1942
1850001-1853991	UK enlistments, Oxford	November 1942
1860001-1869800	UK enlistments, Cardington	October 1942-May 1943
1869801-1869808	Belgian enlistments	October 1942
1869809-1889800	UK enlistments, Cardington	from May 1943
1889801-1890000	Belgian and Dutch enlistments	May 1943
1890001-1899799	UK enlistments, Euston	January 1943
1899800-1899999	Belgian and Dutch enlistments	June-October 1943
1900000-1910000	UK enlistments, Northern Ireland	September 1943-November 1945
2000000-2199999	WAAF enlistments in UK	May 1941-August 1942
2200000-2212749	UK enlistments, Padgate	October 1942
2212750-2212999	Dutch enlistments	December 1942
2113000-2229353	UK enlistments, Padgate & Birmingham	October 1942-September 1943
2229354-2235000	UK enlistments	August 1945
2235001-2244800	UK enlistments, Euston	November 1943
2244801-2245000	Dutch and Belgian enlistments	December 1943-January 1945
2245001-2339995	UK enlistments, various centres	November 1943-September 1947

2788000-2791999	Belgian enlistments	March 1944-August 1946
2792000-2794300	Polish WAAFs in UK	June 1943
2795000-2796999	Dutch enlistments	March 1945
2990001-2991700	WAAFs in Middle East	May 1943
2991701-2992000	WAAFs in Cyprus	October 1943
2992001-2995000	WAAFs in Middle East (Palestinians, Greeks, Czechs, Yugoslavs)	May-August 1943
2999001-2999500	WAAFs in Middle East	
3000000-3014917	Ex-ATC cadets, Cardington and Padgate	May 1943
3020001-3026705	Ex-ATC cadets, Edinburgh and Penarth	May 1943
3030001-3044830	Ex-ATYC cadets, Euston and Doncaster	May 1943
3045001-3054173	Ex-ATC cadets, various centres	May 1943-September 1946
3055001-3099999	Ex-ATC cadets, various centres	May 1944-November 1945
3200001-3230000	Ex-ATC cadets, various centres	June 1943-August 1945

Examples

US citizen James Neale Thorne (605508) falls into the block 'Enlistments in Canada, May 1942-October 1943.

Roald Dahl (774022) was a local enlistment in the Middle East in the November 1939-July 1940 block.

Neville Bowker (779035) was a Rhodesian who enlisted in Iraq or the Middle East between May-July 1940.

Philip Stanley Kendall (785014), Patrick Alfred Schade (785018) and Cyril Lionel Francis Talalla (785048) all enlisted in the Far East — Ceylon, Malaya, Singapore, Hong Kong, etc — in summer 1940.

John Raymond Stewart Modera (791162) enlisted in the Middle East about November 1940.

Francis Scott Banner (1365780) enlisted in Edinburgh in August 1940.

Royal New Zealand Air Force Numbers

Paul Sortehaug has clarified the system of numbering employed by the RNZAF. Between the years 1938-48 direct entrant officers, including those transferred from other services, were numbered in the series NZ1001 onwards. All other recruits were numbered in a series which started at 100 each year, following the numbers denoting the year within the century e.g. NZ40100 onwards for 1940 entrants, NZ43100 and onwards for 1943 entrants, and so on. On commissioning this number was retained.

Examples

Evan Dall Mackie (NZ41520) joined the service in 1941 and was the 520th recruit of the year.

John Rutherford Clark Kilian (NZ1043) joined the service pre-war.

Reginald Jack Hyde (NZ2440) has a number which signifies the transfer of an officer from one service (the RAF) to another (the RNZAF).

The Poles

Because a substantial number of the pilots dealt with herein were of Polish nationality and had, perhaps to a greater degree than any of the other nationalities who served with or alongside the RAF, already seen action and achieved early victories with their own air force, some brief detail of the circumstances in which they entered and served within that air force are now described.

To enter the *Szkola Podchorazych Lotnictwa* (Air Force Cadet Officers' School) at Deblin, school leaving examinations similar to GCE standard required to have been passed. Upon passing the entrance examination of the SPL, the new entrant had first to attend a "unitary course" in the *Szkola Podchorazych Piechloty* (Infantry Cadet Officers' School) at Rozan, or a first-line infantry unit, for basic military training. Training at the SPL followed either as a pilot or observer/navigator. Prior to commissioning, cadet officers (with nominal NCO ranks) were posted to first-line units for a period of operational training.

Commissioning took place with considerable ceremony, usually on Polish Army Day — 15 August. Pilots were selected for the appropriate arm of the service (fighters, bombers or army co-operation) before commissioning. "Classes" at Deblin were numbered by the year of commissioning; thus the 1st Class was that of 1927, and the 8th Class that of 1934. A change in training sequence then occurred, the 9th Class being that commissioned in 1936, the class of 1939 therefore becoming the 12th. With war imminent, the 13th Class time schedule was compressed, and commissions were awarded nominally on 1 September 1939 — the last before the war. Included in this class were future notables Gladych, Horbaczewski, Drobinski, Poplawski and Retinger. The 14th Class was only midway through training at this time, but many of its members escaped to complete their training in the UK; included in their number were Blok, Sologub and Potocki.

However, as in several other air forces a pilot could be of non-commissioned rank as low as szeregowy (Private). One route for such personnel was the *Szkola Podficerow Lotnictwa dla Maloletnich* (Air Force NCO School for Minors) in Bydgoszcz. (The Polish term *podoficer* literally means sub-officer.This is not precisely an NCO, for every rank below commissioned officer is *podoficer*.)

The alternative route for both officers and other ranks, but particularly for air force ground personnel and observer/navigators, was to train at an operational unit. Air Regiments (*Pulk Lotniczy*) had their own training Eskadras, which operated as both elementary flying training units and for operational training.

Before the war there were six operational bases in Poland, each numbered as a *Pulk Lotniczy*. *1 Pulk Lotniczy* was at Warsaw, *2* at Crakow, *3* at Poznan, *4* at Torun, *5* at Lida (now in Belarus) and *6* at Lwow (now Lviv in the Ukraine). Each Pulk had two, three or four *Eskadra Mysliwska* (fighter units) as well as bomber and army co-operation/reconnaissance units. The Eskadra Mysliwska was the basic unit, similar to a Luftwaffe Staffel or Armée de l'Air Escadrille — larger than an RAF Flight, but smaller than a Squadron. *Eskadra* numbers related to the parent *Pulk*, and consisted of three digit numbers, where the first was '1', the second related to the *Pulk*, and the third to the *Eskadra* in the *Pulk*.Thus the first *Eskadra Mysliwska* of *1 Pulk Lotniczy* was No *111*; the second *Eskadra Mysliwska* of *6 Pulk Lotniczy* was No *162*, and so on.

Two or three *Eskadras* formed a *Dywizjon* (commonly abbreviated to *Dyon*) — similar to a Luftwaffe Gruppe or Armée de l'Air Groupe, but between an RAF Squadron and Wing in size, although later in the war Polish squadrons with the RAF were to be referred to as *Dywizjon* in Polish records. The fighter *Dywizjon* was usually the third (or in one instance, the fourth) in the *Pulk*, first and second being reserved for bombers and other types of aircraft. Thus fighter *Dywizjon* were Nos *III/1*, *III/2*, *III/3*, *III/4*, *III/5*, and *III/6* respectively.They were based at their regimental bases with the exception of *III/5 Dywizjon* (*151* and *152 Eskadras*), which were at Wilno (now Vilnius in Lithuania). *1 Pulk Lotniczy* had four fighter *Eskadras*, which made two *Dywizjon*; *111* and *112 Eskadras* formed *III/1*, while *113* and *114* formed *IV/1*.

In Polish, military ranks are written in lower case, commencing with a capital letter only when at the beginning of a sentence. Czech ranks were treated in the same manner, as were those of the Soviet Union.

All PZL aircraft designations used Arabic, rather than Roman, numerals, so for instance, the PZL P.11 fighter should be written thus, and not as P.XI as used previously in *Aces High*.

CHAPTER THREE

New Names

ALLEN Derek Hurlestone   Flying Officer   RAF No. 39840

Derek Allen was granted a Short Service Commission on 5 July 1937, training at 5 FTS, Sealand. He joined 85 Squadron in February 1938, being promoted Flg Off on 10 December 1939. In France he was shot down in flames by Bf 110s of 5/ZG 26 on 15 May 1940, but baled out of Hurricane P2828 south of Ath, returning safely next day. On 18 May however, he was shot down in P2701 by a Bf 110 of I/ZG 26, and was killed. The award of a DFC was gazetted on 30 May.

1940					
10 May		Hs 126	Hurricane I		85 Sqn
„	1/3	Ju 88	„		„
11 May	1/3	Do 17	„		„
„	1/3	Do 17	„		„
13 May	2	He 111s (reportedly)	„		„

TOTAL: potentially 3 and 3 shared destroyed.

BARY Ronald Edward   Wing Commander   RAF No 41818

Ronald Bary was born in New Plymouth, New Zealand, on 9 June 1915, working as a law clerk in the Department of Justice in Palmerston North before being accepted by the RAF for a Short Service Commission in 1938; he left for the UK on 16 December. Initial training was at 1 E & RFTS, Hatfield, and then 11 FTS, Shawbury. In late October 1939 he joined 229 Squadron at Digby, and was in action over Dunkirk in June 1940. In May 1941 the squadron departed for the Middle East, flying off HMS *Furious* to Malta on 21st, and thence to Mersa Matruh. Initially he was attached to 274 Squadron in the Western Desert, and then to the Ferry Pool at Takoradi, West Africa, until 229 Squadron reformed fully in September for the night defence of Mersa Matruh. In early October he was posted to 250 Squadron as a flight commander. He received a DFC in April 1942, and shortly thereafter was posted to 1 METS at El Ballah as an instructor. In January 1943 he was given command of 80 Squadron, which he led until mid June, when he returned to 239 Wing as Wing Leader, leading this unit on fighter-bomber duties over Sicily and Italy. In late January 1944 he was sent back to the UK, attending the Fighter Leaders' School at Milfield, and then becoming an instructor there in July. He subsequently joined the staff of the CFE at Milfield. In December 1944 he returned to Italy to command 244 Wing. On 12 April 1945 he took off with Spitfires of 92 Squadron on a dive-bombing sortie, but as he dived on the target north-east of Imola, his aircraft was seen to blow up and disintegrate. No Flak had been experienced, and it was considered that one of his bombs had exploded due to a faulty fuse. He was awarded a DSO on 12 February 1946, with effect from 11 April 1945. He was subsequently buried in the British Empire Cemetery at Faenza.

1940					
1 Jun		Ju 87 unconf	Hurricane I	Dunkirk	229 Sqn
27 Jun	1/2	Ju 88	„		„
4 Oct	1/3	Ju 88	„		„
12 Dec	1/2	Bf 109E	„		„
1941					
3 Jun		Bf 109 (a)	„		„
17 Jun		Ju 87 Damaged	„		„
20 Nov		Ju 87 Probable	Tomahawk IIB	S Bir el Gobi	250 Sqn
„		Bf 109	„	„	„
4 Dec		Bf 109 Probable	„	SE Tobruk	„
5 Dec		Bf 109 Damaged	„		„
9 Dec	1/2	Bf 110 (b)	„	Bir el Gobi	„
24 Dec		Ju 52/3m on ground	„	Agheila airfield	„

TOTAL: 2 and 4 shared destroyed, 1 unconfirmed destroyed, 2 probables, 2 damaged, 1 destroyed on the ground.
(a) Bf 109E of 2/JG 27, flown by Uffz Reichstein; (b) Bf 110 of 2(H)/14, flown by Fw Günther Ursinus, shared with John Waddy.

BEAZLEY Hugh John Sherard   Wing Commander   RAF No. 73023

Born on 18 July 1916, the son of a judge, Hugh Beazley attended Cheltenham College and Pembroke College, Oxford, joining the Oxford University Air Squadron. As a member of the RAFVR he was called up on 1 September 1939, and was posted to 249 Squadron upon the unit's formation in May 1940, on completion of his own training. He was promoted to command 'A' Flight on 18 September 1940, while on 21 May 1941 he flew off HMS *Ark Royal* to Malta with the unit. On 19 January 1942 he led Hurricane fighter-bombers in an attack on Comiso airfield, Sicily, where his aircraft, BV174, was hit by ground fire. He managed to return to Malta, where he crash-landed. In February 1942 he was posted to the Middle East, where he later became a flight commander in 89 Squadron, flying Beaufighters at night. He was awarded a DFC on 7 March 1944, and was released from the RAF in 1946 as a Wg Cdr.

1940						
8 Jul	1/3	Ju 88 (a)	Hurricane I	P3055 GN-N		249 Sqn
15 Aug		Bf 110 (b)	„	P3855 GN-P		„
2 Sep		Bf 110 Probable	„	P2988(c)		„
5 Sep		Bf 109 Probable	„	V6635		„
6 Sep		Ju 88 Probable	„			„
7 Sep	1/4	Do 17 (d)	„	V6628		„
15 Sep		Do 17 (e)	„	V6635		„
19 Sep	1/2	Do 17 (f)	„	V6559		„
26 Sep		Do 17 Damaged	„	V6622 GN-C		„
27 Sep	1/3	Bf 110 (g)	„	V6559		„
1941						
8 Jun	1/2	BR 20M Probable	Hurricane II		Malta	„
12 Dec		Bf 109 Damaged	„		„	„
1942						
19 Jan	2	Ju 88s Probable on ground	„	BV174	Comiso, Sicily	„
4 Feb	1/3	Ju 88 Damaged (h)	„		Malta	„

TOTAL: 2 and 4 shared destroyed, 3 and 1 shared probable, 2 and 1 shared damaged, 2 probables on the ground.
(a) Aircraft of 9/KG4; (b) Aircraft of II/ZG 76; (c) Shot down himself by Bf 110 of 5/ZG 26; (d) Aircraft actually a Bf 110 of Stab I/ZG 2; (e) Aircraft of II/KG 3; (f) Possibly aircraft of I/KG 77 — claim may have been on 18th, rather than 19 September; (g) Possibly an aircraft of V(Z)/LG 1; (h) Possibly an aircraft of 2/KGr 806, which crash-landed on return to Sicily.

BENNETTS B.R.   Lieutenant   SAAF No. 103758

Bennetts served in the Western Desert with 2 SAAF Squadron during summer 1942. He was posted to 601 Squadron later in the year to fly Spitfires during the advance from Alamein. On 17 March 1943 he was seen to attack Ju 87s in EP309, but broke away and was attacked and shot down by two Bf 109s. He had been hit in the legs, and was further injured seriously when the aircraft crashed. No further information regarding this pilot has been discovered.

1942						
29 Aug		MC 202 (a)	Kittyhawk I	DB-W	10m SSW El Alamein	2 SAAF Sqn
2 Nov	2	Bf 109s	Spitfire VC	BP959	forward area	601 Sqn
7 Nov	1/2	Bf 109	„	BR192	Matruh-Sidi Barrani road	„
„	1/2	Ju 87	„	„	„	„
10 Dec		Bf 109 Damaged	„	ER283	Marble Arch a/fld	„

TOTAL: 3 and 2 shared destroyed, 1 damaged.
(a) May have been claimed as a MC 200; pilot baled out.

BOARDMAN Hubert Stanley   Flight Lieutenant   RAF No. 126590

Boardman served as a Sgt in 600 Squadron during the mid war period. He was later posted to 153 Squadron after being commissioned in early 1944, and on 1 February claimed a Ju 88 and a probable over a convoy off Oran during an evening patrol sortie. It appears that this probable may subsequently have been confirmed. He and his radar operator, Flt Sgt J.R.Mordan, were to claim three further victories over convoys, for which Boardman received a DFC during June. On 7 August 1944, as they pursued a Ju 88 which they had damaged off Alghero, Sardinia, contact with them was lost and Beaufighter ND314 was reported missing. Boardman's promotion to Flt Lt was announced in September. In *Aces High* he was included on the list of pilots claiming four victories.

1944						
1 Feb		Ju 88	Beaufighter VIF	V8844	off Oran	153 Sqn
„		Ju 88 Probable*	„	„	„	„
11/12 Apr	2	Ju 88s	„	ND314	over convoy	„
30/31 May		Ju 88	„	„	„	„
7/8 Aug		Ju 88 Damaged	„	„	NW Alghero	„

TOTAL: possibly 5 destroyed, 1 damaged.
* May have been confirmed later.

CASTELAIN Noel   Sous Lieutenant   RAF No. F

Noel Castelain was born at Niort (Deux-Sevres), France, on 30 May 1917. He volunteered for the Armée de l'Air in November 1936, and in June 1939 entered the school for junior officers, gaining his wings as a pilot in December 1939. He was then posted to the Ecole de Chasse at Avord, but following the fall of France in June 1940, was posted to the south. Here on 18 June he decided with others at Saint Jean-de-Luz to join the British, departing on a cargo vessel on 19th to join the Forces Aeriennes Francais Libre. Here he exaggerated his degree of flying training in order to get into action, and on 20 July was posted to 6 OTU, Sutton Bridge. On 10 August he was posted to Odiham, from where the following month he joined a sea convoy to Dakar for Operation 'Menace'. When this failed, he was put ashore at Davola, Cameroun, with other pilots and three crated Dewoitine

D-520 fighters. This detachment of French pilots was then flown across Africa to Ismailia in an RAF DC 2. Here in December 1940 Free French Flight 1 was formed with Hurricanes. In late March 1941 the flight was sent to Greece on attachment to 33 Squadron. After a few defensive patrols over Athens, the flight returned to Egypt, then being sent to join 73 Squadron at Tobruk. Here Castelain claimed his first victory. On 19 October 1942 he volunteered to join the French Groupe 'Normandie' in Russia, where he flew Yak 1s. During a three month period he claimed six further victories. However, on 16 July 1943, after claiming his final success, he and Albert Littolf, with whom he had served in FF Flight 1 in Africa, and a third pilot, were shot down and killed near Krasnikovo in combat with FW 190s of JG 51.

1941						
11 Apr	1/2	Ju 87	Hurricane I	V7853	Tobruk	att 73 Sqn
1943						
3 May	1/3	Hs 126	Yak 1		Spas Demansk	Gr Normandie
15 May		Bf 110	„		Mouliatino	„
„	1/2	FW 189	„		Marinka	„
13 Jul		Bf 110	„		Ksin	„
14 Jul		FW 190	„		Dolgaja	„
16 Jul		Bf 110	„		Krasnikovo	„
TOTAL: 4 and 3 shared destroyed.						

CLIFT Douglas Gerald   Flight Lieutenant   RAF No. 41828

Born on 15 March 1919, Douglas Clift joined the RAF in January 1939. He trained at 5 E & RFTS, Hanworth, and 11 FTS, Shawbury. After undertaking a Hurricane conversion course, he joined 79 Squadron in November 1939. He was promoted flight commander in early 1941, but in July was posted to CFS, Upavon, on an instructor's course. He then volunteered for the MSFU, serving with the unit until October 1942. He ended the war in South East Asia, attached to the RIAF. With the conclusion of hostilities, he served with 34 Squadron until its disbandment in August 1947. He later served in Germany and Singapore, and spent some years at the Royal Radar Establishment, Malvern. Following a year as an adviser to the Imperial Iranian Air Force, he served at West Drayton on the 'Linesman' project. He retired from the RAF on 2 July 1974 as a Sqn Ldr.

1940				
16 May		FW 189 (a)	Hurricane I	79 Sqn
17 May	1/2	Do 17 (b)	„	„
27 May		Bf 110	„	„
15 Aug		Bf 110	„	„
30 Aug	1/4	He 111	„	„
1 Sep		Bf 110 Probable	„	„
1941				
24 Mar		He 111 Probable	„	„
TOTAL: 3 and 2 shared destroyed, 2 probables.				
(a) Aircraft of 9(H)/LG 2; (b) Aircraft of 4/KG 76.				

COOK Harry   Flight Lieutenant   RAF Nos. 754199 (NCO); 126096 (Officer)

Listed in the 1994 volume as a pilot with four victories, further research shows Harry Cook's total to be higher. He joined the RAFVR in 1939, qualifying as a pilot in June 1940 and being posted to 7 OTU. In August he joined 266 Squadron as a Sgt, and then on 12 September moved to 66 Squadron, where he claimed five and one shared victories. Early in 1941 he was posted back to the OTU (now 57) at Hawarden as an instructor, but shortly thereafter a Master trainer collided with his aircraft, the propeller knicking his skull. Surviving this event, he was commissioned in June 1941, and in 1942 served with 234 Squadron. He then voluneered for service with the CAM ships of the Merchant Navy during 1942-43, before joining 41 Squadron as a Flt Lt, 1943-44. He was demobilized in 1946.

1940					
15 Sep	1/2	He 111 (a)	Spitfire I	West Malling	66 Sqn
24 Sep		Bf 109E	„	Channel	„
27 Sep		Bf 110	„		„
„		Bf 110 Damaged	„		„
30 Sep		Bf 109E	„	in sea off Dover	„
27 Oct		Bf 109E (b)	Spitfire IIA		„
26 Nov		Bf 109E	„		„
TOTAL: 5 and 1 shared destroyed, 1 damaged.					
(a) The He 111 crash-landed at West Malling; Cook landed nearby and took the pilot's binoculars: (b) Aircraft of JG 53.					

COOKE Charles Alfred   Squadron Leader   RAF Nos. 580219 (NCO); 43634 (Officer)

Born on 7 June 1912, Charles Cooke was a regular pre-war NCO pilot. It appears that he enlisted as a direct entry pilot under training in 1936. He was commissioned on 1 April 1940 and posted to 66 Squadron. On 4 September 1940 he was shot down by Bf 109Es, baling out of R6689 over Ashford, Kent, with burns to his face and hands. He returned to the unit on 21 September and was promoted flight commander on 10 October. He left the squadron in December, but a year later he took command of 264 Squadron on Defiants. When the unit re-equipped with Mosquito IIs in May 1942 and the command position became one for a Wg Cdr, he remained with the unit as a flight commander. He was awarded a DFC on 13 October 1942. He stayed on in the RAF after the war, serving in the Secretarial Branch and becoming a graduate of the Staff College. He retired on 11 July 1958 as a Sqn Ldr, and died on 28 January 1985.

1940						
13 May	2	Ju 87s	Spitfire I		North Sea off Dutch coast	66 Sqn
		Ju 87 Damaged	,,		,,	,,
10 Jul	1/3	Do 17	,,		off Winterton	,,
20 Aug		Bf 110	,,			,,
4 Sep	3	Bf 109Es Probable	,,	R6689		,,
1942						
30/31 Jul		Ju 88 (a)	Mosquito II		N Malvern Wells	264 Sqn

TOTAL: 4 and 1 shared destroyed, 3 probables, 1 damaged.
(a) Aircraft of KüFlGr 106.

COX Neill Dudley   Flight Lieutenant   RAF Nos. 1385775 (NCO); 124417 (Officer)

Born in Weybridge, Surrey, on 12 June 1923, Neill Cox attended Charterhouse School from 1937. He enlisted on 3 March 1941, training in the USA at 4 British Flying Training School from December 1941-June 1942, when he qualified as a pilot, having flown PT-17s, BT-13As and AT-6As; he was commissioned on 19 June. Returning to the UK, in August he was posted to 6(P) Advanced Flying Unit at Little Rissington, and then to 1 FIS on an instructor's course. Promoted Flg Off in December 1942, in May 1943 he was posted to HQ, North West African Air Force, joining 614 Squadron to fly Bisleys on coastal patrol duties. In August he moved to 39 Squadron, newly-converted to Beaufighters, gaining early success with this unit whilst hunting Luftwaffe transport aircraft between Corsica and Italy. He was awarded a DFC on 26 November 1943, and in June 1944 his tour ended. He was promoted Flt Lt and posted to HQ, RAF Middle East in Cairo, and from there the following month to 203 Group as an instructor. On 27 August he was appointed PA to the AOC at HQ, Mediterranean Allied Air Forces, but a few days later returned to Med Allied Coastal AF as a supernumary. On 8 September 1944 the award of a Bar to his DFC was gazetted, which recorded that since the award of his DFC he had claimed a probable victory over a torpedo bomber and had damaged a second during the same engagement; details of this further combat have not been found. He returned to the UK immediately thereafter, being posted to 1 PDC, West Kirby, until January 1945, when he attended 53 OTU, Kirton, to convert to single-engined fighters. At the start of April he went to the Tempest Pool at 83 GSU, and from there to 56 Squadron to take part in the final month's operations over North West Europe. He left the unit in July 1945, and after delayed disembarkation leave, he was posted to Farnborough in September for test flying duties. In December he went to HQ, 41 Group as a supernumary for ferrying duties until July 1946, when he was released.

1943						
23 Sep	2	Ju 52/3ms	Beaufighter X (a)	Elba area		39 Sqn
24 Sep	2	Ju 52/3ms	,, (b)	,,		,,
?		Torpedo Bomber Probable	,, (c)	,,		,,
,,		Torpedo Bomber (c) Damaged	,,			,,
1945						
15 Apr	1/2	Me 262 (d)	Tempest V	NV968 US-G Kaltenkirchen		56 Sqn

TOTAL: 4 and 1 shared destroyed, 1 probable, 1 damaged.
(a) Own aircraft damaged and crash-landed on return to base; (b) Own aircraft hit by return fire and caused to ditch in the sea; rescued; (c) Confirmed as an Arado Ar 234 jet bomber.

CROSLEY R. Michael   Lieutenant Commander

Born in Rockferry, near Liverpool, on 24 February 1920, Mike Crosley was the son of an opera singer. He attended Winchester Cathedral School, then joining the Metropolitan Police after failing to gain entrance to the Royal Naval College at Dartmouth. Following the outbreak of war, he attempted to join the RAF, but found the service temporarily full up at the time. In late 1940 therefore, he volunteered for the FAA instead, and commenced training on 11 November. He was taught to fly on Magisters at 24 EFTS, then completing his training with an RAF SFTS at Netheravon. In July 1941 he was posted to HMS *Hermes* at Yeovilton as a Sub Lt, transitioning onto Hurricanes. He was posted to 813 Squadron on HMS *Eagle* on 28 December 1941 to fly Sea Hurricanes, and first saw action during Operation 'Harpoon', a convoy escort to Malta, during June 1942. In August the carrier took part in Operation 'Pedestal', the largest of the Malta convoy operations, but was sunk early in the operation. The 813 Squadron pilots were returned to Gibraltar on HMS *Argus*. Three months later he took part in the cover for Operation 'Torch', the landings in Algeria and Morocco, now serving with 800 Squadron aboard HMS *Indomitable*, still flying Sea Hurricanes. In early 1943 the unit was disbanded and he was posted to 804 Squadron on HMS *Dasher*, sailing to Iceland to cover Convoy JW 53 to Russia. From here the unit disembarked at Hatston in the Orkneys, where he received an award of the DSC. In June the squadron was also disbanded, and he was posted to RNAS Henstridge — HMS *Dipper* — to convert to Spitfires. He flew several sweeps with RAF wings to gain experience, and in early 1944 was promoted Lt. He was now posted to 3 Naval Fighter Wing at Lee-on-

Solent as Staff Air Gunnery Instructor on Seafires. During June 1944 he took part in gun spotting duties for the warships supporting the Normandy invasion, and here he claimed his final victory, being Mentioned in Despatches on 20 June. In August he was promoted Lt Cdr and given command of 880 Squadron on Seafire IIIs, initially serving on HMS *Furious*. In September the unit moved to HMS *Implacable* to join 24 Naval Fighter Wing with 887 and 894 Squadrons, sailing at the start of 1945 to join the British Pacific Fleet. The vessel arrived in Australia at the end of April, taking part in the final operations against Japan in July-August 1945. After the close of hostilities, Griffon-engined Seafire XVs were received in Australia, but at this stage he sought compassionate home leave, being posted to command 894 Squadron for the journey home on HMS *Indefatigable*, where he arrived in March 1946. Becoming a Lt again, he was posted to St Merryn, where he was to fly Seafire 17s and 47s. He then commanded 718 Squadron, a training unit at Eglinton, Northern Ireland. Subsequently he attended the Empire Test Pilots' School at Cranfield. He remained in the Royal Navy, reaching the rank of Commander,RN. His autobiography, *They Gave Me a Seafire* (Airlife Publishing Ltd), was published in 1986.

1942						
13 Jun		Z 1007bis (a)	Sea Hurricane		Mediterranean	813 Sqn
14 Jun	1/2	Ju 88 (b)	,,		,,	,,
,,						
,,		S 79 Probable	,,		,,	,,
,,		Re 2001 Possible (c)	,,		,,	,,
8 Nov	2	D 520s (d)	Sea Hurricane IIB		Algiers	800 Sqn
1944						
7 Jun		Bf 109	Seafire III		Normandy Beachhead	880 Sqn

TOTAL: 4 and 1 shared destroyed, 1 probable, 1 "possible".
(a) Aircraft of 212ª Squadriglia; Ten Gerolamo Piccioni and crew picked up by British destroyer; (b) Initially claimed as a probable; Ju 88D F6+EH of 1(F)/122, shot down 120 miles west of Trapani; Uffz Emil Schwarz and crew picked up three days later by British warship (two dead), and confirmed shot down by Hurricanes; (c) Aircraft of 150ª Squadriglia, 2° Gruppo CT, flown by Mar Olindo Simionato, force-landed near Korba, Tunisia, with damaged aircraft; repaired and flown back to Sicily two days later; (d) Pilot of one Dewoitine baled out; 5 claims by British pilots — 2-4 lost.

DRAPER John William Petterson   Flight Lieutenant   RCAF No. J10159
John Draper was born in Toronto, Canada, on 15 July 1921. He served as a Private in the Queen's York Rangers Militia during 1937-38, and joined the RCAF on 23 April 1941. He was trained at 1 ITS, Toronto, 20 EFTS, Oshawa and 2 SFTS, Ottawa, qualifying as a Sgt Pilot on 16 January 1941, at which point he was commissioned. In March 1942 he departed for the UK, completing his training at 58 OTU in May and joining 611 Squadron in August 1942. Promoted Flg Off on 1 October, he was then posted to 111 Squadron for service in North Africa, accompanying the unit to Algeria during early November. On 26 January 1943 he shot down one FW 190 in flames, then attacked another head-on, this colliding with the tailplane of his Spitfire and crashing; his own aircraft was not badly damaged. He completed his tour on 3 June 1943, the award of a DFC being announced on 9 July. Following this he served at the Fighter Pilots' Practice Unit until January 1944, when he was flown back to the UK and promoted Flt Lt. After leave in Canada, he returned to the UK in March 1944, undertook a refresher course at 53 OTU, and on 14 June 1944 joined 91 Squadron. He was slightly injured on 25 February 1945 when the engine of his aircraft cut whilst taking off. The Spitfire crashed and somersaulted twice, but nevertheless he was able to walk away. He left the unit in June 1945, serving at Cranfield until 2 August, when he returned to Canada. He was released on 7 January 1946, but subsequently rejoined the RCAF Auxillary, rising to the rank of Grp Capt — Brigadier General following the amalgamation of Canada's armed forces. In *Aces High* he was included in the list of pilots claiming four victories.

1942						
18 Nov		Ju 87 Probable	Spitfire VC		Bone area	111 Sqn
29 Nov		Ju 88	,,		,,	,,
,,	1/4	Ju 88	,,		,,	,,
1943						
26 Jan	2	FW 190s	,,	JG927	Tabarka-Souk el Arba	,,
5 Apr		Bf 109 Damaged	,,	JG876	Hamman Lif	,,
20 Apr		Bf 109 Probable	,,	JK426	La Sebala	,,
1 May		Bf 109	,,	,,	Ras Zebib	,,
1944						
19 Jun		V-1	Spitfire XIV	RM617	N Beachy Head	91 Sqn
24 Jun		V-1	,,	NN654	NW Hastings	,,
28 Jun		V-1	,,	RB161	Channel	,,
9 Jul		V-1	,,	RM620	Goudhurst	,,
12 Jul		V-1	,,	RM621	Newchurch	,,
20 Jul		V-1	,,	RM686	N Tonbridge	,,

TOTAL: 4 and 1 shared destroyed, 2 probables, 1 damaged, 6 V-1s destroyed.

GASSON John Edward   Major   SAAF No. 279804V
Previously included in the four victory list, John Gasson, a member of the SAAF, joined 92 Squadron as a 2nd Lt in early summer 1943. He was promoted 1st Lt in early 1944, Capt in April of that year, and in October he

became commanding officer, leading the unit until July 1945. He was awarded a DFC in June 1944, a Bar to this in June 1945, and a DSO in March of that year.

1943						
10 Jul		Ju 88 Damaged	Spitfire VB	ER470	3m out to sea from Avola	92 Sqn
13 Jul		Ju 88	"			"
19 Sep		Bf 109 Probable	Spitfire VIII	JF510	Grottaglie area	"
1944						
16 Feb		Bf 109	"	JF476	N Anzio	"
25 Feb	1/2	Bf 109	"	JF619	Anzio-Rome	"
19 Apr	1/2	FW 190	"	JF616	NE Cisterna	"
23 Apr		FW 190	"	"	SE Avezzano	"
15 May		Bf 109 Damaged	"	JF619	Arsoli/Highway 6	"
18 May	3	FW 190s Damaged	"	"	Civita Castellana	"
"	2	FW 190s Damaged	"	"	Viterbo airfield	"

TOTAL: 3 and 2 shared destroyed, 1 probable, 7 damaged.

GLEW Norman Vipan   Squadron Leader   RAF Nos. 742507 (NCO); 107955 (Officer)

Born in Derby in November 1916, 'Sticky' Glew joined the RAFVR in 1938 and was posted to 72 Squadron in 1940 as a Sgt. Late in the year he moved to 41 Squadron, but volunteered for overseas service, being posted to the Middle East. En route on the carrier HMS *Victorious* with 260 Squadron, which unit he had joined during 1941, delivery to Gibraltar was delayed whilst the German battleship *Bismarck* was pursued and sunk. Commissioned in August 1941, he remained with the squadron until 1942, being promoted Flg Off in August of that year. He then undertook various training and delivery tasks until March 1944, when he was given command of 1435 Squadron. On 17 May 1944 he was flying a Hurricane in a mock dogfight with a Spitfire over Brindisi, when he crashed and was killed. He was buried in the Bari War Cemetery.

1940						
2 Sep		Bf 110	Spitfire I	P9460	Dungeness	72 Sqn
"		Bf 109E Probable	"		"	"
7 Sep	2	Do 17Zs Damaged	"	K9841	Maidstone/Dartford	"
10 Sep	1/2	Do 17Z	"	P9376	Weybridge	"
"	1/2	Do 17Z	"	"	"	"
23 Sep	1/2	Bf 109E	"	R6881	Folkestone	"
24 Sep		Ju 88 Probable	"		Rochester	"
27 Sep		Do 17	"	X4481 RN-M	Dungeness	"
"		Bf 109E Damaged	"	"	"	"
12 Oct		Bf 109E Damaged	"			"
1942						
2 Jan		Bf 109F Damaged	Hurricane I		12 m S Agedabia	260 Sqn
3 Jan		Ju 87	"			"
2 Apr		Bf 109F Damaged	Kittyhawk I		5m NW Tobruk	"

TOTAL: 3 and 3 shared destroyed, 2 probables, 6 damaged.

HAMBLIN B.W.   Flying Officer   RAF No.126762

Hamblin served with 242 Squadron as a Plt Off in late 1942, taking part in the initial operations over French North-West Africa following Operation 'Torch'. On 2 December 1942 he and another pilot intercepted five S 79 torpedo bombers of 280ª Squadriglia, 130° Gruppo Sil, over the sea to the north of Bizerta.Identifying these as Breda 88s, they attacked and rapidly shot down three. Hamblin attacked a fourth, but ran out of ammunition. As his companion, Plt Off Willie Lindsay, turned to take up the attack, he saw Hamblin's aircraft pouring white smoke. He broke off his attack as he saw Hamblin bale out, but although seen to go down apparently alright, he was not found. In fact their fire at this fourth bomber had been equally effective, as Ten Caresio and his crew went into the sea in flames immediately afterwards, surviving to claim the Spitfire shot down. Hamblin also survived, but was picked up by an Italian motor torpedo boat sent to rescue the bomber crews, and became a prisoner of war.

1942						
15 Nov	1/4	Ju 88 (a)	Spitfire VB		Maison Blanche area	242 Sqn
25 Nov		Ju 87	"	LE-X	Bone area	"
"		Ju 87 Damaged	"	"	"	
26 Nov	1/2	FW 190 (b)	"	"	Mateur-Tebourba	"
"	1/2	FW 190 Damaged	"		"	
28 Nov		Bf 109 Damaged	"	LE-M	Souk el Arba	"
30 Nov		Ju 88	"	LE-C (c)	Bone area	"
2 Dec		Ba 88 (d)	"	ER766	N Bizerta	"
"	1/2	Ba 88 Damaged (d)	"	"	"	"

TOTAL: 3 and 2 shared destroyed, 2 and 2 shared damaged.
(a) Aircraft of III/KG 76; (b) Combat with aircraft of III/ZG2; (c) Belly-landed on return to base after this engagement; (d) S 79sil aircraft of 280ª Squadriglia, 130° Gruppo Aut Sil; 3 and 1 damaged claimed — 4 shot down.

HOBBS Joseph Bedo   Flight Lieutenant   RAF No 41926

From Folkestone, Kent, Joseph Hobbs joined the RAF on a Short Service Commission in November 1938, and on completion of training was posted to 3 Squadron. He saw service in France during May 1940, while in early July 'B' Flight, of which he formed part, became the nucleus of 232 Squadron. He was posted to the Middle East in early 1941, joining 274 Squadron as a Flg Off. He was promoted Flt Lt later in the year, but on 7 December 1941 his was one of three Hurricanes shot down by Lt Marseille, Ofw Espenlaub and Uffz Grimm of I/JG 27, and he was killed. He was aged 26 at the time.

1940						
17 May	½	He 111	Hurricane I	N2535		3 Sqn
19 May	2	He 111s	„	P2351		„
20 May	¼	He 111	„	N2434		„
„	¼	He 111	„	„		„
1941						
15 Jun		Hs 126	„	W9268	Acroma-Fort Capuzzo	274 Sqn
24 Jun		S.79 (a)	„	Z4704	over naval vessels	„

TOTAL: 4 and 3 shared destroyed
(a) Aircraft of 279ª Squadriglia, 131° Gruppo Aut BT, flown by Serg Magg Riccardo Balagna.

HOLDER Maurice Henry   Flight Lieutenant
RAF Nos. 590816 (NCO); 44070 (Officer)

'Blondie' Holder enlisted in the RAF as an apprentice clerk in January 1934, but later volunteered for aircrew duties. He passed out as a Sgt Pilot in January 1936, and was commissioned on 25 June 1940. He served in Singapore, flying Vildebeeste torpedo-bombers with 36 Squadron until the formation of 243 Squadron in March 1941, when he was posted to this unit as deputy 'B' Flight commander. In November 1941 he was deputy commander, Kota Bharu detachment, and then of the Ipoh detachment in December. He saw action during early 1942 with 243 Squadron, and was evacuated to Ceylon following the withdrawal from Malaya. He then returned to the UK, but here he was killed in a flying accident on 16 July 1942, south west of Aston Keynes, Gloucestershire.

1942						
12 Jan	2	Ki 27s (a)	Buffalo I	W8178 WP-V		243 Sqn
17 Jan	sh 3	G3Ms	„	„		„
„	sh 2	G3Ms Damaged	„	„		„

TOTAL: may have been 2 and 3 shared destroyed, 2 shared damaged.
(a) This is according to information recently obtained from the diary of Sgt 'Vin' Arthur, RNZAF; these claims are not included in *Bloody Shambles, Volume I* (Grub Street, 1992).

JASTRZEBSKI Franciszek   Flight Lieutenant/Kapitan   RAF No. P1296

Born on 10 November 1905, Franciszek Jastrzebski trained as a teacher. He joined the Army Reserve and was sent to Officer Cadet School to train as an infantry officer, later transferring to the Air Force and to the Officers' School at Deblin. He was commissioned a 2nd Lt in 1928, and in August 1929 became an observer in the 5th Regiment at Lido. He was posted to the 4th Regiment at Torun in 1931, while in 1935-37 he was an instructor on an advanced bombing and gunnery course at Grudziadz. He then took pilot training, and in 1938 was appointed commanding officer of 132 Eskadra in III/3 Dyon at Poznan. On 16 September 1939 he was released by the High Command and went to Warsaw, but here was wounded and hospitalised. He escaped from the occupying forces and fled through Hungary and Yugoslavia to Lyons in January 1940. Joining the Armée de l'Air, from 19 May he led six pilots in GC II/1, defending Chateaudun. After the collapse, he reached the UK and on 23 July 1940 joined 302 Squadron as 'B' Flight commander. During a Channel patrol on 25 October 1940, he was attacked by Bf 109s and did not return, his Hurricane, V7593, falling into the sea. His body was later washed up on the island of Sylt; after the war his body was exhumed and reburied in the Kiel War Cemetery. He was awarded the Virtuti Militari, 5th Class, in December 1940, the Cross of Valour in December 1943, and three Bars to this in October 1947. He was also awarded a Croix de Guerre by the French, all his awards being announced posthumously.

1939						
2 Sep		Ju 86	PZL P.11			132 Esk
8 Sep		Bf 110	„			„
10 Sep		Bf 109	„			„
1940						
May/Jun		1 and 1 shared				
15 Sep	sh	Do 17	Hurricane I			302 Sqn
18 Sep		Do 17 Probable	„			„

TOTAL: 4 and 2 shared destroyed, 1 probable.

KOSINSKI Kazimierz   Flight Lieutenant/Kapitan   RAF No. P0296

Kosinski was born on 26 August 1906, joining the 3rd Class of the SPL, Deblin, from which he was commissioned as an observer in 1929. He then served with the 13 Eskadra Towarzyszaca (Army Co-operation) with the 1 Pulk Lotniczy in Warsaw. He subsequently trained as a pilot, and was posted to the 2 Pulk at Kracow, serving in the 122 Eskadra where he became a member of the unit's display aerobatic team. In 1938 he was posted to the Centrum Wyszkolena Lotnictwa Nr 1 at Deblin, to command a training platoon. In September 1939 he evacuated to Rumania and hence to France. Here he led a 'Chimney Flight' known as ECD Ko (short for Kosinski) in defence of the SNCAC aircraft factory at Bourges, where Curtiss H-75A fighters from the USA were being assembled. He set out to escape to England in June, arriving on 7 July 1940. On 9 September he was posted to 307 Squadron as a flight commander, but as this unit was intended for night fighting, he volunteered to fly by day, and on 10 October was transferred to 32 Squadron. He was posted to 308 Squadron on 22 December, where on 1 February 1941 he was awarded the Cross of Valour. He was then moved to 72 Squadron on 24 July, and on 30 October received a Bar to his Cross. He transferred to 302 Squadron in November 1941, becoming a flight commander, but on 26 January 1942 he was shot down into the sea near Brest in Spitfire AA747, and was killed. He was posthumously awarded the Virtuti Militari, 5th Class.

1940					
5 Jun	$3x\frac{1}{5}$	He 111s	Curtiss H-75A		ECD Ko
,,	$2x\frac{1}{5}$	He 111s Damaged	,,		,,
1941					
29 Aug		Bf 109	Spitfire V	W3511	72 Sqn
		Bf 109 Probable	,,		,,
1 Oct		Bf 109	,,	P8783	,,
,,		Bf 109 Probable	,,	,,	,,

TOTAL: 2 and 3 shared destroyed, 2 probables, 2 shared damaged.

LUCAS Norman John   Flying Officer   RAF No.80398

He joined the RAFVR early in the war and on completion of training was posted to 19 Squadron as a Sgt. On 4 November 1941 he moved to 266 Squadron, where he was soon commissioned. With this unit on 9 August 1942 he shared in the first victory to be credited to the Hawker Typhoon. It was to be more than a year before he again achieved a success, by which time he had been promoted Flg Off. Prior to this he had been obliged to bale out of EJ901 south of Lizard Point, Cornwall, as a result of an engine failure. He was to claim two further shared victories subsequently, but when he was awarded a DFC, gazetted on 28 March 1944, the citation mentioned only these two latter claims. Meanwhile he had undertaken his final sortie on 9 February 1944, leaving the unit in early March, tour-expired.. No further information regarding this pilot has been found.

1942						
9 Aug	$\frac{1}{2}$	Ju 88	Typhoon IB	R7696	ZH-C 50 m off Cromer	266 Sqn
1943						
15 Oct		FW 190 (a)	,,	JP906	ZH-L 40m SSE Start Point	,,
,,	$\frac{1}{2}$	FW 190 (a)	,,	,,		
30 Dec	$\frac{1}{2}$	Ju 52/3m	,,	JP969	ZH-D 10m W Ile de Groix	,,
1944						
9 Feb	$\frac{1}{2}$	Do 24	,,	JP925	ZH-J nr Evreux	,,

TOTAL: 1 and 4 shared destroyed.

(a) FW 190A-4 WNr 694 'Black 11' (Oblt V.Klein) and FW 190A-3 WNr 367, 'Black 9'(Oblt H.Sell), both of NAGr 13.

MARTYN William Haig   Lieutenant Commander

Born in Calgary, Canada, in December 1915, William Martyn joined the RAF in October 1936, later transferring to the Fleet Air Arm. He served with 801 Squadron during 1940, flying Skuas, taking part in dive-bombing attacks on Calais in July. He was awarded a DSC in November 1940, then serving with 758, 759 and 760 Squadrons on training duties until 1942, when he served with 800 Squadron during the Operation 'Pedestal' convoy to Malta. He subsequently commanded Seafires on HMS *Indomitable*, and then HMS *Ruler* in 1945, operating in the Okinawa area. Postwar he worked for Canadian National Railways Freight Transport Department; he died in April 1975.

1940						
16/7Apr	$\frac{1}{3}$	Do 18 (a)	Skua		North Sea	801 Sqn
26 Apr	$\frac{1}{2}$	He 111 (b)	,,	7C	Aandalsnes	,,
31 May		Bf 109E (c)	,,	L3030		
1942						
12 Aug		Ju 88 (d)	Sea Hurricane	V7416	Mediterranean	800 Sqn
,,	$\frac{1}{2}$	Ju 88 (d)	,,	,,	,,	,,

TOTAL: 2 and 3 shared destroyed.

(a) 18G K6+FH of 1/KüFlGr 406 flown by Lt zur See Max Keil; (b) He 111P 5J+CN of 5/KG4, flown by Fw Richard Gumbrecht, crash-landed; (c) Aircraft of 3/JG 20 flown by Uffz Werner Francke, who was killed — shot down by Telegraphist/Air Gunner, Leading Airman L.W.Miles, with his rear-firing Lewis gun; (d) Aircraft of I or II/KG 1.

MASTERMAN Cedric Audley   Wing Commander   RAF No. 37199

Cedric Masterman joined the RAF on a Short Service Commission in 1935. Initially he flew Hawker Audax aircraft on army co-operation duties in India, but then took an engineering course in order to obtain a Permanent

Commission. At the outbreak of war 225 Squadron was formed from 'B' Flight of 614 Squadron, and equipped with Lysanders, and he joined this unit as a Flt Lt. It appears that he assisted the Finns in taking over the Lysanders supplied to them by the RAF during their Winter War with the Soviet Union, for in the 1941 New Year's Honours List he received an OBE for the aid he had provided to this nation. In mid 1940 he joined 13 Squadron as a Sqn Ldr when this unit returned from France and exchanged its Lysanders for Blenheims. In 1941 he became a fighter pilot, commanding 232 Squadron during June-July, and then joining 72 Squadron. Promoted Wg Cdr in April 1942, he was posted to Malta as a prospective Wing Leader, but due to the shortage of Spitfires he became Air Advisor to the Governor, Lord Gort. In October 1942, aged 28, he was given command of 227 Squadron, usually flying with Plt Off Gordon Burnside as his navigator. His tour ended in December 1942, when he was awarded a DFC and posted to Egypt.

1941							
22 Nov	1/3	Bf 109	Spitfire VB	AD183	5m SE Gris Nez	72 Sqn
,,	1/3	FW 190	,,	,,	,,	,,
1942							
13 Nov		S 81	Beaufighter VIC	EL234 A	Sicily-Tunisia	227 Sqn
,,	1/2	S 81	,,	,,	,,	,,
14 Nov	1/2	S 79 (a)	,,	,,	off Bizerta	,,
20 Nov		Ca 314 (b)	,,	X8080 C		,,

TOTAL: 2 and 4 shared destroyed.
(a) Actually an S 75 transport aircraft; (b) Two of these aircraft were initially identified as "Ju 88s or S 79s", and were both shot down; they were Ca 314s, one from 173ª Squadrilgia RST (Serg Magg G.Battista Bosio) and one of 58ª Squadriglia, 32° Gruppo, 10° Stormo BT.

MELLOR Frank   Flight Sergeant   RAF No. 1230374
Frank Mellor enlisted in the RAFVR in early 1941, and subsequently served as a Sgt with 111 Squadron during the Tunisian Campaign, being promoted Flt Sgt in early May 1943. On 3 July 1943 he formed part of the escort for Spitbombers of 126 Squadron to attack Biscari, Sicily. Bf 109s attacked, and he failed to return. The award of a DFM was gazetted on 20 June 1944, but with effect from July 1943.

1943						
17 Feb		Bf 109 Damaged	Spitfire VC	JK310	Pont du Fahs	111 Sqn
24 Feb	1/2	FW 190	,,		E Beja	,,
28 Feb	1/3	Bf 109	,,	JK310	NE Beja	,,
4 Mar		Bf 109 Damaged	,,		Beja	,,
5 Apr	1/2	Bf 109	,,	JG914	in sea off Hamman Lif	,,
20 Apr		Bf 109 Damaged	,,	JG/K806	S Bizerta	,,
1 May		Bf 110 Probable	,,	,,	E Ras Zebib	,,
6 May		Bf 109	,,	,,	La Marsa airfield	,,
24 Jun		Me 210	Spitfire IX	EN518	off Cap Passero	,,

TOTAL: 2 and 3 shared destroyed, 1 probable, 3 damaged.

MELVILLE-JACKSON George Holmes   Flight Lieutenant   RAF No. 80842
Born on 23 November 1919, he joined the RAF at the outbreak of war, being posted to 236 Squadron as a Coastal Command long range fighter pilot on 9 July 1940. In August 1941 he was posted to 272 Squadron, accompanying the unit to Malta. In August 1942 he joined 248 Squadron, where on 20 April 1943 he received a DFC as a Flt Lt for at least four aircraft shot down. He was released from the service in 1946, joining the RAFVR in 1949. He subsequently rejoined the RAF, becoming a Wg Cdr on 1 January 1958. He retired on 29 September 1968.

1942					
15 Aug		BR 20	Beaufighter (a)		248 Sqn
13 Oct		Ju 88	,,	WR-D	,,
1943					
9 Feb	1/3 of 3	Ju 88s	,,		,,

TOTAL: 2 and 3 shared destroyed.
(a) He crash-landed at Luqa on return due to damage suffered during this engagement.

MILLS Jack Percival   Flight Lieutenant   RAF Nos. 742477 (NCO); 64890 (Officer)
Jack Mills enlisted in the RAFVR in November 1938. He was posted to 43 Squadron in early July 1940, but on 13 September moved to 249 Squadron at North Weald as a Sgt. He was commissioned in April 1941, and in May accompanied the unit to Malta, flying off HMS *Ark Royal* to the island on 21st. On 5 August 1941 he was posted to the Malta Night Fighter Unit (later 1435 NF Flight). Following a spell as an instructor at 71 OTU, he joined 73 Squadron in July 1943, remaining with this unit until January 1944. He was subsequently awarded a DFC, gazetted on 7 April 1944. He was released from the service as a Sqn Ldr in 1947.

1940					
13 Aug		Bf 109E	Hurricane I		43 Sqn
18 Aug		Ju 87	,,		,,

6 Sep		Bf 109E	,,		,,
27 Sep	¹/₃	Ju 88	,,	P5206 GN-L	249 Sqn
,,	¹/₃	Ju 88	,,	,,	,,

TOTAL: 3 and 2 shared destroyed.

NICHOLLS Charles William Kelvin   Wing Commander   RAF No. 34224

Charles Nicholls was included in the original 1966 version of *Aces High*. Some doubt still remains regarding his final total of claims, but he is re-included here for the avoidance of doubt. Born in Palmerston North, New Zealand, on 7 October 1913, he joined the RAF in 1934 and served in the Middle East before the war. During 1940 he served in 73 Squadron as a flight commander in France, where it is reputed that he claimed six victories. He then became a test pilot at the A & AEE during 1940-41, then commanding the Handling Squadron at ECFS, Hullavington, in 1942-43. Transferring to the RNZAF, he returned home in 1943 to become commanding officer of the OTW, Ohakea, and then commander of the RNZAF Fighter Wing on Bougainville, Solomon Islands, as a Wg Cdr during 1944. He was awarded a DSO for his leadership in the fighter-bomber role, then becoming SASO, Northern Group. Returning to the UK to serve with the RAF again, he was SASO 46 Group, Transport Command, 1945-46, then commanding 24 Communications Squadron, 1946-48. During 1948-49 he was Air Attache in Nanking, China. Awarded an OBE, he retired as a Grp Capt in 1958, and died in early 1996.

1940			
23 May	Bf 110	Hurricane I	73 Sqn
24 May	Bf 110	,,	,,
3 Jun	Bf 110 unconfirmed	,,	,,

TOTAL: 2 destroyed, 1 unconfirmed destroyed, plus possibly 3 further claims of which no details are available.

NOWAK Tadeusz   Flying Officer/Porucznik   RAF No. P76704

Born on 2 June 1914, Nowak joined the SPL at Deblin for the 11th Class, receiving his commission in 1938. Posted to the 2 Pulk Lotniczy in Kracow, he flew with the 121 Eskadra in September 1939. He reached France via Rumania, and from there went to the UK. On 10 July 1940 he was posted to 253 Squadron, seeing action during the Battle of Britain. On 17 October 1940 he crashed Hurricane P3537 due to engine failure. He transferred to 303 Squadron on 13 November 1940, and on 21 January 1941 moved to 315 Squadron as it was forming. He was awarded the Virtuti Militari, 5th Class, on 1 February 1941. He was shot down over Dover during a 'Circus' to Gosnay on 21 September 1941, his Spitfire, AB927, falling into the sea where he was drowned. His body was later washed ashore near Dieppe and was buried at Quiberville. Posthumously he was awarded the Cross of Valour and two Bars, the second being announced on 31 October 1947. He has previously been included in the four victory list in *Aces High*.

1939					
3 Sep	¹/₂	He 111	PZL P.llC		121 Esk
1940					
30 Aug		'Do 215' Probable	Hurricane I	P2883	253 Sqn
31 Aug		He 111	,,	,,	,,
4 Sep		Bf 110 (a)	,,	,,	,,
13 Sep		He 111 Damaged	,,	N2455	,,
29 Oct		Do 17	,,	V6637	,,
1941					
19 Aug		Bf 109E	Spitfire II	P7839	315 Sqn

TOTAL: 4 and 1 shared destroyed, 1 probable, 1 damaged.
(a) Bf 110C-4 of III/ZG 26, either WNr 2104 2N+FP (crashed at East Clandon) or WNr 3101 2N+CBN (crashed at West Horslet).

NOWAKIEWICZ Eugeniusz   Flight Lieutenant/Porucznik
RAF Nos. P783583 (NCO); 1913 (Officer)

Eugeniusz Nowakiewicz was born at Jaslo, Poland, on 2 January 1920. He entered the Szkola Podoficerow Lotictwa dla Maloletnich at Bydgoszsz, qualifying in 1939 and joining the 2 Pulk Lotniczy in Kracow, where he flew with the 123 Eskadra as part of the Brygada Poscigowa. On 18 September 1939 he flew his fighter to Cernantsi, Rumania, subsequently reaching France where he served with a Polish section led by *porpil* Wladyslaw Goethel in GC II/7. With this unit he became the top-scoring Polish pilot of the Battle of France, with three and two shared victories. After the Armistice, he flew to North Africa, and from there reached England on 16 July 1940. On 20 August he was posted to 302 Squadron, but on 8 November he was wounded in combat with a Bf 109 and crash-landed at Detling in P3935. Awarded the Virtuti Militari, 5th Class, on 23 December 1940, he was commissioned on 1 June 1942. On 23 July 1942 he was shot down by ground fire at Pont de Brique, near Boulogne, and force-landed Spitfire VB BL549, WX-E. He was aided to escape by the French Resistance and Polish immigrants, planning to try and steal a Ju 88 with five other escapees, and fly to England. The day before undertaking this plan, they were arrested by the Gestapo, and he spent the next six months in the infamous Fresnes prison. Finally moved to a POW camp, he was transferred to Stalag Luft III at Sagan. Following the long march of winter 1944-45, as the Germans moved prisoners westwards in the face of the advancing Soviets, he was liberated at Lübeck on 2 May 1945. Returning to the UK, he undertook refresher flying training at the PAF Depot at Blackpool, but was released in 1947. He settled in Manchester, running a private business; he is known to have died since.

1940					
11 May		He 111	Morane MS 406	959	GC II/7
1 Jun	1/3	He 111	Dewoitine D 520	62	,,
11 Jun		He 111	,,		,,
14 Jun		Hs 126	,,	62	,,
15 Jun	1/2	Do 17	,,	,,	,,
,,	1/2	He 111 Damaged	,,	,,	,,

(This is the official PAF listing; French records differ somewhat on the dates)

1940					
18 Oct		Ju 88 Probable	Hurricane I	P3205 WX-E	302 Sqn
1941					
13 Mar	1/2	Ju 88 Damaged (a)	,,	Z2523 WX-G	,,
8 May		Bf 109	Hurricane II		,,

TOTAL: 4 and 2 shared destroyed, 1 probable, 2 shared damaged.
(a) This Ju 88 of 4(F)/121, WNr 0419, 7A+LM, flown by Uffz Egon Schmidt, was in fact lost.

O'BRIEN Joseph Somerton   Squadron Leader   RAF No. 34171

The son of a Major, killed in France in 1917, Joseph O'Brien trained on HMS *Conway* for a career in the Merchant Navy. After several years at sea, he obtained a Short Service Commission in the RAF in March 1934. After training at 3 FTS, Grantham, he was posted to 3 Squadron in March 1935. In September the unit was despatched to the Sudan during the Abyssinian Crisis, but on return to the UK he was transferred to 23 Squadron in July 1936, where he was a flight commander when war broke out, and was promoted Sqn Ldr on 1 June 1940. Whilst obtaining his first victory during the night of 18/19 June 1940, his Blenheim was hit by return fire, and shot down. He managed to bale out, but his observer, Plt Off King-Clark, and his gunner, Cpl Little, were both killed. Soon after this he was sent to the Pembrey Operations Room, but on 1 July he joined 92 Squadron as a supernumary Sqn Ldr. Meanwhile on 30 July the award of a DFC was gazetted for his night victory. According to R.M.B.Duke-Woolley, who served with 23 Squadron, on one occasion after he joined 92 Squadron, a Do 17 flew over the airfield one morning at 2,000 feet. He reported that O'Brien leapt into a Spitfire without helmet or parachute, gave chase and shot the Dornier down. However, no confirmation of this has been found in 92 Squadron's records, and for that reason this has been discounted. On 17 August 1940 O'Brien was posted to command 234 Squadron, where he immediately claimed a number of successes. On 7 September however, he became involved in a combat with Bf 110s near Weybridge. Reportedly, he hit one, but was then hit by another. His Spitfire, P9466, was seen to return to Biggin Hill, but here he baled out, the aircraft then crashing at St Mary Cray. When found, he was dead, his left arm severed at the shoulder and his left eye shot out.

1940						
18/19 Jun	1/2	He 111 (a)	Blenheim IF	YP-H	nr Cambridge	23 Sqn
21 Aug	1/2	Ju 88	Spitfire I		Middle Wallop/ Southampton	234 Sqn
24 Aug		Bf 109E	,,		Isle of Wight	,,
6 Sep	2	Bf 109Es	,,		N Beachy Head	,,
7 Sep		Bf 110 Probable	,,	P9466	Weybridge area	,,

TOTAL: 3 and 2 shared destroyed, 1 probable.
(a) Aircraft of KG 4, shared with a Spitfire pilot of 19 Squadron.

POPEK Mieczyslaw   Warrant Officer/Chorazy   RAF No. P782474

Born on 30 October 1916, Popek served as an NCO in the 5 Pulk Lotniczy in Lida/Wilno before the war. During September 1939 he flew with the 152 Eskadra, but on 10th of that month was shot down near Minsk Mazowiecki, and crash-landed his PZL P.11. He escaped to France via Rumania, and flew in a defence flight at Cognac. In the UK he was posted to 303 Squadron in February 1941, serving in this unit for two years. He received the Cross of Valour on 10 September 1941. He then volunteered for the Polish Fighting Team, which went to North Africa as 'C' Flight of 145 Squadron. He returned to the UK on conclusion of the campaign in Tunisia, and was posted to 16(Polish) SFTS at Newton as a flying instructor, although he managed to undertake some operational flights with his old unit. On 15 January 1944 he was killed in the crash of Miles Master DL941 at Tollerton, during a night flight. He received two Bars to his Cross of Valour and a posthumous award of the Virtuti Militari, 5th Class.

1941						
5 May		Bf 109 Damaged on the ground	Spitfire II	P8085 RF-J		303 Sqn
1942						
4 Apr		FW 190	Spitfire VB	AD116	St Omer	,,
3 Jul	1/2	Ju 88 (a)	,,	BL670 RF-K	nr Horncastle	,,
19 Aug	1/2	FW 190	,,	,,	Dieppe	,,
1943						
8 Apr		Bf 109 Damaged	Spitfire IX	EN315 ZX-6	Tunisia	PFT/145 Sqn
20 Apr		MC 202	,,	EN268 ZX-7	W Pantelleria	,,

28 Apr	MC 202	„	EN315 ZX-6	Cap Bon area	„
3 Oct	FW 190 Damaged	„	MA222 RF-A S	Lille	303 Sqn

TOTAL: 3 and 2 shared destroyed, 2 damaged, 1 damaged on the ground.
(a) Ju 88A-4 WNr 140016, M2+BK of 2/KüFlGr 106, crashed at Limes Farm, Baumber, Lincolnshire; Fw H.Majer and crew killed. NB He also claimed a share in the destruction of Ju 88A-4 WNr 140017, M2+KK of the same unit, which crash-landed at Odlings Farm, Aswardby, Lincolnshire, the crew becoming POWs. However this was credited to two other pilots.

SEWELL R.P.W.   Flying Officer   RCAF No.

'Percy' Sewell accompanied 601 Squadron to Malta aboard USS *Wasp* in May 1942. This Canadian pilot served on the island, and thereafter in the Western Desert and in Tunisia. He was promoted Flg Off between September 1942 and March 1943. Nothing else is known regarding his background or subsequent career. He does not appear to have been decorated for his undoubted achievements.

1942						
9 May	$1/2$	Ju 87 Damaged	Spitfire VB		Malta	601 Sqn
10 Jun		MC 202 (a)	„		„	„
12 Jun		Bf 109 Damaged	„			„
22 Aug		Bf 109 Damaged	„	BE392	SW Burg el Arab	„
2 Sep		Bf 109	„	BR478		„
1943						
13 Mar		MC 202 Probable	„	ER776	W Medenine	„
7 Apr		Bf 109 Probable	„	ER220	Chikera	„
„		Bf 109	„	„	„	„
4 May	$1/2$	Bf 109	„	ER517	Kelibia	„
12 Jul		Ju 87 (b)	„	ER556	Augusta area	„

TOTAL: 4 and 1 shared destroyed, 2 probables, 2 and 1 shared damaged.
(a) Aircraft of 378ª Squadriglia, 151° Gruppo, 51° Stormo CT, flown by Mar Lorenzo Serafino; (b) Originally claimed as a Probable, but upgraded on the evidence of ground forces witnesses; 6 claims confirmed; 3 Ju 87Ds of 121° Gruppo Tuffatori actually lost.

SIMS James Ayscough   Flight Lieutenant   RAF Nos. 562604 (NCO); 43944 (Officer)

Born on 2 October 1912, he appears to have enlisted as an Aircraft Apprentice in 1928, being retrained as a pilot and posted to 3 Squadron in September 1939 as a Sgt. After serving with this unit in France in May 1940, he was commissioned on 21 June, and the following month, with the rest of 'B' Flight, formed the nucleus of 232 Squadron. Promoted Flg Off on 25 April 1941, and Flt Lt on 25 April 1942, he remained in the RAF after the war, being confirmed in the rank of Flt Lt on 1 September 1945. He retired on 25 March 1959 as an Acting Sqn Ldr, and died in 1977.

1940						
12 May	2	Ju 87s	Hurricane I	L1681		3 Sqn
19 May		He 111	„	N2435		„
20 May	$1/4$	He 111	„	P3318		„
„	$1/4$	He 111	„			„

TOTAL: 3 and 2 shared destroyed.

SZTRAMKO Kazimierz   Warrant Officer/Chorazy   RAF No. P782842

Born in 1914, he served with the 1 Pulk Lotniczy in Warsaw before the war. In September 1939 he flew with the 113 Eskadra, where unconfirmed accounts report that he claimed two victories, although these were not apparently officially credited to him. He escaped to France via Rumania, where he flew with GC II/10. After the Armistice, he flew across the Mediterranean to Algiers, travelled by train to Casablanca in Morocco, and thence by sea to the UK. In September 1940 he joined 8 B & GS as a staff pilot. In April 1941 he was posted to 317 Squadron, and in March 1943 joined the Polish Fighting Team in North Africa. He returned to the UK in July, and in November was posted to 308 Squadron, where he served until February 1944. In July 1944 he joined 315 Squadron, remaining with this unit until it was disbanded in December 1946. Unconfirmed reports indicate that he was commissioned on 9 June 1945. He was awarded a DFM by the British, and a Cross of Valour with three Bars. He emigrated to Canada after the war, where he died on 21 December 1995.

1939						
1 Sep	$1/3$	'Ju 86' (a)	PZL P.11			113 Esk
„		He 111 (a)	„			„
1940						
7 Jun		Bf 109E	Bloch MB 152			GC II/10
1942						
19 Aug	$1/3$	He 111	Spitfire VB	AD295 JH-C	Dieppe	317 Sqn
1943						
22 Apr		MC 202	Spitfire IX	EN267 ZX-5	off Cap Bon	PFT/145 Sqn
„		Bf 109G	„	„	„	„
6 May		Bf 109	„	EN286 ZX-8	N Tunis	„

TOTAL: 4 and 1 shared destroyed (possibly 5 and 2 destroyed).
(a) Not officially confirmed.

WESOLOWSKI Marian   Squadron Leader/Kapitan   RAF No. P0603

Born in Poland on 25 August 1913, he was a pilot in the 5 Pulk Lotniczy at Lida/Wilno, and in September 1939 was deputy commander of the 151 Eskadra, supporting the Army Narew. On 9 September, whilst on a courier flight for III/5 Dywizjon, he crash-landed his PZL P.7A fighter, but was unhurt. Escaping to France, he joined the 'Chimney Flight' at Bourges, flying Curtiss H-75As, where he made several claims. He then reached the UK, where he joined 308 Squadron, becoming commanding officer on 11 December 1941. He was killed in a flying accident at Woodvale on 9 January 1942 in Spitfire II P8206. He was awarded the Virtuti Militari, 5th Class, and Cross of Valour with Bar.

1940						
24 May	$\frac{1}{3}$	He 111	H-75A			ECD Ko
„	$\frac{1}{3}$	He 111 Damaged	„			„
„	$\frac{1}{3}$	He 111 Damaged	„			„
5 Jun	$\frac{1}{5}$	He 111	„			„
„	$\frac{1}{5}$	He 111	„			„
„	$\frac{1}{5}$	He 111	„			„
„	$\frac{1}{5}$	He 111 Damaged	„			„
„	$\frac{1}{5}$	He 111 Damaged	„			„
1941						
14 Aug		Bf 109E	Spitfire IIA	P8655	NE France	308 Sqn
29 Aug		Bf 109 Damaged	„	P8547	Hazebrouk	„
21 Sep		Bf 109	Spitfire VB	W3798	NE France	„

TOTAL: 2 and 4 shared destroyed, 1 and 4 shared damaged.

WILSON C. Denis W.   Flying Officer   RCAF No. J.

'Denny' Wilson flew with 411 Squadron during 1945, making several claims during the closing weeks of the war. Subsequently he served as a volunteer with the Israeli IDF/AF, flying with 101 Squadron. He claimed two aircraft shot down here, and in the past has been listed with four victories (see *Aces High*, page 659). However, prior to these two latter successes, he sighted an Egyptian aircraft whilst he was on a supply flight in a Spitfire with no ammunition. On seeing his aircraft, the Egyptian pilot immediately baled out, and according to Wilson, he was credited with this as a victory.

1945					
16 Apr	Ju 88 (or He 111)	Spitfire IXE	RR201	nr Grabow	411 Sqn
29 Apr	FW 190 Damaged	Spitfire IXB	MK303	Lauenburg area	„
2 May	Bf 109	Spitfire IXE	ML396	N Lubeck	„
1948					
??	u/i Egyptian a/c	Spitfire IX			101 Sqn
31 Dec	G 55 (a)	„	2015	Sinai	„
„	Spitfire (b)	„	„	Falluga	„

TOTAL: 5 destroyed, 1 damaged.
(a) Pilot baled out; (b) Aircraft was escorting a transport aircraft; shot down with machine guns only.

CHAPTER FOUR

Corrections and Additions to
Listed Pilot Biographies

Explanation of the method in which corrections and additions to the biographical notes contained in *Aces High* have been undertaken here, is as follows:-

i)   Where no correction or addition to the rank and/or service number(s) has occurred, the surname and forenames are listed as the header to the item.

Where a name, rank and/or service number, or numbers, are provided, but no other information follows, this indicates that the only correction or addition relates to these items.

ii) Additional information is provided in two sections. Where there is additional information or corrections to the text detailing the pilot's service, background, etc, this is provided first, in standard typeface.

Corrections and additions to the claim lists provided in *Aces High* are set out after any more general information, and in a smaller typeface for ease of identification, as was used in the original book.

iii) Whereas in *Aces High* individual aircraft letters were provided following serials where they were known, but without the unit code letters, here the latter have been included where appropriate.

iv) In a number of cases research has shown that various pilots entered the RAF at an early age, either as Boy Entrants or as Aircaft Apprentices. Since it has not always been clear in which capacity they first served, I have referred in each case to them as Aircraft Apprentices. It is fully appreciated that several may actually have joined as Boy Entrants.

AANJESEN Ola Gert

Additions to claim list:
Identities of the aircraft flown are as follows:-

1943			
22 Jun	Spitfire IX	MA228	
8 Sep	,,	BS508	
3 Oct	,,	BS249	
25 Nov (not 23rd)	,,	MA870	
29 Dec	,,		FN-Q
1945			
14 Jan	,,	NH516	AH-O

ACWORTH Richard Alvin

He was commissioned in 1937. In summer 1941 he served as an instructor at 71 OTU, Gordon's Tree, Sudan, returning to 112 Squadron on 27 October 1941. In early 1942 he was posted back to the UK, joining 55 OTU from No 1 RAF Depot as a Flt Lt instructor on 26 March. He was promoted Acting Sqn Ldr in August, being posted as a supernumary to 118 Squadron on 30 April 1943. In late 1944 he joined 80 Squadron in 2nd TAF as a supernumary Sqn Ldr, but on 1 October was wounded when an Me 262 of KG(J) 51 dropped anti-personnel bombs on Grave airfield.

Additions to claim list:
1940
20 Nov —   one of the CR 42s was probably that flown by Sottoten Carlo Agnelli of 96ᵃ Squadrilgia, 9° Gruppo, 4° Stormo CT, who was killed.
1941
27 Feb —   Hurricane I flown was V7288, as on 28th.

ADAMEK Mieczyslaw   RAF No P782849 (NCO); P2095 (Officer)

Upon reaching France in 1939, he was posted to GC II/10 of the Armée de l'Air, flying Bloch MB 152s. From October 1940 until March 1941 he served at 10 Bombing and Gunnery School, Dumfries, then joining 303 Squadron on 28 April 1941. He was awarded the Cross of Valour on 10 September 1941, and the Virtuti Militari, 5th Class, on 4 March 1942. He was posted to 58 OTU as an instructor on 20 March 1942, and was commissioned on 1 January 1943. Posting to 317 Squadron occurred on 3 November 1943. His aircraft was hit during a sortie over Dreux on 8 May 1944, but he managed to get back to within five miles of the English coast before baling out. However, he was too low and his parachute did not open. His body was recovered by a minesweeper, and landed at Newhaven, Sussex. His son, Micky, was born two days after his death. He also received three Bars to his Cross of Valour, and an Air Medal with two Bars.

Corrections to claim list:
His victories in 1939 were actually:-
4 Sep	$\frac{1}{4}$	Bf 110
6 Sep	$\frac{1}{5}$	Ju 87

On 23 June 1941 one of the Bf 109Es he claimed was credited as a 'probable'.
REVISED TOTAL; 5 and 2 shared destroyed, 1 probably destroyed, 1 destroyed on the ground.

AGAZARIAN Noel le Chevalier

He was buried in the Knightsbridge War Cemetery, Acroma, Libya. He did not claim two Bf 109Es on 12 August 1940, but may have been credited with a further Bf 110 destroyed or 'probable'. On 15 September 1940 he shared a Do 17 shot down with John Curchin. His total would therefore appear to be 5 or 6 and 3 shared destroyed, 4 and 1 shared damaged.

AIKMAN Alan Frederick

Corrections and additions to claim list:
1942
16 Nov	$\frac{1}{2}$	S 79
,,	$\frac{1}{4}$	S 79

All claims 12-20 November in Spitfire VBs, not VCs.
1943
13 Jan	Spitfire VB	ER652

5 April-17 July all claims in Spitfire VC JK649.

AITKEN The Honourable John William Maxwell

He was born on 15 February 1910 (not 5 February).

ALEXANDER Richard Lear   RCAF No. R67881; USAAF No. O-885165

The claim for a FW 190 destroyed on 19 August 1942 was later downgraded to a 'probable'. His total was thus 5 destroyed. He died in Piper City, Illinois (not Florida).

REVISED TOTAL: 5 destroyed, 1 probable.

ALLAN John Watson   RAF Nos. 741760 (NCO); 89617 (Officer)

He was Mentioned in Despatches on 1 January 1945.

Corrections and additions to claim list:
1943
11/12 Jul, not 12/13 Jul; claims that night and on 29/30 July made in Mosquito HK131.

ALLARD Geoffrey   RAF Nos. 563859 (NCO); 44551 (Officer)

Promoted Flt Lt 8 September 1940.

Revised claim list for May 1940:-
1940
10 May	$\frac{1}{3}$	He 111 unconfirmed	N2319		N Lille
,,		He 111 (a)			Contescourt
,,		He 111 unconfirmed	,,		S Cambrai
11 May	2	He 111s	,,		
12 May	2	He 111s	,,		
15 May		He 111			
16 May		He 111			

(a) Aircraft of III/KG 51.
(b) He may have made further claims. Unless this is the case, his total appears to have been 16 and 5 shared destroyed, 1 and 1 shared unconfirmed destroyed, 2 probables.

ALLEN Hubert Raymond
Line 4 of the biographical notes in *Aces High* should read: "His final posting was as Officer i/c Flying at a 2nd TAF airfield..."

Correction to claim list:
The serial recorded for the aircraft flown on 14 November 1940 has been incorrectly recorded; X7492 was a DH Dominie!

ALLEN James Alan Sandeman   RAF Nos. 914547 (NCO); 172079 (Officer)

ALLEN John Lawrence
He was commissioned in the RAFO on 9 August 1937, and attended 8 FTS from 21 August. He crashed and was injured during a training flight on 18 June 1938, but subsequently completed his training and joined 54 Squadron on 5 December 1938, then transferring to a Short Service Commission. On 24 July 1940 the engine of R6812 was hit by fire from a Bf 109E. Allen attempted to reach the coast, but the Spitfire stalled and spun in at Cliftonville.

ALLEN Percy Frank
He joined the RAFVR in June 1939; he was promoted Flt Lt on 27 June 1943.

ANDREW James Richard   RAF Nos. 1126043 (NCO); 172188 (Officer)
Andrew was from Sheffield. He enlisted in October 1940 and was commissioned on 6 December 1943. He was aged 23 when killed in 1945, and is commemorated on the Singapore Memorial.

Additions to claim list:
All his claims were made whilst flying Spitfire IXs.

ARIES Ellis Walter RAF Nos. 741835 (NCO); 79555 (Officer)
He enlisted in the RAFVR on 23 July 1938.

ARMSTRONG H.A.   RCAF No.

Additions to claim list:
His claims in the period 27-31 March 1943 were all made whilst flying Hurricane IIB HW309.

ARMSTRONG Hugo Throssell
He was killed in Spitfire BS435, FY-F.

ARTHUR Charles Ian Rose

Additions to claim list:
Aircraft flown were as follows:-

1943		
29 Jun	Spitfire VB	JK656
14 Aug (not 12th)	„	NA295
1944		
7 May	Spitfire IX	MJ407
16 May	„	MJ401
14 Oct	„	PL319

ARTHUR Wilfred Stanley
After the First Libyan Campaign he was rested, serving as an instructor at 71 OTU, Sudan. He returned to 3 RAAF Squadron in September 1941 for a second tour.

Correction and additions to claim list:
1940
12 Dec — Aircraft of 84ª Squadriglia, 10° Gruppo, 4° Stormo CT; Serg Onorino Crestani POW.
The Hurricane in which he claimed a victory on 14 April 1941 is listed as P37325 on the combat report, not V7734 as shown.

ASHTON John Henry   Wing Commander   RAF Nos. 745057 (NCO); 77456 (Officer)
John Ashton enlisted in the RAFVR in February 1939; he was commissioned in February 1940. Posted to 85 Squadron from 6 OTU on 2 March 1940, he was shot down on 15 May by Bf 110s of 5/ZG 26, baling out of L1964 south of Ath, and returning to the unit. He was evacuated on 17 May. Subsequently, he remained with 145 Squadron during the summer of 1940, but on 7 November was shot down over the Isle of Wight by Bf 109Es of JG 2, surviving unhurt. It was reported that he flew in Yugoslavia during 1944, but this has not been confirmed.

He ended the war newly-promoted Wg Cdr, but was then demobilised, joining the family business, Beck & Moss, in Stoke-on-Trent. He died in 1988.

Additions to claim list:
1940

13 May	2	He 111s	Hurricane I		85 Sqn

TOTAL: 4 destroyed, 1 unconfirmed destroyed.

ASKEY Michael Wilmot Hamilton   RCAF No. J19049

Although born in Saskatoon, he lived in Winnipeg, Manitoba, before the war. He was killed in a flying accident in JF563 on 28 October 1943, and is commemorated on the Alamein Memorial.

Additions to claim list:
1943

7 Mar		Spitfire VB	EP689	
20 Apr	am	Spitfire IX	EN446	
20 Apr	pm	”	EN147	E Kelibia

(not 30th) — 2 MC202s of 1° Stormo CT were shot down and a third crash-landed

28 Apr			EN333	
15 Jul		Spitfire VC	JL182	Augusta

ATCHERLEY David Francis William   Group Captain

This was not 'Batchy' (Richard), but his twin brother. He was born in York in 1904, attending the Royal Military College, Sandhurst. He was commissioned into the East Lancashire Regiment in 1924, but in 1927 transferred to the RAF, receiving a Permanent Commission in 1929. He served on the North-West Frontier of India from 1931-35, receiving the India General Service Medal and Clasp. He took command of 85 Squadron in November 1938, leading this unit until January 1940. After his crash in 25 Squadron, he was posted to 57 OTU as a Wg Cdr on 24 October 1941, being promoted Grp Capt on 9 March 1942; on 2 April he was appointed to command RAF Fairwood Common, where he remained until posted to North Africa. In 1952 he was appointed AOC, 205 Group, in the Middle East, but on 7 June of that year he disappeared whilst flying a Meteor PR 10 (WB161) of 13 Squadron from Fayid to Nicosia, Cyprus. He was an Air Vice-Marshal at that time.

Additions to claim list:
1939

23 Nov	½	He 111 Damaged (a)	Hurricane I		85 Sqn

(a) This was an aircraft of 1(F)/122.
(b) The aircraft claimed during the night of 16/17 June 1941 is believed to have been a Ju 88A WNr 5210, 4D+LH, of 1/KG 30.

ATHERTON Geoffrey Charles

He transferred to the RAF after the war and was granted a Permanent Commission in 1947. He served at CFE, West Raynham, on the staff of the Day Fighter Leaders' School, 1948-49. He died in Launceston, Tasmania.

AUDET Richard Joseph

From Lethbridge, Alberta, he was killed in Spitfire IX MK950 near Münster.

AYERST Peter Vigne

He is believed to have died on 18 December 1992.

Correction to claim list:
The Hurricane flown on 3 and 4 November 1942 was a Mark IIC, not a IIB.

AYRE Harold Woolgar

He was awarded an AFC in January 1944, as a Flt Lt.

BABBAGE Cyril Frederick   RAF Nos. 742134 (NCO); 89298 (Officer)

He later undertook a further tour of operations on Mosquitos, during which he was twice shot down. After the war he qualified as an A.I. instructor following a course at CFS, but subsequently became an Administrative Officer, in which role he served at RAF Stradishall in 1956.

Correction to claim list:
His victory against the FW 190 of II/JG 26, claimed as a "Curtiss Hawk", occurred on 18 September 1941, not 19 September.

BACHE Knut RAF No. N71920

He was shot down and killed whilst strafing Moiselles airfield on 7 May 1944.

BADER Douglas Robert Stuart

Corrections and additions to claim list:
Hurricane V7467, flown during September 1940-January 1941, carried the letter 'D'. The Spitfire IIA flown during June and early July 1941 carried DB, but was NOT V7467 as shown.

BADGER Ivor James   RAF Nos. 563629 (NCO); 42975 (Officer)

He was posted to the Middle East in November 1941. He returned to the UK in September 1942. Date of death was 30 January 1995.

Additions to claim list:

1940						
19 May	Bf 109	Hurricane I				87 Sqn
„	Bf 109 unconfirmed	„				„
1942						
17 Jun	Bf 109F Damaged	Hurricane IIC	BN357	Sidi Rezegh		73 Sqn
3 Jul	Bf 109 Damaged	„	BN403	Alamein		„
11 Jul	„	„		E Ras el Shaqiq		„

NB. The 'He 114' claimed on 19 May 1941 was an Arado Ar 196 of 5/196.
REVISED TOTAL: 4 destroyed, 1 unconfirmed destroyed, 5 damaged.

BADGER John Vincent Clarence

He attended the Belfast Academical Institute, then enlisting in the RAF as an Apprentice in 1928; he was selected for Cranwell in September 1931. He attended 11 Group Pool as a Sqn Ldr for a refresher course in January 1940.

Corrections to claim list:
The claims for two Do 17s on 21 July 1940 appear to be in error, and his total is therefore now believed to be 6 and 2 shared destroyed.

BAILEY James Richard Abe

RAFVR June 1939; commissioned 26 September 1939. Attended 1 ITW, Cambridge and 3 ITW, Hastings, then Cranwell in January 1940. He was then posted to 5 FTS, Sealand, followed by 1 School of Army Co-operation, Old Sarum, and in June 1940 to 5 OTU, Aston Down. In 1943 he was attached to the 415th Night Fighter Squadron, USAAF (not 615th). When at 54 OTU, 60 OTU was formed from within this unit, and he became CFI. Whilst flying out to North Africa, he spotted and strafed a U-Boat. He flew several patrols with locally-based Beaufighter units before being posted to 600 Squadron.

BALDWIN John Robert   RAF Nos. 908634 (NCO); 122337 (Officer)

BALFOUR Robert Hamish

He died on 28 June 1995.

BALL George Eric

He was killed when Meteor F.3 EE448 dived into the ground at Fairmile, Devon.

Correction to claim list:
The Spitfire flown on 26 May 1940 appears to have been N3198, rather than L3198.

BALLANTYNE James Hamilton

Correction to claim list:
1942
11 Oct —   the MC 202 was flown by Serg Paolo Pedretti of the 353ª Squadriglia, 20° Gruppo, 51° Stormo CT, who crash-landed.
12 Oct —   the claim for an MC 202 may have been a 'probable'.

BAMBERGER Cyril Stanley   RAF Nos. 810024 (NCO); 116515 (Officer)

BANKS Wilfred John

Corrections to claim list:
The Spitfire IX flown on 28 June and 7 July 1944, listed as MH132 in the first case and MH182 in the second, appear both to be incorrect; the aircraft on each occasion is believed to have been NH182. MH132 and MH182 were in a block of serials allocated to Ansons.

BANNER Francis Scott

After serving with 243 Squadron, he was posted to 73 OTU as an instructor, before joining 145 Squadron. He returned to the UK and served at Air Ministry before being posted to 57 OTU as a Flt Lt in November 1944. A month later he was sent to Vickers Supermarine.

Revised claim list:
1943

30 Mar		Bf 109	Spitfire V	ER895	Djebel Abiod	243 Sqn
10 Apr	1/2	Bf 109	„	ES176 SN-D	W Tebourba	„
„		Bf 109	„	„	Oued Zarga	„
13 Apr	1/2	Bf 109 Probable	„		E Beja	„
4 Jul		Bf 109	Spitfire VC	JK189 SN-L	NE Catania	„
13 Jul		Bf 109 Probable	Spitfire IX	EN148 SN-E	Catania	„
„		Bf 109 Damaged	„	„	„	„
„	1/2	Do 217	„	„	„	„
3 Aug		Bf 109	Spitfire VC	JL139 SN-J	W Bronte	„
„		Bf 109 Damaged	„	„	„	„

REVISED TOTAL: 4 and 2 shared destroyed, 1 and 1 shared probable, 2 damaged.

BANNOCK Russell

Corrections to claim list:
1945

5/6 Jan	He 111 at				Husum airfield (not Josum)
23/24 Apr					MV548/Z (not NV548)

BARBER Maurice Clinton Hinton

He was transferred from the Southern Rhodesian Air Force to the RAFVR for the duration of hostilities as a Flg Off on 21 March 1940. Six SRAF officers were transferred at this time, and were allocated service numbers 83205-83210. Barber was given 83209, but was later renumbered 80027, which may have been his original SRAF number. He was promoted Sqn Ldr on 1 December 1941.

Corrections to claim list:
1942

21 Aug	Bf 109 Probable may only	LD-K(Not ET995)
	have been a Damaged	N Gabel Kalelch
1 Oct		AK907 LD-I Kittyhawk I was ET995

BARCLAY Richard George Arthur   RAF Nos. 754320 (NCO); 74661 (Officer)

He was a member of the Barclays banking family; he joined the RAFVR in June 1939. His diaries were published by William Kimber in 1976, edited by Humphrey Wynn, under the title *Fighter Pilot: A Self-Portrait* by George Barclay; the book was republished by Crecy Books in 1994.

Additions to claim list:
1942

16 Jul	Hurricane IIBF	
17 Jul	„ U	El Alamein area

BARGIELOWSKI Jakub   RAF No. P794457

Born in Grabowo in the Lublin region, he entered the air force in 1937, and in September 1939 began fighter pilot training at Ulez. Captured by the invading Soviet army later in the month, he was sent to the White Sea area to work in a stone quarry until May 1940. He was then despatched to a Siberian gulag, where he was kept for 14 months, suffering from blindness, dysentery and scorbatic paralysis due to starvation. Released after the German invasion of the Soviet Union and transferred to Arkangelsk via Moscow, he arrived in Scotland on 13 November 1941. He required more than a year to recover his health before re-commencing flying training. On 20 January 1943 he joined 16 (Polish) SFTS, and was then posted to 41 OTU on target-towing duties. On 28 September 1943 he attended 61 OTU for fighter training, and on 24 January 1944 joined 315 Squadron, where he remained until April 1945. After a brief spell at the PAF Depot at Blackpool, he returned to 61 OTU as an instructor, and in July 1945 was posted back to 315 Squadron. On 17 November 1945 he moved to 303 Squadron where he served until the unit was disbanded. In May 1948 he emigrated to Australia, setting up a jewelry business. He was still living there in retirement at the time of writing.

Additions to claim list:
1944

18 Jul	1/3	V-1	Mustang III	PK-B	
11 Aug	1/2	V-1	„	PK-F	SW Canterbury
15 Aug		V-1	„	PK-V	N Ashford

NB. He also claimed an "Me 109 on fire" off the Norwegian coast on 28 December 1944, but no formal report was filed.
REVISED TOTAL: 5 destroyed, 3 damaged, 1 and 2 shared V1s destroyed.

BARNES William Lawrence LeCoq

Son of Colonel Barnes of Maiden Newton, Dorset. He was commissioned in the Royal Navy before the war, and was promoted Acting Lt on 16 June 1939. He was 24 when killed.

BARNHAM Dennis Alfred   RAF Nos. 903456 (NCO); 60760 (Officer)

Born on 3 June 1920 in Feltham, Middlesex, he was attending the Royal Academy of Art when war broke out, and joined the RAFVR on 4 September 1939, already having obtained a private pilot's licence before the war for flying autogyros. He commenced flying training in July 1940 at 25 EFTS, Belvedere, Salisbury, Southern Rhodesia. In September he moved to 20 SFTS at Cranbourne, Salisbury, then returning to England to attend 57 OTU, Hawarden. He flew out of Malta in a Hudson to Gibraltar on 22 June 1942, and then to the UK in a Sunderland. In mid July he served as o/c 'C' Flight, 57 OTU until March 1943, when he attended the Instructors' Flying School at 2 IFS, Montrose. 5 PAFU at Ternhill followed in May, and then CGS, Sutton Bridge (28 Course). In August 1943 he joined 17 PAFU, Calverley until February 1944, when he was temporarily attached to the RAF College SFTS, Cranwell, now as a war artist. Further attachments followed in this role, to Biggin Hill, 660 Squadron and 84 Group. In June 1944 he joined the Department of Public Relations, Air Ministry, flying around in a Spitfire to various locations. In September he returned to 57 OTU for a refresher course, and then joined 126 Squadron on 20 December. Nine days later he was hospitalised with a duodenal ulcer, which led to his being invalided out of the service on 17 April 1945. He undertook some civil flying after the war, also returning to the Royal Academy. He then taught for a while at the Epsom School of Art before becoming Art Master at Epsom College. Here he remained until 1972, also running the air section of the School CCF. A brain tumour led to early retirement and a move to Dorset, where he painted until his death on 16 April 1981.

Revision of claim list:

1942	
21 Apr	In his logbook he claims the Ju 88 destroyed whilst flying 'J1'.
	He claims the Bf 109 on this date as "damaged/destroyed ?"
24 Apr	He claims this Ju 87, but notes that it was "given to Takali". The aircraft flown
	on this date is believed to have been BP975, rather than BR975.
14 May	He claims in his logbook a Bf 109 "probable/destroyed ?", a Ju 88 shared with
	Ingram and a Ju 88 "given to AA", all while flying Spitfire 'U' "with white spots".
21 May	He does not mention any claims on this date, nor any claims for Italian aircraft.

BARNWELL David Usher   RAF Nos. 976822 (NCO); 61052 (Officer)

He was from Stoke Bishop, Bristol, and joined the RAFVR in December 1939. He was shot down by Sottoten Bruno Paolazzi of the 96ª Squadrilgia, 9° Gruppo, 4° Stormo CT.

Additions to claim list:

1941		
4/5 Sep	Hurricane II	3574
8/9 Sep	,,	2680
14 Oct —	the MC 202 credited to him was in fact damaged; it was an aircraft of the 96ª Squadriglia, 9° Gruppo,	
	4° Stormo CT flown by Ten Annoni.	

BARR Andrew William

He was awarded an OBE.

Corrections and additions to claim list:

1941			
13 Dec	The Bf 110 may have been claimed as a Bf 109		
1942			
1 Jan	One of the two Ju 87s may have been claimed as a Probable		
11 Jan	MC 200 may have been claimed as a G-50		
8 Mar	The MC 200 and the Probable may have been claimed as MC 202s		
22 May			AL199 (not AK199)
1 Jun			CV-W
9 Jun			AK992 (not AK756)
16 Jun			AK756 (not AK745)
24 Jun	G-50	Kittyhawk	AK756

BARRICK John Frederick

He died on 6 September 1997 in Chickasaw, Alabama.

Correction to claim list:
His last claim should read Nakajima Ki 43 Damaged (a)

BARTHROPP Patrick Peter Coleman

Believed shot down by Oblt Karl Willius of I/JG 26 on 17 May 1942. He led a formation of 24 Meteor F.8s from Waterbeach in the 1953 Coronation Review Flypast.

BARTLEY Anthony Charles

He also served briefly in 61 OTU as a Flt Lt instructor in June 1941.

BARTON Anthony Richard Henry   RAF Nos. 30104; 81623

It appears that he transferred from the RN to the RNVR. He was promoted from Temporary Sub Lt to Temporary Lt in April 1940, but on 6 July 1940 became a Plt Off in the RAF. His initial RAF service number, 30104, was probably a holding number with dual RN/RAF rank pre war. He is buried in Totteridge Churchyard, North London.

Corrections and additions to claim list:
1942

9 Apr		2, not 1 Ju 88 Damaged
22 Apr		Ju 87 and Ju 87 Probable, rather than 2 Damaged
24 Apr	$1/2$	Ju 88 rather than a Probable
14 May		Bf 109 and one Probable, rather than just a Probable

REVISED TOTAL: 8 and 1 shared destroyed, 4 and 1 shared probables, 8 damaged.

BARTON Robert Alexander

In December 1941 he joined 58 OTU, but the following month became o/c Training at 52 OTU. In December 1942 he was posted to 9 Group HQ for Air Staff duties as a Wg Cdr. He was Mentioned in Despatches on 1 January 1945.

Corrections and additions to claim list:
1940

15 Aug		P3055
24 Aug	he may only have claimed the shared Bf 109 on this date	
2 Sep	he was flying V6625, US-K, newly taken over from 56 Squadron on this date.	
11 Sep	he claimed damage to only one He 111, flying P3579	
15 Sep	the 2 Do 17s appear to have been claimed as Probables, flying V6693	
27 Sep		V6729
29 Oct		V7538

REVISED TOTAL: may therefore have been 10 and 4 shared destroyed, 3 and 1 shared probables, 6 damaged.

BARWELL Eric Gordon   RAF Nos. 741745 (NCO): 77454 (Officer)

BAYNE Alfred William Alexander

He was a Flg Off instructor at 11 Group Pool in June 1939, becoming i/c 'B' Flight in March 1940 when it became 6 OTU. He was shot down on 25 August 1940, baling out of V7407 into the sea off Portland, and may have been the victim of Hpt Hans-Karl Mayer of I/JG 53, who has been credited with shooting down the Belgian pilot, Jacques Philippart, on that date.

Additions to claim list:
The Bf 109E claimed on 5 September 1940 was flown by Hpt Fritz Ultsch, Gruppenkommandeur of III/JG 54. The Bf 110 on 11 September was flown by Lt Rudolf Volk of 6/ZG 26.
2 Oct —   this claim may have been a $1/2$ share rather then $1/5$. It was a Do 17Z-3 WNr 2659, U5+DM of Stab/KG 2, which crashed near Wickham Market, South Norfolk; Oblt Hans Langer and his crew were taken POW.

BAYNHAM Geoffrey Theodore

He was commissioned in November 1938, and was posted from 53 OTU to 10 Group on 22 September 1941, returning on 26 November.

Corrections and additions to claim list:
1943

25 Apr	Bf 109 Damaged	Spitfire VB	ES146	Pont du Fahs	152 Sqn
8 May	"		ES142	W Delibia	"
25 Jul		Spitfire VC	JL240	Gulf of Milazzo	"

BAZIN James Michael

Bazin was born during 1913. He was promoted Flt Lt in September 1940, and was awarded an AFC in 1942. On completing training at 16 (Bomber) OTU, he then attended 1660 Conversion Unit and 5 Lancaster Finishing School, before being posted to 49 Squadron in May 1944. After a little over one month he was appointed to command 9 Squadron. He flew 25 operational sorties on Lancasters.

Additions to claim list:
1940

10 May	$1/3$	He 111 (not individual victory)			
11 May	$1/5$	He 111 (plus individual claim for He 111 as shown in *Aces High*)			
14 May		E/a (possibly)			
15 Aug		He 111	Hurricane I		607 Sqn

REVISED TOTAL: potentially this accounts for 5 and 2 shared of his citation total of 10.

BEAMISH Francis Victor

He was allocated a 249 Squadron Hurricane, GN-B, V6615, until this was damaged in action on 18 September 1940. He then flew V7507 until this was damaged in the collision on 7 November 1940. He was lost in Spitfire VB W3649, FV-B.

Corrections to claim list:
1940

12 Jul	the Do 17 was shared, and was claimed whilst flying P3304	
18 Aug		P3871

REVISED TOTAL: 9 and 1 shared destroyed, 11 and 1 shared probables, 5 damaged.

BEAMONT Roland Prosper

Wg Cdr Beamont has indicated some corrections to the biographical notes included in *Aces High*, pages 119-120. These are best dealt with by the provision of a duly modified version:- 'Bea' Beamont was born in Chichester, Sussex, on 10 August 1920, seeking to join the RAF on completion of his education. Poor at maths, he failed to obtain selection for Cranwell, but finally managed to gain a Short Service Commission in January 1939. On qualifying as a pilot he was sent to 11 Group Fighter Pool, St Athan, on 13 October 1939. He was posted to France in November to join 87 Squadron, travelling out with his father, who had rejoined the army. When the 'Blitzkrieg' began in May 1940 he was able to claim his first successes during two weeks of fighting before he was sent to London on leave, during which time the unit was withdrawn, and he rejoined it at Church Fenton on its arrival in England. Following action during the summer of 1940, and then six months of night operations, he was posted as part of a flight from the squadron stationed at St Marys in the Scilly Isles to hunt Luftwaffe flyingboats. Awarded a DFC in June 1941, and rated as "*Exceptional as a Fighter Pilot*" in his logbook, he was posted to 79 Squadron in South Wales, but was court martialled for taking a WAAF up in his Hurricane, and was admonished. In December 1941 he was rested, being posted to Hawker Aircraft as a production test pilot on Hurricanes and the early Typhoons, He then flew Typhoons operationally, going first to 56 Squadron in May 1942 as a supernumary Flt Lt, and then to 609 Squadron, where he became commanding officer ten weeks later in October 1942. A dedicated proponent of the Typhoon, he developed night intruding activities, leading 609 in specialised 'train-busting' sorties. He was awarded a Bar to his DFC in January 1943 and a DSO in May. In this latter month he completed his second tour and returned to Hawkers, again testing Typhoons and now also Tempests. In March 1944 he was promoted Acting Wg Cdr at 23, and went to Castle Camps to head a mixed Tempest and Typhoon Wing. He was to meet enemy aircraft in the air again for the first time in two years over Normandy in June, but his Wing (150) was then involved in the interception of V-1 flying bombs, against which he became one of the top scorers, personally claiming 26 and five shared, whilst the Wing was credited with 683 in total. He received a Bar to his DSO in July. In late September 1944, the threat over, the Wing moved to Brussels, and then to Volkel, where it became 122 Wing in 2nd TAF. Immediately after arrival he claimed a further victory, but in early October was about to be posted back to Hawkers again. He had flown 491 operational sorties, 94 of them over hostile territory, so he decided to bring the latter total up to 100, and then accept the posting. However on 12 October, whilst attacking Rheine airfield, his Tempest was hit by Flak and he had to crash-land, becoming a POW until the camp was overrun by the advancing Russians in May 1945. After some delay in getting away from the latter, he returned to the UK and began forming a Tempest II Wing at Chilbolton to go to the Far East as part of 'Tiger Force', but the war with Japan ended before it could be despatched. He then became commander of the Air Fighting Development Squadron at CFE, before leaving the RAF to join Glosters as an experimental test pilot. He later became Chief Test Pilot with English Electric, where he flew the prototype Canberra jet bomber, the P-1 — later developed into the Lightning fighter — and the TSR 2. He made three record Atlantic crossings in the Canberra, including the first ever both ways in one day. He also joined the RAuxAF, commanding 611 Squadron from 1949-51. In 1955 he was Manager, Flight Operations with English Electric, and in 1960 became a Special Director. In November 1965 he became Director, Flight Operations at BAC, Preston, receiving a CBE in 1969. He later held the same position with Panavia, but resigned his BAC directorship in 1978 to concentrate on the development of the Tornado MRCA. After delivery of the first production Tornado to NATO, he retired to Wiltshire, where he was living at the time of writing. In 1977 he had been created Deputy Lieutenant of Lancashire. A biography, *Against the Sun* (Cassell) by Edward Lanchbery was published in 1955, and in 1969 his own autobiography of the war years, *My Part of the Sky* (Patrick Stephens Ltd) was published. He has written eight other aviation titles and many magazine articles.

Corrections and additions to claim list:
1940

14 May	Bf 110	Hurricane I	L1963	Valenciennes	87 Sqn
15 May	Do 17	,,	,,	Louvain	,,
17 May	Ju 88	,,	,,	nr Lille	,,
15 Aug			V7285 (not R7295) LK-L		
3 Sep	Ju 88 Damaged	,,	,,	nr Cirencester	,,
4 Sep	t/e e/a Damaged	,,	,,	nr Bath	,,
12 Oct	Bf 109E Probable	,,	,,	S Portland	,,
1941					
5 Apr	Ju 88 Damaged	,,	,,	S Exeter	,,

1942
4/5 Sep
1944

Date		Type	Aircraft	Serial/Code	Location	Wing
4/5 Sep				R7752 PR-G		
28 May		Ju 188 on ground	Tempest V	JN751 R-B	Cormeilles	150 Wg
16 Jun	½	V-1	„	EJ525 R-B	nr Faversham	„
17 Jun	½	V-1	„	„	N Hastings	„
18 Jun		V-1		JN862 E	10m N Hastings	„
„	½	V-1	„	„	Rye area	„
19 Jun		V-1	„	JN817 T	Tonbridge	„
23 Jun		V-1	„	EJ525 R-B	nr Tonbridge	„
„	½	V-1	„	M	N Hastings	„
27 Jun		V-1	„		nr Ham Street	„
„	2	V-1s	„	EJ525 R-B	N Hastings	„
28 Jun		V-1	„	„	London	„
29 Jun		V-1	„	„	nr Ashford	„
„		V-1	„	„	Ashford	„
4 Jul		V-1	„	JN751 R-B	nr Hastings	„
5 Jul		V-1	„	„	N Eastbourne	„
9 Jul		V-1	„	„	NW Rye	„
10 Jul		V-1	„	„	Ashford	„
11 Jul		V-1	„	„	N Hastings	„
19 Jul		V-1	„	„	NW Rye	„
22 Jul		V-1	„	„	Bexhill	„
„		V-1	„	„	Rye	„
„		V-1	„	„	Hastings-Eastbourne	„
26 Jul	½	V-1	„	JF-M	Hailsham	„
27 Jul		V-1	„	R-B	NW Bexhill	„
„		V-1	„	„	N Tenterden	„
„ (after dark)		V-1	„	„	N Pevensey	„
28 Jul („)		V-1	„	„	N Hastings	„
„ („)		V-1	„	„	N Tenterden	„
10 Aug		V-1	„	„	E Ashford	„
16 Aug		V-1	„	„	N Ashford	„
22 Aug		V-1	„	„	nr Sevenoaks	„

REVISED TOTAL: 9 and 1 shared destroyed, 2 probables, 4 damaged, 1 destroyed on the ground, 26 and 5 shared V-1s destroyed.

BEARD Donald Rowland (not Ronald) Warrant Officer

Born on 24 November 1917 in Sandbach, Cheshire, he attended Sandbach Grammar School, then joining the Post Office and qualifying as an automatic telephone engineer. He enlisted in the RAFVR in September 1939 as an electrician, but remustered as aircrew at the end of 1940. He undertook all his training in the UK, at EFTS, Desford, SFTS, Hullavington, and 57 OTU, Hawarden, where he was on the same course as George Beurling. He was posted to 74 Squadron at Gravesend, moving with the unit to Llandbedr for the defence of Liverpool, and then to Northern Ireland. Returning to England, he was posted to the Middle East, joining 73 Squadron in summer 1942. The first Ju 88 he shot down, crashed in front of a cheering crowd of soldiers. After shooting down the second, he struck the surface of the sea, which broke off the tips of his Hurricane's propeller, the compass and radio also being damaged by the impact. He managed to return, navigating by the stars. At the end of his tour he was posted to HQ, Middle East, Egypt, and thence to Rhodesia on a CFS course, being promoted Wt Off. Here he found a MET Flight of old Hurricanes at Cranbourne, Salisbury, but then became involved as a target drogue-towing pilot for air gunners under training, flying Fairey Battles in this role until after D-Day. He also married in South Africa. Posted home to the UK, he served at Fighter Command HQ at Stanmore, then at APS, Hawkinge, and finally at Charterhall. Near Christmas 1945 he left the RAF to return to South Africa. Here he began a crockery and cutlery importing business, until quotas were introduced. Prevented from continuing the business, he worked for Telenews, an electronic newspaper, as Sales Director until this was sold, when he joined Thompson Newspapers in Rhodesia. Following the declaration of UDI, he moved back to South Africa, working for the *Sunday Express* in Johannesburg, and then for the *Star*. Following an illness, he joined the Atlas Aircraft Corporation, preparing technical publications for the SAAF. His second wife was then killed in a motor accident, so he returned to the UK, where he was living in retirement near Sandbach at the time of writing.

Additions to claim list:

1942

Date	Aircraft	Serial
27 Oct	Hurricane IIC (not Mark IIB)	HL972
16 Dec	„	HL909

The victories claimed in April and May 1943 were claimed in Hurricane IIC HL725.

BEARD John Maurice Bentley   RAF Nos. 740502 (NCO); 89588 (Officer) — not 98588

On 6 February 1941 he was despatched to the RAF aircraft depot at White Waltham for ferrying duties, as 249 Squadron was about to receive Hurricane IIs. Next day he crashed whilst flying a Spitfire and was removed to hospital. He did not return to the unit or to operations, going to 52 OTU on recovery.

Corrections to claim list:
1940

2 Sep	Do 17 Damaged (not destroyed)	P2863
6 Sep		V7313 US-F (an ex-56 Squadron machine)
18 Sep		P3834 (not P3615 — which was flown on subsequent dates)

28 Sep — the Bf 109E he shot down was flown by Hpt Rolf Pingel, Gruppenkommandeur of I/JG 26, who had just shot down A.G.Lewis of 249 Squadron; Pingel baled out into the sea and was rescued by the Luftwaffe ASR service.

BEAUMONT Walter   RAF Nos. 740000 (NCO); 76308 (Officer)

He enlisted in the RAFVR and was commissioned on 10 December 1939. He appears to have been a member of the family of Viscount Allendale of Yorkshire.

BELC Marian

His date of birth was 27 June 1914 (not 1941). He commenced elementary flying training in 1935, and advanced training in 1936. Qualifying as a fighter pilot, he was posted to 143 Eskadra Mysliwska. This unit was disbanded in November 1937, and he was sent to 152 Eskadra at Wilno. In September 1939 he operated in support of Army Modlin as a *plutonowy* pilot (Corporal). On arrival in France he was posted to ECD I/55, a section equipped with Bloch MB 152s and Koolhoven FK 58s (not GC II/1). He reached the UK and joined 303 Squadron on 2 August 1940. Contrary to earlier reports, he was not shot down on 30 September — he escorted another damaged Hurricane from which the pilot baled out. After the 1940 fighting he was sent to Cadet Officers' School and commissioned on 21 May 1941, then returning to 303 Squadron. He was nearly shot down by Oberstlt Adolf Galland on 21 June 1941, but at the last moment Galland was attacked and obliged to force-land by Boleslaw Drobinski. Belc was awarded the Virtuti Militari, 5th Class, on 10 September 1941, and the Cross of Valour with two Bars.

Additions to claim list:
1940

26 Sep				RF-U	
5 Oct				RF-M	
7 Oct (a)				RF-O	
1941					
15 May	1/2	Ju 52 Damaged on ground	Spitfire II	P8099	303 Sqn
„		Minelayer *Dirk* damaged on water	„	„	„
24 Oct				RF-S	

REVISED TOTAL: 7 destroyed, one shared damaged on the ground.

BELL Maxwell Heron

He enlisted in the RAAF during 1940.

BENHAM Douglas Ian   RAF Nos. 745064 (NCO); 104443 (Officer)

Additions to claim list:
1942

29 Nov	Spitfire VB	EP951
4 Dec	„	ER676

BENNIONS George Herman (not Harman)   RAF Nos. 563057 (NCO); 43354 (Officer)

During September 1940 'Ben' Bennions was obliged to force-land at Hornchurch on 11th and at Lympne on 20th, whilst he belly-landed at Rochford on 7th (not 15 August, as previously recorded); his aircraft was also damaged by Bf 109s on 18th. During the Battle of Britain he flew 17 different Spitfires, 14 of them in September alone. On 1 October he was shot down in X4559 over Henfield, Sussex (not Hatfield), baling out semi-conscious, wounded in the face, head, right arm and right leg. He was taken to Horsham Base Hospital initially, later transferred to the Queen Victoria Hospital at East Grinstead. In 1943 he went out to North Africa in charge of a party of groundcrew of 219 Squadron, then being posted as liaison officer with the Spitfire-equipped US 31st and 52nd Fighter Groups. After being wounded again when the landingcraft going ashore at Ajaccio was bombed, he was in hospital in a convent for a short time, and was then air evacuated home to the UK via North Africa in November 1943. He had been Mentioned in Despatches during 1942. He was retired on a 50% disability in 1946, becoming welfare officer of a building contractor for a short time. He received training on an emergency teacher training scheme during 1948, becoming a teacher of wood and metal work. He was recalled into the RAF briefly during the Suez crisis of 1956, but apart from that, has lived and worked in North Yorkshire since the war, where he continues to live in retirement at the time of writing.

Additions to claim list:
1940

30 Sep	Bf 109E Probable	Spitfire I	EB-B	41 Sqn

NB. His claims in July and August were made in EB-J; He flew K on 5th (first claim) and 9-15 September, L (second claim) on 5th and 6th, A on 17th and 18th, and J on 23rd and 28 September.

BENSON James Ghillies   RAF Nos. 754580 (NCO); 81365 (Officer)

Born on 17 July 1914 in Tufnell Park, North London, he was educated at Westminster School and then worked for Esso Petroleum before enlisting in the RAFVR in June 1939. After his service with 141 Squadron, he was posted to an Operational Conversion Unit in Scotland before joining 62 OTU. (Correction to text in *Aces High*); line 15 "...was promoted Wg Cdr, while Brandon became a Sqn Ldr." Line 16 "...to form 1692 Bomber Support Training Unit which Benson..." After the war he returned to Esso, becoming aviation manager and a marketing manager. He retired in 1974, retaining an interest in gliding and hot air ballooning.

Corrections and additions to claim list:
Dates should read:-
1940
22/23 Dec
1942
15/16 Feb
4/5 Jun
1943
14/15 Apr
3/4 Jul
1944
12/13 Jun and onwards

27/28 Jun		V-1	Mosquito XIX	MM630 RS-E	Calais-Le Touquet	157 Sqn
2/3 Jul		V-1	„	MM670 RS-H		„
5/6 Jul		V-1	„	MM630 RS-E		„
6/7 Jul	2	V-1s	„	„	Eastbourne	„
17/18 Jul		V-1	„	„	SE Dungeness	„

BERG Rolf Arne

Correction to claim list:
1942
2 Oct   The victory was claimed in Spitfire AA936 FN-L, not AR936.

BERRY Frederick George

Born on 4 January 1914, son of a physical training instructor in the Royal Regiment of Fusiliers, at Fort William, Calcutta, India, Frederick Berry became an Aircraft Apprentice at Halton in August 1929. Qualified as an AC1 Rigger in 1932, he was posted to 5 FTS, Sealand. He was promoted LAC in August 1933, and in March 1934 was posted to 24 Squadron, Hendon. In January 1935 he undertook further training at Halton, but volunteered for pilot training and was selected in July 1936. He trained at 9 FTS, Thornaby, and then in February 1937 joined 43 Squadron as a Sgt. In August 1939 he was posted to 1 Squadron, accompanying this unit to France. He was promoted Flt Sgt on 1 April 1940.

BERRY Joseph   RAF Nos. 1177137 (NCO); 118435 (Officer)

Joseph Berry was born on 28 February 1920 in Tursdale, County Durham. His family moved to Hampeth, near Felton, Northumberland, from where he attended Duke's School, Alnwick, matriculating and joining the Civil Service, where he entered the Inland Revenue as a tax officer. He was posted to Nottingham in this role, where he joined the RAFVR in August 1940. On completion of training he was posted to 256 Squadron on Defiants, but on 4 November 1941 he was obliged to abandon T4053 due to engine failure over the west coast. His gunner, 746874 Flt Sgt E.V.Williams, baled out too, but was blown out to sea and drowned. Berry was commissioned on 14 March 1942, marrying five days later, but later in the year was posted to 255 Squadron, serving with this unit in the Mediterranean area, where he was to claim three victories. The first Bar to his DFC was awarded on 4 August 1944, and he was promoted Sqn Ldr on 10th of that month. He is buried in Holland.

Additions to claim list;
1943

8/9 Sep		Me 210	Beaufighter VIF	S Capri	255 Sqn
9/10 Sep		Me 210	„	Lago Paolo	„
23/24 Oct		Ju 88	„	S Volturno River	„

(all claims made with Flg Off I.Watson as radar operator)
1944

12/13 Aug	2	V-1s	Tempest V	EJ590 L	501 Sqn
13/14 Aug		V-1	„	„	„
15/16 Aug	2	V-1s	„	„	„

| 19/20 Aug | V-1 | „ | EJ584 Q | | „ |
| 30/31 Aug | V-1 | „ | EJ596 C | Faversham | „ |

REVISED TOTAL: 3 destroyed, 59 and 1 shared V-1s destroyed.

BERRY Ronald   RAF Nos. 740170 (NCO); 78538 (Officer)

It appears that 'Ras' Berry enlisted in the RAFVR in April 1937, and was commissioned on 1 December 1939. On 29 June 1943 he joined 53 OTU as o/c Training Wing at Kirton-in-Lindsey. In April 1944 he served at HQ, ADGB. He was awarded an OBE on 1 January 1946, and became a CBE in 1965. It was recorded in *Aces High* that he had died in 1991. This was incorrect, for which apologies are offered; at the time of writing he was believed still to be alive, although in poor health.

Corrections to claim list:
1940

28 Aug —	claim made in P9459 XT-N, not R6751	
31 Aug —	R6626 was XT-Y	
17 Sep	½ Bf 109E Probable (not individual claim)	X4347
27 Sep	½ Bf 109E Probable (not individual claim)	
27 Oct		P7309
7 Nov	Bf 110 shared by 11 pilots, not four	P7449
8 Nov		„
17 Nov		P7489
23 Nov		P7449 (both claims)

NB. The Spitfire VC shown as the aircraft flown on 23 November 1940 for the claim for the CR 42 Probable, should be dropped to relate to the next claim, made on 9 November 1942.
1943
All claims in 1943 made in Spitfire IXs.

31 Jan		should read Spitfire (not Sptifire)
2 Mar	Spitfire IX	EN240
26 Apr	„	EN137

REVISED TOTAL: 14 and 10 shared destroyed, 7 and 2 shared probables, 17 damaged, 7 destroyed on the ground.

BEURLING George Frederick

On 27 May 1943 he arrived at the Central Gunnery School as a Flg Off. Here on 8 June he was accidentally fired on during a mock dogfight, baling out of Spitfire IIA P7913 when the engine caught fire. The engine and other wreckage of this aircraft was recovered by aviation archaeologists during 1985.

Corrections and additions to claim list:
1942

6 Jul (b)	
12 Jul	
23 Jul	BR565 was U, not V
1943	BR135 (not BF135)
24 Sep	MA585 KH-B
30 Dec	MH883 VZ-B

NB. In 1943 MA585 carried 29 swastikas on the cowl in front of the cockpit; MH883 carried 30.
Note (b) states that Serg Magg Pecchiari was picked up from the sea. This is not the case; he was killed in this engagement.
Note (f) to the claim list notes in *Aces High* should read "Actually a Re 2001 of 358ª Squadriglia, 2° Gruppo CT."

BEYTAGH Michael Leo ffrench

He was posted to 52 OTU as a Flt Lt, o/c 'E' Squadron on 17 December 1941. He moved to 53 OTU as Sqn Ldr CFI on 31 December 1941, and on 18 January 1942 to 55 OTU.

Addition to claim list:
1940

| 5 Sep | Ju 88 Damaged | Hurricane I | V7209 | | 73 Sqn |

BIRD-WILSON Harold Arthur Cooper

Correction to biographical notes in *Aces High*; line 3 should read "...causing him to crash, seriously injuring...". On release from hospital he attended the 12 Group Fighter Pool in January 1940 for operational training before joining 17 Squadron. He joined 56 OTU as an instructor in November 1940. On 17 January 1941 he was posted to 55 OTU, then joining 234 Squadron on 10 March 1941. After the war he joined CFE at West Raynham in July 1952 as a Wg Cdr, to replace Wg Cdr John Baldwin, who had been sent to Korea. He also departed for Korea in February 1953 on a fact finding tour, and here he requested permission from the USAF to fly on F-86 operations, despite having strict instructions from the AOC, Fighter Command, Sir Basil Embry, not to fly. Permission was refused, so he persuaded the commanding officer of 77 Squadron, RAAF, to allow him to fly one of that unit's Meteor F.8s, undertaking six fighter-bomber sorties over North Korea.

Corrections and additions to claim list:
1940

| 19 May — | the claim may have been for a Bf 109 destroyed unconfirmed, rather than damaged, in which case his total |

would be increased by one.
Notes: the Do 17 shared on 18 May was a Do 17P of 4(F)/14; the Hs 126 shared on 21 May — not with two other pilots, but with five — was 5D+DK of 2(H)/31Pz.

BIRKSTED Kaj

'Birk' Birksted was born on 2 March 1915 in Boston, USA, where his father had a business. As a boy he was sent home to Denmark to be educated. On completion of his schooling he joined the Danish Naval Air Force, training as a pilot during 1936-37. He was Watch Officer at Copenhagen Naval Air Station on 9 April 1940 when the German invasion occurred, and a week later, having drunk with the airfield guards until they were insensible, he escaped by boat to Sweden. Here he was imprisoned in Malmo, as he had no passport or money. Provided with a temporary passport by the Embassy, he made his way to Norway, from where on 6-7 May 1940 he sailed on the destroyer HMS *Wolverine* to the UK. At that early stage of the war there was no provision for foreigners in the RAF and he was refused. In a fit of anger he signed on the Danish-captained MS *Tasmania* as a greaser, sailing for Burma. On arrival at Capetown he received a telegram ordering him to the 'Little Norway' air force training camp that had meanwhile been set up near Toronto, Canada, for pilot training. He arrived back in the UK from there six months later, initially joining 43 Squadron, and then 331 (Norwegian) Squadron on its formation on 21 July 1941. On leaving 331 in April 1943 he spent two months as an instructor at the Fighter Leaders' School, returning to North Weald in July 1943 and taking over 132 (Norwegian) Wing in August. He was awarded a DFC on 25 August 1942 and a DSO on 26 November 1943. In March 1944 when his second tour ended, he was attached to 11 Group Combined Control Centre at Uxbridge as an Operations Planner, working on the air defence for the Normandy landings. After his return to Denmark in 1945 he became an adviser to the War Minister in regard to the formation of an independent Danish Air Force, of which he became the first Inspector General. The award of the Norwegian War Cross with Swords was made on 21 July 1944, while after the war he received the Haakon VII Freedom Cross. Not comfortable in the Danish forces due to jealousy towards his wartime achievements, he resigned. In 1953 he joined the international staff of NATO in Brussels, where he remained until his retirement in 1980, serving on the European Aerospace Committee. He then settled in Hampstead, North West London, with his English wife. He died on 23 January 1996.

Corrections to claim list:

1942		
29 Nov		BS547 FN-T (not BN547)
1944		
14 Sep		BS548 (not B5548)

BISDEE John Derek   RAF Nos. 741770 (NCO); 76575 (Officer) — not 76573

He enlisted in the RAFVR in July 1938. From 14 September-21 October 1945 he was o/c RAF Luqa, Malta.

Corrections and additions to claim list:

1940		
7 Oct		R4560 is not correct.
1942		
21 Apr	Spitfire V	BP954 D

BJORNSTAD Bjorn   RAF No. N373 (or N374)

He was posted from 331 Squadron to 57 OTU as an instructor in May 1943. In August 1943 he joined 332 Squadron, while in January 1944 he went to the Fighter Leaders' School as an instructor with the rank of Captain.

BLACKADDER William Francis

Corrections and additions to claim list:

1940	
11 May —	Both claims made 20 miles NE Brussels — not over France
18 May —	His Hurricane, P2571 AF-G was damaged by return fire from Do 17Zs of II/KG 76, and he force-landed at Vitry
26 Sep —	The He 111 claimed on this date was probably a Bf 110C, 5F+CM of 4(F)/14.

BLAKE Arthur Giles

Born in 1917 in the Slough area of Buckinghamshire, Arthur Blake attended Slough Grammar School, where he became a lifelong friend of Richard Cork. Together they joined the Windsor Rugby Club and the Eton Excelsior Rowing Club, the latter in 1936. In 1934 Blake followed Cork to work for Naylor Brothers of Slough, having remained two years longer at school than the latter. In 1938 both applied for commissions in the Royal Navy together, with a view to flying in the Fleet Air Arm. Both were offered Short Service Commissions, entering Greenwich Naval College together for basic training, and then attending Pilots' Course No 6 from 2 May 1939 as Midshipmen (A). Both became Sub Lts, and in late August were posted to the RAF's 20 EFTS, Gravesend, followed by 1 FTS, Netheravon, in early November. Both gained their pilots' badges in March 1940 and were posted to HMS *Raven* at Southampton, for deck landing and other training with 759 and then 760 Squadrons. In June 1940 they were sent with a group of other newly-qualified Naval pilots, including Dennis Jeram, Francis Dawson-Paul and 'Jimmie' Gardner, to 7 OTU, Hawarden, for operational training on Spitfires, then going on loan to the RAF. When killed on 29 October 1940, he had been recommended for the award of a DFC. He was buried at St Mary's Church, Langley, Buckinghamshire, aged 23.

Corrections to claim list:
1940
17 Sep — this claim was made in a Spitfire II, not a Mark I.

BLAKE Minden Vaughan

Correction to claim list:
Above the final claim, dated 19 August, insert "1942".

BLAKESLEE Donald James Mathew   USAAF No. O885264

He joined the Army Reserves in October 1938 as a 2nd Lt of Infantry, but obtained a discharge on 13 September 1940 to join the RCAF. He transferred to the USAAF as a Capt on 29 September 1942, becoming a Major on 1 January 1943 and a Lt Col on 7 July. He became a full Colonel on 8 March 1944. He transferred to the Regular Army as a Lt Col on 5 July 1946 until the USAF became a separate service. He took command of the 27th Fighter Escort Group on 7 December 1950, leading the unit until 3 March 1951. He returned to the unit, which had become the 27th Wing, on 6 July 1952 and flew F-84 Thunderjets with the unit over Korea. He remained in command until August 1954. He later commanded the 312th Fighter-Bomber Wing during 1955, and was promoted Colonel in March 1963. He retired from the service in April 1965.

Corrections and additions to claim list:
1941
18 and 22 November, and 8 December — claims made in Spitfire AD421, YO-H
1942
28 April and 30 May — claims made in Spitfire BL753 YU-H
27 June - 19 August — claims made in Spitfire EN951
1943
15 Apr P-47C WD-F
1944
7 Jan-29 May — claims made in P-51B WD-C

23 Mar	FW 190 Damaged	P-51B	4th FG

REVISED TOTAL: to include 10 and 1 shared damaged.

BLATCHFORD Howard Peter

Attended Concordia College and Eastwood High School.
   Correction — the penultimate line of the biographical notes in *Aces High* should read "...Obfw Hans Ehlers." (not Obffz)

Addition to claim list:
1940
2 Oct — this was a Do 17Z-3 WNr 2659, U5+DM of Stab/KG 2, which crashed near Wickham Market, South Norfolk; Oblt Hans Langer and crew POW.

BLOK Stanslaw   RAF No. P1681

Blok was born in Wejherowo, near Gdansk, in 1919. He joined the Polish Air Force in 1938, escaping with a group of cadet officers led by the class commander, Witold Urbanowicz, to France via Rumania and the Mediterranean. Subsequently he reached the UK. He was trained at 16 (Polish) EFTS at RAF Newton, and then at 60 OTU, being posted initially to 65 Squadron. He then moved to 315 Squadron and was commissioned at the end of 1941. In early 1942 he became involved in a fight over a girl dated by his friend. It turned out that the opponent was the girl's husband, and both pilots were posted to the far north of the British Isles, Blok serving with 164 Squadron. He returned to 315 Squadron at the start of 1943, but on 3 February of that year, having claimed an FW 190 during 'Circus 258', his Spitfire was severely damaged. He attempted to bale out, but the cockpit canopy jammed and he was forced to fly back across the Channel, which he succeeded in doing. He remained with the unit until the end of the war, staying on in the UK thereafter, living in Lidell. He died some years ago. He was awarded the Virtuti Militari, 5th Class, and the Cross of Valour and Bar.

Corrections and additions to claim list:

21 Sep				AD134 (not AB134)	
1942					
31 May	½	Ju 88 Damaged	Spitfire V	R6801	164 Sqn
1943					
3 Feb			Spitfire IX	BS409 PK-B	
13 May			„	BS411 PK-J	

| 15 May 1945 | „ | EN172 PK-K |
| 21 Feb | Mustang III | KH492 |

BLOMELEY (not BLOMLEY) David Henry

From Stafford, David Blomeley was the son of a headmaster, attending King Edward's School, Stafford, in 1933-34. He then worked for South & Stubbs, agricultural valuers and surveyors in the town until he entered the RAF, receiving his Short Service Commission in March 1938. He attended 7 EFTS, Desford, 11 FTS, Shawbury, and then joined 1 Squadron on Hawker Furies. He was posted to 92 Squadron on 8 March 1940, then to 25 Squadron ten days later, and on 8 April to 151 Squadron. He was attached to 607 Squadron in France, 13-28 May, then returning to 151, but on 8 June he was shot down by Flak in Hurricane P3315, and baled out over Amiens. Evading capture, he escaped from Cherbourg at the end of the month with the survivors of the 51st Highland Division. His logbook was lost due to enemy action, but it appears that he claimed five victories with 607 Squadron and two more with 151 Squadron in late May. He took part in the fighting of summer 1940, claiming in his logbook to have taken part in the shooting down of a number of aircraft, but this is not confirmed by squadron records or available combat reports. On 16 August 1940 he was shot down again, baling out of Hurricane 4181. He was then posted to 9 FTS, Hullavington, as an instructor on Masters. He later undertook an instructor's course at CFS, Upavon, then serving at 1 SFTS, Netheravon, from November 1941 to the end of January 1942, followed by 17 AFU, Watton, from January to March 1942. In mid March he moved to 60 OTU at East Fortune, and then in July to 287 Squadron, an AA co-operation unit, flying Defiants. In January 1943 he attended 51 OTU and in early April joined 605 Squadron to undertake intruder operations on Mosquitos. Here he crewed with Flg Off Birrell, the pair intercepting and shooting down four aircraft between August and November. On the night of 17/18 August, during the Bomber Command raid on the German secret weapons base at Peenemunde, they flew to Jagel airfield where they were attacked by a single-engined fighter believed to have been a Bf 109. This overshot, allowing Blomeley to shoot it down into water. He then attempted to photograph the tail, which could be seen, sticking out of the water. He received an immediate award of the DFC in October. At this time his Mosquito, UP-O, carried 14 swastikas painted on the nose, nine of which he claimed to be confirmed. He left the unit in February 1944, going to 60 OTU at High Ercall as CFI until mid April, and then to 13 OTU as Gunnery Leader and instructor. On 13 June 1945, still with the unit, he force-landed a Mosquito, while in July he conducted service trials of the Tempest II at Middleton St George. He left the RAF in March 1946, training as a forester at the Forest of Dean Foresters' School. In early 1950 he was invited to rejoin the RAF, again becoming an instructor. He served at 1 FRS, Finningly, December 1950-February 1951, then attended 124 Course at CFS, Rissington, until June 1951. He then instructed on Meteors at 203 AFS, Driffield, until December, when he moved to 208 AFS, Merryfield, and then in July 1952 to 209 AFS, Weston Zoyland. During this period he received an A1 instructor's category, allowing him to test other instructors, and undertook much low level display work. During 1953 he took part in the Queen's Coronation Review Flypast, and received the Queen's Commendation during the year. In November 1955 he attended the Bomber Command Jet Conversion Course, then joining 40 Squadron at Wittering on Canberras in May 1954. He was awarded an AFC during 1954. In February 1955 he was posted to 138 Squadron at Gaydon as 'B' Flight commander on Valiant bombers. In October 1956 the unit moved to Malta for the Suez operation, during which he undertook two bombing raids on airfields at Fayid and Almaza in Egypt, before returning to Marham in December. He was then offered promotion, but in a non-flying role, so instead he retired and at age 44 emigrated to New Zealand, where he joined the NZ Forest Service. He also became a Rescue Team Leader and volunteer ambulance driver. In 1985 he returned home to the UK to retire, settling in Devon. He died in 1991.

Corrections and additions to claim list:
1940

| 13 - 28 May — | Possibly five claims with 607 Squadron in France. | | | | |
| 2 Jun | Bf 109E | Hurricane I | P3275 | Rouen area | 151 Sqn |

9 July - 5 August — Possibly some claims — not confirmed.
REVISED TOTAL: 6 known claims; personally claimed 14, 9 of them confirmed. Full details cannot be provided.

BOBEK Ladislav   RAF Nos. 788011 (NCO); 133995 (Officer)

BOCOCK Eric Percy William   RAF Nos. 903477 (NCO) ; 61215 (Officer)

He was posted to 72 Squadron from 58 OTU in April 1941. After service with 234 Squadron he was sent out to join the Spitfire Wing in Australia, commanding 549 Squadron there from January 1944 until 1945. He took part in the longest-ever Spitfire operation on 27 November 1944, escorting USAAF B-25s to Timor in the Dutch East Indies. He was killed when Meteor EE490 of the Central Gunnery School broke up during a slow roll near Scarborough, Yorkshire, on 13 September 1946.

BODDINGTON Michael Christopher Bindloss
RAF Nos. 740604 (NCO); 88017 (Officer)

After the war he is reputed to have become somewhat eccentric, and impecunious. He lived for a time on a caravan site in Cumbria, but having researched the cheapest place in the world to live, emigrated to New Guinea during the 1970s, where he subsequently died.

Corrections and additions to claim list:
1940
4, 5 and 6 Sep — the serial X3057 reported as the aircraft flown on these dates is not correct. The correct serial is believed
            to have been N3057.
1943

6 Jul	Bf 109 Damaged	Spitfire VC	JK260 LE-K	Syracuse area	242 Sqn
10 Jul	,,	,,	,,	Gela-Cap Scoldini	,,

All remaining claims in 1943.

BODIE Crelin Arthur Welford
He was granted a Short Service Commission just before the outbreak of war, and appointed Acting Plt Off on 23 October 1939.

Additions to claim list:
1940

8 Aug	1/3	He 111	Spitfire I		66 Sqn

REVISED TOTAL: 5 and 6 shared destroyed, 1 unconfirmed destroyed, 8 and 2 shared probables, 3 and 1 shared damaged.

BODIEN Henry Erskine   RAF Nos. 566662 (NCO); 45720 (Officer)
Born in Hackney, East London, in 1916, he joined the RAF in September 1933 as an Aircraft Apprentice at Halton, and trained as a fitter. He was later accepted for pilot training, and on 28 October 1940 arrived at 6 OTU from 48 (Coastal) Squadron for fighter training as a Sgt. Commissioned in May 1941, the award of his DFC was gazetted on 7 April 1942, and he was promoted Flt Lt on 1 May 1943. During 1943 he was an instructor at 51 OTU, and in December commanded 551 Training Squadron of that OTU as a Sqn Ldr. On 13 February 1944 he was posted to 21 Squadron in 2 Group on Mosquito fighter-bomber duties, flying Day Rangers. He was awarded a DSO for these activities, gazetted on 5 September 1944. He remained in the RAF after the war, becoming a substantive Sqn Ldr on 1 August 1947. He was attached to the USAF in Korea, 1950-51, and flew B-26 Invaders on night interdiction sorties, being awarded a US Air Medal. On his return he commanded 29 Squadron from May 1951-January 1952. In April 1953 he relinquished his RAF commission on transfer to the RCAF. Details of his career thereafter are not known.

BOITEL-GILL Derek Pierre Aumale
Derek Boitel-Gill was born in 1911, rather than 1909. He was educated at Milburn Lodge School and Steyne School, Worthing. After his recall to service in April 1940, he attended 5 OTU as a Flt Lt before joining 152 Squadron. During June he was posted briefly as an instructor on Defiants, but rejoined the squadron at the end of the month. On 1 July 1941 he was posted to 59 OTU as o/c Flying Wing, being promoted Wg Cdr on 26 August 1941.

BOOT Peter Victor   RAF Nos. 740531 (NCO); 76455 (Officer)
He enlisted in the RAF about July 1937 and was commissioned on 1 December 1939. He then attended 6 OTU before being posted from there to 1 Squadron in France on 23 March 1940. He left 1 Squadron on 19 October 1940 to become an instructor at 5 OTU, but on 22 February 1941 was despatched to CFS on an instructors' course. On 8 September 1941 he joined 4 SFTS as a Flt Lt to instruct.

Corrections and additions to claim list:
1940

12 May		Bf 109 Damaged — own aircraft damaged by a Bf 109E of 2/JG 27.	
14 May	1/2	Bf 110 — rather than full individual victory.	

REVISED TOTAL: 5 and 1 shared destroyed, 2 damaged.

BOSMAN Andrew Christiaan
Correction to biographical notes in *Aces High*: In 1941 he served as a Captain in 4 SAAF Squadron, not 3 SAAF Squadron as stated.

Addition to claim list:
1944
27 May — the Bf 109G of 1° Gruppo CT, RSI, was flown by Serg Magg Giorgio Leone of 2ª Squadriglia, who was killed.

BOUDIER Michel   RAF No. F30159

BOUGUEN Marcel   RAF No. F30155
His claim for a FW 190 Probable on 17 August 1943 is believed to relate to an aircraft of 4/JG 26 (Blue 17, Wnr 410001) in which Uffz Karl Hadraba was killed when he crashed near Fruges following this combat. He was awarded a DFC in April 1944.

BOULTER John Clifford

Corrections and additions to claim list:
1940
23 Sep —   Flying N3267, not X4248.
30 Sep —   Bf 109E was destroyed rather then Damaged, according to the Squadron ORB; the aircraft was reported last
              seen on fire.
7 Nov   1/11 Bf 110   Spitfire II   P7436   10m NE Rochford   603 Sqn
17 and 23 Nov — P7359 and P7597 were Spitfire IIs, not Mark Is.
REVISED TOTAL: 5 and 1 shared destroyed, 3 and 1 shared probables.

BOUSSA Adolph Lucien   RAF No. 101465; Belgian No. 28112

His birthplace was Glain-les-Liège. He became a pupil pilot in the 67th intake of the Force Aerienne Belge on 12
December 1931. He had reached the rank of Capitaine by 1940. He arrived in the UK on 1 June 1941, being
posted to 131 Squadron on 30 August, moving to 79 Squadron on 22 October, 118 Squadron on 4 January 1942,
615 Squadron on 7 January, 234 Squadron on 18 February, 130 Squadron on 28 February, 124 Squadron on 4
March, and finally reached 350 Squadron on 28 March 1942. His service in Occupied Europe was confined to
France (Brittany area), rather than Belgium. Upon his return from these clandestine duties, he applied in February
1945 to be posted to command 350 Squadron again, but was considered by the Air Ministry to be too old. He
received an MC in November 1943 for his SOE service during 1944. He died at Clayes (Eure et Loire) on 13
March 1967 (not 12 March).

BOWES Roderick Russell Herbert

Bowes from Springfield, South Australia, was born in Windsor, Victoria, on 22 January 1916. A clerk before the
war, he enlisted on 9 November 1940, attending 1 ITS, 3 EFTS and 2 SFTS in Australia, qualifying as a pilot in
March 1941. He was posted to the UK in June, where he attended 52 OTU in September 1941, then joining 79
Squadron at the end of October.

Corrections and additions to claim list:
1942
15 Dec   Hurricane IIC   BN786
1943
5 Mar   „   HV831
17 Mar   „   HV653 NV-F
The 'Oscar' claimed damaged was apparently subsequently confirmed
27 Mar   „   „
30 Mar   „   BN679
5 Apr   „   HV653 NV-F
REVISED TOTAL: 6 and 1 shared destroyed, 2 damaged.

BOWKER Neville   RAF Nos. 779035 (NCO); 89773 (Officer)

Bowker was born in 1918 in the Orange Free State of South Africa, but was brought up in Southern Rhodesia.
He joined the SAAF, but transferred to the RAF in mid 1940, being commissioned in the RAFVR. He attended
70 OTU at Nakuru, joining 112 Squadron on 14 February 1941.

Corrections and additions to claim list:
1941
15 Mar —   this claim was actually made on 14 March.
11 May —   this claim was definitely confirmed destroyed in the Command Intelligence Summaries.
5 Dec —   the G-50 was an aircraft of 352ª Squadriglia, 20° Gruppo, 51° Stormo CT, from which Ten Aldo Vitali baled
              out to become a POW.
REVISED TOTAL: 10 and 1 shared destroyed, 3 probables, 2 damaged.

BOWMAN Henry Cecil Francis   RAF Nos. 903366 (NCO); 111776 (Officer)

Henry Bowman joined the RAFVR in September 1939; he had not been a member of this service earlier, when
obtaining his private pilot's licence. His body was washed up on the coast off Ford, Sussex, about 25 August 1942,
and was buried at Burwash on 29 August.

BOYD Archibald Douglas McNeill (not NcNeill)

He was granted a direct entry RAFVR commission as an Acting Plt Off on 18 October 1938.

Corrections and additions to claim list:
1941
16/17 May —   this was a Ju 88A-5, WNr 4230, V4+IR of 7/KG 1.
Claims on 30 June/1 July, 24/25 August and 18/19 September 1943 were all made whilst flying V8882 FK-X; the claim on
6/7 September 1943 was made in V8881 FK-L.

BOYD Alan Hill

Addition to claim list:
1940
13 Dec — one of the CR 42s claimed was flown by Cap Antonio Larsimont Pergameni, commanding officer of the 97ª Squadriglia, 9° Gruppo, 4° Stormo CT, who crash-landed.

BOYD John Livingstone

He was shot down and killed on 14 May 1942 either by Ten Carlo Seganti or Sottoten Leonardo Venturini, both of the 358ª Squadriglia, 2° Gruppo Aut CT.

BOYD Robert Finlay

After service with 58 OTU during late summer 1941, he was posted in October of that year to 57 OTU, being promoted Wg Cdr. He then went to Tangmere as Wg Cdr Flying on 14 December 1941. He was Mentioned in Despatches on 1 January 1945, and died on 22 February 1975.

Corrections to claim list:
1941
17 Jul — claim made while flying Spitfire VA P8740, not R8740.
After his claim on 12 April 1942, should be inserted:-
1943
15 Mar Ju 88 Damaged etc

BOYLE Brian John Lister

He was not, as stated, the first SAAF pilot of the war to be decorated; he was the first SAAF fighter pilot to receive a decoration.

Corrections to claim list:
1941
Regarding the claims of 10,13 and 15 February, it is believed that the correct serial for the Hurricane he was flying on these dates was V7711, not N7711.

BOYLE John Greer

Known as 'Beryl', he attended 5 OTU on 22 May 1940 and was posted to 611 Squadron on 9 June, subsequently being transferred to 41 Squadron.

BRABNER Rupert Arnold

Rupert Brabner was born on 29 October 1911 in Chelsea, London, attending Felstead School, Essex, and St Catherine's College, Cambridge, gaining an MA. He then went into banking and in 1937 became an elected member of the London County Council, subsequently becoming the Conservative Member of Parliament for Hythe in July 1939. He joined the RNVR (FAA) in 1939. He was awarded a DSO during 1942 and a DSC the following year. From June 1943-July 1944 he was Technical Assistant to the Fifth Sea Lord at the Admiralty, then becoming Assistant Government Whip in Parliament in July 1944. In November he was appointed Parliamentary Under-Secretary of State for Air, but on 27 March 1945 was lost with several other senior officers when the Liberator "Commando" (formerly Winston Churchill's personal transport aircraft) crashed into the sea near the Azores. He is commemorated on the Fleet Air Arm Memorial at Lee-on-Solent.

BRADSHAW Anthony   RAF Nos. 1021614 (NCO); 144012 (Officer)

BRAHAM John Robert Daniel

Since 1994 a new biography of this pilot has been published under the title *Night Fighter Ace* by Tony Spooner (Sutton Publishing, 1997).

BREITHAUPT William Ranson   RCAF Nos. R123142 (NCO); J17271 (Officer)

He joined 54 OTU from 6(P) AFU as a Sgt on 29 July 1942. He and Flg Off Kennedy were shot down in Mosquito II DZ254.

BRETHERTON Bruce Albert

His claim during the night of 6/7 July 1943 was made when flying with Flg Off T.E. Johnson as radar operator. His subsequent claims were all made with Flt Lt W.T. Cunningham in this role.

Additions to claim list:
1944
30/31 Jul   KW190 YD-A
3/ 4 Aug   (c)   KW198 YD-Q

8/9 Aug   (b)   KW190 YD-A
(b) F6+DP was WNr550209: (c) Aircraft of 6(F)/122.

BRIGHT Vernon Maxwell
He was posted to 55 OTU as an instructor with the substantive rank of Flg Off in March 1941.

BROAD Charles Ernest   RAF Nos. 1058486 (NCO); 121529 (Officer)
There is a possibility that his claim for a Bf 109F damaged on 1 June 1942 may have been upgraded to 'Destroyed', although this is not indicated in his logbook.

BROADHURST Harry
He attended Portsmouth Grammar School. His service with the Royal Artillery was as a member of the Territorial Army. In 1956, when newly-appointed AOC-in-C of Bomber Command, he went on a tour of Australia and New Zealand in a new Avro Vulcan bomber, XA897, of 230 Operational Conversion Unit. On return in bad weather on 1 October, the pilot attempted to land at Heathrow, but undershot in low cloud and driving snow, and thereupon ejected. Before following suite, Broadhurst took over the controls and attempted a landing, but was also forced to eject at low level, suffering injuries to his feet and legs. He died in August 1995.

Addition to claim list:
1940
20 May —   the aircraft claimed as a Bf 110 on this date may have been a Do 17 of Stabstaffel/ZG 26, which was damaged
              and in which two of the crew were wounded.

BROOKER Richard Edgar Peter
'Boy' Brooker was born in 1918 in Chessington, Surrey, attending the Royal Masonic School, Bushey, Hertfordshire. He subsequently lived in Ashted, and later in Willington (not Willingdon), Sussex. He was commissioned in the RAF in July 1937. On his return to the UK from the Far East in 1942, he was posted as o/c 1 SLAIS as a Wg Cdr, then becoming temporary commanding officer of 59 OTU. In early 1944 he was on the Staff of the Fighter Leaders' School. When posted to lead 123 Wing in May 1944, he brought with him his Typhoon MN143, RL-7, from the FLS, but on 23 May was obliged to bale out of this into the sea, from where he was rescued by a Sea Otter.

BROTHERS Peter Malam
On leaving 257 Squadron in January 1941, he joined 55 OTU, but in February was despatched to CFS on a course. He left the Tangmere Wing in April 1943 on posting to 52 OTU, moving from there to 61 OTU on 1 August 1943. He now lives in retirement in Devon, not Somerset as stated in *Aces High*.

Additions to claim list:
1940
19 May   Bf 109E unconfirmed   Hurricane I   32 Sqn
1942
26 Mar   Spitfire VB   BM143
29 Apr   „   „
1943
26 Jan   „   BL907
REVISED TOTAL: 16 destroyed, 1 unconfirmed destroyed, 1 probable, 3 damaged.

BROWN Mark Henry
On 12 May 1940 his aircraft was damaged by a Bf 109E of 2/JG 27. A biography, written by his sister, Jean Brown Segall, was published by The Macmillan Company of Canada Ltd under the title *Wings of the Morning*.

Corrections and additions to claim list:
1940
10 May —   the Do 17 was shared with four other pilots, rather than two.
14 May —   the Ju 87 was claimed first, and was an aircraft of I/StG 77 — the Bf 109 was an aircraft of I/JG 53.
17 May —   the Bf 110 was claimed in the Sedan area.
18 May —   the Hs 126 was claimed SE St Quentin.
19 May —   the second He 111 was claimed as unconfirmed destroyed, rather than 'probable'.
1941
8 Feb —   he led 1 Squadron on a 'Rhubarb' to Arques, where he claimed a Bf 109 destroyed on the ground; an aircraft
              of 4/JG 3 actually suffered damage during this attack.

BROWNE Allen Edward
He was posted to the UK in March 1941, attending 56 OTU in August, and then joining 256 Squadron in October. He transferred to 488 Squadron in July 1942, in which unit 188134 Plt Off Thomas Frederick Taylor, RAFVR, became his radar operator. In December 1943 he was posted to 51 OTU as an instructor, rejoining 488

Squadron in July 1944. In September 1944 he was awarded a DFC, as was Taylor, but he was posted to 5 PDC for service overseas, joining 89 Squadron in India in November as a flight commander. He became commanding officer in July 1945, a post he held until September. He left the RNZAF in July 1946, and died on 12 June 1979.

BRUEN John Martin

Corrections to claim list:
1940
3 Jul —   the Breguet Bizerta in which he shared, was credited as destroyed, rather than damaged.
1942
All claims listed in 1942 were made whilst flying with 800 Squadron, not 803 Squadron as indicated.
REVISED TOTAL: 4 and 5 shared destroyed, 2 and 1 shared damaged, 1 shared damaged on the ground.

BRYAN John Michael   RAF Nos. 1195470 (NCO); 102570 (Officer)

Born in South Norwood, South London, in 1922, he subsequently lived in Bedford. He enlisted in the RAFVR in 1940, training in Canada and being commissioned in 1941.

BRZESKI Stanislaw   Flight Lieutenant/Kapitan

Born in Lipniki (not Lipnik), he completed elementary school at Sandomierz in 1933, then undertook a three year course at the Infantry NCO School for Minors at Nisko-on-San in 1936. On graduation he volunteered for air force service. He completed a flying course at the Air Force Training Centre at Deblin, and in 1937 at the Wyzsza Pilots' School. He was then posted to 152 Eskadra, where in 1938 he became a member of the team which represented his regiment at the annual Fighter Aviation Contest, winning first place. On 4 September 1939, while flying PZL P11C 8.110 coded 'A', he was shot down while attacking a second observation balloon. According to unconfirmed accounts he shared in the destruction of an He 111 and damaged another during September. He then escaped via Hungary, making his way to France. Here he was posted to GC II/1, operating in the Orleans area. After the fall of France he reached North Africa, and from there reached the UK via Gibraltar. In October 1940 he was posted briefly to 303 Squadron for operational training before joining 249 Squadron. On 15 February 1942 he and another pilot were instructed to intercept and shoot down an unidentified aircraft, which turned out to be a Liberator I being operated by BOAC on the Lisbon-England route (AM918, registered as G-AGDR). The destruction of this aircraft was categorised as an accident at the subsequent enquiry, which ruled that no blame attached to the Polish pilots. In 1943 he joined 302 Squadron, but was subsequently posted to 303 Squadron as a flight commander. With this unit he was shot down by ground fire on 21 May 1944, becoming a POW. He returned to England after the war, joining the RAF as an air traffic controller. He retired during the 1960s and died on 3 December 1972.

Corrections and additions to claim list:

1939					
1 Sep		He 111 Probable — Delete			
4 Sep	½	Balloon	PZL P11C	8.110 'A'	152 Esk
9 Sep		He 111 — Delete			
1941					
10 Feb				R4178	
10 Jul				V7339 GN-X	
6 Dec	(a)			W3424 JH-Q	
1942					
25 Apr				AA758 JH-V	
26 Jul		FW 190 (confirmed, not probable)		AR340 JH-P	
19 Aug				AR332 JH-S	

REVISED TOTAL: 7 and 3 shared destroyed, 1 and 1 shared observation balloons destroyed, 2 probably destroyed, 1 damaged, 1 aircraft destroyed on the ground.
(a) This was Ju 88D-2 WNr 0398, 4U+CH of 1(F)/123; Ofw K.Raasch and crew killed.

BUCHANAN George Andrew Forsyth   RAF Nos. 1250002 (NCO); 60080 (Officer)

He joined the RAF in May 1940. On return to the UK from Malta, he was posted to 61 OTU as an Acting Flt Lt from 2 PDC on 6 July 1942. On 25 July 1943 he was posted from Air Ministry to 51 OTU to study synthetic training devices prior to being posted to Washington. He was released from the RAF in January 1946 and apparently rejoined the BSAP, but left again on 10 May 1946 with the rank of Trooper to rejoin the RAF.

Correction and alteration to claim list:
1942
10 May —   Ju 87 listed as damaged, may in fact have been a probable.
16 May —   the MC 202 was probably a Re 2001 of 150ª Squadriglia, 2° Gruppo Aut CT flown by Sottoten Carlo Grillo, which was Damaged.

BUCHANAN John Kenneth

He attended Portsmouth Grammar School; he was commissioned in the RAF on 3 May 1937, and became a Plt

Off on 1 March 1938. He undertook two tours on bombers, and was already an Acting Wg Cdr when awarded a Bar to his DFC on 7 April 1942. He was awarded a Croix de Guerre (Belge) on 1 February 1944, but was shot down on 16th of that month in Beaufighter FL467 'J', with Wt Off R.C. Howes as navigator; Howes was subsequently rescued after Buchanan had died.

BUNTING Bobby   Flying Officer
Born on 18 July 1922 in Melbourne, Victoria, he attended Hampton High School, then training as a telecom mechanic at the Royal Melbourne Technical College; he also became a Cadet in the 2nd Cavalry Signals in July 1938. He joined the RAAF on 19 July 1941, undertaking his initial training at the SFTS at Deniliquin, New South Wales. He was then posted to the UK for advanced training at Ternhill, then attending 52 OTU, Aston Down, in December 1942. In January 1943 he was posted to Gibraltar, being engaged for some months in ferrying Spitfire Vs, VIIIs and IXs to North Africa. On 25 August 1943 he was posted to 93 Squadron at Castelli, Sicily. The following month he landed at Salerno with Flt Sgt W.W.Downer and the Wing Engineering Officer to mark out an airfield from which the unit would operate. Having gained his first successes in the Rome area, on 27 March 1944 he attacked over 50 Bf 109s and FW 190s single-handed, but his aircraft was hit many times and he was wounded in the right leg by a cannon shell. He received a DFC in May whilst recuperating, returning to the unit in June, and moving with it to Corsica. Here he undertook last light patrols, having had some training in night flying in the UK. During one such sortie on 27 July he intercepted a reconnaissance Me 410 escorted by two FW 190s, making for the Corsican ports. He managed to turn it back and to shoot down one of the FW 190s, for which he was awarded a US DFC. On 11 August he took part in the destruction of a Giant Wurzburg radar station east of Marseilles, also undertaking patrols over the South of France invasion fleet during the month. He was commissioned at Lyon-Bron on 12 September 1944, but at the start of October was posted to Ismailia Training School in Egypt as an instructor, then becoming a gunnery instructor at ABGS, El Ballah. He returned to Australia in December 1945, and was discharged in February 1946. Obtaining a Diploma from the Australian School of Pacific Administration at St Lucia University, he joined the Papua New Guinea Administration field service in August 1946 as a Patrol Officer. He served in various districts, rising to District Commissioner. He became First Secretary of the Territory Intelligence Committee, acting as Territory Anthropologist, 1966-67. Rendered redundant when PNG obtained self-government in 1974, he retired to Queensland to write short stories about New Guinea. From 1977-1983 he fought a long battle with melanoma, from which he successfully recovered. At the time of writing he was living in retirement in Queensland. He was also a war poet, one of his poems gracing the Introduction to this volume.

Corrections to claim list:
All his claims were made whilst flying Spitfire IXs, not Marks VII and VIII as indicated in *Aces High*.

BUNTING Edward Nigel
Nigel Bunting was an Oxford BA. It seems that when shot down and killed, he was not flying with his regular radar operator, but with Flg Off E.Spedding, with whom he was buried at St Remy, 21 miles south west of Caen, France.

BURBRIDGE Branse Arthur
RAF Nos. 1377411 (NCO); 100067 (Officer) — not 10067

Correction and additions to claim list:
1941

8 Jul	VY-H
13 Aug (day)	VY-R
23 Aug	VY-B

4/5 Nov — the Bf 110 claimed during this night was an aircraft of II/NJG 1, flown by Oblt Franz Runzek; two of the crew baled out.
12/13 Dec — The Ju 88G was an aircraft of 6/NJG 4 flown by Uffz Heinrich Brue, who was killed with his crew.

BURGES George

Corrections and additions to claim list:
1940
2 Nov — the CR 42 was an aircraft of 72^a Squadriglia, 17° Gruppo, 1° Stormo CT, in which Serg Abramo Lanzarini was killed.
23 Nov — both claims made while flying Hurricane V7548 (not N7448).
1941
18 Jan — both claims made while flying P3731 (not N3731).
19 Jan — first claim made while flying P3730 (not N3730); N7446, listed as flown for the second claim, was a Miles Master; the correct identity of this Hurricane has not been determined.

BURKE Patrick Lampard
He left 93 Squadron as a Flt Lt on 8 August 1941 to instruct at 51 OTU.

BURNELL-PHILLIPS Peter Anthony   Flight Lieutenant   RAF Nos. 37848 (pre-war Officer); 745892 (NCO on re-enlistment); 88212 (wartime Officer)

He attended Air Service Training Ltd at Anstey for initial training. In June 1936 he then trained at 11 FTS on Harts and Furies, joining 54 Squadron in January 1937 on Gauntlet IIs, and later on Gladiators. In January 1939 he was classified in his logbook as 'Above Average'. In April 1939 he undertook an instructor's course with the RAFVR, in June being posted to 32 ERFTS at West Hartlepool. In October he undertook 61 Instructors' Course at CFS, Upavon, and in December went to 7 FTS. He had been promoted Flt Lt by the time of his death.

Additions to claim list:
1940		
15 Aug		P2912
9 Sep		"
26 Sep		3937
4 Oct		2586

BURNEY Henry George

He joined 112 Squadron on 8 August 1941. He was lost in Kittyhawk IA AK772, GA-Y, carrying the name 'London Pride'. This had been an aircraft frequently flown by Sqn Ldr C.R.Caldwell.

Addition to claim list:
1942
14 Feb —   the MC 200 claimed as a Ba 65 was an aircraft of 363[a] Squadrilgia, 150° Gruppo Aut CT.

BURRA-ROBINSON Lance Amigo Percy   RAF Nos. 915237 (NCO); 89384 (Officer)

Born on 25 February 1917 in Bournemouth, son of Capt P.D.Robinson of the 9th Northumberland Fusiliers and Mrs E.L.Dimond, he lived in Wooler, Northumberland, before the war, being educated at Stowe (1933-35) and Trinity College, Cambridge (1935-39). He enlisted in the RAFVR in February 1940, gaining his wings in December and being promoted Sgt. He was commissioned at the end of the year and sent to 1 School of Army Co-operation on a course. He was then retained for flying duties at the school, which became 41 OTU in September 1941. Promoted Flg Off in December 1941, Acting Flt Lt in June 1942 and Flt Lt in December 1942, he then attended 1526 Flight on a BAT course in January 1943, before undertaking the Central Gunnery School Gunnery Instructors' Course at Sutton Bridge. In April he returned to 41 OTU as an air combat instructor. At last in November 1943 he attended 59 OTU for operational training. Following this, he joined 122 Squadron on 1 February 1944, and then 65 Squadron on 15 July 1944, being promoted Acting Sqn Ldr on 9 September. On 1 January 1945 he was posted to 61 OTU on completion of his operational tour. He attended 1335 Conversion Unit at Molesworth in August 1945 for conversion to Meteors, then joining HQ, 12 Group, as Sqn Ldr Operations on the Day Air Staff. He left the service at the end of 1946. On 1 July 1959 he relinquished his commission, retaining the rank of Sqn Ldr. In April 1940 he had married Nancy Bowes Lyon, daughter of the 15th Earl of Strathane and Kinghorne, a relative of Queen Elizabeth, the Queen Mother; they were divorced in 1950.

BURTON Howard Frizelle

He attended Bedford School. He was lost not while flying to England, nor on 13 June 1943. On conclusion of the Tunisian Campaign, a number of unit commanders, including Burton, were flown home to England on leave. Whilst returning to North Africa on 3 June 1943 in a Hudson VI, FK386 of 1 OADU, flown by Grp Capt R.G.Yaxley, DSO,MC,DFC, the aircraft was intercepted and shot down by a Ju 88C of V/KG 40. Amongst those lost were Burton and Sqn Ldr O.V.Hanbury, DSO,DFC and Bar, commanding officer of 260 Squadron. (See biographical notes on Hanbury in *Aces High* and as expanded herein).

BUTLER Roy Thomas   Flying Officer RAF Nos. 1384335 (NCO); 196074 (Officer)

Roy Butler was born in Southend-on-Sea, Essex, on 19 March 1922. He attended Southend Technical College and South East Essex Technical College, and from 1939-41 worked in the Body Design Office of Briggs Motor Bodies, Dagenham. He took his pilot selection examination in October 1940 and entered the RAFVR in June 1941, beginning training at 8 ITW, Newquay. He was sent to 35 SFTS, North Battleford, Canada, for flying training, qualifying in April 1942, and being promoted Sgt. He returned to the UK in November 1942, attending 54 OTU, and then being posted to 29 Squadron in March 1943. The following month he returned to 54 OTU for low level intruder training, following which he was promoted Flt Sgt. In June he collected a new Beaufighter at Lyneham and flew it out to North Africa. In August he joined 108 Squadron, which in October was absorbed into 46 Squadron. In May 1944 he was promoted Wt Off. He returned to the UK in December 1944, and in March 1945 was commissioned and posted to 51 OTU at Cranfield. At the end of the war he undertook a conversion course on Dakotas, joining 1334 Transport Flight in India. He was released in 1946, returning to automotive design. In 1950 he went to the USA to work for the Ford Motor Company, returning to the UK in 1966 as Chief Engineer, Ford Europe. He retired in 1980 to live in Florida, where he continues to live at the time of writing, spending a few months each year in the UK.

BUTTERFIELD Samuel Leslie

Born in Leeds, West Yorkshire, in 1913, he was brought up in Stamford, Lincolnshire. He enlisted as an Aircraft Apprentice at Halton in September 1929. He is buried in the Boulogne War Cemetery.

Corrections and additions to claim list:

1940						
19 May	$^1/_5$	Hs 126 (a)	Hurricane I	P2673	S Tournai	213 Sqn
"	$^1/_3$	Hs 126 Damaged	"	"	"	"
20 May	$^1/_5$	Hs 126 (b)	"	P2834	Arras	"

Note — these claims replace those listed for these days in *Aces High*.
REVISED TOTAL: 5 and 3 shared destroyed, 1 unconfirmed destroyed, 1 shared damaged.
(a) Aircraft of 2(H)/41; (b) Aircraft of 2(H)/23Pz.

CAINE John Todd

Died during 1995.

CALDWELL Clive Robertson

After the end of the war the RAAF discovered that Caldwell had been flying in alchoholic spirits to Morotai, which had then been sold via his batman to US servicemen at a substantial profit. He was court martialled and reduced to the rank of Flt Lt. He petitioned the Governor General against the sentence, but when this failed, he left the service in February 1946. He then commenced an export-import business, achieving considerable success. He died on 5 August 1994.

Corrections and additions to claim list:
Since publication of *Aces High* it has been possible to inspect a copy of Clive Caldwell's logbook. A new claim list derived from this, with comments as appropriate is set out below:-

1941						
6 Jun	$^1/_2$	Z1007 (a)	Tomahawk IIB	AK349		250 Sqn
26 Jun		Bf 109	"	AK1419	3m W Capuzzo	"
"		Bf 109 Damaged	"	"	N Capuzzo	"
30 Jun		Bf 110 (b)	"	AK346	in sea, near	"
"	2	Ju 87s	"			"
9 Jul		G-50 (c)	"	"	1m S Bir Taieb	"
12 Jul		Bf 109 Damaged	"	AK376	over ships	"
3 Aug		Bf 109 Damaged	"	AK416	Bardia-Capuzzo	"
10 Aug		Bf 109 Damaged	"	AK511		"
14 Aug		Bf 109 Probable	"	AK504	over ships	"
16 Aug	$^1/_2$	G-50	"	"	off Bardia	"
19 Aug		Bf 109 Damaged (d)	"	"	Gambut-Sidi Omar	"
25 Aug		Bf 109 Damaged	"	AK493		"
28 Aug		Bf 109E unconfirmed (e)	"	"	over ships	"
29 Aug		Bf 109F	"	"	"	"
14 Sep	2	Bf 109s Damaged	"	AK498	Escort duties	"
26 Sep		Bf 109 Damaged	"	AK324		"
27 Sep		Bf 109F	"	"	10-12m NW Bardia	"
30 Sep		Bf 109 Damaged	"	"	over ships	"
18 Oct		Bf 109 Damaged	"	AK498	"	"
11 Nov		Bf 109F Damaged	"	"		"
22 Nov		Bf 109F (f)	"	"		"
"		Bf 109E Damaged (f)	"	"	Trigh Capuzzo	"
26 Nov		Bf 109F Damaged	"	"		"
28 Nov		Bf 109 Probable	"	"		"
30 Nov		Bf 109 Probable	"	"		"
5 Dec	5	Ju 87s (g)	"	"	nr El Gobi	"
14 Dec		Bf 109F Damaged (h)	"	"		"
17 Dec		Bf 109F Probable	"	"		"
18 Dec		Bf 109 Damaged	"	"		"
19 Dec		Bf 109 Probable	"	"		"
22 Dec		Bf 109F (i)	"	"	Agedabia area	"
"		Bf 109E (i)	"	"	"	"
"		Bf 109F Damaged (i)	"	"	"	"
28 Dec	2	Ju 87s on fire on ground	"	"	Agedabia	"
1942						
8 Jan		Bf 109 Damaged	Kittyhawk IA	AK658		112 Sqn
26 Jan		Bf 109 Damaged	"	"		"
21 Feb		Bf 109F	"	"		"
23 Feb		Bf 109F Damaged	"	"		"
6 Mar		Bf 109F Damaged (j)	"	AK900		"
9 Mar		Bf 109 Probable (j)	"	"		"
11 Mar		Bf 109F	"	AK968		"
"		Bf 109F Damaged	"	"		"

12 Mar	Bf 109F Probable (k)	„	AK766		„
14 Mar	Bf 109F (l)	„	AK772		„
„	MC 202 (l)	„	„		„
23 Apr	Bf 109	„	AK766	Tobruk	„
1943					
2 Mar	Zero	Spitfire VB	BS295		1 Wg
„	Light Bomber	„	„		„
2 May	Zero	„	BS234		„
„	Hap	„	„		„
20 Jun	Zero	„	S295		„
„	Betty Probable	„	„		„
28 Jun	Betty Probable (m)	„	BS234		„
30 Jun	Zero	„	BS295		„
„	Betty Probable (n)	„	„		„
17 Aug	Dinah	„	LJ394		„

Comparison with previous listings, derived from squadron Operations Record Books and combat reports (where available) indicate some differences:
(a) This claim has been credited to Flt Lt J.Hamlyn in all other accounts, and does not seem officially to have been credited to Caldwell as a share.
(b) In the ORB he is credited with a half share in this Bf 110, whereas in his logbook he lists it as an individual victory.
(c) The ORB lists this claim as occurring on 7 July, rather than 9th.
(d) The ORB lists this claim as being made on 18th, rather than 19 August.
(e) This claim was subsequently classified as a probable.
(f) These claims were listed in the ORB for 23 November, rather than 22nd. Comparison with Luftwaffe records indicates that the former appears indeed to have been the correct date. Although the ORB shows the second claim of the day to be destroyed, and whilst it is known that the pilot, Lippert, did indeed bale out, the logbook clearly lists this as Damaged only.
(g) Whilst the ORB also lists a MC 200 Damaged on this date, there is no mention of this in the logbook — possibly because it was totally overshadowed in Caldwell's mind at the time by his claims for five Ju 87s.
(h) The ORB lists claims for two Bf 109s Damaged on this date, whilst in the logbook only one is mentioned.
(i) The ORB lists one Bf 109 on 20 December and one Damaged on 22nd. In the logbook there are no claims listed for 20th, but two destroyed and one Damaged on 22nd.
(j) The ORB lists one Bf 109 Damaged on 8 March; the logbook lists one Damaged on 6th and one Probable on 9th.
(k) This claim is listed in the ORB as occurring on 13 March, rather than on 12th.
(l) Caldwell records in his logbook that the pilot of the MC 202 baled out and became a POW. He makes no mention of this claim being shared. He lists a Bf 109 as the other claim of the day, whereas the ORB records both aircraft claimed as Macchis.
(m) The second claim on this date for a Probable has not been listed before.
(n) The 'Betty' listed was previously recorded from the ORB as a confirmed victory, whereas the logbook lists it as a Probable; this accords with Caldwell's seven Japanese victory flags shown on his Spitfire VIII during 1944.

Additionally, the ORBs list several claims which do not appear in his logbook — notably:-
1941
24 Dec   Bf 109 Damaged
1942
14 Jan   Bf 109 Damaged

If the claim for a share in the Z1007 on 6 June 1941 is discounted, the number of confirmed claims whilst with 250 Squadron amounts to 17, two of them shared, which appears to accord as a total at that time. He added five more with 112 Squadon, and then seven (rather than eight) against the Japanese. This appears to arrive at a total of 29, two or three of them shared, which equates reasonably well with the victory markings on his Spitfire later in the war. There are however, a few anomalies between his logbook and unit records, as can be seen.

It is noteworthy that at the end of August 1941, his logbook contains an entry written by Sqn Ldr J.E.Scoular, his commanding officer, which stated: *"An extraordinarily keen fighter pilot who is apt to let his keeness get the better of him. Needs more practice in leading and will turn out a very good pilot. At the moment he is purely an individualist."*
REVISED TOTAL: Appears to be circa 25 or 26 and 2-4 shared destroyed, 11 probables, 25-28 damaged, 2 destroyed on the ground.

CAMPBELL Francis   Flight Lieutenant RAF Nos. 1373373 (NCO); 162831 (Officer)

Born in Lanarkshire, Scotland, on 21 September 1920, he attended Our Lady's High School, Motherwell, until 1939, and then worked for Shotts Ironworks Company as an engineer from 1939-41. He enlisted in the RAFVR in July 1940, being called up on 28 January 1941 for training as pilot/wireless operator/air gunner, and as an Aircrafthand. Initial training was undertaken at 5 Recruit Centre, West Kirby, and then in April at 1 Receiving Wing, Babbacombe, followed in June by 1 Training Wing, Torquay. In August he was promoted LAC and sent to 51 Group Pool, from where on 5 November he went to 8 SFTS, Montrose, to complete pilot training, a spell at 59 OTU, Crosby-in-Eden following in February 1942. In April he was promoted Sgt, and shortly afterwards Flt Sgt, before joining 232 Squadron in June. On 25 September he was posted to 93 Squadron, accompanying this unit to North Africa in November. His award of the DFM was gazetted on 28 May 1943, and on 8 June he left the unit for the UK, via Malta. After a short spell at personnel centres, he joined HQ, 9 Group in August, then bring posted in mid September to 3 Flying Instructors' School, Hullavington. During November he was commissioned, returning to HQ, 9 Group, on 17th of that month. At the start of January 1944 he joined 2

Tactical Exercise Unit at Grangemouth, where he stayed until April as an instructor. He then undertook No 12 Junior Commanders' Course at the Officers' Advanced Training School, Cranwell, before joining 83 Group Support Unit for flying duties with 111 Mustang Wing, being posted to 122 Squadron. In May he was promoted Flg Off, and on 12 June returned to 83 GSU for posting to 132 Squadron. After claiming his final victories with this unit, he was posted to 91 Squadron on 17 November 1944, but a month later went to 57 OTU, Eshott, as an instructor. In June 1945 he moved to 61 OTU, Keevil, and then at the start of September to 587 Squadron, an anti-aircraft co-operation unit. Promoted Flt Lt in November, he moved to 691 Squadron on similar duties in June 1946, but on 9 August he was released from the service.

CARBURY Brian John George

It appears that in 1948 he was involved in the illegal ferrying of aircraft to Israel. A pilot listed as B.J.Carbury had his British Pilot's Licence suspended at that time for such activities.

Corrections to claim list:
1940
14 Sep		X4323 (not X4324)
10 Oct		X4490 (not X4164)
25 Dec	Spitfire II (not Mark I)	

CAREY Frank Reginald

Corrections to claim list:
Note — all claims listed from 9 July 1940-18 August 1940 were claimed whilst he was serving with 43 Squadron, not 3 Squadron as incorrectly indicated in the listing in *Aces High*.
1940
6 Aug —   should read 8 Aug.

CARLSON Donald

He was born in Owhango (not Ourhango), King Country, New Zealand. He was just within the maximum age limit of 25 when he joined the RAF in August 1937. Although engaged initially primarily as an instructor once he had completed training, he served briefly with 245 Squadron during 1940, where he was injured in an accident. After service with 74 Squadron as a flight commander, he was posted to 58 OTU as an instructor in August 1941, before taking command of 154 Squadron in March 1942. On 30 July 1942 his squadron escorted Hurricanes to bomb St Omer airfield. Here a large force of Luftwaffe fighters intercepted, eight Spitfires and three Hurricanes being lost. He remained in the RAF after the war in the Fighter Control Branch, retiring as a Sqn Ldr on 7 May 1958. He died on 17 August 1983.

CARPENTER John Michael Vowles

John Carpenter did not die as reported; he was still alive at the time of writing this further volume. He was born on 9 April 1921; at the end of December 1939, on completion of training, he was posted to 11 Group Pool before joining 263 Squadron. During 1944 he was seconded to Hawkers as a test pilot (not Chief Test Pilot), testing Typhoons and Tempests. After his postwar service with 80 Squadron, he served at HQ, Fighter Command, and on radar duties. Following his retirement from the service, he operated hotels in Bermuda and South Africa. His first wife died in 1974 after a long illness. His second wife, who he had met during the war, died in 1989, also following a long illness. Subsequently he returned to the UK to live in retirement in the West Country.

Additions to claim list:
1941
30 Jun —	aircraft of 86^a Squadriglia, 7° Gruppo, 54° Stormo CT; Ten Armando Cibin killed.
4 Sep —	probably an aircraft of 90^a Squadriglia, 10° Gruppo, 4° Stormo CT in which Serg Luigi Contarini was killed.
8 Nov —	aircraft of 96^a Squadriglia, 9° Gruppo, 4° Stormo CT, in which Serg Magg Luigi Taroni was killed.

CARTRIDGE David Leslie

He was born in Bristol, attending Bristol Grammar School. He enlisted in 1937, being commissioned on 26 March 1938. He retired as a Wg Cdr.

Corrections to claim list:
1943
9 Feb —   his claims on this date were not for a single Ju 88, but for 1/3 shares in three.
REVISED TOTAL: 2 and 3 shared destroyed.

CARTWRIGHT Henry

Born in 1915 in Wigan, Lancashire, he worked as a foreman-beater before enlisting in May 1938. During his combat on 16 May 1940, his Hurricane, N2483, was damaged by return fire from the aircraft which he had attacked. He was then attacked by Oblt Karl-Wolfgang Redlich of 1/JG 27, following which he force-landed at Braue-le-Comte.

Revised claim list:
1940

12 May	$\frac{1}{4}$	He 111	Hurricane I			79 Sqn
14 May	$\frac{1}{2}$	Ju 88	,,			,,
,,		Ju 88	,,		Louvain	,,
16 May		FW 189 (a)	,,	N2483		,,
20 May	$\frac{1}{3}$	Hs 126 (b)	,,		near Arras	,,
,,		Do 17 Damaged	,,		Arras	,,
27 May		Bf 110 unconfirmed	,,		W Boulogne	,,

REVISED TOTAL: 1 and 3 shared destroyed, 1 unconfirmed destroyed, 1 damaged.
(a) Not an FW 198, as he claimed; an aircraft of 9(H)/LG 2; (b) Aircraft of 3(H)/12Ps.

CASBOLT Charles Edward
Flight Lieutenant RAF Nos. 565529 (NCO); 47700 (Officer)
Born in Southend in 1914, he worked as a shop assistant before joining the RAF. He enlisted in September 1931, becoming a Fitter (Aero Engines); he was later selected for pilot training. In August 1941 he was awarded a DFM, and in September was posted to 71 OTU as an instructor. He was commissioned on 8 February 1942, joining 250 Squadron on 3 April that year. He was promoted Flt Lt on 21 December 1943.

Additions to claim list:
1940
19 Nov — aircraft of 361^a Squadriglia, 154° Gruppo Aut CT; Ten Attilio Maneghel killed.
1941
20 Feb — one of the G-50s claimed was an aircraft of 361^a Squadriglia, 154° Gruppo Aut CT in which Ten Alfredo Fusco was killed.

CHADBURN Lloyd Vernon
He was awarded a DSO on 7 September 1943 and a Bar to this on 14 January 1944. He was promoted Wg Cdr on 16 May 1944, and was killed in MJ824, five miles north of Caen.

CHALUPA Stanislaw Jozef
He was born in Zaraz, near Chrzanow in the Kracow region, and entered the Artillery Reserve Cadet Officers' School at Wlodzimierz Wolynski on leaving school. In January 1936 he moved to the Air Force Flying School at Deblin, receiving his commission in 1938 and being posted to the 2 Pulk Lotniczy in Kracow. In September 1939 he flew in the 123 Eskadra of the Pursuit Brigade (Brygada Poscigowa), according to his diary claiming a shared victory on 3 September. He escaped to France via Rumania. The claims noted in his diary for the May-June 1940 period differ slightly from those in Armée de l'Air records, primarily in that he recorded a Ju 88 shot down on 11 May and a Bf 109 plus a single Ju 87 on 8 June. The formal records have been employed in this case however. He was wounded in combat during June. With 302 Squadron he was injured in a crash-landing on 20 September 1940 and was forced to cease operational flying. He was awarded the Virtuti Militari, 5th Class, on 21 December 1940, and on recovery from his injuries returned to 302 Squadron as Operations Room Controller. After his navigation course in 1945 he returned to 16 SFTS, Newton, as Navigation Instructor. In 1995 he returned from Canada to his native Poland, where he was living in Kracow at the time of writing.

Corrections and additions to claim list:
1939

3 Sep	$\frac{1}{3}$	Bf 110	PZL P7A		123 Esk
1940					
21 Aug —	delete				
24 Aug		Ju 88 Probable	Hurricane I	P3934 WX-T	302 Sqn
15 Sep			,,	P3923 WX-U (both claims)	

REVISED TOTAL: 3 and 4 shared destroyed, 2 and 2 shared probables.

CHAMBERS Hansford Ward
He attended 61 OTU after arriving in the UK, before being posted to 154 Squadron. In September 1943 he was posted to HQ, 203 Group, and then to RAF El Ballah as a gunnery instructor. He returned to New Zealand in August 1944, and was released on 17 October 1944, returning to his farm in Waikato. He died on 6 August 1977.

Additions to claim list:
1943

3 Apr		ER673	
10 Jul		EN304 LE-D S Comiso	

CHANDLER Horatio Herbert
He attended No 6 Course at 6 OTU, Sutton Bridge, in late April 1940, before joining 501 Squadron.

CHARLES Edward Francis John

After the war he continued to serve in the RCAF, but in 1949 was found slumped over his desk at the RCAF base at St Huberts, Quebec. Diagnosed as suffering from acute shizophrenia, believed to be caused by wartime stress, he was given treatment, making an apparent recovery. This proved to be brief, and he suffered a relapse, being released from the service in March 1951 as incurable. He then spent 35 years in Shaughnessy Veterans' Hospital, Vancouver, where he remained until his death on 5 November 1986.

CHARNEY Kenneth Langley   RAF Nos. 1375017 (NCO); 112709 (Officer)

Born in Buenos Aires, Argentina, Ken Charney attended Aldenham School, Elstree, Hertfordshire, from 1934-36. He joined the RAFVR in August 1940, remustering as a pilot in April 1941, promoted Sgt. He joined 91 Squadron in June 1941, and was commissioned in November. He was posted out to Malta in May 1942, joining 185 Squadron in June. Here he was promoted Flt Lt in July. He returned to the UK in November, being posted to 53 OTU as an instructor. Posted to 122 Squadron in August 1943, he moved to 602 Squadron in November, being promoted Sqn Ldr. At this time he was granted an Extended Service Commission. During February-March 1944 he attended 2 Air Support Training Course at Milfield. He was to remain in command of 132 Squadron until April 1946, when he was posted to HQ, Air Command, South East Asia. He remained in the Far East for some time, serving with Palembang Air Command, Sumatra, and then Air HQ, Ceylon, until early 1947, when he returned to the UK. He then served at HQ, 63 Group, from May 1947-February 1948, subsequently attending Aircrew Training at Lübeck, BAFO, Germany. In April 1948 he became an instructor, and in October was awarded a Permanent Commission. He served at Sylt in Germany from May 1949-June 1951, then attending the Staff College Course at Bracknell. Various postings in France followed, and then he was posted to CFE on Ground Attack Tactics in May 1954. He then served as an Aide de Camp to the British Ambassador in Baghdad from January 1957. In December 1957 he joined HQ, Task Force 'Grapple X', where he remained until July 1959. Promoted Wg Cdr, he then joined HQ, Flying Training Command, until September 1960, when he left for the Indian Ocean as commanding officer, RAF Christmas Island, where nuclear bomb tests were being conducted. In March 1962 he returned to RAF Germany, joining HQ, 2nd Allied TAF in June 1963. In 1964 he became Air Attache in Djakarta, Indonesia, as a Grp Capt. He remained there until 1969, returning to the UK at the start of 1970 to retire. He then lived in Andorra, but suffered from cancer, which his wife believed had been caused by exposure to radiation during his period on Christmas Island. When he died on 3 June 1982, his weight had fallen to only five stone (70 lbs).

CHARNOCK Harry Walpole

He served in 57 OTU in November 1943, prior to joining 61 OTU. He was posted to AFDU in January 1944.

CHASE Frederick John Allison   Wing Commander RAF No. 72283

Born on 18 April 1910 in Kings Lynn, Norfolk, he lived in Cambridge, attending the University there and serving in the University Air Squadron, 1929-33. He was commissioned in the RAFVR in April 1938, and was called up on 2 September 1939, being despatched to 13 EFTS, White Waltham, on a flying instructor's course. In October he was posted to an IT Wing as a supernumary, and ten days later was promoted Flg Off, becoming an Acting Flt Lt in November, although he relinquished this rank in May 1940. Meanwhile he was posted to 217 Squadron, Coastal Command, at Carew Cheriton in December 1939 for flying duties. On 8 June 1940 he attended 1 (Coastal) OTU at Silloth on a conversion course, but in October was posted back to the Cambridge UAS as adjutant, in October becoming a substantive Flt Lt. In September 1941 he joined 54 OTU, Church Fenton, as a navigation instructor, but six months later as an Acting Sqn Ldr, he became a flying instructor. Finally in June 1943 he was posted to 68 Squadron for operational experience, then joining 264 Squadron in October 1943 as a flight commander, with 146285 Flg Off Alexander Frederick Watson as his radar operator. Chase's tour ended in October 1944, and he was then posted as a Wg Cdr to 85 Group. In August 1945 he was released from the service, and in 1948 became Assistant Master at Rugby School. On 8 February 1949 he became a Flg Off, RAFVR Training Branch, then commanding the Officer Cadet Contingent of the School CCF as an Acting Sqn Ldr. He relinquished this rank in October 1951, but retained his previous rank of Wg Cdr in the RAFVR.

CHISHOLM Roderick Aeneas

He was born at Bridge of Allan, Scotland. He was Mentioned in Despatches on 1 January and 14 June 1945. He died in December 1994.

CHISHOLM William Lawrence

He also served at 1 METS as an instructor in late June 1943, before leaving the Middle East for Canada.

Additions to claim list:

1942				
4 Jul			Hurricane IIC	BN291
24 Jul			„	BN359
1 Aug			„	„
19 Aug			Spitfire V	BR492
30 Aug			Bf 109F	„	BR474
„	½	Bf 109F	„	BR525
1 Sep			„	„

28 Sep	½	Bf 109	"	BR476		
7 Oct			"	BR525		
27 Oct			"	BR576		
1943						
8 Jan			"	ER345		
7 Mar (a)			"	ER821		

(a) The MC 202 claimed on this date was an aircraft of 168ª Squadriglia, 16° Gruppo, 54° Stormo CT, flown by Serg Alberto Calistri, who was killed.

CHRISTIE George Patterson

Corrections and additions to claim list:

1940						
10 Apr	⅓	He 111	Hurricane I	L1608	Scapa Flow	43 Sqn
13 Jun			Spitfire PR	P9385		212 Sqn
1 Aug			Hurricane I	P3090		242 Sqn
30 Aug			"	"		
4 Sep			Spitfire I	X4052 (a)		
5 Sep		Bf 109E Damaged	"	K9944 (b)		
14 Nov			"	P7425		
26 Nov			"	P7522		
27 Nov			"	P7525		
29 Dec			"	P7669		

REVISED TOTAL: 6 and 1 shared destroyed, 3 probables, 2 and 1 shared damaged.
(a) Slightly wounded in left arm and right leg by splinters; (b) After making this claim he was shot down by another Bf 109E and baled out.

CHRISTIE Werner RAF No. N1071

Correction to claim list:

1943		
17 Jun		EN177 (not EW177)

CHUDEK Aleksandr

The aircraft AB271 in which he was shot down and killed was a Spitfire VB, not a Mark IX.

Corrections and additions to claim list:

1941					
16 Sep		Bf 109F Probable	Spitfire VB	AB892 PK-H	

(This claim was not confirmed destroyed, as shown in *Aces High*)

1943					
17 Aug	2	FW 190s (a)		BS451 RF-M	
6 Sep				MA299 RF-E	

REVISED TOTAL: 9 destroyed, 1 probable, 1 damaged.
(a) Only one German aircraft was lost in this engagement; FW 190A-4 WNr 2386 of JG 26, flown by Lt Jorg Kiefner was shot down by fire from three Polish pilots, Chudek being one of them.

CHURCHILL, Walter Myers

He was a Cambridge University BA. Walter Churchill is buried at Syracuse, Sicily.

Revised claim list:

1940						
12 May	⅓	Hs 126 (a)	Hurricane I	P3318	near Diest — St Trond	3 Sqn
13 May	⅓	He 111 (b)	"	N2351	Louvain — Wavre	"
14 May	3	Ju 87s (c)	"	L2825	Sedan area	"
"		Ju 87 unconfirmed	"	"	"	"
15 May		Bf 109E	"	L1899	Louvain area	"
"		Bf 109E unconfirmed	"	"	"	"

REVISED TOTAL: 4 and 2 shared destroyed, 2 unconfirmed destroyed.
(a) Aircraft of 1(H)/23; (b) He 111P of 3/KG 54; (c) the squadron claimed 11 Ju 87s; I(St)/TrGr 186 lost eight.

CLEAVER, Gordon Neil Spencer

On 19 May 1940 his Hurricane, L1690, was damaged by debris from an He 111 and he crash-landed south of Lille. In early 1942 he was 'Ops III' at HQ, 10 Group.

Addition to claim list:

1940						
18 May	½	Do 17	Hurricane I	L1690	Douai area	att. 3 Sqn

CLERKE Rupert Francis Henry

Prior to joining the RAF, he attended university, obtaining an MA. During 1944 he commanded the Bomber Support Development Unit from its formation in April, on 4 July flying the unit's first sortie with Flt Lt J.R.Wheldon. He died in 1988.

CLISBY Leslie Redford

His DFC was awarded posthumously, in contravention of regulations which permitted no posthumous awards other than the Victoria Cross. This occasioned some considerable dispute at the time, and was acceded to only because his family had already been advised. It appears that he was shot down in Hurricane P2546 by Bf 110Cs of I/ZG 26 and crashed south of Sedan on 14 May 1940. He is buried in Chaloy War Cemetery, France.

Revisions to claim list:
1940

11 May	$\frac{1}{2}$	Bf 110 (d)	
„	$\frac{1}{3}$	Bf 110 (d)	
„	$\frac{1}{2}$	Bf 110 (d)	
12 May		Bf 109E	
„	2	"Arado biplanes" (e)	
13 May		Bf 110	N2326
„		He 111 (f)	
„		He 111 (g)	

REVISED TOTAL: appears to have been 8 and 3 shared destroyed.
(d) 8 or 9 claims were submitted against Bf 110s by the unit; I/ZG 2 lost two; (e) These aircraft appear to have been Hs 123s or Hs 126s; (f) Aircraft of KG 55; (g) Aircraft of 8/KG 55 which force-landed west of Druzy on the west bank of the Maas. This is the aircraft which he landed alongside to secure five prisoners. The Luftwaffe crew were subsequently released by advancing Panzers. Clisby's Hurricane had been damaged, and was abandoned.

CLOSTERMANN Pierre Henry

Further combat reports have been discovered relating to some of his claims in 1945, which affect his claims list:

1945

28 Mar	This Fi 156 was claimed destroyed on the ground, not in the air.
2 Apr	Add—2 Ju 188s Damaged on ground.
3 May	The FW190 was destroyed on the ground, not in the air.
„	Add 2 FW 190s Damaged on the ground.

REVISED TOTAL: 11 destroyed (plus possibly 5 additional), 2 probables (plus possibly 3 additional), 9 damaged, 4 destroyed on the ground (plus possibly 3 listed by Clostermann on 3 May 1945 as air victories), 4 damaged on the ground.

CLOWES Arthur Victor   RAF Nos. 563046 (NCO); 44780 (Officer)

'Darky' — not 'Taffy' — Clowes had no connection with Wales. He joined the RAF as an Aircraft Apprentice at Halton in January 1929. The French aircraft which collided with his Hurricane on 23 November 1939 was a Curtiss Hawk 75A, not a Morane 406. He was Mentioned in Despatches on 11 July 1940. In North Africa he attended a short refresher course at 1 METS before taking command of 94 Squadron. During a Mess party later in 1943 he was accidentally blinded in one eye, which put an end to his operational flying. He died of cancer of the liver, and is buried in Brampton, Cambridgeshire.

Additions to claim list:
1940

14 May —	the Bf 109E claimed was an aircraft of 4/JG 53.				
„ —	the Ju 87 was an aircraft of 2/StG 77, shot down over the Le Chesne area.				
15 May	Bf 110 (a)	Hurricane I		NW Rheims	1 Sqn

REVISED TOTAL: 10 and 1 shared destroyed, 1 shared unconfirmed destroyed, 3 probables, 2 damaged.
(a) Four Bf 110s of III/ZG 26 were claimed; two were actually shot down and two more were damaged and crash-landed.

COATE Edward Ernest

Ern Coate was born on 13 August 1908 in Lakes Entrance, Victoria. An engineer before the war, he enlisted in the RAAF on 13 October 1940, initially attending 2 ITS. In December he was posted to 8 EFTS, after which he was despatched to the UK in February 1941. Here he completed his pilot training at 2 SFTS, and then went to 3 School of General Reconnaissance via 3 PRC, in July 1941. He attended 2 (Coastal) OTU in October, and in February 1942 joined 236 Squadron as a coastal fighter pilot. In March he was sent out to the Middle East, initially joining 252 Squadron, He was transferred to 227 Squadron on 4 June 1942, and then to 272 Squadron on 27 June. He was posted home in May 1943, arriving in Australia on 1 June, where he became an instructor at 5 OTU. In July 1944 he was posted to RAAF HQ, while in October he commenced a course at the RAAF Staff School, returning to the HQ in January 1945. He was demobilised on 16 May 1945.

COBLEY Peter Charles   RAF Nos. 1293718 (NCO); 102296 (Officer)

He joined the RAFVR in July 1940 and subsequently served with 252 Squadron in early 1942, before joining 272 Squadron. He was promoted Flt Lt on 23 July 1943.

Additions to claim list:
1940

20 Feb	He 111 Damaged	Beaufighter IC	BT-U	W Mersa Matruh	252 Sqn
15 Jun		„	BT-O		
28 Nov		„	T5037 BT-E		
21 Dec		„	BT-J		

REVISED TOTAL: Add 1 damaged.

COCHRANE Arthur Charles
Attended Vernon High School, British Columbia.

COCHRANE Homer Powell
He may also have claimed two S 79s on 4 August 1940. He became a Sqn Ldr on 1 July 1944. In the original text in *Aces High* line 9 should read "...525 Transport Squadron."

Additions to claim list:
1941
13 Mar — two of the three CR 42s claimed were aircraft of 375ᵃ Squadriglia, Gruppo Aut CT, Serg Gualtiero Bacchi and Sottoten Enzo Torrini both being killed.

COCK John Reynolds
The Hurricane in which he was shot down on 11 August 1940 was V7233. It was salvaged from the sea on 30 August 1983; he had returned to the UK to be present on the occasion.

Corrections and additions to claim list:
1940
10 May — the Bf 110 claimed damaged may have been a second Do 17.
    „ — it was recorded in *Aces High* that the claim on this date for a Ju 88 may have been a Do 17, shared with another pilot. It was in fact a shared claim, but it is now believed that the victim was an He 111P of III/KG 54.
12 May — the He 111 claimed on this date is believed to have been an He 111H of 4/LG 1 flown by Oblt Kurt Söhler, which crashed NW of Lille.
14 May — the Bf 109E listed on this date was actually claimed on 13 May.
19 May — the Hs 126 was an aircraft of 1(H)/11Pz flown by Obgefr Karl-Heinz Kramer, lost in the Cateau-Cambrai area.

COEN Oscar Hoffman   RAF No. 62244; USAAF No. O-885105; O335955; 8746A
Oscar Coen graduated from the University of Wisconsin in 1939, entering the US Army Air Corps as an Aviation Cadet on 15 May 1940. He commenced training in Texas, but on 3 September was discharged on the basis of "flying deficiency". He joined the RCAF a week later, completing his training by December 1940, and in January 1941 was despatched to the UK. Here he was commissioned a Plt Off on 6 February, attending 56 OTU the following month before joining 71 'Eagle' Squadron on 19 April 1941. Promoted Flt Lt on 30 May 1942, he was awarded a DFC on 4 August 1942 and Mentioned in Despatches on 1 January 1943. He transferred to the USAAF as a Captain on 15 September 1942, and was promoted Major on 30 December that year, followed by Acting Lt Col on 4 October 1943. By this time he had completed his tour, serving for a time as an instructor at 53 OTU, RAF. After his return to the US he was confirmed as a Major on 1 November 1943, becoming a Lt Col again on 1 August 1944 and a full Colonel on 2 August 1945. He went onto the Reserve on 15 July 1946 as a 1st Lt ACRA, but rejoined the USAF, becoming a Captain in October 1948. During 1949 he completed the Senior Officer Military Management Course at the Air Command Staff School at the Air University. He also took the All Weather Interceptor Course and the Disaster Control Operations Officer Course, the latter in 1960. He served as Chief Air ROTC at the University of Wisconsin, and then commanded a jet fighter squadron. Later appointments included Assistant Air Mission Chief to Venezuela, Air Force Senior Advisor to the New Hampshire Air National Guard, and finally Group Operations Staff Officer, Wing Executive Officer and then Wing Deputy Commander for Operations at Kincheloe Air Force Base, Michigan. Promoted Major in October 1951 and Lt Col in August 1958, he retired on 31 May 1962 from the 507th Fighter Wing, Air Defence Command at Kincheloe, being promoted full Colonel on his retirement.

Corrections to claim list:

1943					
22 Jan		FW 190	Spitfire V	BL545 MD-L St Omer	336th FS
1944					
21 Jan	½	FW 190 Damaged	P-47	42-75389 R St Leger airfield	356th FG
10 Feb		„	„		
11 Feb		„	„		

No change to total.

COGHLAN John Hunter
John Coghlan was promoted Flg Off on 3 September 1938. He went to France with 56 Squadron on 18 May 1940. Some confusion surrounds his death however. Following his posting to the Parachute Practice Unit, on the night of 17/18 August 1940 he flew Lysander 'C' of the Unit's Special Duty Flight to France with an unidentified passenger aboard. This aircraft is believed to have been R2625, the fate of which is not recorded. It is known however, that it had been modified for night flying and that the rear guns had been removed. It is also believed that his last flight was made from North Weald, where the PPU's Special Duty Flight subsequently became 419 Flight. It was from this airfield that the first signal recording the loss of the Lysander emanated. It is also believed that rather than crashing into the sea, he had delivered a French agent to the Boulogne area, where he and the agent were either captured and shot by German troops, or killed whilst seeking to resist or escape. Final confirmation of the exact circumstances of his fate have not been discovered, but he is buried at Boulogne.

Corrections and additions to claim list:

1940					
18 May		Bf 109E	Hurricane I	N2400	near Mauberge	56 Sqn

| | ½ | He 111 unconfirmed (b) | ,, | ,, | 20 miles SE Lille | ,, |
| 19 May | | He 111 Damaged | ,, | ,, | near Mauberge | ,, |

13 Jul — the second claim on this date should read "He 113" (not He 112)
REVISED TOTAL: 4 and 1 shared destroyed, 1 and 1 shared unconfirmed destroyed, 4 damaged/inconclusive.
(b) This aircraft was from the Stabsstaffel/KG 1, and crash-landed at Graux, SW Naumur.

COLE Robert Bruce   RAF Nos. 9299432 (NCO); 66483 (Officer)

Cole volunteered for the RAF in September 1939 and was called up for training in June 1940. He was promoted Flt Lt on 2 April 1943. After the war he became a Sqn Ldr on 1 January 1950, and in 1955 was a Wg Cdr, DFC & Bar, AFC, commanding the Tactics Branch of the All-Weather Wing of the CFE. He was killed on 16 January 1956 when he crashed at Sudbrooke in Canberra PR 7 WT529.

COLEMAN George Byrne Stanislaus

Coleman was born on 4 September 1908, working initially as a salesman before being commissioned in the RAF as a Plt Off on 13 September 1929. He trained as 5 FTS, Sealand, then joining 16 (Army Co-operation) Squadron in September 1930. In January 1932 he was posted to 463 (Torpedo Bomber) Flight on HMS *Courageous*, where he served with future VC, then Flg Off Eugene Esmonde. In May 1933 he went to the RAF Base at Gosport on Fleet work, but on 13 September 1934 was transferred to the Class A Reserve of Officers, becoming an airline pilot. He was promoted Flt Lt in April 1937, and was mobilized on 1 September 1939, being seconded to a civil flying school as an instructor for the rest of the year. At the start of 1940 he moved to 15 EFTS, Redhill, and in March attended the Flying Instructors' Course at CFS, gaining a Category B classification. On completion of this course he remained at CFS as a supernumary until January 1941. He was then posted to 8 SFTS, Montrose, until May 1941, when he joined 6 AACU, Ringway. Finally in August he attended 60 OTU, East Fortune, in September joining 256 Squadron. In December he was posted to 456 Squadron, RAAF, but in mid March 1942 was sent to the Middle East. He moved from 89 Squadron to 46 Squadron on 21 May, immediately following his service on Malta, while in November 1942 he joined 272 Squadron. On 11 January 1943 he was slightly injured in a flying accident, when 272 Squadron's "hack" Beaufort, DW761, collided with a Harvard during take off from Heliopolis. He was promoted Acting Sqn Ldr on 16 January 1943, but relinquished this rank on posting home to the UK in May. Here in July he went to 2 Torpedo Training Unit, Castle Kennedy, as an instructor, moving in August to 9 (Coastal) OTU, Crosby-on-Eden, in a similar role. In March 1944 he returned to the Mediterranean, joining 600 Squadron. On 20 October he became a flight commander and was again promoted Acting Sqn Ldr. He returned to the UK in mid April 1945, and resigned his commission at the end of September. He then returned to airline flying, but was killed in a flying accident.

Corrections and additions to claim list:

1942			
4 Sep		V8227	S Amriya
1943			
17 Mar		EL323 'M'	
1945			
20 Jan	*	V8734 'M'	Italy

* The claims on this date were made with Flg Off W.R.Frumar, RAAF, acting as his radar operator; one of the aircraft claimed was a Ju 87D-5 of 3/NSGr 9 flown by Obfhr Peter Stollwerk.

COLEMAN Patrick Tuisley   RAF Nos. 1386814 (NCO); 190247 (Officer)

Born on 7 July 1922 in Southend-on-Sea, Essex, he attended Southend High School, then working as a clerk at the Bank of England, 1939-41. He was recommended for pilot/observer training with the RAFVR in March 1941, enlisting as an AC 2 Aircrafthand/Pilot, but was placed on the reserve until July. He commenced training at 4 ITW, Paignton, in August, and in September became an LAC u/t Pilot (Group 2), being selected for Arnold Scheme training in the USA. Travelling out via Canada, he reached Maxwell Field, Alabama, as a Sgt on 16 October 1941, qualifying as a pilot on 17 May 1942. He returned to the UK in June, and in July was posted to 5(P) Advanced Flying Unit at Ternhill. He was promoted Flt Sgt in May 1943, and on 1 March 1944 was posted to the 13 Group Communications Squadron. A month later he attended 1 TEU, Tealing. Promotion to Wt Off followed, and on 7 June 1944 he joined 41 Squadron to fly Spitfire XIIs. He was commissiond on 12 December 1944 as a Plt Off, becoming a Flg Off on 12 June 1945. On 27 July his DFC was gazetted. On 8 August 1945 he was posted to the Transport Command Aircrew Holding Centre at Morecambe. He was attached to 44 Group at Melton Mowbray for ferry training, 17 August-11 September, but was then granted three months compassionate release. He was recalled to the active list at HQ, Fighter Command, on 23 February 1946, but was released on 6 July. He returned to the Bank of England until 16 January 1952, when he relinquished his commission and rejoined the General Duties Branch of the RAF as a Flg Off. Promoted Flt Lt in November 1956, he then transferred to the Secretarial Branch (Intelligence); in January 1957 his service was extended for a further five years, and then for two more in January 1962. However, he died on 10 August 1962.

Corrections to claim list:

| 1944 | | |
| 3 Sep | | Spitfifre XII (not XIV) (a) |

1945
All further victories in Spitfire XIVs.
(a) FW 190 of II/JG 26.

CONWAY Alfred (not Arthur) Gordon   RAF Nos. 1295392 (NCO); 104547 (Officer)
In 1948 when he served with 222 Squadron, it was equipped with Meteor F.4s, not F.3s.

COLLOREDO-MANSFELD Franz Ferdinand
RAF Nos. 1385480 (NCO); 112005 (Officer)
He had lived in Welham, Massachussets, prior to joining the RAF. He was aged 33 at the time of his death, and was buried in the Boulogne War Cemetery.

Corrections to claim list:
1943
13 Jan —   the Spitfire flown was BS541 (not B5541).

COLLYNS Basil Gordon RNZAF No. 391368 (not RAF)

Corrections to claim list:
Claims from 20 June 1944 onwards were made whilst flying with 19 Squadron (not 65 Squadron).

COMELY Peter Woodruff
He was commissioned in April 1939, training at 11 FTS. He was detached from 145 Squadron to 87 Squadron on 16 May 1940.

CONRAD Walter Allan Grenfell

Correction to claim list:
The Hurricane IIB in which he made his claims in February 1942 was BG631, not DG631.

CONSTABLE-MAXWELL Michael Hugh
Michael Constable-Maxwell was not dead at the date of publication of *Aces High* in 1994; he remained alive at the date of writing this current volume. He was born into a wealthy and noble Scottish family, one of six sons and two daughters. He attended Ampleforth College, 1927-36, and then Hertford College, Oxford, where he read History and joined the University Air Squadron. He spent two months in Poland during 1938, and in spring 1939 applied for a Permanent Commission in the RAF. He was accepted on 28 August, but spent the first months of the war with the Queen's Own Cameron Highlanders. He was granted his commission on 7 October 1939, but with seniority from 7 July 1938, and on receipt of this, relinquished his territorial commission with the Camerons on the same day, joining the RAF on 10th. He was then posted to 9 FTS, Hullavington, with many other UAS pupils. In March 1940 he was posted to 7 Bombing and Gunnery School at Stormy Down, Porthcawl, before joining 56 Squadron on 20 April. With 84 Squadron in 1945 he took part in some operations against Indonesian guerillas in Java from October 1945 — March 1946. During his time at Ampleforth he did some teaching and also commanded the RAF contingent of the school's CCF as a Flg Off. On his return to the RAF as a Sqn Ldr he attended an Officers' Administration Course and then a flying refresher course at 22 FTS, Syerston, in January 1953. In March he attended 209 Advanced FS at Weston Zoyland, learning to fly Meteors, and then in July went to 228 OTU, Leeming, on Meteor NF 11s. On 12 November he joined 23 Squadron at Coltishall on Vampire NF 10s, taking command of the squadron in January 1954 when the previous CO was killed, and converting the unit to Venom NF 2s. He then became o/c Flying at Coltishall, commanding this airfield's "all-weather" Wing until January 1956. A refresher course on instructing at CFS, South Cerney, followed, and then in April he took command of the Oxford UAS. In March 1960 he was posted to command RAF Gan in the Indian Ocean until the end of that year, when he returned to the UK as Air Liaison Officer to the GOC, Chester, in Western Command. He married on 20 January 1962, obtaining a three month leave of absence to study military problems in Africa. On return in April 1962 he went to HQ, Scottish Command, until his retirement from the service. A biography of he and his WW I fighter pilot brother, Gerald Maxwell, was written by Alex Revell under the title *The Vivid Air* (William Kimber, 1978).His cousins included David Sterling, founder of the Special Air Service, Lord Lovat, commander of the Lovat Scouts Commando unit, who wrote *March Past*, and Fitzroy Maclean, who served in Yugoslavia, attached to Tito's headquarters, and who wrote *Eastern Approaches*. Details of Robert Maxwell's career will also be found in *Above the Trenches* (Grub Street, 1990).

CONSTANTINE Alexander Noel
He joined the RAF in May 1938 and attended 9 E & RFTS, Anstey, initially. In July he undertook ground training at Uxbridge, then going to 8 FTS, Montrose, for his main flying training until March 1939.Postings followed to

1 Air Observers' School, North Coates, as a staff pilot until September, and then 4 AOS, West Freugh. A period in hospital and convalescing occupied October-November, following which he attended 10 BGS, Warmwell. On 4 December 1939 he was posted to 141 Squadron on Defiants. On 28 April 1941 he moved to 23 Squadron to fly Havocs. A course at 1 Blind Approach School in May-June was followed by a posting to 60 OTU at East Fortune as an instructor. In October 1941 he joined 264 Squadron, flying Defiants again, but a month later moved to the similarly-equipped 125 Squadron, and then in December to 87 Squadron on Hurricanes. In January 1942 he was despatched to India on HMAS *Monarch of Bermuda* and HMAS *Awatea*, joining AHQ, New Delhi, on arrival. On 30 April 1942 he was posted to command 273 Squadron in Ceylon on Hurricanes, remaining there until June 1943, when he moved to 136 Squadron, converting to Spitfires late in the year. In April 1944 he was posted to HQ, ACSEA as Wg Cdr Tactics, but returned to the UK in June 1944 to attend the Fighter Leaders' School at Milfield. He returned to HQ, ACSEA, in October 1944, where he served until June 1945. He then went home to Australia, joining HQ, RAAF Airboard, Melbourne, until the end of July 1945. A return to HQ, ACSEA, at Kandy followed on 3 August.

COLLARD Peter

From Ashted, Surrey, Peter Collard joined 11 Group Pool for fighter training on 12 September 1939 as a Flg Off. He was aged 24 at the time of his death, his body being washed ashore at Oye-Plage, east of Calais.

COOPER-SLIPPER Thomas Paul Michael

His date of birth was 11 January 1921. After service in the East Indies in 1942, he spent six months in various hospitals in India and South Africa.

Corrections and additions to claim list:
The date of the 1943 claim was 15 June, and the Spitfire flown was a Mark IX.

CORK Richard John

His prewar life was similar to that of his close friend, Arthur Blake, as detailed in the notes on the latter earlier in this volume. On 14 April 1944 he had taken off before dawn to check whether prevailing poor weather would allow an exercise to take place. He advised that it would not, but could not land back on the carrier as the deck was full of aircraft awaiting take off. He flew instead to China Bay, arriving before dawn. He passed over the runway once to ascertain whether the airfield, which was generally closed at that time of day, was clear. Finding the flarepath lit, he then landed, but met an unlit Corsair which was just taking off to join *Illustrious*, head-on. Both aircraft were burnt out. Cork had been flying JT347, carrying his initials RC, as Wing Leader. An excellent and well-illustrated biography, detailing not only his own life, but also that of Arthur Blake, had just been published at the time of writing, entitled *Naval Fighter Pilot: Lt Cdr R.J.Cork, DSO,DSC,RN*, written by A.H.Wren (Heron Books of Lichfield, 1998). This contains a number of excellent illustrations, including a photograph depicting Dennis Jeram, Arthur Blake, Francis Dawson-Paul and 'Jimmie' Gardner with Cork.

COSBY Ivor Henry

On 15 May 1943 he moved from 51 OTU to 60 OTU whilst an instructor, at this time with the rank of Flt Lt. He commanded 151 Squadron during 1955, and died of cancer in September 1994.

Corrections and additions to claim list:
The 141 Squadron victory board indicates that his claim, recorded as 15/16 April 1942, in fact occurred on 15/16 February. The claim of 25 August was noted as being confirmed destroyed.

1944				
15/16 Jul	V-1	Mosquito XIII (b)	481	264 Sqn
19?20 Jul	V-1	"	610	"

REVISED TOTAL: 5 and 1 shared destroyed, 2 damaged, 2 V-1s destroyed.
(b) with Flt Lt E.R.Murphy as radar operator.

COTTINGHAM Leonard

He commenced his Halton apprenticeship in September 1931.

COWPER Robert Barson

During the engagement of 11/12 July 1943, the mine or bomb being carried by the Ju 88 was not jettisoned; it exploded whilst still attached to the aircraft.

Addition to claim list:

1944			
27/28 Jul	V-1	Mosquito XVII	456 Sqn

REVISED TOTAL: 6 destroyed, 1 damaged, 1 V-1 destroyed.

COX David George Samuel Richardson   RAF Nos. 745136 (NCO); 101041 (Officer)

Corrections to claim list:

1941		
27 Jun		Spitfire II (not VII)

12 Aug		„	P8241 (not R8241)	
1942				
26 Jul		Spitfire V (not IX) BM345		

COX Graham James   RAF Nos. 564573 (NCO); 41668 (Officer)

Graham Cox actually joined the RAF in 1930, being commissioned in 1939. Following his final operational tour, he worked as a forward controller in Italy during the late months of the war. He was awarded a DSO on 10 October 1945. He was later killed in a flying accident in a Cessna whilst flying over Canada's Northern Territories; bad weather caused the aircraft to become uncontrollable due to icing.

CRAIG John Teasdale

'Bobby' Craig enlisted as a Halton Apprentice in January 1930, later being selected for pilot training. He was despatched to France on 18 May 1940. On 21 January 1941 he was posted to 56 OTU as a Sgt instructor. He is buried at Witton-le-Wear, which is in County Durham, not on the Isle of Man as recorded in the 1994 *Aces High*.

Additions to claim list:

1940					
18 May		Bf 110 (b)	Hurricane I	L1607	111 Sqn

REVISED TOTAL: 6 destroyed, 4 probables, 8 damaged.
(b) His own aircraft was damaged and he crash-landed north of Vimy; his victim was a Bf 110C of I/ZG 26.

CRAWFORD-COMPTON William Vernon   RAF Nos. 905967 (NCO); 65500 (Officer)

As a Grp Capt he commanded Gamil airfield, Egypt, immediately following the seaborne invasion during the Suez operation of November 1956.

Corrections to claim list:

1941			
13 Oct		Spitfire VB	P8786 (not P87886)

CREW Edward Dixon

He attended 5 OTU in June 1940, prior to joining 604 Squadron. Whilst operating against V-1s during summer 1944, he flew with Sgt Jaeger, Wt Off Croysdill, Capt Hughes and Flg Off Da Costa as radar operators. On 25 June 1944 an exploding V-1 split open the nose of Mosquito XIII MM499, causing he and his radar operator to bale out near Worthing, Sussex.

Corrections and additions to claim list:

1940						
11 Aug	1/2	He 59 (a)	Blenheim IF	L6728		604 Sqn
11 Sep	1/2	Do 18 on sea (b)	„			„
1944						
All claims made in Mosquito XIIIs, not Mark XIIs.						
18/19 Apr		Me 410 (c)				
20/21 Jun		V-1	Mosquito XIII	MM499	N Dungeness	96 Sqn
24/25 Jun		V-1 (d)	„	„	S Hastings	„
27/28 Jun		V-1	„	„	„	„
28/29 Jun	2	V-1s	„	MK426		„
2/3 Jul	3	V-1s	„	MM985		„
5/6 Jul	3	V-1s	„	MM591	over sea	„
6/7 Jul		V-1	„	MM511		„
9/10 Jul		V-1	„	„	Worthing	„
20/21 Jul	2	V-1s	„		over sea	„
22/23 Jul		V-1	„	N5985	6 m N Newchurch	„
„	2	V-1s	„	„	over sea	„
28/29 Jul		V-1	„		„	„
3/4 Aug	2	V-1s	„	N5985	6 m S Dover	„

REVISED TOTAL: 12 and 1 shared destroyed, 1 shared destroyed on the sea, 5 damaged, 21 V-1s destroyed.
(a) Crew and another pilot forced this floatplane to land on the sea and completed its destruction there; (b) Reportedly this flyingboat was being towed by an E-Boat when attacked; (c) This aircraft was shot down with the assistance of Wt Off W.R.Croysdill as radar operator. It was flown by Oblt Richard Pohl, a highly-decorated pilot of KG 2, who was killed when the aircraft crashed in St Nicholas Churchyard, Brighton. The navigator/air gunner, Fw Wilhelm Schubert, baled out into the sea and was drowned. (d) Crew and his radar operator baled out when their own aircraft was damaged by the explosion.

CROMBIE Charles Arbuthnot

The serial numbers for the Beaufighters flown during the September-December 1942 period were extracted from Crombie's logbook. All those listed from 23/24 September — 27/28 November were Mark IFs, not Mark VIFs. V8158, listed as flown on 17/18 December 1942 was a Mark IIF, recorded as being used only for training in the UK; this entry must therefore have been in error.

CRONIN Laurance Francis Marshal

Corrections to claim list:
1943

26 Mar	Spitfire IX	EN195 FL-C (not FN195)
25 Jul	Spitfire VC	JL188 (Not Spitfire IX EN490)
14 Sep	Spitfire IX	MB531 (not MB807)

1944

6 Mar and 13 Mar	Spitfire VIII	JF630 FL-C
12 Apr		JG314

CROSS Robert Walter   RAF Nos. 924906 (NCO); 173280 (Officer)

He was commissioned on 22 September 1943.

Additions to claim list:
1943

23 Jan	Hurricane IIB	HM-E

1944

9 Feb	Spitfire VIII	HM-E
16 Mar		HM-J

CROWLEY-MILLING Denis   RAF Nos. 740885 (NCO); 78274 (Officer)

He was born in St Asaph, Flintshire. He attended 5 OTU in April 1940, before joining 615 Squadron. During his tours he undertook 290 patrol sorties, 101 sweeps, 30 dive-bombing and ten intruder strafing attacks, for a total of 431 sorties. He died on 1 December 1996.

Corrections and additions to claim list:
1940
31 Aug (not 30th)

17 Sep	$1/2$	Ju 88	Hurricane I	242 Sqn

1941

8 Feb	$1/4$	Do 17 (not $1/3$)	
1 Apr	$1/2$	Ju 88 Probable (not Damaged)	

1942

19 Aug		Bf 109F (not Probable)
„		FW 190 Damaged
„		Bf 109F Damaged

REVISED TOTAL: 4 and 2 shared destroyed, 1 and 1 shared probables, 3 and 1 shared damaged.

CULLEN Richard Nigel

Additions to claim list:
1940

30 Dec			Gladiator II	N5786

1941

28 Jan			„	N5817
9 Feb			„	„
10 Feb			„	N5810
20 Feb			„	N5817
27 Feb		CR 42	Hurricane I	V7137	Valona
28 Feb	$1/2$	BR 20 (not whole)	„	V7138

„		„	„

REVISED TOTAL: 15 and 1 shared destroyed, 2 probables, 1 damaged, 1 destroyed on the water.

CUNDY William Ronald

With 452 Squadron in the Darwin area, he usually flew Spitfire VIII A58-435, QY-T.

Corrections to claim list:
1942

26 Oct	Kittyhawk II	FL288 (not FL2887)

CUNNINGHAM John

His victory on 19/20 November 1940 was not, in fact, the first for a Beaufighter as stated. This was achieved on 25/26 October 1940 by Sgt A.J.Hodgkinson. Hodgkinson is listed in *Aces High* as flying a Blenheim on that occasion (see pages 330-1), but this is in error, and is corrected herein under the relevant entry.

Corrections to claim list:
1943

13/14 June and thereafter	Mosquito XII(NB) DZ302/G VY-R

1944

20/21 Feb and 23/24 Feb	Mosquito XVII (not XVIII)

NB. This aircraft had been constructed as a Mark II, but converted to Mark XII standard — hence the /G at the end of the serial.

CUNNINGHAM Wallace RAF Nos. 741899 (NCO); 80545 (Officer)
Known as 'Jock', not 'Jack'. He attended 5 OTU in June 1940 before joining 19 Squadron.

CURCHIN John
He was not shot down on 4 June 1941, but collided with a Bf 109 of Stab/JG 53, flown by Fw H.Ruhl, and crashed.

Addition to claim list:
1940

15 Sep	½	Do 17	Spitfire I	E London	609 S

REVISED TOTAL: 8 and 5 shared destroyed, 1 shared unconfirmed destroyed, 1 probable, 1 damaged.

CURRANT Christopher Frederick RAF Nos. 580097 (NCO); 43367 (Officer)
He entered the RAF in January 1936. He was Mentioned in Despatches on 14 January 1944.

Addition to claim list:
1940
On 21 or 22 May he claimed an He 111 unconfirmed near Arras. His Hurricane was hit by return fire and he crash-landed, making his way to Calais on foot for return to the UK by sea.
REVISED TOTAL: 10 and 5 shared destroyed, 1 unconfirmed destroyed, 2 probables, 12 damaged.

CURRY John Harvey

Additions to claim list:
1942

26 Jun		BR301
1 Sep		BP988
7 Sep		BR478
„	Bf 109F Damaged	„
11 Sep		BR481
29 Sep		BR469
3 & 11 Oct		BR583
20 Oct		BP852
21 Oct		AB345
23 Oct		BR583
26 Oct (a)		AB345

REVISED TOTAL: 7 and 1 shared destroyed, 2 probables, 4 damaged.
(a) An aircraft of 90ª Squadriglia, 10° Gruppo, 4° Stormo CT which Serg Amleto Monterumici crash-landed.

CURTIS Victor Farley RAAF No. 400039 Flying Officer
Vic Curtis was born on 11 November 1918 in Melbourne, Victoria. He was a motor finance collector prior to joining the RAAF on 29 April 1940. He attended 3 EFTS and 1SFTS in Australia, followed by 1 Bombing and Gunnery School in December 1940. The following month he joined 24 RAAF Squadron, but in August 1941 was despatched to the Middle East, where he joined 3 RAAF Squadron on 25 September. At the end of his tour he returned home to Australia, being posted to 2 OTU, Mildura, on 20 October 1942. He was killed on 6 January 1943, it is presumed in a flying accident whilst an instructor.

Addition to claim list:
1942
8 Mar — claims made against the 150° Gruppo Aut CT, which lost three pilots in this engagement.

CWYNAR Michal RAF Nos. P782851 (NCO); P1903 (Officer)
Michal Cwynar was not dead in 1994. His brother, Grp Capt Stanislaw Cwynar, VM, KW, who had flown PZL Los bombers in Poland in 1939, and then commanded 300 (Polish) Bomber Squadron in the UK, died on 9 August 1982. His death was mistakenly believed to have referred to Michal Cwynar. Michal was born in the East Carpathian village of Orzechowka in the Lvov area. In 1933 he entered the air force school for juniors, undertaking a three year course as a pilot, engine and airframe mechanic. During 1934 he undertook an elementary gliding course, and in 1935 undertook his elementary flying training at Radon. That autumn he was sent to No 1 Air Force Base, Okecie, Warsaw, where he flew Potez XV and XXV, Breguet XIX and Lublin R XIII aircraft. In 1936 he attended the Advanced Flying School and was selected for fighters, now training on MS 61, PWS 26, and finally on PZL P 7 aircraft. In autumn 1936 he was posted to 113 Eskadra in the Warsaw Pursuit Brigade. From May to December 1938 he was one of seven pilots chosen to be based at Sarny, a strip in the east of the country, covering construction of fortifications to the eastern frontier. Deputy commander of this detachment was A.Gabszewicz, from 114 Eskadra. At the end of August 1939 the Pursuit Brigade eskadras were

dispersed to landing grounds near the capital prior to the German invasion. Following a move to south-east Poland during 10-12 September, he crossed into Rumania on 17th, where he was interned in Bucharest. False passports identifying he and other pilots as civilian mechanics, were provided by the Polish embassy, and the group were moved to Constanza on the Black Sea, and thence on the Greek vessel *Patria*, to Syria. They then sailed on the *Strasbourg* to Marseilles. In December 1939 he arrived at the Armée de l'Air base at Lyon-Bron for training on French fighters, and in April 1940 joined GC III/10 on Morane 406s at Le Luc. This unit had moved to Toulouse to convert to Dewoitine D 520s when the Italian attack on Southern France occurred, and was then evacuated to North Africa. The senior Polish officer organised all Poles at Casablanca, and from there they went by sea to Gibraltar. Eventually all arrived at Liverpool, and were despatched from there to Scotland by train, and then to a new Polish Depot in Blackpool. Cwynar was then posted to 15 FTS, Carlisle, where the PZL Chief Test Pilot, Capt Orlizski was an instructor. Here he flew Fairey Battles, being posted to 10 BGS, Dumfries. He then attended 55 OTU at Usworth, and in April 1941 was posted to 315 Squadron. Commissioned in June 1942, he was rested in May 1943, going to 58 OTU, Balado Bridge, as an instructor, and then in October to 61 OTU, Rednal. In November he rejoined 315 Squadron, where he served until September 1944, becoming a flight commander in June. On 8 June his Mustang was hit by Flak, forcing him to jettison his bombs and bale out near Caen. On 5 September, whilst on an armed reconnaissance in the Cologne-Hamburg area, he was slightly wounded by Flak. Posted to the Depot in Blackpool, he then moved to 16 (Polish) SFTS at RAF Newton in January 1945. In May, after the close of hostilities, he rejoined 315 Squadron, now at Andrews Field, but in July took command of 316 Squadron. In October he was posted to the 133 Wing HQ at Andrews Field. He moved to Turnhouse in December, transferring to the RAF at this time, and then to Wick, where he remained until 27 March 1946. He was then posted as adjutant to the CFI at Hethel until December 1946. He was then moved to PRC, Framlingham until August 1947, and then to Leeming until November. He then attended a Link Trainer Instructor's Course at South Cerney, returning to Leeming. As he was no longer able to fly, he left the RAF in September 1948 to live in Dumfries, Scotland. Here he began a business upholstering motor coaches, which he built into a successful concern. He also constructed a house on the bank of the River Nith, where he was still living in retirement at the time of writing. He was awarded the Virtuti Militari, 5th Class, the KW and three Bars, the Silver Cross of Merit with Swords, the DFC (8 September 1945), the AFM and Bar, and the Croix des Combattants Volontaires (in 1947).

Corrections and additions to claim list:

1939						
1 Sep		Ju 87	PZL P11C		W Warsaw	113 Esk
4 Sep		Bf 110 (a)	”			”
1941						
14 Aug		Bf 109E (b)	Spitfire II	P7613 PK-Z	Ardres	315 Sqn
16 Sep		Bf 109E	Spitfire VB	AB914 PK-R	N St Omer	”
1943						
3 Feb		FW 190	Spitfire IX	EN123 PK-T		”
1944						
19 Jul	½	V-1	Mustang III	PK-Z	3m NW Tenterden	”
20 Jul	½	V-1	”	PK-U		”
22 Jul	½	V-1	”	PK-N	5m NW Ashford	”
”	½	V-1	”	”	2m SE Tenterden	”
24 Jul		V-1	”	PK-Z		”
30 Jul		Bf 109F	”	”	Escorting Beaufighters	”
”	½	Bf 109F	”	”	to Norway	”
6 Aug		V-1	”	”	6m N Tonbridge	”

TOTAL: 5 or 6 and 1 shared destroyed, 1 or 2 probably destroyed, 2 and 4 shared V-1s destroyed.
(a) His own records indicate a Bf 110 destroyed or probably destroyed on 4 September; Polish records indicate an He 111 Probable on 6 September. It is likely therefore that his 1939 total was 1 and 1 probable, but may have been 2 destroyed; (b) This is recorded in the 315 Squadron ORB as occurring on 12 August, when he was flying Spitfire II P8582, PK-R.

CZERNIN Count Manfred Beckett

He attended the 12 Group Pool at Aston Down for operational training in December 1939, before being posted to 504 Squadron. On 16 May 1940, shortly after joining 85 Squadron, his Hurricane, L1630, was hit by fire from a Bf 109E of 3/JG 76, and he force-landed. He returned on foot to Lille-Seclin after three days.

Corrections and additions to claim list:
1940
19 May — (i) He claimed two Do 17s; one Do 17Z was lost by 9/KG 76, flown by Oblt Rudolf Strasser.
   (ii) The He 111 he claimed was an He 111P of 6/KG 4, which was also attacked by another pilot. Flown by Uffz Johann Kettner, it came down north west of Cokeren.
   (iii) The second He 111 claimed, was claimed as damaged, not unconfirmed destroyed.
20 May — The Hs 126 was an aircraft of 3(H)/14.

DADDO-LANGLOIS William Raoul RAF Nos. 1164369 (NCO); 100625 (Officer)

The service number 36426 listed in *Aces High* related to his father, Grp Capt W.J.Daddo-Langlois. Raoul was 21 when killed.

Additions to claim list:
1942

6 Jun (a)	Spitfire VC	BR107 C-22
4 Jul	"	BR170 B
11 Jul	"	BR565 U

(a) 152ª Squadriglia, 2° Gruppo Aut CT lost four pilots during this combat.

DAFFORN Robert Chippindall   RAF Nos. 740804 (NCO); 81674 (Officer)

He attended 11 Group Pool for operational training before joining 501 Squadron on 14 September 1939. He was commissioned on 13 July 1940 with seniority from 25 April.

Corrections and additions to claim list:
1940

11 May —	the Do 17 was a Do 17Z of 2/KG 2; two aircraft from this unit were claimed during the engagement; one was actually lost and one damaged.
24 Aug —	Regarding the Ju 88 claimed damaged, it is reported that Dafforn saw this aircraft in a damaged condition and fired at it until it went down into the sea. Fighter Command Combats & Casualties record only two Ju 88s damaged by the squadron at this time. It does however appear to have been an aircraft of 5(F)/122 which was lost off the Kent coast at the time recorded — 1330 hours approximately. This does not appear to have been credited to Dafforn other than as a Damaged however.

DAHL Roald

Corrections and additions to claim list:
1941

8 June	½	Potez 63 Probable (a)	Hurricane I	V7148		80 Sqn
15 Jun				Z4194	12 m W of Fleet	"

REVISED TOTAL: 4 destroyed, 1 shared probable
(a) Not an individual confirmed victory as listed in *Aces High*.

DALEY William James Jr.   RAF No. 101457; USAAF No. O-885103

Born on 30 November 1919, and qualified as a pilot on 5 January 1941.

DALTON-MORGAN Thomas Frederick

Attended 6 OTU as a Flt Lt in June 1940 before joining 43 Squadron.

DANIEL Edward Gough RAF Nos. 1181645 (NCO); 61310 (Officer)

From Barrington, Somerset, he was aged 23 when killed.

DANIEL Stephen Walter   RAF Nos. 629264 (NCO); 46874 (Officer)

He enlisted in December 1938, and was commissioned in October 1941. He was shot down by Flak on 27 December 1944 and crash-landed, suffering slight wounds. On 21 August 1945 he was awarded a DSO, not a DFC as stated at the top of page 209 in *Aces High*.

Corrections and additions to claim list:
1943

26 Mar	Spitfire IX	EN391 RN-7 (not EN3917)
8 Jul	Spitfire VC (not IX)	JG793
11 Jul	"	JK173
12 Jul	"	JK429(c)

(c) This aircraft is listed as missing from a sweep over Sicily on this date; it may have been lost whilst flown by another pilot later in the day.

DARLEY Horace Stanley

On return from France in 1940, he attended 5 OTU before joining 65 Squadron. He was later Mentioned in Despatches.

DARLING Edward Vivian   RAF Nos. 740608 (NCO); 65979 (Officer)

He was born in 1914 in Wellington, Madras, India, but lived later in Wembley, Middlesex. He enlisted in the RAFVR as an AC2 in December 1936, training as a pilot, and attending 12 Group Pool, Aston Down, as a Sgt in January 1940 for operational training before joining 41 Squadron. He was posted to 53 OTU as an instructor on 27 November 1941 (rather than in early 1942, when it is recorded in *Aces High* that he was rested).

DAVENPORT Robert Monroe

Davenport was not, as recorded, a Canadian. He was a US citizen, born in Russellville, Arkansas, who lived in Arlington, Virginia, before the war. He enlisted in the RCAF on 4 October 1941, undertaking his flight training by the end of August 1942. He was despatched to the UK the following month as a Sgt, attending 58 OTU from 29 December. Promoted Flt Sgt on 31 January 1943, he joined 401 Squadron the following month. He was commissioned on 23 June 1943, and promoted Flg Off on 23 December that year. On 9 January 1944 he was shot down over Europe, but was able to evade capture and returned to the UK by 10 April. A month later he rejoined his unit, where he became a flight commander on 17 September. His claims included 60 motor vehicles destroyed during strafing attacks. He returned to Canada on 31 March 1945, where he was released from the service on 11 October.

DAVID William Dennis

Dennis David left school at the age of 14 to work as a clerk in the City of London in the firm of a family friend. He completed his flying training at the Royal Navy Air School at Ford in early 1939 before joining 87 Squadron in February. He was posted to 213 Squadron on 16 September 1940 (not 16 October), and to 152 Squadron on 23 November. On 24 March 1941 he went to 55 OTU as a Flt Lt instructor, and from there to 59 OTU on 19 June as Assistant CFI. He returned to 55 OTU on 23 November 1941 to become Wg Cdr Training, moving with the OTU to Annan in April 1942. After his return to the UK from the Far East, he served at HQ, Reserve Command, from July 1946-September 1948, then being sent out to Libya as station commander, RAF El Adem from September-November 1949. From then until March 1951 he was i/c Flying, 324 Wing, in the Mediterranean area, then returning to the UK to HQ, 18 Group, Coastal Command, until April 1953. A spell at the RAF Flying College, Manby, was followed by two years at the Air Ministry, May 1954-56. His next posting was as Air Attache in Budapest, where he was able to assist many fleeing the country following the unsuccessful rising in Hungary during the autumn of 1956. Awarded a CBE, he retired from the service in May 1967, becoming director of an engineering company. He was to serve in this role with several other companies until about 1980. Since then he has been involved in work for a number of service charities.

Corrections and additions to claim list:
His logbook for 1940 shows a provisional total at the end of his service in France as four Heinkels, two Dorniers, a Bf 110, a Ju 87 and four probables. He was however "awarded" 14 confirmed in France. A note made in August 1940 records that he could account for 11 confirmed and approximately 12 "doubtful" in France. Later in August he recorded 14 confirmed and 14 unconfirmed, and at the end of his 1940 fighting, he arrived at a total of 18 confirmed and 14 unconfirmed. This considerably exceeds the 27 claims that have been found for him, or that can be identified.

1939		
2 Nov		He 111 Damaged — this was an aircraft of 2(F)/122 which suffered 30% damage; David's own Hurricane was damaged by return fire, and Plt Off Mackworth who was with him, was obliged to force-land.
1940		
10 May		He 111 — this was an He 111H of II/KG 53, one of four attacked by four Hurricanes; two of the Heinkels crash-landed due to damage.
,,	½	Do 17 ⎱ six Do 17Zs of III/KG 2 were attacked by David and Sgt G.L.Nowell, who claimed two or three Do 17 ⎰ between them. One crash-landed near Trier, and a second was damaged, but reached its airfield.
11 May		Ju 87 — six claims made against Stab and I/StG 2, which suffered six losses, three crashed and three crash-landed.
		Do 17 — this was one of three Do 17Ms of StabSt/StG 2, flying with the Ju 87s, all of which were lost.
14 May	½	He 111 ⎫ He 111Ps of I and III/KG 27, initially attacked by 85 Squadron; six and one probable claimed He 111 ⎬ — three actually shot down and one damaged. He 111 ⎭
,,	½	Bf 109E-(not a full victory as previously recorded); this may have been an aircraft of I/JG 27.
16 May		Bf 110 Probable — this is in addition to the Ju 87 claimed on this date; the Hurricane flown on this date was V7207, not N7207.
15 Aug		

REVISED TOTAL: in the light of the obvious confusion regarding his service in France, his total remains uncertain. He undoubtedly claimed seven confirmed victories over England during the summer of 1940 to add to those claimed in France.

DAVIDSON Henry John   RAF Nos. 741340 (NCO); 61945 (Officer)

He joined the RAFVR in February 1938.

Revised claim list:

1940						
15 Aug	⅓	Bf 110	Hurricane I	P2866	Ringwood area	249 Sqn
2 Sep	½	Bf 110	,,	P3579	Sutton Valence	,,
5 Sep		Bf 109E Probable	,,	P3667	Sheerness	,,
7 Sep		Do 17	,,	V6534	1m S Gravesend	,,
		Bf 109E Damaged	,,	,,	NE London	,,
27 Sep	½	Bf 110	,,	,,	near Redhill	,,
,,		Ju 88	,,	,,		,,
29 Oct		Bf 109E	,,	,,	North Weald area	,,

REVISED TOTAL: 3 and 3 shared destroyed, 1 probable, 1 damaged.

DAVIDSON Robert Tremayne Pillsbury

As a Wg Cdr he flew 51 sorties in F-86s over Korea on attachment to the 335th Fighter Interceptor Squadron of the 4th Fighter Interceptor Wing, USAF, September-December 1952, claiming damage to two MiG 15s. It was for this that he was awarded a US Air Medal.

Addition to claim list:
1941

17/18 Dec		Hurricane I	Z4718 RS-T

REVISED TOTAL: 3 or 4 and 2 shared destroyed, 2 probables, 4 damaged.

DAVIS Charles Trevor

Born in 1920, he was educated at the County School, Whitby, North Yorkshire.

DAVISON Michael Metcalfe   RAF Nos. 1380826 (NCO); 101089 (Officer)

He became a Training Captain with an airline after the war, in which role he was killed in a flying accident on 29 February 1964.

Corrections and additions to claim list:
1942

3 Sep		Beaufighter VIF	X8165
4 Sep		„	„
26 Oct (c)		Beaufighter IF	B
1943			
10 Jul		Beaufighter VIF	BT294 D (not BT2294)
12 Jul		„	BT299 B
23 Jul		„	BT300 C
26 Jul		„	BT287 A
1944			
19/20 Jul	V-1 (d)	Mosquito XIII	519

(c) Mllo Roberto Costantini (not Constantini) was a pilot of 101° Gruppo, 5° Stormo Assalto;(d) with Lt Col Fell, USAAF, as radar operator.

DAW Victor George   Wing Commander

He commanded 187 Squadron on Dakota IVs as a Wg Cdr, September 1945-March 1946.

Addition to claim list:
1940
19 May —   the Bf 110 claimed was a Bf 110C of 5/ZG 26, flown by Oblt Artur Niebahr.

DAY Robert William Rouviere

In line 7 of the biographical notes in *Aces High*, it is recorded that he engaged six Japanese fighters on 9 July 1945; this should read "...9 January 1945". On 19 February 1945 he was advised of the award of a DFC, but the next evening he was injured in a motor accident, and transferred from the Command. He is known to have died of a heart attack in about 1978.

Additions to claim list:
1944

15 Feb	Spitfire VIII	FL-T
1945		
9 Jan	„	JG567

DAYMOND Gregory Augustus   RAF No. 84657; USAAF No. O-885115

He was born on 14 November 1920 as Fred Beaty, growing up in Glendale and Van Nuys, California. He was working in France when war broke out, and reached England with the fall of that country. He joined the RAF in August 1940, aged 19, and changed his name in order to safeguard his US citizenship, due to the US still being neutral. Following his transfer to the USAAF, he returned to the US to instruct on tactics and as a technical advisor on two films. He ended the war in the Pentagon, having been awarded the US Silver Star, DFC with Oak Leaf Cluster and Air Medal with two Oak Leaf Clusters, together with a Croix de Guerre from the French, and was released on 3 August 1945 as a Major. In 1957 he moved to Lido Isle to begin a career with Interstate Electronics of Anaheim, California, having taken a degree in Physics at CalTech after leaving the forces. He retired in 1981, and died in Newport Beach, California, on 17 December 1996.

DEALL John Howard   RAF Nos. 778411 (NCO); 80361 (Officer)

His award of the DSO was gazetted on 14 September 1945.

DEAN Ernest Henry

Dean was born in Fulham, London, on 21 October 1917, being educated at Chelsea Central School and Emmanuel School, where he served in the OTC. On 15 March 1937 he entered the Civil Flying School, Hanworth, which had become 5 E & RFTS, receiving a Short Service Commission for four years. In June he attended 11 FTS, and in September 1937 qualified as a pilot, being posted to 151 Squadron in January 1938. Three months later he joined 80 Squadron as it was about to depart for the Middle East, where in September 1938 he was promoted Flg Off. In April 1940 he was posted to 33 Squadron, becoming a flight commander in June on the outbreak of war with Italy. On 17 March 1941 he was Mentioned in Despatches, but at the end of April, after the withdrawal from Greece, he was sent to HQ, Middle East, to the Rest Pool as a supernumary. In July 1941 he was posted to 71 OTU, Ismailia, as an instructor, remaining there until October, when he was posted to 30 Squadron. On 1 December 1941 he was promoted Temporary Sqn Ldr, and on 12 February 1942 joined 274 Squadron as a supernumary, becoming commanding officer the following month. On 13 July 1942 he returned to HQ, ME, and was sent to the rear HQ in Egypt to train as a fighter controller. In this role he joined HQ, 252 Wing, and then in December 1942, to HQ, 219 Group. He was awarded a Greek DFC on 29 December 1942. In September 1943 he became 29 Sector Ops Room Controller, and then in November a controller at 217 Group. On 20 March 1944 he joined 335 (Greek) Squadron for flying duties, while in June 1944 he was posted to Air HQ, Levant, on a War Course. On 6 October he joined the Air Staff at Air HQ, Egypt, in Cairo. A year later he went to HQ, ME, as a supernumary, but from here was at last sent home to the UK. Following leave, he worked as an Acting Wg Cdr in charge of 19 Recruit Centre until April 1946, when he went to 1 Recruit Centre for administrative duties, reverting in June to his substantive rank of Sqn Ldr. He then served at 3 Radio School until April 1947, and then at Wing Visual Inter-Service Training Research Establishment as an instructor. He moved to RAF Rudloe Manor in May 1947 as SAdO. On 1 April 1948 he relinquished his war substantive rank and was promoted Acting Sqn Ldr, on 16 June 1948 taking command at HQ, 62 Group (V). He went onto the 'A' Class Reserve in November 1950, retaining the rank of Wg Cdr.

Additions to claim list:
1940

14 Jun (a)		Gladiator I	L9046
30 Jun		"	"

(a) Aircraft of 93ª Squadriglia, 8° Gruppo, 2° Stormo CT; Serg Edoardo Azzaroni killed.

DEANESLY Edward Christopher
He died on ?? 1998.

DEERE Alan Christopher
Al Deere died in late September 1995, his last wish being that his ashes be scattered over the Thames Estuary from a Spitfire of the RAF Memorial Flight.

DE HEMRICOURT DE GRUNNE Count Rodolphe Ghislain Charles
RAF No. 82158; Belgian No. 41717
He was born in Etterbeek, Brussels. In Spain he claimed ten and four probables. On return to Belgium he entered the Aviation Militaire Belge as a 2nd Lieutenant in 1940, serving with the 2e Escadrille, Ière Groupe, 2e Regiment.

Corrections to claim list:
1940

17 Aug		Believed to have been R4081 (not P4081).

REVISED TOTAL: 11 and 1 shared destroyed, 4 probables, 1 damaged.

DE L'ARA Louis George Charles   Flight Lieutenant
RAF Nos. 740976 (NCO); 132072 (Officer)
He was born in Poona, India, in 1914. His home in England before the war was Poole, Dorset. He enlisted in the RAFVR in June 1937, and was commissioned after his service on Malta. On 17 August 1944 he was promoted Flt Lt.

Addition to claim list:
1942

13 Oct —	the shared MC 202 was an aircraft of 352ª Squadriglia, 20° Gruppo, 51° Stormo CT in which Mllo Maurizio Iannucci was killed.

DEMOZAY Jean-Francois   RAF No. F297; French No. 3058

DENHOLM George Lovell

Corrections to claim list:
1940

20 Oct		Spitfire IIA (not Mark I)
11 Nov		"
29 Nov		"

DENIS James RAF No. F30511

As a Wt Off he was posted to 6 OTU in July 1940, and then to Odiham in August. He was accompanied to Dakar for Operation 'Menace' by several other French pilots and by three crated Dewoitine D 520s. When 'Menace' failed, he and the other pilots were put ashore at Domala, Cameroun, with the crated fighters, and from there were flown across Africa to Ismailia, Egypt, in an RAF DC-2 to form Free French Flight 1 with Hurricanes. Swiftly, further operational training followed at 70 OTU, Nakuru, and then a posting to 274 Squadron on 12 March 1941 for the formation of the Flight. Initially this was then attached to 33 Squadron in Greece, but after a few defensive patrols over Athens, it withdrew on 5 April. On return to Egypt it was sent to reinforce 73 Squadron at Tobruk on 10 April, and here he at once claimed the first victory for the Flight over a CR 42. During 24 days based within the perimeter of the Tobruk fortress, the unit flew 167 sorties, claiming ten and two probables, of which Denis claimed six. He was awarded a DFC in September 1941, and was promoted Capitaine, becoming a flight commander in the new Groupe 'Alsace' in January 1942. Health problems caused him to cease operational flying, and he served with the Free French HQ at Beirut, and subsequently in Algiers. He died during the 1990s.

Revised claim list:
1941

10 Apr	CR 42	Hurricane I	V7716	Tobruk	FFF1 att 73 Sqn
14 Apr	Ju 87	„	W9198	„	„
22 Apr	Ju 87	„	„	„	„
„	½ Ju 87	„	„	„	„
„	Bf 109E	„	„	„	„
23 Apr	Bf 109E (a)	„	AS990	„	„
21 May	Bf 109E (b)	„	V7859	Capuzzo-Tobruk road	„

REVISED TOTAL: 6 and 1 shared destroyed.
(a) Aircraft of 3/JG 27 flown by Obfhr Hans-Joachim Marseille; crash-landed and 100% destroyed; pilot safe; (b) Aircraft of 3/JG 27, again flown by Obfhr Marseille; crash-landed again, this time suffering 40% damage; pilot safe.

DETAL Charles Firman Joseph RAF No. 148947; Belgian No. 50438

Detal was born on 28 March 1914 at Profondeville. He was a pupil pilot of the 70^e Promotion of 7 May 1934, and was posted as a Sgt to 5^e Escadrille, IIIe Gruppe of the 2^e Regiment, flying Fairey Fox VICs. He was shot down and badly wounded on 10 May 1940 (not 16th), and was taken prisoner whilst in hospital at Maastricht. Removed to a hospital in Brussels on 28 August, he escaped on 25 November and managed to reach Switzerland, where he was interned. He subsequently gained his release and made his way through France and Spain, being interned again in each of these countries for a time. He finally reached the UK on 13 March 1942. He was awarded a DFC on 15 February 1944, and was killed 300 yards north of North Scoton Hall, Newbiggin-by-Sea, Northumberland, whilst on rocket firing training.

DEXTER Peter Grenfell

He is buried at Samer Communal Cemetery, eight miles south east of Boulogne, France.

DICKS-SHERWOOD Eric Sidney Flight Lieutenant
RAF Nos. 778164 (NCO); 80256 (Officer)

Born in Salisbury, Southern Rhodesia, on 6 January 1917, he was educated at Prince Edward School, Salisbury, until 1931. He worked as a plumber prior to enlisting in the RAFVR on 9 July 1940. He was promoted Sgt in November 1941, and was commissioned whilst serving with 266 Squadron. At the end of April 1942 he was posted to Duxford to the ME Pool as a section leader, joining 603 Squadron on Malta on 9 May. On 26 August 1942 he was posted to Egypt, serving at 1 ME Training School, El Ballah, as an instructor. On 4 September he joined the Defence Flight at RAF Heliopolis, while on 12 October he went to 94 Squadron. In April 1943 he moved to 238 Squadron (the opposite way round to the postings recorded in *Aces High*), and then to 145 Squadron, followed a few days later, by a move to 92 Squadron. On 1 November 1943 he was posted to 2 Base Personnel Depot, and from there to the Advanced Flying Unit at Setif as Chief Gunnery Instructor, being promoted Flt Lt. In February 1944 he was sent home to Rhodesia to become an instructor at 25 SFTS of the Rhodesian Air Training Group. In April he attended 33 Flying Instructors' School, RATG, on an instructors' course, and was granted a Category 'B' (SE) Licence. On 28 July he joined 20 SFTS, RATG, as an instructor. He relinquished his RAFVR commission on 24 September 1945, reporting as a serving member of the SRhoAF with effect from that date.

Corrections and additions to claim list:
1943

28 Jul		Spitfire VC	JL388 (not Spitfire VIII) Augusta

DINI Antonio Simmons RAF No. 40609

Dini was born on 17 January 1918 (not 7 June). He studied engineering at the Christchurch Technical College, also playing rugby for the First XV, 1935-36; he was also Senior Athletic Champion, 1935. He spent five years as a military cadet in the College aircraft squadron, and was a member of a number of radio and model aircraft clubs. He then became a junior mechanic at the Automatic Telephone Exchange, P & T Dept, Christchurch. He applied for a Short Service Commission in the RAF in March 1937, departing for the UK on 1 December that year. Initially he attended Civil Flying School at Hatfield, being commissioned on 26 March 1938. He completed his training at 3 FTS, Shillingford, in October, and was posted to the School of Naval Co-operation. In May 1939 he joined 750 Squadron, Fleet Air Arm, on loan, but in July was posted to 66 Squadron. In December 1939 he joined 3 Receiving Centre, Padgate, for temporary administrative duties. For the next five months he served briefly with 610, 607 and 605 Squadrons of the Auxillary Air Force. He was killed in a flying accident in Kent, and buried in the Borough Cemetery, Folkestone. He had been recommended for an immediate award of the DFC, but this was cancelled upon his death in the wake of the furore over the posthumous awards to Clisby and Soden.

Corrections and additions to claim list:

1940				
10 May		He 111 Damaged — this was an aircraft of II/KG 1.		
„	1/2	He 111	AF-P	
„		He 111	P2572 AF-B	
„		He 111 Damaged	P3535 AF-C	nr Orchies — this was an aircraft of III/KG 54.
11 May	1/5	He 111	P2536 AF-R	NE Brussels — this was an aircraft of 1/LG 1.
13 May		Bf 109E	„	nr Diest — this was an aircraft of 8/JG 3.
16 May		Do 17 Damaged	P2874 AF-B	
17 May		Do 17	„	Probably an aircraft of 6/KG 76, also attacked by others.
„	1/2	He 111	P2536 AF-R	nr Binche
„	1/2	He 111	„	
18 May	2	Do 17s Damaged	P2797 AF-E	Cambrai

His own aircraft was damaged by Bf 109Es of II/JG 26, and he crash-landed at Vitry.
REVISED TOTAL: 3 and 4 shared destroyed, 5 damaged.

DIXON Henry Peter   RAF No. 90283

Educated at Marlborough College and Sidney College, Cambridge, where he gained an engineering degree, he served with the University Air Squadron, and on graduation joined 607 Squadron in December 1936. From August 1937 he spent 18 months in Calcutta on the engineering staff of the Cleveland Bridge and Engineering Co, working on the foundations for the New Howrah Bridge. He returned to the UK in March 1939. On 11 May 1940 he was reported missing; he had followed enemy aircraft too far into Germany, and ran out of fuel on his way back, being obliged to land at Tirlemont. Whilst he was searching for petrol, his Hurricane, P2573, AF-A, was bombed and destroyed, and he was obliged to return by road 24 hours later. On 1 June he baled out of a burning aircraft, having his burns dressed on the Mole at Dunkirk whilst awaiting evacuation. He was believed lost when the ship bringing him to England was sunk.

Corrections to claim list:

1940						
11 May —	the He 111 recorded as Damaged, was in fact claimed Destroyed.					
15 May —	the two He 111s were shared.					
16 May	1/5	Do 17 "Possible"	Hurricane I	P2536 'R'		607 Sqn

REVISED TOTAL: 2 and 3 shared destroyed, 2 unconfirmed destroyed, 1 shared "possible".

DODD Wilbert George

Corrections to claim list:

1942				
8 May		Hurricane II	GL-H	
10 May	First claim	Spitfire V	BR291	
„	Second claim	„	GL-H	
6 Jun		„	GL-E	
6 Jul	First Bf 109	„	BR303	
7 Jul		„	AB469	

DODDS James   Flight Lieutenant   RAF Nos. 989725 (NCO); 139938 (Officer)

Born in Knightswood, Glasgow, on 22 July 1921, he was educated at Hyndland High School until 1939. He enlisted on 9 May 1940, being called up on 1 July as an AC 2 Aircrafthand/Pilot. Promoted LAC u/t pilot on 24 August, he completed his training and was promoted Sgt on 13 January 1941, and Flt Sgt on 1 October. On 1 September 1942 he became a Wt Off, and was commissioned on 26 November 1942 whilst serving with 26 AACU. His award of the DFM was gazetted in January 1943 (not July). He became a Flg Off in May 1943 and a Flt Lt in November 1944. He returned to the UK in May 1945, being posted initially to HQ, Fighter Command, and then in June to 124 Squadron. On 1 April 1946 he moved to 56 Squadron, whilst on 23 October 1946 he was released, his formal final day of service being 3 February 1947. He rejoined as a Flg Off in the

General Duties Branch of the RAFVR in May 1948 for five years, becoming a Flt Lt again in March 1951. On 6 May 1953 his service was extended for a further five years in the VR, his commission finally being relinquished on 6 May 1958.

Corrections and additions to claim list:
1941			
1 Dec	Hurricane IIB	Z5117	
4 Dec	„	Z2835	
6 Dec	„	„	
8 Dec (a)	„	„	
14 Dec	„	Z5130	
31 Dec	„	Z2831	
1942			
23 Jan	„	Z5435	
24 Jan	„	„	
27 Feb	„	Z5469	
2 Mar	„	Z5148	
13 Mar	„	BD173	

5 Jun (not 1 Jun)   Bf 109F Damaged
12 Jun —   the second Bf 109F was claimed Damaged, not Destroyed.
REVISED TOTAL: 13 destroyed, 6 probables, 8 damaged.
(a) The MC 202 claimed was an aircraft of 97ª Squadriglia, 9° Gruppo, 4° Stormo CT, which was in fact only damaged; it was flown by Serg Alfredo Bombardini.

DOE Robert Francis Thomas
See top line of biographical notes on page 224 of *Aces High*. He was not awarded an Indian DSO, there being no such decoration. He was awarded a DSO whilst serving with 10 Squadron, RIAF.

Addition to claim list:
1940		
4 Sep		X4036 AZ-G

DOGGER Ragnar   RAF No. N1779

DOHERTY Eric Steele
He was sent from New Zealand to the UK in April 1942, attending 53 OTU in September after a period at 5(P) AFU. He joined 242 Squadron in June 1943. Sent back to the UK in late 1944, he joined HQ, Fighter Command, briefly, and was then sent to 53 OTU as an instructor in late October. In May 1945 he was despatched home to New Zealand, being released in October 1945. He then worked in insurance, joining the Territorial RNZAF in December 1948 and serving until November 1952. He suffered a car accident in Brisbane while visiting Australia shortly after his retirement, and died of his injuries on 19 June 1980. Reportedly he shared with three others in shooting down a Ju 88 prior to the Sicily landings; after his final two victories in June 1944, the squadron ORB recorded his total as 7¼ destroyed. However, detail of this claim has not been found.

Additions to claim list:
1943			
6 Jul		LE-J	Syracuse
25 Jul		LE-A	off Cap Rascolmo
1944			
10 May		LE-D	Albinia
25 May		LE-L	
19 Jun		LE-J	Piombino

DOLEMAN Robert Daniel   RAF Nos. 1250915 (NCO); 61504 (Officer)
Born in Dublin in 1921, Doleman lived in Chelmsford, Essex, prewar. He enlisted in June 1940, and was commissioned in February 1941. He was promoted Flt Lt in February 1943, receiving his DFC in March 1945 and DSO on 21 September 1945, at which time he was an Acting Sqn Ldr.

Additions to claim list:
1944					
3/4 Jul	2	V-1s (b)	Mosquito XIX	MM643 RS-F	157 Sqn
14/15 Aug		V-1	„	MM678 RS-A nr West Malling	

24/25 Dec — two of the Bf 110s claimed were from NJG 1; G9+OT of 9 Staffel flown by Hpt Heinz Strunning (56 victories); the crew baled out successfully; and G9+GR of 7 Staffel; the pilot survived.
(b) With Flg Off Brooks as radar operator.

DOLL John Christopher Shaboe   RAF Nos. 901699 (NCO); 87445 (Officer)
Born in Knightsbridge, London, on 8 September 1919, the son of a doctor and of concert pianist Kathleen Chabot, Chris Doll moved with the family to Horsham, Surrey, in 1937. He had been educated at Westminster

School until that year, and enlisted in the RAF on 3 September 1939, having previously been accepted for a Short Service Commission that July. He was commissioned a Plt Off with the RAFVR on 29 October 1940, and in November attended 56 OTU before joining 43 Squadron the following month. He moved to 258 Squadron on 21 July 1941, and then to 610 Squadron on 13 August. On 17 November he was posted as a flight commander to the newly-formed 131 Squadron, and on 12 June 1942 he claimed to have sunk an armed trawler off Le Havre. He was posted as Sector Gunnery Officer at Biggin Hill on 14 January 1943 as an Acting Sqn Ldr, then going to 58 OTU as an instructor in February. On 1 September 1944 he joined 91 Squadron. On 3 March 1944 the unit re-equipped with Spitfire XIVs, and on 26 April he was scrambled to 40,000 feet in one of these, climbing to 44,500 feet after two FW 190s. In combat with these, he was wounded and passed out, regaining consciousness at 7,000 feet in time to crash-land, and was removed to hospital. On 13 October 1944 he was posted to RAF Clevely, Blackpool, and on 23 February 1945 became PA to the AOC of 11 Group, AVM Cole Hamilton. He was granted three months leave on 1 August 1945 to join J.Arthur Rank Films as an assistant cameraman, and on 1 November 1945 was demobilized. From 1946-54 he worked for MGM as a camera assistant and operator, and then 1954-55 as a production assistant at BBC TV. He became a producer of film programmes and documentaries for the BBC 1955-70, when he became a freelance. During 1968 he was producer/director of the *"Battle for the Battle of Britain"* documentary. During 1970-85 he produced and directed a number of documentaries including *"The Life of Sir Francis Chichester"*, and *"Prince Charles"*, the latter for BBC 2 in 1975. He also produced a series on *"Pilots Royal"*, including Princes Charles, Philip and Bernhard of the Netherlands. He then became executive producer with Willis World Wide. In 1988 his wife died and two years later he married the US author Elise Piquet. He was living in Brighton in retirement at the time of writing. His brother, Sir Richard Doll, is an eminent epidomologist, who was made a Companion of Honour in 1996.

Corrections and additions to claim list:

1942			
19 Aug	$\frac{1}{4}$	Do 217 — Chris Doll confirms that this Probable claim was subsequently confirmed.	
1943			
19 Sep			MB851
23 Sep			MB842
24 Sep			,,
20 Oct			,,

REVISED TOTAL: 4 and 1 shared destroyed, 1 damaged.

DONAHUE Arthur Gerald
He was born on 29 January 1913.

Additions to claim list:

1940					
8 Aug	Bf 109 Damaged	Spitfire I			64 Sqn
1941					
7 May & 17 Aug			DL-O		
26 Sep			DL-R		
1942					
11 Sep			BL511	Ostende	91 Sqn

DONALDSON Arthur Hay
He was born in Weymouth, Dorset, and educated at Kings School, Rochester, and Christ's Hospital School. He lived in Marlborough before the war. In January 1941, prior to joining 242 Squadron, he undertook refresher operational training at 56 OTU. He was awarded an AFC on 1 July 1941, and a DFC the following month. Flown out of Malta on 31 October 1942 with a number of other wounded or tour-expired pilots in a Liberator transport, he was one of the survivors when the aircraft crashed into the sea next morning whilst attempting to land at Gibraltar. He was promoted Grp Capt on 1 July 1953, and retired in March 1959. He died on 5 October 1980.

Additions to claim list:

1942	
2 Sep (a)	
11 Oct	BR254 T-S
14 Oct	BR130 T-3

(a) Sottoten Emanuele De Seta was a pilot of 353[a] Squadriglia, 20° Gruppo, of the 51° Stormo CT.

DONALDSON George Millar

Additions to claim list:

1941

28 Feb — the G-50 confirmed may have been flown by Ten Italo Traini of 394[a] Squadriglia, 160° Gruppo Aut CT, who was killed.

9 Mar — one of the CR 42s claimed may have been an aircraft of 369[a] Squadriglia 22° Gruppo Aut CT in which Mllo Marino Vanini was killed.

14 Mar — claims made against aircraft of 393[a] Squadriglia, 160° Gruppo Aut CT.

DOUGLAS William Anderson
He left 611 Squadron in September 1944, being posted to 57 OTU via HQ, ADGB. In April 1945 he was appointed Wg Cdr Flying at Coltishall.

Addition to claim list:
1942
6 Jul — the MC 202 claimed damaged was probably the aircraft flown by Cap Riccardo Spagnolini, commander of the 351ª Squadriglia, 155° Gruppo, 51° Stormo CT.

DOVELL Ronald Leonard
Born in 1920 in Willesden, north west London, he lived in Kensal Rise, Kensington, and worked as a clerk before joining the RAFVR in August 1940.

DOWDING Harry James
He had not died, as reported in *Aces High*, but was living in retirement.

DOWNER William Watson   RCAF Nos. R132482 (NCO); J86143 (Officer)

DOWNING Alwyn Berriman   RAF Nos. 1380768 (NCO); 145321 (Officer)
Berry Downing was born on 3 October 1922 in Wimbledon, South London. Thereafter the family lived in Staines, and then Camberley, Surrey; he was educated at Salesian College, Farnborough, Hampshire. On leaving school he worked in Lloyds Bank, Cranley Branch, also joining the LDV (precursor of the Home Guard) on the outbreak of war. He was intended to go to the Royal Naval College at Dartmouth, but the minimum age was raised to 18 years 6 months, so instead he volunteered for the RAFVR in October 1940 on reaching 18, requesting immediate service. Initially he was engaged on guard duties until he could be fitted into the aircrew training programme, which followed at 19 EFTS, Sealand, and then departure to Canada, to 32 SFTS, Moose Jaw. On return he was posted to 60 OTU, East Fortune, where he teamed up with Sgt John Lyons as his radar operator. In May 1942 both were posted to 141 Squadron until October, when they were sent to Ferry Command, ultimately flying a Beaufighter out to join 600 Squadron in North Africa, although for much of the spring of 1943 they were attached to 153 Squadron. During the night of 31 January/1 February 1944, they suffered engine failure in V8766 and were obliged to bale out into the sea. Downing was rescued, but Lyons, who had just been commissioned, drowned. Following this, Downing flew no more operations with the unit, being sent home to the UK during February. He was posted first to TFU, Defford, in March, where he flew many types until August 1944, when he was moved to Fairwood Common. In February 1945 he joined 169 Squadron to fly Mosquito VIs and XIXs on bomber support duties. With the conclusion of the European war, he joined 141 Squadron in June on Mosquito XXXs, but in September moved to 1382 TUC to convert to Dakotas. In May 1946 he went to 1333 (TS) CU, and was then flown out to India in an Avro York. Here he joined 76 Squadron, equipped with Dakota IVs and Beaufighter Xs, and then the next month moved to 62 Squadron. He was then released to BOAC, where he was to serve for many years, initially flying Dakotas and Yorks, and later, Argonauts, Hermes IVs, C.4s and CL 44s. During the early 1950s he was attached for two years to Aden Airways. Finally, in 1966 he commenced flying VC 10s, becoming a Senior Captain on these. By 1977 he had flown over 18,000 hours. Meanwhile, in 1974 he had bought a smallholding in Cornwall, where from 1977 he, his wife and five daughters practised "self-sufficiency" living until he became ill with cancer. He died from this scourge on 22 September 1995.

DOYLE Joseph John
Correction to claim list:
1949
7 Jan — these final claims were made in a Mustang, not a Spitfire IX.

DRAKE Billy
Although born in London, son of an English father and Australian mother, Billy Drake lived in a number of different countries in which his father, a doctor, practised. At his own request, he was educated in Switzerland before entering the RAF. See page 12 for his claims list.

DRAPER Bryan Vincent   RAF Nos. 741507 (NCO); 76309 (Officer)
He enlisted in the RAFVR in April 1938. He was posted to the 11 Group Pool for operational training in December 1939 on completion of training, and on 22 January 1940 to 2 Ferry Pilot Pool.

DRIVER Kenneth Weekes

Addition to claim list:
1940
17 Dec   274
1941
5 Feb —   aircraft of 412ª Squadriglia Aut CT; Ten Giovanni Consoli killed.
10 Feb —   aircraft of 412ª Squadriglia Aut CT; Mllo Arturo Martini killed.

DROBINSKI Boleslaw Henryk

Before joining the Polish Air Force, he trained as a glider pilot at Goleszow, near Cieszyn, during 1934. He joined 65 Squadron on 22 August (rather than 12 August) 1940. He received his DFC on 19 September 1941, being awarded the Virtuti Militari and the KW and two Bars by General Sikorski during a visit by the latter to 303 Squadron on 28 October 1941. On 8 October 1943 he was posted as a flight commander to 317 Squadron (not 21 October). When he took command of 303 Squadron on 26 September 1944 the unit was still flying a mixture of Spitfire Vs and IXs. Not until April 1945 did it convert to Mustang IVs. He died on 26 July 1995.

Corrections and additions to claim list:
1941
15 May   ½   Ju 52/3m Damaged on ground
                      Set fire to SS *Senateur Louis Barfleur,* a merchant vessel
18-25 Jun   Spitfire II   P8335 RF-R
21 Jun —   the Bf 109F claimed on this date was an F-2, WNr 5776 of Stab/JG 26 flown by Oberstlt Adolf Galland, who
              crash-landed at Berck, the aircraft suffering 40% damage
3 Jul   P8461 (not P8507)
24 Oct-13 Mar 1942   Spitfire VB   AB929 RF-R
REVISED TOTAL: 7 destroyed, 1 and 1 shared probables, one shared destroyed on the ground.

DRUMMOND John Fraser

Born in Liverpool in 1918, he attended Llansaintffraid Grammar School and Wellington School, Somerset. When he and Plt Off Williams' Spitfires collided on 10 October 1940, he baled out with injuries to an arm and a leg, but was too low for his parachute to open.

Correction to claim list:
1940
2 Jun   Hurricane I   N2543 (not W2543)

DUKE Neville Frederick   RAF Nos. 923780 (NCO); 61054 (Officer)

Corrections and additions to claim list:
1941
30 Nov —   the G-50 was an aircraft of 378ª Squadriglia, 155° Gruppo Aut CT in
              which Serg Magg Girolamo Monaldi was killed.
4 Dec —   the MC 200 was probably the 384ª Squadriglia, 157° Gruppo Aut CT
              aircraft in which Sottoten Arrigo Zancristoforo was killed.
22 Dec   Bf 109F   Tomahawk IIB   AK354 GA-L W Magrun, near coast   112 Sqn
   „   Ju 52/3m Probable (not shared)
1942
14 Feb —   MC 200s of 363ª Squadriglia, 150° Gruppo Aut CT were engaged in this
              combat and three of the unit's pilots were reported missing.
1943
8 Jan (j)   Zidan
11 Jan —   he claimed the shared victory first, not second as shown in *Aces High* in Spitfire VB EP338 (not
                                   ER336) QJ-S NNW Tamet
21 Jan   S Castel Benito
1 Mar   ER821 QJ-R (not ER281) NW Medenine
3 Mar   Oudref area
4 Mar   W Medenine
7 Mar   Bf 109F   ER821 QJ-R nr Medenine
                  Bf 109F   BR519 QJ-T nr Neffatia
25 Mar   15 m W Gabes
29 Mar   Spitfire VC   ES121 QJ-R
REVISED TOTAL: 27 and 2 shared destroyed, 1 probable, 6 damaged, 2 shared destroyed on the ground, 1 shared probably destroyed on the ground.
(j) Aircraft of 74ª Squadriglia, 23° Gruppo, 3° Stormo CT; Serg Giorgio Pettazzoni killed.

DUKE-WOOLLEY Raymond Myles Beecham

He claimed 124 Squadron's first victory on 17 December 1941.

DU MONCEAU DE BERGENDAEL Count Yvan Georges Arsene Felician
RAF No. 87700; Belgian No. 39493

He was born in Fulham, London. On leaving the Belgian cavalry he initially became an observer in the 3rd Regiment at Evere, then a pupil pilot of the 83^e Promotion on 3 June 1940. His cousin, Yves Du Monceau de Bergandael, who was born on 24 October 1915 at Folkestone, England, was a pilot from 1936, flying CR 42s with the 4^e Escadrille, IIe Groupe of the 2^e Regiment.

DUNCAN Andrew

Corrections and additions to claim list:
1940
1 Nov —   this victory was credited to Robin Pare, not to Duncan.
1942
31 May   AN523 R
REVISED TOTAL: 4 and 1 shared destroyed, 1 probable, 2 and 10 shared destroyed on the ground, 1 damaged on the ground.

DUNCAN-SMITH Wilfred George Gerald   RAF Nos. 748014 (NCO); 85684 (Officer)

The 4th and 5th lines of the biographical notes on page 237 of *Aces High* should read "..Commissioned during September 1940, he was awarded a DFC in June 1941..." He joined the RAFVR in April 1939. His Spitfire sortie on 31 December 1950 was not the last in which the Spitfire fired its guns against a hostile target whilst in RAF service; that occurred the following day during an attack on the same objective. On 29 August 1952 he was awarded a Second Bar to his DFC for distinguished service in Malaya. He died on 11 December 1996.

Additions to claim list:
1943

Date	Aircraft	Serial	Notes
3 Jun	Spitfire VC	JK650 T	
26 Jun	"	JK611 M	off Scalambria
11 Jul (e)	"	JK650 DS	
25 Jul	Spitfire IX		
29 Aug	"	MA281	
1944			
22 Jan	"		
29 Feb	"	DS	
20 Mar	"		
5 Jun	"		

(e) Aircraft of 386^a Squadriglia, 21° Gruppo Aut CT; Ten Germano Gennari killed.

DUNDAS Hugh Spencer Lisle

Born at Barnborough, Yorkshire. He was shot down on 8 May 1941, force-landing at Hawkinge, the 68th victory of Oberstlt Werner Mölders of JG 51. In 1948 he became air correspondent with Beaverbrook Newspapers, and in 1950 he stepped down as commanding officer of 601 Squadron when promoted by Beaverbrook. He then undertook a number of editorial and management posts, but left in 1960. In 1970 he became Managing Director of Rediffusion, and in 1973 Managing Director of BET, the parent company of Rediffusion. From 1978-85 he was Chairman of Rediffusion, while in 1981 he also became Deputy Chairman of BET, becoming Chairman of that company the following year. He also became a Director of Thames Television in 1968, chairing that company from 1981-87. Additionally, he served on the RAF Benevolent Fund from 1987-90, and also chaired the Prince's Trust and Home Farm Development Trust. In 1969 he was appointed Deputy Lieutenant of Surrey, and High Sheriff in 1989. In 1950 he married the daughter of the 1st Baron Oaksey and 3rd Baron Trevethin, and sister of Lord Oaksey, the *Daily Telegraph* racing correspondent. He died on 10 July 1995.

DUNN Patrick Hunter

On 12 April 1941 he took command of 'B' and 'C' Flights of 70 OTU, which was renamed the Fighter OTU, becoming 71(ME)OTU in June 1941. In October 1941 when a Grp Capt arrived to take command, he became CFI. He became SAO of 203 Group for a brief period from 23 February 1942. He was later to become a Fellow of the Royal Aeronautical Society.

Additions to claim list:
1940
8 Aug —   engagement with 9° Gruppo, 4° Stormo CT, which lost 8 pilots.
9 Dec —   claims against CR 42s — Serg Magg Guglielmo Biffani of the 73^a Squadriglia, 9° Gruppo, 4° Stormo CT became a POW; 2 other pilots crash-landed.
1941
5 Jan —   aircraft of 23° Gruppo Aut CT; Sottoten Sante Schiroli and Sottoten Leopoldo Marangoni both killed.

DUNN William Robert
RAF No. 60510; USAAF and USAF Nos. O-39084; O-534445; 954520

The son of a doctor, Bill Dunn began learning to fly as a teenager. He worked on various ranch and horse-ranging jobs initially, and took part in rodeos before joining the army. He was discharged in 1937 at the end of his service, returning to school, and in 1939 began work as a commercial artist. He went to Canada in September 1939 to join the RCAF, but as no US volunteers were being accepted at that time, he entered the army instead. He was sent with his unit to the UK for service in France, but it arrived too late, just in time to be evacuated from Brest. He was, however, promoted Sgt due to his past military experience. On 16 August 1940 four Ju 87s attacked Borden Camp, and he fired at these with a Lewis gun from a gun pit. One crashed and one, flown by a Feldwebel Clausen, crash-landed. Other guns had also been firing, but his bullets had been seen to hit both aircraft, and he was considered to have been primarily responsible for their demise. In October 1940 a message was passed around calling for pilot volunteers for the RAF, to which he responded, being accepted and commissioned as a Plt Off on 13 December. He did not attend EFTS due to his previous flying experience, and on 6 February 1941 attended 5 SFTS on Masters, where by mid April he had achieved 'Above Average' rating. No vacancies at OTUs were available at this time, and he was posted direct to 71 Squadron, although soon after his arrival he was sent to the OTU at Debden for operational training. He subsequently recorded in his autobiography that during August 1941 he was shot down in flames during the mid part of the month, baling out into the Channel, from where he was rescued. The relevant date of this reported episode has not been discovered. When claiming his two victories on 27 August, his Spitfire was shot up and he was wounded in the right leg, landing at Hawkinge and being removed to the Royal Victoria Hospital, Folkestone. On recovery he returned to the squadron, but soon after this, he left for the US on leave; he was then posted as an instructor to 31 B & GS, Picton, Ontario, Canada, in early 1942. During the summer he moved to 1 OTU, Bagotville, Quebec, where he was promoted Flt Lt. In late 1942 he was given command of 130 Squadron, RCAF (not 130 Squadron, RAF, as indicated in *Aces High*). In the USAAF with the 53rd Fighter Group he acted as a gunnery officer on P-39s, then P-51s. In October 1943 he volunteered to join the 406th Fighter Group, which was being formed on P-47s for service with the 9th Air Force in the UK. Promoted Captain, he arrived back in England in March 1944 as Assistant Group Operations Officer. Here he attended a course at the Fighter Leaders' School, and claimed that prior to D-Day he shot down two FW 190s "unconfirmed" and one probable. He was promoted Major on 13 July 1944. Following leave in the US, he attended the Command and General Staff School at Fort Leavenworth, Kansas. In March 1945 he was flown out to India, and from there via Burma to China, to the HQ of the 14th Air Force. He flew on two B-24 missions here, then becoming air base commander at Liuchow until the end of the war. Subsequently he worked on air transport duties, then joining the Chinese 4th Fighter Group as advisor on P-51s during the the civil war. On 15 November 1946, now a Lt Col since January, he was granted a regular commission. In total he had flown 82 missions in the CBI theatre, 28 of them with the 4th Fighter Group. Awarded Chinese decorations, he returned to the US in June 1947, where a marriage he had entered into during the war broke up. He became Chief, Operations Plans, at HQ, 10th Air Force, San Antonio, Texas, and then Senior Air Instructor to the South Dakota National Guard at Sioux Falls, flying P-51s and A-26s. Later in the year he went to HQ, 2nd Air Force at Omaha, Nebraska, as Deputy Director of Operations. In early 1948 he joined the 82nd Fighter Wing as Deputy Wing Commander, while in August of that year he went as fighter advisor to the Imperial Iranian Air Force at Teheran, where he flew Hurricanes and P-47s. In June 1949 he was passsed over for promotion; passed over a second time after reappraisal, he obtained his discharge on 27 September 1949 as a Lt Col. He then rejoined on 14 November 1949 as an NCO, being graded Technical Sergeant. He became an operations NCO with the 42nd Bomb Squadron, 11th Bomb Group, 71st Bomb Wing, Strategic Air Command. Later he worked as an advisor to the Brazilian Air Force with the Joint Brazil-US Military Commission, first as a Master Sergeant and then a Wt Off. He returned to the US in April 1954 as War Plans Officer, 33rd Air Division, Air Defence Command at Tinker Air Force Base, Oklahoma. He was promoted Chief Wt Off, and in June 1956 became a Lt Col in the Air Force Reserve by order of the President. After four years he joined the 51st Fighter Interceptor Wing on Okinawa which was flying F-86Ds, and from 1960, F-102s. In 1961 he returned to the US to the Central Air Defence Force as War Plans Officer. He then served in the Philippines with the 84th Aircraft Control and Warning Squadron in the 405th Fighter Wing. In 1964 he joined Pacific Air Force HQ, Hawaii, for three years as War Plans Officer to SEATO. In 1965 he went to Vietnam, where he was awarded a Bronze Star by Commander, 7th Air Force, for action during an attack on a hotel by the Viet Cong. Returning once again to the US in June 1968, he was posted to HQ, Aerospace Defence Command, Colorado Springs, as War Plans Officer. He retired five years later on 1 February 1973 as a Chief Warrant Officer, but was promoted Lt Col on his final day of service. He then settled in Colorado Springs where he died on 14 February 1995 as the result of a massive stroke.

DUNNING-WHITE Peter William

On 6 April 1940 he attended 5 OTU before joining 29 Squadron. On 4 July 1940 he commenced a refresher course at 6 OTU , then being posted to 145 Squadron.

Correction to claim list:
1940
8 Aug —   claimed Ju 87, not Ju 88.

DUPERIER Bernard

His real name was Baron Bernard Sternberg de Armella. He designed the Armella-Senemaud AS 10 Mistral aircraft in 1934, which was built and test-flown as F-ANJQ, but was not a success.

DURNO Leslie Duncan

A member of the RNVR; Durno's Corsair was hit in its oil tank by AA fire whilst over Talangbetoetoe, Palembang, on 29 January 1945. He was obliged to bale out during the return flight to the Fleet, when his engine seized up, and he was never found, being presumed dead.

Addition to claim list:
1944

19 Oct		JT383 7D

DUTTON Roy Gilbert

He resumed fighter flying in March 1946 when posted to command 46 Squadron, which he led until July. In late 1953 he was station commander at RAF Waterbeach.

Corrections and additions to claim list:
1940

18 May		He 111*	Hurricane I	N2495
„		He 111 unconfirmed*	„	„
„	½	He 111*	„	„
19 May		He 111	„	N3314

* Five Heinkels were claimed destroyed and four more were the subject of unconfirmed claims. Three were actually lost by I and II/KG 4.
REVISED TOTAL: 13 and 6 destroyed, 1 unconfirmed destroyed, 2 probables, 8 and 1 shared damaged.

DU VIVIER Daniel Albert Raymond Georges Leroy
RAF No. 82159; Belgian No. 50017

He was a pupil pilot in the 75ᵉ Promotion of 1 May 1937. By 1940 he was a Sgt with the 4ᵉ Escadrille, IIᵉ Groupe, 2ᵉ Regiment of the Aviation Militaire. He did not in fact serve with 229 Squadron during 1940, following his arrival in the UK. He left the service in 1947 as a Lt Col to work for Shell.

Corrections and additions to claim list:
1940
Claims of 27 Sep — 12 Dec — delete (these were made by Plt Off R.A.L. Duvivier of 229 Squadron, who was not the same person).
1941

10 May		Hurricane IIB	Z3079
28 May		„	Z3031 FT-A
1942			
25 Apr		Hurricane IIC	BN230 FT-A

REVISED TOTAL: 3 and 2 shared destroyed, 1 damaged.
(b) The Ju 88 was VB+KM of 2(F)/ObdL.

DYGRYN-LIGOTICKY Josef D.

He is buried at Westwell, Kent.

DYMOND William Lawrence

Born on 11 November 1917, he was educated at Richmond County School, Surrey. He entered the RAF on direct entry pilot training in September 1935. He was despatched to France on 18 May 1940.

Additions to claim list:
1940

18 May		L1522

DYSON Charles Harold

He was commissioned on 13 October 1937 and promoted Flt Lt on 11 December 1945. He retired from the Secretarial Branch, having received an MBE.

Revision to claim list:
1940

11 Dec		S-79
„		CR 42 Probable
„	6	CR 42s
19 Dec	2	CR 42s

REVISED TOTAL: 9 destroyed, 1 probable.

EAGLE William Geoffrey   RAF Nos. 1168509 (NCO); 143448 (Officer)

Line 2 of the biographical notes on page 245 of *Aces High* should read "On 2 March 1942 he was shot down by Bf 109Fs of I/JG 27..." He joined 274 Squadron from No 5 Course at 71 OTU in June 1941. On return to the

UK he served at 55 OTU until 30 September 1942, when he was sent on a Flying Instructors' Course at Hullavington. He was commissioned on 23 November 1942. After his second tour he was seconded to de Havilland Propeller Division, not Hawkers. He was undertaking a 50 hour endurance test in Typhoon SW519, which was fitted with an experimental four bladed dry barrel hydromatic propeller. When he took off on 30 May 1945 the port undercarriage fairing door failed to close fully. He was seen to undertake what were described as "vigorous manoeuvres" over his fiancee's place of work, when the door became detached and struck the tailplane, causing structural failure. He was buried in Brockenhurst Cemetery.

Addition to claim list:
1942
17 Mar   Hurricane IIB   Z5382

ECKFORD Alan Francis
On 5 May 1941 whilst serving with 253 Squadron, he engaged an FW 200 50 miles north of Skeabrae in the Orkneys. Although he raked it with gunfire, he did not see specific damage, and made no claim. He died in 1990, rather than 1991 as recorded in *Aces High*.

EDGHILL Douglas Frank Kitchener
Born in Market Harborough, Leicestershire, on 9 January 1915, he worked as a tithe rentcharge clerk in a local firm of estate agents before entering the RAF in May 1935 as an AC2 u/t Clerk Accounts, serving at Home Aircraft Depot, Henlow. Promoted LAC in August 1936, he was posted to Cardington in January 1937, where in August he was recommended for training as an Airman Pilot. He was accepted the following year and commenced training in June 1938, first at 10 E & RFS, Filton, and then 2 FTS, Brize Norton. Promoted Cpl in October, he obtained his flying badge in December 1938, and was promoted Sgt in April 1939, remustering as Pilot/Clerk Accounts. He was then posted to 2 Air Observers' School, Warmwell, on 4 September 1939. In December 1939 he joined 92 Squadron, but at the start of February 1940 moved to 229 Squadron. When wounded on 31 May 1940, he was flying Hurricane P3553; he suffered a fractured right arm and a bullet wound to his left elbow. He remustered to Clerk Accounts on 21 November, but on 27 March 1941 was commissioned in the RAFVR, rejoining 229 Squadron. He was briefly attached to 450 Squadron, RAAF, in June 1941, but returned to 229. Returning from combat on 7 September (not 6th) in Hurricane W9326, he fractured his spine in the landing crash. After treatment in hospital, he was posted non-effective sick, and was sent to South Africa on medical grounds in January 1942. In August he returned to the UK, where on 25 December 1942 he was obliged to resign his commission due to his injuries. He died on 10 February 1961.

Addition to claim list.
1940
31 May   P3553

EDINGER Charles Emanuel
Not a Canadian, but a US citizen, Edinger was born in Onaway, Michigan, on 17 April 1916. He joined the RCAF on 12 May 1941, undertaking flight training between July 1941 and February 1942, when he was commissioned. He then became a flying instructor at Camp Borden until May 1943. Promoted Flg Off in October 1942, he was finally posted to the UK in July 1943, but it was December before he was sent to 51 OTU for operational training. He was promoted Flt Lt in February 1944, and in June joined 410 Squadron, where he served until April 1945. Returning to Canada in September, he was released from the service on 26 October 1945.

EDNER Selden Raymond   RAF Nos. 64860; USAAF No. 36629A
Born on 26 June 1919 in Fergus Falls, Minnesota, Edner was to receive a US DFC and four Air Medals. He transferred to the regular service in July 1946.

EDWARDS Frederick Edward Fitzgerald
Edwards was born in Adelaide, South Australia, on 4 June 1922, working as a clerk until he enlisted in the RAAF on 8 November 1941. He was trained at 2 ITS and 8 EFTS, then being sent to Canada to complete his flying training at 1 SFTS in September 1942. He reached the UK in early 1943, being held at 11 PD & R Centre from February-May, when he attended 17(P)AFU. The following month he was posted to Grangemouth, where he remained for a year (apparently employed on instructional duties). In May 1944 he was posted to 3501 Servicing Unit, and in June to 26 Squadron, a tactical reconnaissance unit. 11 days later, on 13 June, he was moved to 130 Squadron, in time to see action against the V-1s, and then later with 2nd TAF over north-west Germany. He returned to 11 PD & R Centre in September 1945 at the end of his tour, returning to Australia in November. He was released on 11 February 1946.

Addition to claim list:
1944
20 Aug   ½   V-1   Spitfire XIV   SW Dover   130 Sqn
REVISED TOTAL: 2 and 4 shared destroyed, 1 damaged, 1 V-1 shared destroyed.

EDWARDS Henry Grahame

Addition to claim list:
1942
21/22 Dec | | Beaufighter VIF | X8022 (not Mark IF)

EDWARDS James Francis

He was an instructor at 1 METS in late June 1943, following his tour with 260 Squadron.

Additions to claim list:
1942
23 Mar | | | AK858
1944
Jan-Feb — Spitfire VIII QJ-F was JF502.

EKBERY Joseph Scarisbrick   RAF Nos. 1379909 (NCO); 145863 (Officer)

Corrections and additions to claim list:
1943
7 Apr | | | ER783 | Medjez area
26 Apr | | | EF326 | Teboursouk area
6 Jul | | Spitfire VB | JK365 (not Mark IX)

ELIOT Hugh William

He was posted to 73 Squadron from 6 OTU on 27 April 1940. His radar operator in 255 Squadron was 109499 Flt Lt Allan Barker, DFC. In 256 Squadron he usually flew with 145760 Flt Lt Denis Revill Ibbotson, DFC, but when shot down and killed, Flt Lt W.T.Cox was lost with him in HK178; Eliot was still only 23 at the time of his death. He is buried in the Argenta Gap War Cemetery in Italy.

Potential addition to claim list:
1940
16 May — his claims on this date may only have been for two aircraft damaged, rather than destroyed. This would potentially reduce his total to 6 and 1 shared destroyed.
1944
10/11 Jan | | | SW Vis

ELLIS John

His personal Spitfire JE, when he was a Wg Cdr, is believed to have been JK533.

Correction to claim list:
1940
3 Jul — the shared Do 17 was confirmed
REVISED TOTAL: 13 and 2 shared destroyed, 1 probable, 2 damaged.

ELLIS Ronald Vernon

'Monty' Ellis joined the RAF in January 1933 as a Halton Apprentice, and was later selected for pilot training. He joined 73 Squadron on 12 July 1940 (not on 7 June). On 2 December 1940 he flew from Takoradi across Africa to Egypt, where initially he was involved in the defence of Alexandria. He rejoined 73 Squadron at the end of September 1942 as a Flt Lt, subsequently becoming commanding officer on 17 February 1943. He died on 3 June 1988.

Corrections and additions to claim list:
1940
11 Sep | sh | Bf 110 | Hurricane I | | | 73 Sqn
15 Sep | sh | He 111 | ,, | | | ,,
,, | sh | He 111 Probable (not damaged) | ,, | | | ,,
27 Sep | sh | Bf 110 | ,, | | | ,,
1941
14 Apr | | | V7249
REVISED TOTAL: 3 and 4 shared destroyed, 1 probable.

ELSDON Thomas Arthur Francis

'Jimmy' (not 'Jimmie') Elsdon was the eldest son of Sqn Ldr T.W.Elsdon, RNAS and RAF. He was shot down twice during 1940, baling out safely on the first occasion, but crash-landing at Biggin Hill on 7 September after being wounded; he was removed to Farnborough Hospital. He returned to operations in July 1941 as a supernumary with 257 Squadron, but was again slightly wounded during an engagement with two Bf 109s over the Channel on 24 July; this time he was able to land safely at Hawkinge. On arrival in India with the first Hurricanes in January 1942, he took part in a formation flight over Delhi to raise civilian morale, before flying down to Rangoon on 23rd of the month. He flew out the last serviceable Hurricane from Akyab to India on 27 March 1942. He married a former WRAF Squadron Officer in May 1950, their two children both entering the service in due course. His daughter Rosemary was a Nursing Sister aboard SS *Canberra* during the Falklands operations. His son, who, as reported, was killed during the Gulf War (on 17 January 1991, not 20th as previously recorded) was commanding officer of 27 Squadron at the time, and was twice Mentioned in Despatches.

Corrections and additions to claim list:
1940
| 1 Sep | 2 | Bf 109Es (not Bf 110s) |
| 4 Sep | | Ju 88 (in addition to the 2 Bf 110s) |

REVISED TOTAL: 8 destroyed, 1 unconfirmed destroyed, 2 damaged.

ENSOR Philip Stephen Baddesly

He was born in 1920 and educated at Bradfield College. He was posted to 12 Group Pool at Aston Down on 10 December 1939, prior to joining 229 Squadron.

ERIKSEN Marius

He was shot down by Hpt Dietrich Wickop. Kommandeur of II/JG 1. It is possible that he had hit Wickop's FW 190 before falling himself, as the former then crash-landed, having been wounded.

ETHERTON John Hill   RAF Nos. 1173750 (NCO); 63093 (Officer)

Etherton was born in Liverpool in 1921 and lived in Bracknell, Berkshire, before the war. He enlisted in the RAFVR in 1940, and was commissioned in 1941 on completion of training. He was promoted Flt Lt on 23 March 1943.

Additions to claim list:
1941
| 17/18 Dec | Beaufighter IF (not VIF) |
| 20/21 Dec | Beaufighter VIF |

EVANS Charles Leo (not Les) Glandore

He commanded HMS *Eagle* in 1958.

EVANS Kenneth William Samuel (not Samuels)

RAF Nos 745888 (NCO); 125320 (Officer)

He received his Permanent Commission whilst at Moreton-in-Marsh, before being posted to Germany in 1955. He had intended to return to flying, but was never able to obtain the necessary medical grading following his motorcycle accident.

Correction to claim list:
1942
| 13 Jul | Spitfire VC | BP992 (not BK992) |

EYRE Anthony

Tony Eyre joined 615 Squadron in June 1938, between then and February 1940 flying 33 hours in Gauntlets, 101 hours in Gladiators and 6 hours 30 minutes in Hurricanes. He was on leave in the UK when the 'Blitzkrieg' commenced on 10 May 1940, arriving back with the unit on 14th. During July his aircraft was shot-up twice, on 14th and 22nd, while it was also hit by a single bullet on 26 August. He left the squadron in May 1941, serving at HQ, 9 Group, at Preston until January 1942. On 29 January he was posted as Wing Leader, North Weald. On 8 March 1942 the Wing provided close escort to six Bostons to Commines. He was captured immediately after his aircraft had crash-landed. Released on 2 May 1945, he served at 106 PRC, Cosford, until July, then at HQ, 11 Group. He managed quite a lot of flying during this period, including Spitfires of various Marks, and Tempest IIs and Vs. His last recorded flight on 24 January 1946 was his first in a Meteor III.

Corrections and additions to claim list:
1940
16 May	Hs 126	Hurricane I	L1992	Lille-Louvain	615 Sqn
20 Jul —	these claims may have been made on 22 July. His logbook is not clear.
26 Aug —	the second Bf 109E, claimed as a probable, may have been credited as a damaged.
28 Aug —	The Do 17 may have been a probable, rather than confirmed.

REVISED TOTAL: Eyre's logbook lists his final total as 7 and 2 shared destroyed, 3 probables and 8 damaged. This appears to indicate that he may have classified his claims on 19 May as damaged, rather than unconfirmed destroyed.

FAIRBANKS David Charles

David Fairbanks was born on 22 August 1922 in Ithaca, New York State, the son of a Cornell University professor. In February 1941 he managed to convince his widowed mother to allow him to join the RCAF, where he qualified as a pilot on 21 November 1941 at 9 SFTS, Summerside, Prince Edward Island. He was then despatched to 6 CFS, Trenton, to train as an instructor, thereafter instructing at 13 SFTS, St Hubert, until February 1943. He was then sent to the UK to complete advanced training and attend OTU, before joining 501 Squadron on 12 January 1944. When shot down on 28 February 1945, he broke his nose against the gunsight whilst crash-landing in NV943, north of Osnabruck. He was then rescued from a crowd of angry civilians by a German Flak officer, following which he received a week of ill-treatment before being transferred to POW camp. Released by Allied troops in April 1945, he returned to Canada in July, and was released from the service in October. He then attended Cornell University, gaining a degree in mechanical engineering, subsequently joining the staff of Dominion-Bridge in Canada, where he also joined the RCAF Auxillary. In 1951 he moved to Sperry Gyroscope, where he remained for four years, two of them spent in the UK, where he flew Meteors with 504 Squadron. In 1955 he became a test pilot with De Havilland Canada, remaining with the RCAF Auxillary until 1959, when work pressure caused him to resign. He became a Canadian citizen, and in early 1976 was awarded the McKee Trophy for service to Canadian aviation. He was reported to have died "of natural causes".

FALKOWSKI Jan Pawel (not Paivel)
With the defence flight at Cognac he flew Koolhoven FK 58 fighters.

Corrections and additions to claim list:
1941

16 Jun	Hurricane II (not Mark I)	Z2984
14 and 19 Aug		P8540 PK-K
21 Aug		P8648 PK-M
16 and 21 Sep		W3619 PK-F
24 Oct		W3944 PK-A
1943		
22 Aug		MA304 RF-H
6 and 23 Sep		MA524 RF-F (b)

(b) According to his logbook on 6 September 1943 he was flying Spitfire IX BS451 RF-M; however the squadron ORB recorded MA524 RF-F.

FARNES Paul Caswell Powe   RAF Nos. 741447 (NCO); 88437 (Officer)

FARQUAR Andrew Douglas
He was posted to 53 OTU on 2 June 1941 as CFI, moving to 61 OTU on 23 June and then to 58 OTU on 4 August.

FAURE Johannes Morrel (not Morkel)
He died in early 1995.

Additions to claim list:
1942

23 Jul	Hurricane II	282 AX-F
1 Sep	Spitfire VC	BR491 (not BR389)
2 Nov		HL892 AX-H
27 Nov		204 AX-F
1943		
19 Jul		JK393 AX-X

FEARNLEY Fredrik Arild Sverdup   RAF No. N223
At the end of his first tour he was posted to 58 OTU as an instructor in January 1943. He returned to 331 Squadron in June of that year.

FEARY Alan Norman
His service number indicates that he enlisted in the RAFVR in 1938, rather than 1936.

Corrections and additions to claim list:
1940

18 Jul	½	Ju 88 Unconfirmed (not ⅓)		L1008 PR-K	
12 Aug				N3223 PR-M	
25 Aug				R6691 PR-J	
7 Sep and rest of combats				X4234 PR-B	
24 Sep —	the two claims recorded against Do 17s were actually made against Bf 110s.				
26 Sep		Bf 109E Damaged	Spitfire I	X4234 PR-B Southampton	609 Sqn

REVISED TOTAL: 5 destroyed, 1 shared unconfirmed destroyed, 1 probable, 5 damaged.

FECHTNER Emil

Correction to claim list:
1940
27 Sep — the Hurricane flown is listed as L2713. This was in fact a Wellesley bomber, lost in East Africa. The correct identity of his aircraft is P2715 NN-S.

FEJFAR Stanislav B.

After reaching the UK, he attended 6 OTU from 17 August 1940, before joining 310 Squadron. His diary records his total as 7 and 2 shared destroyed; the two additional claims have not been discovered, and this may be in error. The aircraft flown in 1942, BL973, was RY-S; this code has been incorrectly set in the "location" column in *Aces High*.

FENWICK Harry Elmore

Reports regarding his fate on 21 June 1944 differ. One states that, whilst on beachhead patrol in Spitfire NH207, he engaged enemy aircraft, but was shot down in error by "friendly" AA, and crashed west of Oucelles, near landing ground B.6. A second report claims that he was shot down by P-47s of the US 9th Air Force.

FERIC Miroslaw

He was born at Travnik, near Sarajevo, in Yugoslavia. In 1919 his family arrived at Ostrow Wielkopolski, Poland. He entered cadet school in 1935, and was commissioned on 15 October 1938, when he was posted to 111 Eskadra of the 1 Pulk Lotniczy (1st Regiment) in Warsaw. In September 1939 he fought in the Pursuit Brigade, and during this time on one occasion baled out of a severely damaged aircraft. He escaped through Rumania, reaching France at the end of October 1939. After conversion to Morane 406 fighters, he joined the fighter section of Kapt Kazimierz Kuzius at Tours, Nantes and La Rochelle. Evacuated to Britain, he joined 303 Squadron with the initial batch of pilots on 2 August 1940. He was decorated with the Virtuti Militari, 5th Class, on 18 September 1940, and with the DFC on 15 December of that year. Eight days later he received the Cross of Valour, followed by a Bar to this on 1 February 1941 and a second Bar on 10 September 1941. He acted as an instructor from October 1941 to January 1942, then rejoining 303 Squadron. He was killed during a routine flight in BL432, RK-K.

Corrections and additions to claim list:
1939
8 Sep   Hs 123 (not shared)
1940
31 Aug — believed to be Bf 109E-7 WNr 5600 of 3/LG 2, which crashed at Chathill Park Farm, Crowhurst. He was flying P3974 RK-J
2 Sep — believed to be a Bf 109E-4 of JG 3 which ditched off the French coast. He was flying RK-E.
6 Sep   RK-E
15 Sep — his second claim is believed to be a Bf 110C-3 of 13/LG 1 which crashed at Hothfield, north of Ashford. He was flying RK-G.
27 Sep and 5 Oct   RK-D
1941
22 Jun   RK-A (named 'Impregnable')
27 Jun   Bf 109F Damaged   Spitfire II   P8385 RK-A   303 Sqn
  „   Bf 109 on ground   „   „   „
REVISED TOTAL: 9 and 1 shared destroyed, 1 probable, 1 damaged, 1 destroyed on the ground.

FERRISS Henry Michael

Addition to claim list:
1940
18 May   L1822

FINLAY Donald Osborne

He originally entered the RAF as a Halton Apprentice in September 1925, gaining a Permanent Commission ten years later. During 1944 he commanded 61 OTU briefly as a Grp Capt. He was awarded his AFC whilst commanding 909 Wing in Thailand in 1945. In 1966 he was involved in a road accident which left him confined to a wheelchair with a broken back, which led to his death in April 1970.

FINUCANE Brendan Eamonn Fergus

Corrections to claim list:
1941
4 Jan   Spitfire I (not Mark II)   X4478
19 Jan - 9 Aug — all claims made whilst flying Spitfire IIs.

FISKEN Geoffrey Bryson

Correction to claim list:
1943
12 Jun and 4 Jul — these claims were made with 14 RNZAF Squadron as stated in the text, not 15 RNZAF Squadron as
     indicated in the listing. All his three final claims were made on 4 July 1943.

FLINDERS John Layton
RAF Nos. 580082 (NCO); 8133 (Officer- RAFVR); 48342 (Officer — RAF)

As a prewar regular airman, 'Polly' Flinders should have been commissioned into the RAF, but when
commissioned on 1 April 1940, it was into the RAFVR with the service number 81333. However the *London
Gazette* on 4 February 1941 announced his commissioning in the RAF, although when promoted Flg Off on 1
April 1941, he was still listed as a member of the RAFVR. Finally, a year later, on his promotion to Flt Lt, he was
listed as RAF, No. 48342. On return to the UK from Canada in March 1945, he served at AFEE, Beaulieu and
AAEE, Boscombe Down, before release. He joined the RAFVR in 1948, serving until September 1953 at 69 RFS,
Desford, 12 RFS, Filton, and 1 SRFS, Redhill. He returned to Canada in 1978.

Corrections and additions to claim list:
1940
18 May —   the He 111 was classified as an unconfirmed destroyed, not a probable; it may in fact have been claimed as
         damaged.
15 and 18 Aug   L2067 (not N2062)
REVISED TOTAL: 5 and 1 shared destroyed, 1 unconfirmed destroyed (or damaged).

FOKES Ronald Henry   RAF Nos. 740109 (NCO); 88439 (Officer)

He was 31 when killed (not 33), and is buried at Banneville le Campagne.

FORBES Athol Stanhope

He was posted from 1 Army Co-operation HQ to 6 OTU for a refresher course as a Flt Lt on 8 July 1940, prior
to joining 303 Squadron.

Additions to claim list:
1940
5 Sep   RF-U
6 Sep   RF-Q
7, 11 and 26 Sep   RF-V
27 Sep   RF-O

FORSTER Anthony Douglas

He was known as 'Bunny'.

Corrections and additions to claim list:
1940

Date		Claim		Location	Unit
10 May	1/3	He 111 unconfirmed (a) Hurricane I	P2573 AF-A		607 Sqn
11 May	2	Ju 88s Damaged	,,		,,
9 Jul		Bf 110 — not damaged, but destroyed — uncertain if confirmed or unconfirmed			,,
15 Jul	1/3	Do 17 Damaged	,,	off Harwich	,,
29 Jul		Bf 110 Damaged	,,	18 miles E Harwich	,,

REVISED TOTAL: remains unclear.
(a) Aircraft of III/KG 1.

FOSKETT Russell George

He was awarded an OBE and Mentioned in Despatches. The Ju 52/3m which he forced to land whilst flying
Spitfire IX MA766 GO-F on 6 June 1944 is believed to have been flown by Polish escapees. He was killed in
Spitfire VB ER489 when it suffered engine failure following a strafing sortie.

Additions to claim list:
1941
24 Nov   Z4744
1942
19 Jun   BN405
10 Jul   BP542
18 Jul   BP235
31 Aug and 3 Nov   BP337
1944
6 Jun   Spitfire IX (not VB)   MA766 GO-F
10 Aug   ,,   MJ328

FOSTER Reginald John RAF Nos. 1238704 (NCO); 106065 (Officer)

Known as 'Jack' or 'Fingers', he was born in Wolverhampton on 16 June 1921, attending Winchester College, 1934-40. He enlisted as a Gunner in the Royal Artillery on 29 September 1939, being placed on the Reserve, and in January 1941 transferred to the RAFVR. After initial training in the West Country, he attended 7 EFTS, Desford, and 12 SFTS, Grantham, qualifying as a pilot and being commissioned in September 1941. He then attended 54 OTU, and in December joined 604 Squadron. Promoted Flg Off in September 1942, he was posted to the Middle East in January 1943, initially joining 89 Squadron. However he was injured in an accident in Beaufighter VIF EL175 on 14 February, and on recovery in March was posted to 108 Squadron. Promoted Flt Lt in September 1943, he and 116700 Flg Off Maurice Frederick Newton were decorated, and then posted home. They served at 51 OTU, Cranfield, as instructors from November, but in December they were posted to Hunsdon, where Foster became a supernumary. January 1944 saw them at 63 OTU, Honiley, for a navigation and radar conversion course, followed by a return to 604 Squadron. On 21 April 1945 Foster was posted to 85 Group Personnel Centre, and then in May to 1668 Conversion Unit, 7 Group, Bomber Command. On 21 May he was sent to Farnborough, where on 28 October 1945 he was promoted Sqn Ldr. He was released on 23 May 1946, and on 1 January 1947 received the award of an AFC for his work at Farnborough.

Additions to claim list:

1943		
20/21 Apr	Beaufighter VIF	V8687 'F'
12/13 Jul	„	BT287 'A'
16/17 Jul	„	BT299 'B'
30/31 Jul	„	BT287 'A'

FOSTER Robert William RAF Nos. 748045 (NCO); 80815 (Officer)

He was born on 19 May 1920.

FOSTER William Morley Culverwel

Additions to claim list:

1945	
4 Jan	JW860 'TH'
12 Apr	JX814 'W-132'

FRANKLIN William Henry

He enlisted as an Apprentice at Halton in January 1929.

FRANTISEK Josef

He enlisted in the Czech Air Force in October 1930, joining Air Regiment 2 on completion of pilot training. By 1935 he was a Corporal in Air Regiment 1, returning to Air Regt 2 as a Sgt in 1937. He did not, as previously stated, serve in the Polish Air Force in 1938-9. He joined a Czech platoon formed in Poland following the German invasion, this unit serving mainly in the east against the invading Soviets; subsequently all Czechs who served in this unit, and who escaped from Poland to the UK, remained with the Poles, since the Czech authorities in exile maintained friendly relations with Stalin. In France Frantisek was posted as a fitter at a Polish air base at Clermont-Ferrand, where he became notorious for being absent without leave, flying all the types of French aircraft he could lay his hands on!

Corrections and additions to claim list:

1940

3 Sep — this claim for an 'He 113' is believed to relate to Bf 109E-11, WNr 6290 of 9/JG 51, which crashed in the Channel.

9 Sep — the Bf 109E claimed on this date is believed to have been E-4 WNr 1617 of 7/JG 27, which crashed at Romans Gate Cottage, Rudgwick.
— the bomber claimed is believed to have been He 111H-2 WNr 5548, A1+DS of III/KG 53, which returned damaged 22%.

11 Sep — the bomber is believed to have been He 111H-3 WNr 5606, V4+FA of Stab/KG 1, which crashed at Camber, near Rye. On this date he was flying RF-S.

15 Sep — his victim on this date is believed to have been Bf 110C-3 of 14/LG 1 which crashed into the Channel; his Hurricane R3089 was RF-S.

18 Sep — V7465 was RF-V.

30 Sep — the Bf 109 claimed is believed to have been an E-1, WNr 3859, '3' of 6/JG 27, which crashed at Grayswood, near Haslemere.

FRASER Joseph Frederick

Born in Colombo, Ceylon, in 1915, his family lived in Cairo, Egypt. He was sent to the UK for his education, attending Malvern College and Pembroke College, Cambridge, where he served in the University Air Squadron. In consequence he was commissioned in the Reserve of Air Force Officers in 1936, transferring to the RAFVR in 1938, and then to the RAF. He was adjutant of 112 Squadron in Egypt in 1939. In June 1941 he was posted to 71 OTU as an instructor, being promoted Sqn Ldr. In November he became Chief Ground Instructor, and he was still with the unit in September 1942. He was promoted Wg Cdr on 1 July 1944, and was Mentioned in Despatches on 14 June 1945.

Corrections and additions to claim list:

1941				
28 Feb	G-50	Gladiator II	Tepelene-coast	112 Sqn
9 Mar	delete CR 42			

FREEBORN John Connell   RAF No. 70854 (not 708854)

He attended E & RFTS, January-March 1938, being commissioned in the RAFO at the end of that period. He then attended 8 FTS until late October, when he joined 74 Squadron. He transferred to the RAF on a Short Service Commission on 17 January 1939. After serving with 118 Squadron in 1943, he instructed for a time at 61 OTU and then 57 OTU, before going to Italy.

Corrections to claim list:

1940
21 May —   Spitfire P8047 was a Mark IIA, part of a batch delivered between June 1940 and July 1941, so could not have been available at this time. This serial was clearly recorded in error.

FRIENDSHIP Alfred Henry Basil   RAF Nos. 742051 (NCO) — not 752051

He joined the RAFVR in September 1938. His posting to 604 Squadron occurred in December 1943, rather than April 1944, and he had first undertaken a conversion course at 51 OTU. His radar operator was Flt Sgt Powell.

Revised claim list:

1940						
12 May	1/3	Hs 126 (a)	Hurricane I	L1591	Louvain/St Trond	3 Sqn
14 May		Ju 87 (b)	,,	N2351	Sedan area	,,
,,		Bf 109E	,,	,,		,,
17 May	1/2	He 111	,,	L1609	nr Charleroi	,,
18 May		Ju 87	,,	N2434		,,
19 May		He 111	,,	P3318 QO-K		,,
20 May	1/4	He 111	,,	N2351		,,
,,	1/4	He 111	,,	,,		,,

REVISED TOTAL: 4 and 4 shared destroyed.
(a) Hs 126 of 1(H)/41, flown by Uffz Heinz Kubik; (b) Ju 87 of I(St)/TrGr 186.

FROST John Everitt

The SAAF Hurricane 289 which he flew on several occasions in 1941 had previously carried the RAF serial P3253.

Corrections and additions to claim list:

1942					
11 Mar —	claim may have been against a Ju 88 rather than an He 111.				
27 Mar —	identified at the time as possibly a 'Do 215' — twin engine, twin tail.				
28 May			AN434 GL-H (not GL-F)		
29 May			AN523		
31 May			385 (not 395); may have been AN prefix.		
3 Jun			AN247 GL-K		
4 Jun			AN 247 (not AM247)		
7 Jun			AN422 GL-B		
8 Jun	Bf 109F Damaged	Tomahawk IIB AN422 GL-B	NE Bir Hakeim		5 SAAF Sqn
9 and 14 Jun		,,			

FULFORD David   RAF Nos. 905533 (NCO); 63787 (Officer)

Correction to claim list:

1942
9 Apr   Z5146 (not Z4146)

FUMERTON Robert Carl

After arrival in the UK, he attended 6 OTU in September 1940 before being posted to 32 Squadron. He was awarded an AFC on 1 January 1946.

GABSZEWICZ Aleksandr Klemens

Szawle, where Gabszewicz was born, is now Siauliai, Lithuania. During World War I his entire family was evacuated into Russia, reaching as far east as Vladivostok. They returned home in 1921, Aleksandr entering cadet school at Komorow in October 1931. Before receiving his commission, he undertook a gliding course in September 1933, then applying for transfer to the Air Force. In August 1934 he was commissioned as an infantry officer, joining the 30th Kaniowscy Fusiliers in Warsaw, commanding the 6th Company. In September 1934 he was posted on a 12 month conversion course at the Air Force Officers' Training Centre at Deblin. Posted thereafter to 1 Pulk Lotniczy, he qualified as a fighter pilot in 1937, and then joined 114 Eskadra. In summer 1938 he was posted to a special KOP flight at Sarnay to intercept Soviet reconnaissance aircraft violating air space in Eastern Poland. During July-August 1939 he led another special section on the Polish-German frontier, but was then appointed tactical officer in IV/1 Division of 1 Pulk. In the early hours of 1 September he took the PZL P.11 of *por* Tadeusz Sawicz of 114 Eskadra, and with *kpr* Andrzej Niewara, shot down an He 111, the first Luftwaffe aircraft to fall in the Warsaw area. That afternoon he was shot down himself, baling out but suffering burns, although he was able to return to his unit next day. Evacuated to Rumania after the Soviet invasion of 17 September, he reached France in October. In early spring 1940 he commenced conversion training at Lyon-Bron, then joining an improvised flight in defence of Lyons, commanding this unit from 1 June, attached to GC III/10. He was awarded the Cross of Valour on 11 June. Following the French surrender, he flew to North Africa, from there making for Gibraltar via Algiers and Morocco. In September 1942 he took command of 58 OTU; he was posted to command 2 Polish Wing at Kirton-in-Lindsey in January 1943, moving south to take over 1 Polish Wing at Northolt in June. His role as commander of 18 Sector was the highest RAF post achieved during the war by a non-British subject. The Sector controlled two Polish Wings, 131 and 133 (previously the 1st and 2nd Polish Wings respectively); it also included 35 Wing of British, Belgian and New Zealand squadrons. He was then leading a unit twice as large as the Pursuit Brigade of September 1939. On 13 March 1944 he received the Virtuti Militari, 4th Class, the highest Polish military decoration, and only the 29th such award to be made. After the disbandment of the RAF sectors, he commanded 131 Polish Wing until May 1945. His other decorations included the Commander's Cross with Star of the Polonia Restituta Order, DSO and Bar, DFC, the Dutch Commodore Order of Orange Nassau and the French Croix de Guerre avec Palmes. After the war he was active with the Polish Air Force Society, of which he was Chairman for over 17 years. He was twice promoted by the Polish authorities in exile; on 1 October 1966 to *pulkownik* (Colonel) and on 1 January 1974 to *general brygady*. He died at Hanley Swan, Worcester, and in 1992 his ashes were taken back to Poland and scattered over Deblin and Poniatow (his first wartime airfield).

Corrections and additions to claim list:

1939				
1 Sep		PZL P.11	'4'	IV/1 Dywijon
1940				
1 Jun	He 111 (not Do 17)	Morane 406 (not Bloch 152)		
1941				
1 Apr			SZ-S	
24 Jul		Hurricane II	Z3573 SZ-D	
1942				
27 Mar			SZ-G	
10 & 27 Apr, 5 & 6 May			SZ-G	
25 Apr			SZ-D	
1943				
4 Apr			L	
4 & 6 Jul, 19 Aug			G	

GARDNER Peter Melvill

On 18 May 1940 his Hurricane, N2464, was hit by return fire from a Do 17Z of 2/KG 76 which he was attacking, and he force-landed, setting fire to his aircraft to prevent it falling into enemy hands. After his capture in 1941, he was held in Stalag Luft III.

Corrections to claim list:

1940				
18 May	1/3	Do 17 (a)	Hurricane I	N2464 (not N2584)

REVISED TOTAL: 8 and 2 shared destroyed, 1 damaged.
(a) Aircraft of 2/KG 76.

GARDNER Richard Exton

From May 1943-August 1944 he commanded 736 Squadron, formed as the School of Air Combat with Seafires. In September 1943 this unit moved to St Merryn to become the Fighter Combat School element of the School of Naval Air Warfare. He then took command of 715 Squadron, which was formed from a nucleus provided by 736, and equipped with Seafires and Corsairs to provide Fighter Air Combat courses and Fighter Leaders' courses. He remained with this unit until December 1944.

GARTON Geoffrey William   RAF Nos. 740288 (NCO); 67034 (Officer)

Born on 3 October 1915 in Grantham, Lincolnshire, he lived in Wigston Fields, Leicestershire, before the war, attending Wyggleston Grammar School. He enlisted in the RAFVR in May 1937.

Corrections and additions to claim list:
1941
21 Apr   V7673

1942			
17 Jun		Kittyhawk I	AK929 (not AK925)
16 Sep	MC 202 (a)		EV136
1 & 11 Nov		Kittyhawk III	FR213

(a) Whilst listed in the ORB as a Probable, his logbook indicates that this was subsequently confirmed.

GAUNCE, Lionel Manley

In the claim list on page 275 of *Aces High*, insert '1941' between the claims listed for 11 Nov and 20 Aug.

GAYNOR John Henry

Additions to claim list:

1942		
3 Jul	Hurricane II	968
22 Jul	„	356
23 Jul	„	2503
31 Aug	„	EP663
27 Nov	Spitfire VB	981 AX-T
1943		
21 Jan (a)	„	193
29 Mar	„	„

(a) Probably an aircraft of 78ª Squadriglia , 13° Gruppo, 2° Stormo CT; Sottoten Ernesto Sagramoso killed.

GAZE Frederick Anthony Owen   RAF Nos. 911051 (NCO); 60096 (Officer)

He made his first claim in a Spitfire HF VI. His brother, Plt Off I.S.O.Gaze, was killed in a flying accident in a Spitfire on 23 March 1941.

Corrections to claim list:
1941 —   this claim was made in a Spitfire II, P8749, not a Mark VB.
1942
6 Sep —   this claim was made in a Spitfire IX, not a Mark VB, and with 64 Squadron, not 616 Squadron.

GENDERS George Eric Clifford   RAF Nos. 754713 (NCO); 120165 (Officer)

He did not join 33 Squadron immediately on completion of training, as indicated in *Aces High*. On 15 November 1940 he joined 73 Squadron as this unit was about to depart for service in the Middle East. From Takoradi, West Africa, he flew one of the unit's Hurricanes, V7558, across the continent to Egypt. On 13 December however, he was posted to 70 OTU for further training, and it was from there that he subsequently joined 33 Squadron. He was known as 'Jumbo'.

Additions to claim list:

1941			
15 Apr (not 14th)			Larissa airfield
23 Apr			S Athens (the Bf 109)
			Piraeus (the Ju 87s)
„			
3 May —	the 2 Ju 88s may have been confirmed, rather than Probables		
17 Jun			Bir Sofafi-Sidi Omar area
1942			
6 Sep	Spitfire V	234	Aboukir area, 60 m out to sea
21 Oct	„	EP407	20 m NE Heliopolis

GENTILE, Don Salvadore   RAF No. 112302; USAAF Nos. O-885109; O-56912

He was born on 6 December 1920, and joined the RAF (not RCAF) in September 1940. He qualified as a pilot on 11 November 1940, then instructing in the UK until posted to 133 Squadron. He transferred to the USAAF as a 2nd Lt, being promoted 1st Lt on 19 January 1943 and Capt on 30 September. Promoted Major on 17 January 1946, he was released on 16 April of that year. He rejoined what had become the USAF in November 1947, but was killed in T-33A 49-905 on 28 January 1951. In 1944 a book, *One Man Air Force*, was published by L.B.Fisher, as told to Ira Wolfert. In more recent years *Don Gentile, Soldier of God and Country* by Mark M.Spagnuolo, was published by College Press (1986).

Additions to claim list:

1943					
12 Mar	FW 190 Damaged	Spitfire VB	BL673	Audruieq area	336th FS
16 Aug	Bf 109 Damaged	P-47C-5RE	41-6529	Paris	„
16 Dec		P-47D-5RE	42-8659 VF-T		
1944					
5 Jan		P-47C-2RE	41-6180		
14 Jan & 25 Feb		P-47D-5RE	42-8659 VF-T		
3 Mar	Do 217 Damaged (not destroyed)	P-51B	43-6705		
„	2 FW 190s (not 1 Bf 109)	„	„		

8 & 18 Mar	43-6913
23 Mar - 1 Apr	43-6572
8 Apr	43-6913

REVISED TOTAL: 21 and 2 shared destroyed, 3 damaged, 5 and 2 shared destroyed on the ground.

GIBB Walter Frame   RAF Nos. 913424 (NCO); 88881 (Officer)
One of the Ju 88s claimed during the night of 5/6 March 1945 was flown by Oberstlt Walter Borchers (Knights' Cross holder with 59 victories) of NJG 5.

GIBBES Robert Henry Maxwell
At Morotai in 1945 he flew Spitfire VIII A58-497, RG-V. In 1994 he published privately his autobiography *You Live But Once.*

Corrections to claim list:
1941

25 Nov		Bf 109F Damaged	Tomahawk IIB	AN374	Sidi Rezegh		3 RAAF Sqn
12 Dec —	this Probable may have been claimed as a Ju 88, rather than a Ju 87						
13 Dec				AM374 (not AN374)			
1943							
22 Jan (a)				FL334 was CV-L, not CV-V			

(a) probably an aircraft of 77ª Squadriglia, 13° Gruppo, 2° Stormo CT; Serg Vittorio Sperati killed.

GIBBS Eric Malcolm   RAF Nos. 562696 (NCO); 43200 (Officer)
He joined the RAF as an Aircraft Apprentice at Halton in September 1928. He was later chosen for pilot training, and on 1 April 1940 was commissioned from Sgt. He was promoted Flt Lt on 1 April 1942.

GIBSON John Albert Axel
On page 280 of *Aces High*, the 7th line of the biographical notes should read "...he returned to operations as a flight commander in 452 Squadron."

GIDDY Peter Radcliffe   RAAF No. 715
Peter Giddy was born in Armadale, Victoria, on 14 March 1919, working as an accountant in Toorok before the war. Commissioned on 5 February 1940, he attended 3 EFTS and 1 FTS, CFS and 1 SFTS to complete his training as a pilot by December 1940. It appears that he was retained as an instructor, but in August 1941 he was posted to the Middle East, where he joined 3 RAAF Squadron on 29 September. In October he was sent to 71 OTU, returning to the squadron on 28 February 1942.

Additions to claim list:
1942

22 Jan —	MC 200 of 364ª Squadriglia, 150° Gruppo Aut CT; Serg Renato Carrari killed
14 Feb —	three MC 200 pilots of 363ª Squadriglia, 150° Gruppo Aut CT missing
8 Mar —	three MC 200 pilots of 150° Gruppo Aut CT missing

GILBERT Humphrey Trench
He qualified as a pilot in June 1938, joining 73 Squadron initially the following September, before going to 17 Squadron. In October he was posted to CFS, Upavon, qualifying as an instructor in December. In January 1939 he was posted to 504 Squadron, Auxillary Air Force, as a flying instructor. In August 1940 he undertook a course at 6 OTU before joining 601 Squadron, where on 16th of that month he was shot down in V7260, baling out safely. He became a flight commander in April 1941, but was temporarily attached to 1422 Flight.

GILBERT John Carlton   Pilot Officer   RAF Nos. 2590631 (NCO); 127785 (Officer)
Born in 1920, he lived in West Kensington, London, before the war. He was commissioned in June 1942, just before he was killed. He is recorded on the Malta Memorial.

Addition to claim list:
1942

| 18 May — | the Re 2001 was an aircraft of 152ª Squadriglia, 2° Gruppo Aut CT; Ten Remo Cazzolli POW. |

GILDERS John Stanley
He was lost on 21 February 1942, not 22 February.

Addition to claim list:
1940

| 15 Sep | He 111 | Spitfire I | | | 72 Sqn |

REVISED TOTAL: 5 and 1 shared destroyed, 3 damaged.

GILLAM Denys Edgar

Addition to claim list:
1940
8 Oct   P2575 YQ-P

GILLIES James RAF Nos. 519573 (NCO); 47317 (Officer)

From Intake, Yorkshire. He was lost in Hurricane IIC HV546/2, not in a Thunderbolt. He is remembered on the Singapore Memorial.

GILLIES Kenneth McLeod

He was lost in Spitfire X4320.

Addition to claim list:
1940

8 Aug	1/3	He 111	Spitfire I		66 Sqn

GILMOUR William MacMillan

He joined the RAFVR in Glasgow on 6 November 1938. He was called up at the start of the war, being posted to 5 ITW, Hastings, in September 1939, and then to 7 OTU at Hawarden in August 1940, before joining 616 Squadron on 28 August. In early October he was moved to 611 Squadron, from where he was attached to 54 Squadron for two weeks in March 1941. In September 1941 he returned to Hawarden to instruct at 57 OTU. He rejoined 611 Squadron in April 1942, and was posted to 111 Squadron at the start of September. He returned to the UK at the end of April 1943, and in May joined 239 Squadron to fly Mustangs on tactical reconnaissance sorties. On 18 June he moved to 174 Squadron, but in July went to 1 SLAIS for a month. He then served at HQ, 83 Group, until May 1944, when he was posted to 19 Squadron. He had been promoted Wg Cdr by the end of the war, but the strain of operations had seriously affected his health. After a period of convalesence, he left the service and joined Westclox as a purchasing agent. During 1952 he worked on defence contracts, and in 1954 spent time in the US and Canada, organising factories in those countries. On return to the UK in June 1954 he became Works Manager, but on 26 October 1955 he died suddenly. The photograph in *Aces High* purporting to illustrate him is in fact of Noel MacGregor, a pilot who served on Malta in 1941.

GILROY George Kemp

He died on 25 March 1995, aged 79.

Corrections and additions to claim list:
1940

18 Jul		He 111 Damaged	Spitfire I	R6755	20m NW Dyce	603 Sqn
24 Jul	1/3	He 111 (not Damaged) — aircraft of 3/KG 26				
28 Oct and 21 Nov			Spitfire II (not Mark I)			

1942
General — in North Africa he flew Spitfire VCs, not Mark VBs.
1943

11 Jan	Spitfire VC	ER727 (not BR727)	
18 Jan	,,	GK-G	
22 Apr	,,	,,	
24 Apr	Spitfire IX	,,	
1 May	Spitfire VC	,,	
5 May	Spitfire IX	,,	
13 Jul	,,	,,	
4 Sep	,,	MA247 ,,	Messina-Reggio (not Reggia)
29 Oct	FW 190 Damaged	,,	,, ,,	25m SE Rome	324 Wg

REVISED TOTAL: 14 and 11 shared destroyed, 2 shared probables, 7 and 3 shared damaged, 3 shared destroyed on the ground.

GIMBEL Edward Lister   RCAF No. J15890; USAAF No. O-887752

He was born on 28 December 1916, joining the RCAF on 9 October 1940, and qualifying as a pilot on 24 September 1941. He was flying Spitfire BS110 when he came down in France on 4 April 1943. He transferred to the USAAF on 24 June 1944, becoming a Captain. It was 4 March 1945 (not 1st) when he was wounded and crashed near Brussels. He was brought down on 16 April 1945 in P-51D-25NA 44-72769.

GLADYCH Boleslaw Michal   RAF No. P1392

As a boy he was expelled from several schools, choosing a military career and joining the Cadet Corps at Lwow. He entered the Deblin flying school in 1938, and was commissioned on 1 September 1939, too late to fly in combat during that month. He led a group of newly commissioned pilots to evacuate the PZL P.7A fighters of the Polish Pilots' School to Rumania. In France he flew with the Polish GC I/145 'Varsovie', and was shot down during one sortie. On 23 June 1941 he was credited with three victories in two sorties. The second sortie ended when he crash-landed in a field near Manston and his aircraft hit a telegraph pole and was totally wrecked, the engine being torn out. He suffered severe facial cuts, a fractured skull and a fractured collarbone. He returned to 303 Squadron in October 1941, but in July 1942 transferred to 302 Squadron. He was then rested for three months, rejoining this unit in December and becoming a flight commander on 17 May 1943. Ending his tour in January 1944, he then flew unofficially with the 61st Fighter Squadron, 56th Fighter Group, of the US 8th Air Force. When his activities (and those of Witold Lanowski, who was with him) became known to the Polish authorities, they attempted to discipline them by recalling them to serve as Liaison Officers with 12 Group in June, threatening otherwise to expel them from the Polish Air Force. Both opted to continue flying with the Americans, and were expelled. In consequence Gladych's final claims were not recognised by the Polish Air Force, and were not included by them in his total — despite having been confirmed by the USAAF. He was never officially accepted into the US service either, but continued to fly operationally with them until the end of the war (although some sources suggest that his status was subsequently sanctioned on 29 October 1944, and he then again became a Polish pilot on exchange to the USAAF). After the war he stayed with US units in the UK, and was involved in some illegal activities, including smuggling gold coins across Europe. He located his brother, a Polish resistance fighter, in a POW camp in Austria, which had been liberated by the Soviets. Since most Polish resistance soldiers falling into Red Army hands were more likely to be sent to Siberia than home to Poland, he used his US uniform and the fact that US flying personnel were also in the camp, to visit and smuggle out his brother to the West. Both brothers subsequently emigrated to the US, where Michal worked for a time in the aerospace industry (including with Lockheed). He also wrote a number of articles regarding his wartime activities which were at least in part, fictitious. Eventually, having obtained a degree in psychology, he became a doctor in Seattle, Washington State, where he was living at the time of writing.

Corrections and additions to claim list:

1941				
23 Jun —	on the second sortie he claimed 2, not 3, Bf 109s in P8338 RF-D			
1942				
5 Jun		AD198 '		RF-W
1943				
10 Jun		AR377		WX-W
1944				
21 Feb		P-47D	42-75393	HV-S
8 Mar			42-75140	HV-M (not HV-U)
27 Mar				HV-O
6 Jun				HV-V
5 Jul			42-26044	HV-Z
12 Aug			"	"
21 Sep			44-19718	HV-M

REVISED TOTAL: 17 destroyed, 2 probables, 1 shared damaged.

GLEN Arthur Allan   RAF Nos. 998543 (NCO); 115232 (Officer)

'Pinkie' Glen was born in Hull, East Yorkshire, on 2 May 1918, being educated at Hymers College, Hull. Prior to joining the RAF he was employed as a clerk with the Hull Food Control Committee. He enlisted as an Aircrafthand Pilot u/t; Air Observer in the RAFVR on 25 May 1940, and was mobilised on 1 July, undertaking initial training at ITW, Paignton, before being sent to the USA to undertake flying training. He qualified as a pilot on 8 January 1941, being promoted Sgt, and was commissioned on 1 January 1942 whilst with 41 Squadron. He arrived back in the UK from Malta in early August 1942, being posted to 52 OTU, Aston Down, as an instructor in September, although he spent six weeks in hospital immediately thereafter. He was promoted Flg Off on 1 October whilst there, and on release was posted to A.V.Roe & Co Ltd on adminstrative and light duties. In January 1943 he joined 11 Group, to train as a sector controller, attending an elementary controller's course in the spring, following which he undertook a GCI course, before becoming a GCI controller at RAF Black Gang, Isle of Wight. On 20 July 1943 he returned to 41 Squadron, attending the Fighter Leaders' School, Charmy Down/Aston Down during August. At the end of the month he was promoted flight commander, and on 5 November 1943 received the Bar to his DFC. He took command of the unit on 20 January 1944, but on 22 February returned to the Fighter Leaders' School, now at Milfield, on a further course. In late May he went briefly to HQ, 10 Group, as a supernumary, and then in June was posted back to Milfield on the staff of the Fighter Leaders' School as a Sqn Ldr. In October he was posted to the Day Fighter Training Squadron of the CFE, at Milfield, although he was at once sent to the Central Gunnery School, Catfoss, on No 56 Pilot Gunnery Instructor's Course, returning on 6 December 1944. A year later he was released from the service.

GLOSTER Michael John   RAF Nos. 1182358 (NCO); 65559 (Officer)

Born in Birmingham in 1920, he attended the Wrekin College at Wellington, Shropshire, and then Birmingham University. He joined the RAFVR in 1940 and was commissioned in 1941. He was promoted Flt Lt on 30 April 1943.

Additions to claim list:

1943				
23/24 Mar	t/e e/a	Beaufighter VIF	Decimomannu, Sardinia	255 Sqn

13 Apr —   on this date his radar operator was Flt Sgt R.C.B.Wall.
REVISED TOTAL: 11 destroyed.

GLOWACKI Antoni

He undertook has basic flying training at the military training base at Lublinek airfield, near Lodz. He served in the 1 Pulk Lotniczy in Warsaw and at the No 1 Air Force Training Centre, Deblin. In July 1940 he attended 6 OTU (not 60 OTU). On 31 August 1940 he was shot down in Hurricane I, V6540, near Gravesend, but survived unhurt. He died on 27 April 1980 in Wellington, New Zealand.

Additions to claim list:

1940					
28 Aug	(a)		P5193	SD-O	
29 Aug —	delete				
31 Aug			V6540	SD-P	
18 Sep			P5193 (not N1572)		
30 Sep	Bf 110 Damaged	Hurricane I	V6545		501 Sqn
1942					
19 Aug		Spitfire VC (not VB)		RF-Q	
1943					
22 Sep		Spitfire VB	BM416		

(a) Believed to have been a Bf 109E-4 of JG 3.

GLOWCZYNSKI Czeslaw   Flight Lieutenant/Kapitan   RAF No. P1495

Born in Bedzin, he entered the Cadet School in 1936 and was commissioned in 1938 from the 11th Class. This included Zumbach, Skalski, Lokuciewski, Feric and Lanowski amongst its graduates. He was posted to the 162 Eskadra, engaging in 17 combats during September 1939. On arrival in England he was posted to 302 Squadron, but on 17 August 1940 was seriously injured in a flying accident in Hurricane P3927 WX-E, not being fit to return to the unit until March 1941. From January 1942 he was adjutant to General Sikorski, and on the latter's death, to General Kazimierz Sosnkowski, the replacement Polish C in C. In 1944 he entered the Wyzsza Szkola Lotnicza (the Polish Air Force Academy), and after graduation was posted on an exchange tour to the US 9th Air Force, flying P-47s with the 390th Fighter Squadron, 366th Fighter Group. He remained in the UK after the war, but in recent years returned to Poland, where he was living in Warsaw at the time of writing. He was awarded the Virtuti Militari, 5th Class, the Cross of Valour and three Bars, the US Air Medal and DFC, and the British DFC.

Corrections and additions to claim list:

1939				
3 Sep —	the 'Ju 86' was a Do 17			
6 Sep —	He 111 Damaged (not $^{1}/_{3}$ Probable)			
1940				
9 Jun	Bf 109E	Caudron C.714		GC I/145
„	Bf 109E Probable	„		„
„	Do 17 Probable	„		„
1941				
30 Dec			AD257 WX-A	

REVISED TOTAL: 5 and 1 shared destroyed, 2 probables, 1 damaged.

GLYDE Richard Lindsay

He was killed in Hurricane P3387.

GODDEN Grenfell (not Stanley)   Flight Lieutenant
RAF Nos. 779030 (NCO); 84996 (Officer)

Although known as 'Stan', his name was actually Grenfell. He was born in Mafeking, South Africa, on 8 October 1914, but he joined the RAF in Iraq on 15 January 1940, training at 4 FTS from February to August, gaining his 'wings' on 24 May 1940. He was commissioned in the RAFVR on 24 August, and was posted to the Training Unit Reserve Pool in the Middle East. On 3 October 1940 he joined 274 Squadron. Shot down in flames in the Tobruk area in V7825 on 1 May 1941, he was reported missing, believed killed, but was subsequently reported to be a POW by the Red Cross. Promotion to Flg Off was announced on 24 August 1941, and to Flt Lt a year later. It appears that he had suffered severe wounds or burns when shot down, for on 16 September 1942 he was repatriated from Germany to the UK, where he was posted to Home Establishment. On 9 March 1945 he was posted as a Category C(EL) flying instructor with the Rhodesian Air Training Group. Here on 15 June he was tested on a Cornell by the EFTS and re-categorised Category B. However on 23 November 1945 he was killed in a flying accident in Harvard IIA EX768 at 20 SFTS, Cranbourne, Southern Rhodesia.

Additions to claim list:

1940			
9 Dec		N2624	Sidi Barrani — Bir Zigdin
11 Dec		„	Sidi Barrani — Sofafi area
14 Dec		V7293	Sidi Rezegh

1941
4 Jan(a)				V7558	5m N Great Gambut	
27 Apr				V7780		
30 Apr				V7825		
1 May	$1/3$	Bf 109 (b)	Hurricane I	,,	Tobruk	274 Sqn

REVISED TOTAL: 7 and 1 shared destroyed, 1 damaged.
(a) CR 42 of 91^a Squadriglia, 10° Gruppo, 4° Stormo CT, flown by Ten Ennio Grifoni, who was killed; (b) this claim is listed on the Form 541 in the Squadron ORB, but is uncertain.

GOLDING Douglas William

Additions to claim list:
1941
23 Nov —	the Bf 109 was listed as "E/F"	LG 122	
12 Dec —	the Bf 109 was an F		Gazala
13 Dec	,,		,,
18 Dec	,,		Mechili
22 Dec	.		El Magrun
30 Dec			Msus airfield
1942			
4 Nov		ET901 KJ-W	
18 Nov		EV347 KJ-K	Brina airfield
,,		,,	20m S Benghazi
3 Dec		EV136 KJ-L	15m SW Mersa Brega
5 Dec		,,	

GOLDSMITH Adrian Philip

The claims that can be listed for Goldsmith from Malta records differ somewhat from those listed in his logbook. This may be because some of the latter were subject to later confirmation. The differences and additions to the listing in *Aces High* for the Malta period are as set out below:

1942
9 May		Z1007 claimed as BR 20
10 May		Bf 109 } as opposed to 2 confirmed and 1 probable
,,	2	Bf 109s Probable } ,,
14 May	$1/2$	Ju 88 (not individual claim)
25 May	$1/2$	Z1007 Damaged (not individual destroyed victory)
30 May	$1/4$	Z1007 Damaged (not $1/2$ destroyed BR 20)
15 Jun	$1/2$	BR 20 (not individual destroyed victory); this aircraft was, as stated, an S 84 of 4° Gruppo BT; it was from that unit's 15^a Squadriglia, flown by Magg Gastone Valentini — three members of the crew were killed.

On this basis his total (including his later Pacific claims) would become 11 and 2 shared destroyed, 3 probables, 7 and 2 shared damaged. This does not however, equate with the citation to his DFC, published on 7 July 1942, which recorded that since being awarded the DFM he had claimed six further aircraft to bring his total to 11. His four Pacific victories would thereby bring his total to at least 15 destroyed, although some of these may indeed have been shared.

GOODMAN George Ernest

'Randy' Goodman was posted to 1 Squadron from 6 OTU on 27 April 1940. He was killed in P2686.

GOODMAN Geoffrey Horace   RAF No. 70799 (not 45491)

He was educated at Queen's College, Taunton, Somerset, and gained a civil pilots' licence during 1935-36. He lived in Wrotham, Kent, prior to the war. He obtained his 'ab initio' flying training with the RAF with 4 E & RFTS, Brough, during September-November 1937, then attending No 8 Course at 8 FTS, December 1937-July 1938; he was commissioned on 24 November 1937 in the RAFO, going onto the Reserve List in September 1938 after his service with 75 Squadron. He may have been employed by the Bristol Aircraft Co thereafter, as he was based at Yatesbury with 10 E & RFTS. He was recalled to active service on the outbreak of war, although he remained with 10 EFTS, as the E & RFTS became, until September 1941 as an instructor. The top line on page 292 of the biographical notes in *Aces High* should read "...including four in one sortie on 4 May, 1944" (not 1941). He received a DFC on 4 April 1944 and a DSO on 13 June of that year. The pilot of similar name with whom it was mentioned he was frequently confused, was 580286 (NCO); 45491 Flt Lt Geoffrey Goodman, who received a DFC on 26 October 1943. The latter will be found in the four-victory claim list.

GOOLD Wilfred Arthur

Additions to claim list:
1944
20 Jan	MA677 AF-T
21 Feb	MA674 AF-N
14 May	JG559 AF-N

GOSLING Leslie Cyril

On 19 July 1943 he baled out of LZ808, X-D, ten miles north of Mount Etna, being seen to land in the sea; he was not found. He is buried in the Catania West Cemetery, Sicily.

Corrections and additions to claim list:

1943		
13 Apr		606 (not 506)
19 Apr		264
7 May		720
13 Jun		233
5 Jul		LZ808 'X-D'
11 Jul	(a)	,,
12 Jul		,,

(a) MC 202 of 96ª Squadriglia, 9° Gruppo, 4° Stormo CT;Ten Otello Gensini baled out.

GOUBY Gabriel Robert   RAF No. F30246

GOUCHER Richard Tannott   RAF Nos. 1197621 (NCO); 103593 (Officer)

GOULD Derrick Leslie

He was born in Exmouth, Devon, in 1919, thereafter living in Madras, India. He was sent back to the UK to be educated, attending Bristol Grammar School.

GRACIE Edward John

After his return from Malta, he instructed at 57 OTU, being posted from there to RAF Ayr, Scotland, in August 1943. When shot down and killed, his navigator, Flt Lt Wilton W.Todd, survived to become a POW. Gracie is buried in Hanover Cemetery, Germany.

GRAHAM Michael   RAF Nos. 1286007 (NCO); 67660 (Officer)

Born in Blackheath, Kent, on 18 July 1922, he enlisted in August 1940, attending 2 ITW and then being held at 50 Group Pool from December to March 1941, when he was sent to 8 SFTS. Promoted Sgt in April 1941, he was commissioned in June, completing his training at 59 OTU. In July he joined 504 Squadron, but in April 1942 he was posted to 611 Squadron. Soon after his arrival on 18 April he was slightly injured in an accident in a Magister. He was promoted Flg Off in October 1942 and posted to 243 Squadron. He completed his tour at the end of May 1943 and was sent back to the UK, where in July he was seconded to Vickers Armstrong as a test pilot. He was promoted Flt Lt in December, and in March 1944 began his second tour with a posting to 602 Squadron. In May he moved to 132 Squadron as a flight commander, where on 12 July he was slightly wounded in combat whilst on a bomber escort sortie. He was awarded a DFC in October, the following month being posted to 17 SFTS for twin-engined conversion. On 30 January 1945 he attended 105 OTU for transport training, and on 8 May joined 11 Ferry Unit. He moved to 147 Squadron on 2 September 1945, where he flew Dakotas. He was released in May 1946, and in July resigned his commission to reside permanently overseas. It appears that he returned to the UK in retirement, where he died of cancer in Malvern, Worcestershire, during the 1992-93 period.

Correction to claim list:
After the claim of 11 April 1943, insert "1944" before the claim on 5 July.

GRAN Martin Yngvar   RAF No. N115

He served as an instructor at 57 OTU in early 1943, returning to 331 Squadron in May. The reference in the second line of the biographical notes on page 296 of *Aces High* to 332 Squadron is incorrect, and should read "331 Squadron".

GRANT Reginald Joseph Cowan

He is buried in Brookwood Military Cemetery, Woking, Surrey.

GRANT Stanley Bernard

He was educated at Charterhouse before attending Cranwell. In February 1941 he was posted from 65 Squadron to 55 OTU as an instructor. After the war he served at the Air Ministry during 1946-47, then with Flying Training Command, 1948-54. He was promoted Wg Cdr in July 1950, and during his last year with the Command flew a Hastings transport to Northern Norway during an exercise. He then served with Fighter Command, 1955-56, following which he went to SEATO in Bangkok, Thailand, as a Grp Capt. He returned to Fighter Command in 1960, while in 1962 he undertook the Imperial Defence College course, being promoted Air Cmdr. 1963-64 were spent at NATO, Fontainebleu, and he then returned to the IDC to become a part of the Directing Staff until 1968. Whilst there he was promoted Air Vice-Marshal on 1 January 1966. During 1968-69 he was Commander,

British Forces, in the Persian Gulf, leading up to his retirement on 6 June 1970. He then lived in France until his death.

Corrections and additions to claim list:
1942

23 Mar	$\frac{1}{2}$	Ju 88 Damaged	Spitfire V		Malta	249 Sqn
„	$\frac{1}{2}$	Ju 88 Damaged	„		„	„
„		Ju 87 Damaged	„		„	„
21 Apr	$\frac{1}{2}$	Ju 88 Probable (not destroyed)				
10 May		Ju 88	Spitfire V		„	„

REVISED TOTAL: 6 and 1 shared destroyed, 1 unconfirmed destroyed, 3 and 2 shared probables, 5 and 2 shared damaged.

GRAY Colin Falkland
He died on 2 August 1995.

Additions to claim list:
1943

2 Mar				EN190 FL-A		
23 Mar	(a)			„		
25 Mar and 3 Apr				„		
18 Apr		Bf 109 Probable	Spitfire IX	EN520	Tunis-Bizerta	81 Sqn
20 and 23 Apr				„		
28 Apr				EN356 'DC'		
14 Jun				EN350 'CG'		
17 Jun			Spitfire IX (not V)	EN534 'Y'		
25 Jul			Spitfire VC	ES112 'UM-U' (not VM-U)		

REVISED TOTAL: 27 and 2 shared destroyed, 7 and 4 shared probables, 12 damaged.
(a) MC 202 of 368ª Squadriglia, 151° Gruppo, 53° Stormo CT; Serg Ugo Dal Pozzo killed.

GREAVES Douglas Haig   RAF Nos. 938887 (NCO); 113989 (Officer)
In November 1940 he was a Sgt at 56 OTU. He moved to 54 OTU on 6 January 1941.

GREEN Charles Patrick

Corrections and additions to claim list:
1940

27 Dec	$\frac{1}{2}$	Do 17 Probable (not $\frac{1}{2}$ Bf 109 Probable)			

1943

5 May		V8672
All other claims in V8700 BQ-F.		
11/12 Aug		8m S Riposta
9/10 Sep		20m NW Naples

The claim on 25 January 1944 was made with 125945 Flt Lt Reginald Joseph Gillies, DFC, as radar operator.

GREEN Wilfrith Peter
He was born in 1914 in Raniknet, India, living as a boy in Abridge, Essex. He was educated at Copthorne School and Bradfield College, Berkshire, joining the RAF in circa 1936. In October 1937 he was posted as an Acting Plt Off to 217 (General Reconnaissance) Squadron. He subsequently served with 240 Squadron, another Coastal Command unit, while in December 1941 he joined 277 Air-Sea Rescue Squadron as commander of the unit's Hawkinge Flight. He was promoted Flg Off in July 1939, Flt Lt in September 1940 and Sqn Ldr on 1 June 1942. When he joined 219 Squadron, Flt Sgt Grimstone was sent on rest; Flt Lt Oxby's pilot had just been posted to the Far East, so the pair teamed up, claiming nine victories together.

Additions to claim list:
1944

18/19 Jun		V-1	10m NW Hastings
„		V-1	10m SW West Malling
23/24 Jun	2	V-1s	off Frinton
„		V-1	nr Worthing
„		V-1	off Hastings
25/26 Jun		V-1	over sea
29/30 Jun		V-1	SSE Beachy Head
19/20 Jul	3	V-1s	over sea
20/21 Jul		V-1	
28/29 Jul		V-1	over sea
8/9 Aug		V-1	20m S Beachy Head

GREENWOOD John Peter Bowtell
Born in Stratford, East London, on 3 April 1921, he was educated at Tiffin's School, Kingston-on-Thames, leaving in 1935. He applied for a Short Service Commission in 1938, forging his father's signature to do so, and was accepted in 1939. He had also claimed that he had matriculated, whereas he had in fact only taken the

General Schools Certificate. In March 1946 on his return to the UK he became Sports and Fire Officer at Tangmere until August, when he joined 130 Squadron where he flew Spitfire IXs and Vampires. In November he was posted to Fassberg in Germany, where he flew Tempest IIs until demobilized in July 1947. He then attended the London School of Printing, intending to follow a career in printing. So qualified, he emigrated to Australia in May 1950, undertaking printing in Brisbane, picking grapes, etc. Subsequently he worked as an airline pilot in Adelaide, then undertook crop spraying and more printing work, before becoming a newsagent in Perth. Finally he ran a general store and newsagents in Gnowangerup, Western Australia, until his retirement, when he moved to South Australia, where he was living at the time of writing.

Additions to claim list:

1940				
18 May			L1712	
19 May			,,	
23 May			L1663	
30 Aug			P3714	
9 Sep —	(shared with eight others)		P3537	
23 Oct	Bf 109E	Hurricane I	V7499	253 Sqn
7 Dec	Bf 109E Damaged	,,	,,	,,

REVISED TOTAL: 4 and several shared destroyed, 1 unconfirmed destroyed, 2 probables, 1 damaged.

GREGORY Donald Swift   RAF Nos. 565558 (NCO); 47849 (Officer)

Born in Northampton in 1915, he lived in Nottingham, attending Worksop Central School. He enlisted as an Aircraft Apprentice in September 1931, later being selected for pilot training. He served as an instructor at 71 OTU in late 1941 as a Wt Off, and was commissioned on 7 March 1942, joining 250 Squadron a month later.

Additions to claim list:

1940		
28 Nov and 4 Dec		N5776
21 Dec		N5854
1941		
9 Dec	Gladiator I	K6138

GRIBBLE Dorian George

Correction to claim list:
1940
24 Jul (not 25 Jul)

GRICE Douglas Hamilton

He attended 5 OTU in late June 1940. Douglas Grice died during March 1999.

GRIER Thomas

He attended 6 OTU in May 1940.

GRIFFITHS Albert Michael   RAF No. 1382927

From Carmarthen, North Wales, he enlisted in October 1940. He crashed at Syracuse on 16 July 1943, and was 26 years old when killed.

Addition to claim list:
1943
12 Jul —   the 2 aircraft claimed as MC 200s were actually G.50bis of 159° Gruppo, 50° Stormo Assalto.

GRIFFITHS Glyn   RAF Nos. 991242 (NCO); 135394 (Officer)

Granted a Short Service Commission on 17 September 1938, his commssion was terminated on 27 August 1939. He rejoined about April 1940, becoming a Sgt. He then attended 5 OTU during that month, and was posted to 17 Squadron. The reason for his departure from the service and re-enlistment after the outbreak of the war as an NCO is not known, but is presumed to have a disciplinary content.

GROVES John Lawson

Groves was born in St Margarets, Middlesex, on 22 April 1918, and was educated at Temple College, 1929-35. He then worked as a clerk with the National Provincial Bank in the City of London until May 1939, when he attended an elementary flying course at Civilian School, Perth (11 E & RFTS). He was commissioned in the RAF on 8 July 1939, completing his training with 4 FTS, Habbaniya, Iraq, qualifying as a pilot on 24 November 1939. In February 1940 he attended a navigation course at the Navigation Training Squadron, which was located at 102 MU, Abu Sueir, before going to the Training Unit Reserve Pool for operational training in June 1940, and then to 112 Squadron in July. He was promoted Flg Off on 20 February 1941, and left the squadron for HQ, Middle East, on 1 May 1941, where he became a Flt Lt on 6 October. He was ill for a period from December 1941-

February 1942, during which time he received his DFC on 30 January 1942. At the start of April 1942, having meanwhile returned to the UK, he joined 30 MU, Sealand, as a test pilot, but on 16 May he was posted to 59 OTU, Crosby-on-Eden, as an instructor. On 21 June 1942 he became lost in unexpectedly very bad weather conditions whilst on a flight in Hurricane P3170, and crashed into the sea in Doone Bay, near Kirkudbright, Scotland, losing his life.

GRUNDT-SPANG Helmer (not Helner) Gustav Einer   RAF No. N416

He was posted from 331 Squadron to 57 OTU in May 1943 as an instructor. In November 1943 he moved to HQ, RNorAF, subsequently returning to 331 Squadron in late 1944.

Corrections to claim list:	
1942	
9 Nov	BS445 (not B5445)
1943	
22 Jan and 2 Feb	BS530 (not B5530)
15 Feb	BS470 (not B5470)

GUNNIS Herbert Horatio Kitchener   RAF Nos. 968182 (NCO); 61508 (Officer)

'Alec' Gunnis was born in Mansewood, Glasgow, in 1916, and lived in Alloa, attending Alloa Academy. He joined the RAFVR in September 1939 as a u/t pilot, and was commissioned during 1941. He was promoted Flt Lt on 2 March 1943, and later in the war was awarded a Bar to this DFC, which was gazetted on 22 July 1945. He also served with 603 Squadron, apparently in the Mediterranean area in 1943, when the unit was equipped with Beaufighters. After the war he emigrated to Canada, where he was believed to be living in retirement in Ontario at the time of writing.

Corrections and additions to claim list:	
1942	
18 Jan	T4834 was BT-F (not BT-C)
11 Mar	T4880

GUTHRIE Giles Connop McEachern   Lieutenant Commander

Born on 21 March 1916, he was educated at Eton and Cambridge. A pre-war civil pilot, he won the Portsmouth-Johannesburg Air Race of 1936. He was a Traffic Officer with Imperial Airways, 1938-39, entering the Fleet Air Arm on the outbreak of war, and rising to the rank of Lt Cdr. After the war he became Managing Director of Brown, Shipley & Co; Deputy Chairman of North Central Finance; Director of Prudential Assurance, Radio Rentals, and other companies, and Chairman and Chief Executive of BOAC, 1964-68. He was also a Board Member of BEA, 1959-68, and of the Air Registration Board, 1964-68. He then became Chairman of Air Transport Insurance, 1969-71. He was also a merchant banker, and from 1955 a Justice of the Peace. Knighted, he ultimately retired to Jersey, Channel Islands. He is believed to have died.

GUY Leonard Northwood

It is believed that Guy was not shot down by Bf 109s, but that the wingtip of his aircraft struck the water whilst he was chasing a Ju 88 at low level, following an attack on Thorney Island. The Ju 88 pilot, Otto Schmidt, subsequently reported that the "Spitfire" pursuing him had crashed into the water; Guy is the only missing pilot unaccounted for on that date.

Additions to claim list:	
1940	
13 Aug —	the Bf 110 claimed, crashed at North Baddesley, north of Southampton
15 Aug —	the Ju 88, shared with Flt Lt Sir Archibald Hope, crashed at West Tisted, near Alresford, Hampshire.

HADDON John Arthur Munro   RAF Nos. 1186211 (NCO); 103567 (Officer)

Corrections and additions to claim list:	
1943	
13/14 Jan*	V8625
17/18 Aug (not Jan)**	V8872
* with Sgt F.C.Wilkinson as radar operator.	
** with 158981 Flg Off Robert (not Ralph) James McIlvenny as radar operator.	

HAGGER Ronald Arthur   RAF Nos. 909740 (NCO); 60538 (Officer)

Born in Golders Green, North West London, on 13 December 1916, he worked as a clerk before the war. Selected for a Short Service Commission, he was due to commence training in October 1939, but this was delayed by the outbreak of war. He therefore enlisted as an AC 2 in December 1939, but was placed on the Reserve. Recalled on 17 June 1940, he attended 5 ITW and then was held at 51 Group Pool until August, when he was posted to 7 SFTS, moving to 9 SFTS the following month. He qualified as a pilot in December, being promoted Sgt, but was commissioned in January 1941. After attending 61 OTU, he joined 56 Squadron in February. Promoted Flg Off in January 1942, he was ordered to the Middle East in July, but instead went from 2 PDC to 609 Squadron on 10 September. In November he was sent to Manston pending overseas duty, and in November was sent out to East Africa Command. Finally in December he reached the Tunisian Front, where he joined 81 Squadron. He was promoted to Flt Lt, becoming a flight commander in February. In April 1943 he joined 72 Squadron, but at the start of June ended his tour. He returned to the UK in September 1943, going to HQ, Fighter Command, and then to the USAAF as a Liaison Officer. In November he was attached to the 361st Fighter Group at Bottisham. On 1 May 1944 he was posted to HQ, Technical Training Command, as a test pilot, where he remained until 16 August 1946, when he was posted to 164 Squadron. The following month this unit was renumbered 63 Squadron, but on 10 September he was slightly injured in a flying accident in Spitfire XVI TE453, when he crashed north of Attanbuttel, Germany, during a practice armed reconnaissance. He was released from the service in December 1946.

Additions to claim list:
1943
| 6 May — | first two claims of the day | EN250 |
| „ — | third claim (FW 190 Damaged) | EN358 |

HAINE Richard Cummins   RAF Nos. 580010 (NCO); 43147 (Officer)
Line 11 of the biographical notes on page 306 of *Aces High* is incorrect. He did not claim two victories with 96 Squadron, as the list of claims clearly indicates.

HAINES Leonard Archibald
The OTU in which he served during 1941 was 53 OTU.

Correction to claim list:
1940
| 15 and 28 Nov | Spitfire II (not Mark I) |

HALL John Anthony Sanderson   RAF Nos. 1375850 (NCO); 107269 (Officer)

HALL Peter Francis Locker
From Opotiki (not Opotoki).

HALLETT Nigel George   Lieutenant Commander
On 8 May 1941, after his first engagement, he ditched in the sea, he and his observer being rescued. From September to November 1941 he served as an instructor at 768 Squadron, a deck landing training unit. He then commanded 884 Squadron from November 1941-March 1943, following which he commanded 759 Squadron, a training unit comprising the Advanced Flying School of No 1 Naval Air Fighter School, until the end of the year. May-September 1945 he commanded 887 Squadron, flying Seafires from HMS *Indefatigable* with the British Pacific Fleet. During the war he was awarded a DSC and two Bars. He was promoted Air Group Commander, 7th Carrier Air Group on *Indefatigable*, continuing in this role until March 1946. Remaining in the Navy, he became a Captain in December 1957. He retired to live in East Sussex.

HALLOWES Herbert James Lampriere   RAF Nos. 563179 (NCO); 45010 (Officer)
He was commissioned on 29 November 1940, but with seniority from 18 September. He was posted from 65 Squadron to 56 OTU as an instructor, going from there to 122 Squadron. In late 1944 he was a Wg Cdr at 57 OTU, while in March 1945 he was posted to North Weald as deputy station commander.

Correction to claim list:
1940
1 and 7 Jun — the Hurricane flown on these dates, and shot down on 7 June was N2585 (not L2585).

HAMAR Jack Royston
He worked in the family groceries and wholesale provisioners store in Knighton before joining the RAFO. He undertook his post-entry initiation with 10 E & RFTS during May-July 1938, being commissioned on 9 July. He then completed his training at FTS by March 1939, when he was posted to 151 Squadron. On 16 May 1939 he transferred to the RAF on receiving a Short Service Commission. His DFC award was one of two made to pilots posthumously at this time (the other being Leslie Clisby of 1 Squadron). This was in conflict with policy and led to considerable altercation, no such further awards being permitted. He had, however, been aware of the forthcoming award of the decoration prior to his death. A chapter of Dilip Sarkar's book *Through Peril to the Stars*, is devoted to Hamar.

Additions to claim list:
1940
17 May — the Ju 87 claimed unconfirmed on this date was an aircraft of III/StG 51. His Hurricane was damaged by return fire from a Ju 87 of IV(St)/LG 1.

29 May —	according to Ken Wynn, his claim on this date may have been for a half share in a Ju 88 unconfirmed.
9 Jul —	again according to Ken Wynn this day's claim may have been for a half share of a Bf 110 destroyed (rather than damaged).
14 Jul —	from the same source, it is suggested that his claim on this date may have been for a Bf 109E Probable, rather than destroyed.

HAMILTON Claud Eric

Correction to claim list:
His final claim was made during the night of 11/12 April (not March) and was for a Ju 87, not a Ju 88; this was an aircraft of 9/StG 1.

HAMLYN Ronald Fairfax   RAF Nos. 580244 (NCO); 45277 (Officer)

He was on a charge on 24 August 1940 for a disciplinary infringement, but was allowed to fly. He died in 1991.

HAMMOND Derek Harold

He was commissioned in December 1940. The award of the Bar to his DFC was made in September 1944.

Additions to claim list:

1941					
12 Dec	½ of 4 Ju 52/3ms Damaged; all claims on this date made in 'V' in the Derna area.				
31 Dec	¼	Fi 156	'V'	Ras Lauf	272 Sqn
1942					
11 May			'B'	over Convoy 'Rivet'	

REVISED TOTAL: 1 and 2 shared destroyed, 1 probable, 1 and 4 shared damaged, 15 shared destroyed on the ground.

HAMMOND Ronald Frank

When lost on 1 December 1942, his was one of three Beaufighters shot down by aircraft of 8/JG 2.

Corrections and additions to claim list:

1942					
4 Jul		BV 138 forced to land	Beaufighter IC	T4846 WR-Z W Goosen Island	248 Sqn
27 Sep	½	Ju 88 Damaged	Beaufighter VIC	EL362 WR-X	"
13 Oct		Ju 88 (not shared)		WR-Q	
29 Nov (not 22nd)				WR-Y	

REVISED TOTAL: 3 destroyed, 1 forced to land, 1 probable, 1 and 1 shared damaged, 1 or 2 destroyed on the ground, possibly 1 damaged on the ground.

HAMPSHIRE Keith Macdermott

On arrival in the UK in late summer, he was posted to 60 OTU, moving to 51 OTU in September before joining 456 Squadron. He was awarded a DFC on 12 May 1944, but did not receive a Bar to this.

HANBURY Osgood Villiers   RAF Nos. 742867 (NCO); 81357 (Officer)

Born in Richmond, North Yorkshire, on 13 September 1917, he went to Germany after completing his education in order to learn the language. On his return he worked for Shell at Teddington, also joining the RAFVR in early 1939. He trained at 12 E & RFTS until March at Wick, then going to 13 E & RFTS at White Waltham, where he trained until August 1939. Called up full time at the outbreak of war, he attended 1 ITW at Cambridge from November to January 1940, and then 11 FTS, Shawbury. In July, having qualified as a pilot, he was posted to 1 School of Army Co-operation at Old Sarum, and then in August to 13 Squadron to fly Lysanders. Requirement for fighter pilots caused his almost immediate posting to 7 OTU, Hawarden, followed by his arrival at 602 Squadron on 4 September. Assessed 'above average' at the end of his time with this unit, he flew off HMS *Furious* to Malta on 14 June 1941, and then on to Mersa Matruh, Egypt, two days later. Within a week he was in action over Syria, strafing Baalbeck airfield on 23 June. Here he was attacked by three Vichy French Dewoitine D 520s, being wounded in the shoulder; he landed his damaged Hurricane, Z4608, at Haifa. When rested in July 1942, he was posted to 211 Group at Amriyah, helping plan the conversion of fighter units to fighter-bombing. He returned to the UK for a brief leave on conclusion of the Tunisian Campaign, where he got married. It was whilst being flown back on 3 June 1943 in Hudson FK386, piloted by Grp Capt R.G.Yaxley, DSO,MC,DFC, with Wg Cdr H.F.Burton, DSO,DFC and Bar, and a number of other officers, that the aircraft was intercepted and shot down with the loss of all on board, by a Ju 88C of 15/KG 40 flown by Lt Hans Olbrechte. Unbeknown to Hanbury, his new bride had become pregnant, and was to give birth to a son, Christopher, who was never to see his father.

Additions to claim list (extracted from his logbook):

1941		
14 Dec —	claim was for a Ju 87, not a Ju 88	Z4804
1942		
3 Apr		AK867
25 Apr		AK801
6 Jul		ET575

HANCOCK Allan John   RAF Nos. 903543 (NCO); 120710 (Officer)

He enlisted in September 1939, but was called up in early summer 1940. He completed his flying training at 7 FTS before being posted to 56 OTU in early November 1940.

Addition to claim list:
1942
11 Apr and 10 Jun   BM966 was AK-T

HANKS Peter Prosser

He was educated at Worksop College, Nottinghamshire, and was commissioned in the RAF on 7 October 1935. In August 1945 he commanded 287 Wing in Italy.He served as Wg Cdr Flying at Wunstorf, Germany, during 1948, being posted later in that year to command the Day Fighter Leaders' School at CFE, West Raynham, until 1949. In 1956 he was SASO, RAF Levant. He retired to South Africa, where he died in Westville Hospice, Natal, on 31 January 1986.

Corrections to claim list:

1940				
10 May		the Do 17 claimed was an aircraft of 8/KG 3, flown by Fw Helmut Hoffmann		
„	$\frac{1}{2}$	Do 17 (or He 111) Hurricane I	N2380 'S'	1 Sqn
11 May	$\frac{1}{2}$	Bf 110 (d) „	NE Rethel	„
„	$\frac{1}{3}$	Bf 110 (not a single Bf 110 as reported)		
13 May	$\frac{1}{3}$	He 111 (not a single victory as reported)	SE Vouziers	
14 May (not 15th) 2 Bf 110s (e)			Berry au Bac	
25 Jul	(a)			
1941				
28 Mar		Hurricane I (not Mark II)		

REVISED TOTAL: 11 and 4 shared destroyed, 1 and 3 shared probables, 6 damaged, 2 probably destroyed on the ground.
(a) Some controversy surrounds this Ju 88 of II/KG 51, which was credited to Hanks. The crew of the aircraft was briefed to attack Hucclecote aircraft factory in Gloucester. It was intercepted by two Hurricanes from the Ferry Pool at Kemble, Plt Off Alec Bird firing at the bomber and following it into cloud, where the two aircraft collided. Two 5 OTU Spitfires then arrived, one flown by Hanks, who attacked the Ju 88 as it emerged from cloud, as the crew were preparing to bale out. Bird meanwhile, was killed when his damaged Hurricane crashed. Apparently when the circumstances were explained to Hanks, he withdrew his claim. On this basis his total would be reduced to 10 and 4 shared destroyed.
(d) two Bf 110s of I/ZG 2 were lost; 8 or nine claims were made by 1 Squadron; (e) he was then shot down by Bf 110Cs of I/ZG 26 south of Sedan.

HARDS Maurice Sydney   RAF Nos. 742199 (NCO); 122062 (Officer)

He joined the RAFVR in 1938; he was promoted Sqn Ldr on 26 July 1944.

Addition to claim list:
1943
16 Dec   JF570   Between Ortona and Orsogna

HARDY Owen Leslie

He was awarded an AFC.

HARKER Alan Stuart   RAF Nos. 740826 (NCO); 63791 (Officer)

Known as 'Budge'. He died on 6 August 1996, aged 80.

HARRIES Raymond Hiley   RAF Nos. 902509 (NCO); 87447 (Officer)

He was a dental student (not medical student), but left his studies to join Prudential Assurance as a District Agent in Canterbury. He joined the RAFVR in September 1939. He was posted from 43 Squadron to 52 OTU on 8 July 1941. He is reported to have claimed five V-1 flying bombs shot down during summer 1944, when he was Wing Leader of 135 Wing, but details of only one of these claims has been found. The award of a Belgian Croix de Guerre was made on 14 June 1945.

Addition to claim list:
1944
25 Jun   V-1   Spitfire IX   135 Wg
REVISED TOTAL: 15 and 3 shared destroyed, 2 probables, 5 and 1 shared damaged, (possibly also 5 V-1s destroyed).

HARRINGTON Archibald Allan   1st Lieutenant
RCAF No. J9422; USAAF No. O-885992

He joined the RCAF in March 1941, completing his pilot training in December of that year. Posted to the UK as a Plt Off a year later, he attended 54 OTU before joining 410 Squadron in June 1943. He had transferred to the USAAF on 14 April 1943 meanwhile. He remained with the squadron until 28 December 1944. After the war he transferred to the regular Army Air Force, becoming a Captain on 25 October 1948. He transferred to the

Reserve on 30 January 1951, finally retiring from this as a Lt Col in August 1963. In US service he also received a DSC and eight Air Medals.

HART Kenneth Graham
After completing his flying training, he arrived at the 11 Group Pool in December 1939. In March 1941 he was posted as a Flg Off to 59 OTU to instruct, moving soon afterwards to 55 OTU, and then in July to 60 OTU. In early November he was posted to the Middle East. On conclusion of his tour in February 1942, he went to 71 OTU in the Sudan as a Flt Lt instructor. He was posted to 94 Squadron on 10 August 1941, but returned to 71 OTU on 20 September.

HARTEN John Wilbert Edmund   RCAF Nos. R90818 (NCO); J16665 (Officer)

HAVERCROFT Ralph Edward   RAF Nos. 740168 (NCO); 114000 (Officer)
Corrections to claim list:
1940
23 May - 14 Aug	N3285 was QJ-R
18 Sep	X4069 (not S4069)
13 Nov	N3125 (not P3125)

1941
21 and 26 Jun   Spitfire I, converted to Mark VA standard X4476 (not R4476)

HAW Charlton   RAF Nos. 745249 (NCO); 117992 (Officer)

HAY Ronald Cuthbert
He was commissioned on 1 September 1935, undertaking flying training at Rochester and Netheravon.

HAYLEY-BELL Dennis
Born on 30 June 1916 in Knightsbridge, London, he was educated at Wellington College. He enlisted in the Queen's Royal Regiment as a Private in 1934, being promoted Lance Corporal the following year. In December 1936 he bought himself out and in March 1937 attended civil flying school at Anstey, thereafter joining the RAF and receiving a commission as an Acting Plt Off on a four year engagement in May 1937. He attended 3 FTS, South Cerney, obtaining his 'wings' in July 1937, and in November was posted to 269 (General Reconnaissance) Squadron on Avro Ansons. He was promoted Flg Off in March 1938 and the following month qualified as a first pilot. During August-December 1938 he attended the School of General Reconnaissance on a course, while from January to April 1940 he attended a conversion course on Hudsons at 1 OTU. In October 1940 he was promoted Flt Lt and posted to 55 OTU, then joining 420 Flight on night fighting duties; he was awarded a DFC on 22 November. January-February 1941 saw him attending the Blind Approach School, and on 24 April he joined the Fighter Experimental Establishment after his service with 93 Squadron. He was promoted Sqn Ldr in December 1941 and in January 1942 joined 604 Squadron, moving in March to 255 Squadron as a flight commander. In September 1942 he was posted to 54 OTU as an instructor, going from there to 68 Squadron on 21 April 1943. On 12 May he moved to 96 Squadron and then on 29 June to 125 Squadron, these postings all being as a flight commander. Having returned to 68 Squadron and become Acting Wg Cdr, he completed his tour on 9 August 1944, relinquishing his acting rank, and was seconded to BOAC as a transport pilot. He was released from the RAF on 12 February 1946.

HAYSOM Geoffrey David Leybourne
Born in 1917, he was educated at Natal University College and Edinburgh University, where he obtained a BSc.

HAYTER James Chilton Francis
Corrections and additions to claim list:
1940
26 Oct   V6921 (not B6921)
1942
2 Jul —   the MC 202 which shot down his Hurricane, and which he in turn shot down, is believed to have been an aircraft of 90^a Squadriglia, 10° Gruppo, 4° Stormo CT, the pilot of which, Sottoten Italo Alessandrini, became a POW. Listed in *Aces High* as having occurred between 17-22 June, Italian records indicate that this engagement probably took place on 2 July.
10 Jul   BE487 NH-F
18 Jul   Bf 109E Damaged (not destroyed)
REVISED TOTAL: 5 destroyed (plus 1 not claimed), a probable, 4 damaged.

HAYTON Gilbert McLean   RAF No. 42503 (not RNZAF)

Hayton was born on 12 May 1917 in Hawera, New Zealand. A brilliant scholar, he graduated from university before the war with a BCom, and qualified as an accountant. He then entered the teaching profession, becoming an assistant master at Wellington College, NZ. In April 1939 however, he obtained a Short Service Commission in the RAF, and in May left on the SS *Rangitane* for the UK. Trained as a bomber pilot, he served with 98 Squadron, and then with 12 Squadron in France during May 1940, flying Fairey Battles. Transferring to fighters, he served briefly with 19, 266 and 66 Squadrons, before joining 255 Squadron in December 1940. Posted to the Middle East in February 1942, he joined 89 Squadron in March. HMS *Laconia* on which he was bound for the UK, was sunk by *U-156*; his date of death was registered as 20 October 1942. The award of a DFC was gazetted on 18 September 1942.

Correction to claim list:
Claims on Malta made in Beaufighter IF X7750 'B' (not X7250).

HEARNE Peter Joseph   RAF Nos. 1333300 (NCO); 129957 (Officer)

HEDGECOE Edward Richard

Born in London in 1910, Hedgecoe lived in Brookmans Park, Hertfordshire. He was commissioned in the RAFVR in the Accounts Branch, but on 20 August 1940 he transferred to the GD Branch, dropping rank from Flg Off to Plt Off in order to become a pilot. During the night of 24/25 May 1944 he opened fire on a Ju 88 at 700 feet range, closing to 300 feet to fire again. The aircraft then exploded, the Mosquito flying through the blast, which caused the airframe fabric to catch fire. He ordered Flg Off Bamford to bale out, but the flames went out. He hauled Bamford back into the cockpit and landed safely. Norman Bamford, who was from Sevenoaks, Kent, took part in ten victories with various pilots, but was later killed in a flying accident. In 85 Squadron Hedgecoe flew with Flt Sgt J.R.Whitham, who he had teamed up with at the FIU. The Bf 110 they shot down during the night of 6/7 December 1944 was an aircraft of 8/NJG 4, flown by Hpt Helmut Bergmann, a Knights' Cross holder with 36 victories. Hedgecoe is buried in North Mimms Cemetery, Hertfordshire. The award of a DSO was gazetted in October 1945.

HEGLUND Svein RAF No. N126

The OTU at which he instructed at Eshott during 1943 was No 57. In recent years he completed his autobiography of the war years, *Hok over Hok* (Wings Forlag A/S, 1995). He was working on the translation of this into English for publication by Grub Street during a long illness, completing the task the day before he died — 18 June 1998.

Corrections and additions to claim list:
1943
4 Sep —   these claims were made on 3 Sep, not 4th.
3 Oct   Bf 109G (destroyed, not damaged)
1944
4/5 Dec   Mosquito XXX   VY-B
24/25 Dec   „   VY-A
1945
5/6 Jan   „   VY-B
REVISED TOTAL: 15 and 1 shared destroyed, 5 probables, 6 and 1 shared damaged.

HENNEBERG Zdzislaw Karol

He entered the cadet school at Deblin in 1932 and was commissioned as an observer in 1934, joining the 1 Pulk Lotniczy in Warsaw. The following year he completed a flying course at Deblin and then attended an advanced course at Grudziadz; on completion of this pilot training he joined the 111 Eskadra. In 1937 he became an instructor at the Deblin Central Flying School, also becoming a well-known sports flyer in the Warsaw Flying Club, representing Poland at the gliding championships at Rhon, Germany. In September 1939 he operated with the Deblin Group, an 'ad hoc' unit of flying instructors. He then made his way to Rumania, and subsequently to France. Here during the 'Blitzkrieg' he flew in an Escadrille de Chasse et de Defence — known as 'Chimney Flights' — in defence of the Bloch aircraft assembly plant at Chateauroux. On 18 June 1940 he led his flight of one Bloch 152, two Bloch 151s and a Caudron-Simoun across the Channel to RAF Tangmere, the only Polish unit to fly its aircraft to the UK. He was awarded his Virtuti Militari, 5th Class, on 18 September 1940, not 23 December; the DFC was awarded on 15 December, although gazetted on 16 October. He was killed in Spitfire II P8029 (not in a Hurricane).

Additions to claim list:
1940
31 Aug   V7290 RF-H
2 Sep   RF-D
7 Sep   YO-N (a)
11 Sep   (b)   RF-H

15 Sep	RF-A
27 Sep	RF-D
5 Oct	RF-J

(a) This Hurricane was borrowed from 1 RCAF Squadron, also based at Northolt. (b) the bomber claimed on this date is believed to have been He 111H-2 WNr 5304, V4+RW of 6/KG 1, which crashed at Camber, near Rye.

HEPPELL Philip Whaley Ellis   RAF Nos. 745110 (NCO); 86370 (Officer)
He joined the RAFVR in early 1939. On completing his tour with 616 Squadron in 1941, he served as an instructor at 61 OTU before being posted out to Malta.

HERRICK Michael James
He is buried at Frederikshaven, Denmark.

Corrections and additions to claim list:
1940
He may have made one claim during December. This is believed to have been for a Ju 88 Damaged during the night of 12/13th. If correct, this increases his total of aircraft damaged to three.
1941
21/22 Jun — this claim was against a Ju 88C-4 fighter of 1/NJG 2, WNr 0827, R4+JH.

HESSELYN Raymond Brown
He was born in Dunedin, not Invercargill, and was brought up in Oamaru, North Otago. He was based at Biggin Hill during the early 1950s, while from 1960-62 he was Sqn Ldr Admin Plans at HQ, Fighter Command. His funeral at RAF Uxbridge was supported by the Queen's Colour Squadron of the RAF Regiment as Guard of Honour and bearer party.

Addition to claim list:
1942

5 May	Bf 109 Damaged	Spitfire V	Malta	249 Sqn

REVISED TOTAL: 18 and 1 shared destroyed (plus possibly 2 more on 3 October 1932), 2 probables, 8 damaged.

HETHERINGTON Erik (not Eric) Lawson
RAF Nos. 758132 (NCO); 102091 (Officer)
He enlisted in the RAFVR about July 1939. His DFC citation, gazetted on 3 November 1942, recorded that he had shot down a Ju 88 in October (probably the 'Probable' of 14th) and had destroyed two other aircraft.

Corrections to claim list:
1942

10 May —	this claim may have been a probable, rather than destroyed			
7 Jul	Ju 88 Damaged	Spitfire V	BR347 'T-Z' Malta	249 Sqn
17 Oct			Comino-St Paul's Bay area	

HEWETT Edward William Foott   RAF Nos. 580333 (NCO); 49250 (Officer)
Hewett enlisted in June 1936. He was commissioned on 5 July 1942 from Wt Off, and promoted Flt Lt on 5 July 1944. He received the award of an AFC on 8 June 1944. He is believed to have died in a house fire.

Additions to claim list:
1940

4 Dec	N5858

1941

27 Feb	V7589

HEWITSON John Loch

Additions to claim list:
1942

11 Mar			AN448 GL-H	
27 Mar			„	
29 Mar	Bf 109F Damaged	Tomahawk IIB	„ Gazala	5 SAAF Sqn
4 Jun			AN452 GL-M	
13 Jun			AN525 GL-H	

REVISED TOTAL: 5 destroyed, 1 damaged, 5 and 1 shared damaged on the ground.

HIBBERT Walter James   RAF Nos. 1168883 (NCO); 120487 (Officer)

Addition to claim list:
1943

4 Jan		Spitfire VC	BR591 MK-D

HIGGINSON Frederick William   RAF Nos. 563147 (NCO); 44630 (Officer)

He entered Halton in January 1929.

HILL George Urquhart

Additions to claim list:
1943

Date		Aircraft	Serial	Location
4 Feb			ER500	
23 Feb			ER698	Sbiba-Sbeitla
28 Feb			597	
5 Apr				
10 Apr (not 8th)			JK281	
11,12 and 20 Apr			"	
21 Apr			"	La Sebala airfield
23 Apr			JK426	
1 May			JG746	
6 May			JK389	
3 Jul		Spitfire IX	EN303	
11 Jul	(a)	"	EN518	
13 Jul		Spitfire VC	JG937	
"	Ju 88			5m S Syracuse
"	FW 190			Noto-Augusta

(a) aircraft claimed actually a G-50bis of 159° Gruppo, 50° Stormo Assalto — six lost in this combat.

HILL Howard Perry

Corrections and additions to claim list:
1940

26 Jul —	this claim may have been confirmed				
15 Sep		Bf 109E Probable	Spitfire I	Maidstone	92 Sqn
"	1/2	Do 17 (as listed)			
"	3	He 111s (not 2)			

REVISED TOTAL: 4 or 5 and 1 shared destroyed, 1 and 1 shared probable, 1 shared damaged.

HILLARY Richard Hope   RAF Nos. 754280 (NCO); 74677 (Officer)

HILLS Hollis Harry   RCAF No. J5803; USN No. 243201

HOARE Bertie Rex O'Bryen   RAF No. 37853 (not 37858)

He lived at Hove, Sussex, before the war, gaining his education at Harrow School and Wye Agricultural College. He was awarded a Bar to his DFC on 5 June 1942. His navigator in 23 Squadron was 580808 Wt Off John Frederick Potter, who received a DFC on 30 October 1942, and who had earlier been a bomber navigator. Hoare was posted to 51 OTU from 23 Squadron on 23 September 1942, moving to 60 OTU on 15 May 1943, where he formed the unit's 2 Squadron. He then moved to command 51 OTU, and in July 1943 became o/c Training Wing. Whilst with 605 Squadron he flew with 131832 Flg Off Robert Campbell Muir, who was awarded a DFC on 28 April 1944.

Corrections and additions to claim list:
1941

Date		Aircraft	Serial
21/22 Apr	FW 200 (a)	Havoc I	BJ495 YP-W
1944			
29/30 Aug			PZ176 (not PX176)

(a) initially claimed as an unidentified four-engined aircraft, and then as an FW 200, this victim appears in fact to have been a Ju 88A-5 of IV/KG 1, WNr 5198, which crashed near Rosières after being attacked by an intruder, Fw E.Weber and his crew being killed.

HODGKINSON Arthur John   RAF Nos. 565887 (NCO); 45353 (Officer)

'Hodge' Hodgkinson was a member of the regular RAF, born in Hampstead, North London, who had joined as an Aircraft Apprentice in January 1932. He made the first confirmed claim to be achieved in a Beaufighter during the night of 25/26 October 1940. He was lost with Sgt V.Cropper in Mosquito VI NJ640, YP-H, whilst attacking an airfield in the Rome area.

Corrections and additions to claim list:
1940

Date	Aircraft	Serial
25/26 Oct	Beaufighter IF	R2097 (not Blenheim IF)
1943		
15/16 Mar		DZ233 YP-T (g)
26/27 Apr		DZ231 YP-R (h)

(b) The aircraft listed in *Aces High* was He 111P-2 WNr 2801, G1+GR of 7/KG 55; (g) with Wt Off Woodman as navigator; (h) with Flg Off L.S.Andrews as navigator.

HODGSON William Henry
He was initially commissioned in the RNZAF on a short service basis of five years, but this was transferred to the RAF on 13 April 1940.

HOGAN Henry Algernon Vickers
He was Sector Commander, Northern Sector (HQ, Linton-on-Ouse), 1952-53.

HOLDEN Kenneth
On 26 November 1939 he attended 11 Group Pool for operational training.

HOLLAND Robert Hugh
On receiving his Permanent Commission, he attended 11 Group Pool before being posted to 92 Squadron.

HOLMAN Frank (not Francis) Street   Flight Lieutenant   RAF No. 40176
From Umtali, Southern Rhodesia, he received a Short Service Commission on 13 October 1937. He was promoted Flg Off in March 1940, and Flt Lt in March 1941. It appears that he did not die at once when he crashed on 19 April 1941, but lived until the next day. He had been recommended for the DFC, but this was disallowed due to his death, and he received instead a Mention in Despatches. He was buried in Phaleron War Cemetery, Greece.

Addition to claim list:
1940

31 Oct		P3725	Mersa Matruh

HONOR Dudley Sandry Garton
It is reported with satisfaction that Dudley Honor had not died, as recorded in *Aces High*, but at the time of writing was living in retirement in Devon. During his service with 88 Squadron in France in 1940, he took part in front line reconnaissances and dive-bombing attacks on bridges over the River Meuse. It was for these actions that he was awarded a DFC, although only gazetted in November 1940. He did not attend a fighter OTU, but was posted direct to 145 Squadron in August, transferring in November to 85 Squadron for night operations on Hurricanes and Defiants. In January 1941 he was posted to the Middle East, flying a Hurricane off HMS *Furious* to Takoradi, and then across Africa to Egypt, where he joined 274 Squadron. He later commanded 262 Wing, the first Desert fighter wing. In February 1942 he went to Air HQ, Egypt, as GTI, and later commanded the Heliopolis Fighter Sector. In December 1942, following the advance from Alamein, he commanded 17 Sector, Benghazi, until 1943, when he moved to No 1 MORU on Malta for the invasions of Sicily and Italy. In 1944 he returned to the UK as Wg Cdr Training, 14 Group. He then became Air Attache, South America, covering Colombia, Venezuela and Ecuador. He was promoted Grp Capt in 1946, but the next year resigned from the RAF to become 1st UK Civil Air Attache in South America, accredited to Argentina, Uruguay, Chile, Bolivia and Brazil. In 1951 he became Director, Latin America, with Bristol Aeroplane Co. In 1960 he became Director, Latin America, for Canadair, and later Manager, Air Canada, South America, until his retirement, when he returned to settle in the UK.

Additions to claim list:
1941

15 May	W9269
17 Jun	Z4614

HOPE Sir Archibald Philip, Bart
In France in May 1940 he took part in the destruction of a Do 17Z of 2/KG 76 on 18th, but his Hurricane, N2605, was damaged by return fire, and he force-landed near Grevillers. Two days later N2546 was damaged by Flak, and this time he was obliged to force-land at Merville. In August 1943, as a Wg Cdr, he commanded 57 OTU following his service at Drem. Promoted Grp Capt in February 1944, he became station commander at RAF Exeter.

Addition to claim list:
1940

18 May	½	Do 17Z	Hurricane I	N2605		601 Sqn

REVISED TOTAL: 1 and 2 shared destroyed, 2 unconfirmed destroyed, 3 and 1 shared probable, 4 damaged.

HOPEWELL James
Hopewell's service number indicates that he enlisted as an Aircrafthand, not as an Apprentice. He served with 616 Squadron from December 1939-October 1940, then briefly with 66 Squadron, before joining 73 Squadron. In November 1940 he was posted to 151 Squadron where he remained until May 1941. Whilst with this unit, he crashed in Defiant N3388 when the aircraft ran out of fuel; he survived, but his gunner, Sgt Wallace, RNZAF, was killed. He then served at 54 OTU for a short period before joining 219 Squadron in June 1941. In August he

moved to 264 Squadron, and then in September went to 1452 Flight, a Turbinlite Havoc/Hurricane night fighting unit. It was with this unit that he was killed.

Corrections and additions to claim list:
1940

28 Aug	Bf 110	Spitfire I
30 Aug — delete		
2 Sep	Do 17 (not Bf 110)	

HOPKIN William Pelham
Before joining 54 Squadron, he attended No 6 Course at 6 OTU.

HORBACZEWSKI Eugeniusz
After serving his initial three months of training from September 1937, he joined the Training School at Deblin on 2 January 1938 for the 13th Class, and was commissioned as a fighter pilot on 1 September 1939. He was one of several pilots instructed to evacuate PZL P.7A fighters of the Polish Pilots' School at Ulez to Rumania. From here he reached France via the Mediterranean, and is believed to have flown with a Polish flight at Bordeaux. He reached the UK on 21 June 1940 and attended 58 OTU, then being posted to 303 Squadron in August 1941, where he remained for over a year. Here he was in conflict with Sqn Ldr Jan Zumbach, who had him posted away to 302 Squadron in September 1942, following an accident in which a Spitfire was written off. Apparently 'Dziubek', as he was known, swore that he would exceed Zumbach's total of aerial victories (at that time 12 and one shared, compared with Horbaczewski's three).He was posted back to 58 OTU, this time as an instructor, until he volunteered for the Polish Fighting Team. Following the disbandment of the Team he flew further sorties with 145 Squadron, and subsequently with 601 Squadron, before joining 43 Squadron on 6 July 1943. On 27 July in Spitfire V MA345, FT-G, he attacked a Bf 109, which was finished off by two other pilots. On return to base, according to the Operations Record Book, he forewent his share of the claim. On 9 August he became commanding officer of the squadron. He returned to the UK on 13 October 1943, and in February 1944 took command of 315 Squadron in 133 Wing. His final engagement on 18 August 1944 was against II/JG 26, and possibly also elements of I or III/JG 2. This combat over Beauvais cost II/JG 26 eight aircraft lost and one damaged, with seven pilots killed and one badly wounded. Horbaczewski was posthumously promoted to the Polish rank of Major. His nickname 'Dziubek' translates as 'Little Beak' — a reference to his large and rather hooked nose.

Corrections and additions to claim list:
1942

4 Apr				AA940 was RF-E		
19 Aug				AR366 was RF-L		
1943						
28 Mar				EN267 ZX-5		
2 Apr				EN315 ZX-6		
6 Apr				EN459 ZX-1 (b)		
22 Apr				EN315 ZX-6		
27 Jul	1/3	Bf 109 (c)	Spitfire V	MA345 FT-G		43 Sqn
4 Sep			Spitfire IX	MA259 FT-7		
15 Sep			Spitfire VIII	JF571 FT-13 (not Mark IX)		
16 Sep			Spitfire V	MA345 FT-G		
1944						
12 Jun				FB166 was PK-G		
19 Jul	1/2	V-1	Mustang III	,,	3m NW Appledore	315 Sqn
,,	1/2	V-1	,,	,,	,,	,,
20 Jul		V-1	,,	,,	1m S Hythe	,,
29 Jul	1/2	V-1	,,	,,	,,	,,
,,	1/2	V-1	,,	,,	,,	,,
30 Jul		(d)	,,	,,	,,	,,

REVISED TOTAL: 16 and 1 shared destroyed, (plus 1 shared destroyed, not claimed), 1 probable, 1 damaged, 1 and 4 shared V-1s destroyed.
(b) This was Skalski's aircraft; after claiming the Bf 109, this aircraft was hit by another and the engine was set on fire. Horbaczewski glided down to force-land at Gabes, the fire stopping en route; (c) not claimed; (d) During this engagement the Polish pilots claimed six Bf 109s shot down. One pilot was seen to bale out and may have been picked up by German ASR. JG 5 lost four Bf 109G-6s, three of 11 Staffel and one from 12 Staffel.

HORRICKS Garth Edwards

Corrections and additions to claim list:
1942

23 Feb	Z5140 GN-C
10 Apr	BD826 HA-A (not GL-A)
21 Apr	BG905 GL-J (not GL-V)
26 Apr	Z4942 GL-V

1943		
8 Dec		JF336 AN-C (not AN-O)
1944 (insert)		
14 Feb		JF964 AN-T

HOULE Albert Ulric

Corrections and additions to claim list:

1942				
4 Sep		BP128 AK-W		
26 Oct		HL887 (not AL887) AK-W (not AH-W)		
1943				
8 Jan		Spitfire VB		
1944				
28 Jan	FW 190	Spitfire VIII	JF457 AN-A	417 Sqn

REVISED TOTAL: now appears to be 12 and 1 shared destroyed, 1 probable, 7 damaged, if the claim of 28 January 1944 is correct; this may however have been treated as a squadron victory.

HOULTON John Arthur

On 21 December 1944, when his tour with 485 Squadron ended, he was posted from HQ, 12 Group, to 53 OTU as an instructor. He died on 16 April 1996.

HOWARD Donald Ridgewell   Flight Lieutenant
RAF Nos. 1315987 (NCO); 124165 (Officer)

'Podge' Howard was born on 9 February 1923. He trained in the USA in Georgia and Alabama from October 1941-April 1942, when he was commissioned. It appears that he was retained as an instructor until July 1943, although during April-May 1943 he was also involved in some air testing duties. Returning to the UK, he was posted to Swanton Morley, where from September-December he served with the BSDU. It seems that he was then posted to 54 OTU, where in April 1944, as a Flg Off, he was tried by Court Martial. The nature of his offence is not disclosed, but he appears to have been exonerated, for shortly thereafter he joined 239 Squadron. In the RAF after the war he was promoted Sqn Ldr on 1 January 1953, and retired on 9 February 1966 (not 1967), having been awarded an AFC. He died on 17 June 1979 in Florida, a victim of cancer of the pancreas.

HOWARD-WILLIAMS Peter Ian

He did not go from 19 Squadron to 610 Squadron in early 1941 as recorded in *Aces High*, but to 118 Squadron, where he remained until April 1942. He then served with 276 Squadron on Air-Sea Rescue duties for a few weeks, before joining 2 Delivery Flight at Colerne in May, where he was to remain until February 1943. In that month he commenced his second operational tour, this time with 610 Squadron, although he served with 2 (Fighter-Reconnaissance) Squadron for a short period, April-June 1943, then returning to 610 Squadron until November. From November to March 1944 he served with 11 APC, and then during March and April with 3 FIS. In April 1944 he became an instructor at 57 OTU, Eshott, and then in May with 27 OTU, Lichfield. Here he stayed until March 1945. From March-September 1945 he was at HQ, 91 Group, Abingdon, on training duties, followed by a spell at the Air Ministry until June 1946. He then served with 601 Squadron until April 1947. Service at 61 (Reserve) Group, Kenley, followed, but in May 1947 he went to the British Embassy in China, where he remained until May 1950. He then returned to Cranwell as Senior Admin Officer. In October 1952 he undertook a course at 201 AFS, Swinderby, then in January 1953 being posted to No 1 ANS, Hullavington. April 1954-March 1957 saw him with another spell at Air Ministry, and then came his final posting to the British Embassy in Paris. Following his retirement from the service, he purchased the 'Pandora Inn' at Restornguet Creek, near Falmouth, Cornwall, and ran this for a time. He then opened and ran a toy shop in Falmouth, also becoming involved in sailing for the blind. He retired in 1979, living for the next 12 years in Spain, before returning to the UK when he became ill.

Corrections to claim list:

1941		
6 Aug		P8584 (not P8535)
15 Oct		AD209 (not AD202)

HOWELL Frank Jonathan

When Frank Howell was killed on 9 May 1948, he suffered a fractured skull, not decapitation. His family have asked that this correction is stressed.

HOWES Harold Norman

He enlisted in the RAFVR in December 1937, and was called up on 1 September 1939.

HOWITT Geoffrey Leonard   RAF Nos. 741018 (NCO); 81037 (Officer)

HUBBARD Thomas Edward

He was posted to France on 18 May 1940. During his first action next day, he was shot down by a Bf 109E of 1/JG 77 after claiming the He 111, and force-landed P2684 at Noyelles, south of Arras. He set the aircraft on fire to stop it falling into enemy hands. On 24 September 1941 he transferred to the Administration and Special Duties Branch.

Addition to claim list:
1940

19 May	P2684

HUGHES Dennis Lawrence   RAF Nos. 745296 (NCO); 84913 (Officer)

Born on 10 August 1923, he enlisted in the RAFVR in early 1939. His radar operator during all his successful engagements was 128548 Flt Lt Richard Haslewood Perks, DFC. Hughes retired with DFC,AFC,MBIM, and died on 17 December 1989.

Additions to claim list:
1944

22/23 May		Dortmund
24/25 May	DZ309	Aachen

1945
16/17 Mar (not 17/18) — the Ju 188 claimed was in fact a Ju 88 night fighter of I/NJG 5, flown by Maj Werner Hoffmann, a Knights' Cross holder with 52 victories.

HUGHES David Price

On 11 July 1940 he was posted from the School of Army Co-operation to 6 OTU as a Flg Off, before joining 238 Squadron.

HUGHES Frederick Desmond

He received a Direct Entry Commission in the RAFVR on 3 October 1939.

Corrections and additions to claim list:
1940

26 Aug	L7028
15/16 Oct	N1621

1942
4 Nov should read   Beaufighter VIF
1943
12/13 Feb (not 12/13 Jan)

HUGHES Paterson Clarence

He transferred from the RAAF to the RAF on 19 February 1937.

Correction to claim list:
1940

7 Sep	X4009 (not V4009)

HUGHES-REES John Anthony   RAF Nos. 745790 (NCO); 113942 (Officer)

He enlisted in the RAFVR in April 1939. Between December 1939 and 25 May 1940 he completed his flying training at 22 EFTS, Cambridge. On completion of his tour in March 1942, he was posted to 53 OTU as a Plt Off instructor. In June he undertook a gunnery course at the CGS, then being posted to the Middle East, where he joined 73 OTU.

HUGO Petrus Hendrik

Corrections and additions to claim list:
1940

20 May					Arras-Douai-Lens	
17 Jul	1/2	Do 17 Damaged	Hurricane I		S Redhill	615 Sqn
1943						
29 Jun			Spitfire VB	EN534 EF-Y		
18 Nov			Spitfire VC	MA433	Tivat harbour	

HULL Bernard John   RAF Nos. 1169226 (NCO); 126860 (Officer)

He was born in 1921 in Eltham, living in Kingston Vale, Surrey, before the war, working as a hotel clerk. He enlisted in July 1940.

HULL Caesar Barrand

Born on 23 February 1913 into a farming family, he was taught at home until 1926, when he was sent to the

Transvaal to board at St John's College, Johannesburg. He then returned to the family farm at M'Babore, Swaziland, before going to work for a mining company. In 1934 he was in the Springbok boxing team for the Empire Games at Wembley, London. He sought to join the SAAF, but experienced initial difficulty in gaining acceptance, as he did not speak Africaans. He became a cadet in the Transvaal Training Squadron of the Reserve Training School, but was not permitted to transfer to the regular SAAF due to his language problem. He therefore obtained a Short Service Commission in the RAF in 1935.

Correction to claim list:
1940
4 Sep   V6641 (not P6641)

HUMAN Johan Daniel Wilhelm

Corrections and additions to claim list:

1942		
11 Mar	Tomahawk IIB	AM401 GL-F (not Kittyhawk)
27 May	Kittyhawk I	AL186 DB-G
30 May and 7 Jun	,,	,,
11 Jul	,,	ET80 DB-G
1943		
22 Apr	,,	EV327

HUMPHERSON John Bernard William

He was born in 1916 and educated at Brighton College. He was not posted to 90 Squadron as stated in *Aces High*. He was in fact posted to the RAE, Farnborough. On 22 June 1941 he flew a DB-7 to West Rainham, accompanied by Flt Lt (Dr) W.K.Stewart of the RAF Physiology Laboratory to investigate the oxygen system of the Boeing Fortress Is with which 90 Squadron was equipped. They took off in a Fortress flown by Flg Off J.C.M.Harley, with Humpherson acting as 3rd Pilot, to record temperatures in the cockpit. The aircraft entered cumulo nimbus cloud, where a structural failure was experienced. It was subsequently believed that the crew suffered from anoxia, for the aircraft went out of control. Dr Stewart managed to bale out, but seven others on board, Humpherson included, were killed.

Corrections to claim list:
His claims on 10 May 1940 appear to have been for two He 111s unconfirmed, both shared with two other pilots.
REVISED TOTAL: 3 destroyed, 2 shared unconfirmed destroyed, 2 probables, 3 damaged.

HUMPHREY Andrew Henry

On leaving 58 OTU, he attended a course at No 1 Specialised Low-Level Attack Instructors' School, Milfield, before being posted to the Middle East to join 6 Squadron. He was to help convert this unit from Hurricane IIDs with 37mm cannon, to rocket-firing Hurricanes. He was awarded an AFC on 1 June 1943. In January 1944 he became an instructor at 5 ME Training School, training pilots on rocket-firing Beaufighters and Hurricanes. This led to the award of a Bar to his AFC on 1 January 1945. At the end of the war he was a Sqn Ldr in the Far East. He became a Wg Cdr in 1951, receiving a Second Bar to his AFC in 1955, and was promoted Grp Capt two years later. He was for a time Air ADC to the Queen. His later postings included o/c RAF Akrotiri, Cyprus, 1959-61; the Imperial Defence College, 1961; Director, Defence Plans, 1962-65; AOC, Air Force, Middle East, 1965-67; Air Member for Personnel, MOD, 1968-70; AOC, Strike Command, in the 1970s.

HUNTER Philip Algernon

Born in 1913 in Frimley, Surrey, he attended King's School, Rosslyn House, Felixstowe, and Bishops Stortford School. In 1936 he was on the instructing staff at the RAF College, Cranwell, while from October 1939-January 1940 he commanded the new 254 Squadron on Blenheim IFs, before joining 264 Squadron.

HURST John   RAF Nos. 741220 (NCO); 121463 (Officer)

John Hurst was born in Strood, Kent, in 1918. He joined the RAFVR in January 1938.

HUSSEY Roy Jack Hubert   RAF Nos. 1312369 (NCO); 145116 (Officer)

He is buried in Coxley Churchyard, Christchurch, Sussex.

Corrections and additions to claim list:

1943			
8 Jul			Spitfire VC
11 Jul			Spitfire IX
12 Jul			,,
13 Jul			,,
14 Jul	$\frac{1}{2}$	Bf 109 (not individual)	Spitfire VC
18 Jul			,,
20 Sep			Spitfire IX

19 Dec		Spitfire VC	
30 Dec (not 19th)	FW 190 Damaged	,,	
1944			
24 Jan		Spitfire IX	

REVISED TOTAL: 9 and 5 shared destroyed, 1 probable, 4 and 1 shared damaged, 1 destroyed on the ground.

HYDE Reginald Jack   RAF Nos. 741834 (NCO); 115301 (Officer); RNZAF No. 2440

He was posted to 12 Group Pool, Aston Down, on 30 October 1939, before joining 66 Squadron. When on the RNZAF Reserve after the war, his reserve number was 2440.

Additions to claim list:
1940					
11 Jul	1/2	Do 17 Damaged	Spitfire I		66 Sqn
4 Oct	(a)				

REVISED TOTAL: 5 destroyed, 1 probable, 1 and 1 shared damaged.
(a) The MC 200 was an aircraft of 79ª Squadrilgia, 6° Gruppo, 1° Stormo CT; Ten Mario Nasoni was killed.

IBBOTSON Desmond   RAF Nos. 1107760 (NCO); 129238 (Officer)

Born in 1921 in Harewood, Leeds, East Yorkshire, he was educated at Harrogate Grammar School, and then at Seddon Memorial College in New Zealand. He became an instructor at the Gunnery School at RAF Ballah at the conclusion of his first tour, but was despatched to 103 MU for special flying duties, 7-23 September 1943. He then went to Air HQ, ADEM. After his return to 601 Squadron, and his further successes, he was killed in a flying accident in a Spitfire on 19 November 1944. He is buried in Assisi War Cemetery, Italy.

Corrections and additions to claim list:
1942
2 Nov   AB289 (not AB286)
1943
29 Apr — this MC 202 was an aircraft of 86ª Squadriglia, 7° Gruppo, 54° Stormo CT, from which Cap Ugo Diappi baled out.

INGALLS Bruce Johnston

He was lost in Spitfire JF748.

Corrections and additions to claim list:
1943				
12 Jul		Spitfire IX		Syracuse-Augusta
12 Sep		,,		
1944				
7 Feb	1/2 (not individual claim) (a)			N Rome
16 Feb			MH562	

(a) this claim was made for a "long-nose" FW 190; the identity has not been ascertained, but the date and the location both rule out the possibility that this could have been an FW 190D.

INGLE Alec   RAF Nos. 740349 (NCO); 83980 (Officer)

INGRAM Mervin Robert Bruce

Corrections and additions to claim list:
1942		
31 Oct		BR361 (not BR 261)
1943		
3 Aug		JK991 GK-L
18, 19 and 22 Sep		LZ970 UM-U

INNISS Aubrey Richard De Lisle

Corrections and additions to claim list:
1940				
23 Sep	1/3 (not individual claim)	Blenheim IF	ND-K	
1942				
29 Nov	Ju 88 Probable	Beaufighter		248 Sqn
1943				
29 Jan	sh (not individual claim)			
10 Mar	1/3 (not individual claim)			

REVISED TOTAL: uncertain.

JAMESON George Esmond

On 18 July 1943 he and Flg Off Crookes were posted from 125 Squadron to 51 OTU as instructors.

JAMESON Patrick Geraint

He was Mentioned in Despatches on 14 January 1944 and 14 June 1945. On return from the Staff College in Palestine, he undertook a course on Vampire jet fighters, then holding staff and fighter school appointments until 1952, when he became commanding officer of RAF Wunstorf, Germany, in 2nd TAF. In 1954 he became SASO, 11 Group, Fighter Command, and in 1956, Deputy SASO, 2nd TAF. He became a member of the HQ Staff for Operation 'Grapple', the RAF's megaton nuclear bomb trials at Christmas Island. He was made a CB in 1959. Following his retirement, he suffered from tuberculosis as a result of his wartime service. On recovery, he returned to New Zealand, where he died in September 1996.

JAMIESON David Robert Charles

Jamieson was born in Brighton, Sussex, in 1919, but emigrated with his family to Canada, living in Toronto. He joined the RCAF in 1940, and was commissioned in 1943.

JANUS Stefan

Born in 1911, he entered the Polish military, being commissioned as an infantry officer. In 1934 he completed a flying training course at the Officers' Central Flying School in Deblin, and in 1935 undertook an advanced course. In 1938 he returned to Deblin as an instructor. In September 1939 he led a group of cadets across the border into Rumania, and thence to France. In the UK he was posted to 308 Squadron, becoming a flight commander in May 1941. On 9 November 1941 he took command of 315 Squadron. He had to bale out of Spitfire IX BS241, UZ-J, over France on 26 January 1943, following a collision over the Gravelines area with Wt Off Jasinski of 306 Squadron, becoming a POW for the rest of the war. He died on 11 November 1978.

Corrections and additions to claim list:

1941		
22 Jul	Spitfire IIB	P8320
29 Aug	"	P8516
21 Sep		W3820
24 Oct		AB930 ZF-J
8 Dec		AB931 (not AD931)

JASPER Clarence Murl

Jasper was born on 29 March 1915 in Ottawa, Kansas, a US citizen. In 1933 he enlisted in the US Navy, hoping for flight training, but became a gun pointer on a cruiser. After the outbreak of war in 1939, he left the Navy to enlist in the RCAF, gaining his 'wings' on 13 March 1941. He then became an instructor for the next two years. He arrived in the UK, attending 60 OTU in October 1943, and then joined 418 Squadron in December. He returned to Canada in August 1944 after undertaking 39 sorties, becoming an instructor in 8 OTU on Mosquitoes until the end of the war. He continued to fly many types of aircraft until 1975, when he was grounded following a heart attack.

Corrections and additions to claim list:

1944		
19/20 Jun		Channel
27 Jun	TH-K	
9/10 Jul		20m S Beachy Head

JAY Dudley Trevor

Correction to claim list:
TOTAL: 7 and 2 shared destroyed (not 7 and 1 shared).

JEFFREY Alistair John Oswald

The first Spitfires reached his squadron in February 1940, and on 25 March, whilst flying K9844 near Church Fenton, he heard a loud crack; there had been a structural failure in the rear fuselage. He rolled the aircraft over and baled out. Subsequently he frequently flew P9421, SH-F.

JEFFREY Peter

He died during spring 1997.

Corrections to claim list:
1941
20 Nov-9 Dec — claims made with 234 Wing (not 324 Wing).

JEFFRIES Charles Gordon St David

Initially posted to 253 Squadron, on 14 May 1940 he was sent to France to join 3 Squadron. Later in the day he was shot down in L1908 by Bf 110s of I/ZG 2, returning on foot three days later after force-landing in flames.

After the war he commanded 30 (Communications) Squadron on Ansons for Government and Service use, while in 1959 he commanded 543 Squadron on Valiant PR 1s, having been promoted Wg Cdr in January 1955.

Corrections and additions to claim list:
1940
14 May $\frac{1}{2}$ Bf 110 (not individual claim)   L1908
1941
4 Jul   (a)
29 Sep (not 30th)
REVISED TOTAL: 2 or 3 and 3 shared destroyed, 2 or 3 probables, 2 damaged, 6 shared destroyed on the water, 4 shared damaged on the water.
(a) The MC 200 was probably the 76ª Squadriglia, 7° Gruppo, 54° Stormo CT aircraft in which Ten G.Paolo Mantovani was killed.

JEKA Jozef
He was born in Tupadly, near Wladyslawowo in the Wejherowo district, near Gdansk. He undertook flying training in 4 Pulk Lotniczy at Torun. He was commissioned on 1 November 1941 and promoted Flg Off a year later. Between May and August 1943 he served with 306 Squadron (not 308 Squadron). He was 'A' Flight commander in 316 Squadron from 4 August 1943, while subsequently he held a similar position in 308 Squadron until shot down in Spitfire IX ML254 on 21 May 1944. At the time of the Korean War he was engaged with several other Poles by the American services for a secret operation whereby a pilot was to be parachuted into Soviet-controlled Eastern Europe to steal a MiG 15 and fly it to West Germany. Specialised training was given in Bavaria, but at an advanced stage the project was cancelled when several MiGs were obtained, delivered by defectors. Jeka then volunteered for other clandestine missions which involved flying over Warsaw Pact countries. He is listed as "killed in the line of duty" at Wiesbaden in April 1958. It is believed that he was lost in a take-off crash at the start of such a mission on 13th of that month.

Additions to claim list:
1940
15 Sep   P3219
26 Sep   L1998
27 Sep $\frac{1}{2}$ Bf 110 (not 1 Damaged)   P3219
30 Sep
7 Oct   L1889 "
1941
17 Jun   UZ-B
27 Jun   UZ-C
16 Aug   UZ-B
1943
19 Aug   LZ989 SZ-J
REVISED TOTAL: 7 and 1 shared destroyed, 3 damaged.

JERAM Dennis Mayvore
He was commissioned Midshipman, RN, on 1 May 1939, and attended 7 OTU in June 1940 before joining 213 Squadron. From April-June 1947 he commanded 791 Squadron, a Fleet Requirements, air-sea rescue and communications unit, until it was disbanded.

JOHNSON Carl L.
An American citizen from Banks, Oregon, Carl Johnson joined the RAFVR. He was killed on 23 November 1942, aged 32.

Corrections and additions to claim list:
1942
25 Sep   Beaufighter VIF (not Mark IF)   X
14 and 22 Nov   EL232 J

JOHNSON James Edgar   RAF Nos. 754750 (NCO); 83267 (Officer)
He was employed as Assistant Surveyor with Poulton Urban District Council before entering the RAFVR. In Korea he flew about 12 sorties in B-26s on reconnaissance missions, and in F-80 fighter-bombers during the October-December 1950 period.

JOHNSON James Robert Feir
On leaving 418 Squadron and receiving a DFC, he also received a demotion, losing his acting rank. His AFC was awarded for his work at the Mosquito OTU at Debert, Nova Scotia.

JOHNSON Paul Gilbert
Paul Johnson was a US citizen, born on 5 March 1920 in Bridgeport, Connecticut, and a resident of Bethel in

the same state. He joined the RCAF on 11 October 1941, undertaking flying training from January-November 1942, receiving a commission on 23 October 1942. He arrived in the UK in December 1942, and in March 1943 was despatched to 52 OTU. Promoted Flg Off in late April, he was posted to 421 Squadron in June 1943. He remained with that unit, apart from a leave at the end of 1943, until his death on 18 July 1944, when he hit a tree five miles east of Mezidou in Spitfire IXB MK809. He attempted to recover, but his aircraft went out of control at 7,000 feet when he was just north west of Caen, and crashed.

JOHNSON William John   RAF Nos. 754371 (NCO); 115410 (Officer)
Line 5 of his biographical notes in *Aces High* should read "He attended 6 OTU, Aston Down,..." He was awarded a Bar to his DFC in October 1944, gazetted on 1 December that year. He died in February 1996.

JOHNSTON George Robert Arthur McGarel
He resided in High Wycombe, Buckinghamshire, before the war. In 1952 he was o/c the Police Reserve Air Wing in Tanganyika.

Corrections to claim list:
1941

9 Dec	Ju 88		Hurricane IIC	Sidi Omar	73 Sqn
1942					
9 Feb		"	BD957 (not BP9570)		
19 Feb	Bf 109 Damaged		Hurricane IIB	E Martuba	
31 Aug (not 30th)				Amriya area	

REVISED TOTAL: 10 and 2 shared destroyed, 2 probables, 3 damaged, 3 damaged on the ground.

JOHNSTON Hugh Anthony Stephen   RAF Nos. 1160634 (NCO); 88723 (Officer)
Line 4 of the biographical notes in *Aces High* should be corrected to indicate that he attended 56 OTU (not 5 OTU) before joining 257 Squadron on 20 January 1941.

JOHNSTONE Alexander Vallance Riddell
The Hurricane OTU he joined in September 1943 was 56 OTU, where he was posted from HQ, 9 Group. When he retired in 1968, he was made a CB, not a CBE.

JOLL Ian Kenneth Sefton
He was posted from 604 Squadron to 54 OTU in July 1941 as an instructor. Promoted Flt Lt in December of that year, he was then posted to 153 Squadron on 9 April 1942.

Corrections to claim list:
Between 4/5 July 1941 and 21/22 September, insert 1943, viz:-

4/5 Jul	He 111
1943	
21/22 Sep	Do 217

JONES Edward Gordon
He was born in Lancashire and brought up in India (not born in India). After the withdrawal from Greece, he served in Egypt, Palestine and Cyprus with 80 Squadron. During 1945 he commanded 121 Wing at Volkel, Holland. In 1961-63 he was AOC, Germany (not ADC). In the final line of the biographical notes on page 262 of *Aces High*, delete "OBE".

Additions to claim list:
1940

27 and 28 Nov	Gladiator II	
1941		
28 Feb		N5823

JONES Frank Everett

Addition to claim list:
1942

6 Jun —	the Re 2001 was an aircraft of 2° Gruppo Aut CT.

JONES Norman Garston   RAF Nos. 1056288 (NCO); 115275 (Officer)

Additions to claim list:
1943

19 and 25 Jul	JK829
17 Sep	MA526

JONES Ripley Ogden   RAF No. 100520 (not RCAF)

He obtained his private pilot's licence whilst on holiday in England in August 1936, and graduated from Harvard University in 1938. He then joined the US Navy and was commissioned an Ensign, becoming a Naval Aviator at NAS Pensacola, Florida, in 1939. In 1941 he served as a spotter aircraft pilot on the battleship USS *Texas* until May, when he requested release in order to join the RAF. He arrived in England on 2 June 1941, and was commissioned a Plt Off in September. After attendance at an OTU, he was posted to 611 Squadron, from where he subsequently left for Malta.

JONSSON Thorstein Elton

Additions to claim list:

1942				
19 Nov	Ju 88 Damaged	Spitfire VC	Bone area	111 Sqn
1943				
18 Jan		ER500		

REVISED TOTAL: 8 destroyed, 1 probable, 3 damaged.

JORSTAD Nils Kolbjorn   RAF No. N214

He took part in the handling trials of the Spitfire XIV at Boscombe Down. He was forced to bale out of one of the prototypes, JF318, when the engine caught fire at 30,000 feet on 23 September 1943.

JOWSEY Milton Eardley

Corrections and additions to claim list:

1943		
7 Mar		ER613 (not ER474)
18 Apr	(a)	
14 Jul		believed to be EN416 (not EN333/7)
15 Jul — should read MC 202 (not MC 2O2)		

Note re 18 April-14 July; in the case of all Spitfire IXs the number shown behind the serial (i.e. EN143/12) was not part of the serial; it was carried on the fuselage instead of an individual aircraft letter in order to differentiate the aircraft from the Mark Vs which the unit was also using at this time. Hence each should read, for instance, EN143 QJ-12.

(a) the MC 202 claimed on this date is believed actually to have been an MC 200 of 162° Gruppo Assalto.

JOYCE Ernest Leslie

He was posted from 8 FTS to 56 OTU on 9 December 1940, and from there to 3 Squadron on 20 January 1941. It was from this unit that he was sent to the Middle East. He was buried ten miles south-south west of Dreux, at Mariville.

Corrections and additions to claim list:

1942

First three claims made in Hurricane IIBs, not Mark IICs.

25/26 May and 9 Jun			BN156 QO-L		
3 Jul			BP177 QO-L		
4 Jul	Bf 109 Damaged	Hurricane IIC	,,	Alamein	73 Sqn
7 Jul			BP167 QO-L		
2/3 Sep	Bf 110 Damaged	Hurricane IIC	,,	W LG39	,,

REVISED TOTAL: 9 destroyed, 2 probables, 5 damaged.

JUDD Michael Thomas   Group Captain

Michael Judd was born in Sutton Scotney, near Winchester, Hampshire, on 19 September 1917. He joined the RAFVR, and was one of the first group to receive commissions in this service on 16 November 1937. Called up in 1939, he attended 7 FTS, Peterborough, from October to 29 January 1940, qualifying as a pilot on 1 December 1939, and immediately being promoted Flg Off. In March 1940 he was posted to 1 Air Armaments School, Manby, as a staff pilot, and then in May attended CFS on an instructor's course. Qualifying as an instructor on intermediate training aircraft in June, he joined 8 SFTS, Montrose, where he was promoted Flt Lt in November. In September 1941 he was sent to the Middle East, joining 73 OTU, Sheik Othman, Aden, as an instructor. In mid December he was sent to AHQ, Western Desert, from where at the end of the month he joined 238 Squadron. The award of an AFC for his training work was announced on 1 January 1942. On 24 February 1942 he was slightly wounded in combat in Hurricane Z4862. He led 250 Squadron from 5 April — 23 July 1942, then being posted to 239 Wing. He returned to 250 Squadron in early September, leading it again until 23 November, when he was posted away, sick. On recovery he served briefly at AHQ, East Africa, but in January 1943 was promoted Acting Wg Cdr and was attached to the RAF Delegation, Washington, USA. He returned to the UK in early 1944, briefly joining 83 GSU, before taking over 15 (F) Wing as Wg Cdr Flying. In May he went to 22 Sector HQ, and then in July to 143 Wing, transferring to 121 Wing on 31 October. On 22 January 1945 he was promoted Acting Grp Capt, joining Main HQ, 2nd TAF. He received an Air Efficiency Award on 20 September 1945, and was released on 13 November. He was Mentioned in Despatches on 1 January 1946, and finally relinquished his commission in the RAFVR on 1 July 1959, retaining the rank of Grp Capt.

Additions to claim list:
1942

6 Jun		AL157 LC-B
22 Oct	Kittyhawk III	

JULIAN Ivon
He reached the UK in November 1940 after training at 2 FTS in New Zealand. He then attended 56 OTU before joining 232 Squadron on 6 January 1941.

KAIN Edgar James
In regard to page 366 of *Aces High*, the Press identified him from the citation to his DFC published in the *London Gazette*. On page 367, lines 1-3, reference to his being shot down by French AA should be deleted; this related to fellow-New Zealander 'Bill' Kain, who was also serving with 73 Squadron at this time. Line 367 should read "...Kain was one of the only original pilots..." Line 13 should be corrected to note that he was killed on 7 June 1940, not 6th. His mother and sister were en route to the UK for his wedding. They had reached the USA when advised of his death. He is buried in Choloy War Memorial.

Corrections and additions to revised claim list:
1940

10 May	Do 17 (g)	P2535 K	Rouvres (not Metz)
11 May	Bf 110 unconfirmed (h)	„	Mourmelon
„	Do 17		
12 May	Hs 126 (i)		
14 May	Bf 109E (j)		N Sedan
15 May	Bf 110 unconfirmed		
17 May	Bf 110 unconfirmed (k)	P2559 D	
„	Bf 109E (l)	„	
19 May	Do 215 (m)		
„	Ju 88 (n)		
„	Bf 110		
25-27 May as before			
5 Jun	Bf 109E (p)		nr Rheims

REVISED TOTAL: 16 or 17 destroyed, 3 unconfirmed destroyed, 1 or 2 damaged.
(g) Do 17 of 9/KG 3; pilot Oblt Gottfried Hagen; (h) Aircraft of I/ZG 2; (i) Aircraft of 3(H)/21; (j) Aircraft of I/JG 76; pilot Lt Rudolf Ziegler; (k) probably Do 17Z of II/KG 3; (l) Aircraft of I/JG 76; pilot unhurt; (m) Do 17Z of II/KG 3 damaged; (n) Aircraft of I or II/KG 51; (p) Possibly this aircraft was only claimed damaged.

KARUBIN Stanislaw
He was born in Warsaw, and trained at the Szkola Podoficerow Lotnictwa dla Maloletnich in Bydgoszcz. He was posted in 1939 to the 111 Eskadra. In France he served in ECD I/55 in May 1940, defending Étampes; this unit was equipped with Koolhoven FK 58s, Bloch MB 152 and Arsenal VG 33 fighters.

Additions to claim list:
1940

31 Aug		R2688 RF-F
5 Sep		P3975 RF-U
6 Sep		N7290 RF-H
30 Sep	(a)	V7504 (not V7505) RF-G
5 Oct	(b)	P3901 RF-E

(a) Believed to be Bf 109E-1 WNr 6384 '3' of 6/JG 53, which crashed in the Channel; (b) Believed to be Bf 109E-1 WNr 4865 '2' of 1/JG 3, crashed at Russell Farm, Bethersden.

KAYLL Joseph Robert

Corrections to claim list:
1940

16 Aug	R4221 (not P4221)

TOTAL; should read: 7 and 1 shared destroyed, 1 unconfirmed destroyed (not 2).

KEELE Brian Rushworth   RAF Nos. 1386254 (NCO); 110837 (Officer)

KEIGHLY-PEACH Charles Lindsay
After service with 3 Squadron in 1926, 'KP' as he was known, served at HMS *Columbine*, a destroyer base at Port Edgar, Firth of Forth. He joined HMS *Eagle* in 1927. With Submarine *M-2*, he flew the vessel's Parnall Peto aircraft. He then spent two years with HMS *Centaur*. He next served on HMS *Glorious* with 408 Flight, flying Nimrods (not *Courageous* and Flycatchers). In 1933 408 and 409 Flight amalgamated to form 802 Squadron on *Glorious*. 1935-37 saw him on the staff of Rear Admiral (Destroyers), before two years on HMS *London*. In his role as Naval Assistant (Air) from 1941-43, he helped ensure that future commanders of aircraft carriers were aircrew officers, this policy taking effect late in the war. In 1944 he commanded HMS *Heron*, the Naval Fighter School at

Yeovilton. On HMS *Troubridge* from 1947, he was Captain (D), Third Flotilla. He died in early 1995, after a long illness. His son flew Sea Furies with 807 Squadron aboard HMS *Theseus* during the Korean War, becoming the third generation of Keighly-Peaches to be awarded a DSO.

Addition to claim list:
All claims in N5517.

KEITH George Noel

Corrections and additions to claim list:

1943					
3 Apr			EN351 (not FN351)		
24 Apr	Bf 109 Damaged	Spitfire IX	EN291	N Pont du Fahs	72 Sqn
18 Jun		Spitfire V(not IX)	JK429 (not EK429)		
12 Jul		Spitfire IX	JK637 (not JK429)		

REVISED TOTAL: 8 and 1 shared destroyed, 2 probables, 3 damaged.

KELLETT Ronald Gustave
He died on 1 November 1998.

Correction to claim list:

1940		
31 Aug		R4178 RF-G
5 Sep		RF-A
6 Sep	(a)	"
15 Sep	(b)	RF-V
26 Sep		V6681 (not C6681) RF-D
5 Oct		RF-G

(a) The Do 17 claimed is believed to have been Ju 88A WNr 8104, F1+HP; (b) Believed to have been a Bf 110C-3 of 13/LG 1, which crashed in the Channel.

KELSEY Howard Charles   RAF Nos. 1191586 (NCO); 112445 (Officer)

Corrections and additions to claim list:

1943
23/24 Dec   (not 22/23) This Ju 88 was an aircraft of 4/NJG 1; Oblt Finster, the pilot, was killed; the radar operator was wounded and the gunner baled out.

1945
2/3 Feb and onwards   RS575 3P-V (not R5575)

KENDALL Philip Stanley   RAF Nos. 785014 (NCO); 127038 (Officer)
Born in 1912 in Castleford, West Yorkshire, he lived in the Roundhay district of Leeds, attending Normanton Grammar School and Scarborough College. He joined the RAFVR in 1940, and was to be commissioned on 27 May 1942. He was promoted Flt Lt on 27 May 1944.

Corrections and additions to claim list:

1942					
29/30 Dec			X7931		
1943					
15/16 Jan				50m NNE Bone	
27/28 Apr				20m N Bone	
11/12 May	2	Ju 88s Damaged on ground	Beaufighter VIF	Villacidro airfield	255 Sqn
24/25 May	(c)			near Raf Raf	
1944					
17/18 Jun	(d)				

REVISED TOTAL: 8 destroyed, 1 probable, 2 damaged, 2 damaged on the ground.
(b) with Flt Sgt J.M.C.Talbot as radar operator; (c) with Plt Off D.M.Nedahl as radar operator; (d) Aircraft of NJG 1; crew killed.

KENNEDY Irving Farmer
He died in late 1997 on return to Canada from a visit to the UK.

Correction to claim list:
1943
13 Oct   LZ929 (not LK929)

KENT John Alexander
The final line of the biographical notes on page 372 of *Aces High* should read "....but in March he was rested, becoming CFI at 53 OTU." He was awarded the Cross of Valour by the Poles on 18 September 1940.

Additions to claim list:
1940

9 Sep	(a)	RF-J
23 Sep	(b)	RF-D
27 Sep	(c)	RF-F
1 Oct		RF-D

1941

27 Jun	P8567

(a) The first claim is believed to have been a Bf 110C WNr 3108, 2N+CP of III/ZG 76, which crashed in the Channel; (b) The Bf 109 is believed to have been an E-1 of Stab/JG 3, which crashed into the Channel; (c) Believed to be a Ju 88A-1 WNr 7106, 3Z+GN of 5/KG 77, which crashed at Horham, near Hailsham; it was also attacked by other pilots.

KETTLEWELL George Victor Wildeman

Additions to claim list:
1941

20 & 28 Feb	N5917

KILBURN Michael Plaistowe   RAF Nos. 1165266 (NCO); 116807 (Officer)

Additions to claim list:
1942

19 Aug—12 Dec	BR579 was ON-H

KILIAN John Rutherford Clark   Squadron Leader   RNZAF No. 1043

John Kilian was born in the Queenstown area of Christchurch, New Zealand, on 23 June 1911. He obtained his private pilot's licence in 1933, and joined the RNZAF in September 1937. He was an instructor until late 1941, when he transferred to the RAF and travelled to the UK as a Flt Lt, attending 60 or 61 OTU in early January 1942. On 18 January he joined 401 Squadron, RCAF, but nine days later moved to 485 Squadron. He was posted to 222 Squadron on 30 May, and to 122 Squadron in July. During the Dieppe operation on 19 August 1942 he was slightly wounded whilst on his second sortie of the day. He was rested in November, resuming operations with 504 Squadron in March 1943. He was posted to HQ, 10 Group, in July 1943, and in August to 2 PDC awaiting a passage to New Zealand, where he arrived in November. He attended 2 OTU in May 1944, then joined 19 Squadron, RNZAF, undertaking a tour in the Solomon Islands. He returned to New Zealand in June 1945 to Ohakea, then taking command of 14 Squadron, RNZAF. He left the RNZAF on 28 November 1945. He was awarded a Croix de Guerre by the French for his European operations. Thereafter he became a commercial pilot, carrying tourists and undertaking scenic flights in Otago and South Island. He ultimately retired to farm, and died in July 1989.

Corrections to claim list:
1942

16 Apr	FW 190	Spitfire VB	485 Sqn
24 Apr	FW 190 Damaged (not destroyed)		

REVISED TOTAL: 2 and 1 shared destroyed, 3 damaged.

KILMARTIN John Ignatius

In late May 1940 he instructed at 6 OTU first, moving to 5 OTU on 11 June. In line 19 of his biographical notes on page 374 of *Aces High*, it should read "...He was then posted to 52 OTU for a spell of instructing..." He died on 1 October 1998.

Revisions to part of the claim list for May 1940:
1940

10 May	⅕	Do 17 (a)	Dun-sur-Meuse (not Longuyon)
11 May	2	Bf 110s (b)	Reims (not NW Meziers)
12 May		He 112 unconfirmed	
14 May	2	Ju 87s (not Bf 109Es) (c)	Le Chesne (not Sedan)
15 May		Bf 110(d)	
16 May		No claim listed	
17 May		Bf 110(e)	nr Sedan
„		Bf 110 unconfirmed (e)	„
19 May		He 111 Damaged (not 17th)	

REVISED TOTAL: 10 and 2 shared destroyed, 2 unconfirmed destroyed, 1 damaged.
(a) Do 17Z of 7/KG 3, flown by Uffz Wolfgang Gräfe; (b) 9 claims made; I/ZG 26 lost two Bf 110s; (c) Aircraft of 2/StG 77; (d) Aircraft of ZG 26; (e) Claims for 5 and 2 unconfirmed; V(Z)/LG 1 lost 3 Bf 110s.

KILNER Joseph Richard   RAF Nos. 741005 (NCO); 63783 (Officer)

Born in 1916 in Beckenham, Kent, he lived in Medecine Hat, Alberta, Canada, before returning to England in the late 1930s, where he joined the RAFVR in December 1937. Having been taught to fly, he was attached to 65 Squadron in May 1939 for a few weeks advanced training. He was recalled at the outbreak of war, rejoining the unit.

KING George James   RAF Nos. 904228 (NCO); 136540 (Officer)

He appears to have enlisted in September or October 1939. On arrival in Australia from Java he was attached to 77 Squadron, RAAF, to help form the unit, and was commissioned on 6 May 1942. He returned to the UK in 1943, and at the end of May was withdrawn from 55 OTU, where he was on a course, and was posted to 1 Squadron to fly Typhoons. From there he was posted to 609 Squadron during 1944, and his DFC was gazetted in June 1945. In spring 1946 he was posted out to Italy where in April he took command of 87 Squadron. On 26 June the engine of his Spitfire failed and he attempted a dead-stick landing at Treviso airfield, but crashed, and the aircraft broke up. He was thrown clear, and was taken to 22nd British General Hospital at Mestre, where he died five hours later without regaining consciousness. He was buried in Padua War Cemetery.

KINGABY Donald Ernest   RAF Nos. 745707 (NCO); 112406 (Officer)

His claim on 30 July 1942 was the first confirmed victory for a Spitfire IX.

Correction to claim list:
1941
16 May   R6882 does not seem to have been allocated to 92 Squadron

KINGCOME Charles Brian Fabris

Addition to claim list:
1940
23 Sep   Bf 109E (a)   Spitfire I   92 Sqn
REVISED TOTAL: 9 and 3 shared destroyed, 1 shared unconfirmed destroyed, 5 probables, 13 damaged.
(a) Aircraft of 8/JG 26.

KINMONTH Michael William   Flight Lieutenant

Born in 1922 in Khartoum, Sudan, he lived in Mount Merrion, Dublin, Eire. He enlisted in the RAFVR in 1940, training at 18 EFTS and 3 SFTS, and then attending 54 OTU in May 1941, having received his commission. On return from his tour in North Africa, he was posted as a Flt Lt instructor to 51 OTU. On 11 November 1943 he took off on a ferry flight in Beaufighter IF R2252 with a ground staff Corporal aboard. He was seen to make what was subsequently described as a "dangerous" curved approach to land at Cranfield. A DH Dominie was on its landing approach and flew into the Beaufighter, both aircraft disintegrating, and diving into the ground. Here the wreckage burst into flames, all on board both machines being killed.

KIPP Robert Allan

Corrections to claim list:
1945
12 Apr   Me 410 on ground (not Bf 110)   Kirchheim (not Kursheim)
     ,,   Ju 88 Damaged on ground (not Bf 110)   ,,

KOC Tadeusz

Born on 9 August 1913 at Grabnowo, near Biala Podlaska, he undertook secondary education locally, and also glider training at the PWS aircraft factory's school which was located in that city. Elementary flying training followed at Lublinek, near Lodz, during summer 1934, after which he was drafted for military service and volunteered for training at the Szkola Podchorazych Rezerwy Lotnictwa. He then attended the SPL at Deblin and was commissioned in 1937. Having achieved excellent results, he had the privilege of choosing his own posting, opting for the 161 Eskadra at Lvov. During the 1939 campaign he flew in support of the Army Lodz, and was the only Polish 'ace' credited with the destruction of a Soviet aircraft during the invasion of Eastern Poland — the last victory to be claimed before Poland fell. He escaped via Rumania, Yugoslavia and Greece, arriving in France. He was undergoing conversion training in May 1940, and saw no action, reaching England on the SS *Arandora Star*. In early September he was posted to 307 Squadron to fly Defiants on night fighting duties, but joined a group of that unit's pilots seeking postings to day units. He was sent briefly to No 1 School of Army Co-operation at Old Sarum, then joining 303 Squadron in October. Subsequently he was posted briefly to 245 Squadron, and then joined 317 Squadron during 1941. On 15 March 1942 the unit encountered dense fog on return from a mission, nine Spitfires crashing, only Koc and Sgt Brzeski landing safely. Two weeks later he was appointed flight commander, but in mid 1942 he completed his tour. At the end of the year he was posted to 308 Squadron as a flight commander. On 3 February 1943, during 'Circus 258', he claimed a FW 190 probably destroyed, but was shot down over Dunkirk. He managed to evade capture, returning to his unit on 21 February. He was posted to command 303 Squadron on 23 November 1943, leading this unit until 25 September 1944. He was then posted briefly to 60 OTU as CFI of the Polish Squadron there. He then went to 11 Group as a Liaison Officer. He undertook a course at the Wyzsza Szkola Lotnicza (Polish Air Force Staff College) in 1944/45. He was awarded the Virtuti Militari, 5th Class, the Cross of Valour with three Bars and the DFC. After the war he served with Transport Command for a time, and then emigrated to Canada.

Corrections and additions to claim list:
1939
17 Sep (not 19th)—this was a Soviet aircraft, believed to be a Polikarpov R-5

1941			
8 Nov			W3970 JH-Y
1942			
25 Apr			BL410 (not BL563) JH-D
28 Apr			BL563 JH-S
29 Apr	FW 190 Probable (not Damaged)		"
7 Sep (a)			AD177
1943			
24 Sep (b)			BR629 RF-H

REVISED TOTAL: 3 and 3 shared destroyed, 3 probables.

(a) These two claims for aircraft destroyed were not credited to him officially by the Polish authorities.

KREMSKI Jan Bernard   RAF Nos. P783270 (NCO); P1531 (Officer)

He was born in Werneland, Westphalia, Germany, and brought up in Korolowka, Poland. He studied at Teachers' College in Dzialclowo, but in 1932 joined the air force technical training school at Bydgoszcz, qualifying in 1935 as an airframe fitter. He underwent flying training at Radom-Sadkow, and then advanced fighter training at Grudziadz, subsequently being posted to 121 Eskadra of the 2 Pulk in Kracow. In September 1937 he was a member of the team that won the PAF fighter competition trophy outright for the 2 Pulk. For this he was awarded the Bronze Cross of Merit. He was one of the most successful Polish pilots during the Polish and French campaigns, in summer 1940 flying with ECD Ko at Bourges. It appears that he did not serve with 54 Squadron after arrival in the UK (this was Plt Off Walenty Krepski), but went to 308 Squadron in September 1940. He was commissioned on 16 July 1941, but was killed over Gravelines in Spitfire II P8310. He was awarded the Virtuti Militari, 5th Class, the Cross of Valour and two Bars, and an Air Medal.

Corrections and additions to claim list:

1939				
3 Sep	$^1\!/_2$	Do 17 (not Probable)		
1940				
24 May	$^1\!/_3$	He 111	Curtiss H-75A	ECD Ko (not ELD)
"		2x$^1\!/_3$ He 111s Damaged	"	"
5 Jun		3x$^1\!/_5$ He 111s	"	"
"		2x$^1\!/_5$ He 111s Damaged	"	"
1941				
26 Mar	$^1\!/_3$	Ju 88 Probable (not Damaged)	P2855	
7 Jul			P7886	
22 Jul			P8310	

REVISED TOTAL: 3 and 6 shared destroyed, 1 shared probable, 4 shared damaged.

KROL Waclaw Szczepan

In 1935 he qualified as a glider pilot at Ustianowa Gliding Centre and joined the SPL, Deblin. He was commissioned in 1937 as a pilot and joined the 123 Eskadra of the 2 Pulk at Kracow. In August 1939 he commanded fighter detachments at Wielun and Aleksandrow, near Bielio-Bida, but in September became deputy commander of the 121 Eskadra. In line 10 of the section of the biographical notes on page 381 of *Aces High*, it should indicate that he became CFI at 61 OTU.

Revised claim list in accordance with Polish records:

1939						
5 Sep	$^1\!/_2$	Do 17	PZL P.11C			121 Esk
1940						
24 May		He 111	Morane MS 406		Chatenois	GC II/7
1 Jun		Do 17 Probable	Dewoitine D.520		Portarlieu	"
3 Jun		Do 17	"			"
15 Oct		Bf 109	Hurricane I	P3931 WX-V	Hawkinge	302 Sqn
1941						
13 Mar	$^1\!/_3$	Ju 88 Damaged (a)	Hurricane II	Z2463 WX-U	Worthing	"
8 May		Bf 109F (b)	"		Dover Straits area	"
1942						
5 Jun		FW 190	Spitfire VB	AD313 SZ-X	Fecamp	316 Sqn
1943						
4 Apr		Bf 109	Spitfire IX	EN313 ZX-4	Chiblat	PFT/145 Sqn
20 Apr		MC 202	"	"	S Pantelleria	"
21 Apr		Bf 109	"	"	Cap Bon area	"

REVISED TOTAL: 8 and 1 shared destroyed, 1 probable, 1 shared damaged.

(a) Ju 88 WNr 0408 of 4(F)/121, 15% damaged; (b) Bf 109F-2 WNr 5647, 'Black 3' of 1/JG 3 flown by Lt G.Popel; probably shared with Flg Off Zygmut Kinel.

KUCERA Jiri   RAF Nos. 781568 (NCO); 103533 (Officer)

KUCERA Otmar   RAF Nos. 787658 (NCO); 112548 (Officer)

Line 5 of the biographical notes on page 382 of *Aces High*, should be corrected to indicate that he attended

6 OTU at Sutton Bridge. He died on 6 June 1995 after a long illness with cancer.

Correction to claim list:
1940
15 Nov   V7361 (not V7316)

KUTTELWASCHER Karel Miroslav   RAF Nos. 787969 (NCO); 111519 (Officer)

KYNASTON Norman Arthur   RAF Nos. 969134 (NCO); 89810 (Officer)

Born in 1914 in Hereford, he subsequently lived in Chester. He enlisted in 1939, and was commissioned in 1940.

Additions to claim list:
1944

Date		Type	Aircraft	Serial	Location	Sqn
18 Jun	V-1	Spitfire XIV	RB185		nr London	91 Sqn
	V-1	„	„		Dungeness	„
23 Jun	V-1	„	„		N Hastings	„
„	V-1	„	„		Channel, off Eastbourne	„
30 Jun	V-1	„	„		Hailsham	„
1 Jul	V-1	„	„		NW Maidstone	„
	V-1	„	„		Biggin Hill	„
3 Jul	V-1	„	„		NW Ashford	„
	V-1	„	NH703		NW Tonbridge	„
7 Jul	V-1	„	RB185		N Detling	„
	V-1	„	„		8m W Ashford	„
10 Jul	V-1	„	RWO (a)		SE Sevenoaks	„
„	V-1	„	RB185		4m NE Hailsham	„
11 Jul	V-1	„	„		Maidstone	„
	V-1	„	„		4m NW Ashford	„
19 Jul	V-1	„	RM656		2m SW Maidstone	„
	V-1	„	„		3m W Maidstone	„
23 Jul	V-1	„	„		1m N Gatwick	„
26 Jul	V-1	„	„		10m NW Bexhill	„
27 Jul	V-1	„	RM684		N Staplehurst	„
	V-1	„	„		S Tonbridge	„
28 Jul	V-1	„	RM687		Tenterden area	„

REVISED TOTAL: 4 and 1 shared destroyed, 1 probable, 1 damaged, 22 V-1s destroyed.
(a) Aircraft of the Wing Leader, Wg Cdr R.W.Oxspring.

LACEY James Harry (not Henry)   RAF Nos. 740042 (NCO)

On his return to the UK in May 1946, no flying jobs were available, so he was posted to the Air Ministry Directorate of Accident Prevention. In March 1947 he was able to join 72 Squadron as a Flt Lt to fly Vampires. In May of that year he was granted an Extended Service Commission in the Aircraft Control Branch as a Fighter Controller. He applied for the General Duties (i.e. flying) Branch, and was allowed to stay with 72 Squadron until March 1948. He then attended the School of Fighter Control before being posted to a GCI unit in December 1948. Subsequently he was granted a Permanent Commission in the GD Branch, and in February 1949 undertook a conversion course on Meteors, then joining 43 Squadron as a flight commander. In August 1949 he was posted to Hong Kong as an Acting Sqn Ldr for a tour as a fighter controller, commanding a GCI station in the New Territories. He returned to the UK after 30 months as a Flt Lt ground instructor at the Initial Training School, Jurby, Isle of Man, and later at Kirton-in-Lindsey. He applied for the Pilot Attack Instructors' Course at the Fighter Weapons School, Leconfield, staying on as a flight commander and instructor. In March 1957 he was posted to RAF Germany as a fighter controller, where he befriended ex-Luftwaffe 'Experte', Major Erich Hohagen.

LAKE Ronald George

On leaving the RCAF in September 1945, he attended university in Toronto, graduating in 1949 with a BSc in Mining Geology. In 1950 he joined International Nickel, where he remained until his retirement in 1982; at the time of writing he was living in retirement in St Catherine's, Ontario.

LAMB Deryck Percy   RAF Nos. 937498 (NCO); 112530 (Officer)

Born in 1921 in Newcastle-upon-Tyne, he attended the Royal Grammar Public School and Skerry's College. He enlisted for aircrew in September 1939, and was commissioned in 1941. He was promoted Flt Lt in March 1943.

LAMB Peter Gilbert

Peter Lamb was born in Liverpool, in 1914, attending Durham School. He later settled in the USA, and listed New Orleans as his home address when joining the Auxillary Air Force.

LANE Brian John Edward

He initially flew Gauntlets with 66 and 213 Squadrons before the first Hurricanes arrived in January 1939. On

8 November 1940 he was shot down in error by a Hurricane, and force-landed at Eastchurch. He attended 61 OTU for a refresher course after his service in the Middle East; he did not command this unit as stated in *Aces High*. Neither did he take command of 167 Squadron; he joined this unit as a supernumary Sqn Ldr to regain operational experience. He was lost in VL-U, not 3W-U as stated. Finally, his book was incorporated in Dilip Sarkar's *Spitfire Squadron; No 19 Squadron at War, 1939-41* in its original form — not in edited condition.

LAPKOWSKI Waclaw

He trained in the 8th Class of the Szkola Podchorazych Lotnictwa, and was commissioned on 15 August 1934, joining the 1 Pulk Lotniczy in Warsaw. During September 1939 his 112 Eskadra formed part of the III/1 Dywizjon Mysliwski of the Brygada Poscigowa (Pursuit Brigade). On 17 September, after the Soviet invasion, he flew his P.11C to Rumania, from there reaching France and serving with a fighter section defending an aircraft factory at Romorantin. He joined 303 Squadron on 3 August 1940. On 3 April 1941 he was again wounded in action whilst flying Spitfire II P7567, but recovered to take command of 303 Squadron on 5 May.

Corrections and additions to claim list:
1939				
6 Sep —	delete ¹/₅ Do 17			
1940				
5 Sep			P2985 RF-Z	
1941				
27 Jun	Bf 109 on ground	Spitfire II	P8507	303 Sqn

REVISED TOTAL: 6 and 1 shared destroyed, 1 damaged, 1 destroyed on the ground.

LAPSLEY John Hugh

John Lapsley's father died when he was two years old, and in 1920 he accompanied his stepfather to the Falkland Islands Company, where the latter was an accountant. He returned to England for schooling, subsequently entering Halton as an Aircraft Apprentice at the age of 18. He was granted a cadetship to Cranwell in 1935, and commissioned in 1937. On his return to the UK from the Middle East, he married a WAAF officer. He was posted to 81 Group, the training organisation, and sent as o/c and CFI to 58 OTU at Balado Bridge at the end of May 1942. In November he was posted to 52 OTU as o/c Training Wing, and was promoted Wg Cdr. He remained with the unit until 2 April 1943. Subsequently he commanded a Polish Spitfire squadron for a brief period, before joining 125 Wing. At the end of the war he attended the RAF Staff College before going to the Air Ministry. When with the AFDU, he led the RAF aerobatic display team, which was one of the matters which led to the award of his AFC. He then became Wg Cdr Flying at CFE, West Raynham, in 1951, going from there to Fighter Command HQ in 1953. Following this, he was station commander at RAF Wahn, Germany, followed by various staff appointments. When commanding 19 Group during 1967-68, he had the opportunity to fly Shackletons on a number of occasions. In retirement he was Director-General of the Save the Children Fund for two years. He served on Suffolk Coastal District Council from 1979-87. Sir John Lapsley died on 21 November 1995.

Additions to claim list:
1940			
3 Aug			P2641
9 Dec	(a)		V7293
13 Dec			P2641
14 and 19 Dec			V7293

(a) CR 42 of 82ª Squadriglia, 8° Gruppo, 2° Stormo CT; Serg Magg Francesco Nanin killed.

LARDNER-BURKE Henry Patrick   RAF Nos. 904685 (NCO); 87449 (Officer)

He enlisted in October 1939, beginning his flying training in early 1940. In May 1942 he joined the CGS from 53 OTU, where he had initially been posted after recovering from his wound. On 26 September 1942 he was obliged to bale out of Miles Master III DL684 over Cambridgeshire.

Additions to claim list:
1943
All claims in August and September in Spitfire IXB MH434.

LARICHELIERE Joseph Emile Paul

He attended 6 OTU before joining his first squadron.

Corrections to claim list:
1940
15 Aug — the final claim should read Bf 110 (not BF 110).

LATIMER Jerrard

He was posted from 17 Squadron to 85 Squadron on 17 May 1940. When killed, he was flying as second pilot in Lancaster ED752, ZN-H, and is buried at Sauvillers-Mongival, south-south east of Amiens.

Corrections and additions to claim list:

1940						
11 May				N2403		
19 May		Bf 109E unconfirmed	Hurricane I			85 Sqn
15 Sep	$\frac{1}{2}$	Do 17 (a)		R4089 NN-R		
„	2	Do 17s (a)			„	
18 Sep		and onwards; delete reference to 312 Sqn as shown in *Aces High*; all claims from 31 August 1940-April 1941 while with 310 Squadron.				

1941							
15 May	$\frac{1}{2}$	Do 17	Hurricane IIA	NN-R	N Foreland/Channel	310 Sqn

REVISED TOTAL: 7 and 2 shared destroyed, 1 unconfirmed destroyed, 1 probable, 1 and 1 shared damaged.

(a) Czech sources indicate that he claimed two and one shared on this date, not three shared as shown in *Aces High*.

LATTA John Blandford

He was educated at Oak Bay High School, Victoria, and Victoria College — both in British Columbia.

Additions to claim list:

1940						
14 Jun	2	Bf 109Es	Hurricane I		nr Paris	242 Sqn

REVISED TOTAL: 9 and 1 shared destroyed.

LAUBSCHER Charles James

He was commissioned in the RAFO whilst in England due to his membership of the Oxford University Air Squadron, becoming a Plt Off in Class 'C' by 1937 (technical, accounts and other duties). He was recalled in October 1939 as a Plt Off with special duties in the Admin & SD Branch, but returned to the General Duties Branch as a Flg Off on 24 October 1940.

Corrections and additions to claim list:

1941			
20 Apr	(a)		
1942			
6 Apr-15 Apr	Kittyhawk I (not Tomahawk IIB)		
8 Jun	„		AL134 DB-H
10 Nov	„		ET977 DB-Z
1 Dec	(b) „		ET822 DB-R

(a) One of the CR 42s was an aircraft of 74ª Squadriglia, 23° Gruppo Aut CT; Serg Giuseppe Sanguettoli killed; (b) MC 200 of 92ª Squadrilgia, 8° Gruppo, 2° Stormo CT; Serg Nadio Monti killed.

LAUREYS Francois Pierre (not Pierre F.)   RAF No. F30125

LAWRENCE Arthur George

Correction to claim list:

1942	
23/24 Jul	T7941 was a Tiger Moth, so this serial was clearly in error.

LAWRENCE Keith Ashley

He was not accepted for a Short Service Commission in the RNZAF as stated in *Aces High*. In 1938 he applied to the RAF via the Direct Entry Commonwealth Recruiting Scheme. On arrival in the UK he undertook initial training at 10 E & RFTS, Yatesbury, and was awarded a Short Service Commission. He then trained at 5 FTS, Sealand, before joining 234 Squadron. With 421 Flight he was shot down on 27 November (not 26th). In October 1943 he went to the CGS, Sutton Bridge (not 56 OTU). In February 1945 he returned to operations with 124 Squadron (though not as commanding officer), engaged on dive-bombing attacks. In 1946 in New Zealand, when he went onto the Reserve, he served with the Territorial Air Force as an Air Traffic Controller whilst also opening a shop in Christchurch, before returning to England, as recorded.

Corrections and additions to claim list:

1940	
24 Aug —	this Bf 110 was an aircraft of 5/ZG 2; it ditched in the Channel, Lt Jurgen Meyer being drowned, while Fw Harry Schneider was rescued.He received credit only for an aircraft damaged.
1942	
10 May	BR136

LAWS Adrian Francis   RAF Nos. 514143 (NCO); 45092 (Officer)

Laws was born on 10 August 1912 in East Dereham, Suffolk, living subsequently in Saxmundham in the same county. Initially he worked as a shop assistant with International Stores in the City of London, but enlisted in the RAF on 30 March 1931 as an Aircrafthand/Storekeeper, being promoted LAC in November 1932. He remustered as a pilot on 11 July 1935, whilst serving in the Middle East, and received his flying training at 4 FTS, Abu Sueir. He became a Pilot/Storekeeper with 14 Squadron in April 1936, and was promoted Sgt, while in April 1937 he became a Pilot Equipment Assistant. He had returned to the UK in September 1936, and on completion of training on Demons and Blenheims, was posted to 64 Squadron. He was promoted Flt Sgt on 1 July 1940, and was commissioned on 27 September that year. He had married in September 1939.

LAWSON Walter John   RAF Nos. 563331 (NCO); 43419 (Officer)

Born in January 1913 in Somerset, Walter Lawson joined the RAF as an Apprentice in January 1929. He remustered as a pilot, receiving his wings and being promoted Sgt in December 1936. He was commissioned in August 1940.

Corrections to claim list:
1940

5 Nov		Spitfire II	P7420 (not Mark I)
,,		Spitfire I	R6889

LEARY David Cooper

David Leary was born in London in May 1921. He attended Alleyns School, then entering the RAF as a pilot under training in August 1939; he received a Short Service Commission in October 1939. He attended 6 OTU in May 1940 before being posted to 17 Squadron.

Corrections to claim list:
1940

3 Sep		V7241 (not V2741)

LEATHART James Anthony

Line 8 of his biographical notes in *Aces High* should be altered to read "..., but in September 1940 was posted to the Deputy Directorate of Air Tactics." He died during late 1998.

LEATHER William Johnson

He was Mentioned in Despatches on 1 January 1945.

LE CHEMINANT Jerrold   RAF Nos. 742864 (NCO);126148 (Officer)

Whilst with 92 Squadron he was on one occasion shot down by a Bf 109 over the Channel and baled out onto the Goodwin Sands. He was passed by a launch, which returned at high water full of rescued RAF and Luftwaffe personnel, by which time the sea was up to his chest. In the UK in late 1943 he was attached to the US 8th Air Force to teach German fighter tactics. In 1947 he went on an exchange posting to the USAF at Mitchell Field, Long Island.

Corrections and additions to claim list:
1943

6 Jan		Spitfire VC (not Mark IX)	
1 and 2 Mar		Spitfire IX	EN242
24 Apr		,,	EN250

LEE Richard Hugh Anthony

Lee was born on 12 May 1917 at the Curzon Hotel, Mayfair, London. He was the son of Lt Col Charles F.Lee, who had joined the RFC on 1 March 1914 as a retired Captain, having been invited by General Hugh Trenchard to assist in its build-up; he became Trenchard's adjutant, being Mentioned in Despatches, and receiving the AFC and US Aero Club Medal. He had retired as an Acting Lt Col in March 1919. 'Dickie' Lee was educated at Charterhouse, 1931-35. At Cranwell he represented the College at hockey and soccer, passing out on 30 July 1937 and being posted to 87 Squadron initially. He was the godson of Hugh Trenchard.

Revisions to claim list:
1939

21 Nov		He 111 (a)	Hurricane I	L1898	Boulogne area	85 Sqn
1940						
10 May		Hs 126	,,	N2388 VY-R		,,
,,	1/2	Ju 88 unconfirmed (b)	,,	L1779	Armentières-Forêt de Nieppe	,,
,,	1/3	Ju 88 (c) ,, (d)	,,	,,	NW St Amand	,,
11 May	1/3	Do 17 (e)	,,	,,	,,	,,
,,		Do 17	,,	N2388 VY-R (f)	,,	,,
13 May	2	He 111s (g)	,,	,,	,,	,,
14 May	2	He 111s (h)	,,	,,	,,	,,
15 May		He 111 (g)	,,	,,	,,	,,
16 May		He 111 (g)	,,	,,	,,	,,

APPARENT REVISED TOTAL: 9 and 2 shared destroyed, 1 shared unconfirmed destroyed.

THE DAY FIGHTERS

Top left: G .'Sammy' Allard was one of the "stars" of 85 Squadron both in France and England during 1940. He was killed in a flying accident on 13 March 1941.   *A.C.Brookes*

Top centre: Artist Dennis Barnham saw service on Malta with 601 Squadron in 1942. Subsequently he became an official war artist, before returning to operations late in the war.   *Mrs D.Barnham*

Top right: One of Australia's most successful fighter pilots in the Western Desert, A.W. 'Nicky' Barr claimed 11 victories with 3 RAAF Squadron before becoming a POW. He escaped in 1943, and

was awarded an MC for service with the Italian partisans.   *A.W.Barr via J.Rugner and R.Guest*

Bottom left: No photographs of George 'Ben' Bennions are available, but the man himself has provided this wartime sketch, prepared later in the war.   *G.H.Bennions*

Bottom right: Bobby Bunting, a pilot of the RAAF, saw action over Italy with 93 Squadron during 1944. He also became a war poet, one of his poems being included in the Introduction to this volume.   *B.Bunting*

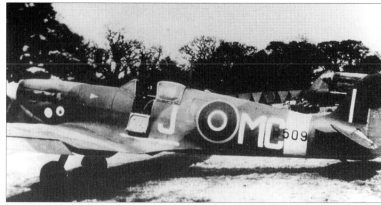

Top left: Argentine-born Ken Charney flew with 185 Squadron on Malta in 1942, later serving in 2nd TAF in Western Europe, ending the war in the Far East in command of 132 Squadron.

Mrs J.Charney

Top right: Spitfire V AB509 JMC of Wg Cdr J.M.'Johnny' Checketts when leading 142 Wing. The maple leaf emblem is for 402 Squadron, RCAF, while the white disc contains the 'Kosciuszko' badge of 303 (Polish) Squadron. Both units formed part of the Wing at this time. *via M.Laird & W. Matusiak*

Middle left: Wg Cdr A. Noel Constantine seen

here in July 1945 in Melbourne on his return to Australia from the Burma Front. *G.Constantine*

Bottom left: With claims for seven Japanese aircraft shot down, A.Gordon Conway was one of the most successful RAF fighter pilots in Burma, where he flew with 136 Squadron. *via B.Cull*

Bottom right: Neill Cox claimed four victories as a Beaufighter pilot with 39 Squadron in the Mediterranean area in 1943. He later converted to single-seater fighters, gaining his final victory over an Me 262 jet over Germany with 56 Squadron (Tempests) in 1945. *IWM*

Top left: With at least 20 victories, Bill Crawford-Compton was one of New Zealand's top fighter pilots. He remained in the RAF after the war, reaching Air rank. *via C.Bowyer*

Top centre: RAF top-scorer in Burma was Bob Cross of 136 Squadron, who claimed three victories whilst flying Hurricanes on this front, followed by six more on Spitfires.

Top right: J.H.'Crash' Curry was a Texan volunteer in the RAF. He saw action over Malta and the Western Desert. *M.Stacey*

Bottom: One of the most successful pilots of the Battle of France was W.Dennis David, who flew with 87 Squadron. He continued to see action throughout the Battle of Britain, and later flew night fighters in the Middle East. *W.D.David*

Top left: One of the least-known New Zealand fighter pilots with the RAF at the start of the war was Antonio Dini, who did well in France with 607 Squadron during May 1940, but was killed in an accident at the end of that month. He is seen here during training at South Cerney with a Blackburn Shark aircraft.   *Dini Family via B.Cull*

Top right: Chris Doll is seen here in the cockpit of his Spitfire, presented on behalf of the people of Bexley, Kent, whilst he was serving with 131 Squadron in 1942. He later flew Spitfire XIIs with 91 Squadron with some success.   *J.C.S.Doll*

Above: Belgium's top-scorer, Count Yvan Du Monceau de Bergendael, seen here as a flight commander in 350 Squadron during 1942.
    R.Lallemant

Above right: This 111 Squadron Spitfire has been painted overall matt black for experimental night operations. Leaning against the wing is its pilot, Sgt Peter Durnford, who was later commissioned and served with 124 Squadron. Shot down by Flak in November 1942, he spent the rest of the war as a POW. The Spitfire is believed to have been W38848.   *111 Squadron Records via W.Matusiak*

Right: Commanding both 605 and 253 Squadrons during 1940, Gerry Edge claimed of the order of 20 victories with these units during the year.   *via A.Lowe*

Top left: J.F.'Stocky' Edwards had been one of the most successful Kittyhawk pilots in the African war. He later flew Spitfires with 92 Squadron in Italy, and then led 127 Wing in Western Europe in 1945. He is seen here with the latter unit, his Spitfire XVI carrying his personal initials.

J.F.Edwards

Top right: R.V.'Monty' Ellis commanded 73 Squadron in North Africa in early 1943. On return to England he became a production test pilot with Vickers Armstrong. *via D.Minterne*

Bottom left: The photograph purporting to show K.W.S. Evans in *Aces High* was in fact of another pilot. This is the man himself, with a Spitfire V of 130 Squadron prior to his departure for Malta in 1942. *K.W.S.Evans*

Bottom right: Paul Farnes, later in the war to become a Sqn Ldr, is seen here relaxing in 1940 as a Sgt with 501 Squadron. One of the unit's Hurricanes can be seen in the background, behind his right shoulder.

J.Scutts

Top left: Czech pilot Stanislaw Fejfar, who claimed victories serving with both the Armée de l'Air and 310 and 313 Squadrons, RAF. He was shot down and killed by Hpt Josef Priller of JG 26 on 17 May 1942.
T.Polak

Top right: Olympic athlete Grp Capt Don Finlay prepares for a flight in a Spitfire while commanding 906 Wing in Burma.
D.Healey via A.Thomas

Above left: One of the top-scorers of the Battle of Britain, mercurial Czech Sgt Josef Frantisek flew with the Poles of 303 Squadron, claiming 17 victories before being killed in a landing crash on 8 October 1940.
via W.Matusiak

Above centre: Geoff Garton served throughout the war, seeing action over France and England with 73 Squadron, moving to the Middle East with this unit in 1941, and then spending much of the rest of the war flying Kittyhawks. He ended the war as Wing Leader of 8 SAAF Wing in Italy.
via D. Minterne

Above right: Johnny Gibson, seen here as a flight commander in 452 Squadron in 1942, subsequently flew in the South Pacific with his native RNZAF. He added one victory over a Japanese aircraft here to the 11 and one shared he had claimed during 1940.

Right: John Greenwood, a Londoner, claimed all his successes with 253 Squadron during 1940. He later emigrated to Australia.
J.P.B.Greenwood

Top left: One of only two pilots to receive a DFC posthumously before such awards were prohibited, was Welshman Jack Hamar of 151 Squadron. Commissioned on 9 July 1940, he killed himself in an aerobatic accident less than two weeks later. *via B.Cull*

Top centre: Flt Lt H.D.Johnson of 91 Squadron with his Spitfire XIV RB 188 'Brumhilde' in summer 1944. He was credited with 13 V-1s shot down and a 14th shared. *P.Hall*

Top right: Norman Jones flew with 152 Squadron over Sicily and Italy throughout summer 1943.

During July he was twice involved in shooting down three aircraft in a single sortie. *N.G.Jones*

Bottom left: E.J.'Cobber' Kain of 73 Squadron, first RAF pilot to claim five victories during the war, examines film recording his exploits with his fiancée, Joyce Phillips. *Kain Family via B.Cull*

Bottom right: I.F.'Hap' Kennedy enjoyed considerable success over the Mediterranean during 1943, adding further to this in France in 1944. With ten and five shared to his credit, he became a doctor after the war. *I.F.Kennedy*

Top left: Wg Cdr Don Kingaby in 1944, when he achieved his final success despite being a staff officer at Fighter Command Headquarters. The ex-Sgt pilot had claimed 21 and two shared by the end of June 1944. *R.Lallemant*

Top centre: One of the RAF's great leaders, Brian Kingcome flew with 92 Squadron during 1940, later leading a Wing in Italy in 1943.

via C.Bowyer

Top right: 91 Squadron's commanding officer, Norman Kynaston, in his Spitfire XII in 1944. Initially claiming four and one shared aircraft shot down, he then achieved considerable success against the V-1s, shooting down 14 and one shared of these. He was lost to Flak on 15 August 1944.

P.Hall

Above left: Originally commissioned as Jerrard Jeffries, he became Jerrard Latimer by a change of name deed poll in January 1941. He achieved success as a flight commander in the first Czech squadron, 310. He later converted to bombers, but was shot down and killed in a Lancaster on 15 April 1943. *via T.Polan*

Above right: South African J.J.'Chris' Le Roux, seen here as a Flg Off with a 91 Squadron Spitfire VB in 1941. Later service in North Africa and with 2nd TAF allowed him to claim a total of 18 shot down, but he was lost on a flight back to England on 29 August 1944. *IWM via P.Hall*

Top left: Albert Lewis prepares to climb into his 85 Squadron Hurricane during summer 1940. After service with this unit in France and England, this South African was posted to 249 Squadron, where on 28 September he was shot down and badly burned. He had claimed 17 victories, 11 of them in just two days. *A.C.Brookes*

Top right: Jean-Marie Maridor with his WAAF fiancée, Jan, in 1944. This gallant French pilot lost his life when his Spitfire XIV was destroyed by the explosion of the seventh V-1 he was involved in shooting down. He had closed in to point-blank range to ensure that it would not crash onto a military hospital *P.Hall*

Middle left: Willie Lindsay saw all his operational flying with 242 Squadron in North Africa and from Corsica. *W.R.M.Lindsay*

Bottom left: Ex-Aircraft Apprentice Alfred Marshall joined 73 Squadron in May 1940, later obtaining great success in North Africa with the unit and 250 Squadron. Like several others, he was killed in an unnecessary flying accident on 27 November 1944. *D.Minterne*

Bottom right: Don McBurnie in his 450 Squadron Kittyhawk in the Western Desert during 1942, where he claimed five and one shared victories. *D.H.McBurnie*

Top left: J.K.U.B.McGrath of 601 Squadron when awarded the DFC in August 1940.
via B.Cull

Top right: John Morgan is seen here in the cockpit of his Spitfire V, QJ-S, of 92 Squadron in North Africa in September 1942. By early 1943 he had claimed seven and one shared destroyed when his tour ended. Subsequently he commanded 274 Squadron in Italy, but was brought down by ground fire in February 1944, becoming a POW.
J.M.Morgan

Above left: Czechoslovakia's leading day fighter pilot, Frantisek Perina, claimed all but one of his victories with the French Armée de l'Air in 1940. His operational service with the RAF was relatively brief, as he spent much time as a gunnery instructor.
F.Perina

Above right: Seen here as a flight commander in 64 Squadron in autumn 1943, Greek-Rhodesian Johnny Plagis had recently claimed his 13th victory at this time. He would add four more before the end of the war.
J.A.Plagis

Right: After service during 1940-42 over England and France with 501, 91 and 234 Squadrons, Don McKay served in the Middle East, where he is seen in June 1942 as a Flt Lt.
J. Scutts

Top left: Czech Raimund Puda claimed one and two shared with the French unit Groupe de Chasse II/4, and then two further shares with 310 Squadron over England in September 1940. He served as an instructor for the rest of the war. *via T.Polak*

Top right: Michael Robinson, seen here when commanding 609 Squadron in early 1941, claimed 18 victories before being shot down and killed as Wing Leader of the Tangmere Wing on 10 April 1942.

Middle left: Graham Robertson flew with RCAF units from 1941-44, rising from Sgt to Sqn Ldr. During this period he claimed four and one shared victories. *Mrs J.S.Robertson*

Above left: R.J.H. 'Robbie'Robertson served with 72 Squadron in the UK and North Africa, claiming five and one shared. He was shot down on 20 December 1942, suffering injuries to his face which led to the loss of his right eye. *R.J.H.Robertson*

Above right: Charles Samouelle achieved considerable success over Libya with 92 Squadron during 1942-43. He later served with 41 and 130 Squadrons in 2nd TAF late in the war, increasing his total to ten and one shared destroyed. This photograph was employed during the war for public relations purposes, providing the cover for a book on notable RAF pilots. *Samouelle Family*

Top left: Canadian Dallas Schmidt was an outstandingly successful Beaufighter pilot with 227 Squadron, operating over the Mediterranean with this unit in late 1942, where he claimed eight and one shared victories. *J.W.Ginns via R.C.Nesbit*

Top centre: Donald Scott flew with 73 Squadron in France and over England during 1940. He went with the unit to the Middle East in November 1940, but here he soon became an instructor. *D.Minterne*

Top right: Previously a BBC announcer, John Selby flew with 73 Squadron in the Western Desert becoming commanding officer in October 1942. He later commanded 23 Squadron on Mosquito intruders. *D.Minterne*

Bottom left: RNZAF pilot Bob Spurdle claimed ten victories over Europe and the South Pacific. He is seen here in 1942 when serving with 91 Squadron, with a presentation Spitfire V. *P.Hall*

Bottom centre: J.H.'Jack' Stafford, a Tempest pilot with 486 Squadron, RNZAF, claimed two and three shared aircraft and eight V-1s shot down. *J.H.Stafford*

Bottom right: Jas Storrar began his operational flying with 145 Squadron in May 1940, ending the war as a Wing Leader on Mustangs. He is seen here with 73 Squadron in 1941 as a Flg Off. After the war he became a successful vet in Chester. *D.Minterne*

Top left: Malta pilot Arthur Varey, seen here as a Flg Off with 66 Squadron in 1944.   *A.W.Varey*

Top centre: Described as a "Greek millionaire playboy", Basilios Vassiliades flew Mustangs with 19 Squadron and then Tempests with 3 Squadron, claiming eight or nine and two shared before being shot down by ground fire and killed on 25 March 1945.

Top right: Patrick Woods-Scawen of 85 Squadron, who was shot down and killed on 1 September 1940, one day before his younger brother, Charles, who was flying with 43 Squadron. At the time of his death, Patrick had claimed ten and three shared, Charles having been credited with seven and one unconfirmed.   *A.C.Brookes*

Above: Top-scorer of the North African war for the RAF was Wg Cdr Lance Wade, a US volunteer from Texas. On 26 February 1943 he was obliged to crash-land after being hit by Flak; he was flying Wg Cdr Ian Gleed's Spitfire VB, IR-G, at the time, and here ruefully surveys his Wing Leader's damaged aircraft.   *M.Stacey*

Left: Peter Wykeham-Barnes flew in the Middle East with 80, 274 and 73 Squadrons during 1940-41. He later led 23 Squadron on Mosquito intruders, ending the war in command of 140 Wing, 2nd TAF. One of the RAF's outstanding leaders, he claimed 14 and three shared destroyed. After the war he rose to become Air Marshal Sir Peter Wykeham, also writing several aviation books.   *D.Minterne*

PAIRS

Top left: Successful pair of 85 Squadron pilots after the Battle of France in 1940, were Dickie Lee (left) and Albert Lewis. Lee - Trenchard's godson – was lost on 18 August 1940, having claimed nine and three shared. *A.C.Brookes*

Top right: Outstanding pilots of 74 Squadron during summer and autumn 1940 were Flt Lt J.C.Mungo-Park (left) and Flg Off H.M.Stephen. *I.Piper*

Above left: Two of 249 Squadron's notables of 1940 display the unit's pets. Bill Millington holds a duck, whilst T.F 'Ginger' Neil nurses a puppy. *A.R.F.Thompson*

Above right: Two of New Zealand's greatest with the RAF. Al Deere (left) and Colin Gray both remained in the RAF as career officers. Deere claimed 21 shot down (two of them shared and three unconfirmed), while Gray was New Zealand's top-scorer with 27 and two shared. *via C.Bowyer*

Right: Two great Fleet Air Arm pilots who served in Douglas Bader's 242 Squadron during summer 1940, before their posting to 252 Squadron. Dickie Cork (left) was a RN pilot, while R.E. 'Jimmie' Gardner was RNVR ("Wavy Navy"). Both went on to further success with their own service, Cork having claimed nine and two shared before his death in a landing accident on 14 April 1944, while Gardner claimed six and four shared.

GROUPS

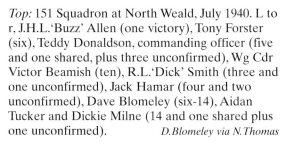

Top: 151 Squadron at North Weald, July 1940. L to r, J.H.L. 'Buzz' Allen (one victory), Tony Forster (six), Teddy Donaldson, commanding officer (five and one shared, plus three unconfirmed), Wg Cdr Victor Beamish (ten), R.L. 'Dick' Smith (three and one unconfirmed), Jack Hamar (four and two unconfirmed), Dave Blomeley (six-14), Aidan Tucker and Dickie Milne (14 and one shared plus one unconfirmed).   *D.Blomeley via N.Thomas*

Above left: 85 Squadron at Lille, France, in May 1940. Third from left is Sqn Ldr J.O.W. 'Doggie' Oliver; third from right is Sgt G. 'Sammy' Allard.
                                    A.C.Brookes

Middle right: 85 Squadron personnel at Debden satellite field in August 1940. L to r John Bickerdike, Patrick Woods-Scawen (ten and three shared), James Lockhart, Dickie Lee (nine and

three shared), Len Jowitt, Beaber (M.O.) and Ernest Webster.   *A.J.Brookes*

Bottom right: Pilots of 3 Squadron with a Hurricane at Hawkinge at Christmas 1939. On the left is C.A.C. 'Bunny' Stone, while on the right is Walter Churchill. The pilot in the centre has not been identified.   *I.Piper*

wall), Flt Lt Brian Van Mentz (seven and one shared plus one unconfirmed).   *A.Long*

Top right: 91 Squadron at Hawkinge, 1941. L to r, Flt Lt J.J.'Orange' O'Meara (11 and two shared plus one unconfirmed), Sgt 'Olly' Cooper, Flt Lt Tony Lee-Knight (five and one shared), Flg Off P.P.C.'Paddy' Barthropp (two and two shared), Sgt Goodwin and Flg Off J.J.'Chris' Le Roux (18).
                                    P.P.C.Barthropp via P.Hall

Above: 'B' Flight, 124 Squadron, 1942. L to r, Belgian pilot, Bob Larcher, W.J'Jesse' Hibbert (four and two shared), M.P.'Slim' Kilburn (six and one shared), Czech pilot, Allan Scott (five), Eddie Bracken, Arne Austeen (five and one shared).
                                                A.H.Scott

Top left: Pilots of 222 Squadron at dispersal at Coltishall in early 1941. Seated from left are Flt Lt Eric Thomas (four and one shared), Sqn Ldr Love, Plt Off Klee, Plt Off J.M.V.'Chips' Carpenter (eight), unknown, Plt Off Roy Marsland (with pipe) and three unknowns. Standing are the Squadron Intelligence Officer and (writing on the

Left: 136 Squadron in Eastern India, March 1944. L to r, Flg Off D.J.Barnett (one victory), Flt Sgt F.E.Wilding (four), Sqn Ldr A.N.Constantine (three), Flt Lt A.G.Conway (seven), Flg Off D.E.W.Garvan (four).   *Dept of Air via G. Constantine*

A GALAXY OF NIGHT FIGHTERS

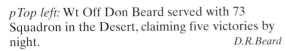

pTop left: Wt Off Don Beard served with 73 Squadron in the Desert, claiming five victories by night.   *D.R.Beard*

Top centre: J.G. Benson, seen here early in the war, rose to the rank of Wg Cdr, claiming victories over ten aircraft and six V-1s, most of them whilst serving with 157 Squadron.   *A.Long*

Top right: After gaining three victories by night in a Beaufighter, Joe Berry flew Tempests with a special Flight of the Fighter Interception Unit, becoming top-scorer against the V-1s, most of his claims against these also being made at night.
Mrs J.Manser

Above left: Due to the loss of his logbook in France in 1940, David Blomeley's final score is uncertain. With 605 Squadron in late 1943 he painted 14 swastikas on the nose of his Mosquito. He is seen here (left) with his navigator, Flg Off 'Jock' Birrell.
I.Piper/N.Thomas

Above right: Roy Butler (left) and his radar operator, Wt Off R.F.Graham, claimed all their five victories with 46 Squadron during a period of one week over the Aegean Sea in late 1944.
R.T.Butler

Above: One of the RAF's most notable night fighters, Wg Cdr John Cunningham (rt), seen here with his radar operator, C.F.'Jimmie' Rawnsley, with their Mosquito.   *A.Brookes*

Top left: 'Berry' Downing survived a ditching in the Mediterranean in early 1944, but his radar operator, John Lyons, was drowned. Downing later became a senior BOAC Captain, flying many hours on VC 10s. *Mrs S.Downing*

Top right: R.J.'Jack' Foster (left) with his radar operator, Maurice Newton, flew with 604 and 108 Squadrons in England and the Middle East, claiming nine victories. *J.Haddon*

Above left: A group of 605 Squadron's successful pilots in early 1944. On the right is the squadron commander, Wg Cdr Bertie Hoare (nine victories); on the left is flight commander Sqn Ldr Richard Mitchell (five and three shared victories in the air, six on the ground), whilst in the middle is Flt Lt Alan Wagner (nine victories and 2 V-1s). *I.Piper*

Above right: A successful pair of night intruder pilots with 1 Squadron during 1942; Sqn Ldr J.A.F, Maclachlan (left), the commanding officer, flew with an artificial hand, having lost his own limb during an air battle over Malta. On the right is Flt Lt Karel Kuttelwascher, a Czech pilot. Between

them, these two had claimed 20 victories during April-July 1942. Both had just been awarded the Czech War Cross when this photograph was taken. *via C.Bowyer*

Above: Wg Cdr Desmond Hughes when commanding 604 Squadron in summer 1944. He was one of the RAF's most successful night fighters, 15 of his 18 and one shared victories being claimed during the hours of darkness. *J.Haddon*

Top left: Bill Maguire claimed five victories with 5 Squadron before being posted to the FIU. Here e claimed his final success, but was killed in a rash on 17 February 1945. *A.Brookes*

Top centre: A.Maurice Pring served in the Middle East and then in India as a night fighter, claiming even victories. He was shot down and killed uring a day sortie in a Hurricane to intercept a ajor Japanese raid on Calcutta on 5 December 943. *via B.Cull*

Top right: Wg Cdr Gordon Raphael, a Canadian, rst saw action as a bomber pilot. Later serving as fighter with 85 Squadron, he was to become the ost successful exponent of the Douglas Havoc ircraft, claiming six of his seven victories whilst ying these. He was killed in a mid-air collision on April 1945. *A.Brookes*

Bottom left: Wg Cdr Richard Mitchell (rt) and his navigator, Flt Lt S. Hatsell, DFC, when commanding 605 Squadron in 1944. Mitchell had earlier flown as a Spitfire pilot over Malta. The nose of his Mosquito, UP-B, carries a dozen swastikas, denoting both air and ground victories. *I.Piper*

Middle right: Flt Lt Ken Rayment claimed six victories in the Mediterranean area with 153 Squadron, and a V-1 with 264 Squadron over England. Later becoming a senior BEA pilot, he died as a result of the crash of a Viscount aircraft at Munich, carrying the Manchester United football team in 1958. *S.G.Rayment*

Bottom right: Nevil Reeves saw service in the Middle East, on Malta, and with Bomber Command's 100 Group on bomber escort duties. He claimed 14 victories, all by night. *via A.Long*

Top left: A most notable trio in the Middle East sit on the bonnet of a captured Kubelwagen. Left to right are Nevil Reeves, Douggie Oxby (later to become the RAF's top-scoring radar operator, having taken part in 21 successful engagements) and Merv Shipard (13 victories), with whom Oxby flew at the time. All were serving with 89 Squadron at this time.   *via A.Long*

Top right: Flt Lt Alan Wagner's Mosquito VI is marked with his victory tally shortly after joining 605 Squadron in 1943. This includes two Japanese aircraft which he claimed over Ceylon in April 1942. He is joined here by his navigator, Flg Off E.T.'Pip' Orringe. He was to claim at least four more victories and two V-1s. On 16 July 1944 he flew into the ground in fog whilst pursuing a V-1, and was killed.   *I.Piper*

Middle left: Leslie Stephenson (left) and his radar operator, George Hall, claimed six victories with 153 Squadron in the Mediterranean area, and then four more over Europe with 219 Squadron. They are seen here on 24 May 1943, having just shot down three Ju 88s during the previous night.   *J.Haddon*

Middle right: Flt Lt Laurie Styles of 153 Squadron with the unit's bantam cockerel mascot at Maison Blanche, Algiers, in February 1943. He later served as a flight commander in 600 Squadron, where he raised his total to five victories.   *J.Haddon*

Right: Johnny Surman of 604 Squadron was credited with five victories, three of them during the night of 6/7 August 1944.   *J.Surman*

Bottom right: Bernard Thwaites claimed at least five victories whilst flying with 85 Squadron, 1943-44.   *A.Brookes*

Top left: Ernest Williams (left), a Rhodesian, flew as an intruder pilot in Mosquitos both over the Mediterranean with 23 Squadron, and then over Europe with 605 Squadron, joined throughout by his navigator, Flg Off Francis Hogg, DFC, RCAF. He also flew against the V-1s with the FIU Tempest Flight, claiming 11 of these bombs shot down to add to his seven victories against aircraft and three on the ground. *I.Piper*

Top right: Staff of the Night Fighter Leaders' School, CFE, West Raynham, 1947. Seated l to r at the front are Flt Lt Roy Lelong (seven victories in the air, ten and three shared on the ground, and three V-1s), Sqn Ldr Jack Haddon (four victories) and the commanding officer, Wg Cdr Derek Pain (five victories). *J.Haddon*

Bottom left: Peter 'Prune' Williamson (left) with his radar operator, Sgt Dennis Lake, serving with 153 Squadron in North Africa, where they claimed five victories. Williamson later claimed four more over Europe with 219 Squadron, flying with another radar operator. He remained in the RAF, retiring in 1978 as an Air Vice-Marshal. *J.Haddon*

Bottom right: 153 Squadron at Maison Blanche, Algiers, in July 1943 when the unit had achieved its 50th victory. Standing, l to r, are Wg Cdr W.Moseby (two victories), Flg Off Peter Williamson (nine victories), Sgt Sherbrooke, Flg Off Jack Haddon (four victories), Flt Sgt Grew (two victories), u/k, u/k, Sgt Cheetham, Flg Off N.Barker, Flt Lt G.Evans, Sqn Ldr G.McLannahan, Sqn Ldr Laurie Styles (five victories), Flg Off Leslie Stephenson (ten victories) and Flg Off Ken Rayment (six victories). Squatting in front are Sgt Thompson, Flg Off D.Bovey (I.O.), u/k, Flg Off H.West, Sgt J.Ayliffe and Flg Off L.Smith. *J.Haddon*

A PLETHORA OF POLES

Top left: Following some years of imprisonment in Soviet labour camps, Jakob Bargielowski required more than a year to recover his health before training as a pilot. Flying Mustangs with 315 Squadron, he claimed victories over five aircraft and three V-1s (two shared) during 1944.

J.Bargielowski via W.Matusiak

Top centre: After action over Poland in 1939, Stanislaw Brzeski served with 249, 317 and 302 Squadrons, claiming a total of seven and three shared in the air, plus one on the ground and one observation balloon shot down.

S.Bochniak via W.Matusiak

Top right: Aleksandr Chudek claimed nine victories with 315 and 303 Squadrons, including one of the first FW 190s in September 1941. He was shot down and killed over France on 23 June 1944.

W.Matusiak

Bottom left: In action throughout the war, Michal Cwynar was credited with five or six and one shared aircraft, two and four shared V-1s shot down.

M.Cwynar

Bottom right: One of the most highly-decorated senior Polish pilots of the war was Grp Capt Aleksandr Gabszewicz. When appointed to command 18 Sector of Fighter Command, he achieved the highest RAF post of the war for a non-British subject. He also claimed eight and three shared aerial victories.

J.Szymankiewicz via W.Matusiak

Top left: One of the "bad boys" of the Polish Air Force, B. Michal Gladych was officially credited by his own service only with the 14 victories he claimed whilst on official duty up to June 1944. However, he was credited by the USAAF with a further four, plus five on the ground, whilst continuing to fly unofficially with the 56th Fighter Group after that date. *via W.Matusiak*

Top centre: Eugeniusz 'Dziubek' Horbaczewski was another pilot who fell foul of higher authorities at times. After service with 303 Squadron and with the Polish Fighting Team in North Africa, he commanded 43 Squadron, RAF, and then led 315 Squadron on Mustangs during the Normandy Invasion. Having claimed 13 and one shared aircraft, one and four shared V-1s, he took part in a fight on 18 August 1944 when 16 Luftwaffe fighters were claimed shot down, three of them by him. However, he was then shot down and failed to return. *M.Cwynar*

Top right: Waclaw Krol saw action over Poland, in France with the Armée de l'Air, over Western Europe with 302 and 316 Squadrons, and in North Africa with the Polish Fighting Team. He was credited with eight and one shared destroyed.
Kopanski via W.Matusiak

Bottom left: Antoni Glowacki (left) and Stefan Witorzenc both flew with 501 Squadron during 1940. With this unit Glowacki claimed five victories in a day on 24 August. Both later served with Polish squadrons, Glowacki ending the war with eight and one shared victories, and Witorzenc with five and one shared.

R.Gretzyngier via W.Matusiak

Bottom centre: After service in France as an attack pilot, Michal Maciejowski reached England, flying with 249 Squadron during 1940-41, and then with 317 and 316 Squadrons. He claimed ten and one shared destroyed. *via W.Matusiak*

Bottom right: One of the senior Polish pilots in England, Grp Capt Mieczyslaw Mümler had gained the majority of his victories in 1939 and in June 1940 over Poland and France. He was to add one more with 302 Squadron in summer 1940, raising his total to four and three shared. Thereafter most of his time was spent as an instructor, and then as station commander at RAF Northolt. *via W.Matusiak*

Top left: After initial service over Poland, Karol Pniak flew with 32 and 257 Squadrons during the Battle of Britain. He later served with the Polish Fighting Team in North Africa. He claimed six and two shared victories. *via W.Matusiak*

Top centre: Poland's top-scorers keep a critical eye on their compatriots. Stanislaw Skalski (left) was credited with 18 and three shared destroyed, while Witold Urbanowicz (rt) received credit for 18 shot down and nine destroyed on the ground - the latter all in China when flying with the US 10th Air Force. The pair were reported never to have been on the best of terms with each other so this is a rare photo! *via W.Matusiak*

Top right: Another Pole who saw action over both Poland and France before reaching the UK, was Eugeniusz Szaposnikow. During autumn 1940 he claimed eight victories with 303 Squadron to add to one earlier shared claim. *via W.Matusiak*

Bottom left: Henryk Szczesny claimed two victories in 1939 with the Deblin Instructors' Group, followed by four and one shared with 74 Squadron during 1940. On 4 April 1943, leading the Northolt Wing, he brought down two FW 190s to raise his total to eight and three shared. The second of these was destroyed by collision however, and he baled out to spend the rest of the war as a POW. *M. Trzebinski via W.Matusiak*

Bottom right: Swiss-born Pole Jan Zumbach became one of the Polish Air Force's top-scorers by the end of 1942, claiming 12 and two shared. He led 133 Wing on Mustangs during 1944-45. *J.B.Cynk via W.Matusiak*

(a) He 111 WNr 1567 of Stab/KG 4, crashed in sea ten miles north of Cap Gris Nez; (b) Believed to be an He 111P of Stab/KG 27; (c) He 111 of LG 1; (d) L1779 was badly damaged by return fire from an He 111P of Stab II/KG 27; (e) Do 17Z of I/KG 76 damaged; (f) N2388 was then hit by Flak near Maastricht and he baled out; (g) These various claims are believed to have been made by him, but remain an estimation; (h) As for (g); in this engagement with KG 27 four were claimed — three were actually lost.

LEE-KNIGHT Roland Anthony
He was born in 1917 in Fareham, Hampshire, and attended Bedford Modern School.

LEFEVRE Peter William
In late October 1942 he was posted to the Central Gunnery School as Chief Instructor, Fighter Wing, as a Sqn Ldr.

Corrections to claim list:
1940
3 Sep —   the Ju 88 claimed was in fact a Blenheim of 25 Squadron, which he shot down in error.
REVISED TOTAL: due to the above, 4 and 5 shared destroyed, 1 shared probable, 1 damaged.

LELONG Roy Emile
He was posted to the UK in May 1942, and was commissioned on 28 June 1943. In Korea he flew F-86s with the 4th Fighter Interceptor Wing, being awarded a US Air Medal for his service there. He commanded 43 Squadron from January 1953-August 1955, forming an aerobatic team. He was awarded an AFC, but retired as a Sqn Ldr on 13 October 1957. He died of a heart attack in 1977.

Corrections and additions to claim list:

1944				
25/26 Jun	V-1	Mosquito VI		605 Sqn
4/5 Jul	V-1	,,		,,
8/9 Jul	V-1	,,		,,
1945				
14 Feb and thereafter — unit should read FEF.				
24/25 Mar	Ju 52/3m on ground	,,	Putnitz	FEF
,,	2	Me 410s on ground	,,	,,	,,
,,	Do 24 Damaged on ground	,,	,,	,,
,,	He 111 Damaged on ground	,,	,,	,,
,,	Ju 52/3m Damaged on ground	,,	,,	,,

REVISED TOTAL: 7 destroyed, 1 probable, 3 damaged, 10 and 3 shared destroyed on the ground or water, 1 probable on the water, 17 and uncertain number of shared damaged on the ground or water, 3 V-1s destroyed.

LE ROUX Johannes Jacobus
Born in Heidelberg, Transvaal, he attended 6 OTU in May 1940, but on 16th was the subject of a Court Martial enquiry for low flying. The same day however, he was reported posted to 85 Squadron in France. Due to the destruction of that unit's records a few days later, his arrival is not recorded. It is surmised therefore that he did not fly Battles in France, but Hurricanes (briefly). Since he does not appear again until later in 1940, it is assumed that he was wounded soon after his arrival, only resuming operational flying on recovery.

Additions to claim list:
1943
14 and 18 Jan   597
3, 6 and 23 Apr   JG746

LEROY DU VIVIER Daniel Albert Raymond Georges   RAF No. : Belgian No. 50017
                                                          (see DU VIVIER, D.A.R.G.L.)

LEU Rudolf Morris
Known as 'Blue'.

Addition to claim list:
1942
14 Feb —   363ª Squadrilgia, 150° Gruppo Aut CT lost three MC 200 pilot during the engagement on this date.

LEWIS Albert Gerald
Before joining the RAF, he undertook a one year civil engineering course at Roberts Heights SAAF base during 1937. He wanted to be a pilot, so applied for a position with the Rand Flying Club. Before joining 85 Squadron he attended 12 Group Pool at Aston Down in October 1939, for operational conversion to Hurricanes. During the fighting in France he claimed seven victories (not nine), flying back to England on 20 May. On 27 September 1940 he was shot down, it is believed, by Hpt Rolf Pingel of I/JG 26, who was in turn shot down by J.M.B.Beard,

also of 249 Squadron. Lewis was flying V6617, GN-R, in which he had claimed all his victories whilst with the unit. On recovery he served with 57 OTU (not, it seems, 52 OTU as stated in *Aces High*). Having been evacuated back to the UK following his injuries in April 1942, he joined 56 OTU as a Sqn Ldr in April 1943, becoming CFI. In August of that year he was posted to HQ, 9 Group.

Corrections and additions to claim list:

1940		
12 May		VY-E
19 May —	the first two Bf 109Es appear to have been aircraft of II/JG 2, which lost at least two such machines in these circumstances.	
18 Aug	Bf 110 was confirmed destroyed, not Probable	VY-D
31 Aug		VY-N
15 Sep —	all further claims in Hurricane I V6617	GN-R
17 Sep	Bf 109E Damaged	

REVISED TOTAL: 16 destroyed, 2 and 1 shared probables, 2 damaged.

LINDSAY Vernon Mearns Lill

Additions to claim list:

1942		
7 Jun		AL173 DB-Q
13 Jun	(a)	AL134 DB-H
11 Nov		EV356 DB-A
18 Nov		EV162 DB-I

(a) MC 202 of 71ª Squadriglia, 17° Gruppo, 1° Stormo CT; Ten Sergio Morandi killed.

LINDSAY William Roy Mackintosh   Flight Lieutenant
RAF Nos. 1369510 (NCO): 116434 (Officer)

Willie Lindsay was born in Glasgow on 31 January 1921. He attended Kelvinside Academy, Glasgow High School and the Royal High School, Edinburgh. He worked for two years in a private bank and then two more in a shipping company. When war broke out he failed to be selected for aircrew at his first attempt in September 1940, but succeeded on his next try three months later. He was deferred for call-up until June 1941, when he attended 4 ITW at Paignton, followed by 3 EFTS, Watchfield, and 5 SFTS, Ternhill, qualifying as a pilot and being commissioned in April 1942. He then attended 53 OTU at Llandow until June, and was posted to 242 Squadron on 1 July. During his time with the squadron he was to fly aircraft 'N' during all his engagements. Following service in North Africa and over Sicily, his tour ended in September 1943, and he became an instructor at the Middle East Gunnery School, El Ballah, Egypt. In December he was selected to command a test flight, the Spitfire Floatplane Flight, at Fanora on the Great Bitter Lake, testing the suitability of the float-equipped Spitfire V for use in the Aegean. He returned to El Ballah in January 1944, then in April rejoined 242 Squadron, which was by then based in Corsica. After operations over France and Italy, the unit was disbanded in October 1944, when he returned to the UK, becoming a gunnery instructor at the CGS, Catfoss. He was Mentioned in Despatches. In 1945 he was posted to 57 OTU, Eshott, and in June 1945 to 12 FU, Melton Mowbray. On demobilisation, he returned briefly to the shipping business, but then commenced a career with a manufacturer of wire ropes. He rose to Technical Director before his retirement in 1984, when he founded (and at the time of writing, still operates), a consultancy in regard to these products. He still lives in Glasgow.

Additions to claim list:

1942		
2 Dec	Spitfire VB	EP545 LE-N
1943		
29 Mar	„	EP909 LE-N

LINNARD Sidney

Addition to claim list:

1941		
7 Dec —	372ª Squadriglia, 153° Gruppo Aut CT lost three MC 200 pilots killed in this engagement.	

LITTOLF Albert   RAF No. F30141

On 25 June 1940 he and two other pilots from his unit flew D 520s from Toulouse to an airfield near Southampton. On 20 July he was sent as a Wt Off from Free French HQ in London to 6 OTU, and then on 10 August to Odiham to join EC 1, which was forming. In September the pilots of this unit, with the three D 520s, which had been crated, went aboard a convoy to take part in Operation 'Menace', the proposed occupation by the Free French of Dakar. When this did not prove possible, the elements of EC 1 were put ashore in Cameroun, from where the pilots were flown in an RAF DC-2 across Africa to Ismailia during December 1940. Here they helped form Free French Flight 1 with Hurricanes. In March Littolf and other members of the unit attended 70 OTU at Nakuru for further operational training, then being attached to 33 Squadron at the end of the month, and flying to Greece. Here they made a few sorties in defence of Athens, before being evacuated back to Egypt. It was on return that they were attached to 73 Squadron at Tobruk.

Corrections and additions to claim list:

1941					
14 Mar	Ju 87	Hurricane I	V7856	Tobruk	att 73 Sqn
,,	Ju 87 Probable	,,	,,	,,	,,
22 Apr — Delete					
23 Apr	Ju 87	,,	V7228	,,	,,
,,	Bf 109E	,,	,,	,,	,,

REVISED TOTAL: 6 and 8 shared destroyed, 1 shared probable, 1 damaged.

LIVINGSTONE David Franklin
He died at Tokanui, New Zealand, on 17 May 1984.

LLEWELLYN Reginald Thomas   RAF Nos. 565271 (NCO); 47380 (Officer)
He attended 12 Group Pool, Aston Down, from 31 December 1939. After the war he commanded 208 Squadron from February-June 1946.

LOCK Eric Stanley   RAF Nos. 745051 (NCO); 81642 (Officer)
He is believed to have been born on 19 April 1919. He joined the RAFVR in February 1939.

LOFTS Keith Temple

Corrections and additions to claim list:

1940				
May —		it appears likely that his two claims in France were for aircraft damaged only.		
15 Sep			V6566	
27 Sep	1/3	Bf 110 (not individual victory)	,,	
15 Oct	1/2	Do 17 Probable (not Damaged)		
(not 16th)				

REVISED TOTAL: 3 and 4 shared destroyed, 1 and 1 shared probable, 6 and 1 shared damaged.

LOFTUS Douglas Haig

Addition to claim list:

1943		
19 Apr		344 I

LOKUCIEWSKI Witold   Squadron Leader/Pulkovnik
He was born in Novocherkask-on-Don, but was brought to Poland in 1918, his family settling in Wilno. In 1935 he entered the Cavalry Reserve Officers' School, and the following year moved to the air force academy at Deblin, receiving his commission in 1938. His first posting was to the 1 Pulk Lotniczy in Warsaw. The reports of his claims on 6 September 1939 are not confirmed by documentary evidence. He flew to Rumania on 17 September 1939 after the start of the Soviet invasion, thence travelling to France via Yugoslavia and Italy. Here he flew with a fighter section in defence of an aircraft factory at Romoratin. On 13 March 1942 he was shot down in Spitfire V BL656, RF-B. After the war he rejoined 303 Squadron at the end of November 1945, and was promoted Major on 1 January 1946.

Corrections and additions to claim list:

1939					
1 Sep	1/2	Ju 87 Probable	PZL P.11		112 Esk
1940					
10 Jun		He 111	Morane MS 406		ECD Romoratin
7 Sep				P3975 RF-U	
11 Sep				L2099 RF-O	
15 Sep				P2903 RF-Z	
1941					
20 Apr				P7546 RF-T	
18 Jun				P8333	

REVISED TOTAL: 8 destroyed, 3 and 1 shared probables.

LONGLEY Harold Watson
Born in New Plymouth on 18 October 1921, Harold Longley joined the RNZAF on 30 November 1941, embarking for the UK after initial flying training, on 22 June 1942. He attended 12 SFTS, August 1942-January 1943, and was then held at 11 PDRC until March 1943, and then at 12 (P)AFU until July. He finally attended 54 OTU, July-October 1943, then being posted to 488 Squadron as a night fighter. He remained with the unit until posted to FIU's special Tempest Flight. When this was incorporated into a reformed 501 Squadron on 8 August

1944, he went instead to 3 TEU until October, and then to 83 GSU, finally being posted to 3 Squadron for day operations on Tempests. He left the unit in July 1945 to return home, reaching New Zealand in October. He was released on 16 January 1946, but postwar joined the Territorial RNZAF, serving with 4 (Otago) Squadron. He ran a business in Nelson during the 1950s, and died on 23 December 1992. It is noted that during the closing days of the war he claimed an unidentified aircraft which is believed to have been an He 162 Volksjager jet, but dropped this claim after a dispute.

Corrections and additions to claim list:

1945				
2 May		Ar 234 or Me 262 Damaged	Tempest V	3 Sqn
3 May		Ju 52/3m	„	„
„		Do 24 on water	„	„
„		Do 24 Damaged	„	„
„		Bf 110 on ground	„	„
„	2	He 115s Damaged on water	„	„

REVISED TOTAL: 3 and 1 shared destroyed, 2 damaged, 3 destroyed on the ground or on water, 2 damaged on water.

LORD Geoffrey
He died in March 1995.

Corrections and additions to claim list:

1944			
23 Aug	½	V-1 (not individual claim)	

REVISED TOTAL: 5 and 1 shared destroyed, 1 damaged, 1 V-1 shared destroyed.

LOTT Charles George
On return from the USA, he was Grp Capt o/c 81 (Training) Group from March 1943, then Grp Capt Training at HQ, 9 Group. After his course at Manby in the early 1950s, he was o/c Caledonian Sector, based at Turnhouse, Edinburgh, from May 1952.

Correction to claim list:

1940	
7 Jun	P3386 (not N3386)

LOUD William Walter John   RAF Nos. 1178867 (NCO); 136179 (Officer)
It appears that he enlisted in September-October 1940. He was commissioned on 30 October 1942. In December 1943 he was posted from HQ, 9 Group, to 53 OTU as a Flt Lt instructor.

LOVELL Anthony Desmond Joseph
He was known as 'Lulu' whilst in 41 Squadron.

Additions to claim list:

1942	
26 Oct	EN980 V-W
1944	
3 and 15 May	ADL
15 Jun	MH667

LOVETT Reginald Eric
He was born in Hendon, North London, in 1913, attending Christ's College, Finchley, for his education. On 10 May 1940 he attacked Do 17s of 4/KG 2, but was hit by return fire and crash-landed near Conflans with burns to his face and a cut over his left eye. He was pulled out of P2804 'E' just before it blew up.

Additions to claim list:

1940
10 May —   the shared damaged claim for an He 111 in fact related to a Do 17; he was flying P2804 E.

LOWE Ivan Laurence Firth
He was commissioned Acting Sub Lt (A) on 21 November 1938 in the Royal Navy, beginning flying training at 20 E & RFTS, Gravesend, on 6 March 1939.

LUCAS Percy Belgrave   RAF Nos. 911532 (NCO); 100626 (Officer)
'Laddie' Lucas was created a CBE. He died on 20 March 1998 after a long illness.

Correction to claim list:

1942	
6 Jun	BR109 C-30 (not GR109)

LUMA James Forest   1st Lieutenant   USAAF No. O-885995

Additions to claim list:
1944
21/22 Jan	TH-D
13 Feb	TH-X
6 Mar	TH-Y
21 Mar	TH-U

LUNDSTEN Leif   RAF No. N1072
He was awarded a DFC in August 1943, but was reported missing from a beachhead patrol over Normandy on 9 June 1944 in Spitfire IX MK966.

LYALL Archibald   RAF Nos. 740218 (NCO); 81047 (Officer)
He enlisted in the RAFVR in early 1937.

LYNCH John Joseph
John Lynch was born on 3 February 1918. He saw service with the USAAC before joining the RAF.

Additions to claim list:
1942
11 Dec	EP835
14 Dec	EP140
17 Dec	EP343
1943	
7 Feb	BR373
7 Apr	EP829
10 May	JK465

MacDONALD-HALL Robert

Correction to claim list:
TOTAL: 1 and 6 shared destroyed (not 1 and 5 shared).

MacDONNELL Aeneas Ranald Donald
Before joining 64 Squadron in July 1940, he underwent brief operational training at 5 OTU from 30 June.

MacFADYEN Donald Aikins
Since publication of *Aces High*, Don MacFadyen is reported to have died.

MACIEJOWSKI Michal Miroslaw
He entered the Air Force Reserve Cadet Officers' School, graduating in January 1936. As a reserve pilot he flew with the 3 Pulk Lotniczy at Poznan, being mobilised in August 1939. He escaped to France via Rumania. On 22 February 1941 he transferred to 317 Squadron which was forming at Acklington. On 9 August 1943, during a sortie over France, he collided with the aircraft flown by Ppor Kondracki (he was not shot down), baling out of Spitfire IX BS302 to become a POW. He joined 309 Squadron in November 1949, remaining with the unit until its disbandment.

Corrections and additions to claim list:
1940
29 Oct —	this was Bf 109E-4 WNr 5593 3X-N of 4/LG 2 which crashed at Langenhoe Wick; Ofw Josef Harmeling became a POW. Maciejowski was flying P3463 GN-L.	
7 Nov —	this was Bf 109E-4 WNr 677 'Yellow 1' of 3/JG 26; Ofw Wilhelm Müller was reported missing; this aircraft was shared with several other pilots. Maciejowski was flying V6534.	
„ —	delete 2 Bf 109E Probables	
28 Nov —	apparently not credited	V6855
5 Dec		V6614
1941		
10 Jan —	this aircraft was erroneously recorded by the Polish Air Force as being destroyed on the ground. It may have been Bf 109E-7 WNr 1964; Maciejowski flew V6615 GN-B	
10 Feb		V6614
6 Dec —	apparently not credited	
30 Dec		AA762 JH-W
1942		
19 Aug —	first two claims	AD295 JH-C
„ —	shared Do 217	BL927 JH-L

1943
4 May   BS463 SZ-G
11 Jun   BS403 SZ-K
REVISED TOTAL: 10 and 1 shared destroyed, 1 probable, 1 damaged.

MacKAY John
He was born John MacKay Mahachak.

MACKENZIE John Noble

Additions to claim list:

Date		Claim		Location	Sqn
9 Sep		Bf 109E	Spitfire I		41 Sqn
15 Sep	1/3	Do 17 (a)	„		„
23 Sep		Bf 109E (not Probable) (b)			
7 Oct	1/3	Do 17	„	SE Maidstone	„

NB His DFC citation on 2 November 1940 recorded that he had claimed seven aircraft destroyed, which appears to confirm the additions to the claim list, which have been extracted from his logbook.
REVISED TOTAL: 8 and 2 shared destroyed, 2 probables, 2 damaged.
(a) Shared with two others and confirmed by 'A' Flight; (b) claimed as a probable but confirmed destroyed by AA Command.

MACKENZIE Russell Merriman   RAF No. 40245; RNZAF No. 2366
Educated at Christchurch High School, he travelled to the UK to join the RAF in August 1937, being commissioned on 23 August of that year. He served with 108 (Bomber) Squadron in September 1938, but in October was sent to CFS, Upavon, on an instructors' course, then instructing at 8 FTS in Scotland from December 1938-April 1941. He was sent to 56 OTU before joining 141 Squadron in June 1941 to become a night fighter. In September he moved to 409 Squadron, RCAF, as a flight commander, but in March 1942 was posted to North Africa, where he joined 89 Squadron. In May he moved to 46 Squadron, but in February 1943 he was given command of 227 Squadron on day operations. In October 1943 he completed his tour and joined 201 Group, where he received his DSO on 12 November 1943. In January 1944 he moved to RAF HQ, Levant, and then in May to HQ, RAF Middle East. He attended the Staff College at Haifa during the year, then becoming involved in training again, as Chief Instructor at 79 OTU in Cyprus during 1945. In May 1945 he returned to the UK, from where he was sent home to New Zealand in April 1946. As recorded in *Aces High*, he had transferred to the RNZAF in January 1944, but he was now demobilised. He rejoined the RAF in June 1947, and in the 1950-53 period was o/c Flying as a Wg Cdr at Leuchars, Scotland, flying Meteors. He served with HQ, Fighter Command, 1954-57, and then HQ, FEAF, 1957-58. He then retired as a Wg Cdr and returned home to settle in Christchurch, New Zealand.

Corrections and additions to claim list:
1942

Date		Claim		Serial	Location	Sqn
28 Apr		He 111 (not Probable) (a)				
8 Jul				X7638		
31 Jul/1 Aug		Z1007 (not He 111)		X7837		
7 Sep				X8137		
1942						
27 May		Ju 88 (not shared) (b)		EL467 B		
23 Jul	1/2	Arado Damaged	Beaufighter VIC	Y	Crete	227 Sqn

REVISED TOTAL: 5 destroyed, 2 shared damaged.
(a) This was originally claimed as damaged, but was upgraded to destroyed; (b) There is no mention in the squadron records that this claim was shared.

MACKIE Evan Dall
He was born in Waihi, not Otorohanga. He died on 28 April 1986. His biography, *Spitfire Leader*, was published by Grub Street in 1997, written by Max Avery with Christopher Shores.

Corrections and additions to claim list:
1943

Date	Serial
7 Apr	JK189 SN-L
9 Apr	ER564 HD
10 Apr	JK189 SN-L
13, 16 and 18 Apr	ES347 SN-A
27 and 28 Apr, 8 May and 5 Jul	JK715 SN-A
11 Jul	JK666 SN-V
12 and 13 Jul, 11 Sep, 15 Oct	JK715 SN-A
3, 5 and 16 Dec	JF570
1944	
27 Jan, 2 Feb	JF709
1945	

4 May — only one shared Fi 156 on the ground.
REVISED TOTAL: 20 and 3 shared destroyed, 2 probables, 10 and 1 shared damaged, 3 and 1 shared destroyed on the ground.

MACLACHLAN James Archibald Findlay

He lived in East Grinstead, Surrey, before the war. In October 1941 he was attached briefly to 3 Squadron to gain some experience of night intruder operations, before taking command of 1 Squadron. He was 24 when killed, and was buried ten miles north of Lisieux, France.

Addition to claim list:
1941
9 Jan — during this engagement two MC 200 pilots of 6° Gruppo, 1° Stormo CT were shot down; Mllo Ettore Zanandrea was killed and Cap Luigi Armanino baled out.

MACLENNAN Ian Roy

Correction to claim list:
1942
14 Nov   V-V (not V-U)

MACQUEEN Norman Carter   RAF Nos. 968025 (NCO); 86689 (Officer)

He was born in Walsall, Staffordshire, in 1920, subsequently living in Rhyl, Flintshire. He joined the RAFVR in September 1939 and was commissioned in 1940. The award of a DFC was gazetted on 1 May 1942. He is buried in the Capuccini Naval Cemetery, Malta.

MAGUIRE William Hudson   RAF Nos. 740249 (NCO); 62249 (Officer)

He enlisted in the RAFVR in early 1937. On 17 February 1945 the aircraft suffered engine problems on take-off from Ford, and crashed at Rustington, near Littlehampton. Maguire, Flg Off D.Lake, DFM, who was with him, and three civilians were all killed.

Corrections and additions to claim list:
1943
15/16 Oct — the Ju 188E-1 was 3E+FL (not BL)
8/9 Nov — this was WNr 10244 of KG 2; Major Wilhelm Schmitter, holder of the Knights' Cross with Oak Leaves, and his navigator, Uffz Felix Hainzinger, were both killed when the aircraft crashed into Shinewater Marsh, Eastbourne.

MAGUIRE William Ivan Hartley   RAF Nos. 778508 (NCO); 80455 (Officer)

Born in 1921 in Bulawayo, he lived in Salisbury, Southern Rhodesia, attending Park Town Public School and Prince Edward Senior School. He joined the RAFVR in 1940, remustering as a pilot the following year. He was commissioned on 25 October 1942, and became a Flt Lt on 25 January 1945.

Corrections and additions to claim list:
1943
23 Jun   EN528
16 Jul   EN492 (not EN496)
5, 9 and 10 Sep   LZ893
10 Sep — should read Bf 109Gs (not BF 109Gs)
11 Nov   MA580

MAHON Jackson Barrett

He was born on 5 February 1921. He obtained his RAF 'wings' in September 1941, before leaving for the UK.

MAILEY Walter Henry Arthur

He enlisted on 19 August 1940 (not 1941), commencing training at 2 ITS. In October he was despatched to Southern Rhodesia, arriving in December. Here he attended 25 EFTS and 20 SFTS, then being sent to the Middle East, where he arrived at the Reserve Pool in May 1941. He attended 71 OTU in June and joined 3 RAAF Squadron the following month. On completion of his tour he returned to Southern Rhodesia in April 1942, being posted initially to 25 EFTS as an instructor. In June he attended 33 Flying Instructors' School, in July going to 20 SFTS, where he remained until late January 1943. He then moved to 21 SFTS for a short period, returning to 20 SFTS during February. He was sent home to Australia in April, 1943, arriving in May and becoming an instructor at 2 OTU in June. Three months later he was posted to 2 Fighter Sector HQ. In November he moved to 113 Fighter Sector HQ, and then in March 1944 to 55 Op Base Unit. In July he joined 105 Fighter Control Unit, where he remained for the next 12 months. Finally, in July 1945 he returned to 2 OTU. He was released on 17 October 1945.

MALAN Adolph Gysbert

He joined 58 OTU on 9 August 1941 as o/c Flying Training.

Addition to claim list:
1940

24 Jul	¼	Do 215 Probable	Spitfire I	off Dover	74 Sqn

REVISED TOTAL: 27 and 7 shared destroyed, 2 and 1 shared unconfirmed destroyed, 3 and 1 shared probables, 16 damaged.

MALFROY Camille Enright

Before the war he represented New Zealand in the Davis Cup. His service number suggests that he became an Auxillary Air Force or Special Reserve pilot; he appears to have seen some service with 501 Squadron in May 1935. He was mobilized in August 1939, and was posted to the 11 Group Pool on 13 September. From there he returned to 501 Squadron, where he was promoted Flt Lt on 12 March 1940. On 12 May his Hurricane, L1914, was hit by fire from a Bf 110 of I/ZG 2, and he was obliged to force-land at Mourmelon. On return to the UK from France he was posted to 5 OTU as an instructor on 18 June, moving to 7 OTU on 27th. He became a flight commander in this unit, which became 57 OTU, returning to 501 Squadron in February 1941. In August 1942 he was posted to the Air Ministry from 61 OTU. He was listed in New Zealand newspapers as having claimed four victories.

Additions to claim list:
1940

8 Jun		Bf 109E	Hurricane I		501 Sqn
„	2	Bf 109Es unconfirmed	„		„

REVISED TOTAL: 2 destroyed, 2 unconfirmed destroyed.

MALLINSON James Robin

Born in 1920 in Norwood, South London, he lived at Halstead, near Sevenoaks, Kent, becoming a student physical training instructor before enlisting in July 1940. He was aged 22 when killed, and is commemorated on the Malta Memorial.

Additions to claim list:
1940

9 Nov			Spitfire VB	ER536
28 Nov				ER601
1 Dec	½	'Ba 88'		ER176
„		other claims on this date		EP545

MANGER Kenneth

Kenneth Manger was born on 25 February 1917. He worked in various jobs before joining the RAFO. After attending 5 E & RFTS during the opening months of 1938, he was commissioned on 26 March, beginning full training at 3 FTS on 9 April. Graduating as a pilot, he was posted to 17 Squadron at the end of October. He then transferred to the regular RAF on a Short Service Commission on 17 January 1939.

Corrections and additions to claim list:
1940

17 May —		these were aircraft of IV(St)/LG 1
18 May	¼	Bf 110 unconfirmed (rather than ⅓ Damaged); this was an aircraft of 5/ZG 26
29 May —		it is possible that the second Do 17 claimed on this day, was classified as Damaged, rather than destroyed.
31 May —		the second Bf 109E was credited as unconfirmed destroyed, not Damaged.

REVISED TOTAL: 4 and 3 shared destroyed, 1 and 1 shared unconfirmed destroyed, 2 and 1 shared damaged.

MANN Jack

Jackie Mann had not died as reported when *Aces High* was published in 1994. He did however, die on 12 November 1995.

MANSFELD Miroslav Jon   RAF Nos. 787518 (NCO); 69453 (Officer)

In June 1952 he served as adjutant of 651 Squadron as a Flt Lt, at Ismailia, Egypt.

Additions to claim list:
1940

13 Nov	V7361	
1941		
27 Jan	V6696	S Montrose
12/13 Oct	R2248 WM-S	
1942		
30 Apr/1 May	V8246 WM-H	off Happisburg
10/11 Dec	V8253 WM-W	
1943		
15/16 Mar	V8562	
1944		
14/15 May	ND211 WM-K	

27 Jul			Mosquito XIX	MM683 WM-C		
24 Oct			,,	,,		

MARIDOR Jean-Marie   RAF No. F30114

He was born on 24 November 1921. Contrary to reports, it appears that he was not awarded a Bar to his DFC.

Additions to claim list:
1944

18 Jun		V-1	Spitfire XIV	RB161	5m N West Malling	91 Sqn
22 Jun	½	V-1	,,	RB180	E Bexhill	,,
,,	½	V-1	,,	,,	Tonbridge	,,
30 Jun		V-1	,,	RB188	Biddenden	,,
5 Jul		V-1	,,	NH698	4m S Cranbrook	,,
,,		V-1	,,	NH654	5m SW Canterbury	,,
3 Aug		V-1 (a)	,,	RM656	Benenden	,,

REVISED TOTAL: 3 and 1 shared destroyed, 2 probables, 3 damaged, 5 and 2 shared V-1s destroyed.
(a) His aircraft was damaged by the explosion of this V-1 and crashed; he was killed.

MARLAND Rainford Gent   RAF Nos. 745750 (NCO); 62657 (Officer)

He enlisted in the RAFVR in April 1939. Posted to the Middle East in November 1941, he was killed the following month whilst attempting to force-land.

MARPLES Roy

He was born in 1920 in Muswell Hill, North London, but lived at Bramhall, Cheshire, attending Stockport Grammar School and Manchester University. He attended E & RFTS in early 1938, being commissioned in the RAFO on 26 March. He then trained at 8 FTS, joining 19 Squadron on 29 October 1938. He transferred to the regular RAF on 8 May 1939 on a Short Service Commission. He was killed in MK373, crashing at Lower Chancton Farm, near Washington, Sussex, after colliding with MK346 of 329 Squadron.

Corrections and additions to claim list:
1942

8 Jul —	the shared victory was a Bf 109F		Z5235

1943

12 Jan		Spitfire VB	ER166

MARRS Eric Simcox

Educated at Dauntsey's School, West Lavington.

MARSHALL Alfred Ernest   RAF Nos. 565286 (NCO); 47124 (Officer)

Born in Portsmouth in 1915, he enlisted as an Aircraft Apprentice in January 1931. He was posted direct to 73 Squadron in France from 6 OTU on 13 May 1940. He joined 71 OTU as an instructor in November 1941 and was commissioned at the end of December that year. In January 1942 he was posted to 73 OTU, but returned to 71 the following month, before being posted to 250 Squadron. He is buried in Hitchin Cemetery, Hertfordshire.

Additions to claim list:
1941

3 Jan				TP-D		
5 Jan				TP-A		
7 Apr	sh 3	Ju 52/3ms on ground (d)	Hurricane I	Z7560 TP-F	Mechili airfield	73 Sqn
9 Apr am	½	G 50 Probable	,,	V7562 TP-A		,,
,, pm		Ju 52/3m (e)	,,	,,	nr Derna	,,
,,	sh 6	Bf 110s on ground (f)	,,	,,	Derna	,,
11 Apr				V7560 TP-F	W Tobruk	,,
22 Apr				V7353 TP-M	over Tobruk	,,
23 Apr		(g)		,,	15m W Tobruk	,,

REVISED TOTAL: 16 and 2 shared destroyed, 2 probables, 1 damaged, 1 V-1 destroyed, 17 shared destroyed on the ground.
(d) Ju 52/3ms of III/KGzbV 1; (e) Ju 52/3m of III/KGzbV 1; (f) Bf 110s of III/ZG 26; (g) on landing after claiming the Ju 87, he was strafed by Bf 109s and wounded in the head and shoulder.

MARTIN Richard Frewen

He joined 6 OTU as an instructor on 14 June 1940. On recovery from his wound in 1941, he was posted to 71 OTU, moving at the end of the year to 73 OTU. In April 1942 he was posted to HQ, 206 Group, and from there to 250 Squadron.

Additions to claim list:
1940

13 May	¼	Do 17 (c)	Hurricane I		nr Reims	73 Sqn
14 May		(d)				

REVISED TOTAL: 5 and 3 shared destroyed, 2 unconfirmed destroyed, 1 damaged.
(c) Do 17P 4N+FH of 1(F)/22, flown by Oblt Rudolf Sauer; (d) I/StG 76 lost two Ju 87s and two damaged against claims for four and one unconfirmed destroyed.

MASON Ernest Mitchelson

An 'Imshi' Mason Memorial Trophy was put up by his mother in 1949, to be competed for annually by squadrons of MEAF Command for efficiency in weapons training.

Additions to claim list:
1940-41
All claims with 274 Squadron, 9 December 1940-26 January 1941, made in P3722
1941

30 Jan		P3723
13 Apr	Hurricane II	Z2838
26 Aug	Hurricane I	Z4561

MASON Frank   RAF Nos. 748162 (NCO); 115320 (Officer)

Born in Barrow-in-Furness, Cumberland, in 1912, Frank Mason attended Blackpool High School, and then lived in Luton, Bedfordshire. He enlisted as an Aircraft Apprentice in 1928, but left the service in 1934. He re-enlisted for pilot training in the RAFVR in May 1939. He was promoted Flt Lt on 14 July 1943, serving in 53 OTU as an instructor. He was released from the service in January 1946.

Additions to claim list:

1941	
8 Dec	Z4786
1942	
26 Mar	BE556
21 Jul	BN126

MATHEWS John Owen   RAF Nos. 1378335 (NCO); 67630 (Officer)

'Jimmy' Mathews was born in Muswell Hill, North London, working before the war for Prudential Assurance (not Insurance). He returned to 51 OTU as an instructor for a second time in July 1943, being promoted Flt Lt the following month. While he received a DSO, Sqn Ldr Penrose did not, although recommended for one. Mathews' award was dated 26 October 1945.

Addition to claim list:

1944						
6/7 Jul		V-1	Mosquito XIX	TA392	RS-K	157 Sqn
24/25 Jul	2	V-1s	„	MM671	RS-C	„
7/8 Aug	2	V-1s	„	TA401	RS-D (a)	„

24/25 Dec — the Ju 88G shot down on this date was an aircraft of 5/NJG 2; the crew baled out.
(a) Own aircraft damaged when the second of these bombs blew up.

MATTHEWS Gerald Peter Hugh

He received a Queen's Commendation for Valuable Services in the Air in January 1956.

Corrections and additions to claim list:

1940		
17 Jun (not 18th) sh He 111 (not ½ Ju 88)		
1942		
3 Jul		BP177
1 Sep		BR235
3 Sep (not 2nd)		„
11 Sep		AR287
29 Sep		978
21 Oct	Spitfire VB	618
23 and 27 Oct		BR477
1943		
2 Dec	Spitfire VC	

MAYERS Howard Clive

He was commissioned directly into the RAFVR as a Plt Off on 11 March 1940; he may have been a member of the RAFO in the 1930s, leaving in mid decade. His Spitfire was shot down by Bf 109Fs of III/JG 53. It is possible that he was lost in a Ju 52/3m over the Mediterranean, rather than on a ship.

MAYNE Ernest   RAF Nos. 82478 (NCO); 46329 (Officer)

His NCO number was an original RFC issue, granted between April-October 1917, which he retained on formation of the RAF. He was an instructor at 56 OTU in 1941.

Correction to claim list:
1940
26 and 27 May — R9871 and P9871 are both believed in fact to relate to K9871, flown on both occasions.

McBURNIE Donald Hindle
He died in early 1995.

Correction to claim list:
1942

1 Jul	AK634 (not AL634)

McCOLPIN Carroll Warren   USAAF Nos. O-32591; 3514A
He learned to fly in 1928, later graduating from Golden Gate University. He joined the RAF in November 1940, being granted his 'wings' on 6 February 1941. He attended 56 OTU in April 1941 before joining 607 Squadron. He commanded the 407th Fighter Group from 9 September 1943-18 June 1944, and then the 404th Fighter Group from 27 June-25 November 1944. He was promoted Lt Col on 10 January 1944 and full Colonel the following 25 May. On leaving the 404th, he was Director of Combat Operations with 29th TAC. After the war he commanded the 335th Fighter Group from March 1946. He was promoted Brigadier General on 23 April 1960, and Major General only ten weeks later. He retired from the USAF in April 1968.

Corrections to claim list:
1944

27 Aug	Y8-A (not YB-A)

McDOWALL (not McDOWELL) Andrew   RAF Nos. 802602 (NCO);89299 (Officer)
His number indicates that he enlisted in the Auxillary Air Force pre war, rather than in the RAFVR. He was Mentioned in Despatches on 14 January 1944. In May 1945 he became a test pilot with Rolls-Royce, testing that company's engines in Meteors and other jets. In December 1944 two Lockheed YP-80s had been sent to the UK for tests, the second going to Rolls-Royce as a Nene engine testbed. This aircraft, 44-83027, was written off in a forced landing at Syerston by McDowall due to a fractured engine fuel pipe on 14 November 1945. He died in Derby, Rolls-Royce's home town.

McELROY John Frederick
On return from Malta he served with 57 OTU until 5 December 1942, when he was posted to 276 Air-Sea Rescue Squadron. In July 1943 he moved to 56 OTU. He died in Victoria, British Columbia, on 24 October 1994.

Corrections to claim list:
1942

7 Jul	UF-S (not VF-S)
16 Oct	EP132 was J (not F)
22 and 27 Oct	EP708 (not EP201) U

McGREGOR Gordon Roy
Mentioned in Despatches, 1 January 1945.

McGREGOR Hector Douglas
He attended 5 OTU for a refresher course before joining 213 Squadron on 28 May 1940. He was Mentioned in Despatches on 14 January 1944 and 1 January 1945, and was created a CBE on 14 June 1945.

McINTOSH Lawrence

Corrections and additions to claim list:
1943

13 Jul	Spitfire VC
13 Sep onwards	Spitfire IX

McKAY Donald Alistair Steward   RAF Nos. 740115 (NCO); 113322 (Officer)
In 1943 he served at Aboukir MU, Egypt, as a test pilot.

Corrections and additions to claim list:
1940

12 May	(a)			
29 Jul —	the claim for a Ju 87 was apparently confirmed, according to Fighter Command Combats & Casualties.			
15 and 27 Nov, 17 Dec	Spitfire IIA			
1942				
12 Feb		BL241 AZ-E		
3 Nov	Bf 109 Damaged	Hurricane IIC		274 Sqn

REVISED TOTAL: 15 (plus 1 and 1 shared, details not available) destroyed, 3 unconfirmed destroyed (details not available), 5 damaged.
(a) 3 claims made against He 111s of II/KG 55; one lost and one damaged.

McLEOD Henry Wallace
From 1928-1934 he served with the 5th Saskatchewan Regiment, and then with the Regina Rifle Regiment until 1939.

Additions to claim list:
1942

26 Sep		BR236
11 Oct —	2 damaged claims	,,
,, —	2 confirmed claims	BS161
12 Oct		AR420
13 and 14 Oct		BR236
16 Oct		EP541
22 Oct		BS161

McMULLEN Desmond Anthony Peter
In November 1941 he joined 55 OTU as a Flt Lt from 257 Squadron, where he had briefly served. On 5 December he moved to 57 OTU, while on 16 May 1942 he was posted to 124 Squadron. He did not become a Wing Leader in North Africa due to illness caused by operational exhaustion. On 8 August 1943 he joined 53 OTU as a Sqn Ldr, but in September 1943 was posted to HQ, 93 Group, for fighter liaison duties, reverting to Flt Lt rank. On 23 June 1944 he broke his leg playing rugby at 53 OTU.

McNAIR Robert Wendell
Corrections and additions to claim list:
1942

22 Apr	BP968 N
22 May	BR176 C-25
25 May	BR109 C-30
10 Jun	BR107 C-22
1943	
20 Jun	EN398

McPHARLIN Michael George Hurschell
RCAF No. C1530; USAAF Nos. O-885107; 89764
Born on 13 June 1913 in Blue Island, Illinois, he joined the RCAF on 2 June 1940, but was discharged on 17 July and transferred to the RAF. After training he was posted from 56 OTU to 71 Squadron initially, but then moved to 403 Squadron, RCAF, for about six months. He then returned to 71 Squadron.

Restatement of 1944 claims:
1944

19 May	1/2	Bf 109	P-51B	6N-Z	Lubeck-Schwerin	334th FS
,,		Bf 109 Damaged	,,	,,	,,	,,
28 May		Bf 109 Damaged	,,	,,	Magdeburg area	,,
,,		Bf 109	,,	,,	,,	,,
29 May		Do 18 on water	,,	,,	Direnau	,,
6 Jun		FW 190 Damaged	,,	,,	Evreux	,,

REVISED TOTAL: 1 and 4 shared destroyed, 1 shared probable, 3 damaged, 1 destroyed on the water.

MEAGHER Patrick Edward
Born in 1910 in Haulbowline, County Cork, Ireland, he lived in Neston, Cheshire. In 1931 he joined the Territorial Army as a 2nd Lieutenant in the 67th (7th London) Field Brigade RA (TA). He resigned his commission on 29 April 1933 on receiving a six year Short Service Commission in the RAF. In February 1940, by then a Flt Lt, he ferried one of 12 Blenheim IVs to Finland, delivering the aircraft to Jukajarvi airfield. It is believed that he then served with a Special Duties Flight at Christchurch, Sussex, during summer 1940, claiming one victory whilst with this unit. He was promoted Wg Cdr on 1 September 1941, and his DSO was gazetted on 6 October 1944. Doubt remains over his postwar career; an ex-member of 211 Squadron reports that he became Manager of Cardiff Airport during the late 1940s, and was present at a reunion in 1947. Other sources indicate that he might have been drowned in a swimming accident in the Far East in late 1945.

Addition to claim list:
1940

2 Sep	'Do 215'	Spec Duties Flt

REVISED TOTAL: 10 destroyed, 2 probables, 1 damaged, 2 destroyed on the ground, 1 probably destroyed on the ground, 2 damaged on the ground.

MEAKER James Reginald Bryan

Bryan Meaker, as he was known, did not go to Norway in 1940 as reported in *Aces High*. He was posted to 263 Squadron from 46 Squadron on 18 May 1940, he and 'Bobbie' Oxspring being held as stand-by pilots. He was not required however, and was posted to 249 Squadron almost at once.

Corrections and additions to claim list:
1940

15 Aug			P3123	
24 Aug —	delete ; this was not a victory; he witnessed Flt Lt Barton's success.			
2 Sep			P5206	
5 Sep	Do 17 Damaged	Hurricane I	„	249 Sqn
6 Sep			„	
15 Sep			V6566	
27 Sep			V6635	

REVISED TOTAL: 6 and 2 shared destroyed, 1 shared probable, 3 damaged.

MEHRE Helge Olrik

In the photograph of this pilot in *Aces High*, he is described as leader of 132 (Norwegian) Wing in June 1944. He was not in fact Wing Leader at this time, but commanding officer of the Wing.

MELLERSH Francis Richard Lee   RAF Nos. 1382170 (NCO); 105145 (Officer)

35 of his claims against V-1s were made with 130790 Flt Lt Michael John Stanley, DFC, as his radar operator, who also took part in the shooting down of three aircraft. Mellersh died of cancer in December 1996.

Corrections and additions to claim list:
1944

20 Jun		MM577
24 Jun		HK572
28 Jun		HK372
2, 5 and 6 Jul		MM577
18 Jul		MM377
22, 25, 26, 27 and 30 Jul, and 3 Aug		MM577
7/8 Aug	Spitfire IX	473
11, 15,24 and 27 Aug, and 23 Sep	Mosquito XIII	MM577

METELERKAMP Peter Carel Rex

Correction to claim list:
1942

23 Jul	Z5348 (not ZS348)

MILLER Reginald Arthur   RAF Nos. 928613 (NCO); 123201 (Officer)

MILLER Wilfred Handel   RAF Nos. 1526934 (NCO); 169022 (Officer)

He was commissioned on 27 October 1943.

MILLINGTON William Henry

He joined 79 Squadron on 14 June 1940 from 6 OTU.

Additions to claim list:
1940

27 Sep	V6614
7 Oct	V6692
25 Oct	P3463
28 and 29 Oct	V7677

MITCHELL Richard Angelo   RAF Nos. 742943 (NCO); 62259 (Officer)

Born in Croydon in 1910, he lived in Putney and Hove before the war. He enlisted in the RAFVR in February 1939, having attended 5 E & RFTS, Hanworth, since December 1938. In October 1939, having been mobilized, he completed his training at 12 EFTS, Prestwick, then going to 3 EFTS, Hamble, and then Watchfield, where he served from December 1939 to September 1941. During this period he was commissioned in March 1941. It appears, since he had already obtained his private pilot's licence in 1935, that he was retained at these units as an instructor in elementary flying. On 22 September 1941 he was posted to 5 SFTS, Ternhill, until October, and then to 57 OTU, Hawarden, prior to joining 64 Squadron in December 1941. He was posted briefly to 277 Air-Sea Rescue Squadron during March, then joining the Merchant Ship Fighter Unit at Abbotsinch. After one month however, he was posted to Malta aboard USS *Wasp*, flying off on 9 May and joining 603 Squadron on the island. On return to the UK in September 1942 he joined the Air Staff at Air Ministry, where he remained until

August 1943. A brief posting to HQ, Fighter Command, was followed by two weeks at AFDU, Wittering, in September, and then a course at 1530 BAT Flight. At the end of September he attended No 7 Course at 60 OTU, High Ercall, including a spell at the OTU's Chedworth Gunnery Flight. On 27 November he was posted to 605 Squadron. In April 1944 he returned to 60 OTU as an instructor until 20 September, when he returned to the squadron. He was lost in Mosquito VI UP-B with 151901 Flt Lt Stanley Harry Hatsell, DFC. He is buried in the Hanover War Cemetery.

Corrections and additions to claim list:
1942
10 Jul   (a)
23 and 28 Jul — claims with 249 Squadron (not 603 Squadron)
1944

15 Mar			UP-B	
5 Apr	3	u/i e/a on ground		Metzon
„	3	u/i e/a Damaged on ground		„
11 Oct			UP-B	Zagreb

REVISED TOTAL: 5 and 3 shared destroyed, 3 probables, 9 damaged, 6 destroyed on the ground, 4 damaged on the ground.
(a) The MC 202 was an aircraft of 352ª Squadrilgia, 20° Gruppo, 51° Stormo CT; Sottoten Dante Dose was killed.

MODERA John Raymond Stewart   Flight Lieutenant
RAF Nos, 791162 (NCO); 118474 (Officer)

From Nairobi, Kenya, he enlisted in late 1940 to train as a pilot in Southern Rhodesia. He was commissioned in January 1942, and promoted Flt Lt on 2 December 1943. During the combat in which he was engaged on 15 December 1942, a second Ju 52/3m was claimed shot down by his navigator/gunner, Plt Off Hodges, operating a Vickers 'K' gun from the upper fuselage 'blister'.

Additions to claim list:
1942

8 Dec		Beaufighter VIC	
15 Dec	Ju 52/3m (d)		W
1943			
4 Jan	Ju 88 Damaged	„	227 Sqn
27 and 29 May		EL460 U	

REVISED TOTAL: 3 and 3 shared destroyed, 2 probables, 2 and 1 shared damaged.
(d) Second Ju 52/3m destroyed on this date (as well as the one Probable and one Damaged already listed in *Aces High*); this claim made by the navigator/gunner.

MONTET Pierre   RAF No. F30984

MONTGOMERIE Leighton John

Born on 13 May 1922 at New Plymouth, New Zealand, he worked on his father's farm at Sentry Hill, Taranaki, until 3 October 1939, when he applied to join the RNZAF. He undertook initial training at ITW, Levin, from April 1941, and then at 2 EFTS, New Plymouth. In September he was shipped to Canada, where he completed his flying training at 6 SFTS, Dunville, Ontario, obtaining his 'wings'. In February 1942 he was posted to the UK, going to 17 (P)AFU at Watton, Norfolk, to fly Masters for a few weeks until he attended 57 OTU, Hawarden, in late April. At the end of June 1942 he joined 485 Squadron, but on 22 October was flown to Gibraltar in a Liberator to join 81 Squadron, undertaking 189 sorties with the unit over Tunisia and Sicily. On 1 September 1943 he was posted to 73 OTU, Abu Sueir, as an instructor until 18 March 1944, when he joined 92 Squadron in Italy. He was Mentioned in Despatches and awarded a DFC on 3 July 1944. He crashed at Rosignano, and died at 0300 hours on 27 August. Initially he was buried in the US Military Cemetery at Follonica, but he was later reinterred to the Florence British Empire Cemetery.

Corrections and additions to claim list:
1943

7 Aug	Spitfire VC (not Mark IX)	
1944		
13 May		JF493
15 May		JF493 (not JF443)

MOORE Leslie Albert   RCAF Nos. R122957 (NCO); J17857 (Officer)

He lived in Plainfield, New Jersey, USA, before the war. He was killed whilst strafing a train, when his aircraft was hit by debris from this and crashed 15 miles south east of Munster. He is buried in the Reichswald Forest War Cemetery.

MORE James Winter Carmichael

He died at the age of 34, aboard the SS *Rakuyo Maru*. He is commemorated on the Singapore RAF Memorial.

Corrections and additions to claim list:
1940

10 May —	the He 111 he claimed was an aircraft of 3(F)/121, flown by Oblt Kaspar Scheurich, which crashed in the Metz-Thionville area.			
11 May	$^1/_2$ Do 17 Damaged(a) Hurricane I	P2813 H (a)		73 Sqn
15 May —	the $^1/_2$ He 111 he claimed near Grandpré, south east of Vouziertes, was A1+LK of 2/KG 53, flown by Oblt Walter Klaue.			

(a) This aircraft was a Do 17Z of II/KG 76; his Hurricane was hit by return fire and was written off on return to base, due to the damage suffered.

MORFILL Percy Frederick   RAF Nos. 564749 (NCO); 47655 (Officer)

MORGAN John Milne

He was born in London, and commenced training as a pilot at the Blackburn Flying School at Brough, East Yorkshire, in 1935. He was commissioned in the RAFO in July 1937, obtaining a Short Service Commission in the RAF the following year, after which he completed his training at the Ternhill FTS. He then went to a Fighter Pilot Pool from which he was despatched on various short supernumary postings in 10 Group, before attending 52 OTU, Aston Down. He served briefly with 56 Squadron before joining 609 Squadron in 1941 as a Flt Lt. He was transferred from this unit to 92 Squadron for service in the Middle East. He did not serve in 238 Squadron as indicated in *Aces High*. After completion of his tour with this unit, he joined the staff of 219 (F) Group at Alexandria, and was involved in the ill-fated Dodecanese operations during 1943, managing to escape from the island of Kos when the Germans re-invaded, making his way back to Egypt via Turkey. After his return from POW camp at the end of the war, he served at Air Ministry and MREU, BAOR, gathering information on missing aircrew. He then attended the School of Land Air Warfare at Old Sarum and undertook liaison with Southern Command of the Army in Salisbury. After commanding 208 Squadron, he served as Air Attache in Paris, following which he undertook a staff appointment with 11 Group and Northern Sector of Fighter Command. A posting to 2nd TAF in Holland followed, and he then became Air Attache in Lima, Peru, covering Chile, Bolivia, Colombia and Panama, until 1962. On leaving the RAF he joined the Foreign and Commonwealth Office as a Queen's Messenger,later becoming temporary airfield manager at Compton Abbas in Dorset, where he reestablished the airfield's Flying Club in 1976. At the time of writing he had been living for some years in retirement in Dorset, chiefly involved with dogs and horses, but was about to move to the Channel Islands.

Corrections and additions to claim list:
1941

23 Nov — delete	
1942	
4 Jul	BM984
27 Jul	BN126
27 Aug-9 Oct	BR525
7 Dec (not 8th) and & Jan 1943	EP338

REVISED TOTAL: 7 and 1 shared destroyed, 1 shared probable, 6 damaged.

MORRIS Douglas Griffith

Educated at St John's College, Johannesburg, he was the brother of E.J.Morris. He was awarded a DFC in October 1941.

MORRIS Edward James

Born in Benoni, Transvaal, brother of D.G.Morris, he lived in Vryheid, Natal, before the war, and trained on the training ship *General Botha*. In May 1943 he was Chief Instructor at 71 OTU.

MORRIS Thomas Charles   Flying Officer

Tom Morris was born in Eastbourne, Sussex, on 25 October 1911, his family then living in Portsmouth. He entered Halton as an Aircraft Apprentice in August 1928, qualifying as an electrician three years later. He served in the UK and India until July 1935, when he remustered as a pilot, training at 4 FTS in the Middle East. Having qualified as a Sgt Pilot in April 1936, he joined 29 (F) Squadron at Amriya, flying Demons and Gordons. Posted to the UK, he joined 151 Squadron, but in March 1938 was posted to 80 Squadron, and returned to the Middle East, serving in Palestine where he was awarded the General Service Medal with Clasp. He converted to Hurricanes in June 1940 and became a member of the unit's Hurricane Flight, which subsequently formed the nucleus for 274 Squadron. He was promoted Wt Off in April 1941, and was awarded a DFC (not DFM) in August. In January 1942 he was posted to 71 OTU as an instructor, where in February he was commissioned. In June he was at 1 Middle East Training School, El Ballah, but he then returned to the UK, going to 8 Air Gunnery School, Evanton. On 26 August 1943 he was flying with a student on a low level gunnery exercise when the engine of their Martinet failed, and they crash-landed in a field near Dornoch. However, Morris died of his injuries next day and was buried in Milton Cemetery, Portsmouth.

Additions to claim list:		
1940		
9 Dec		V7300
12 Dec (not 13th)		P3723
1941 (not 1942)		
4 Jan		V7293

MORRISON Donald Robert

He did not, as recorded in *Aces High*, return to the UK to join the RAF after the war. He died on 28 January 1994.

MORTON James Stors   RAF Nos. 72026 (RAFVR); 90727 (RAF)

Born in Blackheath, South London , on 24 April 1916, he attended Pembroke College, Cambridge, where he joined the UAS in February 1936. In November 1937 he received a commission in the RAFVR on completing his degree. He then worked for Fife Coal Company at Cowdenbeath Colliery as a trainee manager, and joined 603 Squadron in May 1939, being granted a commission in the RAF. He was called up in August 1939, and was Mentioned in Despatches on 29 February 1940. A year later he was posted to the Manchester UAS as an instructor, moving in March to Sheffield UAS. In August 1941 he returned to 603 Squadron as a controller, before going to 54 Squadron in October. In January 1942 he attended 51 OTU for a night fighter course, then taking command of 1460 (Turbinlite) Flight in March. This unit became 539 Squadron in September 1942. In November 1943 he joined 54 OTU as an instructor until August 1944, when he attended the Army Staff College, Camberley. In December he joined the staff of HQ, Fighter Command, where he remained until November 1945.

Corrections and additions to claim list:			
1940			
28 Sep		L4409 is incorrect	
1943			
16/17 Aug	(d)	V8868	off Bone

(d) This victory was claimed with Flg Off C.Bailey as radar operator.

MOULD Peter William Olber (not Olbert)

He became an Aircraft Apprentice at Halton in December 1933, subsequently being granted a cadetship at Cranwell — hence his nickname 'Boy' (Boy Entrant). At Cranwell he became a triple 'Blue' at rugby, cricket and athletics. After his service with 1 Squadron, he became an instructor at 6 OTU on 28 May 1940, moving to 5 OTU on 28 June. He was 24 when killed in 1941.

Corrections and additions to claim list:					
1940					
10 May —	the He 111 claimed was an aircraft of 5/KG 3				
14 May	½	Bf 110	Hurricane I		1 Sqn
19 May	½	He 111	,,		,,

REVISED TOTAL: 8 and 3 shared destroyed, 1 unconfirmed destroyed, 5 damaged, 6 shared destroyed on the water, 4 shared damaged on the water.

MOYNET Andre   RAF No. F30612

MUIRHEAD Ian James   RAF Nos. 563513 (NCO); 43362 (Officer)

Born in 1913, he enlisted as an Aircraft Apprentice in September 1929.

MÜMLER Mieczyslaw

Trained as an artillery officer, he transferred to the 11 Pulk Mysliwski (11th Fighter Regiment) in 1926 for flying training. He commanded the 132 Eskadra at Poznan from 1929-1937, and in 1938 was promoted to command III/3 Dywizjon Mysliwski. He was commanding the division in September 1939, supporting the Poznan Army. His was the only fighter division to retain its operational capability until 17 September, when the Soviet invasion from the east occurred. He entered Rumania and made his way to France, where he organised the 2nd Polish fighter unit there. After his pilots had been detached in sections and sent to French units from the Lyon-Bron centre, he flew with GC II/7. On 1 June 1940 he shot down an He 111 just short of the Swiss border, observed by a flight of Swiss fighters. Evacuated to the UK after the fall of France, he organised and commanded the first unit there — 302 Squadron — from 26 July-5 December 1940. He became Chief Flying Instructor at 58 OTU, Grangemouth, in February 1941, also spending some time at 55 and 61 OTUs prior to October 1942, when he took command of RAF Northolt. He was released from the service in late 1946 (not in 1948). He died on 5 September 1985.

Corrections and additions to claim list:
1939
6 Sep — delete

8 Sep		'Ju 86'	PZL P.11C			III/3 Dyon
12 Sep		He 111	„			„
„	½	He 111	„			„
13 Sep		Hs 126	„			„
1940						
1 Jun		He 111	D.520	119		GC II/7
15 Jun	½	Do 17	„	„		„
„	½	He 111 Damaged	„	„		„
18 Sep		Do 17	Hurricane I	P3588 WX-J	Thames Estuary	302 Sqn
1943						
3 Feb		FW 190 Damaged	Spitfire VB			Northolt Wg

REVISED TOTAL: 4 and 3 shared destroyed, 1 and 1 shared damaged.

MUNGO-PARK John Colin
Educated at Liverpool College.

MURPHY Francis
His first vistory was not the first credited to 486 Squadron, and occurred on 19 December 1942, not 17th as stated in *Aces High*. He was later awarded an OBE. He died in 1998.

Corrections to claim list:
1942			
19 Dec	½	Bf 109F (a)	
„	½	Bf 109F (a)	
1943			
16 Feb		(b)	
29 Apr		(c)	

REVISED TOTAL: 3 and 2 shared destroyed, 1 probable.
(a) Both aircraft of 4(F)/123; WNr 10246 'White 7', Lt Karl Raucheisen missing; WNr 10189 'White 1', Oblt Karl Ruck missing; (b) Ju 88D-1 WNr 1243 4U+MH of 1(F)/123 missing; Fw Willi Klunze and crew all lost; (c) Bf 109G-4 WNr 14773 'White 7' of 4(F)/123; Fw Willi Quante missing.

MURRAY Frederick Thomas

Correction to claim list:
1944	
29 Dec	MJ851 (not MJ051)

NASH Peter Alfred   RAF Nos. 1160247 (NCO); 113759 (Officer)
When called up in July 1940, he attended 5 ITW at Babbacombe, Devon, until September, then learning to fly at 13 EFTS. Attendance at 5 SFTS, Ternhill and Sealand, followed during October 1940-March 1941, then 53 OTU, Heston, until May 1941, when he was posted to 65 Squadron.

Corrections and additions to claim list:
1941		
18 Sep		W3371 PR-T
13 Oct		AD202 PR-U
1942		
25 Mar		AB335 F
28 Mar (not 27th)		„
9 May		BR108 C-20
17 May		BR195

NEIL John William

Corrections and additions to claim list:
1942		
3 and 22 Jul		BP326 HN-T
2 Sep —	first 2 claims	BP326 NH-T
„ —	third claim	BP742 NH-X
2 Nov		„

NEIL Thomas Francis   RAF No. 79168 (not 71968)

NELSON William Henry
Educated at King Edward VII Public School and Baron Byng High School, Montreal, and Strathcona Academy High School, Outremont, Canada.

NELSON-EDWARDS George Hassall

Born in Stafford, 'Hal' or 'Neddy' as he was known in the RAF — George later — was a successful rower at university. He obtained a Direct Entry Commission into the RAFVR on 26 September 1939, attending 6 OTU at Sutton Bridge before joining 79 Squadron in July 1940. It was on 29 September 1940 that he was brought down in the Irish Sea by return fire from an He 111 (not 27th). On his return claims had already been submitted for the aircraft, which he believed he had shot down, and he was granted only a probable. In July 1941 he was posted to 504 Squadron as a flight commander, while in November he went to 52 OTU, Aston Down, as 'D' Flight commander. He was given command of 93 Squadron in June 1942, remaining with the unit until 13 February 1943, when he was awarded a DFC and posted to Combined Operations HQ the following month as Air Planner. In June he was attached to the Army Staff College until late in the year, when he underwent a Mustang conversion course at 41 OTU, Hawarden, then being made commanding officer of 239 Squadron on these aircraft. The unit was disbanded in February 1944 however, and as an Acting Wg Cdr he became RAF Liaison Officer to HQ, US 9th Air Force. In late 1944 he suffered from jaundice. At this stage he bought a public house, although remaining in the RAF, being posted to the staff of RAF Sudbury for training duties. Demobilised in January 1946, he ran the pub and also a hotel after his father died, but in November 1946 he rejoined the RAF on an Extended Service Commission. After a brief course at 1 Flying Refresher School, he attended CFS, Little Rissington, on an instructors' course, but was then retained as Chief Ground Instructor. He was then posted to the Organisation Directorate at Air Ministry until August 1951. In September 1951 he went to HQ, 2nd TAF, as Wg Cdr Organisation, while in April 1952 , following a Vampire Refresher Course at Chivenor, he became Wg Cdr Flying at Oldenburg, leading 124 Fighter/Ground Attack Wing. In 1953 he attended the Day Fighter Leaders' Course at West Raynham, and led a wing in the Coronation Review Flypast that June. In July 1953 he took a Sabre conversion course, and in December was posted to command the Oxford UAS. In April 1956 he attended 8 Course at the Flying College, Manby, then going to Air Ministry as OR 23 on Fighter Requirements in December. He now purchased another pub in South Wales and at the end of 1959 gave notice of his intention to resign his commission. His final posting was as Air Liaison Officer with the Army's Eastern Command, but he left the RAF in September 1960. After taking a Cordon Bleu cookery course, he ran the 'Trewen Arms' in South Wales as a pub and restaurant. He then bought a second restaurant in the area, the 'Swan Inn', which he ran until 1982-83, when he retired. He then lived in Cyprus, where he died on 21 September 1994, shortly before his autobiography, *Spit and Sawdust* (Newton) was published.

Addition to claim list:
1943
5 Jan   Bf 109 Damaged (a)
(a) It appears that the pilot of this aircraft was later reported to be a POW, so this claim may subsequently have been confirmed.

NESS David Edward

Additions to claim list:
1944

12 Jul			EJ522 US-F	NW Winchelsea	
28 Jul			EJ536 US-R	10m N Robertsbridge	
30 Jul			EJ534 US-O	8m N Hastings	
4 Aug	2	V-1s	Tempest V	EJ547 US-A	E Robertsbridge	56 Sqn

REVISED TOTAL: 5 and 1 shared destroyed, 4 and 1 shared V-1s destroyed.

NEWHOUSE Peter Saxton   Flight Lieutenant
RAF Nos. 748791 (NCO); 112423 (Officer)

Born in Bradford, West Yorkshire, in 1920, he lived in Newcastle-under-Lyme, Staffordshire, and was educated at Wolstanton County Grammar School. He joined the RAFVR as a u/t pilot in June 1939, and was commissioned in November 1941. Promoted Flg Off in October 1942, he joined 51 OTU as an instructor in December 1943, being promoted Flt Lt shortly thereafter.

NEWTON Percy (not Percival) Arthur   RAF Nos. 779507 (NCO); 81017 (Officer)

He enlisted in Rhodesia as a Sgt, and was commissioned almost at once, on 26 May 1940. He was promoted Flg Off on 26 May a year later, and Flt Lt on the same date in 1942.

NIBLETT John   RAF NOs. 655985 (NCO); 47516 (Officer)

He was born in Harrow, Middlesex, and lived in Horsell, Surrey. He joined the Royal Army Service Corps in 1940, but transferred to the RAF when there was a call for aircrew volunteers in spring 1941. He was commissioned in December 1941.

NICHOLLS Henry Treweeke   RAF Nos. 902530 (NCO); 174073 (Officer)

He was commissioned on 12 March 1944.

NICHOLLS John Hamilton   RAF Nos. 1056935 (NCO); 116982 (Officer)

Additions to claim list:
1943

10 Oct	JF413
28 Nov	JF362

NITSCHKE Richard Hastings

He has no known grave, and is commemorated on the Alamein RAF Memorial.

Addition to claim list:
1941
12 Dec —   he was engaged with MC 202s of 1° Stormo CT on this occasion.

NIVEN John Brown   RAF Nos. 748727 (NCO); 109061 (Officer)

Born in Edinburgh in 1920, he attended James Gillespie's College and George Heriot's School in that city, enlisting in the RAFVR in June 1939. He was commissioned in 1941. During 1943 he served as an instructor at 52 OTU, being promoted Flt Lt on 25 July, and joining 322 Squadron on 10 August. In January 1945 he was posted to RAF Rednal to 53 OTU as CFI.

NORRIS Stanley Charles

He died in 1991.

NORTH Harold Leslie

He was posted to 43 Squadron from 11 Group Pool on 17 November 1939.

NOWELL Gareth Leofric   RAF Nos. 740099 (NCO); 146389 (Officer)

Amendments to text in *Aces High*; 3rd line of the biographical notes onwards "..White and Poppe who subsequently moved to Guildford. His apprenticeship was then transferred to the parent company, the Daimler Motor Co of Coventry. In 1932..." (to the 7th line) "...subsequent career. In 1937 (not 1936) he joined the new RAFVR,..." During the fighting in France and immediately thereafter, he was twice recommended for the DFM, then for a Bar to this, and then for a second Bar, which did not materialize.

Corrections to the notes following the Provisional Total at the end of the claim list:
(b) On this occasion he landed wheels-down; (c) He crash-landed wheels-up; (e) He advises that identification of the aircraft he attacked was uncertain. Finally, he advises that his May 1940 logbook was compiled later, with the aid of Dennis David, as wingman to whom he had undertaken most of his flights at this time.

NOWIERSKI Tadeusz   Group Captain/Podpulkownik

Nowierski was born in Warsaw on 22 June 1907; he volunteered for the Polish Air Force in 1929, completing his flying training at the 1 Pulk Lotniczy in Warsaw. As an NCO he graduated from the Cadet Officers' School, and was then commissioned in 1935, joining the 24 Eskadra Liniowa (Light Bomber) of the 2 Pulk Lotniczy in Kracow. In September 1939 he flew PZL P.23 Karas light bombers with this unit. He then escaped via Rumania to France, but moved to the UK in early 1940. He was posted to 609 Squadron on 5 August 1940 with another Polish pilot, the unit ORB recording: *"..neither could speak English but both rapidly acquired efficiency on Spitfires."* On 5 October he was obliged to bale out of N3223 due to mechanical failure. British records credit him with five and two shared destroyed whilst with 609 Squadron, although for some reason the PAF later in the war downgraded his total to three. Having considered the list of 609 Squadron's claims, there appears no justification for this in regard to at least two claims made on 25 September. On 21 January 1941 he joined 316 Squadron, where he became a flight commander on 10 August 1941. His DFC was awarded on 10 June 1941, and the Virtuti Militari, 5th Class, on 5 July. He led 308 Squadron until 5 May 1942, when he became deputy commander of the 1st Polish Wing at Northolt. He instructed at 58 OTU in 1943, then commanding 2nd Polish Wing at Kirton-in-Lindsey, and then Heston. At the end of the war he attended a staff course at Fort Leavenworth, USA, returning to Poland in 1947. He did not rejoin the air force there, but in 1948 was arrested for political reasons, following false accusations. He was released two years later, thereafter working as a taxi driver. He died in Warsaw.

Corrections and additions to claim list:
1940

13 Aug —	this Bf 109E is believed to have been 'Black 9' of 5/JG 53, Fw Pfannschmidt taken POW; his Spitfire, L1082, was PR-A
7 Sep —	this Do 17 may have been reclassified as a Probable.
25 Sep —	the PAF appear to have missed, or discounted these claims. They are included in the 609 Squadron records, and are therefore included in his total here; his Spitfire, N3223, was PR-M.
30 Sep —	this Bf 109E is believed to have been WNr 4861 of 5/JG 2, which crashed at Sydling St Nicholas, Gefr Dollinger being killed. The PAF appear to have missed or discounted the Probable claim on this date.
15 Oct —	this Bf 109E is believed to have been an E-1, WNr 3279 'White 10' of 4/JG 2; Gefr Pollach POW.
2 Dec —	Do 17 7T+KL was WNr 3618; the crew of Lt Helmut Anders were killed.

1941
13 Feb —   the Ju 88 is believed to be an A-1, WNr 4176, of KGr 806.
1942
19 Aug   BL860 JH-T
REVISED TOTAL: According to RAF records, as before. According to PAF records, 3 destroyed, 1 probable, 6 and 1 shared damaged, 1 V-1 destroyed (no details).

OFFENBERG Jean Henri Marie   Belgian No. 42184
Pupil pilot in the 77[e] Promotion of the Aviation Militaire Belge, he graduated on 1 March 1938.

OGILVIE Alfred Keith
Known as 'Skeets'.

Corrections and additions to claim list:
1941
19 Mar   P8430 (not P4830)
16 May   Spitfire II
22 May   Spitfire II
17 and 21 Jun   Spitfire VB

OLIVE Charles Gordon Chaloner   RAF No. 36469 (not 39469 or 37869)
He left 65 Squadron in March 1941 to become a controller at Tangmere until posted to form 456 Squadron in June. He relinquished command of this unit due to ill health in March 1942. Posted to HQ, 81 Group, he joined 55 OTU as a supernumary Sqn Ldr, then moving to 58 OTU in October to command the section at Balado Bridge. In December 1942 he was promoted Acting Wg Cdr and o/c Training Wing at Grangemouth. He transferred to the RAAF on 3 June 1943 as a Sqn Ldr, and in October returned to Australia (not March 1942), where he again became an Acting Wg Cdr on 1 April 1944. After the war he became an executive of Rheem Australia until his retirement in 1972.

OLIVER John Oliver William
After claiming two He 111s on 13 May 1940, on his next flight 'Doggie' Oliver was shot down by a Bf 109E of 8/JG 3, flown by Lt Winfried Schmidt; he baled out of P2821 near Tirlemont. He was fired on by Belgian troops as he fell in his parachute, but survived unhurt to return to 85 Squadron that afternoon. In July 1943 he was a Grp Capt at HQ Fighter Command, and was Mentioned in Despatches on 14 January 1944. In July 1944 he was at HQ, 84 Group, 2nd TAF. In 1955, still a Grp Capt, he served with HQ, 18 Group, following which he became Assistant Chief of Staff, Ops, at Allied Forces Northern Europe, NATO, in 1959.

Corrections and additions to claim list:
1940

10 May	1/3	He 111 Unconfirmed	Hurricane I		nr Hazebrouk	85 Sqn
11 May	2	He 111s	,,	P2821		,,
12 May		He 111	,,	VY-A		,,
,,		Do 17	,,	,,		,,
13 May		He 111	,,		nr Lille	,,
,,		He 111	,,		Hazebrouk	,,

REVISED TOTAL: 7 destroyed, 1 shared unconfirmed destroyed.

OLVER Peter   RAF Nos. 758173 (NCO); 84963 (Officer) — not 84693
Before the war he undertook various short jobs before joining the Derbyshire & Nottinghamshire Electric Power Co as Power Development Officer. He joined the RAFVR in March 1938, but had done little flying before he was called up on the outbreak of war. He attended 7 OTU in September 1940 before joining 611 Squadron. He was promoted Flt Lt in October 1941, then volunteering for service in the Middle East. When shot down in July 1943, he was wounded and burned, and spent some time in hospital in Sicily and Naples before being despatched to Germany, where he was sent to Stalag Luft III. On his return in 1945, he underwent a refresher course on Harvards, then joining Technical Training Command in charge of 3 Wing, Wilmslow. He later served at Chivenor, flying Spitfire XIVs, but in 1947 was released at his own request as a Sqn Ldr; in September he moved with his family to Kenya to farm. He returned to the UK in 1963, farming in Devon until his retirement.

Corrections and additions to claim list:
1940

11 and 29 Nov		Spitfire IIA				
1942						
26 Jun	Bf 109F Damaged	Hurricane IIB	BN141	'Charing Cross'	238 Sqn
29 Jun	Bf 109F Damaged	,,	BN139	S Sidi Heneish	,,
15 Jul			U		
16 Jul			X		
,,	Ju 87 Damaged	,,	,,		,,
7 Aug			BP283 U		

2 Nov		BP401
1943		
21 Jan		318 AX-A
17 Apr	(a)	„
5 May and 11 Jul	Spitfire IX	EN448

REVISED TOTAL: 4 and 2 shared destroyed, 3 and 1 shared probable, 7 and 2 shared damaged, 3 destroyed on the ground.
(a) The shared claim for an MC 205 actually related to an MC 202 of 169[a] Squadrilgia, 16° Gruppo, 54° Stormo CT, in which Sottoten Danilo Leoncini was killed.

ORTMANS Victor Marcel Maurice   Belgian No. 42178

He graduated as a pilot from the 75[e] Promotion of the Aviation Militaire Belge on 1 May 1937. He flew a Fairey Fox VIII in 1940.

Addition to claim list:
1940

27 Sep	P3039 was RE-D and carried the name 'BiBi' on the fuselage.

ORTON Newell

He was the first pilot to be awarded both a DFC and Bar during World War II. (A WW I pilot, Louis Arbon Strange, who had been awarded an MC and DFC in that earlier war, received the first Bar of WW II, for flying an unarmed liaison aircraft of 24 Squadron from Merville to Hendon whilst under attack.)

OSLER Malcolm Stephen

Addition to claim list:
1943

2 Oct	JF417

O'SULLIVAN Kevin Thomas Anthony   RAF Nos. 1383455 (NCO);127032 (Officer)

He was born on 29 December 1920 in Tooting, South London, living in nearby Wandsworth and attending Clapham Xaverian College. He joined the RAFVR in 1941, and was commissioned on 29 May 1942. He remained in the RAF after the war, being Mentioned in Despatches on 1 January 1946. He subsequently served in Borneo, gaining the Queen's Commendation for Valuable Services in the Air. He ended his flying in 1965, becoming an Air Traffic Controller. He was posted to CFS, Little Rissington, but whilst there he died on 21 February 1968 of shotgun injuries to the head, that were considered to have been deliberate.

Additions to claim list:
1943

11/12 May		V8518
27/28 May	(a)	V8510

(a) Both were aircraft of 9/KG 54, B3+BT and B3+LT.
NB. All his claims in 1943 were made with Sgt W.G.Hood as his radar operator.

OTTEWILL Peter Guy   RAF Nos. 565387 (NCO); 46451 (Officer)

Peter Ottewill joined the RAF in January 1931 as an Aircraft Apprentice. He remustered as a pilot, gaining his 'wings' at 9 FTS, Hullavington, in September 1938, following which he was posted to 43 Squadron. As a consequence of his claims in early June 1940, he was later Mentioned in Despatches. On 7 June, during a late sortie, he was shot down — probably by a Bf 109E — and eventually reached England, where he underwent plastic surgery for the next 12 months. He then returned to flying duties, and was commissioned in June 1941. In September he joined 289 Squadron in Army Co-operation Command, although this unit became a special Fighter Command Training Squadron. In April 1942 he joined 165 Squadron, becoming a flight commander in June. He then undertook a Pilot Gunnery Instructors' Course at Sutton Bridge, gaining 'Above Average' classification, and in July took command of 1490 Fighter Gunnery Flight at Acklington, and then Ayr. Here he learned that a Beaufighter of 406 Squadron was on fire in a bomb dump, having crashed there. He went in and rescued the two occupants despite being badly burned himself in doing so. He was recommended for the George Cross by Wg Cdr 'Zulu' Morris, Sqn Ldr George Denholm and Sqn Ldr J.R.C.Young, but was awarded the George Medal. In October 1943 he commanded 14 APC at Ayr, then attending the RAF Staff College from August-December 1944. In January 1945 he commanded RAF Matlaske, Norfolk, where Spitfire XVIs were based, while in June he was sent to Rome to the Air Division of the Allied Commission to Austria as pilot and Air Liaison Officer to General Sir Richard McCreery, the British Commander-in-Chief. In August 1945 he accompanied 'J' Mission to Vienna as ALO to Marshal Koniev, the Soviet C-in-C, for McCreery. He was given command of 253 Squadron of the Desert Air Force in June 1946, serving with this unit at Treviso, Italy, and Zeltweg, Austria. A year later he returned to the UK to command 257 Squadron on Meteors at Horsham St Faith. In November 1948 he was posted to Air Ministry as Ops Training, Day Fighters. March 1951 brought an exchange posting to the RAAF, and he commanded 75 Squadron, RAAF, at Williamstown, New South Wales, flying Nene-powered Vampires. In February 1952 he commanded the Williamstown OTU, then going to Korea to join 77 Squadron, RAAF, on Meteors. He was awarded the AFC in January 1953. Returning home, he joined Tactical Operations Branch in the Air Ministry in August 1953, working with Grp Capt J.E.'Johnnie' Johnson. In July 1958 he attended the US Air War College in Montgomery, Alabama; a year later he served at the Pentagon as Air Executive Officer to Air Chief Marshal Sir George Mills, Head of the UK NATO Military Commission, and to Lord Louis Mountbatten, Chairman of the UK Chiefs of Staff. Promoted Grp Capt in 1966, he took command of the Aircrew Training Centre at RAF South Cerney, Gloucestershire, in July 1962. At the time of writing he was living in retirement in Surrey.

Notes to claim list:
(d) He confirms that he did claim three aircraft shot down on 1 June 1940.

OWEN Alan Joseph   RAF Nos. 1332018 (NCO); 155788 (Officer)

He was commissioned on 11 March 1943. In February 1944 he was posted from 63 OTU to 51 OTU. Both he and McAllister were awarded Bars to their DFCs on 9 March 1945; Owen was later also awarded an AFC. 1448826 Flg Off James Samuel Victor McAllister, DFC & Bar, DFM, took part in all the victories claimed, becoming one of the most successful radar operators in the RAF. From Carrickfergus, County Antrim, Northern Ireland, he was born on 7 November 1918. An agricultural scientist after the war, he was President of the Northern Ireland area RAFA and Aircrew Association. Awarded an OBE in 1972, he died in October 1995.

OXSPRING Robert Wardlow

His date of death was 8 August 1989.

Corrections and additions to claim list:

1942						
26 Jul			Spitfire V (not Mark IX)			
26 Nov	1/5	Ju 88 (not Damaged)	Spitfire VB			
29 Nov						
30 Nov			Spitfire VC			
1943						
1 Mar	1/2	Bf 109G (a)	Spitfire IX	EN116	Beja area	72 Sqn
1944						
23 Jun	1/2	V-1	Spitfire XIV	NH714 RWO	Redhill-Edenbridge	24 Wg
29 Jun		V-1	"	"	Tenterden area	"
6 Jul		V-1	"	"	Balloon barrage area	"
8 Jul		V-1	"	"	2m S West Malling	"
19 Jul (not 16th)		V-1	"	"	S Ashford	"

REVISED TOTAL: 13 and 2 shared destroyed, 2 probables, 12 damaged, 4 and 1 shared V-1s destroyed.

PAGE Alan Geoffrey

He obtained a Direct Entry Commission to the RAFVR on 3 October 1939, due to his UAS membership. He received the Bar to his DFC on 22 August 1944, whilst serving with 132 Squadron.

Text correction to claim list, after Total:
(b) should read Bf 110G (not BF 110G).

PAIN Derek Sydney

Born in 1918 in Purley, Surrey, he lived at Hove, Sussex, attending Alexander House School, Broadstairs, Kent. He enlisted as a u/t pilot in 1936, and was commissioned in August of that year. It is believed that he took part in test flying connected with the early development of airborne radar, for he received a commendation for valuable service in January 1941, an AFC following in April, at which time he was a Flt Lt. He was promoted Sqn Ldr on 1 December 1941, and when despatched to Malta in 1942, it was to command the detachment of 89 Squadron on that island. He flew there with Sgt John Victor 'Jackie' Briggs, DFM, as his radar operator, the two then failing to return from a sortie over Sicily on the night of 7/8 November 1942. They were subsequently to report that their Beaufighter, T5161, had suffered engine failure, although the Italians recorded that it had collided with a barrage balloon cable. Taken prisoner, Pain later managed to escape and evade in Italy, which had by then been invaded, making his way to Allied lines. It appears that he had been reported "missing, believed dead", which accounts for the late gazetting of his DFC, which was stated to be with effect from 6 November 1942. After the war he commanded 219 Squadron as a Wg Cdr, October 1945-February 1946, then serving with the Night Fighter Leaders' School, CFE, until 1948. Attached to the USAF at Wright Patterson Air Force Base, Dayton, Ohio, he was reported killed while testing a jet bomber either in late 1949 or early 1950.

Additions to claim list:

1941		
16/17 Jun	X7554	
1942		
2/3 Mar		Jebel Mariyut

4/5 Nov	(c)		T5161		

(c) This was a Z 1007bis of 265ª Squadriglia, 88° Gruppo Aut BT.

PAIN John Francis

Corrections to claim list:

1941					
20 Apr		Hurricane II	Z3032		
1942					
25 May	MC 200 Damaged	Hurricane IIC	BM157	NE Tmimi	73 Sqn

REVISED TOTAL: 7 and 1 shared destroyed, 10 probables, 7 damaged.

PALLISER George Charles Calder

Corrections and additions to claim list:

1940		
15 Sep		P3615
26 Sep (not 21st) ⅓ Do 17 Damaged (not individual claim)		V6614
27 Sep		V6614
21 Oct —	delete	

REVISED TOTAL: 4 and 7 shared destroyed, 2 shared probables, 1 and 1 shared damaged.

PALMER Cyril Dampier

His service number suggests that he was a Cranwell cadet, probably June 1936-December 1937. This is likely to confirm that, although born in the USA, he was a UK or Commonwealth subject, rather than a US citizen. He was posted to 1 Squadron in 1938. In late May 1940 he joined 6 OTU as an instructor.

Corrections and additions to claim list:
1940
14 May —   this was an aircraft of I/JG 53.
17 May —   the Bf 110 was unconfirmed. Claims were made for 5 and 2 unconfirmed in this
            engagement; V(Z)/LG 1 lost 3. His Hurricane, P2820, was hit during the
            fight, and he baled out near Reims.
19 May —   claims made for 5 and 3 unconfirmed He 111s; III/KG 27 lost 5 in this engagement.
REVISED TOTAL: 1 and 2 shared destroyed, 1 unconfirmed destroyed.

PARE Robin

Additions to claim list:

1940				
1 Nov	Ca 133	Gladiator II	Gallabat area	1 SAAF Sqn
1941				
25 Mar	(a)			
1942				
5 Mar			AN383 N	
3 Jun			AN384 V	

REVISED TOTAL: 6 destroyed, plus 1 not confirmed due to his loss, 1 shared damaged, 1 and 3 shared destroyed on the ground, 6 shared damaged on the ground.
(a) CR 42 of 412ª Squadriglia Aut CT; Serg Pietro Morlotti killed.

PARGETER Reginald Clive

Born in Eastbourne, Sussex, in 1919, he then lived in Stanmore, Middlesex. He attended the University of London, joining the UAS, and was commissioned in the RAFVR in June 1939, being called up in September. It is likely that he was involved in flying instruction during the early years of the war, since he was already a Flt Lt when he joined an operational unit in July 1942. At the end of his first tour with 29 Squadron, he and 78542 Flt Lt Robert Lonsdale Fell returned to 51 OTU as instructors, going back to 29 Squadron in late 1943.

PARK Geoffrey Rosser (not Roger)   RAF Nos. 740298 (NCO); 78710 (Officer)

Although born in South Africa, he lived in Middleton-on-Sea, Bognor Regis, Sussex, just before the war. He enlisted in the RAFVR in 1937, being commissioned in 1940. Promoted Sqn Ldr in September 1943, he returned to Cape Town in May 1944 after an absence of five and a half years. He then made his way to the Middle East, where in September he became commanding officer of 272 Squadron. His Beaufighter was shot down by Flak whilst on a shipping strike over the Adriatic Sea on 15 October 1944, and he was killed.

PARKER Bernard James   RAF Nos. 923736 (NCO); 61488 (Officer)

PARKER Gartrell Richard Ian   RAF Nos. 550085 (NCO); 47140 (Officer)

His radar operator was 1398201 Wt Off Donald Ling Godfrey, DFC, DFM. Parker was Mentioned in Despatches for his air-sea rescue work, receiving two more Mentions later in the war. As a test pilot with Blackburn Aircraft, he was obliged to eject from the prototype Buccaneer, XK486, during 1961. However, he and his observer were killed in 1963 when Buccaneer XN952 crashed during a test flight.

Corrections and additions to claim list:

1944			
14/15 Jun		HK248	10m N Gravelines
21/22 Jun		„	10m S Dungeness
25/26 Jun		HK344	„
27/28 Jun		HK250	mid Channel

PARKER Thomas Campbell

'John' Parker as he was known, was born in Southampton, gaining his education at Bromley County School, Kent. He worked in his father's business until joining the RAFO, then commencing training at 3 E & RFTS on 23 September 1937. He was commissioned on 24 November 1937, attending 8 FTS the following month, then joining 29 Squadron on 9 July 1938. He was placed on the Reserve on 23 September 1938, but applied for a Short Service Commission, which was granted. After a refresher course with 79 Squadron in February 1939, he was commissioned in the RAF on 1 September. On 12 May 1940 he was shot down by return fire from a Do 17Z of 8/KG 77 which he was attacking, and he was obliged to bale out. Six days later his aircraft was again hit by fire from a Do 17Z, this time an aircraft of 5/KG 76, but on this occasion he was able to return to base. However on 20 May his Hurricane, P2634, was hit by ground fire, and this time he crash-landed west of Arras, returning on foot. In February 1941 he was posted to 52 OTU at Debden, then Aston Down, as an instructor. On 10 April 1942 he took command of 242 Squadron, following which he undertook a publicity tour, talking to future aircrew, before being posted to India, where he served first on the staff of 224 Group before joining 67 Squadron. In August 1944 he returned to HQ, 224 Group, as a Wg Cdr, subsequently returning to the UK just before the Japanese surrender. He remained in the RAF, attending the Fighter Leaders' School at CFE before taking command of 63 Squadron, the last Spitfire fighter unit in the RAF, which converted to Meteors in April 1948. He then led the Odiham Vampire Wing, before being posted to Canada in July 1949 to attend the RCAF Staff College. Two years with the Air Defence Staffs at Ottawa and St Hubert followed, before he returned to the UK in 1951. Service on the Staff of Eastern Sector, 12 Group, followed, and then as i/c Admin Wing at Waddington. His last full posting was to HQ, Allied Forces, Central Europe, at Fontainbleau in October 1958. He returned to the UK in March 1961, retiring from the service in September 1962.

Corrections and additions to claim list:

1940					
12 May	1/4	He 111		Hurricane I	79 Sqn
16 May		(a)			
18 May	2	Do 17s Damaged		„	„

REVISED TOTAL: 2 and 4 shared destroyed, 1` unconfirmed destroyed, 3 damaged.
(a) Correction to note in *Aces High*; this was an FW 189A of 9(H)/LG 2, a number of which were being employed for operational assessment in the Wavre area. 3 were claimed shot down in this engagement; 2 were actually lost.

PARKINSON Colin Henry

Correction to claim list:
(a) The MC 202 in which he shared on 23 June 1942 was an aircraft of 155° Gruppo, 51° Stormo CT (not 22° Gruppo).

PARNALL Denis Geach   Flight Lieutenant

Born in 1915, Parnall came from St Gennys, Cornwall. He joined the RAFO in December 1936, transferring to the RAFVR on 1 January 1938, and the regular RAF on a Permanent Commission in September 1938, but with seniority from 3 June 1937. He was almost certainly a university entrant, and probably served in a UAS before joining the RAFO. Permanent Commissions were normally reserved for Cranwell or university entrants. It seems that he saw service with 263 Squadron in Norway during May 1940. He joined 249 Squadron as a Flg Off in July 1940, becoming a Flt Lt at once. He was shot down by Bf 110s, crashing by the A-12 road near Furness Farm, Furze Hill, Margaretting, Essex.

Corrections and additions to claim list:

1940					
26 May		He 111 (e)	Gladiator		263 Sqn
8 Jul	1/3	Ju 88 (a)	Hurricane I	P3615	249 Sqn
15 Aug				„	
2 Sep		(b)		V6559	
7 Sep		(c)		„	
11 Sep		(d)		„	
15 Sep				„	

REVISED TOTAL: 2 and 4 shared destroyed, 2 probables, 1 damaged.
(a) 1/3 shares (not 1/6) — believed to have been an aircraft of 9/KG 4 (not StSt/LG 1); (b) Bf 110 of Stab II/ZG 76; (c) He 111 of III/KG 53; (d) He 111 of 3/KG 3; (e) confirmed as destroyed due to discovery of a crashed aircraft at the time; in fact believed only to have been damaged.

PARROTT Peter Lawrence

At the end of December 1939 he was posted to 11 Group Pool for fighter training, then on 22 January 1940 to 2 Ferry Pilots' Pool. On 12 May 1940 he received the news that his brother, a Whitley pilot, was missing, whilst next day his Hurricane, P3535, AF-C, was hit by Bf 109Es of 1/JG 21 over Louvain, and damaged. On 17 May he was sent back to England on leave.

Corrections and additions to claim list:
1940
10 May   P2536 AF-R
3rd and 4th claims on this date were for ½ He 111 and ⅓ He 111 unconfirmed (not 1 and 1 Damaged)
11 May   P2572 AF-B
1943   (a)   Spitfire VC   JG937
1944
17 Feb   MJ118
REVISED TOTAL: 4 and 5 shared destroyed, 1 and 1 shared unconfirmed destroyed, 1 shared probable, 4 and 2 shared damaged.
(a) The shared MC 200 was in fact a Re 2002 of 5° Stormo Assalto.

PARSONS Claude Arthur

He attended 6 OTU in May 1940 before joining 610 Squadron. He did not shoot down a Skua on 9 July 1940 in the belief that it was an ex-French Navy V-156F (that was Sgt H.H.Chandler of the same unit on 24 July).

Corrections to claim list:
1940
9 Jul —   delete
Claims for 15 September and onwards were made whilst with 66 Squadron, not 610 Squadron as indicated on the list in *Aces High*.

PARSONSON John Edward

'Jack' Parsonson was born on 20 November 1914 in Smithfield, Orange Free State. He joined the Active Citizen Force Militia in 1935 whilst working in a bank, becoming a 2nd Lieutenant with 1st City Regiment, Queenstown Contingent. In March 1937 he was selected for Permanent Force Course 367G, being commissioned on 1 March 1939 and serving with the Field Artillery. Permanent Force officers were also able to learn to fly, which he did. On the outbreak of war in September he was posted to the Coastal Artillery, but in January 1940, due to pilot shortage, he was allowed to transfer to the SAAF. In August 1941 he was flown up to Nakuru, Kenya, to convert to Mohawks, and was based with a detachment of these at Aiscia. After the conclusion of the East African war he returned to the Union as an Armaments Officer, taking over this role from Peter Metelerkamp in March 1941 when the latter was posted to the Middle East. He managed to obtain a posting to this area in July 1942, and joined 2 SAAF Squadron. On 3 November (not 1st) his aircraft was hit by ground fire, and he force-landed behind Axis lines due to leaking glycol, as the Afrika Korps was in retreat. He managed to walk through in the dark and was eventually picked up by a South African Armoured Car unit when near exhaustion. He was promoted to command 5 SAAF Squadron on 17 December 1942, initially on Tomahawks, and then on Kittyhawks again, usually flying GL-X with this unit. As a POW he was transferred to Stalag Luft III at Sagan, where he was involved in digging the tunnel for the Great Escape. His was one of the last numbers drawn however, and he was not able to take part in the escape as a consequence, which may well have saved his life. After the war he was flown to England, and thence, after leave, to Italy, where he was promoted Lt Col and made Wing Leader of 8 SAAF Wing. This was disbanded in November 1945, and he then commanded Shandur airfield until late December, when he returned to South Africa. Reverting to the rank of Major, he was initially based at Waterkloof Air Station until he attended the SAAF Staff College, then holding a number of staff appointments. He had married the daughter of General 'Boetie' Venter, a WW I fighter pilot (see *Above the Trenches*) who had ended WW II at the head of the SAAF. However, Parsonson did not take to the peacetime force and resigned in 1954 to become a tobacco farmer in Rhodesia. He divorced in 1964, and married Joan Oliver, an Englishwoman. They remained on the farm at Darwendale until 1981, when, having seen out the terrorist war, he decided that he had had enough of tobacco farming, and returned to Cape Province. Here he acquired 15 acres of land and built an A frame cottage, subsequently developing this into a fine house. His health then began to fail, requiring a heart by-pass operation, and he also began to suffer considerably from arthritis and osteoporosis. In 1991, now very ill, he was sent home from hospital, but the house he had built in the country was no longer suitable, he and his wife moving to a retirement village near Hermanus. He spent his last months writing an autobiography of his wartime experiences, but on 15 August 1992 he was readmitted to hospital, where he died next day. *A Time to Remember* was published posthumously by Aviation Usk in the USA.

Additions to claim list:
1941
5 Oct   2522
1942
29 Aug   ET1019 DB-G
9 Oct   DB-R
26 Oct   EV326 DB-F
1 Dec   ET904 DB-F

1943
19 and 22 Apr   ET510 GL-X

PASZKIEWICZ Ludwik Witold   Flying Officer/Kapitan

Born on 21 October 1907 (not 28th) at Wola Galezowska, south of Lublin, he studied at Warsaw Technical University. He was called up for military service in 1931, completing a flying course at the Szkola Podchorazych Rezerwy Lotnictwa, then serving in the 1 Pulk Lotniczy in Warsaw as a cadet officer/Lance Corporal. In 1932 he entered the SPL, and was commissioned on 15 August 1934, returning to the 1 Pulk. After advanced flying training he joined the 112 Eskadra. In August 1939 he departed for France with the Polish Military Purchasing Mission to test-fly French fighters, and was there when the German invasion commenced. During 1940 he led a Polish section in GC II/8 until evacuated to the UK, where he joined 303 Squadron as one of the original pilots on 2 August 1940. He was decorated with the Virtuti Militari, 5th Class, by General Sikorski on 18 September 1940.

Corrections and additions to claim list:
1940
30 Aug   (a)   R4217 RF-V
7 - 26 Sep   V7235 RF-M
(a) Actually claimed as a 'Do 215'; this aircraft was in fact a Bf 110C, WNr 3615, M8+MM of 4/ZG 76, which crashed at Barley Beans Farm, Kimpton.

PATON Donald Pearson   RAF Nos. 1383387 (NCO); 103595 (Officer)

He was born in Nagasaki, Japan, in 1914, but his home was in London. He enlisted in the RAFVR in 1940, being commissioned in August 1941 and attending 54 OTU in October of that year. He was promoted Flt Lt on 16 August 1943. His radar operator was 134562 Flg Off John William Alec McAnulty, DFC.

PATTERSON Thomas Lawrence   RAF No. 41316

He was commissioned as a Plt Off in August 1937, becoming a Flg Off in September 1940.

PATTLE Marmaduke Thomas St John

He attended Keetman's Hoop Secondary School, South West Africa, and Victoria Boys' High School, Grahamstown.

Additions to claim list:
1940
8 Aug   K7971
2 Dec and 10 Feb 1941   N5832
1941
20 and 27 Feb   V7724

PATTULLO (not PATTULO) William Blair

He accepted the offer of a Short Service Commission just before the outbreak of war, and was commissioned as an Acting Plt Off on 27 April 1940.

PAUL Harold George

Born on 11 November 1916, he was commissioned on 18 May 1937 (not July 1938). On 10 June 1940 he joined 5 OTU as an instructor, but moved to 6 OTU two days later. He died on 8 January 1994.

PAVEY Alan Francis   RAF Nos. 656281 (NCO); 119252 (Officer)

He was born on 7 September 1919, son of a WW I MC holder. He was buried three miles from Port Audemer.

PAXTON Thomas G.   RAF No. 1053584

Although an Australian, Paxton's service number indicates that he joined the RAFVR in the UK.

Correction to claim list:
1941
26 Jun   AK446 (not AK466)

PAYNE A.D.

Known as 'Jammy'. No further information regarding this pilot has been discovered despite widespread enquiries. He remains one of the 'mysteries'.

Correction to claim list:
1940
15 May   should read Bf 110 rather than Do 17.

PAYNE William John   Warrant Officer   RAF No. 754956

Born in Stroud, Gloucestershire, on 21 June 1921, he was a pupil auctioneer before the war. He joined the

RAFVR on 16 August 1939 as a u/t pilot, becoming a Sgt on mobilization on 1 September. He commenced training at 3 ITW, 54 Group, then 9 SFTS from July-October 1940, following which he was sent to CFS on an instructor's course, which he failed. On 25 November therefore, he was posted to 57 OTU, and thereafter he joined 610 Squadron on 10 February 1941. On 3 June he was posted to 92 Squadron, but on 14th was slightly injured while attempting to land his damaged Spitfire, X4342, at Hawkinge after a sweep over France. During June he claimed five Bf 109s shot down (not six). On 1 July 1941 he was promoted Flt Sgt, but on 4th was sent to 53 OTU as an instructor. He was promoted Wt Off on 1 August 1942, and on 30 September was sent to PRU, Benson, as a supernumary. He was posted to 540 (PR) Squadron on 6 November 1942, and to 541 Squadron a month later. On 13 January 1943 he failed to return from a sortie over the south-west coast of Norway in Spitfire PR IV R7044. He is commemorated on Panel 134 of the Runnymede Memorial.

PAYTON James Joseph   RAF Nos. 656543 (NCO); 145149 (Officer)

(He is incorrectly placed alphabetically in *Aces High*; his biographical notes should follow, rather than precede, T.G.Paxton and the two Paynes). Ex-Army officers who transferred to the RAF were allocated regular service numbers from a pre-war block initially. Those who were members of the Territorial Army were later commissioned into the RAFVR; Jim Payton was commissioned on 21 January 1943 (not 1941).

Corrections and additions to claim list:
1944

7 Aug		JN816	10m E Tunbridge Wells

PEACOCK-EDWARDS Spencer Ritchie

Corrections to claim list:
1941
13 Apr
1942 (insert)
5 Apr

PEART Alan McGregor

Addition to claim list:
1944

17 Apr and 14 May	JG349

PECK James Elvidge   USAAF No. O-885951

Born on 14 June 1921. On his return to the UK from Malta, he joined 53 OTU in August 1942 as a Flt Lt. He was awarded a US DFC and three Air Medals after his transfer to the USAAF. He was killed in P-38J-15 43-28337.

PEDLEY Michael George Foxter

He was born on 17 November 1915 in Bourne End, Buckinghamshire, and was educated at Stubbington House, Fareham, and the Nautical College, Pangbourne. He joined the RAF in August 1935, being commissioned a year later. He served at HQ, 27 Group, as Personal Assistant to the AOC in early 1938, then becoming an instructor at 15 FTS from June 1939, following service with 2 Squadron. He was awarded a Dutch AFC on 15 March 1945, and from July 1953-January 1954 commanded RAF Linton-on-Ouse. Following his retirement from the RAF, he joined the Mirror Group Newspapers, and became financial advertising manager. Following retirement from this career, he took up parachuting at the age of 70, also flying microlights and paragliders. He died on 9 December 1995.

PEGGE Constantine Oliver Joseph

He was not sent out to Burma in June 1945 to command 607 Squadron as indicated in *Aces High*. He took command of 131 Squadron in October 1944 as it was about to leave for India, leading the squadron until its disbandment in June 1945. It was then that he moved to Burma to take over 607 Squadron.

Corrections to claim list:
1940

18 Aug	K9975 (not L9975)

PEPPER George   RAF Nos 1066720 (NCO); 104585 (Officer)

PERINA Frantisek   RAF No. 83231

He trained as a locksmith initially, then training as a pilot, 1929-31. He then joined the 2nd Air Regiment at Olomouc for fighter training. Having become a fighter pilot, he undertook an aerial photography course in 1934 and an instrument flying course in 1937. In April 1938 he joined the 52 Letka (Flight) of the 2nd Air Regiment, becoming one of the outstanding pilots and best shots. On 24 June 1939 he got married, and two days later crossed the border into Poland, hidden on a train. He was sent to the Kracow Czech Military Camp, and from there to Gdynia, where he sailed for France on the SS *Chrobry*. Initially he joined the Foreign Legion, but in September 1939 was sent to the fighter base at Chartres. On 30 November 1939 as a Sgt Chef, he was one of the first group of Czechs to complete the fighter course there, then being posted to GC I/5. On 3 June 1940 he was wounded in combat with a Bf 110 and force-landed, being transferred to hospital. He escaped from here on 7 June and reached Paris, from where he found his unit and flew to Algiers with it on 21 June. On 2 July he was commissioned Lt, and six days later sailed from Casablanca, Morocco, on the SS *David Livingstone* to the UK, reaching Cardiff on 5 August. He was sent to the Czech Depot at Cosford and was commissioned as a Plt Off in the RAFVR, joining 312 Squadron on 5 September 1940. He remained with this unit until July 1942, when he attended 9 Pilots' Gunnery Course at Sutton Bridge, then becoming Sector Gunnery Leader at Exeter, Ibsley, Turnhouse and Coltishall in turn until April 1944. He had been promoted Flt Lt on 17 August 1942 and Sqn Ldr on 25 March 1944. In April 1944 he became an Intelligence Staff Officer at ADGB for the Czech Inspectorate. On 18 October 1944 he was detached to the CGS, Sutton Bridge, to gain experience at the Bomber Wing there, and was then sent to HQ, Fighter Command. In March 1945 he attended the Night Vision School at Upper Heyford, going to the Czech Depot in July 1945, and then home to Czechoslovakia. Here he became Chief Gunnery and Bomber instructor at the Military Air School at Prostejov, August 1945-April 1947. On 3 January 1949 he was appointed to command the Air Gunnery Pilots' School at Malacky, Slovakia, but shortly afterwards he was discharged by the Communists, and on 17 April 1949 made his flight to Germany in an M-10 Sokol. On 1 December 1949 he rejoined the RAF as a Flg Off and was posted to Cardington, Bedfordshire, as adjutant. In 1951 he moved to RAF Grimsby, but in 1955 emigrated to Canada, and from there to the USA in 1959. In September 1991, following the 'Velvet Revolution', he was promoted to the rank of Colonel, Retired, in the Czech Air Force, and in 1993 retired to the new Czech Republic to live in Prague. Here in July 1994 he was again promoted to the Retired rank of Major General, which carried considerable pension benefits. His decorations included four Czech War Crosses of 1939, three Czech Gallantry Medals,the Czech Memory Medal with France and Great Britain Clasp, Czech Distinguished Medal, the French Croix de Guerre with seven palms, two Gold and two Silver Stars, the Legion d'Honneur, and from the British, the 1939-45 Star with Battle of Britain Clasp, the Aircrew Europe Star and the British War Medal.

PETERSON Chesley Gordon   USAAF Nos. O-885114; O-36633; 9383A

PHILIPPART Jacques Arthur Laurent   Belgian No. 36329
He graduated from the Aviation Militaire Belge's 67^e Promotion on 30 November 1931. From 1939-40 he was an instructor at the Duerne Flying School, Antwerp. There is some doubt as to whether his was the aircraft shot down by Hpt Hans-Karl Mayer, who may have shot down A.W.A.Bayne rather than Philippart in this combat.

Corrections to claim list:
1940 25 Aug — his final victory may have been a Bf 109E rather than a Ju 88.

PHILLIPS James William Bristowe (not Bristol)
RAF Nos. 561185 (NCO); 47878 (Officer)
Born in Lucknow, India, in 1910, his home in England was in Sandown, Isle of Wight. He enlisted as an Aircraft Apprentice in January 1927, later being selected for pilot training. He is buried in Littlehampton.

PIERI Donald Mathew   RCAF Nos. R98120 (NCO); J9430 (Officer)
A US citizen, Don Pieri was born in Pecos, Texas, on 15 April 1919, then living in Elmhurst, Illinois. He attended Glenbard High School and Ohio State University, where he studied Mechanical Engineering. He also served as a Cadet at a Civilian Military Training Camp at Sparta, Wisconsin. He joined the RCAF in Toronto on 19 April 1941, attending 9 EFTS, St Catherine's and 2 SFTS, Uplands, qualifying as a pilot and being commissioned on 18 December 1941. He then attended CFS, Trenton, subsequently becoming an instructor at 14 SFTS, Aylmer. In October 1943 he was posted to 130 Squadron, RCAF, at Bagotville becoming a fighter pilot with this unit here, and later at Goose Bay. He was posted to the UK in April 1944, where he attended 57 OTU, August-October, and then went to 83 GSU, from where he was posted to 442 Squadron. He joined 412 Squadron on 18 March 1945. When he baled out, he did not become a POW as stated in *Aces High* (page 495). He was reclassified as 'Missing, believed killed' in November 1945, his fate never being ascertained, and his body not being found.

PIETRASIAK Adolf   RAF Nos. P784763 (NCO); P2093 (Officer)
He was born in Kosmin, near Deblin. Initially he trained as an airframe fitter with basic flying training, but later took an advanced course, following which he was posted to the 122 Eskadra in Kracow. He reached the UK on 27 June 1940, training at 58 OTU before joining 303 Squadron. However, during the summer of 1941 he flew with 92 Squadron, subsequently transferring to 308 Squadron. On 19 August 1941, after claiming a Bf 109 shot down, he was shot down in France. Avoiding capture, he returned to England via Spain and Gibraltar. In August 1942 he was posted to 317 Squadron, but in December attended the Polish Officers' School at Cosford, being

commissioned on 1 January 1943 (not in 1941 as stated in *Aces High*). He then became an instructor at 58 OTU until September 1943, when he rejoined 308 Squadron.

Corrections to claim list:
1941
2 and 4 Jul   W3245 (not W3248)

PIETRZAK Henryk

Born in Ruda Pabianicka (not Pabjanicka). He underwent his flying training with the 143 Eskadra, where on 2 July 1936 his PZL P.7A collided in mid air with that of kpr Zygmunt Najchman, who was killed instantly. Pietrzak was able to land his crippled aircraft in a field, for which he received a special commendation. In 1939 he was a flying instructor at the SPL in Deblin, flying PZL P.23 Karas bombers, and on the outbreak of war he was posted to an 'ad hoc' Karas Eskadra formed from the newly-commissioned 13th Class. Having reached France via Rumania and the Mediterranean, he flew with GC III/9 in the Lyon/Dijon area during the 1940 campaign. Following his tour with 306 Squadron, he flew with the Intensive Flying Development Flight at High Post, testing the initial Spitfire XIIs EN221 and EN222, prior to the introduction of this type into RAF service.

Additions to claim list:

1941					
16 Aug			UZ-N		
1942					
9 Oct			UZ-J		
31 Dec			EN128 UZ-N		
1944					
19 Jul	2	V-1s	PK-A Newchurch area		315 Sqn
22 Jul	1/2	V-1	"		"
23 Jul		V-1		2m W Lympne	"
28 Jul		V-1	PK-U 10m off Le Touquet		"

REVISED TOTAL: 7 and 2 (a) shared destroyed, 1 probable, 1 damaged, 4 and 1 shared V-1s destroyed.
(a) The PAF did not credit him with his claim of 25 September 1944 for a 1/3 share in a FW 190 destroyed.

PINCHES Maurice Henry   RAF Nos. 526493 (NCO); 49207 (Officer)

Born in 1918 in Shrewsbury, Shropshire, he lived in nearby Much Wenlock. He joined the RAF as an Aircrafthand/Armourer in November 1935, but remustered as a pilot after the outbreak of war, being trained to fly in Rhodesia, and commissioned from Sgt on 1 August 1942. He died on 24 October 1944.

Correction to claim list:
1944
17 May —   the 2 Ar 196s were damaged on water, rather than on land.

PINCKNEY David John Colin

In *Aces High*, page 497, it is mentioned that it had been believed that he had claimed two victories in Burma, but recent research had not confirmed this. The period of December 1941-January 1942 when he was operating with 67 Squadron was confused, and it is still possible that some records were lost. In *Wings Over Burma* by J.Helsdon Thomas (Merlin Books Ltd, 1984), the author, who was an engine fitter with 67 Squadron during this period, recorded that Pinckney told him that he had shot down one and possibly shot down, or damaged, a second on 23 December. He also recorded that Pinckney was believed to have shot down three Type 97 fighters (Ki 27s) before he was killed on 23 January 1942. If these claims are correct, Pinckney's total would be increased to seven destroyed.

Corrections and additions to claim list:

1940					
20 Oct-23 Nov — all claims in Spitfire IIAs (not Mark Is)					
1941					
23 Dec		e/a (a)	Buffalo	Rangoon	67 Sqn
		e/a Damaged (a)	"	"	"
1942					
23 Jan.	3	Ki 27s (a)	"	S Burma	"

REVISED TOTAL: 7 destroyed, 3 probables, 3 damaged, 1 destroyed on the ground.
(a) Provisional.

PISAREK Marian

He was born in Jasinowo Gorne in the mountains of southern Poland. He joined the Szkola Podchorazych Piechoty, and was commissioned in 1934, seeing service with the 1 Pulk Strzelcow Podhalanskich (1st Highland Fusilier Regiment). In 1935 he completed flying training at Centrum Wyszkolenia Lotnictwa in Deblin, and was posted to the 61 Eskadra Liniowa of the 6 Pulk at Lvov. After advanced training, he joined the 141 Eskadra of the 4 Pulk at Torun, fighting with this unit in September 1939 in support of Army Pomorze; from 3 September he became commanding officer of the unit. On 1 September he and another pilot shot down an Hs 126, beside which Stanislaw Skalski of the 142 Eskadra landed, capturing the maps and documents in the aicraft before the German crew could destroy them. As a result, Skalski is often credited with shooting down this aircraft. Pisarek is reported also to have shot down a PZL P.23 Karas light bomber in error during the campaign, mistaking it for a Ju 87. He arrived in England on 23 June 1940. When shot down on 7 September, his Hurricane crashed on a shelter behind a house in Loughton, Essex, killing three civilians.

Corrections and additions to claim list:

1939				
1 Sep	½	Hs 126	PZL P.11C	141 Esk
2 Sep		Hs 126 (not shared)	"	"
"		Do 17	"	"
4 Sep		Ju 87 Damaged (not destroyed)		"
1940 (insert)				
7 Sep			R4173 RF-T	
15 Sep			RF-V	
5 and 7 Oct			RF-U	
1941				
2 Jul		Spitfire IIB (not IIA)	P7446	
17 Jul			P8676	
22 Jul			P8341 ZF-A	
14 Aug			P8318	
20 Sep			W3702	
21 Sep			AB825	
13 Oct			W3798	

REVISED TOTAL: 11 and 2 shared destroyed, 1 probable, 2 damaged.

PLAGIS John Agorastos

He lived in Gadzema, Rhodesia, before the war.

PLAYER John Howard

He attended the University of Tasmania, obtaining a BSc in Engineering before joining the RAF. His DFC was gazetted on 16 July 1943, as was his radar operator's (81940 Flt Lt Alfred Lammer), who at this time had taken part in the destruction of four enemy aircraft; Lammer was to receive a Bar to his DFC on 29 October 1943, shortly after Player received his DSO. After the war, when 500 Squadron was renumbered as 249 Squadron at Eastleigh, Kenya, on 14 April 1946, equipped with Mosquito FB 26s, Player commanded the unit here and at Habbaniyah, Iraq, until August 1946 when the aircraft were grounded and all the crews were posted away.

PLEASANCE Harold Percival

On 10 July 1940 his was the only survivor of six Blenheim IVs sent to bomb a satellite airfield near Amiens. He was Mentioned in Despatches on 1 January 1945 and awarded an OBE on 14 June of that year.

PLINSTON George Hugo Formby

He was born at Teignmouth, Devon, on 10 November 1918, attending All Hallows School, Honiton, and the Royal Military College, Camberley, from 1931. In 1933 he was commissioned 2nd Lieutenant and served with the 2nd Battalion, Yorkshire and Lancashire Regiment. In April 1935 he resigned his commission and took flying instruction at a civil flying school in Bristol. In October he received a four year commission in the RAF, and in November attended 11 FTS, gaining his 'wings' in January 1936. In November of that year he was posted to 56 Squadron, and in April 1938 was promoted Flg Off. He transferred to 1 Squadron in July 1939 as an Acting Flt Lt, going to France with the unit in September. On 15 December he relinquished his acting rank and joined 607 Squadron, but on 10 May 1940 he was posted to 85 Squadron, on 18th becoming an Acting Flt Lt again; ten days later he was posted to 242 Squadron. He was reported to have done good work over Dunkirk at the head of 'B' Flight. However, when Douglas Bader took over the unit, he seems to have fallen out with the new CO, and it is suspected that, worn out by the May fighting, he was guilty of an act of insubordination when given Bader's "new broom" treatment. Certainly on 30 June he relinquished his acting rank again and had his seniority as a Flg Off reduced from 26 April 1938 to 26 October 1938, being posted to 6 OTU as an instructor. On 20 July he rejoined 607 Squadron, but on 2 August returned to 6 OTU, where he was promoted Flt Lt in March 1941. In July 1941 he joined HQ, 11 Group, from here going to the Merchant Ship Fighter Unit as a volunteer. On 6 April 1942 he transferred to supernumary duties with this unit, and was then posted to North Africa for operations, reaching HQ, 239 Wing on 14 July, and joining 250 Squadron on 17 September, after flying briefly with 3 RAAF Squadron to gain local operational experience. In November 1942 he became an Acting Sqn Ldr and commanding officer of 601 Squadron. On 20 March 1943 he went to HQ, RAF Middle East, transferring the following month to 2 SFTS in South Africa for a BOAC course. In June 1943 he joined 3 Aircraft Delivery Unit for transport flying duties. On 1 August 1944 he moved to 1 ADU, and in February 1945 to HQ(Unit), Transport Command as a supernumary, attending a course at the School of Air Transport. On 27 March 1945 he was posted to No 1 Ferry Unit, but in October he was released from the service.

Corrections and additions to claim list:
1940
11 May   ½   Ju 87 (not individual victory) (b)
   „   Hs 123 (c)
REVISED TOTAL: 6 and 2 shared destroyed.
(b) Ju 87B T6+MS of 8/StG 2; (c) An aircraft of 5(S)/LG 2, which was 20% damaged.

PLISNIER Andre Marie Alfred Frederick   RAF No. 100654; Belgian No. 50036
Andre Plisnier was born on 2 November 1920 at Wandre, Liège. He enlisted on 31 August 1939, joining the Fortress Artillery at Namur. By March 1940 he had already been promoted Sgt, but had volunteered for pilot training. On 14 May he was sent to flying school in France, from where he was moved to Morocco, then making his way to the UK by 5 August 1940. Here he enlisted in the RAFVR eight days later, being posted to 13 EFTS in December, and then 5 SFTS in April 1941. He completed his training at 58 OTU in July, then joining 131 Squadron. He was posted to 350 Squadron in November. He was hospitalized in October 1942, returning to 350 Squadron in February 1943. He then underwent a spell at 2 Tactical Exercise Unit as an instructor, again returning to 350 Squadron on 26 April 1944. Following his attachment to the USAAF, he instructed at the Belgian Training School and at 17 SFTS alternately until March 1946. He then joined the Belgian Inspectorate General for a brief period, before being posted to 525 Squadron in April. He was discharged from the RAFVR two months later, subsequently joining Sabena Airlines.

PLZAK Stanislaw   RAF Nos. 787502 (NCO); 102595 (Officer)
He was shot down over Southend on 28 November 1940 in Spitfire IIA P7566, by Bf 109Es of I/JG 26, surviving unhurt. When killed, he was flying P7771 over Mardyck.

Corrections to claim list:
1940
5 Sep and onwards he served with 19 Squadron, not 1 Squadron as indicated on the listing in *Aces High*.

PNIAK Karol
He volunteered for the air force in 1928, joining 2 Pulk Lotniczy in Kracow, before attending flying school in Bydgoszcz. He returned to Kracow in October 1930, joining the 22 Eskadra Liniowa. In 1931 he underook an advanced fighter course at Grudziadz, and then joined 122 Eskadra Mysliwska, becoming a member of a famous display team — 'Troika' (Three), which appeared at many air shows, undertaking aerobatics with the wingtips connected to each other by ropes. During 1932-33 he won a nation-wide competition for fighter gunnery at Grudziadz, and in August 1936 was posted to the Szkola Podchorazych Lotnictwa at Deblin. Completing the course here, he was posted to the 142 Eskadra at Torun, and was commissioned in August 1939. He flew 32 sorties during September 1939 before escaping via Rumania and Syria to France. Here he was posted to the centre at Salon, and then to Lyon-Bron airbase. However, by January 1940 he had already been sent to England, serving initially at 1 School of Army Co-operation, Old Sarum, from where he was posted to 6 OTU, Sutton Bridge, on 14 July. He was later posted from 306 Squadron to the AFDU, Duxford, on 18 April 1941 (not in November). On return from North Africa he became Chief Fighter Training Instructor at 58 and 61 OTUs. He was shot down four times during the war, twice baling out after suffering wounds. On return to Poland he settled in Szczakowa, near Kracow, working on a co-operative farm. He died on 17 October 1980.

Corrections and additions to claim list:
1939
3 Sep	¼	Hs 126	PZL P.11C		142 Esk
4 Sep		Ju 87 Damaged	„		„
„	⅓	Do 17 Damaged	„		„
1940					
15 Aug		Bf 109E Damaged (not Destroyed)			
„		Do 17 Probable (not Damaged)			
22 Aug	½ (not ⅓) Do 17 Damaged				
24 Aug —	believed to have been a Bf 109E-7 of 7/JG 3 which suffered 25% damage.				
11 Nov			V7296 DT-Z		

REVISED TOTAL: 6 and 2 shared destroyed, 2 probables, 2 and 2 shared damaged.

PONSFORD Ian Reginald   RAF Nos. 1577058 (NCO); 135684 (Officer)
He was commissioned on 16 December 1942, and was awarded an AFC in January 1956.

POPLAWSKI Jerzy
His birthplace was Model, in the Gostynin area, which is located some 70 miles west of Warsaw. He was commissioned as a light bomber pilot from the 13th Class, and it is unlikely that he did in fact, serve in Dyon III/4. On 6 November 1940 he crash-landed in Hurricane P3898.

Additions to claim list:
1941
4 Sep   P8543
16-27 Sep   W3230
13 Oct   AD119
8 Nov   W3798
1942
20 Apr   PK-Y

POTOCKI Wladyslaw Jan

He entered the 14th Class at the SPL in Deblin, thus not having obtained his commission prior to the start of the war. He escaped via Rumania and the Mediterranean to France, but applied to go to the UK, where he arrived in February 1940. In early 1941 he attended 8 EFTS, Montrose, then becoming a staff pilot at an aerial gunnery school, where on one occasion he landed a Defiant after an inexperienced gunner had shot away its control surfaces. He attended 58 OTU in autumn 1941, and was then posted to 306 Squadron, where he was commissioned in spring 1942. In December he replaced Flt Lt Pietrzak at the Intensive Flying Development Flight at High Post, testing the initial Spitfire XIIs, EN221 and EN222, flying these until February 1943. He then rejoined 306 Squadron, becoming a flight commander in June 1944. After commanding 315 Squadron at the end of the war, he commanded 309 Squadron. In 1948 he transferred to the RAF and in 1951 attended the Empire Test Pilots' School. He achieved second place at graduation, and became a test pilot at Farnborough, where he took part in testing Avro Vulcan jet bombers. He then emigrated to Canada, where he tested the ill-fated Avro Canada CF-105 Arrow fighter, becoming the first Pole to fly at Mach 2. He then worked on the Apollo programme in the USA, subsequently being employed by Rockwell on space projects. He retired to live in Columbus, Ohio, where he died on 23 December 1996.

Additions to claim list:
1943
24 Oct   AB212 UZ-V
1944
7 Jun   FZ196

POWELL Robin Peter Reginald

As a Wg Cdr he claimed two V-1s during July 1944. He was injured when his car collided with an army lorry on 10 October 1944, Flt Lt T.D.Tinsey being killed in this same accident. Upon recovery, he commanded 121 Wing of Typhoons from April to August 1945.

Additions to claim list:
1944
5 Jul   2   V-1s   Spitfire IX
REVISED TOTAL: 7 and 2 shared destroyed, 1 unconfirmed destroyed, 3 probables, 4 damaged, 2 V-1s destroyed.

POWELL-SHEDDEN (not SHEDDAN) George Ffolliott

He was originally born George Shedden Ffolliott Powell, but changed his name by deed poll on 9 August 1938. He was commissioned on 19 December 1936. On return to the UK in 1940 he was posted to 6 OTU for a refresher course before joining 242 Squadron as replacement for George Plinston. He died on 31 October 1994.

Additions to claim list:
1940
23 Jul   Ju 88 (a)   Hurricane I   off Great Yarmouth   242 Sqn
REVISED TOTAL: 5 and 2 shared destroyed, 2 shared probables.
(a) Aircraft of 4(F)/122.

POWERS MacArthur Jr.   2nd Lieutenant   USAAF No. O-884149

He was born on 19 March 1916, and graduated as a pilot with the RAFVR in March 1942. He transferred to the USAAF on 3 January 1943, and left the 324th Fighter Group in July, when he was posted to the US. He retired as a Lt Col in May 1963, and died on 3 February 1996.

Additions to claim list:
1942
4 Nov —   two claims made; Ofw Hans Lampater of I/SG 2 baled out of a Bf 109 and killed.
1943
18 Apr   P-40F   20

DE LA POYPE Roland   RAF No. F30616

PRCHAL Eduard Maxmilian   RAF Nos. 787982 (NCO); 112323 (Officer)

As a Sgt he worked as an instructor at 55 OTU in March 1941, moving to 54 OTU in mid June.

PRIHODA Josef   RAF Nos. 787541 (NCO); 110307 (Officer)
Attended 6 OTU in September 1940.

PRING Arthur Maurice Owen (not Own)
RAF Nos. 1258998 (NCO); 143237 (Officer)
He was born in Ealing, West London, in 1921, later moving to Berkhamstead, Hertfordshire. A student engineer before the war, he enlisted in 1940. His DFM was awarded on 16 February 1943. He was buried in Calcutta.

Additions to claim list:
1942
12/13 Oct — apparently he claimed two He 111s, not one. One of these was in fact the Z 1007bis identified in *Aces High*.
REVISED TOTAL: 7 destroyed, 2 damaged.

PROCTOR John Ernest   RAF Nos. 563641 (NCO); 44131 (Officer)
He entered the RAF in September 1929 as an Aircraft Apprentice at Halton. The Bar to his DFC was not awarded during the war. From February 1950-February 1952 he commanded 205 Squadron, flying Sunderlands from Seletar, Singapore, undertaking operations against Communist guerillas in Malaya. He also led a detachment to Iwakuni, Japan, for operations during the Korean War, and it was for his activities here that he was awarded the Bar on 17 April 1951. It appears that he was a Scot.

Corrections and additions to claim list:
1940
12 May   Bf 110 (not He 111) — aircraft of I/ZG 2
15 May —   this was an aircraft of I/ZG 52, which force-landed, 35% damaged.

PROVAN William Wright   RAF Nos. 1433915 (NCO); 124875 (Officer)

PUDA Raimund   RAF Nos 787623 (NCO); 69458 (Officer)

RABAGLIATI Alexander Coultate

Corrections and additions to claim list:
1940
3 Sep —   these were Blenheims of 25 Squadron, attacked in error, not Ju 88s.
1941
16 Aug   Hurricane I (not Mark II)
20 Aug onwards   Hurricane II

RABONE Paul Wattling
He was born in England, son of a New Zealand serviceman and an English girl, who moved to New Zealand with her husband after WW I. In 515 Squadron his radar operator was Flg Off F.C.H.Johns.

Corrections and additions to claim list:
1940
6 Nov   422 Flt (not Sqn)
1943
8 Sep   Mosquito VI (not Mark II)
?? Jul   3   Z.506Bs Damaged on water
1944 (insert)
21 Jun (not 22nd) — this was G9+NS of 8/NJG 1 which had just taken off from Eelde airfield.
          Uffz Herbert Beyer and crew were killed. Rabone was on a Day Ranger sortie.

RADOMSKI Jerzy
In France he served in GC III/10, not II/10. In the RAF he was known as 'George'. Early in 1956 he was an instructor with CFS Basic Flying Instructors' Course at South Cerney. Apparently he had trained as an instructor on rejoining the RAF, and instructed at an FTS until selected as a CFS instructor. Some time later he transferred to the catering branch after an unnecessary crash or accident. He died on 17 December 1978.

Corrections and additions to claim list:
1939
1 Sep   He 111 Damaged (a)   PZL P.11   113 Esk
?? Sep —   delete
1940
1 Jun   1/2   He 111   Morane MS 406   GC III/10
7 Jun —   delete
30 Sep   RF-H
1942
25 Apr and 6 May   BL631 SZ-F
26 Jul   JH-Z

RAE John Arthur
Born in Winnipeg in 1922; enlisted in the RCAF in 1940.

RAE John Donald
In the final line of the biographical notes in *Aces High*, it should read "..as an instructor at 57 OTU" (not 57 TU).

Addition to claim list:
1943
17 Aug — one of his victims was Ofw Hermann Hoffmann, whose Bf 109G-4 crashed west of Fruges.

RAMSEY (not RAMSAY) Charles Maurice RAF Nos 740915 (NCO); 106078 (Officer)
Charlie Ramsey enlisted in the RAFVR during 1937, and was commissioned from Flt Sgt on 19 August 1941. He was awarded a DFC on 15 July 1943 and a Bar to this on 26 July 1945. Postwar he served with KLM as an airline pilot, subsequently retiring to live in Holland.

Corrections and additions to claim list:
1943
25/26 Jan   (c)   V8632
11 Feb   EL187
1944
14/15 May   (d)
(c) With Sgt Morton as radar operator; (d) Aircraft of 1/KG 6, flown by the Staffelkapitän, Oblt von Manswarda.

RANGER Geoffrey Harold RAF Nos. 1150397 (NCO); 60082 (Officer)
Born in Dulwich, South London, in 1918, he then lived in Cheam, Surrey, attending Croydon High School and Whitgift School. He entered the RAFVR in April 1940, and was commissioned in 1941; he was posted to the Middle East in November. He is buried in the Tobruk War Cemetery.

Addition to claim list:
1941
12 Dec — his claim was identified as either a Bf 109 or MC 202. He was involved in a combat with MC 202s of 1° Stormo CT.

RANKIN James
He attended Royal High School, Edinburgh, then lived in Longridge, near Preston, Lancashire, before the war. He was commissioned on 16 April 1935. Promoted Flg Off on 16 October 1937, he served with 825 Squadron on HMS *Glorious*; he became a Flt Lt on 16 October 1939, and a Sqn Ldr on 12 January 1940. On leaving Biggin Hill in July 1943, he became o/c Fighter Wing, at Central Gunnery School until posted to 15 Fighter Wing. In January 1944 he helped form the Fighter Leaders' School at Milfield. He was confirmed in the substantive rank of Wg Cdr in October 1946, retaining the Acting rank of Grp Capt. In February 1948 he went to Dublin as Air Attache. He was promoted Grp Capt on 1 July 1952.

RANKIN Ronald
Corrections and additions to claim list:
1942
14 Sep and 25 Oct   T4983 W (not T)
10-14 Nov
28 Nov   "
3 Dec   T5038 V
12 Dec   EL240 F
17 Dec   T5038 V
                                                         T4983 W

RAPHAEL Gordon Learmouth
He was a nephew of Capt O.M.Learmouth, VC, a posthumous Royal Navy officer of WW I. His service number indicates that he joined the RAF on a Short Service Commission, as the RAFVR was not formed until July 1936. He became a Sgt Pilot in December 1935, and was commissioned on 20 January 1936. His radar operator during many of his engagements was 622688 Wt Off William Nathan Addison, DFC, DFM. Raphael was Mentioned in Despatches on 1 January 1945.

RATTEN John Richard
Correction to claim list:
1943
8 Apr   EN522 (not EW522)

RAWLINSON Alan Charles

The air fighting unit which he formed at the end of his Western Desert service was the Air Fighting School, Egypt, which he commanded in January and February 1942.

Corrections and additions to claim list:
1940		
19 Nov		L9044 is an incorrect serial for a Gladiator
1941		
25 Jan		Gladiator I (not Mark II)
3 Apr —	His logbook records:-	
	2	Ju 87s
		Ju 87 Probable
		Ju 87 Damaged
22 Nov —	His logbook records:-	
	2	Bf 109Fs
	2	Bf 109Fs Damaged

RAYMENT Kenneth Gordon   RAF Nos. 1269670 (NCO); 108000 (Officer)

Ken Rayment was born in Wanstead, Essex, on 11 March 1921, living in Woodford Green, nearby. On leaving school in 1937 he became a Merchant Navy deck officer on the Argentine run. He joined the RAFVR on 15 October 1940, commencing training at 17 EFTS in March 1941. He was then sent to Canada, to attend 32 SFTS at Moose Jaw, where he passed out top of his course. Commissioned in August 1941, he returned to the UK in September to attend 56 OTU at Sutton Bridge. At the start of December 1941 he joined 153 Squadron, but after a few days was sent to 62 OTU, East Fortune, for training as a night fighter. He returned to 153 Squadron in February, but in May 1942 was again posted to 62 OTU, where he remained until August. He rejoined 153 Squadron yet again, going out to North Africa with the unit during December 1942; on 2 June 1943 he was Mentioned in Despatches. He remained at Reghaia from July-September 1943 after leaving the unit, then returning to the UK, where he instructed at 51 OTU, Cranfield, until 19 April 1944. He then joined 264 Squadron, going to France with this unit on 11 August. His last flight in a Mosquito occurred on 20 September 1944, although he remained in France until late November. It appears that he was then seconded to BOAC, flying Lodestars until the end of 1945. In 1946 he transferred to BEA on its foundation, flying Oxfords and then Dakotas until 1947, and then Vikings. In March 1953 he began flying the Airspeed Ambassador, but subsequently he flew the turboprop Vickers Viscount (BEA 'Elizabethan' Class) as a Senior Captain. Considering retirement from flying, he began researching chicken farming. Finding that a fellow pilot was already operating such a farm, he arranged to fly as second pilot on a special charter flight in order to "pick his brains". The flight in question occurred on 6 February 1958, carrying Matt Busby's Manchester United football team home from Munich, Germany. The Viscount crashed in a snowstorm as it was taking off from Munich Airport with the death of many members of the team. Rayment was taken to hospital unconscious, with a broken leg and severe head and internal injuries. Subsequently the leg had to be amputated, but on 15 March, after seven weeks without recovering consciousness, he died — the 23rd fatality of the crash — in the Recht der Isar Hospital, Munich.

Corrections and additions to claim list:
1942			
24 Dec		V8631 (c)	Tunis Bay
1943			
16/17 May	He 111 (not Ju 88) (d)	EL166	20m N Bone
„	Ju 88 (as stated) (d)	„	15m N Bone
23/24 May	S 79 (not He 111 Probable)		45m NW Bone
24/25 May	(d)		Bone
23/24 Jun	(d)	EL179	Djidjelli
1944 (insert)			
10/11 Jul	(e)		10m N Portsmouth

REVISED TOTAL: 6 destroyed, 1 damaged, 1 V-1 destroyed.
(c) Plt Off Lanning as radar operator; (d) Sgt, later Plt Off H.D.Ayliffe, radar operator; (e) Flg Off Bone radar operator.

RAYNER Roderick Malachi Seaborne

On 6 November 1939 he shot down a French Potez 63 in error; fortunately, the crew survived.

Corrections and additions to claim list:
1940					
15 May		Bf 110 (a)	Hurricane I		87 Sqn
16 May	½	Bf 109E (b)	„		„
„ (not 17th)		Bf 110		Brussels area	„
19 May —	Do 17 claim made in P2683. He was then attacked by Fw Adolf Borchers of 1/JG 77				
	and his aircraft was damaged whilst near Tournai; he force-landed on return.				
20 May		Bf 110 (as listed) (c)	„		„
„		Bf 110 Damaged (c)	„		„
„		Bf 109E (as listed)	„		„

REVISED TOTAL: 8 and 2 shared destroyed, 2 damaged.
Aircraft of II/ZG 76; (b) Aircraft of I/JG 27; (c) Aircraft of I/ZG 26 involved in this engagement.

READ James Alfred Avory
He was commissioned on 5 April 1937. He died on 12 December 1979.

Additions to claim list:
1943

13/14 Jul		BT299 B	E Syracuse
14/15 Jul		BT300 C	E Catania (Z 1007)
		,,	NE Syracuse (He 111)
16/17 Jul		,,	E Syracuse
20/21 Jul		,,	

REES Stewart William
Born on 30 September 1923 in Cunderdin, Western Australia, he was a student in Fremantle when he enlisted in the RAAF on 7 December 1941. He trained at 5 ITS, 9 EFTS and 6 SFTS in Australia during 1942, being despatched to the UK in early 1943, attending the Aircrew Officers' School in April, 12(P) AFU in May, 1536 Beam Approach Training Flight in July, followed by 54 OTU, and then back to 12(P) AFU in August. Finally in February 1944 he was despatched to Italy to join 600 Squadron, where he served until January 1945. He then returned to the UK, becoming an instructor at 54 OTU in March. In June 1945 he was posted to RAF Cranfield, and in September to the RAF Police HQ. He left for home in November, where he arrived the following month, being released on 15 February 1946.

Additions to claim list:
1944
22/23 Dec — Ju 87D-5s E8+FK flown by Ofhr Hans Kölster and E8+KK flown by Fw Edgar Gerstenberger.

REEVES McKenzie   RCAF Nos. R143774 (NCO); J87156 (Officer)
On 28 March 1945 he was flying Spitfire XVI SM302 when hit by Flak. He was heard to report this over the R/T and announce that he intended to bale out, but had not done so when the aircraft crashed ten miles east of Haltern. He is buried in Nederweert War Cemetery, Holland.

REEVES Nevil Everard   RAF Nos. 748096 (NCO); 110797 (Officer)
Born in 1920 in Naunton, Upton-on-Severn, Warwickshire, he attended Hanley Castle Grammar School, Worcester. He enlisted in the RAFVR in spring 1939, subsequently being commissioned in late 1941. His DFC award date was 11 February 1943, the Bar to this on 14 May 1943, and his DSO was gazetted on 24 October 1944. His radar operator, 630959/54654 Plt Off Arthur Alexander O'Leary, was awarded a DFC and two Bars and a DFM. In 1946 Reeves served as an advisor with an RAF mission in Egypt.

Corrections and additions to claim list:
1943
26/27 Feb   Beaufighter IF (not Mark VIF)
1944
27/28 May — this was a Bf 110, G9+CR of 7/NJG 1; Uffz Joachim Tank was slightly wounded, the
              other two members of the crew being killed.
6/7 Dec   Mosquito XIX (not Mark XXX)

REID Donald George

Additions to claim list:
1942

2 Jun	GL-D
6 and 7 Jun	GL-A

REID Leonard Stanley
On arrival in the UK at the end of 1942, he was posted to 55 OTU as an instructor.

REID Wilmer Harry

Correction to claim list:
1943
27 Jul   1/3 (not 1/2)

RETINGER (not RETTINGER) Witold   Squadron Leader/Kapitan
Born on 4 April 1918 in Wiener Neustadt, Austria, of Polish parentage, he was educated in Dzisna, joining the SPL in Deblin as a member of the 13th Class. He was commissioned on 1 September 1939 as a fighter pilot, and almost at once escaped via Rumania and Malta to Marseilles. In France he joined the ECD He (led by Zdzislaw Henneberg) in defence of the Bloch assembly plant at Chateauroux, from where on 18 June 1940 he flew a Bloch

151 to Tangmere, England, with the rest of the flight. He was sent to 55 OTU, then to 308 Squadron. In 1942 he was posted as a flight commander to 303 Squadron, returning as commanding officer to 308 Squadron on 21 March 1944, leading the unit until November of that year. He then acted as Liaison Officer at 11 Group HQ. He was awarded the Virtuti Militari, 5th Class, the Cross of Valour and two Bars, and the DFC (the latter on 17 August 1944). Released after the war, he emigrated to South America, subsequently moving to the USA. He worked for Swissair, and then for Pan American Airlines for 25 years, becoming Transport Department Manager. He died of cancer in New York on 22 June 1982.

Additions to claim list:
1941		
7 Jul	P7629	
13 Oct	AB935	

REYNOLDS Robert Edward   RAF Nos. 1336622 (NCO); 125444 (Officer)

He was born on 2 March 1921 in Norwich, Norfolk, subsequently living at The Hyde, Hendon, North London. He enlisted on 4 April 1941, undertaking his flying training in Canada, and was commissioned in the RAFVR on 3 July 1942 whilst at 41 SFTS. Returning to the UK, he attended 3(P) AFU, South Cerney, and 42 OTU, Ashbourn, during the autumn; on 3 January 1943 he was promoted Flg Off, and in May was posted to North Africa. Here he joined 13 Squadron, flying Blenheim Vs (Bisleys) on coastal patrol and anti-submarine work, in May. There is no indication in the unit records that he was engaged with enemy aircraft at any time whilst operating with the squadron. In August 1943 he was posted to 242 Group Communications Flight, whilst in October he became PA to the AOC of the Group. On 1 December he joined 255 Squadron, being promoted Flt Lt on 3 July 1944. At the end of August he went to 338 Wing as a supernumary, and was posted from there to 210 Group, once again undertaking communications flying. He returned to the UK in November, and in February 1945 joined 54 OTU, Charterhall, as an instructor. On 30 April 1945 he was classified as permanently unfit for full flying duties, and in June was transferred to the Special Duties Branch of the RAFVR, then being trained for flying control work, attending 145 Flying Control Course at RAF Watchfield. In September he was posted for such duties to Manston, moving in November to Spilsby and in January 1946 to Andover. He was released in August 1946.

Corrections and additions to claim list:
1944		
7/8 Jul		Ancona
27/28 Jul		Rimini
1/2 Aug	KW154 YD-R	15m NE Ancona

(c) Ju 88A-4 F6+NP of 6(F)/122 (not 6(G)/122).

REYNOLDS Richard Henry

Born on 12 October 1923, he became a Wt Off Air Cadet in the Cambridge Squadron of the ATC, and won the Marshall's Flying School Challenge Board as Best Cadet of the Year, 1939. In 1941 he joined the Royal Navy under the 'Y' Scheme and was commissioned a Midshipman. He was loaned to RAF Fighter Command for a period, flying sweeps from Culmhead. He then served with 24 Wing (887 and 894 Squadrons) on HMS *Indefatigable*, but did not serve on HMS *Chaser*, as was incorrectly indicated in *Aces High*. He was awarded a DSC and Mentioned in Despatches. He served with 889 Squadron, but land-based at Schofields, Australia, training 24 ex-RAAF pilots on deck landings prior to their proposed transfer to the RANVR. From 1946 he was an instructor at the School of Naval Air Warfare, winning the Boyd Trophy. During the period 1947-51 he became a Diploma Graduate of the Empire Test Pilots' School, then undertaking test flying in the USA, and at Farnborough and Boscombe Down, for which he received an AFC. He undertook general service 1951-53, and then participated in an exchange with the US Navy, 1953-55, serving with Experimental Squadron VX-3. He was promoted Lt Cdr during 1954. On return to the UK he became commanding officer of 811 Squadron, then Lt Cdr Flying on HMS *Eagle*. Promoted Cdr in 1957, he commanded the Fleet destroyer HMS *Context*, and then became Commander (Air) on HMS *Ark Royal* until 1961. For the next three years he served as Fleet Plans Officer, Staff of the C-in-C, Far East. He returned to the UK in 1964 as Fleet Air Arm Drafting Commander and Directorate General of Naval Manning. 1971-76 saw him as Senior Naval Officer, Liverpool, and Directorate, Naval Public Relations. Having flown 5,000 hours in more than 100 different types of aircraft, he retired at the age of 53 and attended a Business Management Course at London Polytechnic. At the time of writing he was living in retirement in an Officers' Home in South Devon.

Corrections and additions to claim list:
1945		
1 Apr		'Zeke' recorded as Damaged, was destroyed (a)
4 May	1/2	'Zeke' (not 'Hamp')

REVISED TOTAL: 3 and 3 shared destroyed.
(a) He advises that the 'Zeke' listed as Damaged actually crashed onto HMS *Indefatigable* after he had gained hits on the port wing. It destroyed part of the ship's island structure, killing his cabin mate amongst others.

RIGLER Thomas Charles   RAF Nos. 904492 (NCO); 114032 (Officer)

He joined the service in October 1939. During June 1941 he flew W3215, the Marks & Spencer presentation Spitfire, 'The Marksman'. He was presented with a framed photograph of this aircraft by Marks & Spencer shortly before his death in 1986.

RILEY William

On 11 November 1939 he was posted as a Flg Off to 12 Group Pool, Aston Down, on a course, prior to joining 610 Squadron. He did not move to 145 Squadron from 302 Squadron in October 1940 as was recorded in *Aces High*, and widely elsewhere; the pilot who claimed with this unit on 7 November 1940 was a Flt Sgt or Plt Off Riley. Bill Riley was aged 25 when killed.

Corrections and additions to claim list:

1940						
21 Aug	(a)			R4095 WX-M		
19 Sep	1/3	Ju 88 (b)	Hurricane I			302 Sqn
7 Nov —	delete					
1942						
11 Jul		Ju 52/3m	Beaufighter IC	T4880 Q	Tobruk/Crete	272 Sqn

REVISED TOTAL: 9 and 3 shared destroyed, 1 or 2 probables, 1 damaged.
(a) This is recorded in the ORB as 'inconclusive', and may not have been treated as a probable; (b) Believed to be Ju 88A-1 WNr 2151, 3Z+GH of I/KG 77, shot down north east of Brandon; Uffz Dorawa and crew killed.

RIPPON Anthony John

On 9 September 1940 he joined 6 OTU from 4 Ferry Pilots' Pool.

ROBERTSON Frederick Neal

On 30 October 1939 he attended 12 Group Pool, Aston Down, for operational training.

ROBERTSON Graham David

On leaving the RCAF, he joined International Harvester Co in 1947, becoming Assistant Sales Manager, Hamilton, in 1964. In 1965 he became General Manager, Fed-quip Inc, and in 1968 became Vice President, Sales. He became President and Chairman of this company, which dealt with heavy construction, logging and mining equipment. In 1978 he became President and Chairman of the Canadian Association of Equipment Distributors, and Director of Fed-quip Inc. He was on the Board of Trade, Toronto. In 1943 he had married an English girl, who he had met in 1941. He died of leukemia in Toronto in 1987.

ROBERTSON Ronald James Harold   RAF Nos. 1253458 (NCO); 123304 (Officer)

Correction to claim list:
1942
25 Nov and onwards   Spitfire VC (not Mark VB)

ROBINSON Douglas Neville

Correction to claim list:
(a) Me 410A-1 U5+HE of 14/KG 2.

ROBINSON McClellan Eric Sutton

Additions to claim list:

1942	
2 Nov	HV314
1943	
14 Jan	960
25 Mar	116
2 Apr	ER171 AX-D
21 Apr	666

ROBINSON Michael Lister

He left 111 Squadron in September 1939, joining 11 Group Pool as a Flg Off instructor. Promoted Flt Lt on 24 September, he was posted to 85 Squadron on 16 March 1940 (not 87 Squadron). Evidence indicates that he claimed three Bf 109s on 6 September 1940, rather than one.

Addition to claim list:
1940
6 Sep   3   Bf 109Es (not 1)
REVISED TOTAL: 18 destroyed, 4 and 1 shared probables, 8 and 1 shared damaged.

ROLLS William Thomas Edward   RAF Nos. 745542 (NCO); 116492 (Officer)

ROOK Michael
On 28 April 1940 he joined No 6 Course at 6 OTU for operational training.

Corrections and additions to claim list:
Insert 1941 above 6 Oct

1942					
9 Nov	½	Ju 88 Probable	Hurricane IIC	Algiers harbour	43 Sqn

REVISED TOTAL: 2 and 1 shared destroyed, 1 and 1 shared probable.

ROSS Jack Kenneth   RAF Nos. 745307 (NCO); 79163 (Officer)
He was born in 1916 in Hornsea, East Yorkshire, but lived in Epsom, Surrey. He enlisted in the RAFVR in early 1939, and was commissioned in May 1940, attending 6 OTU from 18th of that month.

Additions to claim list:

1940					
2 Oct	sh	Do 17 (a)	Hurricane I	Wickham Market	17 Sqn
6 Oct	sh	Do 17 (b)	,,	,,	,,

REVISED TOTAL: 2 and 4-5 shared destroyed, 2 probables.
(a)This victory may have been credited only to H.P.Blatchford and A.W.A.Bayne; it was an aircraft of Stab/KG 2, Do 17Z-3 WNr 2659, U5+DM, which crashed at Pulham, south Norfolk, Oblt Hans Langer and his crew all becoming POWs; (b) Do 17Z-3 of III/KG 76 WNr 4221, F1+FN; all crew killed. (This aircraft was also claimed by pilots of 249 Squadron).

RUCHWALDY Desmond Fred
He lived in Hurstpierpoint, Sussex. He was killed in a flying accident on 21 May 1945, and is buried in Haycombe Cemetery, Bath.

Additions to claim list:

1944					
12 Jul		V-1	Mustang III	FB112 DV-R	nr Lydd	129 Sqn
,,		V-1	,,	,,	nr Lympne	,,
19 Jul		V-1	,,	FB395 DV-Y	3m NW Hastings	,,
22 Jul		V-1	,,	FZ184 DV-Z	,,	,,
18 Aug		V-1	,,	FB178 DV-R	15m off Boulogne	,,
29 Aug		V-1	,,	,,	sea, Boulogne-Dungeness	,,
,,	½	V-1 (a)	,,	,,	N Brenzett	,,
,,		V-1	,,	,,	1m off Boulogne	,,
,,		V-1	,,	,,	5m E Dungeness	,,

REVISED TOTAL: 7 destroyed, 3 probables, 6 damaged, 8 and 1 shared V-1s destroyed.
(a) Shared with AA.

RUDLAND Clifford Percival   RAF Nos. 745446 (NCO); 65998 (Officer)
He joined the RAFVR in 1938 (not 1939). He died in March 1996.

Correction to claim list:
REVISED TOTAL: 2 destroyed, 7 destroyed on the ground, 1 damaged on the ground.

RUSSEL Blair Dalzell

Correction to claim list:

1940		
25 Sep		P3647 was YO-U (not YO-V)

RUSSELL Ian Bedford Nesbitt
He joined the RAF on a Short Service Commission on 18 May 1936, training at 11 FTS, Wittering. Normally this would have involved four years service, followed by four years on the Reserve. The reason for his early release is not known, but he was not on the Air Force List in August 1939, although he was recalled in September as a Flg Off. He was posted to 245 Squadron, but on 14 May 1940 was despatched to France to join 607 Squadron. Later that same day the unit met 15 Hs 123s and 45 Bf 109Es over Louvain, claiming ten shot down for the loss of four Hurricanes. In fact two Hs 123s of II(S)/LG 2 were lost, but none of the escorting Bf 109s of II/JG 2 failed to return. It is believed that he was credited with four of the victories claimed on this date.

Corrections and additions to claim list:

1940					
14 May — possibly 4					
15 May	½	He 111 (not Do 17) (a)	Hurricane I	P2619 AF-D	607 Sqn
,,	½	He 111 (not Do 17) (a)	,,	,,	,,

(a) Aircraft of 9/KG 51 were involved in this action; Russell's Hurricane was hit by return fire and he was slightly wounded, undertaking a crash-landing.

RUSSELL Noel
He was promoted Flt Lt on 6 September 1944.

RUTKOWSKI Kazimierz
He was born in Warsaw in 1912, entering the Deblin SPL in the 12th Class, and being commissioned in 1939. During September he flew with the 36 Eskadra Obserwacyjina in the 3 Pulk, in support of Army Poznan. He escaped via Rumania to France, and thence to the UK, joining 306 Squadron on 4 September 1940. On 8 December he suffered serious burns in an accident in his Hurricane however. On 19 May 1941, having recovered and returned to the unit, he was shot down into the Channel in Hurricane Z3065, but baled out and was rescued. He served with 317 Squadron from May-August 1942, then commanding 306 Squadron until 13 March 1943. He received the Virtuti Militari, 5th Class, in October 1942 and the DFC in December. From March 1943- October 1944 he held a staff position at Northolt, during which time he regularly flew unofficially with the 61st Squadron, 56th Fighter Group, of the US 8th Air Force as part of a group of Polish pilots. On 11 December 1944 he became Wing Leader, 133 (Polish) Wing, holding this post until 30 January 1945. Due to reorganisation, he then became deputy commander until 17 July 1945. He entered the Wyzsza Skola Lotnicza in August 1945, studying there until April 1946. After release he settled in the UK. He also received the Cross of Valour and three Bars, and a US Air Medal.

Additions to claim list:
1941		
16 Jun		UZ-J
18 Dec		UZ-L
30 Dec		UZ-K
1942		
19 Aug —	first sortie	BL690
,, —	second sortie	AD451 JH-N
1943		
21 Jan and 15 Feb		UZ-K
1944		
18 Oct	(a)	FB360 SZ-K
7 Dec		HB886 PK-A

(a) One of six claimed by the Wing. These were in fact five Bf 109s of JG 102 on a training mission led by Ofhr Helmut Haugk in 'White 141'. In fact only Haugk's aircraft was actually shot down, the other four Messerschmitts all being crash-landed at once by their student pilots, as soon as the Mustangs attacked, to avoid being shot down!

RYDER Edgar Norman
He did not go direct from 56 Squadron to Kenley as Wing Leader in 1941. He left 56 Squadron to join 53 OTU as CFI on promotion to Wg Cdr, on 22 June 1941. He was posted from there to Kenley on 30 September 1941.

SABOURIN Joseph Jean Paul

Additions to claim list:
1942						
1 Jun	½	Ju 88 Damaged	Spitfire VB	326 ZX-A	Gambut	145 Sqn
8 Jun			,,	321 ZX-N		
12 Jun				339 ZX-M		
8 and 16 Sep				986 ZX-X		

SAGE Paul Christopher Wendover   RAF Nos. 1251728 (NCO); 113425 (Officer)
He was born in Stamford Hill, North East London, in 1914, living in Southgate, North London. He attended Bishop's Stortford College, Hertfordshire. He enlisted in the RAFVR, being commissioned from Sgt on 25 November 1941. In May 1942 he completed his first tour with 89 Squadron, and when subsequently awarded a DFC, the citation recorded that he had undertaken *"coastal fighter work including convoy patrols and night attacks on targets in Cyrenaica and Sicily during which one enemy aircraft was destroyed"*. This victory has not been found, and this may possibly relate to the destruction of an aircraft on the ground. His radar operator in 46 Squadron was Flt Sgt — later Plt Off — John Cockburn. The pair left 46 Squadron at the start of November 1943, returning to the UK where Sage was promoted Flt Lt on 25 November, and Cockburn Flg Off. Subsequently they were posted to 487 (NZ) Squadron, a Mosquito VI intruder unit forming part of 2 Group, 2nd TAF. On 22 February 1945 they took off from B-87 airfield, France, at 1110 hours during Operation 'Clarion' — a sustained attack on the German transport system; during this sortie their aircraft, HR356, was shot down and both were killed.

Additions to claim list:
1942	
29/30 Jun	X7745
28/29 Jul	X7709
1943	
14/15 Feb	EG-U

SAGER Arthur Hazelton

Before the war he worked in mines for two years before and between university. He then became a deckhand on a freighter for six months in 1938, reaching the UK. He worked for a time as a lift boy in a block of flats near Buckingham Palace, and then as a junior reporter. After the war he became assistant to a university professor, and then a producer of talks on public affairs for CBC. Subsequently he became assistant to a cabinet minister in Ottawa, and then executive of a fisheries association on public relations and conservation. He next became Director of Alumnii, International House, and a lecturer at university. He finally spent 20 years as an official of the United Nations, serving in New York, Africa and Rome, mostly dealing with assistance to developing countries. Following this post, he retired, and at the time of writing was living in France.

Additions to claim list:
1943

15 Jun	FW 190 Damaged	Spitfire IX	Fecamp	421 Sqn
22 Sep	FW 190 Damaged	Spitfire VB	Evreux	416 Sqn

REVISED TOTAL: 4 and 2 shared destroyed, 1 probable, 5 and 1 shared damaged, 1 damaged on the ground.

ST JOHN Peter Cape Beauchamp

He was posted to 5 OTU, Aston Down, on 23 March 1940, before joining 74 Squadron.

ST QUINTIN Perry Robert   RAF No. 40946

SAMOUELLE Charles James   Squadron Leader
RAF Nos. 1375201 (NCO); 113341 (Officer)

He was born in Islington, North London, leaving Acland Central School at 16 to work as a bell-hop in the Savoy Hotel. At the age of 17 he married a girl a year older than himself, then taking a job as a cocktail-fixer. Twin girls were born before he enlisted in the RAFVR in August 1940. He commenced training at IRW, Babbacombe, and ITW, Paignton, then undertaking his initial flight training at 6 EFTS, Brooklands Aviation, Sywell. He was posted to Canada in April 1941, attending 32 SFTS, Moose Jaw. He returned to the UK in August 1941 as a qualified pilot, attending 53 OTU, Llandow, and then joining 92 Squadron as a Sgt. He was commissioned in November 1941, accompanying the unit to the Western Desert in February 1942. Here during July he was, with others, initially attached to 80 Squadron until Spitfires became available. On one occasion he was shot down in error by his own wingman whilst strafing, and was captured by Italian troops; however, he managed to escape and return to his unit. When his tour ended in January 1943, he was sent to Heliopolis by Hudson, and then in a Liberator to the UK. In March he was posted to Air Ministry, and in June he commenced public relations duties, visiting over 100 factories to give talks. In September he was posted to 53 OTU, Hibaldstow, as CO of the unit's 2 Squadron, remaining there for a year. On 1 October 1944 he joined 41 Squadron as a flight commander, and on 22 January 1945 was posted to 130 Squadron as a Sqn Ldr. During this period he undertook much strafing of MET. At the end of the war he accompanied 130 Squadron to Norway. In August 1945 he returned to the Air Ministry to undertake PR duties again, and was seconded to the National Savings Scheme until his release in April 1946. He then became Deputy to the District Commissioner of the National Savings Committee, South East Region. He considered opening a nightclub, but rationing and catering restrictions made this impossible, and in July 1947 he was recalled to the RAF, undertaking an air traffic controllers' course. In September he was posted as Senior Controller at Hendon. He returned to flying in late 1948, joining 99 Squadron to pilot Avro Yorks during the Berlin Airlift. In November 1949 he commenced a flying instructors' course at CFS, and in May 1950 became a flight commander at 3 FTS, Feltwell, on Harvards. April-December 1952 he served as Chief Ground Controller at 14 FTS, Holme-on-Spalding Moor, then serving as squadron commander at 21 SAFS, Finningley, on Meteors, December 1952-February 1953. He spent the next 15 months on a Work Study Course at the College of Aeronautics, Cranfield, becoming the first RAF officer to receive such training. He then returned to the Air Ministry as Work Study Officer until June 1956, when he took up a similar post with 2nd TAF in Germany. During October-November 1958 he attended CFS, Little Rissington, and then served at 6 FTS, Ternhill, November 1958-April 1959. Subsequently he served as Wg Cdr Flying, Bruggen; CO Flying Training, Dishforth; CO of the Joint Services Warfare School, Old Sarum, and then at High Wycombe. He received an OBE in 1971, and retired, as stated, in February 1975. He then joined the training staff at British Steel. In 1980 he fell and broke his shoulder very badly, following which he took retirement. He died of kidney failure in March 1997.

Corrections and additions to claim list:
His logbook provides some corrections and additions to the previous claim list, which are recorded below:-
1942

17 Jul			BN126 EY-P
27 Jul	2	Ju 87s Damaged (not 1)	BM389 EY-C
19 Aug		Bf 109 (not Probable)	BR523(not BR323) QJ-E
"		Bf 109 Probable (not Damaged)	"
23 Aug			BR520 QJ-L
1 Sep	4	Bf 109s Damaged in two sorties	BR479 QJ-E
(not 3)			
3 Sep (not 2nd)			"

29 Sep (not 28th)			BR520 QJ-L	
7 Oct			,,	
9 Oct			BR479 QJ-E	
29 Oct			BR521 QJ-E	
2 Nov			,,	
9 Nov	Bf 109 Damaged	Spitfire VC	,,	
1943				
7 Jan	Bf 109F	Spitfire VC	,,	
11 Jan	½ MC 202	,,	,,	
13 Jan		,,	,,	
21 Jan		,,	ER528 QJ-E	
1945				
2 Mar			AP-B	
19 Mar			,,	
18-24 Apr			AP-F	

REVISED TOTAL: 10 and 1 shared destroyed, 4 probables, 11 damaged, 1 destroyed on the ground, 2 damaged on the ground.

SAMPSON Ralph William Fraser

Correction to claim list:
1944
7 Aug   Spitfire VII (not Mark VB)

SANDERS James Gilbert

On page 531 of *Aces High* in the biographical notes, the OTU in which he served in September 1941 was 53 OTU.

Correction to claim list:
1939
29 Dec   N2308 (not K2308)

SANDERS Philip James

His birthplace was Brampton, Chesterfield, Derbyshire (not Cheshire). The report of his accident on 20 September 1940 is incorrect. This occurred on 23 October, and was not due to combat damage. His batman had used 100 octane fuel to clean an oil stain off his tunic. The burns suffered when he attempted to light a cigarette were in fact relatively minor.

Correction to claim list:
1940
9 Sep   He 111 (not Probable)
REVISED TOTAL: 6 destroyed, 1 unconfirmed destroyed, 2 probables.

SANDERSON John G.

Addition to claim list:
1942
22 Oct —   This is believed to have been an MC 202 of 90ᵃ Squadriglia, 10° Gruppo, 4° Stormo CT from which
                Mllo Antonio Sacchi baled out.

SATCHELL William Arthur John   Group Captain

He was born in Grimsby, Lincolnshire, and attended Denstone College. He joined the Leicester Yeomanry (TA) as a Trooper, serving from 1926-30. He acted as i/c 60/63 Wing at Merville in May 1940, just as the German attack commenced. He returned to the UK via Boulogne on 21 May, and was then sent to 5 OTU on a refresher course before being posted to 603 Squadron as commanding officer. From here he was transferred to 302 Squadron. On leaving Malta, he was posted to the Middle East, where in June 1943 he commanded 73 OTU as a Grp Capt. In late 1950 he was awarded the Polonia Rostituta by the Polish Government-in-Exile in London — the highest award possible. In 1954 he was station commander at RAF Cardington, the recruit entry and kitting-out base.

SAUNDERS Cecil Henry

Additions to claim list:
1942

3 Aug			583 ZX-T	
3 Sep	Bf 109 Probable	Spitfire VB	BP987	145 Sqn
11 Sep			AR287	
22 Oct			AB502	
25 Oct			EP692	

REVISED TOTAL: 5 and 2 shared destroyed, 3 probables, 3 damaged.

SAUNDERS John Henty William

In September 1941 he served briefly with 71 OTU as a Flt Lt instructor, but returned to 3 RAAF Squadron during the month.

SAVILLE Eric Cowley

He attended 71 OTU in September 1941 before joining 2 SAAF Squadron. He is buried in Naples, Italy.

Additions to claim list:
1942
5 Sep   EV368
22 Oct   FR214

SCHADE Patrick Alfred   RAF Nos. 785018 (NCO); 147354 (Officer)

He was posted to 52 OTU as a Flt Sgt instructor in September 1942 (not 62 OTU), and after being commissioned was moved to the AFDU in July 1943. On 31 July 1944, as a result of his collision, his aircraft crashed at Sandhurst Lane, Bexhill, Kent. He is buried in Uxbridge, Middlesex, which was listed as his home during his RAF service.

Additions to claim list:
1942
26 Jun   (c)
1944

Date		Claim	Aircraft	Serial	Location	Squadron
17 Jun	½	V-1	Spitfire XIV	RB180	20m N Hastings	91 Sqn
1 Jul		V-1	„	NH701	Horsmonden	„
7 Jul		V-1	„	RM620	3m NW Rye	„
16 Jul		V-1	„	RM656	SE Dymchurch	„

REVISED TOTAL: 12 (or 13 and 1 shared) destroyed, 2 (or 3 and 1 shared) probables, 2 damaged, 3 and 1 shared V-1s destroyed.
(c) 2 claims made against MC 202s for one loss; aircraft of 155° Gruppo, 51° Stormo CT, Mllo Gino Runci.

SCHMIDT Dallas Wilbur

Correction to claim list:
1942
13 Nov   EL236 Z(not J)

SCHRADER Warren Edward

Addition to claim list:
1943
17 Dec —   the two Bf 109Gs were aircraft of 10/JG 27, flown by Lt Holger Lummerding and Fhr Friedrich Thiel.

SCHWAB Lloyd Gilbert

He died on 15 February 1960.

SCOTT Allan Hugh   RAF Nos. 1119429 (NCO); 143726 (Officer)

SCOTT Desmond James

From 8 FTS he was posted to 56 OTU on 9 December 1940; he moved to 3 Squadron on 20 January 1941. He was Mentioned in Despatches on 1 January 1945. He remained in the RAF until 1947, ultimately serving in Bomber Command. He then became an air adviser to the Greek Air Force until 1949. He died in October 1997.

SCOTT Donald Stuart

He attended 6 OTU in March 1940 before joining 73 Squadron.

Corrections and additions to claim list:
1940
13 May   ¼   Do 17 (not ⅓ e/a) (a)
14 May   (b)
    „   Ju 87 Damaged
15 May   (c)
REVISED TOTAL: 6 and 2 shared destroyed, 1 unconfirmed destroyed, 4 damaged.
(a) This was Do 17P 4N+FH of 1(F)/22, flown by Oblt Rudolf Sauer, shot down west of Reims; (b) Aircraft of I/StG 76; (c) Engagement with I/ZG 2; 3 and 1 unconfirmed claimed — 2 actually lost.

SCOTT Ernest

He was born on 30 December 1917, and educated in York. He worked as a fitter in an engineering works until he joined the RAF as an Aircrafthand in 1935. He was selected for pilot training, attending 15 FTS and qualifying as a pilot on 1 May 1939. He joined 222 Squadron in October 1939 (not June 1940). From 1975 efforts to excavate his aircraft by enthusiasts were refused by the Ministry of Defence on the basis of his parents' wishes. The family were traced, his sister and others then seeking permission to excavate, but these requests were also refused. An appeal was then made to HRH Prince Charles, following which excavation was undertaken by a Ministry team. Scott's remains were found still in the cockpit, and were buried with full military honours in Margate Cemetery, Kent, on 1 February 1991.

Correction to claim list:
1940
3 Sep   X4275 (not Y4275)

SCOTT-MALDEN Francis David Stephen   RAF Nos. 754343 (NCO); 74690 (Officer)

He enlisted in the RAFVR in June 1939, and was commissioned on 3 October of that year.

Correction to claim list:
1940
23 and 29 Nov   Spitfire IIA (not Mark I)

SCOULAR John Evelyn

On return from France in 1940 he instructed at 6 OTU from 24 June as a Flt Lt. He was Mentioned in Despatches on 1 January 1945.

Corrections and additions to claim list:
1940
23 Apr				Senon-Reims
11 May —	He 111s of II/KG 53 were involved in this action.			
13 May		He 111 (not Damaged)	N2721 W	Reims area
15 May	½	He 111 (not individual victory) (d)		
19 May		He 111 (e)		
„	½	He 111 (not individual victory) (e)		

REVISED TOTAL: 14 and 3 shared destroyed, 1 unconfirmed destroyed, 3 damaged.
(d) A1+LK of 2/KG 53, attacked near Grandpre and crashed SE Vouziers; Oblt Walter Klaue, pilot; (e) Believed to be Ju 88s of I and II/KG 51. 4 and 1 unconfirmed claimed; 2 shot down and 2 damaged in fact.

SELBY John Beauchamp   Group Captain
RAF Nos. 901085 (NCO); 88705 (Officer)

He was born in Chelsea, London, and educated at South Place, Bexhill, and the Oratory School, Reading. On leaving school he sold advertising in the London *Evening Standard* newspaper, then moving to Manchester to become a BBC radio announcer. He tried to get into films before enlisting in September 1939. He was commissioned in December 1940 and posted to 253 Squadron in the Orkneys, before joining 73 Squadron in North Africa; he took command of this unit on 1 October 1942. On leaving 23 Squadron, in late 1943 he joined the SOE and was parachuted into Yugoslavia as air liaison expert to Tito, joining Brigadier Fitzroy MacLean. He later returned to North Africa to train a Yugoslav Hurricane squadron for the Balkan Air Force. He returned to Yugoslavia during 1944, being landed by submarine on this occasion; he was subsequently decorated by Tito. Late in the war, as a Grp Capt, he commanded a base in the Middle East, and after the end of hostilities, accompanied MacLean's mission to Austria. He returned to the BBC in 1947, becoming Director of European Programmes with the Overseas Service. He then opened a garage business in Rome, but returned to the UK to become Managing Director of Gresham Linley in the City of London. In 1954 he went back to the Middle East as export manager for Turner Newall, based in Baghdad. In 1970 he set up as a business consultant in Geneva, Switzerland, until 1978, when he retired to the South of France. He died in 1990. He was described as having been *"large, plump and jolly"*.

Corrections and additions to claim list:
1942
25/26 May	(b)		BM975 F		
8 Jun			BE568		
28/29 Jun	(b)				
3 Jul	Ju 87 Damaged	Hurricane IIC	BE554	Alamein	73 Sqn
7 Sep	e/a Probable	„	BN410	Maaten Bagush airfield	„
„	e/a Damaged	„	„	„	„

REVISED TOTAL: 5 destroyed, 1 probable, 2 damaged.
(b) These two claims have been listed as 'probables'. However, detailed research indicates that they were both confirmed, and this corresponds with his DFC citation, as well as with the identification of the second victim.

SEWELL Alfred Jack

He was killed on 3 October 1943 over Yarmouth, Maine, USA, when his Corsair I, JT190, collided with his wingman.

SEWELL Herbert Scott   RAF Nos. 745811 (NCO); 86667 (Officer)

He enlisted in the RAFVR late 1938/early 1939. He was promoted Flt Lt on 12 October 1942, having been posted from RAF Ouston to 53 OTU. He received an AFC.

SHAW Harry   Flying Officer   RAF Nos. 1491400 (NCO); 182110 (Officer)

Born in 1924, he was commissioned in June 1944, receiving promotion to Flg Off on 18 December, and to Flt Lt on 18 December 1947. His DFC was gazetted on 8 May 1945, but with effect from 15 January of that year.

Corrections and additions to claim list:

1944						
4 Jul		V-1	Tempest V	JN875 US-P	10m W Newchurch	56 Sqn
10 Jul		V-1	”	EJ532 US-H	8m N Pevensey	”
12 Jul		V-1	”	EJ548 US-G	N Tonbridge	”
18 Jul	½	V-1 (a)	”	”	10m S Maidstone	”
28 Jul		V-1	”	JN875 US-P	edge Tunbridge Wells	”
5 Aug	½	V-1 (b)	”	JN867 US-H	E Hastings	”
”	½	V-1 (b)	”	”	SW Tunbridge Wells	”
27 Aug		V-1	”	EJ548 US-G	nr Ham Street	”
28 Aug		V-1	”	”	”	”
29 Aug		V-1	”	EJ658 US-C	Cranbrook	”
31 Aug		V-1	”	EJ548 US-G	nr Rye	”

REVISED TOTAL: 2 and 3 shared destroyed, 8 and 3 shared V-1s destroyed.
(a) Shared with a Mustang: (b) Shared with Spitfires.

SHAW John Thornhill   Wing Commander
RAF Nos. 748190 (NCO); 108962 (Officer)

He was born in Worksop, Nottinghamshire, and attended Nailsworth College, Adelaide. He joined the RAFVR in May 1939. On return from North Africa, he joined 57 OTU as Chief Instructor before going to 122 Squadron. In January 1945 as a Wg Cdr he served with 55 OTU. In 1953 he led a wing of Venom FB 1s from 2nd TAF during the Queen's Coronation Review of the RAF.

Addition to claim list:

1943		
15/16 and 17/18 Apr		HW750

SHEAD Harold Frederick William

He joined the RAFVR in March 1939.

SHEEN Desmond Frederick Burt

During 1955-56 he was Wg Cdr Flying at Leuchars. Following his service with Transport Command, he went to New Delhi, India, as Air Adviser to the UK High Commissioner. Shortly after his return to the UK, he left the service to join BAC/British Aerospace as Administrator in respect of the BAC 111 and Concorde marketing teams. His spent three seasons flying with the Red Arrows, then flying Jaguars in Germany; he later became an airline pilot with Britannia Airways.

Corrections and additions to claim list:
1940
15 Aug — the claim listed for a Ju 88 should have been for a Bf 110, which he reported carried drop tanks, which blew up.
1941
13/14 Mar   X4596 (not K4596)

SHEPHERD John Bean   RAF Nos. 803581 (NCO); 104447 (Officer)

His service number indicates that he enlisted in the Auxillary Air Force before the war, and possibly commenced training in April 1939, when the AuxAF started training selected NCOs as pilots.

Additions to claim list:

1944					
20 Jun		V-1	Spitfire XIV		610 Sqn
22 Jun	½	V-1	”		”
7 Jul		V-1	”		”
9 Jul		V-1	”		”
12 Jul		V-1	”		”
29 Jul		V-1	”		”
4 Aug	½	V-1	”		”

REVISED TOTAL: 8 and 5 shared destroyed, 1 and 1 shared probables, 2 and 1 shared damaged, 5 and 2 shared V-1s destroyed.

SHIPARD Mervyn Charles

Additions to claim list:
1941
1/2 Nov   X7540
1943
8/9 Jan   Beaufighter IF
16/17 Jan and 2/3 Mar   Beaufighter VIF

SIMPSON Peter James

Educated at Mayfield College School, he was commissioned on 1 April 1939, and was posted to 11 Group Pool on 24 October. He commanded 145 Wing from September 1943-February 1944, and thereafter 135 Wing in June 1944. In May 1945 he was CO of 58 OTU. In late 1956 he led the Tangmere Hunter Wing (1 and 34 Squadrons) to Cyprus for the Suez operation. In 1959 he was Air Attache in Copenhagen, Denmark. He retired on 5 March 1966 (not 1968) and died on 13 November 1987.

Addition to claim list:
1940
18 Aug   P3399

SINCLAIR Gordon Leonard

He was posted to 5 OTU as an instructor on 22 June 1940 before joining 310 Squadron. He was awarded the Czech War Cross in December 1940.

Corrections and additions to claim list:
1940
26 May —   one of these Bf 109Es was unconfirmed (a)
27 May   He 111 unconfirmed   Spitfire I   19 Sqn
   „   'Do 215' unconfirmed   „   „
1 Jun   Bf 109E (not Bf 110)
   „   ¹/₂   Bf 109E (not Bf 110, and not individual victory)
   „   He 111 unconfirmed
   „   Do 17
REVISED TOTAL: 7 and 1 shared destroyed, 4 unconfirmed destroyed, 1 damaged
(a) These Bf 109s were claimed in two seperate sorties. The second was an unconfirmed claim made against an aircraft which had just shot down one of 19 Squadron's Spitfires.

SING John Eric James   Wing Commander

In November 1940 he went to 56 OTU as a Flt Lt instructor. On return from North Africa in 1943, he returned to 56 OTU in November as a Wg Cdr o/c Training Wing. It was 16 Squadron that he commanded from January 1951-February 1952 (not 14 Squadron). He died on 9 March 1996 at Northam, Devon.

SINGLETON Joseph   RAF Nos. 967740 (NCO); 69431 (Officer)

SIZER Wilfred Max

He joined 58 OTU on 28 December 1940, but on 15 January 1941 moved to 56 OTU.

Corrections and additions to claim list:
1940
? May —   delete
19 May   ¹/₃ (not ¹/₂) Hs 126 (b)   Hurricane I   P2834 AK-S   S Tournai   213 Sqn
   „   ¹/₃ Hs 126 Damaged   „   „   „   „
   „   ¹/₃ (not ¹/₄) Hs 126 (c)   „   P2673   W Aalst   „
20 May   ¹/₄ (not ¹/₃) Do 17 (d)   „   P2802   Courtrai   „
   „   ¹/₅ Hs 126 (e)   „   P2673   nr Neuville   „
1943
10 Jul   93 Sqn (not 152 Sqn)
REVISED TOTAL: 7 and 6 shared destroyed, 1 probable, 9 and 1 shared damaged.
(b) Aircraft of 2(H)/41 flown by Uffz Walter Ehremann; (c) Aircraft of 2(H)/41 flown by Uffz Gerhard Meermann; (d) A Do 215B of 3(F)/ObdL, flown by Uffz Erich Luther; (e) Aircraft of 2(H)/23Pz.

SKALSKI Stanislaw

No collective award of the Virtuti Militari was made to the 142 Eskadra in September 1939, as is incorrectly stated in *Aces High*. On first arriving in England, Skalski was posted initially to 1 School of Army Co-operation at Old Sarum, moving on to 6 OTU on 14 July 1940 to prepare for fighter operations. It is not correct that 302 Squadron was not yet operational when he was posted to 501 Squadron. The Polish Fighting Team was organized by *plk* Stefan Pawlikowski, the Polish Liaison Officer with Fighter Command, and was commanded by Wg Cdr Tadeusz Rolski, with Skalski as flying leader. He was also not the first Pole to command an RAF squadron, but the second. Soon after his release from prison, he wrote *Black Crosses over Poland* regarding his experiences during the 1939 campaign. In 1996 a short biography was published in Poland under the title *Miedzy niebem a pieklem (Between Heaven and Hell)*. This is a wordplay, as Polish has the same word for 'Heaven' and 'Sky'. The motto for the book is taken from his own words *"The shorter my speech, the longer you will remember."*

Corrections and additions to claim list:
1939

1 Sep —		delete. This Hs 126 was shot down by other pilots of 141 Eskadra; Skalski landed alongside and removed the maps and documents from it.		
3 Sep	$1/4$	Hs 126 (the second claim on this date was shared, not an individual victory)		
4 Sep	$1/3$	Do 17 Damaged	PZL P.11C	142 Esk
9 Sep —	delete			

1940
30 Aug		SD-B	
1 Sep		P2329	

1941
24 Jul		UZ-K
19 and 21 Aug		UZ-Y
17 Sep		UZ-N

1942
10 Apr		SZ-R	
25 Apr		SZ-S	
3 May		BL646 (not LB646) SZ-R	

1943
28 Mar and 2 Apr		EN459 ZX-1
4 Apr		EN315 ZX-6
6 May		EN267 ZX-5

REVISED TOTAL: 18 and 3 shared destroyed, 2 probables, 4 and 1 shared damaged.

SKINNER Wilfred (not William) Malcolm   RAF Nos. 740078 (NCO); 68722 (Officer)
On 17 May 1941, when commissioned, he was posted to 53 OTU. As a POW, he was held in Stalag Luft III.

SMART Thomas
He was born in 1919, and attended the Birkenhead Institute before entering the RAF. In October 1941 he was posted from 64 Squadron to 58 OTU, but next month was posted to 73 OTU, Aden, as a Flt Lt.

SMIK Otto   RAF Nos. 787314 (NCO); 130678 (Officer)
He is commemorated on the RAF's Runnymede Memorial.

SMITH Alan   RAF Nos. 754069 (NCO); 102999 (Officer)

SMITH Albert Ivan

Addition to claim list:
1942
11 Mar		T4886

SMITH Leonard Alfred   RAF Nos. 1376328 (NCO); 182872 (Officer)
He was born in Bow, East London, in 1920, and worked as a storeman before enlisting in 1940. He was commissioned on 19 June 1944; his DFM was gazetted on 23 January 1945.

Corrections and additions to claim list:
1943

24 Apr		Spitfire VB (not Mark VC) ER787			
25 Apr	Bf 109	„	ES142	Pont du Fahs	152 Sqn
5 May	Bf 109 Probable	„	„	nr Mateur	„
19 and 25 Jul		Spitfire VC	ES308		
17 Sep			JL240		
19 Sep		Spitfire IX	MA501		

1944
5 Nov		LB734

REVISED TOTAL: 6 and 1 shared destroyed, 1 probable, 2 damaged.

SMITH Robert Rutherford
He attended a course at 1 METS in September 1942 before joining 112 Squadron. As a POW he was held in Stalag Luft III.

Correction to claim list:
1942
10 Dec		FL880 (not FR287)

SMITH William Alexander

He was born in Lucknow, India, and was educated in Scotland, reading engineering at Edinburgh University. He left before obtaining his degree in order to join the RAF in May 1937. In February 1942 he replaced A.C.Rawlinson as CO, Air Fighting School, Egypt. When this was expanded into 1 METS, El Ballah, in April 1942 he became i/c Air Fighting Flight until September. He was then posted to AHQ, Egypt, until December, when he went to Malta. On 10 March 1943 he returned to HQ, Middle East, where he remained until June 1944. He was then sent home to the UK, joining HQ, Transport Command. In July he attended 17 SFIS, Cranwell, on a twin engined conversion course, then going to 105 (Transport) OTU in October. He served at 11 Ferry Unit from January-August 1945, then attending 108 (Transport) OTU to convert to Dakotas. He joined 187 Squadron in September 1945, and when this unit was disbanded in December 1946, moved to 53 Squadron. He served in several appointments and commands thereafter, including that of Wg Cdr Flying at Fassberg, Germany, 1951-53, and station commander at Ouston in 1956. He died in RAF Hospital, Ely, on 21 November 1990.

Addition to claim list:
1940
17 Feb   EP257 V-W

SMYTHE George   RAF Nos. 565977 (NCO); 47752 (Officer)

He enlisted as an Aircraft Apprentice in January 1932, later being selected for pilot training.

SNOWDEN (not SNOWDON) Ernest George

RAF Nos. 745043 (NCO); 101031 (Officer)

He enlisted in the RAFVR in February 1939.

SODEN Ian Scovill

Ian Soden was born in 1917 in Winchcombe, Gloucestershire, and attended Woodbridge School, Suffolk. He subsequently lived in London, and at Combe Down, Bath, Somerset. He attended the RAF College, Cranwell, September 1934-August 1936, and was commissioned in December 1937. During the fighting in France on one occasion he jumped from a trench as the airfield was under attack, and leapt into the nearest aircraft, not knowing whether it had been refuelled or not, and took off after the raiders. He flew five times on 18 May 1940, on the fourth occasion shooting down one of three He 111s over the airfield, and then was forced to land. He took off again at 1930 hours in N2437, but was not seen again; he had been shot down near Vitry by Bf 110Cs of II/ZG 76 as he was taking off, and had crashed outside the airfield perimeter, being killed, He was buried at Bioche-St Vaast, near Arras. The C-in-C, 11 Group, noting that he had claimed six victories, made a strong recommendation for the award of the DSO. Fighter Command responded that this was inadmissable unless he had been alive at the date of the recommendation. During June a "quibble" was raised that he had technically been missing, rather than known to be dead at the date. A long correspondence followed, since only Victoria Crosses and Empire Gallantry Medals could be awarded posthumously, On 22 June Archibald Sinclair, the Secretary of State for Air, approved the award as it had already been communicated to relatives. The award of a DFC to Leslie Clisby was approved on a similar basis, but it was noted that these were irregular awards, and the situation should not be allowed to happen again. HM King George VI signed the awards, but noted that there should be no further such, as it would be *"bound to have unfortunate repercussions in the other services"*. The award was gazetted on 26 August 1940.

Corrections and additions to claim list:
1940

17 May	Do 17 (not Ju 88) (a)	N2437	nr Cambrai
„	(b)	„	
18 May	(c)	„	
„	(d)		
„	(e)		nr Louvain
„	(f)		

(a) Do 17Z of 6/KG 76; Lt Otto Grister crashed at Vitry; (b) 4 and 2 unconfirmed claimed; I/KG 54 lost 3 He 111Ps; (c) Do 17P of 3(F)/10 flown by Uffz Horst Liebe; (d) Do 17P of 4(F)/14 flown by Lt Alexander Schreiner; (e) 2 claims made in this engagement; 1 Bf 109E of 6/JG 2 lost, Uffz Wilhelm Mahs; (f) Aircraft of 9/KG 54; Uffz Otto Ellinghaus.

SOGNNES Helge   RAF No. N106

SOLOGUB (not SOLLOGUB) Grzegorz   RAF No. P1624 (not P1627)

Born in 1918, he entered the SPL at Deblin in the 14th Class. He was evacuated to Rumania with a group of other cadet officers in September 1939, reaching France and then the UK, where he underwent further training before being commissioned during 1940. He served as an instructor at 58 OTU after his first tour with 306 Squadron, returning to the latter unit where he became a flight commander in 1944. During the latter part of 1944 he flew in 302 Squadron as a supernumary Flt Lt. He received the Virtuti Militari, 5th Class, in September 1944, and the DFC in August 1942, together with the Cross of Valour and three Bars and a US Air Medal. He settled in Britain after the war and is believed to have died in 1991.

Additions to claim list:		
1941		
27 Sep		UZ-Y
30 Dec		UZ-O
1942		
16 Apr		UZ-V

SOPER Francis Joseph

He enlisted as an Aircraft Apprentice in September 1928. After service in France, he instructed as a Flt Sgt at 6 OTU from 28 May 1940, being commissioned by November of that year.

Corrections and additions to claim list:		
1940		
10 May	(d)	L1905 H
11 May	(e)	"
12 May	(f)	L1686 (g)
14 May	(h)	
15 May	Bf 110 (i)	
17 May	(j)	L1905 H (k)
19 May		L1925 (l)

REVISED TOTAL: 11 and 4 shared destroyed, 1 shared unconfirmed destroyed, 2 and 1 shared damaged.
(d) Do 17Z of 7/KG 3; Uffz Wolfgang Gräfe; (e) 5 claims; 2 losses by I/ZG 26; (f) 1 Bf 109E of 2/JG 27 lost against several claims; (g) Own aircraft damaged by Bf 109s and force-landed on return; (h) Aircraft of I/JG 53; (i) 5 and 1 unconfirmed claimed — 4 aircraft of III/ZG 26 crash-landed; (j) 5 and 2 unconfirmed claimed — 3 of V(Z)/LG 1 lost; (k) Own aircraft hit 30 times; returned and force-landed; (l) Whilst attacking the first He 111, L1925 was hit in the engine by return fire and he was obliged to crash-land.

SOWREY John Adam

He attended 55 OTU in December 1940, then 56 OTU in January 1941. After serving with 80 Squadron, he was posted to 71 OTU in early 1943, then attending a course at CFS, Salisbury, Southern Rhodesia.

Corrections and additions to claim list:		
1941		
15 Jun a.m.		W9293
" p.m. —	may have been a Probable	
1942		
21 May		AK-M
23 May and 10 Jun		AK-F

SPARKE Philip Donald Julian

He was commissioned in the Royal Navy as Midshipman(A) on 4 July 1938.

SPORNY Kazimierz   Flight Lieutenant/Kapitan

He was born in 1916 and entered the Szkola Podchorazych Rezerwy Lotnictwa, graduating in 1936 as an NCO, and becoming an instructor. In September 1939 he escaped to Rumania, and from there to the UK via France. He completed training at 5 OTU, then being posted to 213 Squadron. On 19 October 1940 he transferred to 302 Squadron where he served until 1942. On return to the UK after service in North Africa, he joined 306 Squadron, and on 7 November 1943 received the Virtuti Militari, 5th Class. He remained with the unit until the end of the war, becoming a flight commander, and receiving a DFC on 9 February 1945. He also received the Cross of Valour with three Bars, and a US Air Medal. He is believed to have died since.

Additions to claim list:		
1941		
4 Sep		WX-B
1943		
7 Apr		EN267 ZX-5
22 Apr		EN261
1944		
24 Jun		UZ-W

SPURDLE Robert Lawrence

He died on 5 March 1994.

SPURGIN Arthur Leslie Mervyn

A tobacconist before the war, he enlisted in the RAAF on 24 May 1940, attending 2 ITS and 5 EFTS before being despatched to the UK to complete his training. Arriving in October 1940, he attended 3 SFTS until February

1941, then 3 PRC, followed by 54 OTU in March. In May he was posted to 68 Squadron (not 29 Squadron), where he remained until posted to the Middle East in early 1942. Here he joined 89 Squadron in April. He completed his tour in August 1943 and was returned to the UK, being posted to 63 OTU as an instructor in September. In April 1944 he began the journey home to Australia where he arrived in July, being posted the following month to 5 OTU. His stay was short, and during the month he moved to RAAF Bradfield Park. In November he was posted to 2 Reserve Personnel Pool, and from there on 10th of the month to 87 Squadron, RAAF, to fly PR Mosquitoes. He remained with this unit until his discharge on 30 October 1945.

Correction to claim list:
1943
7/8 Feb   Beaufighter VIF T8311 (not V8311)

SROM Leopold RAF No. 787682
On 21 October 1940 he attended 6 OTU (which became 56 OTU whilst he was there) as a Sgt.

Correction to claim list:
1942
4 Feb   AD423 (not AD412) NN-Q

STAFFORD John Harry
His birthplace, New Lynn, is near Auckland. He was brought up in Rotorua, a cousin of Eric Doherty, and attended boarding school with Gray Stenborg. He departed for the UK in January 1943, attending 11 PDRC in March, 7(P) AFU in June and 55 OTU in August, before joining 486 Squadron as a Sgt in November. In February 1944 he was posted to the Propeller Test Division of de Havilland as a test pilot, returning to 486 Squadron in April. He was promoted Wt Off in June and was commissioned in July, becoming a flight commander in February 1945. On one occasion he flew through a high tension cable, his Tempest then being hit by light Flak; nonetheless, he managed to return to base. He left the unit for HQ, 83 Group, in May 1945, having just received his DFC, and was then posted to 80 Squadron. He was repatriated in December 1945, and released in 1946. He then married the sister of a 486 Squadron pilot who had been lost in action, becoming a roading contractor for 25 years and director of a real estate practice. In 1970 he gave up roading to concentrate on real estate. At the time of writing he was partially retired, living in Rotorua.

Addition to claim list:
1945
22 Feb — this was WNr 331486 of 13/JG 27; Lt Gerhard Schindler baled out, wounded
12 Apr — the FW 190 claimed was a D-9 model

STAPLES Michael Edmund RAF Nos. 742463 (NCO); 83242 (Officer)
He enlisted in the RAFVR in November 1938, attending 5 OTU in June 1940.

STAPLETON Basil Gerald
He was posted to 58 OTU from 603 Squadron in March 1941.

Correction to claim list:
1940
29 Aug
17 Oct-11 Nov   Spitfire IIA (not Mark I)

STAPLETON Frederick Snowden
He was born in Stamford Hill, North London, and lived in Reading before the war. He attended Downing College, Cambridge. In 1933 he joined the RAFVR as a Sgt, receiving a university entrant commission in the RAF in 1936. He served initially with 3 and 87 Squadrons, and then on the staff of 50 Group during the early months of the war. He attended 58 OTU for a refresher course in April 1941 before joining 54 Squadron. After his service at Hornchurch, he spent the remainder of the war in South Africa as an instructor and CO of 42 Navigation, Gunnery and Bombing School. He then became Deputy Director, Operational Requirements, in 1945. In 1947 he attended the RAF Staff College, then becoming Grp Capt Ops at Fighter Command in 1948. The following year he was a sector commander in Fighter Command, then commanding RAF Wunstorf, Germany, in 1951. In 1953 he became Chief Instructor at the RAF Flying College, Manby, while in 1955 he attended the Imperial Defence College. 1956-58 he commanded Northern Sector, Fighter Command, while in 1958-59 he was SASO, 13 Group.

STARK Lawrence William Fraser RAF Nos. 1058229 (NCO); 148445 (Officer)

STARR Norman John
In 23 Squadron he flew with 116967 Flg Off George Oswald Lace, DFC, as his radar operator. He was serving

with 142 Wing in Holland when killed on 8 January 1945. His brother Harry commanded 253 Squadron during the Battle of Britain, but was killed in action on 31 August 1940.

Corrections and additions to claim list:
1943
7/8 Jan - 2/3 Mar   DD687 YP-E
1944
10/11 Jun — the Me 410 (or Me 210) was claimed on the ground, not in the air
29 Jun (not Jul)   V-1
REVISED TOTAL: 4 destroyed, 1 probable, 2 damaged, 2 destroyed on the ground, 1 V-1 destroyed.

STARRETT Henry John   RAF No. 40188
He was promoted Flg Off on 16 February 1940 and Flt Lt a year later.

Addition to claim list:
1940
31 Oct   P3729

STEEGE Gordon Henry

Correction to claim list:
1941
3 Apr —   V3937 was an Airspeed Oxford I, not a Hurricane; this serial is therefore clearly recorded in error; the correct serial has not been ascertained.

STEERE Harry   RAF Nos. 564595 (NCO); 46016 (Officer)
He was from Wallasey, Cheshire, and entered Halton as an Aircraft Apprentice in September 1930, remustering as a pilot at later date.

Correction to claim list:
1940
27 Sep and 28 Nov   Spitfire IIA (not Mark I)

STEHLIK Josef   RAF Nos. 787701 (NCO); 104693 (Officer)

Corrections and additions to claim list:
1941
18 Jun   Bf 109 Probable   Hurricane IIB   Z3019   312 Sqn

STENBORG Gray
On arrival in the UK he attended 58 OTU in November 1941, then being posted to 11 Group Pool, and in December to 485 Squadron. The following month he was moved to 111 Squadron. In April 1943 as a Flg Off he attended No 5 Fighter Leaders' Course at Charmy Down.

Corrections and additions to claim list:
1942
30 Apr   (a)
1943
23 Sep —   MB620 was a serial allocated to a Firefly I for the Fleet Air Arm; clearly therefore, this serial has been recorded in error.
(a) One of these FW 190s was flown by Oblt Wilfried Sieling of Stab/JG 26, who was killed, crashing near Gravelines.

STEPHEN Harbourne Mackay   RAF Nos. 740095 (NCO); 78851 (Officer)
He was born in 1916 (not 1914). During September 1939 he attended the 11 Group Pool as a Sgt for fighter training. In 1958 he became General Manager of the *Sunday Express* on transfer from Glasgow to London. He moved to Thompson Newspapers at the invitation of Roy Thompson in 1960, becoming General Manager at Grays Inn Road and the *Sunday Graphic*. At the year's end he was sent to Lagos, Nigeria, to run a Thompson publication, the *Daily Express*, for nine months, then returning to London to assist in the transfer of the *Sunday Times* from Fleet Street to Grays Inn Road. In 1963 he became Managing Director of the *Daily Telegraph* and *Sunday Telegraph*, where he remained for 23 years until his retirement.

STEPHENS Maurice Michael

Corrections and additions to claim list:
1940
12 May   Ju 87   L1610
     "   Do 17 (a)
     "   Ju 87 (b)
14 May   Ju 87 (c)   N2546 QO-S
     "   Bf 109   "

	Hs 126 (d)		
18 May	Do 17 (e)	"	S Douai
20 May	Do 17 (f)	P3449	SE Cambrai
"	Hs 126 Damaged (g)		
1941			
9 Dec	Hurricane I (not Mark II) Z4415		
1942			
10 Oct —	second claim	EP338 A(not EP706 L ; that was flown for the first claim only)

(a) Believed to be a Do 17Z of 8/KG 77, flown by Lt Konrad Hengsboch; (b) 8 and 1 unconfirmed claimed; I/StG 2 lost 2; (c) 11 Ju 87s claimed; I(St)/TrGr 186 lost 8; his Hurricane was damaged and he force-landed near Mauberge, later taking off and returning; (d) Aircraft of 1(H)/11; (e) 3 claims — 2 aircraft of 2/KG 76 lost: (f) Aircraft of 5(F)/122, Uffz Karl Beyer; (g) Aircraft of 3(H)/41 badly damaged and force-landed.

STEPHENSON Leslie   RAF Nos. 1132759 (NCO); 118959 (Officer)

Born in Langley Moor, County Durham, in 1921, he enlisted in December 1940, and was commissioned in January 1942. His radar operator was 120955 George Arthur Hall, of Pudsey, Leeds, West Yorkshire. They instructed at 51 OTU in early 1944, before joining 219 Squadron on 3 March.

Additions to claim list:
1943
11/12 May	EL174
23/24 May	V8816

STEVENS Richard Playne   RAF Nos. 740527 (NCO); 87639 (Officer)

Educated at Hurstpierpoint College, Sussex, he served with the Palestine Police before the war, while his NCO service number suggests that he enlisted in the RAFVR in July 1937. It seems likely that he learned to fly at 16 E & RFTS, Shoreham, and then obtained a flying job at Croydon. On 28 October 1940 as a Sgt he was posted from 6 AACU to 6 OTU for operational training before joining 151 Squadron. It appears that the stories regarding his family being killed in the 'Blitz' may have been exaggerated, for it was noted when he was killed that he had married Mabel Hyde of Tunbridge Wells, and left a son.

Addition to claim list:
1941
15/16 Jan	V6934

STEVENSON Peter Charles Fasken

On 18 October 1941 he moved from 55 OTU (as 5 OTU had become) to CFS, Upavon, as an instructor.

STEWARD George Arthur   RAF Nos. 580149 (NCO); 45375 (Officer)

He enlisted in the RAF in 1936.

Corrections and additions to claim list:
1940
19 May — this Bf 109E was an aircraft of I(J)/LG 2.
21 May — this Hs 126 was 5D+DK of 2(H)/31Pz.
6 Oct — this was a Do 17Z-3 WNr 4221m F1+FN of III/KG 76; the crew were killed.
(This aircraft was also claimed by pilots of 249 Squadron).

STEWART Kenneth William

He was posted to the UK in November 1941, attending 6 SFTS from January 1942, then becoming an instructor at 29 EFTS from July 1942. In July 1943 he was posted to 3(P) AFU, and in November to 11(P) AFU. After this long period of instructing, he finally attended 54 OTU in May 1944, teaming up with NZ421827 Flg Off Harold Edward Brumby of Auckland (a pre-war civil servant), the pair joining 488 Squadron in September to commence operations. During the night of 27/28 December 1944 they saw two Ju 87s, but their Mosquito was hit by Flak, and they force-landed at Melsbroek, Belgium. The aircraft turned over and broke up, but they were unhurt. They were repatriated in September 1945 and released in November. After the war Stewart became a barrister and solicitor in Dunedin, but died on 3 August 1960.

Correction to claim list:
1945
24/25 Feb - 7/8 Apr	NT263 (not MT263)

STOKOE Jack   RAF Nos. 748661 (NCO); 60512 (Officer)

When he first joined the RAFVR, he attended 26 E & RFTS.

STOREY William John

On the second sortie of 5 March 1943, he led his flight of six Hurricanes back over Akyab to *"have another look"*.

The Ki 43s seen were all below, and the 135 Squadron pilots were able to bounce the top trio of Japanese fighters, all of which were claimed shot down.

Correction to claim list:
After the claim recorded for 23 February, insert '1943' before the claims on 5 March.

STORRAR James Eric

When he sought to join the RAF, his mother helped him to put up his age by one year, as he was too young. He joined 55 OTU on 9 December 1941, posted in from 57 OTU as a Flt Lt. On 27 May 1943 he attended a Central Gunnery School course. On 15 November 1943 he joined 53 OTU as an air firing instructor, where in December he became CFI (not CF1). During 1946 when commanding 239 Wing in Italy, he occasionally flew a Yak 9, No 72/7087, marked 'JAS'; this was an ex-Bulgarian aircraft, the pilot of which had defected. Upon release, he studied at Edinburgh University to become a vet, finally retiring from this profession in 1990. He died on 29 March 1995, aged 73.

Additions to claim list:

1941				
6 Jan		E		
19 Feb —	first claim			
"	Ju 88 Damaged	V7553"	Benghazi	73 Sqn
1943				
18 Aug-18 Sep		MH358		

REVISED TOTAL: 12 and 2 shared destroyed, 1 unconfirmed destroyed, 2 and 1 shared probables, 3 damaged, 1 and 8 shared damaged.

STOTT John Phillip

He was commissioned Temporary Sub Lt(A) with seniority from 4 June 1943. He was Mentioned in Despatches on 31 July 1945.

Addition to claim list:

1945	
12 Apr	DV119

STRATTON William Hector

He joined 6 OTU as an instructor on 28 May 1940. Postwar in the RNZAF he commanded the base at Ohakea. Subsequently he became Air Member for Personnel, then Head of NZ Defence Staff at Canberra, Australia, followed by a similar post in London. He completed his career as Chief of Air Staff, RNZAF, with the rank of Air Vice-Marshal, CB, CBE.

Addition to claim list:
1940
14 May — the Ju 87 was an aircraft of 2/StG 77, claimed over Le Cheine.

STRICKLAND James Murray

He was born in 1918, returning to the UK to attend King's School, Bruton. He was posted to France on 16 May 1940, where three days later he was shot down in Hurricane P2687 by Bf 109Es of 2(J)/LG 2. He baled out, wounded in one arm, and was shot in the leg by French troops as he parachuted down. He was killed when his Spitfire struck the roof of a dispersal hut at Portsmouth, and crashed into the ground.

STUCKEY Vincent Allan Jackson   RAF No. 41490

Addition to claim list:

1940	
8 Aug	K8022

STYLES Lawrence (not Laurence) Hinton   RAF Nos. 580300 (NCO); 44882 (Officer)

He enlisted in the RAF in August 1936 as a Direct Entry pilot. In March 1953 he commanded an Air Traffic Control unit.

Additions to claim list:

1943	
21/22 Jan	V8630 (b)
24/25 Jun	EL174 (b)
1944	
17/18 Mar	(c)
28/29 Aug and 3/4 Oct	(d)

(b) with Plt Off (later Flg Off) L.Smith as radar operator; (c) with Flg Off J.Ritchie as radar operator; (d) with Flg Off H.J.Wilmer, DFM, as radar operator.

SURMA Franciszek

In 1937 he joined the 12th Class at the SPL, Deblin, following which he was posted to the 2 Pulk in Kracow for operational training. He was commissioned on 31 August 1939. On 20 October 1940 he was shot down in P3893 (not P2983). His decorations included the DFC and the Cross of Valour with three Bars.

Corrections and additions to claim list:

1940					
28 Oct		He 111 Damaged (not Probable)		P3893	
1941					
26 Mar				V6999	
27 Jun	$\frac{1}{2}$	Bf 109E on ground (not Probable)			
„	$\frac{1}{2}$	Bf 109E Probable on ground (not Damaged)			
22 Jul			Spitfire IIB	P8317 ZF-C	
			(not Mark IIA)		
16 Sep				AB930 ZF-J	
20 Sep		Bf 109F and 1 Probable (not 2 confirmed)		AB825	
27 Sep and 12 Oct				AB825	

REVISED TOTAL: 5 destroyed, 3 and 1 shared probables, 1 damaged, 1 shared destroyed on the ground, 1 shared probable on the ground.

SURMAN John Clarke   RAF Nos. 1167383 (NCO); 64929 (Officer)

Born on 12 June 1921 in Guildford, Surrey, Johnny Surman attended the Royal Grammar School, and then worked for Glyn Mills Bank in London. He joined the RAFVR in August 1940, attending ITW at Weston-Super-Mare, and then 10 EFTS. He was commissioned in April 1941 after completing his training at 5 FTS, Ternhill, on Masters. In May 1941 he attended 60 OTU at Leconfield and East Fortune, joining 125 Squadron in July to fly Defiants, and later, Beaufighters. In June 1942 he returned to 60 OTU as an instructor, but in November moved to 54 OTU, Charter Hall. In March 1943 he was posted to 604 Squadron, from where in May he attended an air firing course at 1490 Flight, Ayr, with his radar operator Flt Sgt (later 178927 Plt Off) Clarence Edwin Weston, who was commissioned in early 1944. In October 1944 Surman attended 2 FTS, Montrose, on an instructors' course, and in January 1945 became an instructor at 15(P) AFU, Babdown Farm, near Tetbury, Gloucestershire. He undetook his last flights in May 1945, after which, as redundant aircrew, he was trained for Provost duties with the RAF Police. In mid 1945 he was posted to Hamburg, Germany, where he remained until demobilised in January 1947. He then returned to the bank — by then Williams and Glyns — and entered the International Division which he eventually rose to control. He retired in 1981 and at the time of writing continues to live in Surrey in the same house in which he has resided since 1954.

SUTTON Fraser Barry

On return to the UK in 1945 he served first with 57 OTU, moving in May to 61 OTU.

SWALES Cecil Jack Ormond (not Ormande)

On arrival in the UK in 1941, he first went to 3 PRC, and then in December to 16 Course at 58 OTU. On leaving 185 Squadron in November 1942 he was posted to 1 METS, El Ballah, as a gunnery instructor, then going to CFS, South Africa, in June 1943.

SWEETMAN Harvey Nelson

Sweetman worked as a clerk before the war. After enlisting in the RNZAF, he attended 2 EFTS from May 1940, then sailing for the UK in November. On arrival he attended 58 OTU in December, and in February 1941 joined 234 Squadron; a month later he moved to 485 Squadron. He was commissioned in March 1942 and posted to 486 Squadron as it was forming. On 16 April 1943 his aircraft was hit by Flak over Le Havre and he crash-landed at Selsey Bill on return. His tour ended in July 1943, when he was posted to 59 OTU as an instructor, but a month later he joined Hawker Aircraft. He rejoined 486 Squadron in February 1944. In August 1944 he was recommended for a Bar to his DFC, but this was not awarded. In January 1945 he returned to Hawkers, then attending 3 Course at the ETPS. He returned to New Zealand in February 1946, becoming CFI at Ohakea in June.

Corrections and additions to claim list:

1942					
23/24 Jul	(a)			SA-R	
19 Dec				SA-Y	
1943					
8 Feb				SA-Z	
9 Apr				SA-R	
1944					
16-18 Jun				SA-A	
19 Jun				„	SW Hawkhurst
27 Jun	V-1 (second)		Tempest	JN821 SA-H	N Bexhill

29 Jun	"	NE Rye
30 Jun (not 29th — second claim)	JN801 (not	7-8m N Ashford
	JN810) SN-L	
4 Jul	SA-M	
7 Jul (½ claim)	SA-L	
	SA-D	6m W Ashford (not North)
18 Jul	SA-A	Hastings/Bexhill
9 Aug	SA-F	Hastings area
16 Aug	JN732 (not	12m NW Dungeness
	EJ693) SA-I	

(a) This aircraft was a Do 217E-4 of 5/KG 40, WNr 4279, F8+CN, ; Oblt H.Viess and his crew all became POWs. The victory was credited jointly to Sweetman and 409 Squadron, RCAF.

SZAPOSZNIKOW Eugeniusz

It appears that he was born on 17 July 1917 (not 1916) in Warsaw. There is no sure confirmation that he claimed an He 111 Probable in September 1939, but some accounts indicate this. His Virtuti Militari, 5th Class, was awarded to him by General Sikorski on 18 September 1940.

Additions to claim list:

1940		
31 Aug		V7242 RF-B
7 Sep-7 Oct — all claims		V7244 RF-C
23 Sep —	believed to have been a Bf 109E-7 of 3/LG 2 which landed in France, 7% damaged.	
7 Oct	Bf 109E Damaged (not Probable)	

REVISED TOTAL: 8 and 1 shared destroyed, possibly 1 probable, 1 damaged.

SZCZESNY Henryk

He was posted to SPL in Deblin as an instructor in 1937. His victories in mid September 1939 were gained in a PZL P.11G — a substantially modified P.11 with enclosed cockpit and more powerful engine and armament — rather than a P.24. He died on 25 July 1996 in London.

Corrections and additions to claim list:

1939			
2 Sep	Do 17 Probable	PZL P.7A	Deblin Group
	Do 17 Damaged		"
"		"	
14 Sep		PZL P.11G	
15 Sep		"	
1940			
13 Aug		K9871 ZP-O	
11 Sep		X4167	
5 Oct	Spitfire II (not Mark I) P7363		
1-5 Dec		P7363	
1941			
After 14 Jul insert:-			
1943			
4 Apr		BS514 PH-U	

REVISED TOTAL: 8 and 3 shared destroyed, 1 probable, 2 damaged.

TALALLA Cyril Lionel Francis   RAF Nos. 785048 (NCO); 130674 (Officer)

Born in Malaya in 1921 and educated at the Victoria Institution, Kuala Lumpur, he later lived in Hamilton, Ontario, Canada. He attended 55 OTU in January 1942, and was commissioned from Sgt on 16 July of that year. In November 1943 on leaving 118 Squadron he instructed at 53 OTU.

TALBOT Robert Henry

Additions to claim list:

1940		
19 Dec-5 Jan 1941		P3721
9, 10 and 16 May		V7484
31 May	Z.1007 claim	W9322

TAMBLYN Hugh Norman

He attended Butke Public School, Yorktown, Yorktown Collegiate School and the Provincial Institute of Technology, Calgary.

TAYLOR Edwin Murray   RAF Nos. 742129 (NCO); 85259 (Officer)

He enlisted in the RAFVR in 1938, in February 1941 joining 152 Squadron as a Plt Off from 52 OTU. He was promoted Flg Off on 18 August 1941.

TAYLOR Frederic (no 'k') Frank

Born in 1918 in Newbury, Buckinghamshire, he lived in Hermitage in the same county, attending Bloxham School, Banbury. He was commissioned in the Reserve of Air Force Officers on 24 November 1937, attending 4 E & RFTS, Brough, September-November 1937. On 9 July 1938 he joined 107 (Bomber) Squadron, but on 23 September went onto the Reserve until mobilized in December 1939. He is then believed to have instructed at an E & RFTS. It is likely that he was given brief training on Hurricanes before departing for the Middle East.

Addition to claim list:
1941
26 Feb   V7671

TAYLOR John Stuart   RAF Nos. 911467 (NCO); 60090 (Officer)

The son of the Reverend Percy Taylor of St Olaves, Suffolk, he joined the RAFVR in September 1939. He was aged 23 when killed.

Corrections and additions to claim list:
1942
11 Jul   290 ZX-A
22 Aug   583 ZX-T
12 Sep   986 ZX-X
18 Sep   147 ZX-Y
20-29 Oct   327 ZX-R
1943
12 Jan (b)   EP880
8 Feb   EP579
22 Feb   ER552
26 Feb   EP704
1 Mar   ER199
7 Mar —   first combat   ER228
  „   —   second combat   ER199
12 Jul   EP466 (not EP966)
(b)The MC 200s involved in the engagement were from the 13° Gruppo CT, not from the 16° Gruppo, as shown in *Aces High*. Sottoten Plinio Pellegrini (78ª Sq) and Serg Sergio Vanello (82ª Sq) both killed.

TAYLOR Norman   RAF Nos. 742827 (NCO); 101500 (Officer)

He was born in Chellaston, Derby, in October 1919, joining the RAFVR in January 1939. Following his CAM-ship victory on 1 November 1942, he baled out 550 miles from Gibraltar and nearly drowned. On 29 April 1948 he was in a Harvard T.2B, KF569, when it spun in following an engine failure as it approached Wunstorf, Germany; he and his passenger were killed.

Corrections and additions to claim list:
1940
15 Aug   ½   Ju 88 (destroyed, not damaged)
7 Oct   Bf 110 Damaged   Hurricane I   601 Sqn
1941
25 May —   the Bf 109 claimed was identified as an E model
   „   —   The claim appears to have been credited as a Probable, rather than a Damaged; however, in his logbook he
           lists 2 destroyed on this date — a Bf 109 and a Bf 110. (a)
13 Jun   Z2745 (not Z3030)
16 Jun   „   (not Z3357)
1942
1 Nov   V7070
REVISED TOTAL: 6 (or 7) destroyed, possibly 1 probable, 2 damaged.
(a) The squadron was engaged with III/JG 3, which does not appear to have suffered any losses in this engagement.

TAYLOR-CANNON Keith Granville

He was born in Omahau (not Oamaru), Central Otago, and applied for aircrew training on 6 October 1940 whilst still at school. He began training at ITW, Levin, on 13 April 1941, and then started flying at 1 EFTS, Taieri, in late May. On 22 July he was despatched to Canada, attending 6 SFTS, Dunsville, Ontario, where he was promoted Sgt and qualified as a pilot on 7 November. Shipped to the UK, he was posted to 3 PRC, Bournemouth, and then 56 OTU, Sutton Bridge. He then joined 486 Squadron on 24 March 1942. He became a Flt Sgt on 1 February 1943, having attended a course at 1529 Beam Approach Training Unit, Collyweston. On 20 April he was commissioned, and on 20 October 1943 was promoted Flg Off, whilst on 11 February 1944 he became a Flt Lt. He had flown 239 operational sorties on Typhoons by this date, when the unit converted to Tempests and his tour ended. He then joined 4 TEU at Annan, Dumfries, as an instructor, later moving to 3 TEU in Cumberland, and then to Honiley, Warwickshire. In August he returned to 486 Squadron at 150 Wing airfield, Newchurch, flying 48 sorties from here, 33 of them against V-1s. In September the unit moved to Brussels, Belgium, from where he was to fly a further 102 sorties. On 22 February he was advised of the immediate award of a Bar to his DFC. He was lost on his 361st sortie. Research immediately after the war ascertained that he had been beaten to death by Volksturm and Hitler Youth troops, and buried in a shallow grave; his body has not been found to this day.

Corrections and additions to claim list.
1942
19 Dec (not 17th) ½ Bf 109
      ½ Bf 109 (i.e. 2 shares and not one individual victory on this date)
1944
19 Nov   ½ Me 262 Probable on ground (not in flight)
REVISED TOTAL: 3 and 3 shared destroyed, 1 shared probable on the ground, 1 V-1 destroyed.

THOMAS Eric Hugh RAF Nos. 1293086 (NCO); 39138 (Officer)

Addition to claim list:
1942
5 Jun and 9 Oct   MD-A (carried the name 'Mild and Bitter')

THOMAS Hugh Brian

Thomas was promoted Flt Lt on 8 June 1944. His radar operator was 174685 Plt Off Charles Blackley Hamilton, DFC. During the night of 13 April 1945 their Mosquito was fired on in error by a Lancaster, and one engine was set on fire. They were then attacked by a night fighter, and both baled out, Thomas landing just inland from the Dutch coast, while Hamilton was believed to have fallen into the sea, and was lost. Thomas was repatriated after the war, rejoining 85 Squadron on 15 May 1945.

Corrections and additions to claim list:
1943
15/16 Oct — this was in fact a Ju 88E-1 of 1/KG 6, 3E+HH, flown by Lt Geyr.
30/31 Oct — this was a Ju 88S-1 (not G-1) and was either 3E+KS, WNr 140485, or 3E+AS, WNr 140585, of III/KG 6.
1945
9/10 Apr (not 8/9th)   NT494

THOMPSON Dennis Alfred RAF Nos. 934536 (NCO); 66523 (Officer)

He volunteered for the RAFVR in September 1939, being called up in June 1940. He was promoted Flt Lt on 16 March 1943.

Additions to claim list:
1943
22/23 Jun — with Wt Off White as radar operator
1944
All victories with 141153 Flt Lt Gerald Beaumont, DFC, as radar operator
27/28 Aug — this was an aircraft of NSGr 9.

THOMPSON John Marlow

He was posted to 56 Squadron from 29 Squadron on 15 January 1936. He then flew to France on 18 May 1940, returning to Manston that same evening. He died after a long illness on 23 July 1994.

Corrections and additions to claim list:
1940

18 May	⅓	Hs 126 (b)	Hurricane I	N2549	Cambrai	111 Sqn
„	next 2 claims		„	„		
19 May		(c)	„	L1773		
18 Jul	⅓	Hs 126	„		Channel	„
10-16 Aug				P3524 JU-A		

REVISED TOTAL: 8 and 2 shared destroyed, 3 unconfirmed destroyed, 1 and 1 shared probables, 7 damaged.
(b) Aircraft of 3(H)/41 flown by Uffz Emanuel Müller; (c) After this claim he was attacked by Bf 110Cs of II/ZG 26 and his aircraft was hit in the engine. He force-landed north of Doullens, returning by sea from Boulogne next day.

THOMPSON Peter Douglas RAF Nos. 745492 (NCO); 84697 (Officer)

He was o/c Flying at Biggin Hill in 1955. During 1973 as a Grp Capt he was Military Attache in Lima, Peru.

Additions to claim list:
1941
29 Dec   5326
1942
25 Jan   5147

THOMPSON William Latto Flight Lieutenant
        RAF Nos. 1377878 (NCO); 106659 (Officer) — not 579784

He enlisted in 1936 and was commissioned on 11 September 1941. He was promoted Flt Lt on 11 September 1943.

THORN Edward Rowland   RAF Nos. 562610 (NCO); 46957 (Officer)

He enlisted in September 1928 as an Aircraft Apprentice. In November 1942 he served as an Acting Sqn Ldr at 61 OTU. Following his service with 169 Squadron, he joined 57 OTU in October 1943. He was Mentioned in Despatches on 14 January 1944. He did not leave the service in 1946; it appears that on 14 February of that year he was flying Mosquito VI TA525 of 13 OTU, which flew into high ground at Castle Bolton, Yorkshire, and that he was killed in this accident.

THORNE James Neale   RAF Nos. 605508 (NCO); 175902 (Officer)

He was killed in Mustang III FZ101.

Additions to claim list:
1943	
23 Nov	BM481
1944	
17 Jun	FX935
13 & 26 Jul	FB180
15 Aug	FZ177

THORNTON-BROWN Patrick (not Patric) Glynn
RAF Nos. 745587 (NCO); 81639 (Officer)

He was born in Weston-super-Mare, Somerset, in 1919, but lived in Gloucester and Slough. He joined the Royal Engineers in 1938, but then transferred to the RAFVR in spring 1939 for aircrew duties. He was posted to 263 Squadron in June 1940, having been commissioned.

THOROLD-SMITH Raymond Edward

He was reported killed in Spitfire A58-92 (ex BS231), by an A6M Zero over Port Charles, Northern Territory.

THWAITES Bernard John   RAF Nos. 1375890 (NCO); 66032 (Officer)

He joined the RAFVR in August 1940.

TILLARD Rupert Claude

He was 34 when killed; he is commemorated on the Fleet Air Arm Memorial at Lee-on-Solent.

TILLEY Reade Franklin   USAAF Nos. O-34390; O-885392; 9496A

TINSEY Thomas Davy   RAF Nos. 900612 (NCO); 129721 (Officer)

He was born in 1918 in Edgbaston, Birmingham, and lived in Shrewsbury, Shropshire. He attended the King Edward VI Grammar School and the Collegiate School, Bournemouth. He served in the RAF, June 1936-March 1938, then joining the RAFVR in September 1939. Although still recorded as a Sgt during the Dieppe operations of 19 August 1942, he was commissioned with effect from 28 July, this being gazetted on 29 September 1942. In 165 Squadron he became a flight commander on 3 October 1944. On 10 October however, he was killed when a car driven by Wg Cdr R.P.R.Powell collided with an Army lorry. According to Tony Bartley in his book *Smoke Trails in the Sky*, Tinsley shot down a Bf 109 on 23 or 24 November 1942, then crash-landing, slightly wounded. This would appear to be the fourth victory mentioned in the citation to his DFC. He was described by Bartley as a "huge ex-policeman", which may indicate his employment between March 1939 and September 1939.

Corrections and additions to claim list:
1942						
15 & 19 Nov		Spitfire VC (not Mark VB)				
1944						
29 Jun	½	V-1	Spitfire IX	ML175 SK-P	Tenterden	165 Sqn
1 Jul		V-1	,,	,,	Eastbourne	,,
,,		V-1	,,	,,	S Eastbourne	,,
5 Jul		V-1	,,	,,	Wadhurst	,,
22 Jul		V-1	,,	,,	S Eastbourne	,,
26 Jul		V-1	,,	MK514 SK-Z	SW Faversham	,,

TOPHAM John Groves

He was commissioned on 1 April 1939. At the end of 1942 he was posted to command 54 OTU. In 1968 he was AOC, Air Forces Gulf, as an Air Cmdr.

Corrections and additions to claim list:
1941	
13/14 Jun — this was an He 111H-3 WNr 5652, 6N+FK, of 2/KGr 100	
1942	
6/7 Jul — 19/20 Sep	Beaufighter VIF (not Mark IF)

TOWNSEND Kenneth Norman Varwell

He enlisted in 1933 as an Aircraft Apprentice, qualifying as a fitter. Subsequently trained as a pilot, he already had 250 hours in his logbook when he joined 607 Squadron in April 1940. During 10 May he flew several times, claiming four He 111s and a fifth damaged; his final victim was claimed whilst it was bombing the squadron's airfield at 2140 hours, following which he landed in the dark. Next day he was made Duty Pilot by his flight commander to ensure that he took a rest, although he appears to have managed to fly at least once, making further claims. Accounts of what then happened differ. One records that during the afternoon of 12th he helped provide cover to RAF bombers attacking the Maastricht bridges, where his aircraft was shot down by Flak, and he baled out. An alternative report indicates that on 13 May he was shot down in P2616 near Louvain by Bf 109Es of 1/JG 21, and baled out; the engine of his Hurricane was recovered as the consequence of an excavation in 1992. Whichever of the above reports is correct, he became a POW.

Revised claim list:
1940

10 May 0500 He 111 (a) (may have been a $1/2$ share) Hurricane I		Cambrai		607 Sqn	
„	1430 He 111 Damaged (b)	„	„	„	
„	1435 He 111 (b)	„	„	„	
„	1450 He 111 (b) (c)	„	„	„	
„	2140 He 111	„	„	„	
11 May	2 He 111s unconfirmed	„	N Brussels	„	

REVISED TOTAL: 3 (or 4) destroyed, 1 shared destroyed(if not a full victory), 2 unconfirmed destroyed.
(a) Believed to be an aircraft of 6/KG 1; (b) III/KG 1 lost 7 He 111s in this engagement; (c) This aircraft force-landed at St Quentin where a French Escadrille de Chasse was based. Townsend landed at this airfield and pursued the crew, brandishing his revolver; all were captured; (d) Claims were made for 4 and 2 unconfirmed; I/LG 1 lost 3.

TOWNSEND Peter Wooldridge

He died on 19 June 1995.
Addition to claim list:
1940

31 Aug	P3166 VY-K	

TOYNE William Arthur

He was commissioned on 29 June 1936. On 3 July 1940 he was posted to 6 OTU, which became 56 OTU. He left this unit on 22 March 1941 on posting to CFS, Upavon, on an instructors' course. He died on 25 April 1994.

Corrections and additions to claim list:
1940

11 May —	delete — he did not make a claim. However I/JG 51 did lose 2 Bf 109Es during the engagement. He was flying N2662.			
19 May —	3 and 2 unconfirmed claims were made; I(J)/LG 2 lost 2.			
21 May —	this was 5D+DK of 2(H)/31 flown by Oblt Adolf Köcher.			
26 May	$1/2$ Do 17	Hurricane I		17 Sqn

REVISED TOTAL: 3 and 3 shared destroyed, 2 damaged or inconclusive.

TRACEY Owen Vincent

He is buried in the Halfaya Sollum War Cemetery, Libya.

TREACY Wilfred Patric Francis

He was born in Dublin in 1917, and was educated at St Joseph College, Dublin, and Cistercian College, Roscrea. He was commissioned in March 1936, and Mentioned in Despatches in January 1941. His body was found in the sea off Boulogne, and he was buried there.

TROKE Gordon William

Addition to claim list:
1942

10 Jul —	the MC 202 was claimed during an engagement with the 4° Stormo CT; this unit suffered no losses on this occasion, but several of its aircraft were damaged.

TROUSDALE Richard Macklow

On 18 August 1943 he joined 51 OTU to command the unit's 3 Squadron. He was detached to 488 Squadron in November 1943 for a seven day operational 'refresher'.

TUCKWELL George Arthur Flying Officer

RAF Nos. 917422 (NCO); 134002 (Officer)

Born in 1919 in Newmarket, Cambridgeshire, but resident in Chingford, Essex, he worked as an insurance clerk before enlisting in February 1940. He was commissioned after his Tunisian flying, and promoted Flg Off on 6 March 1943. During the campaign he also attacked E-Boats and other shipping.

Additions to claim list:

1942					
14 Jun				W	
27 Jul	S 81 Damaged		Beaufighter IC	A	272 Sqn
23 Nov				EL227 X	

TULL Desmond Trevor   RAF Nos. 1333455 (NCO); 169425 (Officer)

Born in 1923 in Swindon, Wiltshire, he attended Felixstowe County Secondary School in Suffolk. He was commissioned in January 1943, and promoted Flg Off on 1 May 1944. During the night of 18/19 December 1944, flying an 85 Squadron Mosquito with 169485 Flg Off Peter James Cowgill, DFC, he accidentally rammed Bf 110 G9+CC of Stab IV/NJG 1, flown by Hpt Adolf Breves, as the latter was trying to land at Dusseldorf airfield. Breves managed to land his badly damaged aircraft, but the Mosquito crashed with the loss of both aboard. Tull is buried in the Reichswald Forest War Cemetery.(He did not become a POW as reported in *Aces High*).

TURKINGTON Robert Wilkinson   RAF Nos. 1073648 (NCO); 117519 (Officer)

Born in 1920 in Mhow, India, he lived in Lurgan, County Armagh, Northern Ireland, before the war. He enlisted in 1940 and was trained in the USA. With 43 Squadron he flew during the Dieppe operation of 19 August 1942, where his Hurricane suffered damage. By the end of his tour he had flown 766 operational hours with the unit. On completion of his tour with 601 Squadron, he was posted to British Army HQ in Italy as RAF Liaison Officer. He returned to 241 Squadron subsequently, and was killed in a flying accident with this unit on 29 July 1945. He is buried in the Padua War Cemetery.

Corrections and additions to claim list:

1943	
27 Mar	JG879
1944	
19 Jul	JG494 RZ-Y
21 & 29 Jul	JF351 RZ-U

REVISED TOTAL: 9 and 3 shared destroyed, 1 probable, 4 damaged.

TURNBULL Peter St George Bruce

His body was found in his wrecked aircraft near the KB Mission by a patrol from the 2/12th Battalion on 4 September 1942.

Correction to claim list:

1941	
25 Jan —	L9044 was a Blenheim IV, not a Gladiator. This serial is therefore incorrect; the correct serial has not been discovered.

UMBERS Arthur Ernest

Additions to claim list:

1944						
16 Jun		V-1	Tempest V	JN745	N Dover	3 Sqn
18 Jun	1/2	V-1	"	JN768	sea	"
"		V-1	"		W Cranbrook	"
"		V-1	"	JN796	Dunsfold/Biggin Hill	"
19 Jun		V-1	"			"
20 Jun		V-1	"	JN817	Redhill area	"
22 Jun	2	V-1s	"			"
27 Jun		V-1	"			"
6 Jul		V-1	"	JN817		"
7 Jul		V-1	"			"
8 Jul	1/2	V-1	"			"
11 Jul	1/2	V-1	"			"
16 Jul		V-1	"			"
3 Aug	3	V-1s	"			"
"	1/2	V-1	"			"

REVISED TOTAL: 4 and 1 shared destroyed, 1 and 1 shared probable, 2 and 1 shared damaged, 14 and 4 shared V-1s destroyed.

UNWIN George Cecil   RAF Nos. 590289 (NCO); 46298 (Officer)

The Spitfire he deliberately crashed on 3 March 1939 was K9797.

Correction to claim list:

1940	
5-28 Nov	Spitfire IIA (not Mark I)

URBANOWICZ Witold   RAF No. P76735 (not 76736)

He entered the Szkola Podchorazych Lotnictwa at Deblin in 1930, and was commissioned in 1932 as an observer, joining a night bomber unit of the 1 Pulk. He then applied for pilot training, which he completed in 1933. In October 1936 he was posted to Deblin to become an instructor, where he remained until the outbreak of the war. In September 1939 he led the cadets of the 14th Class to Rumania, and thence by sea to Marseilles. He then volunteered for training in the UK, being posted to 1 School of Army Co-operation at Old Sarum with a number of other Polish pilots. However on 14 July 1940 he was sent to 6 OTU, and thence in August was posted to 145 Squadron. On 8 August he managed to claim his first victory over England with 601 Squadron, although he was never formally posted to that unit. He was awarded the Virtuti Militari, 5th Class, on 18 September 1940. During his service in China with the USAAF he claimed the sinking of 15 riverboats. In 1945 he visited Poland, but the experience of Communist rule discouraged him from resettling there, and he left swiftly, emigrating to the USA. Here he worked for American Airlines, Eastern Airlines and Republic Aviation as an executive in production control. He retired in 1973, becoming a security consultant in the aviation industry until 1994. In 1995 he was promoted General in the Polish Air Force by the new regime, and in May 1996 visited the 1 Pulk Lotnictwa Mysliwskiego 'Warsawa' on the 75th anniversary of the original founding of the 1 Pulk in which he had served. Here he gave his blessing to the young fighter pilots of the unit. He then returned to New York, where he had been living in Queens, but on 17 August 1996 he died in a Manhattan hospital.

Corrections and additions to claim list:

1936				
Aug	Soviet reconnaissance aircraft (a)	PZL P.11		111 Esk
1940				
8 Aug	Bf 110 (not Bf 109) (b)	L1819		601 Sqn (c)
12 Aug	(d)	R4177		
6 Sep			RF-B	
7 Sep			RF-G	
15 Sep	(e)		RF-F	
26 Sep			RF-E	
27 Sep	(f)			
"	(g)			
30 Sep	(h)			
"	(i)			
"	(j)			
1943				
11 Dec		P-40K-1		

REVISED TOTAL: 18 destroyed, 1 probable, 9 destroyed on the ground (no details).
(a) Believed to have been a Polikarpov R-5: (b) Believed to have been a Bf 110C of V/LG 1, which crash-landed in France, 70% damaged; (c) Claimed flying with 601 Squadron, not 145 Squadron; (d) Believed to have been a Ju 88A-1 of KG 51 which crashed in the sea; (e) Believed to have been Do 17Zs WNr 2549, U5+FS and WNr 4245, U5+GS, both of 8/KG 2; (f) Believed actually to have been Bf 110C-2 WNr 3849, L11+GL of 15/LG 1, which crashed near Hailsham, having also been attacked by other pilots: (g) One of the Ju 88s is believed to have been WNr 4117, 3Z+DN, of 5/KG 77; (h) Believed to have been WNr 2693 of II/JG 53, which crashed in the Channel, and '4', WNr 6050 of 4/JG 54, which crashed at Bexhill; (i) Possibly an aircraft of KG 3; (j) Believed to have been Bf 109E WNr 5818 of Stab/JG 26, which crashed at Roundhurst, Northchapel.

URWIN-MANN John Roland

'Jack' Urwin-Mann was educated at Xaverian College, Brighton. He was commissioned on 1 May 1939, and was posted to the 11 Group Pool at the end of December for fighter training, before joining 253 Squadron.

Additions to claim list:

1941					
28 Dec	Bf 110 Damaged	Hurricane IIC	KC-Y	over base	238 Sqn
1943					
28 Jan		Spitfire VC	EP330 HA-I		

REVISED TOTAL: 8 and 2 shared destroyed, 2 unconfirmed destroyed, 2 probables, 3 damaged.

USHER Dennis Charles

Corrections and additions to claim list:

1942					
11 Sep	MC 202 Damaged	Hurricane IIC	BP592	El Alamein	213 Sqn
1943					
12 Jan		Spitfire VB	ER313		
6 and 7 Mar			ER703		
22 Mar			EP440		
27 Mar			ES130		

VAN LIERDE Remi (not Remy)   RAF No. 106250; Belgian No. 44418

He was born on 14 August 1915 in Overboelaere, Belgium, enlisting in the Aviation Militaire Belge on 16 September 1935. Initially trained as an observer, he then became a pupil pilot with the 73^e Promotion on 1 May

1937, and by 1940 was a Sgt in 3^e Escadrille/IIe Groupe/1eme Regiment flying Fox IIIs. He was shot down and wounded on 16 May 1940 and was removed to hospital in Bruges. He escaped from Belgium on 28 September, making his way through France and Spain, being held in the Miranda concentration camp near Burgos whilst seeking to pass through the latter country, from 30 October 1940-14 February 1941. Released, he reached the UK on 20 July, and on 5 September joined the RAFVR. During October he attended 57 OTU, and was then posted to 609 Squadron on 9 January 1942. He was awarded a DFC on 25 June 1943, and on 22 December 1943, on conclusion of his first tour, he attended Central Gunnery School. He was then posted to Manston in February 1944 as Gunnery Leader. On 20 April he joined 3 Squadron, where he operated against V-1s until August, when he was awarded a Bar to his DFC. On 20 August he joined 164 Squadron, flying with this unit on Typhoons until 16 May 1945, when he was posted to 84 GSU; in July he received a Second Bar to his DFC. On 21 August 1945 he took command of 350 Squadron. He was given command of 'A' Wing (ex 160 Wing) of the Belgian service on 1 November 1946, then in December 1950 taking command of the 7th Fighter Wing. He commanded Kamina Air Base in the Belgian Congo, 1959-60, and in 1963 was on the Staff of 7 Wing. In 1967 he commanded Chienes Air Base, but he retired as a Colonel on 1 January 1968. He died at Lessines on 8 June 1990.

Additions to claim list:
1944

Date			Aircraft	Serial	Location	Sqn
16 Jun	1/2	V-1	Tempest V	JN862	S Chatham	3 Sqn
17 Jun	1/3	V-1	"	"	N Tenterden	"
18 Jun	1/2	V-1	"	"	nr Dungeness	"
"	1/2	V-1	"	"	nr Ivychurch	"
23 Jun	3	V-1s	"			"
25 Jun		V-1	"	JN862	Dungeness	"
"	1/2	V-1	"	"	3/4m SW Ashford	"
27 Jun		V-1	"			"
28 Jun		V-1	"			"
29 Jun		V-1	"			"
3 Jul		V-1	"	EJ525	4m N Horsham	"
4 Jul		V-1	"	"	NE Pevensey	"
"		V-1	"		15m N Hastings	"
"		V-1	"		12m N Beachy Head	"
"	2	V-1s	"		4m S Hastings	"
6 Jul		V-1	"	EJ525	nr Tonbridge	"
7 Jul		V-1	"	JN862	Cranbrook area	"
"		V-1	"	"	15m S Dungeness	"
8 Jul		V-1	"			"
10 Jul		V-1	"			"
11 Jul		V-1	"			"
"	1/2	V-1	"			"
12 Jul	3	V-1s	"			"
"	1/2	V-1	"			"
13 Jul		V-1	"			"
26 Jul		V-1	"	JN862	5-6m N Bexhill	"
"	3/4	V-1	"	"	N Hastings	"
"		V-1	"	"	10m N Bexhill	"
27 Jul		V-1	"	"	nr Rye	"
"		V-1	"	"	3m S Tonbridge	"
"		V-1	"	"	5m SE Tunbridge Wells	"
"		V-1	"	"	10m NW Hastings	"
"		V-1	"			"
28 Jul		V-1	"			"
"	1/3	V-1	"			"
2 Aug	2	V-1s	"			"
6 Aug		V-1				"
16 Aug		V-1	"			"

REVISED TOTAL: 6 destroyed, 1 damaged, 1 destroyed on the ground, 35 and 9 shared V-1s destroyed.

VAN MENTZ Brian

Born in 1916, Brian Van Mentz's family name was originally Von Mentz, but the prefix was changed by deed poll to Van. He received at least a part of his education in the UK, attending the City of London Freemen's School, Ashtead, Surrey. He applied to join the RAFVR in 1937, attending 4 E & RFTS, Brough, September-November, and then 8 FTS, December 1937-July 1938. He was granted a Short Service Commission in the RAF on 19 October 1938 (not 1937). When he was killed at the 'Ferry Inn', only two other members of 222 Squadron lost their lives, these being the Adjutant and the Medical Officer.

Corrections and additions to claim list:
1940

14 May	1/3	Ju 88 (not individual victory) (a)	
15 May		Ju 87 (b)	Wavre-Gembloux
"		Hs 126 Damaged (not unconfirmed destroyed)	

18 May   Bf 109 Damaged (c)
REVISED TOTAL: 6 and 2 shared destroyed (one no details), 2 and 1 shared probables, 10 damaged.
(a) Aircraft of 3(F)/122 flown by Uffz Erwin Maxroth; (b) Aircraft of 2/StG 2; (c) Believed to be an aircraft of 1(J)/LG 2 in which Fw Heinz Pöhland was shot down; this may in fact be his missing victory, if subsequently confirmed.

VAN VLIET Cornelius Arthur

Additions to claim list:
1941
2 Aug   Hurricane I
17 Dec   Hurricane II
    „   Bf 109F Damaged   „   1 SAAF Sqn
REVISED TOTAL: 4 destroyed, 1 damaged, possibly 8 or 9 destroyed on the ground in East Africa with 11 SAAF Squadron.

VAREY Arthur William   RAF Nos. 1058700 (NCO); 134000 (Officer)
On 2 August 1944 he was posted to 53 OTU for administrative duties as a Flg Off.

VASSILIADES Basilios Michael   RAF Nos. 1388657 (NCO); 182875 (Officer)
Basilios Vassiliades was described as a "Greek millionaire playboy". He attended 9 EFTS, Anstey, in November 1941, then 31 EFTS, Denington, Canada, in January 1942, and 32 SFTS, Moose Jaw, 14 March-3 July. He returned to the UK, joining 7(P) AFU, Peterborough, on 4 September, and moving to 53 OTU on 13 October 1942, where he remained until 13 June 1943, being retained as an instructor. He then attended Fighter Gunnery School at Hutton Cranswick. He joined 19 Squadron on 21 June (not 23 January), flying Spitfire Vs, then Mark IXs. After being shot down in summer 1944, he was posted to 83 Group Communications Squadron on 5 October 1944, and then 83 GSU, Thorney Island, from 18 October-2 December 1944. His DFM was gazetted on 26 July 1944; an award of the DFC followed on 19 March 1945. A US-constructed 'Liberty' ship was subsequently named after him.

Corrections and additions to claim list:
1944
1 May   Bf 109 Damaged   Mustang III   Reims-Metz area   19 Sqn
                 on the ground
24 Jun —   these claims were made during two sorties. On the first he claimed the FW 190
           shot down and the He 111 damaged on the ground near Evreux. On the second
           sortie he claimed the Bf 109G during an armed reconnaissance
8 Jul —   in his logbook he claims ²/₃ Bf 109 rather than ¹/₂
8 Aug —   in his logbook he claims 2 Bf 109s rather than 1 and 1 Probable
REVISED TOTAL: 8 or 9 and 2 shared destroyed, 1 probable (if only 8 destroyed), 1 damaged, 1 destroyed on the ground, 2 damaged on the ground.

VENESOEN Francois August
Born on 19 October 1920 in Antwerp, Belgium, he was a pupil pilot in the 80ᵉ Promotion on 1 March 1939, but was 'washed out' on 25 May. He then became a Corporal air gunner with IIIᵉ Group/2ᵉ Regiment at Nivelles on Fox VICs, but on 13 May 1940 escaped to France as his country was being over-run. He sailed on the MS *Ettrick* from St Jean-de-Luz, reaching the UK on 23 June 1940. Here on 19 August he joined 235 Squadron as an air gunner on Blenheim fighters. On 20 November he was posted to 272 Squadron, but he was then accepted for pilot training, attending 13 SFTS. He was awarded a DFC on 21 December 1942.

VERITY Victor Bosanquet Strachan
He was born in Timaru (not Timara). In August 1941 he was a Flt Lt instructor at 54 OTU.

Corrections and additions to claim list:
1941
15/16 Mar —   N6923 was a Tiger Moth, not a Hurricane; this serial was therefore recorded in error
1943
17/18 Apr   V8651 C (a)
(a) His radar operator on this date was Plt Off A.W.Farquharson.

VIGORS Timothy Ashmead

Correction to claim list:
1940
31 May —   the He 111 was claimed unconfirmed destroyed.

VINCENT Stanley Flamank
After evacuation from the East Indies in 1942, he served as Deputy Chief of Air Staff, RNZAF, October 1942-March 1943.

VOASE-JEFF Robert

He was educated at Cheltenham College, Gloucestershire. After the opening week of the May 1940 'Blitzkrieg', he was sent home on leave on 17th.

Additions to claim list:
1940
10 May —   this was a Do 17Z of 8/KG 3; his Hurricane was hit by return fire and he force-
    landed at Doncourt.
15 May —   the aircraft involved in this action were Do 17Zs of I/KG 76, the interception
    occurring near Louvain.

WADE Lance Cleo

Corrections and additions to claim list:

1941		
18 Nov		Z4360
22 Nov		V7828
24 Nov		Z4311
1942		
6 Apr & 9 Jun		BN or BP239
28 May		BG974
5-19 Jul		BP186
2 & 11 Sep		HL661
8 Sep		HL721
1943		
26 Feb		AB502 IR-G
1 Mar		ER650 ZX-G
6 Mar		ER486
8-22 Mar		ES252
29 Mar	Spitfire IX	EN269
4 Apr		EN296 ZX-M
7 Apr-10 Jul		EN186
2 Oct-3 Nov		JF472

REVISED TOTAL: 23 and 2 shared destroyed, 1 probable, 13 damaged, 1 destroyed on the ground, 5 damaged on the ground.

WADE Trevor Sidney   RAF Nos. 740760 (NCO); 78984 (Officer)

After undertaking the instructors' course, he instructed at 57 OTU. On 22 March 1942 he attended the Fighter Wing at CGS.

WAGNER Alan Derek   RAF Nos. 740760 (NCO); 65993 (Officer)

He was educated at Whitgift Grammar School, Croydon, and enlisted in the RAFVR in 1937. He attended 6 OTU in late August 1940, before joining 151 Squadron.

WAKEHAM Ernest John Cecil

He was born in Harburton, Totnes, Devon, attending Totnes Grammar School and South Devon Technical College. He joined the RAF as a u/t pilot in February 1939, and was commissioned in January 1940. He flew out to France on 18 May 1940.

Additions to claim list:

1940		
18 May	N2771 SO-O	
19 May		SE Cambrai

WALKER Derek Ronald

Corrections to claim list:

1941	
29 Nov and 13 Dec	Hurricane I (not Mark IIB)

WALKER James Arthur

He went out to France on 18 May 1940. He was posted to the Middle East in late 1941 (not early 1942), initially instructing at 73 OTU, Aden.

Additions to claim list:
1940
18 May —   the claim for the He 111 was made whilst flying L1589 (not P2885).

WALKER James Elmslie

Additions to claim list:
1943

4 and 30 Mar	ER668 SN-S
7 Apr	ER564 HD
9 Apr	ER668 SN-S
10 Apr	ER807 SN-E
11 Apr	ER564 HD
16 Apr	ER668 SN-S
18 Apr	JK113 SN-B
26 Apr	ER668 SN-S

WALKER Peter Russell

He was born on 6 March 1914 and attended Woodbridge School, Suffolk. He was commissioned on 21 October 1935. His promotion to Wg Cdr was on 1 June 1942, and after the war he regained this rank on 1 July 1947. He commanded West Malling in 1953, and was promoted Grp Capt on 1 July 1956, retiring from the service on 6 March 1964.

Corrections and additions to claim list:
1940

10 May	(c)			N2382 B	
11 May	(d)				
15 May	Bf 110 (e)		Hurricane I	L1681	NW Reims	1 Sqn
17 May	(f)				
19 May	(g)				

REVISED TOTAL: 4 and 2 shared destroyed (which accords with his DFC citation), 2 unconfirmed destroyed (which, if added, accords with his DSO citation), 1 damaged.
(c) Do 17Z of 7/KG 3, flown by Uffz Wolfgang Gräfe; Walker's Hurricane was hit by return fire and he crash-landed east of Verdun; (d) Bf 110s of I/ZG 26 were involved in this engagement; 9 were claimed, but only 2 were lost: (e) 5 and 1 unconfirmed Bf 110s were claimed; III/ZG 26 lost 2 and 2 more crash-landed. Walker's Hurricane was hit again, and he force-landed near Vouziers; (f) Claims made for at least 5 and 2 unconfirmed Bf 110s; V(Z)/LG 1 lost 3; Walker's own aircraft was damaged; (g) Claims made for 5 and 3 unconfirmed; III/KG 27 lost 5 in the Soissons-Compiegne-Noyon area.

WALLACE Thomas Young
RAF Nos. 1256954 (NCO); 42929 (Officer 1939) 149635 (Officer)

He was born on 5 October 1916. On arriving in the UK he was granted a Short Service Commission in June 1939 as officer No 42919. He attended 7 E & RFTS, Desford, in July, and then 6 SFTS, Little Rissington, in November. He qualified as a pilot on 25 March 1940 with an 'above average' grading, and was posted to 610 Squadron in June. However, having met a girl in London for whom he fell hard, he went absent without leave for two days. He was court martialled and his commission was terminated. He immediately enlisted in the RAFVR with the rank of Sgt, being posted to 111 Squadron on 17 July. After the Battle of Britain he was posted to Canada, where he instructed Fleet Air Arm pilots until 1943, when he returned to the UK to resume operations. He is buried at Pihen-lez-Guines, France.

WALLENS Ronald Walter

He was born on 1 February 1916, and was educated at Worksop College, Nottinghamshire. He sought to join the RAFO in 1937, attending 11 E & RFTS, June-August, at the conclusion of which he received his commission. He then attended 8 FTS to complete his training, and on 26 March 1938 was posted to 41 Squadron for his operational experience. He then transferred to the RAF on a Short Service Commission on 7 October 1938. He worked on adminstrative duties from 1 August 1945 until released in 1946, then entering the motor trade, and subsequently running a number of public houses and hotels. In 1988 he founded the Torbay Aircraft Museum, and in 1990 published his autobiography, *Flying Made my Arms Ache* (Self Publishing Association). He died on 13 December 1995.

WALMSLEY Harold Edward   RAF Nos. 1383221 (NCO); 139425 (Officer)

He was commissioned on 4 January 1943.

WALTON William Coltart   RAF Nos. 1261966 (NCO); 119499 (Officer)

He joined the RAFVR in mid 1940, completing his training at 56 OTU. He returned to this unit in March 1943 as a Flg Off instructor, from where on 10 October 1943 he was posted to 234 Squadron.

WARBURTON Adrian

He resided in Enfield, Middlesex, before the war. His territorial service was with an Armoured Car Company, TA. He was commissioned in the RAF in January 1939 (not 1938). His decorations were — DFC, 11 February 1941; Bar to DFC, 9 September 1941; DSO, 20 March 1942; Second Bar to DFC, 3 November 1942; Bar to DSO, 6 August 1943; US DFC, 18 January 1944. A biography, *Warburton's War*, by Tony Spooner (William Kimber) was published in 1987.

Corrections and additions to claim list:
1942
21 Sep   EP140 (not FP140)
1943
10 Jul   (h)   att 1435 Sqn (not Flt)
(f) Sgt D.J.Moren DFM; (h) His logbook recorded claims of 9 destroyed, 1 probable and 2 damaged prior to July 1943 (which
appears to include ground claims); the Bf 109 claimed destroyed on 10 July may have been credited as a Probable.

WARD Derek Harland

He flew out of France to England on 20 May 1940. He was killed in BN277, and is buried in the Halfaya Sollum
War Cemetery, Libya.

Corrections and additions to claim list:
1940
19 May $\frac{1}{4}$ Hs 126(not HS 126) (b)
    „ $\frac{1}{3}$ Bf 109E unconfirmed (not individual victory, nor claimed as damaged) (c)
1942
9 Feb   Hurricane IIB   BG751
30 Apr/1 May   Hurricane IIC   BN131 P
1/2 Jun (not 3/4th)   „
10 Jun   Bf 109F Damaged „   „   W El Adem   73 Sqn
2 Jul   Ju 88   „
REVISED TOTAL: 7 and 1 shared destroyed, 1 shared unconfirmed destroyed, 1 probable, 5 damaged.
(b) Aircraft of 1(H)/11Pz flown by Ogfr Karl-Heinz Kramer; (c) claims made for 8 and 6 unconfirmed; II/JG 26 lost 4.

WATERS John Lawrence   RAF No. 39262

Promoted Sqn Ldr 1 December 1941. Awarded the AFC.

WATKINS Douglas Herbert

He left 611 Squadron as a Flt Lt after the Battle of Britain to instruct at 57 OTU. On 12 November 1941 he
returned to 611 Squadron as commanding officer. In 1943 he was o/c Training Wing at 56 OTU as a Wg Cdr,
and in September of that year was posted to the Staff of the new 2nd TAF.

Corrections to claim list:
1940
29 Oct   Spitfire I (not Mark II)
1941
25 Feb   Spitfire II

WATKINS Desmond John   RAF Nos. 1314925 (NCO); 188502 (Officer)

He was commissioned on 24 November 1944.

Corrections and additions to claim list:
1945
20 Apr   RB155 MN-C
30 Apr $\frac{1}{3}$ FW 190   SM814 MN-A
    „   FW 190 Damaged on ground (not destroyed)
REVISED TOTAL: 3 and 3 shared destroyed, 1 damaged on the ground.

WATSON Anthony

Born in Dorchester, Dorset, in 1920, he attended Wells Cathedral School, Somerset, and then resided in
Cambridge.

Corrections and additions to claim list:
1942
11 Nov   Beaufighter VIC (not Mk IC) T5210 B
12 Nov   Beaufighter IC   T5079 G

WATTS Leslie William   RAF Nos. 937674 (NCO); 117728 (Officer)

He was born in Birmingham in 1916, and attended Moseley Grammar School, subsequently living in Sandbanks,
Bournemouth, Hampshire. He joined the RAFVR in September 1939 as aircrew, but in 1940 as a Sgt, remustered
as a u/t pilot. He was commissioned in 1942. On return to the UK from Malta, he served with 52 OTU as an
instructor until April 1943.

WAUGH Lawrence Robertson Stuart

Additions to claim list:
1942
4-23 Jul   BG764 AX-W
11 Aug   698

WAY Basil Hugh
When killed, he crashed into the Channel in R6707; he was buried in Belgium.

WEAVER Claude III
When attending 56 OTU as a Sgt in early 1942, he saw and attacked a Bf 110, but it escaped in cloud. On 8 June 1944 he received a Commendation for Valuable Services in the Air. However, he was not awarded a Bar to his DFM; the register of the Meharicourt Communal Cemetery, where he is buried, listed this decoration, but is in error. He was, however, Mentioned in Despatches, and on 15 October 1994 was inducted into the Oklahoma Aviation and Space Hall of Fame.

WEAVER Percy Stevenson
He attended E & RFTS, October-December 1936, and was commissioned in the RAFO on 21 December 1936. He then trained at 8 FTS from January 1937, and was posted to 56 Squadron on 13 September, three days later being granted a Short Service Commission in the RAF.

WEBSTER John Terrance
He was born in Liverpool in 1916, and attended Liverpool College.

WEDGWOOD Jefferson Heywood (not Haywood)
He is buried in the Capuccini Naval Cemetery, Malta.

Additions to claim list:

1940				
2 Sep	Bf 109 Damaged	Hurricane I		253 Sqn
1942				
27 Jul			BP379	
14 Aug		Spitfire VC (not Mar VB)	QJ-B	
16 Aug			BR476	
19 Aug	(b)		,,	
21 Aug	Bf 109F Probable (not Damaged)		BR175	
31 Aug			BR520	
1 Sep			BR475	
2 Sep			BR476	
2 Nov	Bf 109 Probable	Spitfire VC	,,	92 Sqn

REVISED TOTAL: 10 destroyed (plus 3 — see NB in *Aces High*), 2 probables, 12 damaged.
(b) The pilot of the MC 202 was Ten Rinaldo Gibellini of 73ª Squadriglia, 9° Gruppo; taken POW, he died of his wounds two days later.

WEIR Archibald Nigel Charles
He was educated at Winchester, and at Christchurch, Oxford.

WELFARE Dennis
In the UK in 1943, he instructed at 51 OTU, being posted to 239 Squadron on 4 February 1944.

Corrections and additions to claim list:

1943		
17 Mar	Beaufighter IC (not Mark VIF)	T5038
14 May	Beaufighter VIC	
22 May		EL534

WELLS Edward Preston   RNZAF No. 58786 (not RAF)
In 1954 he commanded RAF Bawdsey, Suffolk, as a Wg Cdr.

WELLS John Christopher   RAF Nos. 561960 (NCO); 45883 (Officer)
He was born in Sheringham, Norfolk, in 1912 and enlisted as an Aircraft Apprentice in July 1927. He became a Sgt Pilot during 1935, serving in Palestine, for which he received the General Service Medal with Palestine Clasp. He was commissioned during 1941, and promoted Sqn Ldr on 28 November 1944. He died in 1968.

WELSH Terence Dean
He was born in Staines, Middlesex, in 1916, and was educated at Ashford County School, also in Middlesex.

WEST Jeffery George
Although listed as having worked as a civil servant before the war, it appears that he had in fact been an accountant in private practice. He was posted to the UK in December 1940, completing his training at 58 OTU in February 1941, joining 616 Squadron in April. In February 1942 he was posted to HQ, RAF Middle East, and

from there to Technical Command, Almaza, in April. In May he joined 71 OTU as an instructor, where he remained until June 1943, when he was posted to 103 MU at Aboukir. He moved to Helwan in November, and then to RAF HQ, Levant, in January 1944. In May 1944 he joined HQ, RAF Middle East again, where he served until his return to New Zealand in October 1945. He was released in January 1946.

Additions to claim list:
1943					
13 Aug	Bf 109 Damaged	Spitfire IX		Nile area	103 MU

REVISED TOTAL: 4 and 2 shared destroyed, 1 shared probable, 3 and 1 shared damaged.

WEST Ronald   RAF Nos. 969308 (NCO); 89405 (Officer)

He was born in Lossiemouth, Scotland, in 1918, attending Lossiemouth Higher Grade Public School and Elgin Academy. He enlisted in the RAFVR in 1939, and was commissioned in 1940. He returned from Malta to the UK in July 1942 and joined 58 OTU, but the following month moved to 3 FIS, Hullavington.

WESTENRA Derrick Fitzgerald

Pre war he served in the Kenya Auxillary Air Unit, but enlisted in the RNZAF in February 1940. He was commissioned in the RAF in November of that year. Postwar he returned to farming, and also became a well-known glider pilot in New Zealand.

Correction to claim list:
After the claim on 5 May 1942, insert '1944' before the claim of 17 May.

WESTLAKE George Herbert   RAF Nos. 740702 (NCO); 84019 (Officer)

In line 16 of the biographical notes on page 627 of *Aces High*, it should state that in March 1944 (not 1943) he dropped rank from Wg Cdr to Sqn Ldr. On 31 August 1940 he attended 6 OTU before joining 43 Squadron. He was Mentioned in Despatches on 14 January 1944.

Additions to claim list:

1941	
9 Jun	Z4194
18 Ju;	Z4223
1942	
10 Jun	BE340 AK-W
12 Jun	BN117
16 Jun	BN184 AK-W
26 Jun	BN139
5 Jul	BN184 AK-W

WESTMACOTT Innes Bentall

During 1939 he served with both 6 and 2 SFTS, then joining 110 Army Co-operation Wing in March 1940. He went to 6 OTU in July. On 31 August 1940 he was shot down in flames by a Bf 110 (not Bf 109) and baled out of V7341 US-O near Little Baddow. On 13 May 1941 he was shot down in Hurricane Z2837 and was wounded in the elbow. Whilst recovering, he undertook two sorties as an observer in Wellington bombers, to Tripoli in August 1941 and to Naples in October. On 16 October 1943 he flew a Bf 109G which had force-landed at Safi, Malta, and had been repaired. During 1946-47 he was Air Attache in Mexico, following which he served at HQ, 11 Group, and at Air Ministry, 1947-51. He was on the staff of the RAF Staff College, 1951-53, then at HQ, Fighter Command, 1954-55. 1955-56 saw him as o/c Flying, Middle Wallop. On 25 June 1957 he flew an Auster AOP 7 into high tension cables near Blandford, Dorset, and crashed, suffering a compound fracture of his right leg and many cuts. His Wg Cdr passenger suffered both legs broken. This was his last flight with the RAF, and he retired on 1 May 1958, then becoming Honorary Secretary of the RAF Benevolent Fund. He died in 1991.

Corrections and additions to claim list:
1940						
13 Aug		Bf 110 Damaged	Hurricane I	US-C	nr Canterbury	56 Sqn
18 Aug				US-R	Rochford Thames Estuary	
26 Aug				V7341 US-O	nr Great Tey	
27 Aug	½	Do 17 (not ¼)		US-R		
30 Aug				US-O		
"		Bf 110 Damaged	Hurricane I	"	nr Luton	56 Sqn
1941						
14 Apr		Maryland (d)			Malta	261 Sqn
1942						
8/9		(e)				

REVISED TOTAL: 3 and 2 shared destroyed, 2 probables, 4 damaged.
(d) He shot down Maryland AR735 of 69 Squadron, flown by Flg Off Adrian Warburton, in error; Warburton carried out a successful crash-landing; (e) This claim may have been shared with a Beaufighter, and may have related to an aircraft of I/NJG 2.

WHALL Basil Ewart Patrick
He was born in 1918 in Brighton, but lived at Amersham Common, Buckinghamshire, before the war. A turner in civil life, he joined the RAFVR in July 1937.

WHITAMORE William Michael   RAF Nos. 1174879 (NCO); 102107 (Officer)
Corrections and additions to claim list:
1942
26 Jun   AK890 (not ET510)
4 Jul (not 13th)   ET510 (not ET1024)
23 Oct   (a)
1943
14 and 25 Jul   Spitfire IX (not Mark VC) EN492 FL-E
(a) MC 202 of 84ª Squadrilgia, 10° Gruppo, 4° Stormo CT; Serg Roberto Ugazio baled out.

WHITBY Alfred (no second name)   RAF Nos. 580256 (NCO); 45721 (Officer)
He left 59 OTU as a Flg Off in September 1941 to join 403 Squadron.

Additions to claim list:
1940

12 May		Do 17 (a)	Hurricane I	N2384	S Luxembourg	79 Sqn
20 May	1/4	Do 215 (not 1/3) (b)				
„		Do 17 (not confirmed)	Arras			

REVISED TOTAL: 3 and 3 shared destroyed, 2 unconfirmed destroyed.
(a) Possibly an aircraft of 4(F)/11; (b) Do 215B of 3(F)/ObdL, which crashed near Tourain, flown by Uffz Erich Luther.

WHITE Derek
RAF Nos. 1387935 (NCO); 111262 (Officer) — also recorded as 111362
He was promoted Flt Lt on 8 November 1943.

WHITE Harold Edward   RAF Nos. 1284643 (NCO); 119508 (Officer)
He served as a Sgt at 54 OTU in July 1941, and was commissioned on 26 March 1942. In May 1943, following his first tour of operations, he was posted to 60 OTU as a Plt Off on No 1 Course. His radar operator was 120723 Flg Off Michael Seamer Allen (not Allan), DFC and Bar.

Corrections and additions to claim list:
1943
15/16 Jul — this Bf 110 was flown by Maj Herbert Rauh of II/NJG 4; Rauh was a 31 victory Knights'Cross holder.
17/18 Aug — the Bf 110 claimed as damaged was WNr 6228, and was actually shot down; it was flown by Maj
            Wilhelm Dormann of III/NJG 1, who baled out, although his radar operator was killed. (Dormann was an
            ex-'Wilde Sau' pilot with 14 victories to his credit).The 'Ju 88' was in fact another Bf 110, flown by
            Lt Gerhard Dittmann of 12/NJG 1; he and his radar were both killed when the aircraft crashed into the sea
            near Leeuwarden.
1944
20/21 Apr (not 19/20th) — the Do 217 was an aircraft of 5/NJG 4, flown by Ofw Karl Kaiser, who baled out, wounded;
            one other crewman baled out, but a third was killed.
10/11 May   DZ726 (not HJ726)

WHITE John
From Motherwell, Lanarkshire, Scotland, he joined the RAFVR in March 1938. He is buried in the Halfaya Sollum War Cemetery, Egypt.

WHITEHEAD Clifford   RAF Nos. 565662 (NCO); 45299 (Officer)
'Kim' Whitehead was born in 1916 in Birmingham; he enlisted as an Aircraft Apprentice direct from school in Sheffield in September 1931. He became a Sgt Pilot in 1938. He was killed in Tiger Moth T8200 whilst serving with 4 EFTS, Brough, and was buried in Nottingham.

Correction to claim list:
1940
10 Jul   P3356 (not L3356)

WHITLEY David
He was from Bedford. He and Turner had been recommended for the DFC and DFM respectively, but these decorations were not awarded due to their deaths in action.

WHITTLE Robert James Clarendon

Corrections and additions to claim list:

1941					
23 Nov		Bf 109(a)	Tomahawk IIB	Tobruk	250 Sqn
,,	2	Bf 109s Damaged (a)	,,	,,	,,
1944					
23 Jan			A29-30 (not A29-356)		

REVISED TOTAL: 11 and 3 shared destroyed, 2 probables, 4 damaged.
(a) These claims are not recorded in his logbook, but are confirmed by the squadron ORB.

WICKHAM Peter Reginald Whalley

He was born in Nairobi, Kenya, on 26 March 1918, and was educated in England at Marlborough College and Farnham Military College. He entered Cranwell in January 1937, being commissioned on 17 December 1938. He was promoted Sqn Ldr on 1 January 1944, and in March 1944 joined 2 TEU as CFI, remaining on strength until 12 September, when he was posted to HQ, ADGB (This appears to conflict with the previous information included in *Aces High* for this period, but is believed to be correct).He was stationed at Duxford in the mid 1950s, becoming a Wg Cdr again on 1 January 1953. At the end of June 1956 he was posted as Air Attache, Berne, Switzerland, as a Grp Capt. He retired from the service on 26 March 1961.

Corrections and additions to claim list:

1940		
29 Jun		K8031
30 Jun		N5783
1943		
25 Jul	Spitfire V (not Mark IX)	

WIGHT Ronald Derek Gordon

He was born in Skelmorie in 1915, but lived at Hale, Cheshire, being educated at Bowdon College, Cheshire, Mostyn School, Parkgate, Wirral, and Wrekin College, Shropshire. He was known as 'Widge'. He was despatched to France on 17 May 1940, returning late on 20th.

Additions to claim list:

1940			
19 May		(a)	P2795
20 May	1/4	Do 17 unconfirmed (not 1/2) (b)	
,,		(c)	
,,		Bf 110 (not unconfirmed)	

REVISED TOTAL: 6 and 3 shared destroyed, 5 and 1 shared unconfirmed destroyed.
(a) The Bf 109E unconfirmed was also claimed whilst flying P2795; the Hs 126 which he shared over Oudenaarde (not Audenarde), was an aircraft of 2(H)/41, flown by Uffz Gerhard Meermann; (b) This was actually a Do 215B of 3(F)/ObdL, which crashed near Tournai, flown by Uffz Erich Luther; (c) The Hs 126 was an aircraft of 2(H)/23.

WIGHT-BOYCOTT, Cathcart Michael

He was commissioned on 28 September 1937. In July 1943 he served as a Wg Cdr at HQ, 9 Group. He was made a CBE in the early 1960s, retiring from the RAF on 1 July 1964 (not 1963). He was in fact still alive when *Aces High* was published in 1994, but has since died in December 1998.

WILDBLOOD Timothy Seddon

He was born in Cairo, son of Brigadier General E.H.Wildblood, DSO; he was educated in England at Wellington College.

WILKINSON John Francis   RAF No.150189

He was commissioned as a Plt Off on 20 February 1943, and was promoted Flt Lt two years later.

WILKINSON Royce Clifford

He was posted to 71 Squadron — the first 'Eagle' Squadron — in October 1940 as a flight commander, moving to 121 Squadron in May 1941. A biography, *Spitfire RCW*, was written and published by Kenneth James Nelson, CD, in 1994.

Corrections and additions to claim list:

1940			
12 May	1/3	Hs 126 (not two 1/5 shares) (b)	
13 May		(c)	N2353 (not N2653)
,,		(d)	,,
16 May		(a)	L1899
19 May		(e)	P3454 QO-A S Lille
20 May		(f)	,,

„	¼ He 111	Hurricane I	„		3 Sqn
„	¼ He 111	„	„		„

REVISED TOTAL: 7 and 3 shared destroyed, 1 damaged.
(a) This aircraft, as identified in *Aces High*, was actually a Bf 110C; it was 2N+HH of 1/ZG 1 flown by Lt Heinrich Brucksch, and crashed at Walen, north of Mechelen; (b) Hs 126 of 1(H)/23, flown by Uffz Wolfgang Ulbrich; (c) The He 111 was possibly an aircraft of 3/KG 54; (d) the 'Arado' was actually an Hs 123; (e) He 111s of KG 54 were involved in this engagement; (f) the Hs 126, an aircraft of 3(H)/14, was damaged.

WILLIAMS Alvin Thomas   RAF No. 40276 (not 905450)
He was awarded a DFC on 6 August 1940.

WILLIAMS Cedric Watcyn
He was aged 30 when killed.

Addition to claim list:
1940

8 Aug	(a)		V7407

(a) This was a Do 17Z of III/KG 76, which crash-landed near Calais.

WILLIAMS Ernest Leopold   RAF Nos. 778679 (NCO); 80424 (Officer)
He completed his training at 54 OTU in September 1941, and in 23 Squadron teamed up with NZ391383 Wt Off Francis Elmslie Hogg, DFC, who had previously served with 488 Squadron. Williams was commissioned on 14 August 1942 from Flt Sgt, and when the pair returned to the UK, they instructed at 51 OTU until May 1943, Williams being promoted Flg Off in February. On 15 May they moved to 60 OTU, and from here were posted to 605 Squadron on 26 September, Hogg now also having been commissioned. It was from here that Williams was posted to FIU's special Tempest Flight in June 1944. In July 1944 Hogg received a Bar to his DFC and in August Williams was promoted Flt Lt. Williams' award of the Bar to his DFC in May 1945 records ten victories in the air. It is uncertain whether this was an error, including his three or four on the ground, or whether he had claimed other successes which have not been found (which appears unlikely). He was still on the RAF Officers List in October 1945, but was not included on the List issued in January 1946, there being no note of his release or retirement.

Corrections and additions to claim list:
1944

12/13 Jun —		these claims were made against aircraft on the ground			
15/16 Jun —		these claims were made against aircraft on the ground			
11/12 Aug		V-1	Tempest V	520 SD-Y	501 Sqn
30/31 Aug		V-1	„	EJ585 SD-A	N Herne Bay	„
7/8 Oct	2	V-1s	„	SD-L	„
11/12 Oct		V-1	„	„	Great Dunmow	„
12/13 Oct		V-1	„	SD-K	„
28/29 Oct		V-1	„	SD-L	„
3/4 Nov		V-1	„	„	„

REVISED TOTAL: 5 or 6 destroyed, 1 probable, 2 damaged, 3 or 4 destroyed on the ground, 3 damaged on the ground, 11 V-1s destroyed (1 no details).

WILLIAMS Gordon Albert

Corrections and additions to claim list:
1943

15 May		HV640	Kangaung (not Kamgaung) airfield
5 Dec		KW774	

WILLIAMS Thomas Draper
He was born in St Helens, Lancashire, in 1919, and lived in Liverpool, gaining his education at Rydal School, Colwyn Bay, North Wales.

Correction to claim list:
1940

15 Sep-11 Oct		Spitfire II (not Mark I)

WILLIAMS William Dudley

Corrections to claim list:
1940

13 Aug	R9900 is not a correct serial for a Spitfire. The correct serial has not been discovered.

1941

14 Mar	Spitfire II (not Mark I)

WILLIAMSON Peter Greville Kaye   RAF Nos. 1384023 (NCO); 107239 (Officer)

Born in Adelaide, South Australia, on 28 February 1923, 'Prune' Williamson enlisted in the RAF (rather than the RAAF) in January 1941 and was commissioned on 17 September of that year. He was promoted Flg Off a year later, and in January 1943 claimed the first victory for 153 Squadron. He was promoted Flt Lt on 17 September 1943, and in 1944 flew with 63933 Flg Off Frederick Ernest Forrest as his radar operator. In May 1956 he served with 11 Group as Air Staff Weapons; having been promoted Wg Cdr on 1 January 1959, he became Organisation and Training, Allied Forces Southern Europe in March. He also attended the RAF Staff College. He was promoted Grp Capt on 1 July 1966, and was to command RAF Wittering. Further promotion followed to Air Cmdr on 1 January 1970, and Acting Air Vice-Marshal on 9 October 1972, following which he went to Training Command as Air Staff, Flying & Officer Training. He was confirmed in the rank of AVM on 1 July 1973, and retired on 28 February 1978, having been made CB and CBE, and added the qualification FBIM. He died on 10 August 1982.

Additions to claim list:		
1943		
13/14 and 15/16 Jan		V8631
29/30 Jan		EL187
11 Mar and 22/23 May		V8494

WILLSON John Ellis   RAF Nos. 700188 (NCO); 89058 (Officer)

He was born in Bowes Park, London, living subsequently in Charlwood, Horley, Surrey. He enlisted in the Class 'F' Reserve (later RAFVR) in 1935, attending E & RFTS, May 1935-May 1936. He then worked as a civilian instructor at 7 E & RFTS from August 1938-December 1939, followed by 6 AONS, Staverton, until June 1941, when he was posted to 419 (Special Duties) Flight. He then served briefly with 138 Squadron at the same airfield, as it converted to Halifax bombers. In October however, he was posted to 60 OTU to train as a night fighter, moving after a few days to 51 OTU. In mid December 1941 he joined 219 Squadron, where he teamed up with 115674 Douglas Campbell Bunch (not Burch) as his radar operator, who was to receive a DFC in July 1943, and a Bar to this as a Flt Lt with 157 Squadron in March 1945, by which time he had assisted in seven victories. From 15 March 1943 however, Willson had commenced flying with Flg Off Holloway, with whom he was to claim the rest of his successes, both being posted to 153 Squadron in August, where they were both killed shortly afterwards.

Correction to claim list:
1943
Last victory 26/27 Aug (not Jul)

WILMOT Laurence Aubrey

Additions to claim list:		
1940		
16 Dec	285	
1941		
13 Feb	V7733	
1943		
28 Aug	Spitfire IX	

WILSON Alistair Forbes   RAF Nos. 1250815 (NCO); 118050 (Officer)

He joined the RAFVR in May 1940. He remained in the RAF after the war, and in 1954-56 commanded 34 Squadron on Hunters, leading this unit to Cyprus for the Suez operation in late 1956.

Corrections and additions to claim list:		
1942		
26 Jul	Hurricane II (not Spitfire V)	
22 Oct		ZX-N
4 Nov		ZX-V
1943		
3 Sep	MA414	
1944		
24 Apr	MH836	
19 Jul	MK629	

WILSON Edward Taylor

Corrections and additions to claim list:	
1944	
19 Oct	FN411 5E
1945	
4 Jan	FN398 RG-G
6 Apr	JX762 (not JX886)

WILSON Frederick Albert William Johnson
RAF Nos. 968452 (NCO); 112324 (Officer)

On completion of training, he was posted from 8 FTS to 56 OTU on 9 December 1940. He then joined 213 Squadron on 28 January 1941. He became a very good golfer in his later years, on six occasions obtaining a "hole-in-one". He died on 12 May 1996 after a brief illness.

Corrections to claim list:
There is some confusion regarding the serials of Hurricanes flown between 8 June and 10 October 1941. Z6991 (8 June) appears correct, but W9520 related to a cancelled Blackburn Botha, W6939 to a Lysander, whilst Z6692 does not seem to have been allocated. These serials were provided from his logbook, and appear therefore to have been recorded in error.

WINSKILL Archie Little   RAF Nos. 740365 (NCO); 84702 (Officer)

Corrections and additions to claim list:

1940		
28 Oct-23 Nov	Spitfire II (not Mark I)	
1943		
7 Apr		ER778
27 Apr		ER914

WINTER Douglas Cyril   RAF Nos. 563735 (NCO); 43372 (Officer)

He enlisted as an Aircraft Apprentice in September 1929.

WITORZENC Stefan

He was born in Lida, Poland, and attended the Stefan Batory University in Wilno. During 1929-31 he completed a course at the reserve officers' school, and subsequently at the SPL in Deblin. Commissioned, he was posted to the 3 Pulk in Poznan, flying with the 31 Eskadra in 1932, and then the 132 Eskadra, 1933-35. During 1935 he then served as an instructor at the Wysza Szkola Pilotazu at Gruziadz, and subsequently at Uly. During September 1939 he flew in defence of the Deblin area with a unit of instructor pilots, then escaping to France via Rumania, and from there to the UK. After initial service at 1 School of Army Co-operation, Old Sarum, he was sent to 6 OTU on 14 July 1940, and then to 501 Squadron on 8 August. He took command of 25 EFTS, Hucknall, on 7 January 1945 (not 7 June), then taking command of 131 Wing on 1 June, retaining this post until 3 July 1947. He returned to Poland in 1948, and was finally permitted to join the Polish Air Force again in 1957, then filling several important posts including that of Head of the Air Training Centre at Modlin. Living in Warsaw, he became Chairman of the Polish Airmen Society in 1992, but died suddenly on 30 December 1994. Posthumously he was awarded the *Krzyz Kowaleski z Gwiazda Orderu Odredzemia Polski* (the Polonia Restitution Order Knights' Cross with Star).

Additions to claim list:

1940		
12 and 15 Aug		SD-H
18 Aug	(a)	SD-D
24 Aug		SD-Z
2 Sep	½ Do 17 (not ⅕)	

(a) Believed to have been the aircraft flown by Hpt Horst Tietzen of II/JG 51, Knights' Cross holder with 27 victories, who was shot down over Whitstable, Kent.

WLASNOWOLSKI (not WLASNOWALSKI) Boleslaw Andrzej

He was born in Kracow, joining the SPL at Deblin in 1937 as part of the 12th Class. In June 1939 he was posted to the 122 Eskadra in the 2 Pulk at Kracow for operational training, and was commissioned on 31 August 1939. He escaped to France via Rumania, and thence to the UK, where he served initially with 1 School of Army Co-operation, Old Sarum. Sent in July 1940 to 6 OTU, he then joined 32 Squadron on 8 August, but his first training flight there ended in a crash-landing, whilst on his first operational sortie on 14 August, he was obliged to force-land in V7223. Next day he claimed his first success over England, but his Hurricane was also hit, and he crash-landed again. On 18 August he hit a tree on landing and damaged R4081. He was transferred to 607 Squadron on 13 September, and on 17th was posted to 213 Squadron. On 1 November 1940 he was advised that he was being posted to a Polish squadron; during that day he scrambled in N2608, AK-V, during a surprise low level attack on the airfield, and was shot down and killed, crashing near Liphook Game Farm, Stoughton.

Additions to claim list:

1940	
15 Aug	(a)
18 Aug	(b) and (c)
15 Oct	(d)

(a) Believed to have been Bf 109E-4 'Black 2' of 5/JG 51, which crashed into the sea; (b) Believed to have been Do 17Z WNr 2504, F1+IH of 1/KG 76, actually attacked by several 32 Squadron fighters; (c) Bf 109E-1 of 7/JG 26, flown by Lt Gerhard Müller-Duhe (5 victories) — also claimed by Flt Lt Peter Brothers; (d) Bf 109E-4 '8', WNr 1588, of 3/JG2, which crashed at Bowcombe Down, near Newport — believed also claimed by Flg Off Noel Agazarian of 609 Squadron.

WOJCIECHOWSKI Miroslaw Ignacy
It is confirmed that he joined the RAF in 1947.

Additions to claim list:
1940

15 Sep	(a)	RF-U
17 Sep	(b)	P3975 RF-U

(a) The second Bf 109 claimed on this date is believed to have been an E-7, WNr 2061, of I/LG 1, which crashed at Hartlip Churchyard, Rainham; (b) Believed to be a Bf 109E-1, WNr 3177, of 9/JG 53, which crashed at Bishopden Wood, Faversham.

WOODHOUSE Henry de Clifford Anthony
He began civilian flying in January 1932, going solo on 1 May. He continued private flying until January 1937, but made his first service flight on 9 April 1934. In September 1934 he joined 58 (Bomber) Squadron at Worthy Down, to fly Vickers Virginias, but in May 1935 was sent on a floatplane course at Calshot. In July he went to RAF Leuchars for a Fleet Air Arm spotter-reconnaissance course on Fairey IIIFs, and then in August to Gosport for deck landing training. In September he joined 820 Squadron with Blackburn Sharks, and from August 1937, Swordfish. In January 1939, now a Flt Lt, he was posted to CFS, Upavon, on an instructors' course, then instructing at 7 FTS, March-November 1939. He then returned to CFS as a Sqn Ldr, o/c 'D' Flight. In early 1941 he attended 54 OTU and 56 OTU, then rapidly undertaking short periods as a supernumary with 17, 145 and 610 Squadrons. In June 1941 he took command of 71 Squadron. On arrival in Rangoon, Burma, he took command of the Burma Fighter Force until the retreat was over, then becoming Wg Cdr Flying at Dum Dum, India, in August 1942. He returned to the UK in December 1942 (not 1943), joining HQ, Fighter Command, at Bentley Priory. He was then posted to Cranfield as o/c, Fighter Leaders' School. Promoted Acting Grp Capt, he then commanded 55 OTU, Annan, in summer 1943, before taking command of 16(F) Wing of Typhoons in the new tactical air force. The Wing was disbanded on 16 April 1944 and as there were no jobs in 2nd TAF for a Grp Capt or Wg Cdr at the time, he reverted to Wg Cdr and attended 18 OTU and then 51 OTU for conversion to bomber aircraft, but in June was posted to 100 Group of Bomber Command on bomber support operations. Whilst still with 51 OTU, he flew some anti-'Diver' operations in an 85 Squadron Mosquito, the last on 10/11 August 1944. However, he was killed in a take-off accident in a Mosquito on 13 August 1944.

WOODMAN Brian Wallace   Pilot Officer
Brian Woodman was born on 17 November 1922 in Devonport, Auckland, and attended Nelson College. He then worked on the family sheep farm on D'Urville Island, Marlborough, New Zealand, having to wait until he had turned 20 before being able to enlist in the RNZAF in July 1942. He undertook initial training before being despatched to Canada in June 1943, where he attended 14 SFTS and the 1 OTU, being graded 'above average'. He was sent to the UK in June 1944, attending 57 OTU in August and reaching 83 GSU in October 1944. Finally he was posted to 130 Squadron in January 1945 to commence operations. He was commissioned on 24 April 1945. After the end of the war, he was posted with the unit to Norway in June 1945, but was returned to New Zealand in October as a Flg Off, and released in February 1946. He then resumed farming, but was subsequently to contract cancer. After several years illness, he died on 19 December 1975.

WOODMAN Ronald George   RAF Nos. 1167403 (NCO); 69464 (Officer)
He was only 46 when he retired from Shell, and to celebrate his 50th birthday in 1964, he cycled more than 4,000 miles around Canada. He died on 28 June 1996.

Additions to claim list:
1944
8/9 May — this was a Bf 110 of I/NJG 4 flown by Lt Wolfgang Martstaller, who had just shot down a Lancaster of 405 Squadron; Woodman crash-landed in a field near his victim, both he and his radar operator suffering slight wounds.
NB. His claims on 4 and 10/11 November were made with Flg Off A.F.Witt as radar operator. On 2/3 January 1945, while attached to 85 Squadron, he flew with 152496 Flt Lt Bertram James Pitt Simpkins, DFC, a successful radar operator from that unit. His final claim was made with 121338 Flt Lt Arthur John Neville, DFC.

WOODS Eric Norman   RAF Nos. 925682 (NCO); 60119 (Officer)
He was born in Buenos Aires, Argentina, on 8 May 1910 (not in England), his family returning to England in 1914. In February 1920 they moved to Canada, settling in Victoria, British Columbia, but moving to Vancouver a few years later. In the RAF his home was listed as being in Harborne, Birmingham.

Corrections and additions to claim list:
1942

27 Aug	BP867 (not TE867) T-E
2 and 16 Oct	AR466 (not TR466) T-R
27 Oct	BR529 T-D
11-14 Dec	AR559 T-W
19 Dec	ER728 (not EP728) T-S

1943

4 Dec	2	Ju 87s (not 1)	ENW

REVISED TOTAL: 11 and 2 shared destroyed, 4 probables, 9 damaged, 1 destroyed on the ground.

WOODS William Joseph

Additions to claim list:
1941

10 Feb	N5917
20 Feb	V7138

WOODS-SCAWEN Charles Anthony

He was educated at Salesian College, Farnborough, Hampshire.

WOODS-SCAWEN Patrick Philip

Like his brother, he was educated at Salesian College, Farnborough, Hampshire.

Corrections and additions to claim list:
1940

10 May		(b)	
"		(c)	
11 May		(d)	
17 May	2	Bf 109Es (not 1) (e)	N2319
19 May		(f)	P2547

REVISED TOTAL: 11 and 3 shared destroyed, 2 unconfirmed destroyed, 1 probable.
(b) No Hs 126 was lost, but it is possible that this aircraft was forced to land; (c) The aircraft attacked was actually an He 111; (d) 2 claims made; I/KG 76 lost one aircraft; (e) During this engagement he was shot down by Bf 109s of I/JG 3 and baled out, slightly wounded; (f) Three engagements on this date; on the first at 1000 he claimed 2 Bf 109s east of Seclin; 8 and 6 unconfirmed were claimed against II/JG 26 and I(J)/LG 2, which between them actually lost 4; at 1550 his third claim was probably against Lt Heinz Schnabel of 1/JG 3, who crash-landed at Philippeville, wounded and with 10% damage to his aircraft; 1610 his unconfirmed claim was made in the Lille area; this was possibly Ofw Walter Leyerer of 2/JG 77, who was shot down and baled out.

WOODWARD Herbert John

He was born in 1916, attending Blackpool Grammar School and Leeds University. He was commissioned in the RAFO on 24 November 1937, attending 8 FTS thereafter, and joining 64 Squadron in July 1938. Two months later he transferred to the RAF on a Short Service Commission.

WOODWARD Vernon Crompton

Additions to claim list:
1940

14 Jun	(a)	Gladiator II	N5783
20 Jun			N5774
29 Jun	(c)		
24 and 25 Jul			N5768
1941			
17 Jun			Z4377
12 Jul			Z4268

(a) The pilot of the Ca 310 was Serg Magg Stefano Garrisi; (c) Sottotten Antonio Weiss of the 160ª Squadriglia, 12° Gruppo, 50° Stormo Assalto actually crash-landed; Sottotten G.Mario Zuccarini (not Buccarini), who force landed, was from 77ª Squadriglia, 13° Gruppo, 2° Stormo CT.

WOOTTEN Ernest Waite

He was awarded an AFC for forming the first jet aerobatic team in the RAF, with Meteors, when commanding 245 Squadron. He also received a Venezuelan Air Force Cross for assistance in forming their Sabre aerobatic team when he was Air Attache based in Caracas, 1959-63.

WRIGHT Allan Richard

Corrections to claim list:
1941
13 Mar and 16 May—R6293 was an Airspeed Oxford, whilst R6923 was a Spitfire. It would appear therefore that the latter was the aircraft flown on both occasions.

WRIGHT Eric William   RAF Nos. 748522 (NCO); 64870

As a Sgt he attended 6 OTU, Sutton Bridge, at the start of June 1940. He was later made a CBE.

WÜNSCHE Kazimierz   RAF Nos. P793443 (NCO); P2096 (Officer)

He was born in Jaroslaw, and entered the Szkola Podoficerow Lotnictwa dla Maloletnich at Bydgoszcz in 1936, graduating from the school's new location at Krosno in 1939 as a fighter pilot. His claim for a share in the destruction of an Hs 126 on 8 September is unconfirmed. He escaped via Rumania, finally reaching France on 11 November 1939, where he joined GC II/8. On arrival in England, he was posted to 303 Squadron on 2 August 1940. When shot down in P3700, RF-E, on 4 September he suffered burns. He undertook an officers' course at Blackpool whilst with 303 Squadron in 1943. He was decorated by the RAF with both a DFM on 15 November 1942, and a DFC on 2 October 1944. He returned to Poland in 1947 and was accepted for continued service as an instructor at the Oficerska Szkola Lotnicza in Deblin, but in 1952 was expelled from the service for political reasons, and repressed. After 1957 he joined the air medical service, also flying air/sea rescue operations, and for this was awarded the Krzyz Kowalski Oderu Odrodzenia Polski in later years. Living in Warsaw, he died on 10 July 1980.

Additions to claim list:
1940				
31 Aug		V7244 (not V7289) RF-C		
5 and 6 Sep		V7289 RF-S		
1942				
3 Jul	¼	Ju 88 — delete (a)		
„		(b)		
1944				
4 Aug	½	V-1	Mustang III	PK-K	315 Sqn

REVISED TOTAL: 4 and 1 shared destroyed, 1 shared unconfirmed destroyed, 1 probable, 1 shared V-1 destroyed.
(a) He claimed a share in Ju 88A-4 WNr 140017, M2+KK of 2/KüFlGr 106, which crash-landed at Odlings Farm, Aswardly, Lincolnshire. In the event it was credited to only two of the four pilots involved: (b) Ju 88A-4 WNr 140016, M2+BK of 2/KüFlGr 106, crashed at Baumber, Lincolnshire, Fw H.Majer and crew all killed — shared with Flt Sgt Mieczyslaw Popek (see New Aces).

WYKEHAM-BARNES Peter Guy

Whilst with 23 Squadron his navigator was 116970 Flg Off Geoffrey Ernest Palmer, DFC. In Korea in 1950 he undertook seven intruder sorties in a B-26B Invader of the 90th Bomb Group, USAF, during August-September. He was made a Fellow of the Royal Aeronautical Society in 1968. Whilst at the AAEE he helped develop swept wing fighters, including the Hawker P1052, Supermarine 510 and the Avro 707 delta testbeds for the Vulcan bomber. He married the daughter of author J.B.Priestley. Sir Peter Wykeham died on 23 February 1995.

Additions to claim list:
1940		
4 Aug	Gladiator II	
8 Aug	Gladiator I	K7916
17 Aug	„	K8051
9 Dec (first two claims)		P2638
„ (remaining claims)		V7300
15 Dec		„
19 Dec		V7293
1941		
5 Jan		V7558
17 Jan		P2641
1943		
7/8 Mar and 19/20 Apr		DZ230 YP-A

WYNN Vasseure H.(not F.)   USAAF Nos. O-886007; O-54589; 1249A

He was commissioned on 9 December 1942, but with effect from 5 November. On return to the UK he instructed at 53 OTU until 30 June 1943, when he transferred to the USAAF as a 1st Lieutenant. He served in Korea, 1950-51, and was promoted Major on 15 December 1951. He received two US DFCs and four Air Medals during World War II, and a DFC and five Air Medals in Korea. He also claimed two aircraft destroyed on the ground.

REVISED TOTAL: 3 and 2 shared destroyed, 2 probables, 3 damaged, 2 destroyed on the ground.

YATES Jack Neville   RAF Nos. 1164392 (NCO); 159463 (Officer)

He was commissioned on 1 August 1943.

Corrections to claim list:
1944

15 and 20 Jan, and 9 Feb—Spitfire MA299 was not despatched to the Far East; it is believed that this was a misprint for MA290, which did serve with 607 Squadron.

YOUNG Michael Hugh

Additions to claim list:

1942	
14 Jan and 5 Jul	BN286 AK-O
16 Sep	BP450

YULE Robert Duncan

He was posted to the 11 Group Pool in October 1939 before joining 145 Squadron. He was killed in Meteor WF695, which struck WK938 whilst trying to avoid a Hurricane, and lost its tail.

Addition to claim list:

1940	
18 May	N2496

ZARY Henry Paul Michael   RCAF Nos. R95580 (NCO); J9261 (Officer)

'Hank' Zary was a Polish-American, born in Manhattan, New York, on 23 November 1918; his parents' full name was Zarytkiewicz. He lived in the Bronx, New York, attending Stuyvesant High School and then New York University, where he gained a BSc in Science and Physical Education, also playing baseball for the university. Between 1935-1941 he worked to maintain himself during his studies, first as a filing and general clerk, and then as an assistant in the university's biology department. He joined the RCAF on 26 February 1941, qualifying as a pilot and being commissioned on 21 November 1941. After a period as an instructor, he was promoted Flg Off and posted to the UK in October 1942, attending 53 OTU before joining 421 Squadron in April 1943. He was promoted Flt Lt in November 1943, and on 25 July 1944, having shot down two Bf 109s, he ran out of ammunition as he fired on a third, and missed. He then dived on this aircraft, which turned sharply to avoid him, stalled and crashed. In November he returned to Canada on leave, but in December was back in the UK, where he went to 83 GSU before being posted to 416 Squadron. He was promoted Acting Sqn Ldr on 17 February 1945 on taking over command of 403 Squadron. He was released from the service on 11 October 1945, but on 11 February 1946 he died in the Royal Laurentian Hospital, Ste Agathe, Quebec, Canada, following a brief but unspecified illness, aged only 27.

ZUMBACH Jan Eugeniusz Ludvik

Completing his education in 1935, he forged documents the following year in order to pass as a Pole, and joined the service, attending the SPL at Deblin in 1936. Commissioned in 1938, he joined the 111 Eskadra in Warsaw. In France he served in ECD I/55, flying Koolhoven FK 58s, MS 406s, Bloch MB 152s and Arsenal VG 33s. He reached the UK on 18 June 1940. From April 1943 he commanded the 3rd Polish Wing at Kirton-in-Lindsey, then graduating from the Wyszsza Szkola Lotnicza (the Polish Air Force Staff College in England). He then commanded 133 Wing from 3 August 1944-30 January 1945. He died on 3 January 1986, and was subsequently buried in the PAF section of the Powazki Cemetery in Warsaw.

Corrections and additions to claim list:

1940		
7 Sep		RF-B
9 Sep	(a) (b)	RF-G
11 Sep		
15 Sep		RF-E
26 and 27 Sep		RF-J
1941		
2 Jul		RF-A
1942		
27 Apr and 19 Aug		RF-D
1944		
25 Sep	(c)	HB868 JZ

(a) Believed to be Bf 109E-4 WNr 0963 of 4/JG 53, ditched in the Channel; (b) Believed to be Bf 109E-4 WNr 6139 '1' of 8/JG 53, which actually crashed at Sundown Farm, Ditcham; (c) Either FW 190A-8 WNr 173856 of Stab II/JG 26 which crashed near Nijmegen, Flg Theodor Borgschulze missing, or WNr 173083 'Black 2', crash-landed near Neuss, Ofhr Bruno Krüpen wounded.

ZURAKOWSKI Janusz

He was born in Ryzawka in Eastern Poland; he attended the SPL in Deblin in 1934, and was commissioned in 1937, joining the 161 Eskadra of the 6 Pulk at Lvov. Six months before the war he was posted as a fighter instructor to the Centrum Wyszkolina Lotnictwa in Deblin, and in September 1939 he flew with an ad hoc instructors' unit in defence of the city. On 24 August 1940 it appears that he was shot down by Lt Zeis of 1/JG 53, not by Oblt Hans-Karl Mayer. In summer 1941 he moved from 57 OTU to 55 OTU, then to 61 OTU at the end of July 1941, and subsequently to 58 OTU. In February 1959, disappointed by the cancellation of the CF 105 programme, he left the aircraft industry and moved to deserted forest areas of Canada, working in forestry and construction industries. He constructed from scratch a lake resort centre, which he ran for many years. In recent years he was accepted into Canada's Hall of Fame for the aircraft industry, and to commemorate Canada's first supersonic flight, in 1996 a special $20 coin was minted, featuring his portrait.

Additions to claim list:
1940

15 Aug	(a)	X4016
5 Sep	(b)	N3279
6 Sep	(c)	"
28 Sep (not 29th) Bf 110 Probable (not shared)		N3191

REVISED TOTAL: 3 destroyed, 1 probable, 1 damaged.

(a) Bf 110C M8+BP of 6/ZG 76, which crashed on the Isle of Wight. This was also attacked by a Polish pilot of 609 Squadron. Zurakowski did not claim two victories on this date; (b) Bf 109E WNr 6252 of 8/JG 53, ditched in the Channel, flown by Fw Ochsenkuehn; (c) Bf 109E WNr 3578, '5', of 7/JG 26, crashed at Swamp Farm, Old Romney.

CHAPTER FIVE

Fighter Pilots Claiming Four Victories

Service No	Name	Rank and First Names	Decorations	Units
113431	ATKINS	Flt Lt John Cyril Edwin	DFC	219 Sqn
40660	BAKER	Wg Cdr Ernest Reginald	DSO,DFC	263 Sqn
NZ40960	BARGH	Flg Off Charles Victor, RNZAF	DFC	67 Sqn
J5983	BARKER	Flt Lt Robert Bruce, RCAF	DFC	442,412 Sqn
562424	BARRY	Flg Off J.E.		29 Sqn
103589	BENN	Flg Off Michael Julius Wedgewood	DFC	153 Sqn
J24513	BERRYMAN	Flt Lt Lloyd Frederick, RCAF	DFC	412 Sqn
131762	BIRRELL	Flt Lt Robert	DFC	605 Sqn
	(plus 3 V-1s)			
562424/145147	BLACK	Plt Off McDougall		54 Sqn
126590	BOARDMAN	Flg Off Hubert Stanley	DFC	153 Sqn
	BOWKER	Flg Off Harlow Wilber, RCAF		412 Sqn
	(plus 1 on the ground)			
60522	BRADWELL	Flt Lt Richard	DFC	108,501 Sqn
	(plus 3 V-1s)			
41898	BROADHURST	Plt Off John William		222 Sqn
124625	BRIDGES	Flg Off Vivian	DFC	239 Sqn
102143	BROWN	Flt Lt Eric	DFC	136 Sqn
370060	BROWN	Sqn Ldr Harry Lennox Innes	DFC	112,616 Sqn
J9068	BROWNE	Sqn Ldr John Danforth, RCAF	DFC	442 Sqn
80139	BURKE	Flt Lt Tom Archibald	DFC	65,602 Sqns
	BUYS	Flt Lt T.F.A., Dutch		611 Sqn
AUS404495	CABLE	Flt Lt William Oswald, RAAF	DFC	250,450,452,457 Sqns
64859	CAMPBELL	Plt Off John Acy, US	DFC	71,258,605 Sqns
J15673	CARTER	Flg Off Arthur Reginald, RCAF	DFC	153 Sqn
J19991	CHOWN	Flg Off Clinton Warren, RCAF	DFC	515 Sqn
AUS408969	CLARKSON	Flg Off K.E., RAAF		611,72 Sqns
1331525	CLAY	Wt Off Philip Henry Thornton	DFC	130 Sqn
70797	CLEGG	Flt Lt Charles Gordon	DSO	46,159 Sqns
120734	CORRE	Flg Off Howard John	DFC	264 Sqn
	(plus 1 V-1)			
J4874	COTTERILL	Flt Lt Stanley Herbert Ross, RCAF	DFC	418 Sqn
85689	COUNTER	Sqn Ldr Cyril Frank	DFC	261 Sqn
AUS404004	COWARD	Flt Lt George Cyril, RAAF	DFC	3 RAAF,250 Sqns
124530	COWELL	Flt Lt Peter	DFC	41 Sqn
130416	CRONE	Flg Off Robert Alexander	DFC	29 Sqn
J5065	CULL	Flt Lt Richard Henry, RCAF	DFC	412,401 Sqn
J7769	CURPHEY	Flg Off L.H. RCAF(US)		112 Sqn
P1290	CZERWINSKI	Sqn Ldr Tadeusz, Polish	KW**	GC I/145, 302,306 Sqn
	(plus 1 and 2 shared V-1s)			
126951	DACRE	Flg Off Kenneth Fraser	DFC	605 Sqn
63418	DAVIES	Flg Off Idwal James	DFC	609 Sqn
76311	DEACON-ELLIOTT	Sqn Ldr Robert	DFC	41,72 Sqns
P	DRECKI	Flt Lt Wladyslaw Maciej, Polish		111 Esk,303 Sqn PFT, 152 Sqn
63785	DREDGE	Wg Cdr Allan Sydney	DSO	253,261,183,3 Sqns
AUS412412	ECCLESTON	Plt Off Hubert Sylvester	DFM	111,79 RAAF Sqns
81368	EDSALL	Flg Off Eric Frank	DFC	54,222,261 Sqns
80274	ELCOMBE	Flt Lt George	DFC	66 Sqn
741332	ELSE	Sgt Peter		610 Sqn
J15118	ETIENNE	Flt Lt Philippe Elwyn, RCAF	DFC	609,79,131, 406 Sqns
	(plus 1 on the ground)			
NZ427480	EVANS	Flg Off Andrew Ralph, RNZAF	DFC	486 Sqn
J15976	FARQUHARSON	Flt Lt Gordon Henry, RCAF	DFC	54,126,416 Sqns
J6364	FOX	Flt Lt Charles William, RCAF	DFC*	412 Sqn
J26866	FRANCIS	Flg Off John Philip Wiseman, RCAF	DFC	442,401 Sqn
62647	FRECKER	Flt Lt Albert Derek	DFC	252 Sqn
62320	FURSE	Sqn Ldr Denis Chetwynd	DFC	406,604 Sqn
J17155	GARLAND	Sqn Ldr John William, RCAF	DFC	80,127,3 Sqns
NZ404863	GARTRELL	Flt Lt Ernest Charles	DFC	232 Sqn
AUS411770	GARVAN	Flg Off Denis Edward William, RAAF	DFC	136 Sqn
39438	GIBSON	Flt Lt Guy Penrose +	DFC*	29 Sqn
121291	GILES	Flg Off David	DFC	255 Sqn
AUS404337	GLENDINNING	Flt Lt Alfred, RAAF	DFC	3RAAF,92,450 Sqns

580286/45491	GOODMAN	Flt Lt Geoffrey	DFC	85,29 Sqns
69475	GRAVES	Sqn Ldr Michael Adrian	DFC	126 Sqn
40108	GRAY	Flg Off William Napier		3,213 Sqns
1180408	HACKFORTH	Sgt S.N.		136,232 Sqns
J6795	HALCROW	Flt Lt Alexander Foch, RCAF	DFC	401,411 Sqns
102147	HALFORD	Flt Lt John Rosher Stirling	DFC	274 Sqn
49529	HAMPSHIRE	Flg Off Cyril Edward		85,111,249,286 Sqns, 422 Flt
82546	HANUS	Flt Lt Josef Jan, Czech	DFC	310,32,245, 125,68,600 Sqns
41405	HARDACRE	Flg Off John Reginald		504 Sqn
103504	HARRISON	Sqn Ldr Reginald Harrison	DFC	406,151 Sqns
1193301	HARROP	Wt Off Sidney James	DFC	600 Sqn
81879	HART	Plt Off Norris, Canadian		242 Sqn
NZ41511	HAY	Plt Off Bruce Hamilton, RNZAF	DFC	3 Sqn
66516	HEAD (plus 7 V-1s)	Flt Lt Norman Sidney	DFC	96 Sqn
128431	HENDERSON	Flg Off Robert Welch	DFC	274,92 Sqns
26138	HEYCOCK	Wg Cdr George Francis Wheaton	DFC	23,141 Sqns
101514	HIGHAM	Flg Off Frederick Jack	DFC	68 Sqn
87028	HILKEN	Flt Lt Raleigh Willoughby	DFC	600 Sqn
120026	HINDLE	Plt Off Thomas		260 Sqn
2005774	HOJEM	Capt Rodney Clayton, SAAF	DFC	2SAAF,5SAAF Sqns
36027	HOWELL	Sqn Ldr Edward Alexander	OBE,DFC	33 Sqn
33469	HOY	Sqn Ldr William	DFC	604 Sqn
P784079	IDRIAN (plus 2 V-1s)	Wt Off Ryazard, Polish		315 Sqn
41292	INNESS	Sqn Ldr Richard Frederick		152,603,222 Sqns
	JACKMAN	Sgt W.J.		603 Sqn
41423	JACOBSEN	Plt Off Louis Reginald	DFC	263 Sqn
754867	JEFFERYS	Sgt George William		43,46 Sqns
47706	JENNINGS	Flt Lt Bernard James	DFM	19 Sqn
AUS	JEWELL	Flg Off W.E., RAAF		3RAAF Sqn
101572	JOWLING	Flg Off Frederick Ernest Wambey		153 Sqn
AUS420957	JUDD	Flg Off Garnett Wolsley, RAAF	DFC	600 Sqn
J644494	KALLIO	Sqn Ldr Oliver Charles, RCAF (US)	DFC	33,145,417 Sqns
42006	KAY	Plt Off Desmond Haywood Siddley	DFC*	264 Sqn
39615	KELLOW	Flt Lt Raymond Alan		213 Sqn
R86106	KERNAGHAN	Sgt Stanley John, RCAF	DFM	252 Sqn
AUS584	KINNINMONT	Wg Cdr Jack Royston, RAAF	DSO,DFC*	21RAAF,453, 86RAAF,
		(also 77RAAF Sqn in Korea)		76RAAF,75RAAF Sqns
NZ41912	KUHN	Sgt Edmund Eric Geddes, RNZAF	DFM	488,605 Sqns
103564	LAING-MEASON	Flt Lt Patrick Beverley	DFC	145,43 Sqns
NZ403964	LATTIMER	Flt Lt Charles Henry, RNZAF	DFC	249,1435,234 Sqns
88855	LAWRENCE	Flg Off Norman Anthony		54 Sqn
39796	LEE	Wg Cdr Patrick Henry	DFC	
61056	LINTOTT	Flt Lt John Peter Morley	DFC	85 Sqn
85649	LOVELL	Flg Off Victor Charles	DFC	89,29 Sqns
J19197	MACKENZIE	Plt Off Donald Murdo, RCAF	DFC	151,410 Sqns
109894	MAIN	Plt Off Basil William		46,126 Sqns
42070	MARCHAND	Plt Off Roy Achille		73 Sqn
70809	MARSHALL	Plt Off James Eglinton	DFC	85 Sqn
83715	MARSTON	Plt Off Kenneth John		56 Sqn
82706	McDOUGALL	Flt Lt Roy		3,73 Sqns
J14006	McCLARTY	Flg Off Malcolm Stanley, RCAF	DFC	442,411 Sqns
AUS403596	McINTOSH	Flt Lt Lawrence	DFC	122,111 Sqns
	McLEOD	Flg Off S.J.		72 Sqn
89763	McRITCHIE	Plt Off Alexander Ian, Australian	DFC	151 Sqn
J15237	McROBERTS	Flg Off Robert Cowan, RCAF	DFC	421 Sqn
J17795	MERCER	Flt Lt George Franklin, RCAF	DFC	610,185,411 Sqns
39746	MEREDITH	Flg Off Richard Vincent		17 Sqn
1164046	MERRIMAN	Sgt Edward William	DFM	610 Sqn
	MITCHELL	Flg Off H.E.		87,89 Sqns
102100	MOORE (plus 23 and 1 shared V-1s)	Flt Lt Arthur Robert	DFC*	56,3 Sqns
66484	MORIARTY	Plt Off Patrick Denis		274 Sqn
1078314	MOSTON	Sgt Sidney Percival	DFM	81 Sqn
42871	MOUNSDON	Plt Off Maurice Hewlett		56 Sqn
AUS404773	NEILL	Plt Off Garth Angus, RAAF	DFM	122,3RAAF Sqns
60104	NEWBERY (plus 8 and 1 shared V-1s)	Sqn Ldr Richard Alfred	DFC*	501,118,610 Sqns
NZ404449	NEWTON	Flt Lt Harold Brassey	DFC	125,600 Sqns
R3384	NITZ	Flg Off Arthur Farrand, RCAF (US)	DFM	250 Sqn

44929	NORFOLK	Flt Lt Norman Robert	DFC	72 Sqn
NZ1316	OLDFIELD	Sqn Ldr John Anderson, RNZAF	DFC	14RNZAF, 18RNZAF Sqns
J5125	OLMSTED	Sqn Ldr William Alfred, RCAF	DSO,DFC*	81,232,442 Sqns
	OLSEN	2/Lt Reidar Haave, Norwegian		331 Sqn
65502	PAGE	Flt Lt Vernon Douglas	DFC	601,610,54,111 Sqns
162949	PANTER	Plt Off K.V.		25 Sqn,FEF
72028	PASSY	Sqn Ldr Cyril Wolrick	OBE,DFC	605,89 Sqns
40423	PATTEN	Sqn Ldr Hubert Paul Frederick		64,79,307,108,604, 1435 Sqns
741920	PEARCE	Sgt Leonard Hilary Borlase		32,249,46 Sqns
127224	PEARSON	Flt Lt Graham Stuart	DFC	65 Sqn
	PEARSON	Flt Lt M.G.		54 Sqn
J7892	PEGLAR	Flt Lt Warren Brock, RCAF	DFC	501,335th US,274 Sqns
J10802	PLUMER	Sqn Ldr Ben Erwin, RCAF	DFC	410,409 Sqns
	(plus 1 on the ground)			
741471	PROCTOR	Sgt Jack		602 Sqn
P10397V	RABIE	Lt Schalk, SAAF	DFC	1SAAF Sqn
62014	RABY	Flt Lt Dennis John	DFC	239 Sqn
J5800	RACINE	Flt Lt Gerald Geoffrey, RCAF	DFC	263 Sqn
	(plus 3 on the ground)			
NZ411937	RAYNER	Flg Off Leonard Adolphus, RNZAF	DFC	18RNZAF Sqn
101092	RICE	Sqn Ldr Graham James	DFC	141 Sqn
60515	ROBINSON	Flg Off Denis Norman		152 Sqn
90062	ROYCE	Wg Cdr William Barrington	DFC	504,260
P76762	ROZYCKI	Plt Off Wladyslaw	DFC	141 Esk,238,307 Sqns
	(1 in Poland)			
NZ41714	RUDLING	Flg Off John David, RNZAF	DFM	136 Sqn
J8136	RUSSELL	Flt Lt Neil Gillespie, RCAF	DFC*	250,203,416 Sqns
47428V	SACHS	Lt Albert, SAAF	DFC	92 Sqn
106175	SANDERS	Flg Off Evatt Anthony	DFC	29 Sqn
105167	SAVAGE	Flg Off Thomas Wood		64,92 Sqns
76161	SCADE	Flg Off Thomas Patterson Kyd	DFC	46,73 Sqns
AUS	SCOTT	Sgt Derek, RAAF		3RAAF Sqn
123465	SCRASE	Flg Off Rodney Diran	DFC	72 Sqn
80102	SHAND	Flt Lt Ian Hardy Robertson	DFC	145 Sqn
566529	SHEPPERD	Sgt Edmund Eric		152 Sqn
42653	SIMMONDS	Plt Off Vernon Churchill		238,118,333 Sqns
41481	SIMPSON	Flg Off Geoffrey Mervyn		229 Sqn
85710	SIMS	Plt Off Mervin Harold, Canadian	DFC	418 Sqn
P0717	SLONSKI	Sqn Ldr Jozef, Polish		306 Sqn
117511	SMART	Flg Off Rae Richard	DFC	605 Sqn
37129	SMITH	Wg Cdr Roddick Lee		151,255 Sqns
AUS401252	SMITHSON	Flg Off John Harold, RAAF	DFC	457 Sqn
90223	SPEKE	Flt Lt Hugh	DFC	604 Sqn
1757066	STIRLING	Plt Off James Colin	DFC	145 Sqn
J7597	TEW	Flt Lt William Richard, RCAF	DFC	132,401 Sqns
AUS420363	TURNER	Flg Off Valton Leslie, RAAF	DFC	56 Sqn
P2094	TURZANSKI	Sgt Michal, Polish		307 Sqn
AUS402684	TWEMLOW	Plt Off Frank MacKay, RAAF	DFC	250 Sqn
85670	VARLEY	Flt Lt George Wallace	DFC	79,247,222 Sqns,MNFU
174839	VLOTMAN	Flt Sgt Christian Johan, Dutch	DFC, Dutch Flg Cr	488 Sqn
P1808	WALAWSKI	Flt Lt Janusz, Polish	DFC	317,316 Sqn
P1291	WAPNIAREK	Flt Lt Stefan		132 Esk,302 Sqn
	(3 in Poland)			
AUS402267	WATSON	Flt Lt Philip Herbert, RAAF	DFC	457 Sqn
126771	WAUD	Flg Off Norman Leslie	DFC	81 Sqn
N206	WESTLY	Capt Erik Leif, Norwegian	DFC	332 Sqn
NZ414367	WHITE	Flt Lt Geoffrey Gordon, RNZAF	DFC	126 Sqn
	WHITING	Sqn Ldr Spencer Rowland, South African	DSO	94,213 Sqns
1015523	WILDING	Flg Off Frank Ernest	DFC	136 Sqn
P47885V	WILDSMITH	Capt Hugh Errol Noel, SAAF	DFC	2SAAF Sqn
69442	WOOD	Flt Lt Cyril Patrick Joseph, Canadian	DFC	403 Sqn
564803	WOODS	Flg Off Eric Joseph		33 Sqn
105174	WOOLLEY	Sqn Ldr Frank Geoffrey	DFC*	602,41,350, 130 Sqns
33338	WORCESTER	Flg Off A Gray		112 Sqn
86684	WRIGHT	Sqn Ldr Geoffrey John		605 Sqn
	(plus 2 V-1s)			
J39819	YOUNG	Flt Lt Forrest Bee	DFC	442 Sqn

* Indicates a Bar to a decoration. + Later Wg Cdr Guy Gibson, VC,DSO,DFC.

CHAPTER SIX

"Diver" — The V-1 Aces

Some detail was published in the 1994 edition regarding the operations flown against the V-1 flying bombs, and it is intended to expand somewhat upon this subject here.

Intelligence gathered from agents, Polish and French Resistance movements, and aerial reconnaissance, had prepared the British authorities for an attack on Southern England by robot weapons. Bombing attacks on the German research establishment at Peenemunde, and on factories believed to be involved in the production of such weapons, had delayed their introduction into service, and therefore their onslaught, quite considerably, whilst prior to the Normandy Invasion of 6 June 1944, much aerial effort had been expended in attacking the launching sites being constructed in the Pas de Calais area of France, between Dieppe and Calais.

During the night of 14/15 June 1944 the first interception of a flying bomb was made over the English Channel just after midnight by Flt Lt J.G.Musgrave of 605 Squadron, and this was shot down. The new weapon was a small monoplane of some 22 feet in length, with a wingspan of around 17 feet. Powered by a single pulse-jet engine mounted above the rear fuselage, it flew at a maximum speed of 500 kilometres per hour and at a maximum height of 2,500 metres, to deliver about 1,870 pounds of high explosive to its target. Level flight was maintained by gyroscopically-activated controls until the machine ran out of fuel, at which point it dived onto whatever lay beneath its line of flight.

After a prolonged and difficult introduction to service, the Fieseler Fi 103, as it was correctly designated, was first launched towards its target area on 12 June. The first day's firing proved a fiasco, with only ten launched, seven of which crashed or blew up at once. The first to reach England fell on Swanscombe, near Gravesend, at 0418 hours on 13 June. Thereafter launch rates increased rapidly, and in the 24 hours between the nights of 15/16 and 16/17 June, 151 were reported by the defences. 144 crossed the coast, and of these 14 were shot down by AA, seven by fighters and one by both jointly. Codenamed 'Diver', but soon dubbed 'Doodlebug' or 'Buzz-bomb' by the Press and public, the bombs proved very inaccurate, their fall being quite haphazard.

Initial response was to extend the assault on the launching sites, whilst fighter aircraft formed the first defence, patrolling over the Channel and South Coast between the Thames Estuary and Newhaven/Beachy Head. 192 heavy AA guns and an equal number of light weapons provided the next line of defence in a belt across central Kent, running from the north bank of the Estuary, through Tunbridge Wells, to Leatherhead in the west. On the eastern outskirts of London, 480 balloons provided the final element, before the capital city itself was reached.

The initial patrols were undertaken by 11 squadrons of fighters, two of them Mosquito-equipped for the period of darkness. It became obvious almost at once that these arrangements were inadequate, and rapidly the guns were increased to 376 heavy and 540 light weapons, whilst the balloon barrage was substantially strengthened to some 1,000 balloons.

Fighter units included the new 150 Wing at Newchurch with its three squadrons of Tempests (56 Squadron was just completing re-equipment from Spitfire IXs at the time), together with the Griffon-engined Spitfires of 41 Squadron (Mark XIIs), 91 and 322 Squadrons (Mark XIVs), and the Mustang IIIs of 129, 306 and 315 Squadrons which formed 133 Wing, withdrawn from 83 Group, 2nd TAF, for the purpose. In order to strengthen the night defences, a special flight of Tempests was formed at Wittering with pilots of the Fighter Interception Unit. This moved to join the other Tempest squadrons at Newchurch.

Over the weeks which followed, further units became involved, including 316 Squadron, a further Polish Mustang unit, which moved south from Coltishall in 12 Group's area, 130 and 610 Squadrons, both recently re-equipped with Spitfire XIVs, 1 and 165 Squadrons with Spitfire IXBs, and 137 Squadron with Typhoons.

By night the number of units becoming involved tended to be wider, and at various times 96, 125, 219 and 456 Squadrons — all ADGB units with radar-equipped Mosquito — and 418 and 605 Squadrons with Mosquito II and VI intruder aircraft, would be joined by 85 Group, 2nd TAF, Mosquitos of 264 and 604 Squadrons, and by aircraft of 85 and 157 Squadrons from Bomber Command's 100 Group. By 15 July 2,579 V-1s had reached England, 1,241 being destroyed by the defences, 1,280 falling in the London area. The percentage destroyed had reached 50% during the week of 9-15 July, mainly by the fighters. By then 13 squadrons of single-engined aircraft and three of Mosquitos were on full-time patrol duties, whilst six more divided their time between defensive operations and the invasion area. On 23 June a Spitfire pilot had 'flipped' a bomb onto its back, causing it to fall out of control. This had been achieved by bringing the wingtip of his aircraft gently up beneath that of the bomb, whereupon the gyroscopic controls tumbled.

The number of bombs reaching their target, coupled with the casualties and damage caused were still too high to be accepted however. A change commenced on 14 July, whereby the guns were moved to the coastal area, where by 19th 412 heavy and 572 light weapons were in place, together with 168 Bofors and 416 20mm Hispanos of the RAF Regiment, 28 light guns of the Royal Armoured Corps, and some rocket batteries. Now the fighters patrolled over the Channel and over central Kent, between the guns and the balloons. The guns were now also receiving stocks of proximity-fused shells. From this point the balance of success shifted to the latter, which increased their results from 16% to 24% of all bombs passing through their area. During the week of 7-14 August they claimed 120 of 305 bombs, for the first time exceeding the claims of the fighters.

August saw the greatest concentration of defence, 592 heavy and 922 light guns, 2,015 balloons, 600 rocket-firing barrels, 15 day and six night fighter squadrons, steadily reducing the number of bombs getting through. Between 16 August and 5 September only 17% of the 1,124 launched reached their target area, while during the last four days of this period, only 28 out of 192 reached London. The climatic night was 27/28 August, when 87 of 97 were brought down, 62 by guns, 19 by fighters, two by balloons and four by balloons and guns combined.

By 5 September however, the Allied armies had overrun the launching areas, and the attack ceased. By this time two more Tempest units, 274 amd 501, had joined the defences — the latter incorporating most of the pilots and aircraft from the FIU Tempest Flight — while 616 Squadron had introduced the first operational Gloster Meteor Is to the fray.

11 days later the assault was resumed, seven bombs crossing the coast. These had been air-launched by Heinkel He 111 bombers operating from airfields in Holland. These could carry out their new role safely only by night, and they and the missiles they launched became the prey of night fighters — including the Tempests of 501 Squadron, and the Mosquitos of 25 and 68 Squadrons. 80 were launched in this manner during late September, 23 of which were destroyed by the defences. In the first half of October 38 of 69 were brought down however. One attack was launched on Manchester during December, catching the defences by surprise, while in March 1945 104 were launched from ramps in Holland, 81 of which were shot down, 76 of them by the guns. The last fell on England on 28 March 1945, and the last to be launched was shot down next day.

Between June 1944 and March 1945 3,957 bombs were claimed to have been destroyed, ADGB squadrons reportedly being credited with 1,847 (all RAF fighters with 1,979), while the guns were allocated 1,866, the balloons 232, and Naval guns 12.

Surprisingly few units other than those specifically allocated to V-1 patrol, enjoyed the opportunity to intercept any of the bombs whilst engaged on their normal cross-Channel activities. Indeed, after the first few days they were officially discouraged from doing so, in order to avoid getting in the way of the formal defenders. An exception was 310 (Czech) Squadron, Flt Lt Otto Smik of this unit claiming three shot down on 8 July 1944.

Following the loss of the Pas de Calais area, and the advance of the British and Canadian armies into Belgium, much of the V-1 attack was then transferred towards the port of Antwerp. Only one would ever be caught by a fighter here, Dutch Flg Off G.F.J.Jongbloed, who had claimed seven and two shared during the previous summer, shooting down one on 28 February 1945 whilst flying a Tempest with 222 Squadron.

The totals claimed by individual squadrons amount to a somewhat higher figure when added together than the numbers set out above. Indeed, the totals of several squadrons have been reported at a wide variety of differing figures. 3 Squadron, for instance, has been listed with anything from 258-305½ bombs shot down! This confusion appears to arise from the system of confirmations employed at the time. A study of squadron operations record books shows frequent sour comment, when claims made were reduced, frequently shares in successes being credited to other units, or to AA batteries when pilots felt quite convinced that only they had been involved.

For instance, 486 (New Zealand) Squadron's claims for 241 V-1s were subsequently reduced to 223, BUT pilots' individual claim totals were allowed to stand. Thus an addition of all the individual totals produces a higher total than the squadron is formally credited with. In the case of the Polish units, the Polish Air Force appears to have downgraded many individual totals, rather than allowing pilots to retain their claims made at the time, and many claims which appear to have been made individually, have been treated as shares subsequently. With this in mind, the list of squadron totals provided below is therefore the best that can be arrived at, but may include claims which were not subsequently confirmed.

It will already have been noted that many of the pilots whose biographical notes appeared in the main body of the book because they had made claims against five or more aircraft, also claimed numbers of V-1s. Indeed such a biography has been provided of the most successful of all the "V-1 Aces", Sqn Ldr J.Berry. Others amongst the most successful, such as Wg Cdr R.P.Beamont, Sqn Ldr R.van Lierde of 3 Squadron and Flt Lt F.R.L. Mellersh of 96 Squadron, are similarly included.

In the 1994 volume a list of all those claiming five or more V-1s was provided, although this suffered badly from some faulty print setting and proof reading. A revised and corrected list is therefore provided at the end of this chapter. Also however, full claim lists of both V-1s and enemy aircraft for all those not subject to full biographies, are included here also, with brief notes regarding each of these pilot.

UNIT CLAIMS AGAINST V-1s

Unit	Aircraft Type	Base	Total Claimed
3 Squadron	Tempest V	Newchurch	288-305$\frac{1}{2}$
486 Squadron	Tempest V	Newchurch	223 (241 claimed)
91 Squadron	Spitfire XIV	West Malling, Deanland	185-189
96 Squadron	Mosquito XIII	Ford, Odiham	165-174
322 Squadron	Spitfire XIV	West Malling, Deanland	108$\frac{1}{2}$
501 Squadron	Tempest V	Westhampnett, Manston, Bradwell Bay, Hunsdon	72-95
FIU	Tempest V	Newchurch	86$\frac{1}{2}$
41 Squadron	Spitfire XII	West Malling, Westhampnett, Friston, Lympne	44$\frac{1}{3}$-81
418 Squadron	Mosquito II	Holmesley South, Hurn, Middle Wallop	79$\frac{1}{2}$ (83 claimed)
129 Squadron	Mustang III	Coolham, Holmesley South,Ford, Brenzett	66-86
56 Squadron	Tempest V*	Newchurch	70-77
316 Squadron	Mustang III	West Malling, Friston	74
605 Squadron	Mosquito VI	Manston, Blackbushe	71
306 Squadron	Mustang III	Coolham, Holmesley South, Ford, Brenzett	60
315 Squadron	Mustang III	Coolham, Holmesley South, Ford, Brenzett	53
165 Squadron	Spitfire IXB	Harrowbeer, Detling, Lympne	50$\frac{3}{4}$
1 Squadron	Spitfire IXB	Harrowbeer, Detling, Lympne	47$\frac{1}{6}$
610 Squadron	Spitfire XIV	Harrowbeer, West Malling, Westhampnett, Friston, Lympne	46$\frac{1}{2}$
157 Squadron	Mosquito XIX	Swannington, West Malling	36$\frac{1}{2}$
456 Squadron	Mosquito XVII	Ford	29
137 Squadron	Typhoon IB	Manston	28-29
25 Squadron	Mosquito XVII	Castle Camps, Coltishall	27
68 Squadron	Mosquito XVII	Castle Camps, Coltishall	19
274 Squadron	Tempest V	Merston, Detling, Gatwick, West Malling	19
85 Squadron	Mosquito XVII	West Malling, Swannington	18
264 Squadron	Mosquito XIII	Hartford Bridge, Hunsdon	18
616 Squadron	Meteor I	Manston, Debden	12$\frac{1}{2}$
219 Squadron	Mosquito XXX	Bradwell Bay, Hunsdon	12
130 Squadron	Spitfire XIV	Westhampnett, Merston, Tangmere, Lympne	11$\frac{1}{2}$
125 Squadron	Mosquito XVII	Hurn, Middle Wallop, Coltishall	5$\frac{1}{2}$
310 Squadron	Spitfire LF IX	Tangmere	3
604 Squadron	Mosquito XII	Hurn, Colerne, Zeals	2
222 Squadron	Tempest V	Gilze-Rijen (Holland)	1

* 56 Squadron's first claim was made by a Spitfire IX pilot.

THE PILOTS

BAILEY H.G.   Pilot Officer   RAAF No. 417290

Born in Adelaide, Australia, on 11 January 1924, he was a student in Booborowie, Southern Australia prior to joining the RAAF. On completion of training in the UK, he was posted to 3 Squadron, flying Tempests during summer 1944. After the unit had moved to Holland to become part of 2nd TAF, he was shot down near Rheine in Tempest EJ653 on 22 February 1945 by Lt Waldemar Soffing of I/JG 26, becoming a POW.

1944							
18 Jun	$\frac{1}{2}$	V-1		Tempest V	JN739	nr Dungeness	3 Sqn
,,		V-1		,,	,,	4m N Eastbourne	,,
23 Jun		V-1		,,			,,

Date		Claim	Aircraft	Serial	Location	Squadron
25 Jun		V-1	„	JN752	NW Dungeness	„
27 Jun		V-1	„			„
5 Jul		V-1	„	EJ582	15m S Beachy Head	„
		V-1	„	JN807	3m off Pevensey	„
6 Jul		V-1	„	„	over sea	„
7 Jul		V-1	„			„
16 Jul		V-1	„			„
18 Jul	½	V-1	„	JN807	N Rye	„
28 Jul		V-1	„			„
2 Aug	2	V-1s	„			„

TOTAL: 12 and 2 shared V-1s destroyed.

BALASSE M.A.L.   Flying Officer   RAF No. Belgian No.

Balasse was a Belgian pilot who served with 41 Squadron. When the unit moved to Holland to join 2nd TAF, he was shot down during the first major engagement there on 23 January 1945, falling victim to an FW 190D-9 of III/JG 54.

1944		Claim	Aircraft	Serial	Location	Squadron
3 Jul		V-1	Spitfire XII	EN609	N Bexhill	41 Sqn
4 Jul	½	V-1	„	EN229	SE Isle of Wight	„
19 Jul		V-1	„	MB880	Dungeness	„
21 Jul		V-1	„		8m S Hastings	„
23 Jul	½	V-1	„	MB798	5m SE Rye	„
26 Jul		V-1	„	EN609	5-8m S Beachy Head	„
29 Jul		V-1	„	„	10-15m from Le Touquet	„
		V-1	„	„	3m SE Woodchurch	„

TOTAL: 6 and 2 shared V-1s destroyed.

BANGERTER B.M.   Flight Lieutenant   RAF No. Belgian No.

This Belgian pilot served in 610 Squadron during summer 1944. He was subsequently posted to 350 (Belgian) Squadron, where he remained for the rest of the war.

1944		Claim	Aircraft	Location	Squadron
24 Jun	½	V-1	Spitfire XIV		610 Sqn
31 Jul		V-1	„		„
28 Aug	2	V-1s	„		„
29 Aug	½	V-1	„	off Dungeness	„
1945					
30 Apr	2	FW 190s	„		350 Sqn
2 May	½	Ar 234	„		„

TOTAL: 4 and 1 shared V-1s destroyed, 2 and 1 shared aircraft destroyed.

BARCKLEY Robert Edward   Flying Officer   RAF No. 138650

A Tempest pilot with 3 Squadron, who was awarded a DFC on 3 November 1944.

1944		Claim	Aircraft	Serial	Location	Squadron
18 Jun		V-1	Tempest V			3 Sqn
19 Jun		V-1	„	JN759	W Horley	„
		V-1	„	JN768	nr Biggin Hill	„
24 Jun		V-1	„			„
7 Jul		V-1	„	JN815	nr East Grinstead	„
9 Jul	2	V-1s	„			„
10 Jul	2	V-1s	„			„
14 Jul		V-1	„			„
	½	V-1	„			„
20 Jul		V-1	„	JN755	5m W Rye	„
29 Aug		V-1	„			„

TOTAL: 12 and 1 shared V-1s destroyed.

BARLLOMIEJCZYK Czeslaw   Warrant Officer   RAF No. P783248

Barllomiejczyk flew Mustang IIIs with 316 Squadron; this Polish pilot was awarded the Cross of Valour and Bar, and the Silver Cross of Merit with Swords.

1943		Claim	Aircraft	Serial	Location	Squadron
24 Jun		FW 190	Spitfire IX	BS302	Nieuport	316 Sqn
1944						
5 Jul		V-1	Mustang III	359 SZ-V	S Folkestone	„
		V-1	„	„	3m SW Mereworth	„
7 Aug	4	V-1s	„	849 SZ-W	mid Channel	„

TOTAL: 6 V-1s destroyed, 1 aircraft destroyed.

BENSTED B.G.   Flying Officer   RAF No.

'Bouncing' Bensted flew Mosquito VIs with 605 Squadron. He was killed in action with his navigator, Plt Off C.L. Burrage, on 2 October 1944.

1944						
23/24 Jun	2	V-1s	Mosquito VI (a)			605 Sqn
27/28 Jun		V-1	„	(a)		„
6/7 Jul		V-1	„	(a)		„
28/29 Jul	3	V-1s	„	(b)		„
14/15 Aug		V-1	„	(a)		„

TOTAL: 8 V-1s destroyed.
(a) With Plt Off C.L.Burrage as navigator; (b) With Flt Sgt C.R.Couchman as navigator.

BEYER Andrzej   Flying Officer   RAF No. P1855

Andzej Beyer was a Polish pilot who flew with 306 Squadron.

1944						
18 May	1/4	He 111	Mustang III	UZ-Z	12m NE Nevers	306 Sqn
7 Jun		Bf 109F	„	UZ-Y	Pont Audennes area	„
17 Jun	1/2	FW 190	„	UZ-N	10m SW Nogent	„
12 Jul		V-1	„	UZ-Y	W Rye	„
24 Jul		V-1	„	UZ-V	NE Hastings	„
26 Jul		V-1	„	„	SE Lydd	„
19 Aug		V-1	„			„
29 Aug		V-1	„		N Dungeness	„

TOTAL: 5 V-1s destroyed, 1 and 2 shared aircraft destroyed.

BOND Peter McCall   Squadron Leader   RAF No. 40073

Peter Bond was granted a Short Service Commission in late summer 1937. Details of his service prior to 1944 have not been discovered. In the summer of that year however, he joined 91 Squadron as a supernumary Sqn Ldr, becoming commanding officer in August. He then led the unit until March 1945.

1944						
18 Jun		V-1	Spitfire XIV	RB161	E Croydon	91 Sqn
„	1/4	V-1	„	„	N West Malling	„
21 Jun		V-1	„	„	Channel	„
27 Jun	1/2	V-1	„	„	N West Malling	„
„		V-1	„	„	Ashford area	„
11 Jul	1/2	V-1	„	RM621	Sevenoaks area	„
14 Jul		V-1	„	RB161	SE West Malling	„
23 Jul		V-1	„	RM624	SE Robertsbridge	„
30 Jul		V-1	„	RM652	S Deanland	„
2 Aug		V-1	„	RM687	N Hastings	„

TOTAL: 7 and 3 shared V-1s destroyed.

BONHAM Gordon Loversidge   Flight Lieutenant   RNZAF No. 402434

New Zealander 'Snowy' Bonham served with 243 Squadron in Singapore during the initial Japanese assault on the area. (A full-page photograph of him will be found in *Bloody Shambles, Vol I* — Grub Street, 1992). On 18 January 1942 during an engagement with Japanese aircraft, one of his knees was shattered by a bullet, but he managed to land his badly damaged Brewster Buffalo, W8164, at Kallang airfield, and was evacuated thereafter to New Zealand. On recovery he was posted to the UK, where he served in the Tempest Flight of the Fighter Interception Unit during the early summer of 1944, when this was formed for anti-V-1 activities, mainly at night. He was also awarded a DFC on 28 April 1944 for his Far Eastern service. During July 1944 when 501 Squadron was virtually reformed with an infusion of FIU Tempest pilots, he was one of those joining the unit. On 27 August he brought down four V-1s, three of them by tipping off balance with the wingtip of his aircraft, after his ammunition had been expended; he was credited with five V-1s destroyed in total. During the hours of darkness on 25 September 1944 he crashed in Tempest EJ560 on return from a sortie, and was killed.

1942						
17 Jan		Bomber	Buffalo	W8164	Singapore	243 Sqn
„		Bomber Damaged	„	„	„	„
1944						
26 Aug	4	V-1s (3 by tipping)	Tempest V	EJ597 SD-D		501 Sqn
27 Aug		V-1	„			„

TOTAL: 5 V-1s destroyed, 1 aircraft destroyed and 1 damaged.

BREMNER Robert Duff   Flying Officer   RNZAF No. 424417

From Taihape, New Zealand, Duff Bremner served with 486 Squadron from October 1943 to March 1945. He was awarded a DFC on 8 May 1945. He died on 3 August 1994.

1944						
29 Jun		V-1	Tempest V	JN821 SA-H		486 Sqn
3 Jul		V-1	„	JN801 SA-L	Rye	„
4 Jul		V-1	„	JN854 SA-G	N Hailsham	„
20 Jul	1/2	V-1	„	JN802 SA-C	2-3m W Maidstone	„
26 Jul		V-1	„	JN803 SA-D	W Dungeness	„
27 Jul	1/2	V-1	„	„	NW Tenterden	„
3 Aug		V-1	„	JN767 SA-B	1m E Battle	„
„	1/2	V-1	„	„		„
6 Aug	1/2	V-1	„	EJ560 SA-M	Tunbridge Wells	„
25 Dec	1/2	Me 262 (a)	„	JN803 SA-D	Aachen area	„
1945						
2 Feb	1/3	Do 217 (b)	„	NV719 SA-E	S Paderborn	„

TOTAL: 5 and 4 shared V-1s destroyed, 2 aircraft shared destroyed.
(a) Aircraft of KG(J) 51; (b) Actually Bf 110G-4 G9+QR of 8/NJG 1.

BROOKE Peter de Leighton   Flying Officer   RAF No. 127949

Peter Brooke was a night fighter pilot in 264 Squadron in 1944, operating with Plt Off J.Hutchinson as his radar operator. Brooke was awarded a DFC on 19 September 1944 for having claimed three aircraft shot down; he also accounted for five V-1s.

1944						
17/18 Jun	2	Ju 188s	Mosquito XIII		Invasion area	264 Sqn
19/20 Jul	3	V-1s	„	HK506		„
23/24 Jul	2	V-1s	„	HK 473		„

TOTAL: 5 V-1s destroyed, 3 aircraft destroyed (1 no details).

BRYAN J.   Flight Sergeant   RAF No.

A night fighter pilot in 96 Squadron, Flt Sgt Bryan undertook most of his operational flying with Plt Off Friis as his radar operator. He was flying with Sgt Jaeger during the night of 25/26 July 1944 however, when they failed to return in Mosquito MM468 and were reported missing.

1944					
25/26 Jun	V-1	Mosquito XIII	HK421	off Eastbourne	96 Sqn
	V-1	„	„	off Beachy Head	„
27/28 Jun	V-1	„		S Dungeness	„
2/3 Jul	V-1	„	HK421	10m N Hastings	„
6/7 Jul	V-1	„	MM468		„
13/14 Jul	V-1	„	„	over sea	„
22/23 Jul	V-1	„	„	„	„

TOTAL: 7 or 8 V-1s destroyed (possibly 1 more was claimed during the period 14-17 July).

BURGWAL R.F.   Flying Officer   RAF No.

A Dutch pilot, Burgwal was 322 Squadron's top-scorer against the V-1s. On 7 July 1944 his Spitfire XIV was scorched by the explosion of the flying bomb he had been firing at. In early August the unit re-equipped with Spitfire IXs for other duties, and began escorting Bomber Command 'heavies' over France. On 12 August, whilst so engaged, he noted that his friend, Flg Off Jonker, had fallen out of formation due to engine trouble. He broke away to provide cover whilst Jonker went down and force-landed, but Burgwal then disappeared and was reported missing.

1944						
18 Jun		V-1	Spitfire XIV	VL-K		322 Sqn
19 Jun	1/2	V-1 (a)	„	VL-D	Hailsham	„
29 Jun		V-1	„	VL-F	Rye-Hastings	„
„		V-1	„	„	E Halden	„
30 Jun	2	V-1s	„	VL-E	NE Hastings	„
4 Jul		V-1	„	VL-F		„
7 Jul	1/2	V-1 (b)	„	VL-C	Ashford-Folkestone	„
8 Jul	5	V-1s	„	VL-G	last NW Rye	„
19 Jul		V-1	„	VL-F	nr Wintersham	„
22 Jul	2	V-1s	„	VL-C	Tunbridge Wells area	„
24 Jul	1/2	V-1	„	VL-K	10m N Rye	„
26 Jul	2	V-1s	„	VL-F	E & NW Hastings	„
„	1/2	V-1	„	„	over sea	„
30 Jul	1/2	V-1	„	VL-C	S of base	„
5 Aug		V-1	„	„	Robertsbridge area	„
„		V-1	„	„	E Uckfield	„
7 Aug		V-1	„	VL-L		„

TOTAL: 19 and 5 shared V-1s destroyed.
(a) Shared with a Tempest; (b) He may have been credited with an individual, rather than a shared success on this date. If so, his total becomes 20 and 4 shared.

BURTON H.   Flight Lieutenant   RAF No.

'Monty' Burton flew Tempests with 501 Squadron, claiming six V-1s.

1944						
19/20 Aug		V-1	Tempest V	EJ603 SD-M		501 Sqn
10/11 Nov	2	V-1s	,,	SD-Z		,,
22/23 Nov		V-1	,,	,,		,,
23/24 Nov		V-1	,,			,,
5/6 Dec		V-1	,,	SD-N		,,

TOTAL: 6 V-1s destroyed.

CALDWELL G.L.   Squadron Leader   RAF No.

Caldwell was a night fighter pilot with 96 Squadron.

1944						
22/23 Feb		Me 410	Mosquito XIII	HK370	W Uckfield	96 Sqn
21/22 Jun	2	V-1s	,,	MM461	off Dungeness	,,
25/26 Jun		V-1	,,	,,	12m N Hastings	,,
19/20 Jul		V-1	,,	HK462	over sea	,,
27/28 Jul		V-1 (a)	,,	,,	,,	,,
9/10 Aug		V-1	,,	MM461	,,	,,

TOTAL: 6 V-1s destroyed, 1 aircraft destroyed.

(a) He may have claimed a second V-1 during this night. If so, his total becomes 7.

CAMMOCK Raymond John   Flying Officer   RNZAF No. 414723

Ray Cammock was a New Zealander from Christchurch. After initial service in the UK with 253 Squadron, he was posted to 486 Squadron in May 1944, gaining considerable success against V-1s. After the unit moved to Europe to join 2nd TAF however, he was shot down by Flak and killed on 6 October 1944, crashing to the east of Deventer in Tempest JN863.

1944						
19 Jun		V-1	Tempest V	JN810 SA-P	10m N Beachy Head	486 Sqn
23 Jun	1/2	V-1	,,	,,	2m N Pevensey Bay	,,
,,		V-1	,,	,,	Edenbridge	,,
24 Jun	2	V-1s	,,	JN808 SA-N	Eastbourne area	,,
25 Jun		V-1	,,	JN804 SA-R	S Maidstone	,,
,,		V-1	,,	,,	5m N Hastings	,,
27 Jun		V-1	,,	JN794 SA-T	N Rye	,,
28 Jun		V-1	,,	JN810 SA-P	Beachy Head	,,
1 Jul		V-1	,,	JN866 SA-U	Bexhill	,,
7 Jul		V-1	,,	JN873 SA-W	7m N Pevensey	,,
11 Jul		V-1	,,	JN803 SA-D	Bexhill	,,
22 Jul		V-1	,,	JN863 SA-R	N Ashford	,,
26 Jul		V-1	,,	EJ523 SA-X	7m N Bexhill	,,
,,		V-1	,,	JN770 SA-V	3-4m SW Ashford	,,
27 Jul		V-1	,,	EJ523 SA-X	4-5m S Tunbridge Wells	,,
,,		V-1	,,	,,	Hastings	,,
6 Aug		V-1	,,	,,	Eastbourne	,,
7 Aug		V-1	,,	JN863 SA-R	Dungeness	,,
15 Aug		V-1	,,	EJ528 SA-P	Rye	,,
29 Aug		V-1	,,	EJ869 SA-R	2m N Tonbridge	,,

TOTAL: 20 and 1 shared V-1s destroyed.

CHISHOLM John Henry Matkellar   Squadron Leader   RAF No. 39652

John Chisholm was granted a Short Service Commission in May 1937. In summer 1944 he was a flight commander in 157 Squadron, flying with Flt Lt E.Wylde as his radar operator. On 15/16 September 1944 they failed to return from a high-level sortie to Kiel in Mosquito MM649, RS-M.

1944					
28/29 Jun	V-1	Mosquito XIII	MM676 RS-W		157 Sqn
30/1 Jul	V-1	,,	TA404 RS-M	off Dieppe	,,
4/5 Jul	V-1	,,	MM676 RS-W	Somme estuary	,,
5/6 Jul	V-1	,,	,,		,,
7/8 Aug	V-1	,,	,,		,,
10/11 Aug	V-1	,,	MM674 RS-T		,,
23/24 Aug	V-1	,,	,,	N Le Touquet W	,,

TOTAL: 7 V-1s destroyed.

CHOLAJDA Antoni   Flight Lieutenant   RAF No. P1595

Antoni Cholajda was a Polish pilot who flew Mustang IIIs with 316 Squadron.

1942						
10 Apr		FW 190 Probable	Spitfire VB	AB735	NE Hardelot	316 Sqn
25 Apr		FW 190 Damaged	,,	AB809	SE Dunkirk	,,
1943						
22 Aug		FW 190 Damaged	Spitfire IX	MA309	W Elbeuf	,,
1944						
8 Jul		V-1	Mustang III	394 SZ-Z	2m W Tilehurst	,,
,,		V-1	,,	,,	N Rotherfield	,,
22 Jul		V-1	,,	376 SZ-Q	2m W Cranbrook	,,
26 Jul	2	V-1s	,,	384 SZ-Z	30m S Rye	,,
14 Aug		Bf 109E (a)	,,	835 SZ-P	5m N Chalons-sur-Marne	
,,		FW 190	,,	,,	,,	,,
18 Aug		V-1	,,	,,	mid Channel	,,

TOTAL: 6 V-1s destroyed, 2 aircraft destroyed, 1 probable, 2 damaged.
(a) Claimed as a "He 113 or Bf 109E".

CHUDLEIGH Richard Neil   Squadron Leader   RAF No. 39712

Chudleigh was granted a Short Service Commission in May 1937, subsequently flying as a night fighter and flight commander with 153 Squadron in North Africa during the winter of 1942/43, with Sgt Ayliffe as his radar operator. In 1944 he and Ayliffe, the latter by then a Flg Off, flew with 96 Squadron, in which unit Chudleigh was again a flight commander. During the night of 7/8 July they claimed six V-1s shot down. On 7 August the pair were posted to 151 Squadron for intruder duties. Chudleigh received the award of a DFC on 3 October 1944.

1943						
23/24 Jan		Ju 88 (a)	Beaufighter VIF	EL187	20m W Phillippeville	153 Sqn
28/29 Jan		Ju 88	,,		50m N Bougie	,,
1944						
18/19 Jun		V-1	Mosquito XIII	HK469	off Dungeness	96 Sqn
23/24 Jun	2	V-1s	,,	MM497	sea, Beachy Head area	,,
3/4 Jul	3	V-1s	,,	HK376	over sea	,,
7/8 Jul		V-1	,,	HK379	SE coast	,,
,,	2	V-1s	,,	,,	Channel	,,
,,		V-1	,,	,,	10m off Le Touquet	,,
,,		V-1	,,	,,	W Dungeness	,,
,,		V-1	,,	,,	10m off Le Touquet	,,
19/20 Jul		V-1	,,	MM459	over sea	,,
20/21 Jul	2	V-1s	,,	HK379	,,	,,

TOTAL: 15 V-1s destroyed, 2 aircraft destroyed.
(a) Aircraft of either II/KG 30 or II/KG 76.

CLAPPERTON Raymond Hedley   Pilot Officer   RAF No. 151700

Ray Clapperton flew with 3 Squadron during 1944. Over Western Europe he was shot down by Flak on 29 September 1944 in Tempest EJ504 whilst south-east of Kronenburg; he survived, but became a POW. The award of a DFC was gazetted on 3 November 1944.

1944						
18 Jun		V-1	Tempest V	JN765	W Hailsham	3 Sqn
20 Jun		V-1	,,	JN738	SW Ashford	,,
22 Jun		V-1	,,			,,
27 Jun		V-1	,,			,,
28 Jun	3	V-1s	,,			,,
4 Jul		V-1	,,	JN755	2m N Hailsham	,,
,,		V-1	,,	,,	2m N Hastings	,,
,,		V-1	,,	,,	3m S Hastings	,,
,,		V-1	,,	,,	3m S Bexhill/Hastings	,,
6 Jul		V-1	,,	JN818	nr Tonbridge	,,
9 Jul	2	V-1s	,,			,,
12 Jul	2	V-1s	,,			,,
19 Jul		V-1	,,	EJ504	10m NNW Hastings	,,
27 Jul		V-1	,,	JN815	nr Maidstone	,,
,,		V-1	,,	EJ504	Tunbridge Wells area	,,
3 Aug	2	V-1s	,,			,,
10 Aug	2	V-1s	,,			,,
20 Aug		V-1	,,			,,

TOTAL: 24 V-1s destroyed.

COLE Robert Walton (or Walter)   Flying Officer   RAF No. 182716

Bob Cole trained to fly in the USA during 1942, at Eagle Field, California. He returned to the UK to fly Typhoon IBs on fighter-bomber operations until late February 1944, when the unit converted to Tempest Vs. He shared his first V-1 with Wg Cdr Roland Beamont on 16 June 1944, claiming 20 and four shared ultimately. The first occasion when he shot down one of these missiles single-handed occurred on 18 June near Ivychurch; he flew through the resultant explosion, which scorched his Tempest, JN759. On the Continent during the autumn he shot down an Me 262 jet, receiving a DFC shortly afterwards, which was gazetted on 1 December 1944. Meanwhile, on 26 November during a sweep in the Munster-Rheine area, he strafed Rheine airfield, destroying a Bf 109, but during a second pass his aircraft was shot down by Flak. He baled out, spending the remaining months of the war in Stalag Luft 1.

1944						
24 Feb	1/3	LeO 45	Typhoon IB	JP534	nr Louvain	3 Sqn
16 Jun	1/2	V-1	Tempest V	JN761	Faversham area	,,
17 Jun	1/2	V-1	,,	JN768	N Ham Street	,,
18 Jun		V-1	,,	JN759	Ivychurch	,,
21 Jun		V-1	,,	JN768	10m NW Hastings	,,
		V-1	,,	,,	off Bexhill	,,
23 Jun		V-1	,,			,,
25 Jun		V-1	,,	JN768	7m N Hastings	,,
29 Jun		V-1	,,			,,
30 Jun		V-1	,,	JN768	NW Tonbridge	,,
		V-1	,,	,,	Tonbridge area	,,
12 Jul		V-1	,,			,,
,,	1/2	V-1	,,			,,
19 Jul		V-1	,,	JN768	nr Appledore	,,
22 Jul		V-1	,,	JN759	SE Kingsnorth	,,
,,		V-1	,,	,,	17m N Pevensey	,,
,,		V-1	,,	,,		,,
29 Jul		V-1	,,			,,
16 Aug		V-1	,,			,,
17 Aug		V-1	,,			,,
19 Aug		V-1	,,			,,
28 Aug	2	V-1s	,,		N Rye	,,
13 Oct		Me 262 (a)	,,	JN868	Grave	,,
26 Nov		Bf 109 on the ground	,,	JN822	Rheine airfield	,,

TOTAL: 20 and 3 shared V-1s destroyed (1 no details), 1 and 1 shared aircraft destroyed, 1 destroyed on the ground.
(a) 9K+FL of I/KG(J) 51, flown by Uffz Edmund Delatowski.
NB His V-1 totals were summarized as:- in JN768 — 11 and 1 shared; JN759 — 5; JN738 — 2; JN815 — 1; JN865 — 1; JN878 — 1 shared; JN761 — 1 shared.

COLLIER Kenneth R.   Flying Officer   RAAF No. 422424
Born in Glebe, New South Wales, on 5 November 1920, Ken Collier worked as a meat inspector in Balmain, New South Wales until his entry into the RAAF. In the UK he was posted to 91 Squadron, where he became the first pilot to 'flick' a V-1 off balance with the wingtip of his Spitfire XIV, undertaking this feat on 23 June 1944. He was subsequently reported missing on 5 December 1944 following an engagement with Bf 109s; he was flying Spitfire IX MK587 at the time.

1944						
22 Jun		V-1	Spitfire XIV	RB188	Epsom	91 Sqn
23 Jun		V-1	,,	NM698	East Grinstead	,,
9 Jul		V-1	,,	RB183	NNW Swanley	,,
,,		V-1	,,	,,	NNW Chatham	,,
20 Jul		V-1	,,	RM685	S Lamberhurst	,,
,,		V-1	,,	,,	N West Malling	,,
29 Jul		V-1	,,	,,	E Tonbridge	,,

TOTAL: 7 V-1s destroyed.

CRAMM H.C.   Flight Sergeant   RAF No.
A Dutch pilot who served in 322 Squadron.

1944				
3 Jul		V-1	Spitfire XIV	322 Sqn
6 Jul		V-1 (a)	,,	,,
8 Jul		V-1	,,	,,
9 Jul	2	V-1s	,,	,,

TOTAL: 5 (possibly 4) V-1s destroyed.
(a) This claim may subsequently have been disallowed.

CRUIKSHANK A.R.   Flying Officer   RAF No.
Cruikshank flew Spitfire XIVs with 91 Squadron during summer 1944. Late in the war the squadron became the first to receive Spitfire XXIs, and during an early sortie in one of these (LA203) on 10 April 1945, he and Flg Off J.A.Faulkner were shot down into the sea off Den Helder by Flak whilst strafing shipping; both pilots were picked up safely.

1944						
17 Jun	½	V-1	Spitfire XIV	NH654	NW Hastings	91 Sqn
1 Jul		V-1	,,	RM615	NNE Dymchurch	,,
5 Jul		V-1	,,	,,	E Dungeness	,,
7 Jul		V-1	,,	RB165	Pluckley	,,
		V-1	,,	,,	W Wormshill	,,
11 Jul		V-1	,,	RB182	Tenterden area	,,
		V-1	,,	,,	SW Tenterden	,,
20 Jul		V-1	,,	NH703	SE East Grinstead	,,
21 Jul		V-1	,,	RM649	W Uckfield	,,
26 Jul		V-1	,,	,,	NE Crowborough	,,
4 Aug		V-1	,,	,,	SW Horsham	,,

TOTAL: 10 and 1 shared V-1s destroyed.

CULLEN James Roy   Squadron Leader   RNZAF No. 416462

Jimmy Cullen, from Waihi, New Zealand, joined 486 Squadron in December 1942, remaining with this unit until September 1944. He was awarded a DFC on 17 November 1944, and following a rest from operations, was posted in February 1945 to command 183 Squadron on Typhoons. On 4 May his Typhoon, SW454, was hit by Flak, obliging him to force-land on Fehman Island, where he was captured. However, he was freed a few days later when hostilities ceased, returning to head his squadron until October. A Bar to his DFC was gazetted on 26 June 1945.

1944						
18 Jun		V-1	Tempest V	JN758 SA-Y	Rye	486 Sqn
23 Jun	½	V-1	,,	JN770 SA-V	Beachy Head	,,
25 Jun		V-1	,,	,,	SW Redhill	,,
		V-1	,,	,,	SW Headcorn	,,
29 Jun		V-1	,,	JN810 SA-P	off Shoreham	,,
3 Jul		V-1	,,	JN863 SA-R	Hastings	,,
4 Jul		V-1	,,	JN770 SA-V	4-6m N Hastings	,,
7 Jul		V-1	,,	EJ527 SA-Q	SE Beachy Head	,,
8 Jul		V-1	,,	JN770 SA-V	Dungeness Point	,,
9 Jul		V-1	,,	JN873 SA-W	S Lloyd	,,
		V-1	,,	,,	S Bexhill	,,
14 Jul		V-1	,,	JN770 SA-V	N Hastings	,,
18 Jul	½	V-1	,,	,,	W Tenterden	,,
	½	V-1	,,	,,	10m N Rye	,,
22 Jul		V-1	,,	EJ537 SA-S	nr Sevenoaks	,,
		V-1	,,	EJ523 SA-X	N Rye	,,
26 Jul	¼	V-1	,,	JN770 SA-V	8m N Pevensey	,,
27 Aug		V-1	,,	,,	Tenterden	,,

TOTAL: 14 and 4 shared V-1s destroyed.

DANZEY Raymond Jack   Pilot Officer   No. 416464

'Dan' Danzey, a native of Auckland, New Zealand, served with 486 Squadron from June 1943 to March 1945.

1944						
17 Jun		V-1	Tempest V	JN809 SA-M	Faversham	486 Sqn
18 Jun		V-1	,,	JN797 SA-K	N Tonbridge	,,
20 Jun		V-1	,,	JN820 SA-L	5m S Eastbourne	,,
23 Jun		V-1	,,	JN797 SA-K	Dungeness	,,
	½	V-1	,,	,,	Hastings	,,
29 Jun		V-1	,,	,,	W Newchurch	,,
		V-1	,,	,,	W Beachy Head	,,
4 Jul		V-1	,,	JN805 SA-E	20m N Eastbourne	,,
7 Jul	½	V-1	,,	JN809 SA-M	10m N Beachy Head	,,
11 Jul	½	V-1	,,	JN821 SA-H	Tonbridge area	,,
16 Jul		V-1	,,	JN803 SA-D	N Hastings	,,
22 Jul		V-1	,,	JN801 SA-L	10m S West Malling	,,
6 Aug	½	V-1	,,	JN803 SA-D	Tunbridge Wells	,,
1945						
23 Jan		FW 190 Probable	,,	NV715 SA-F	Minden area	,,

TOTAL: 9 and 4 shared V-1s destroyed, 1 aircraft probable.

DAVY D.H.   Flight Lieutenant   RAF No. 139507

Flying with 1 Squadron, Davy was the one of the few pilots to claim a substantial number of V-1s shot down whilst flying a Spitfire IX. He remained with the unit until the end of the war, being promoted Flt Lt during March 1945.

1944						
4 Jul	V-1	Spitfire IX	MK846	4m NE Hastings	1 Sqn

22 Jul	V-1	,,	ML117	SSW Ashford	,,
23 Jul	V-1	,,	MK986	8m NE Boulogne	,,
,,	V-1	,,	ML423	SE Ashford	,,
,,	V-1	,,	,,	Kingsnorth	,,
26 Jul	V-1	,,	ML117	10m S Folkestone	,,
,,	½ V-1	,,	,,	5m S Lympne	,,

TOTAL: 6 and 1 shared V-1s destroyed.

DE BORDAS Henri F.   Capitaine   RAF No. F30226

Henri de Bordas, a French pilot, flew with 91 Squadron as a Lieutenant during 1944. At the end of September he was posted to 84 Group Service Unit at the end of his tour, later flying as a flight commander with 329 Squadron in south-west France. The award of a DFC was gazetted on 18 December 1945.

1944						
19 Jun	V-1	Spitfire XIV	NH654	N Beachy Head	91 Sqn
,,	½ V-1	,,	RB181	N Uckfield	,,
25 Jun	V-1	,,	NH654	Tenterden-Ashford	,,
9 Jul	V-1	,,	NH720	Paddock Wood	,,
10 Jul	V-1	,,	RB181	SE Beachy Head	,,
11 Jul	V-1	,,	NH720	E Ashford	,,
19 Jul	V-1	,,	RB165	SE East Grinstead	,,
3 Aug	V-1	,,	RM685	N Mayfield	,,
4 Aug	V-1	,,	RM688	W Tonbridge	,,
7 Aug	V-1	,,	RM686	N Appledore	,,

TOTAL: 9 and 1 shared V-1s destroyed.

DELEUZE R.C.   Flight Lieutenant   RAF No. F

'Lulu' Deleuze was a French pilot who served with 501 Squadron during summer 1944. He was later posted to 274 Squadron as a flight commander. On 25 February 1945 he was last seen near Hamm in Tempest EJ775 after reporting that his aircraft had suffered an engine failure. He did not return.

1944						
7 Aug	V-1	Tempest V	EJ599 SD-W	nr Tenterden	501 Sqn
23/24 Aug	V-1	,,	EJ607 SD-N	15m N Rye	,,
4/5 Sep	V-1	,,	SD-Z		,,
6/7 Oct	V-1	,,	SD-Q		,,
14/15 Oct	2 V-1s	,,	SD-J		,,
21/22 Oct	V-1	,,	SD-Q	N Woodford	,,
17/18 Dec	V-1	,,	SD-V		,,

TOTAL: 8 V-1s destroyed.

DOBIE Ian Alexander   Flight Lieutenant   RAF No. 101056

Commissioned on 29 June 1941, Ian Dobie flew Mosquito night fighters in 96 Squadron with Flg Off E.A.Johnson as his radar operator. In December 1944 when the unit was disbanded, he and Johnson were posted to 85 Squadron, where he added one aircraft shot down to his total of 13 V-1s.

1944						
28/29 Jun	4 V-1s	Mosquito XIII	HK396		96 Sqn
2/3 Jul	V-1	,,	MM437		,,
4/5 Jul	V-1	,,	MM495	over sea	,,
6/7 Jul	V-1	,,	HK438	,,	,,
26/27 Jul	V-1	,,	MM437	,,	,,
29/30 Jul	V-1	,,		,,	,,
6/7 Aug	V-1	,,	MM487	10m off Dungeness	,,
11/12 Aug	V-1	,,	MM437	over sea	,,
30/31 Aug	V-1	,,	,,	E Gris Nez	,,
15/16 Sep	V-1	,,			,,
1945						
8 Mar	Ju 188	Mosquito XVII			85 Sqn

TOTAL: 13 V-1s destroyed, 1 aircraft destroyed.

DREDGE Alan Sydney   Wing Commander   RAF No. 63285

Alan Dredge served with 253 Squadron as a Sgt during 1940, and is credited with four victories with this unit during summer 1940. He was commissioned in March 1941, and the following month was posted to Malta, flying a Hurricane off HMS *Ark Royal* to the island in April; here he joined 261 Squadron. On 6 May his was one of four Hurricanes shot down by Bf 109Es, three of them by Oblt Joachim Müncheberg of 7/JG 26 and one by Oblt Erbo Graf von Kageneck of III/JG 27. It is likely that Dredge was the latter's 14th victim. He crash-landed Z3057 on the airfield in flames, suffering severe burns. In mid July he was evacuated to the UK, where he became a plastic surgery patient of Sir Archie McIndoe at East Grinstead. On recovery, he flew Typhoons with 183 Squadron during 1943, the award of a DFC being gazetted in July of that year. In October he was posted to command 3 Squadron, converting this unit from Typhoons to Tempests during February 1944. He remained with the unit until August, when his tour ended. He was promoted Wg Cdr, and on 5 December 1944 the award of a DSO was gazetted. However, he was killed in a flying accident in a Mosquito on 18 May 1945; he was aged 27 at the time of his death.

1940						
30 Aug	2	Bf 109Es	Hurricane I		Tenterden	253 Sqn
4 Sep		Bf 110	,,		Brooklands area	,,
14 Sep		Bf 109E	,,		Isle of Sheppey	,,
1944						
23 Jun		V-1	Tempest V			3 Sqn
25 Jun		V-1	,,		2m ESE Hawkhurst	,,
6 Jul		V-1	,,	JN812	Faversham/Sittingbourne	,,
12 Jul		V-1	,,			,,
22 Jul		V-1	,,	JN812	1m SE Biddenden	,,

TOTAL: 5 V-1s destroyed, 4 aircraft destroyed.

DRYLAND Rodney   Flying Officer   RAF No. 162837

Dryland served with 3 Squadron, being awarded a DFC on 27 October 1944. He was involved in an engagement with FW 190Ds in the Malmedy area on 24 December 1944, claiming one shot down. His Tempest, EJ747, was then hit by Flak and he was obliged to force-land in German-held territory. He was able to evade capture and return safely to Allied lines.

1944						
27 Jun		V-1	Tempest V			3 Sqn
30 Jun		V-1	,,		4m S Rye	,,
1 Jul		V-1	,,	JN865	Biggin Hill area	,,
5 Jul		V-1	,,	JN818	1m N Rye	,,
,,		V-1	,,	,,	over sea	,,
,,		V-1	,,	,,	E Falmer	,,
,,		V-1	,,	,,	16m S Biggin Hill	,,
,,		V-1	,,	,,	S Eastbourne	,,
8 Jul		V-1	,,			,,
16 Jul	2	V-1s	,,			,,
18 Jul		V-1	,,	JN822	NW Hastings	,,
,,	1/2	V-1	,,	,,	20m N Hastings	,,
19 Jul		V-1	,,	,,	nr Biddenden	,,
26 Jul		V-1	,,	JN865	7-8m N Hastings	,,
28 Jul	1/3	V-1	,,			,,
30 Jul		V-1	,,			,,
6 Aug	2	V-1s	,,			,,
21 Oct	1/2	Me 262 Damaged	,,			,,
26 Nov	1/2	Me262 on ground	,,			,,
24 Dec		FW 190D	,,	EJ747	S Malmedy	,,

TOTAL: 17 and 2 shared V-1s destroyed, 1 aircraft destroyed, 1 shared damaged, 1 shared destroyed on the ground.

EAGLESON Owen David   Flying Officer   RNZAF No. 421689

'Ginger' Eagleson, from Auckland, New Zealand, joined 486 Squadron in November 1943. As a Wt Off he gained much success against V-1s during summer 1944. He was then commissioned, and was active over North-West Europe until practically the end of the war. He was awarded a DFC, gazetted on 8 December 1944. On 2 May 1945 his Tempest, NV722, was hit by Flak and shot down. He survived and was captured, but at once managed to escape. Aprehended again next day, he escaped for a second time on 4 May, but a few days later the war ended. He died on 30 October 1990.

1944						
18 Jun		V-1	Tempest V	JN811 SA-Z	Tonbridge	486 Sqn
,,		V-1	,,	JN804 SA-R	5-10m N Newchurch	,,
,,		V-1	,,	,,	S Rye	,,
23 Jun		V-1	,,	JN794 SA-T	Uxbridge- E Hoathley	,,
,,	1/2	V-1	,,	,,	20m N Beachy Head	,,
27 Jun	1/2	V-1	,,	,,	6m N Hastings	,,
28 Jun		V-1	,,	JN859 SA-S	N Hastings	,,
,,		V-1	,,	JN854 SA-G	S Sevenoaks	,,
3 Jul		V-1	,,	JN873 SA-W	6m N Rye	,,
4 Jul		V-1	,,	EJ537 SA-S	W Dungeness	,,
6 Jul		V-1	,,	JN873 SA-W	N Hastings	,,
7 Jul		V-1	,,	EJ627 SA-Q	Newchurch	,,
,,		V-1	,,	JN873 SA-W	3m W Dungeness	,,
12 Jul	1/2	V-1	,,	EJ527 SA-Q	Dover	,,
14 Jul		V-1	,,	EJ523 SA-X	N Eastbourne	,,
27 Jul		V-1	,,	EJ586 SA-Z	20m N Ashford	,,

3 Aug		V-1	"	JN808 SA-N	N Bexhill	"
"		V-1	"	"	20m S Newchurch	"
4 Aug		V-1	"	EJ528 SA-P	10m N Hastings	"
15 Aug		V-1	"	EJ635 SA-T	15m NW Newchurch	"
16 Aug		V-1	"	"	NNE Rye	"
"		V-1	"	"	5-6m S Maidstone	"
"		V-1	"	"	Ashford	"
19 Nov	½	Me 262 Probable on ground		EJ828 SA-Z	Rheine	"
1945						
28 Apr	½	Ju 352	"	SN136 SA-V	W Plon	
29 Apr		FW 190F	"	SN176 SA-N	Lauenburg area	"
"		FW 190F Damaged	"	"	"	"
2 May		FW 44	"	NV722 SA-Q	SE Schwerin	"
"		Fi 156 on ground	"	"	"	"

TOTAL: 20 and 3 shared V-1s destroyed, 2 and 1 shared aircraft destroyed, 1 damaged, 1 destroyed on the ground, 1 shared probable on the ground.

EDWARDS E.W.   Flying Officer   RAF No. 172958
This pilot flew Mustang IIIs with 129 Squadron.

1944						
12 Jul		V-1	Mustang III	PZ143 DV-P	Ivychurch	129 Sqn
16 Jul		V-1	"	FB125 DV-F	2m S Chatham	"
4 Aug		V-1	"			"
5 Aug		V-1	"			"
7 Aug		V-1	"	FB389 DV-M	6m WNW Folkestone	"
10 Aug		V-1	"	HB862 DV-G	2m NW Newchurch	"
12 Dec	2	Bf 109s	"		Dortmund	"
"	2	Bf 109s Damaged	"	"	"	"

TOTAL: 6 V-1s destroyed, 2 aircraft destroyed, 2 damaged.

EDWARDS M.F.   Flight Lieutenant   RAF No. 133358
Edwards flew Tempests with 3 Squadron during 1944. He was shot down and killed in EJ803 north of Rheine on 29 December 1944 during an engagement with Bf 109s.

1944						
17 Jun	½	V-1	Tempest V	JN793	Folkestone-Hawkinge	3 Sqn
18 Jun		V-1	"	JN735	4m N Rye	"
19 Jun		V-1	"	JN752	304m WNW Dungeness	"
5 Jul		V-1	"	EJ525	Edenbridge	"
"		V-1	"	"	nr Tenterden	"
"		V-1	"	"	Tenterden area	"
6 Jul		V-1	"	EJ582	10-15m S Dungeness	"
12 Jul	½	V-1	"			"
22 Jul	½	V-1	"	JN862	4m NE Rye	"
24 Jul		V-1	"	EJ549	Brenchley area	"
"	½	V-1	"	"	Tenterden area	"
26 Jul	¼	V-1	"	JN521	N Hastings	"

TOTAL: 7 and 5 shared V-1s destroyed.

ELCOCK A.R.   Flight Lieutenant   RAF No.
This pilot flew Spitfire XIVs with 91 Squadron during summer 1944. He was killed in a flying accident on 14 May 1945, immediately after the conclusion of hostilities, when he crashed in one of the unit's new Spitfire XXIs.

1944						
17 Jun	½	V-1	Spitfire XIV	RB177	W West Malling	91 Sqn
30 Jun		V-1	"	RB182	Dungeness	"
4 Jul		V-1	"	"	SW Tenterden	"
7 Jul		V-1	"	RM615	NW Rochester	"
21 Jul		V-1	"	RM685	NW Tonbridge	"
4 Aug		V-1	"	RM734	NW Tunbridge Wells	"
6 Aug		V-1	"	"	NW Burwash	"
7 Aug		V-1	"	RM694	NNE Etchingham	"

TOTAL: 7 and 1 shared V-1s destroyed.

EVANS Colin James   Flight Lieutenant   RCAF No. J3731
Colin Evans was with 418 Squadron from spring 1944, flying with Flg Off Stan Humblestone, RAF, as his navigator. By early August they had flown 34 sorties, but on 17th of that month Evans was posted home to Canada to join 69 OTU.

1944					
16/17 Jun	V-1	Mosquito II		2m W Hastings	418 Sqn

24/25 Jun		V-1		"		off Dieppe	"
"		V-1		"		Channel	"
6/7 Jul		V-1		"		10m SE Dungeness	"
"		V-1		"		15m S Hastings	"
		V-1		"		6m SE Hastings	"
11 Jul	1/2	Bf 110		"		Gardelegen	"
19 Jul		FW 190 Probable		"		Lechfeld	"
22 Jul		Ju 52/3m		"	(a)	Baltic coast, 6m W Putnitz	"
26/27 Jul		V-1		"		10m W Eastbourne	"

TOTAL: 7 V-1s destroyed, 1 and 1 shared aircraft destroyed and 1 probable.
(a) Fin and rudder of their own aircraft damaged by debris as they got so close.

EVERSON L.G.   RAF No.187898
A Tempest pilot with 3 Squadron.

1944						
16 Jun		V-1	Tempest V	JN748	10m N Hastings	3 Sqn
27 Jun	2	V-1s	"		10m S Hastings	"
4 Jul		V-1	"	JN868	10m S Hastings	"
"	1/2	V-1	"	JN865	15m S Dungeness	"
4 Aug		V-1	"			"
6 Aug		V-1	"			"

TOTAL: 6 and 1 shared V-1s destroyed.

FAULKNER J.A.   Flying Officer   RAF No.
Faulkner flew Spitfire XIVs with 91 Squadron during summer 1944. In spring 1945 the squadron became the first to re-equip with Spitfire XXIs, and during the first operational sorties undertaken with these on 10 April 1945, Faulkner and Flg Off A.R.Cruikshank were both shot down by Flak whilst strafing shipping off Den Helder. He baled out of LA229 into the sea, from where he was successfully rescued by the British ASR service.(NB In the Air-Britain register of aircraft serials, LA100-LZ999, this aircraft is recorded as having been shot down by enemy fighters, but this appears to be incorrect).

1944						
19 Jun	1/2	V-1	Spitfire XIV	RM617	N Uckfield	91 Sqn
23 Jun	1/2	V-1	"	RM620	W East Grinstead	"
27 Jun		V-1	"	RB161	SE Dungeness	"
12 Jul		V-1	"	RB173	E High Holden	"
24 Jul		V-1	"	RM654	N Hastings	"
29 Jul		V-1	"	RM688	N Robertsbridge	"
5 Dec		Bf 109	Spitfire IXB		NE Weal	"

TOTAL: 4 and 2 shared V-1s destroyed, 1 aircraft destroyed.

FELDMAN Seymour Bernard   Flying Officer   RAF No. 176091
A US citizen, 'Buck' Feldman joined the RAFVR and served with 3 Squadron on Typhoons and Tempests, first as an NCO and later after being commissioned. At the end of 1944 he was posted to 274 Squadron as a Flg Off, having been awarded a DFC on 21 July. He later flew as a volunteer with the Israeli forces during 1948-49, serving in 101 Squadron, flying Spitfire IXs. Here he gained one victory against the Egyptian Air Force.

1943						
5 Oct	1/2	Ju 88 on ground	Typhoon IB		Courtrai	3 Sqn
1944						
16 Jun		V-1	Tempest V	JN735	Ashford area	"
19 Jun		V-1	"	JN752	Bexhill	"
"	1/2	V-1	"	"	8m SW Ashford	"
20 Jun		V-1	"	JN735	N Eastbourne	"
		V-1	"	JN761	SW Tonbridge	"
23 Jun		V-1	"			"
25 Jun		V-1	"	JN761	sea, 40m SE Hastings	"
28 Jun		V-1	"			"
4 Jul		V-1	"	EJ540	10m S Rye	"
"	1/2	V-1	"	"	3-5m N Hastings	"
8 Jul		V-1	"			"
10 Jul	1/4	V-1	"			"
1949						
5 Jan		MC 205	Spitfire IX	2003	Israel	101 Sqn

TOTAL: 9 and 3 shared V-1s destroyed, 1 aircraft destroyed and 1 shared.

FOSTER J.K.   Pilot Officer   RAF No. 186755
Foster served as a Flt Sgt with 3 Squadron during the summer of 1944.

1944						
31 May		1/5 of 2 Ju 188s on ground	Tempest V			3 Sqn
„		1/5 of 2 Ju 188s Damaged on ground	„			„
16 Jun	1/2	V-1	„	JN745	W Lewes	„
27 Jun	1/2	V-1	„			„
30 Jun		V-1	„	JN745	nr Dungeness	„
12 Jul	2	V-1s	„			„
29 Aug		V-1	„			„
1945						
22 Feb		Bf 109 Damaged	„			„

TOTAL: 4 and 2 shared V-1s destroyed, 1 aircraft damaged, 2 shared destroyed on the ground, 2 shared damaged on the ground.

GOODE J.   Flight Lieutenant   RAF No.

He served with 96 Squadron as a night fighter during 1944, flying with Plt Off Robinson as his radar operator. When the unit was disbanded at the end of the year, they were posted to 29 Squadron.

1944						
18/19 Jun		V-1	Mosquito XIII		Dungeness-Dover	96 Sqn
25/26 Jun	2	V-1s	„	HK406	over sea	„
7/8 Jul		V-1	„	MM557	25m N Somme Estuary	„
19/20 Jul		V-1	„	MM452	over sea	„
20/21 Jul	1/2	V-1	„	HK406	off Hastings	„
4/5 Aug		V-1	„	MM452	over sea	„

TOTAL: 6 and 1 shared V-1s destroyed.

GOUGH William John   Flight Lieutenant   RAF No. 120855

Commissioned on 20 April 1942, Gough served with 68 Squadron during that year as a night fighter pilot. He later served in 96 Squadron, with Flt Lt Matson as his radar operator. When the unit disbanded in December 1944, he was posted back to 68 Squadron. The award of a DFC was gazetted on 2 March 1945.

1942					
23/24 Jun	Do 217	Beaufighter IF		East Coast	68 Sqn
22 Aug	Do 217 Probable	„		E North Coates	„
1944					
1/2 Mar	Me 410	Mosquito XIII	HK499	50m SE Beachy Head	96 Sqn
17/18 Jun	V-1	„	„	off Calais	„
23/24 Jun	V-1	„	„	nr Dungeness	„
7/8 Jul	V-1	„	„	off Dungeness	„
12/13 Aug	V-1	„	MM479	over sea	„
13/14 Aug	V-1	„	MM438	„	„
20/21 Aug	V-1	„	MM479	„	„

TOTAL: 6 V-1s destroyed, 2 aircraft destroyed, 1 probable.

HALL Archibald Robert   Squadron Leader   RAF No. 87453

Commissioned on 9 November 1940, Archie Hall flew with 260 Squadron in North Africa during the winter of 1941/42. He was awarded a DFC on 15 May 1942. Posted back to the UK, he then served in 167 Squadron, whilst in 1944 he was commanding officer of 56 Squadron from May to September. He later commanded 91 Squadron during March-April 1946.

1942						
2 Jan		Bf 109 Damaged	Hurricane I		12m S Agedabia	260 Sqn
14 Jan		Bf 109	„		E Antelat	„
12 Dec	2	FW 190s	Spitfire VB			167 Sqn
1944						
4 Jul		V-1	Tempest V	JN869 US-D	sea 7m E Eastbourne	56 Sqn
26 Jul		V-1	„	EJ541 US-B	6m SW Maidstone	„
17 Aug	2	V-1s	„	„		„
20 Aug		V-1	„	„		„

TOTAL: 5 V-1s destroyed, 3 aircraft destroyed, 1 damaged.

HALL Bevan Mason   Flying Officer   RNZAF No.

Bev Mason, a New Zealander from Kiaranga, served with 486 Squadron from January 1944 as a Flt Sgt, receiving his commission in early July. After the squadron's move to Holland to join 2nd TAF late in the year, he was involved in a fierce engagement with the FW 190D-9s of III/JG 54 on 27 December; whilst several of the German aircraft were shot down, Hall's Tempest, EJ627, SA-E, was shot down by Lt Peter Crump of 10/JG 54, and he was killed.

1944						
18 Jun		V-1	Tempest V	JN809 SA-M	SE Sevenoaks	486 Sqn
23 Jun		V-1	"	"	NW Battle	"
28 Jun		V-1	"		SE Rye	"
30 Jun		V-1	"	JN821 SA-H	23m S Hastings	"
"		V-1	"	JN854 SA-G	S Tunbridge Wells	"
11 Jul	½	V-1	"	JN805 SA-E	N Tonbridge	"
12 Jul		V-1	"	JN821 SA-H	E Bexhill	"
16 Jul	½	V-1	"		Hastings	"
29 Aug	½	V-1	"	JN803 SA-d	N Rye	"

TOTAL: 6 and 3 shared V-1s destroyed.

HART William Alfred   Flying Officer   RNZAF No. 424461

Bill Hart, from Wellington, New Zealand, joined 486 Squadron in May 1944. On 7 October that year, shortly after the unit had moved to the European mainland, his Tempest EJ535 was shot down by Flak south-west of Kevelaer, and he became a POW. The award of a DFC was gazetted on 27 February 1945. After the war he returned to the unit in August 1945, remaining for two months until it was disbanded. He died on 27 March 1988.

1944						
18 Jun		V-1	Tempest V	JN797 SA-K	nr Le Treport	486 Sqn
25 Jun		V-1	"	JN809 SA-M	2m W Newchurch	"
		V-1	"	"		"
27 Jun		V-1	"	JN803 SA-D	W Rye	"
26 Jul		V-1	"	JN732 SA-I	E Rye	"
27 Jul	½	V-1	"	JN754 SA-A	Rye	"
3 Aug		V-1	"	JN732 SA-I	N Pevensey Bay	"
"	½	V-1	"	"		"

TOTAL: 6 and 2 shared V-1s destroyed.

HARTLEY James   Flying Officer   RAF No.

Jim Hartley served with 129 Squadron during 1944, flying Mustang IIIs.

1944						
11 Jul		V-1	Mustang III	FZ130 DV-D	Folkestone	129 Sqn
16 Jul		V-1	"	FZ172 DV-A	10m N Dungeness	"
26 Jul		V-1	"	HB862 DV-G	1-2m NW Tunbridge Wells	"
3 Aug		V-1	"	"		"
7 Aug	2	V-1s	"	"	Dover area	"
10 Aug		V-1	"	"	Folkestone/E Lympne	"
19 Aug		V-1	"	FB125 DV-F	7m S Dymchurch	"
		V-1	"	"		"
28 Aug		V-1	"	HB860 DV-J	2m S Dymchurch	"
		V-1	"	FX924 DV-V	20m SE Dungeness	"
29 Aug		V-1	"	FB138 DV-X	10m S Folkestone	"

TOTAL: 12 V-1s destroyed.

HASTINGS, I.   Pilot Officer   RAF No. 183367

Flying Spitfire IXs with 1 Squadron, he was commissioned in late 1944, remaining with the unit for the rest of the war.

1944						
27 Jun	⅓	V-1	Spitfire IX		nr Wadhurst	1 Sqn
28 Jun		V-1	"	MK846	nr Brentwood	"
5 Jul		V-1	"	MK659		"
11 Jul		V-1	"	NH466	S Godalming	"
"		V-1	"	ML117	15m N Hastings	"

TOTAL: 4 and 1 shared V-1s destroyed.

HEAD Norman Sidney   Flight Lieutenant   RAF No. 66516

Norman Head served as a night fighter pilot with 96 Squadron, with 131662 Flg Off Arthur Charles Andrews as his radar operator. They were awarded DFCs on 2 June 1944.

1944						
2/3 Jan		FW 190	Mosquito XIII		Rye	96 Sqn
21 Jan	2	Ju 88s Probable	"			"
14/15 Mar		Ju 88	"	HK406	Hildenborough	"
		Ju 188	"	"	Channel	"
22/23 Mar		FW 190	"	MM451	off Hastings	"
25/26 Jun		V-1	"	MM492	E Eastbourne	"
3/4 Jul	2	V-1s	"	MK461	over sea	"
7/8 Jul		V-1	"	HK462	20m S Beachy Head	"

8/9 Jul	V-1		„	„	3m inland from Dungeness	„
12/13 Aug	V-1		„	MM438	over sea	„
15/16 Oct	V-1		„	MM460	„	„

TOTAL: 7 V-1s destroyed, 4 aircraft destroyed, 2 probables.

HOOPER Garnet John Michael   Flying Officer   RNZAF No. 413231

'Gus' Hooper, a New Zealander from Reikarangi, was posted to 486 Squadron in March 1944. On 2 February 1945 his Tempest, EJ787, SA-L, was hit by Flak and he force-landed near Kirchdorf, becoming a POW. He managed to escape on 4 April, returning to Allied lines. He was awarded a DFC, gazetted on 14 September 1945.

1944						
22 Jun	1/3	V-1	Tempest V	JN809 SA-M	Wrotham	486 Sqn
27 Jun		V-1	„	JN803 SA-D	3m S Hastings	„
„		V-1	„	„	N Tonbridge	„
6 Jul		V-1	„	JN805 SA-E	nr Friston	„
„		V-1	„	„	16-17m S Beachy Head	„
„	1/2	V-1	„	„	off Beachy Head	„
9 Jul	2	V-1s	„	JN821 SA-H	20m S Beachy Head	„
15 Jul		V-1	„	JN803 SA-D	10m S Hastings	„
20 Jul	1/2	V-1	„	JN797 SA-K	nr West Malling	„
1945						
1 Jan		FW 190	„	EJ750 SA-B	Venlo	„
„		Bf 109 Damaged	„	„	„	„

TOTAL: 7 and 3 shared V-1s destroyed, 1 aircraft destroyed, 1 damaged.

HOWARD Basil   Wing Commander   RAAF No. 404787

Basil Howard was born in Seven Hills, New South Wales, on 6 July 1915, working as a petrol representative before the war. Joining the RAAF, he arrived in the UK on conclusion of his training, and after appropriate operational training, was posted to 96 Squadron as a night fighter pilot. He subsequently moved to 456 Squadron, RAAF, where he became a flight commander, and then in 1944 the commanding officer. Awarded a DFC on 9 February 1945, he survived the war to be killed in an aircraft accident on 29 May 1945. His radar operator was Aus 401721 Flg Off J.R.Ross, on all but his final engagement.

1944						
27/28 Mar		Ju 88	Mosquito XVII	HK323	nr Beer	456 Sqn
7/8 Jun	2	He 177s (a)	„	HK290	off Normandy coast	„
7/8 Aug	2	V-1s	„	HK323		„
11/12 Aug		V-1	„	HK292		„
30/31 Aug	2	V-1s (b)	„	HK232		„

TOTAL: 5 V-1s destroyed, 3 aircraft destroyed.

(a) One of the bombers was carrying a glider bomb; (b) Flying with Aus 404399 Flt Lt Thomas Condon, DFC as radar operator; a third V-1 was claimed, but was disallowed.

JANKOWSKI Tadeusz   Warrant Officer   RAF No. P780386

A Polish pilot, Jankowski served with 315 Squadron during 1944. He was awarded the Cross of Valour with two Bars and the Silver Cross of Merit with Swords.

1943						
20 Apr		FW 190 Damaged	Spitfire IX	BS410	10-15m N Fecamp	315 Sqn
1944						
25 May	1/3	Ar 96	Mustang III	PK-W	Bourges	„
11 Jul		V-1	„	PK-R	Hastings	„
19 Jul		V-1	„	PK-X		„
„	1/2	V-1	„	„	8m NW Tenterden	„
„	1/2	V-1	„	PK-R		„
26 Jul	1/2	V-1	„		Beachy Head-Hastings	„
„	1/2	V-1	„		„	„
„	1/2	V-1	„		„	„
27 Jul	1/3	V-1	„		10m SE Tunbridge Wells	„
30 Jul		Bf 109F	„	PK-V	30m W Lister a/fld,	„
„		FW 190	„	„	Norway	„
28 Aug		V-1	„	„	off Boulogne	„
„		V-1	„	„	10m S Dungeness	„

TOTAL: 4 and 6 shared V-1s destroyed, 2 and 1 shared aircraft destroyed, 1 damaged.

JANSSEN M.J.   Flight Sergeant   RAF No.

Janssen was a Dutch pilot who flew Spitfire XIVs with 322 Squadron during summer 1944.

1944						
29 Jun		V-1	Spitfire XIV	VL-K	S Staplehurst	322 Sqn
5 Jul		V-1 (a)	„	VL-D	Fairfield area	„

		V-1 (a)		„		„	2m SW Dungeness	„
12 Jul		V-1		„		VL-E	over sea	„
„		V-1		„		„	N Upchurch	„
13 Jul		V-1		„		VL-A	Sevenoaks area	„
14 Jul		V-1		„		VL-G	nr Tonbridge	„
28 Jul	1/3	V-1		„		VL-D	over sea	„

TOTAL: 6 and 2 shared V-1s destroyed.
(a) One of these claims was downgraded to a 1/2 share.

JOHNSON Herbert Dennis   Flight Lieutenant
RAF Nos. 741206 (NCO); 119186 (Officer)

Herbert Johnson was commissioned from Flt Sgt on 16 March 1942. By 1944 he was a flight commander in 91 Squadron. The award of a DFC was gazetted on 19 October 1945.

1944							
23 Jun	1/2	V-1	Spitfire XIV	RB188	SE Uckfield	91 Sqn
24 Jun		V-1	„	„	W Hawkhurst	„
28 Jun		V-1	„	RB183	W Hastings	„
„		V-1	„	„	S Hastings	„
29 Jun		V-1	„	NH701	High Holden	„
		V-1	„	RB188	S Battle	„
1 Jul		V-1	„	„	SE Dungeness	„
3 Jul		V-1	„	„	E Lympne	„
		V-1	„	RB165	N Ashford	„
7 Jul		V-1	„	NH697	N Appledore	„
26 Jul		V-1	„	RM684	W Battle	„
28 Jul		V-1	„	„	N Deanland	„
4 Aug		V-1	„	RM686	SE East Grinstead	„
7 Aug		V-1	„	RM684	NW Hastings	„

TOTAL: 13 and 1 shared V-1s destroyed.

JONGBLOED G.F.J.   Flight Lieutenant   RAF No.

Dutch-born Jongbloed served with 322 Squadron during summer 1944, flying Spitfire XIVs. During early 1945 he flew as a flight commander in 222 Squadron, with this unit claiming one of the last daylight successes against a V-1, which had been aimed at a Belgian target.

1944							
19 Jun	1/2	V-1	Spitfire XIV	VL-B	20m N Hastings	322 Sqn
28 Jun		V-1	„	VL-B	NW West Malling	„
29 Jun		V-1	„	VL-K	Tenterden area	„
12 Jul		V-1	„	VL-G	SE Cranbrook	„
16 Jul		V-1	„	„	NW Ashford	„
19 Jul		V-1	„	VL-E	W Hastings	„
„	1/2	V-1	„	„	over sea	„
22 Jul		V-1	„	„	N Hastings/Bexhill	„
23 Jul		V-1	„	„	nr Hawkinge	„
21 Sep		FW 190 Damaged	Spitfire IXB	3W-G		„
1945						
28 Feb		V-1	Tempest V			222 Sqn
25 Mar		FW 190 (a)	„	NV972	2m NE Haselhume	„

TOTAL: 8 and 2 shared V-1s destroyed, 1 aircraft destroyed, 1 damaged.
(a) Aircraft of III/JG 54.

JONKER J.   Flying Officer   RAF No.
A Dutch pilot with 322 Squadron.

1944					
30 Jun		V-1	Spitfire XIV	322 Sqn
3 Jul		V-1	„	„
4 Jul		V-1	„	„
8 Jul		V-1	„	„
24 Jul	sh	V-1	„	„
5 Aug		V-1	„	„

TOTAL: 5 and 1 shared V-1s destroyed.

KALKA William Arthur   Flying Officer   RNZAF No.
'Wacky' Kalka, from Auckland, New Zealand, gained some considerable success against V-1s with 486 Squadron during the summer of 1944 as a Wt Off. After the unit had moved to Holland to operate with 2nd TAF, his aircraft (EJ606) was shot down in error by US anti-aircraft fire on 13 January 1945; fortunately, he managed to bale out safely, and returned to his unit. On 25 March he shot down a balloon and then strafed eight Fi 156 Storch

aircraft on the ground. Whilst so engaged his Tempest, NV981, was hit by Flak — German this time — and he was obliged to bale out north-west of Grave. However, he fell into the River Maas, and although a young Dutch girl who was passing on her bicycle dived in to try and save him, he was drowned.

1944						
23 Jun		V-1	Tempest V	JN801 SA-L	5-6m SW Newchurch	486 Sqn
4 Jul	2	V-1s	„	JN809 SA-M	Beachy Head	„
12 Jul	2	V-1s	„	JN803 SA-D	Bexhill area	„
„	2	V-1s	„	„	Hastings area	„
6 Aug		V-1	„	EJ560 SA-M	Bexhill	„
1945						
25 Mar		Balloon	„	NV981	NW Grave	„

TOTAL: 8 V-1s destroyed, 1 balloon destroyed.

KARNKOWSKI Stefan   Flight Lieutenant   RAF No. P0973

Karnkowski was a Polish Mustang pilot in 316 Squadron, credited with taking part in the destruction of five V-1s.

1943						
14 May		Fw 190 Probable	Spitfire IX	BS302	2-3m N Courtrai	316 Sqn
1944						
18 Oct		Bf 109F	Mustang III	865 SZ-Y	10m NE Aalborg	„
„	½	Bf 109F	„	„	„	„

TOTAL: 2 and 3 shared V-1s (no details), 1 and 1 shared aircraft destroyed, 1 probable.

KLAWE Wlodzimierz   Flight Lieutenant/Kapitan   RAF No. P0387

In Poland in 1939 Klawe flew in 113 Eskadra, claiming one and one probable during the September fighting. Escaping to France, and then to England, this Polish pilot served in 316 and 306 Squadrons.

1939						
? Sep		Ju 87 Probable	PZL P.11			113 Esk
6 Sep		Do 17	„			„
1941						
14 Jul		He 111 Probable	Hurricane I	Z2805	NW Lynton	316 Sqn
1944						
17 Aug		V-1	Mustang III		7m W Ashford	306 Sqn
19 Aug		V-1	„		W Appledore	„
„		V-1	„		W Brenzett	„
„	½	V-1	„		SE Ham Street	„
23 Aug	½	V-1	„	UZ-U	3m N Ashford	„
„		V-1	„	UZ-V	Rye	„

TOTAL: 4 and 2 shared V-1s destroyed, 1 aircraft destroyed, 2 probables.

KLEINMAYER Robert Gordon   Flight Lieutenant   RNZAF No. 411985

'Dutch' Kleinmayer was a New Zealand pilot, serving with 129 Squadron in 1944. The award of a DFC was gazetted on 11 May 1945.

1944						
12 Jul		V-1	Mustang III	FZ172 DV-A	15m N Beachy Head	129 Sqn
31 Jul		V-1	„	FB361 DV-B	30m S Beachy Head	„
3 Aug	½	V-1	„	FB152 DV-L	W Ham Street	„
„	2	V-1s	„			„
4 Aug		V-1	„			„
15 Aug		V-1	„	FB137 DV-C	2m NE Ashford	„
28 Aug		V-1	„	FZ128 DV-A	nr Dungeness	„

TOTAL: 7 and 1 shared V-1s destroyed.

LAWLESS Frank Brewster   Flight Lieutenant   RNZAF No. 411417

'Bruce' Lawless, from Lower Hutt, New Zealand, joined 486 Squadron in July 1943. On 10 June 1944, whilst flying support cover over the Normandy landings, his Tempest JN772 suffered engine failure and he was obliged to ditch in the sea off Dungeness. 18 days later, now intercepting V-1s, JN859 was damaged by the explosion of one of these bombs which he had attacked, and this time he had to force-land near Rye. He completed his tour in August, and was posted to the 84 Group Support Unit. Reverting to Typhoons, he was later to serve briefly with 164 and 183 Squadrons, before becoming a flight commander in 198 Squadron. He then continued to fly operationally until the end of the war, undertaking over 200 sorties. He was awarded a DFC, gazetted on 24 July 1945, and a US DFC.

1944						
23 Jun		V-1	Tempest V	JN859 SA-S	Hastings	486 Sqn
28 Jun		V-1	„		„	„
30 Jun		V-1	„	JN811 SA-Z	„	„
1 Jul		V-1	„	JN770 SA-V	Dungeness	„
4 Jul		V-1	„	EJ537 SA-S	Eastbourne	„

8 Jul		V-1			JN770 SA-V	N West Malling	,,
,,		V-1		,,		Prewhurst	,,
28 Jul		V-1		,,		NNW Beachy Head	,,
,,		V-1		,,		SE Tunbridge Wells	,,
1945							
1 Jan		FW 190	Typhoon IB		MN951 TP-A	Euskirchen	198 Sqn

TOTAL: 9 V-1s destroyed, 1 aircraft destroyed.

LAWSON C.M.   Flying Officer   RAAF No.409843

'Ac' Lawson joined 165 Squadron as an NCO at Peterhead. He flew Spitfire IXBs with the unit during the summer of 1944, achieving notable success against the V-1s in these aircraft. Having been commissioned, he became a deputy flight commander before completing his tour on 12 December 1944.

1944						
30 Jun	V-1	Spitfire IX	MK811 SK-S	Marden	165 Sqn
1 Jul	V-1	,,	,,	S Bexhill	,,
,,	V-1	,,	,,	S Hastings	,,
26 Jul	V-1	,,	ML175 SK-P	Ashford	,,
5 Aug	V-1	,,	,,	Hawkhurst	,,
,,	V-1	,,	,,	Tonbridge	,,

TOTAL: 6 V-1s destroyed.

LEGGAT P.S.   Flight Lieutenant   RCAF No. J

He joined 418 Squadron on 6 June 1944 as a Flt Lt, with Flt Lt Cochrane as his navigator. It is presumed that he had been retained in Canada as an instructor prior to this.

1944						
6/7 Jul		V-1	Mosquito II		over sea	418 Sqn
30/31 Jul	2	V-1s	,,		,,	,,
3/4 Aug		V-1	,,		,,	,,
7/8 Aug		V-1	,,		,,	,,

TOTAL: 5 V-1s destroyed.

MACKERRAS D.J.   Flight Sergeant   RAAF No. 422599

Born in Camperdown, Victoria, on 7 November 1920, Mackerras worked as an engineering draftsman in Pymble, New South Wales before joining the RAAF. He flew with 3 Squadron on Tempests during 1944, but was killed on 6 August when JN759 spun into the ground at Ninfield during a V-1 patrol.

1944						
31 May	1/5 of 2 Ju 188s	on ground	Tempest V			3 Sqn
,,	1/5 of 2 Ju 188s	Damaged on ground	,,			,,
16 Jun	1/2	V-1	,,	JN793	S Chatham	,,
18 Jun		V-1	,,	JN752	nr Biggin Hill	,,
		V-1	,,	JN745	nr Gatwick	,,
23 Jun		V-1	,,			,,
25 Jun		V-1	,,	JN745	N Beachy Head	,,
27 Jun		V-1	,,			,,
3 Jul		V-1	,,	JN968	10m SE Dungeness	,,
11 Jul		V-1	,,			,,
12 Jul	1/2	V-1	,,			,,
14 Jul		V-1	,,			,,
20 Jul		V-1	,,		nr Battle	,,
26 Jul		V-1	,,	JN768	E Tonbridge	,,
		V-1	,,	,,	S Ashford	,,
28 Jul	1/3	V-1	,,			,,

TOTAL: 11 and 3 shared V-1s destroyed, 2 shared aircraft destroyed on the ground, 2 shared damaged on the ground.

MACLAREN W.R.   Flying Officer   RAF No.161788

MacLaren served with 56 Squadron during 1944, where he was credited with shooting down five V-1s and sharing a sixth during the summer. In the autumn the unit moved to Holland to join 2nd TAF, and here on 14 October he force-landed Tempest EJ742, US-T, close to Volkel airfield due to engine failure. On 26 March 1945 he was shot down and killed by Flak, EJ708, US-W, crashing north-east of Dorsten.

1944					
4 Jul	V-1	Tempest V	JN684 US-C	2m SE Redhill	56 Sqn
13 Jul	V-1	,,	JN816 US-W	W Winchelsea	,,
21 Jul	V-1	,,	EJ547 US-A		,,
27 Aug	V-1	,,	JN816 US-W	over sea	,,
29 Dec	FW 190	,,	EJ692 US-R	S Dummer See	,,
1945					
22 Jan	Bf 109	,,	EJ721 US-C	Neede area	,,

| 23 Jan | | FW 190 | „ | EJ708 US-W | 10m NW Rheine | „ |

TOTAL: 5 and 1 shared V-1s destroyed (1 and 1 shared no details), 3 aircraft destroyed.

MAJEWSKI Longin   Flight Lieutenant/Kapitan   RAF No. P0327
A Polish pilot who served with 303 and 316 Squadrons during the war.

1943						
24 Aug	½	FW 190	Spitfire IX	MA754	Lisieux area	303 Sqn
1944						
7 Jul	½	V-1	Mustang III	385 SZ-D	SE Hastings	316 Sqn
„		V-1	„	„	nr Alfriston	„
13 Jul		V-1	„	383 SZ-J	N Hailsham	„
6 Aug		V-1	„	821 SZ-L	15m S Beachy Head	„
„		V-1	„	„	20m S Hastings	„
7 Aug		V-1	„	839 SZ-V	S Hastings	„

TOTAL: 5 and 1 shared V-1s destroyed, 1 aircraft shared destroyed.

MARSHALL William Cyril   Flight Lieutenant   RAF No. 126834
Marshall flew as a flight commander in 91 Squadron. The award of a DFC was gazetted during August 1945.

1944						
29 Jun		V-1	Spitfire XIV	RB181	N Sevenoaks	91 Sqn
3 Jul		V-1	„	RM615	WNW Dymchurch	„
„		V-1	„	NH654	off Hastings	„
7 Jul		V-1	„	NH720	SE Tunbridge Wells	„
„		V-1	„	„	Ham Street	„
9 Jul		V-1	„	NH701	NE Dungeness	„
3 Aug		V-1	„	RM682	E Robertsbridge	„
5 Dec	2	Bf 109s	Spitfire IX		NE Wesel	„

TOTAL: 7 V-1s destroyed, 2 aircraft destroyed.

MASON Henry Maurice   Wing Commander   RNZAF No. 413104
'Morrie' Mason, from Waipawa, New Zealand, joined 486 Squadron from OTU as a Flg Off in January 1944, and was at once in action against the V-1s. He was then posted briefly to 197 Squadron on Typhoons, before becoming commanding officer of 183 Squadron in January 1945. He then received further rapid promotion, in February being appointed Wing Leader of 135 Wing, back on Tempests. He was awarded a DFC, gazetted on 14 September 1945. Returning to New Zealand after the war, he was unable to settle back happily into his previous life as a mechanic, and returned to the UK to join the RAF. On 19 July 1948, returning from France in a Vampire after taking part in the Bastille Day celebrations, he and his aircraft disappeared, and he was listed as missing, believed killed in a flying accident.

1944						
4 Jul		V-1	Tempest V	JN805 SA-E	S Rye	486 Sqn
„	½	V-1	„	JN809 SA-M	S Hastings	„
7 Jul		V-1	„	JN732 SA-I	SW West Malling	„
13 Jul		V-1	„	„	Tenterden	„
„		V-1	„	„	Bexhill	„
14 Jul	½	V-1	„	„	„	„
5 Aug		V-1	„	JN801 SA-L	7-8m S Newchurch	„

TOTAL: 5 and 2 shared V-1s destroyed.

MAY N.S.   Flight Lieutenant   RCAF No. J
He joined 418 Squadron on 6 June 1944 as a Flg Off, with Plt Off T.D.Ritch (who had served with the unit earlier) as his navigator. He was promoted Flt Lt in September 1944.

1944						
22/23 Jun	2	V-1s	Mosquito II		over sea	418 Sqn
14/15 Jul		V-1	„		5m off Le Touquet	„
5/6 Aug		V-1	„		25m off Beachy Head	„
7/8 Aug		V-1	„		nr Brighton	„

TOTAL: 5 V-1s destroyed.

McCARTHY Kevin   Pilot Officer   RNZAF No.
From Auckland, New Zealand, Kevin McCarthy joined 486 Squadron in June 1943. During June 1944 he began achieving rapid success against the V-1s, but on 1 July he was obliged to force-land near Battle due to an engine failure, and was seriously injured, seeing no further operational flying. He died on 24 May 1996.

1944						
16 Jun		V-1	Tempest V	JN801 SA-L	N Rye	486 Sqn
22 Jun		V-1	„	„	Cherbourg	„
„		V-1	„	„	3m S Hastings	„
23 Jun		V-1	„	JN754 SA-A	Willingdon	„

		V-1		"		"	W Newchurch	"
24 Jun		V-1		"		JN803 SA-D	W Eastbourne	"

TOTAL: 6 V-1s destroyed.

McCAW James Hugh   Squadron Leader   RNZAF No. 414311

'Black Mac' McCaw, from Hakataramea, New Zealand, joined 486 Squadron in August 1942, serving with the unit until August 1944. He was promoted flight commander in January 1944, achieving considerable success against V-1s during the summer. Awarded a DFC on 8 August 1944, he was then posted to Napiers as a test pilot, subsequently receiving promotion to Sqn Ldr. He died on 16 December 1996.

1944								
19 Jun		V-1		Tempest V		JN770 SA-V	10m NW Dungeness	486 Sqn
20 Jun	1/2	V-1		"		JN758 SA-Y	N Hastings	"
22 Jun		V-1		"		"	Hastings-Eastbourne	"
"		V-1		"		JN808 SA-N	Hastings-Rye	"
"		V-1		"		JN821 SA-H	4-5m N Newchurch	"
26 Jun		V-1		"		JN558 SA-Y	Dungeness	"
8 Jul		V-1		"		"	Ashford/Maidstone	"
"	2	V-1s		"		"	N West Malling	"
"		V-1		"		"	Biggin Hill	"
11 Jul		V-1		"		EJ523 SA-X	6m N Bexhill	"
12 Jul		V-1		"		EN770 SA-V	6m S Maidstone	"
14 Jul	2	V-1s		"		JN758 SA-Y	10 & 12m N Bexhill	"
15 Jul		V-1		"		JN860 SA-Z	Ashford	"
21 Jul		V-1		"		JN758 SA-Y	Rye	"
26 Jul		V-1		"		JN770 SA-V	2m N Bexhill	"
27 Jul		V-1		"		"	Hastings-Bexhill	"
"		V-1		"		EJ523 SA-X	Ashford	"
30 Jul		V-1		"		"	3-4m NW Mayfield	"

TOTAL: 19 and 1 shared V-1s destroyed.

McKINLEY G.M.   Flying Officer   RAF No. 136433

He flew Spitfire XIVs with 610 Squadron during 1944. On 12 July his aircraft was caught in the blast of his fifth and final V-1, and he was killed, the aircraft crashing at Newhaven.

1944						
22 Jun	1/2	V-1		Spitfire XIV		610 Sqn
7 Jul	2	V-1s		"		"
12 Jul	2	V-1s		"		"

TOTAL: 4 and 1 shared V-1s destroyed.

McLARDY W.A.   Pilot Officer   RAF No.

A night fighter pilot in 96 Squadron, who flew with Flt Sgt Devine as his radar operator. In December 1944, when the unit was disbanded, both were posted to 456 Squadron, RAAF.

1944						
18/19 Jun		V-1		Mosquito XIII	NE Beachy Head	96 Sqn
23/24 Jun		V-1		"	nr Lympne	"
8/9 Jul		V-1		"	15m SE Dungeness	"
20/21 Jul	1/2	V-1		"	off Hastings	"
	1/2	V-1		"	"	"
23/24 Jul		V-1		"	3m SSE Beachy Head	"
5/6 Aug		V-1		"	10m E Hastings	"
13/14 Aug		V-1		"	over sea	"

TOTAL: 6 and 2 shared V-1s destroyed.

McPHIE R.A.   Flying Officer   RCAF No. J

A Canadian pilot who served with 91 Squadron, flying Spitfire XIVs against V-1s during summer 1944.

1944							
18 Jun	1/2	V-1		Spitfire XIV	RB182	W West Malling	91 Sqn
"	1/4	V-1		"	"	N West Malling	"
"		V-1		"	"	Croydon	"
27 Jun	1/2	V-1		"	NH698	N West Malling	"
8 Jul		V-1		"	RB182	N Beachy Head	"
18 Jul		V-1		"	NH705	SSE Tunbridge Wells	"
24 Jul		V-1		"	RM680	SE Mayfield	"
29 Jul		V-1		"	"	SE Tunbridge Wells	"

TOTAL: 5 and 3 shared V-1s destroyed.

MIELNECKI Jerzy Andrzej   Sergeant   RAF No. P2913

A Polish Mustang III pilot who served with 316 Squadron.

1944						
7 Jul	½	V-1	Mustang III	386 SZ-N	5-8m N Bexhill	316 Sqn
„		V-1	„	„	3m N Tonbridge	„
12 Jul		V-1	„	391 SZ-B	5m W Tunbridge Wells	„
„		V-1	„	„	W Reigate	„
23 Aug		V-1	„	845 SZ-Y	5m S Dymchurch	„
„		V-1	„	„	Boulogne-Dungeness	„
24 Aug		V-1	„	„	„	„

TOTAL: 6 and 1 shared V-1s destroyed.

MILLER B.F.   Flight Officer   USAAF No.

'Bud' Miller was an NCO pilot of the USAAF, flying on attachment with the RAF to gain night fighting experience. In summer 1944 he was serving with 605 Squadron, flying Mosquito VIs on intruder operations, with Flg Off J.C.Winlaw, RCAF, as his navigator. Shortly after the commencement of the V-1 offensive against London, he was posted to the FIU, where he joined the Tempest Flight at Newchurch. When this unit formed the nucleus of a reformed 501 Squadron in July, he became a part of this unit, remaining with it for the rest of the year.

1944						
22/23 Feb		E/a	Mosquito VI		Melsbroek	605 Sqn
14 Mar	2	E/a Damaged	„		Brussels	„
22/23 Mar		E/a Damaged on ground	„		Oberolm	„
21/22 Jun		V-1				
20 Jul		V-1	Tempest V			FIU
? Jul		V-1	„			„
11/12 Aug	3	V-1s	„	EJ584 SD-Q		501 Sqn
15/16 Sep		V-1	„	SD-M	Castle Camps	„
„		V-1	„		Bradwell Bay	„
24/25 Sep		V-1	„	EJ558 SD-R	„	„

TOTAL: 9 V-1s destroyed, 1 aircraft destroyed, 2 damaged, 1 damaged on the ground.

MILLER William Lister   Flight Lieutenant   RNZAF No. 402208

A New Zealander from Invercargill, and inevitably known as 'Dusty' Miller, he joined 486 Squadron in October 1943, later becoming a flight commander. On 8 February 1945 he force-landed near Verden when his Tempest, EJ750, was hit by Flak, Although this was in hostile territory, he managed to evade capture and return to Allied lines. The award of a DFC was gazetted on 11 December 1945.

1944					
19 Jun	V-1	Tempest V	JN811 SA-Z	7m N Bexhill	486 Sqn
22 Jun	V-1	„	JN794 SA-T	10m N Hastings	„
23 Jun	V-1	„	JN808 SA-N	N Hastings	„
„	V-1	„	„	7-8m N Pevensey Bay	„
27 Jun	V-1	„	JN811 SA-Z	sea, 10m S Rye	„
„	V-1	„	„	4m S Paddock Wood	„
16 Aug	V-1	„	JN803 SA-D	NW Tonbridge	„

TOTAL: 7 V-1s destroyed.

MOFFETT H.Bruce   Flight Lieutenant   RCAF No. J

A Canadian pilot, Bruce Moffett served with 91 Squadron, making the unit's first claim for a V-1 on 16 June 1944.

1944					
16 Jun	V-1	Spitfire XIV	RM617	Kenley	91 Sqn
19 Jun	V-1	„	NH701	Battle	„
27 Jun	V-1	„	RM620	S West Malling	„
3 Jul	V-1	„	RB165	NW Rye	„
15 Jul	V-1	„	NH701	Wrotham	„
29 Jul	V-1	„	RM726		„
30 Jul	V-1	„	RM682	S Sittingbourne	„
3 Aug	V-1	„	RM726	N Mayfield	„

TOTAL: 8 V-1s destroyed.

MOORE Andrew Robert   Flight Lieutenant   RAF No. 102100

He flew as a flight commander with 3 and 56 Squadrons, achieving considerable success against V-1s, while also claiming four aircraft shot down. He was awarded a DFC on 21 July 1944 and a Bar to this on 27 February 1945.

1944					
8 Jun	Bf 109	Tempest V	JN753	N Rouen	3 Sqn
18 Jun	V-1	„	JN818	5m W Rye	„
19 Jun	V-1	„	JN755	over sea	„
„	V-1	„	„	nr Tonbridge	„
„	V-1	„	„	6m NNW Rye	„
21 Jun	V-1	„	JN818	30m S Hastings	„

Date		Type		Serial	Location	Squadron
4 Jul		V-1	,,	,,	20 yds off Pevensey Bay	,,
		V-1	,,	,,	10-15m N Rye	,,
7 Jul		V-1	,,	,,	8-10m N Hastings	,,
8 Jul	3	V-1s	,,			,,
13 Jul		V-1	,,			,,
18 Jul	1/2	V-1	,,	JN815	N Rye	,,
19 Jul		V-1	,,	JN868	8m N Rye	,,
		V-1	,,	,,	10m N Dungeness	,,
22 Jul		V-1	,,	JN817	over sea	,,
,,		V-1	,,	,,	nr Biddenden	,,
,,		V-1	,,	,,	8m NW Hastings	,,
,,		V-1	,,	JN865	N Bexhill	,,
26 Jul		V-1	,,	,,	5m N Beachy Head	,,
29 Jul		V-1	,,			,,
31 Jul		V-1	,,			,,
10 Aug	2	V-1s	,,			,,
29 Sep	1/2	FW 190 Probable	,,	EJ741 US-C	Emmerich	56 Sqn
28 Nov		He 219 (a)	,,	EJ536 US-B	Munster area	,,
17 Dec		Bf 109	,,	EJ778 US-M	NE Munster	,,
		Bf 109	,,	,,	Grave	,,

TOTAL: 23 and 1 shared V-1s destroyed, 4 aircraft destroyed, 1 shared probable.
(a) Aircraft of 1/NJG 1 flown by Lt Kurt Fischer.

MUSGRAVE John Gothorp   Flight Lieutenant   RAF No. 103571
Commissioned on 6 August 1941, John Musgrave subsequently flew as an intruder pilot with 605 Squadron, Flt Sgt F.W.Samwell acting as his navigator.

1944						
15/16 Jun		V-1	Mosquito VI		21m off Dunkirk	605 Sqn
23 Jun		V-1	,,			,,
1/2 Jul		V-1	,,			,,
5/6 Jul	2	V-1s	,,			,,
9/10 Jul		V-1	,,			,,
25/26 Jul		V-1	,,			,,
30/31 Jul	2	V-1s	,,			,,
15/16 Aug	2	V-1s	,,			,,
26/27 Aug		V-1s	,,			,,

TOTAL: 12 V-1s destroyed.

NASH Raymond Stanley   Squadron Leader   RAF No. 119808
Commissioned on 13 February 1942, Nash served in 91 Squadron during 1943-44, becoming a flight commander. Awarded a DFC on 19 September 1944, he was posted to 61 OTU on 21 November to instruct. In April 1945 he took command of 1 Squadron, where he remained until February 1946, when he was posted to the Middle East.

1943						
4 Mar	1/2	FW 190	Spitfire VB		Calais	91 Sqn
16 Jun		FW 190	Spitfire XII		16m SE Dover	,,
20 Oct		Bf 109G	,,		Rouen	,,
1944						
18 Jun	1/4	V-1	Spitfire XIV	RB169	N West Malling	,,
,,	1/2	V-1	,,	,,	Thames, E London	,,
,,		V-1	,,	,,	Beachy Head	,,
,,	1/2	V-1	,,	,,	NW Beachy Head	,,
25 Jun		V-1	,,	,,	NW Maidstone	,,
27 Jun		V-1	,,	,,	SW Frittenden	,,
29 Jun		V-1	,,	RM615	Newchurch	,,
,,		V-1	,,	,,	NW Lydd	,,
4 Jul		V-1	,,	RB169	Uckfield area	,,
,,		V-1	,,	,,	NW Hastings	,,
5 Jul		V-1	,,	,,	N Beachy Head	,,
7 Jul		V-1	,,	,,	S Dartford	,,
9 Jul		V-1	,,	,,	S Paddock Wood	,,
13 Jul		V-1	,,	,,	S West Malling	,,
22 Jul		V-1	,,	,,	N Bexhill	,,
23 Jul		V-1	,,	,,	SE Dartford	,,
24 Jul		V-1	,,	RM624	N Polegate	,,
28 Jul		V-1	,,	RM735	N Pevensey	,,
2 Aug		V-1	,,	,,	N Hastings	,,
,,		V-1	,,	,,	N Mayfield	,,

TOTAL: 17 and 3 shared V-1s destroyed, 2 and 1 shared aircraft destroyed.

NEIL H.M.   Flying Officer   RAF No. 125704
He served with 91 Squadron during summer 1944, flying Spitfire XIVs.

1944					
29 Jun	V-1	Spitfire XIV	RB173	5m N Newchurch	91 Sqn
1 Jul	V-1	”		NE Tilehurst	”
5 Jul	V-1	”	RB177	NW Newchurch	”
7 Jul	V-1	”	RB183	W West Malling	”
”	V-1	”	RB174	NW Dungeness	”
TOTAL: 5 V-1s destroyed.					

NEWBERY Richard Alfred   Squadron Leader   RAF No. 60104
Commissioned on 15 January 1941, Richard Newbery joined 501 Squadron in March of that year. In spring 1942 he was posted to 118 Squadron as a flight commander, being awarded a DFC on 23 June and a Bar to this a year later on 4 June 1943. Following a rest from operations, he took command of 610 Squadron in January 1944 as it converted to Spitfire XIVs, remaining with the unit until February 1945.

1942					
9 Mar	Bf 109	Spitfire VB		NE France	501 Sqn
4 Jun	FW 190 Probable	”		off Cap Levy	118 Sqn
	FW 190 Damaged	”		”	”
1943					
18 Mar	FW 190	”		North Sea	”
27 Jun	FW 190	”		off The Hague	”
18 Jul	Bf 109	”		Den Helder	”
1944					
20 Jun	2 V-1s	Spitfire XIV			610 Sqn
22 Jun	2 V-1s	”			”
23 Jun	1/2 V-1	”			”
24 Jun	V-1	”			”
”	1/2 V-1	”			”
5 Jul	V-1	”			”
11 Jul	2 V-1s	”			”
TOTAL: 8 and 2 shared V-1s destroyed, 4 aircraft destroyed, 1 probable, 1 damaged.					

NOWOCZYN Witold   Flight Sergeant   RAF No. P781525
A Polish pilot who flew Mustang IIIs with 315 Squadron.

1944					
7 Jun	Bf 109F	Mustang III	UZ-W	10m E Argentan	306 Sqn
24 Jun	FW 190 Damaged	”	UZ-V	Tilliers	”
12 Jul	V-1	”	”	Ashford	”
	V-1	”	”	N Tunbridge Wells	”
16 Jul	V-1	”	”	St Leonards	”
5 Aug	V-1	”		8m N Bexhill	”
15 Aug	V-1	”		4m W Ashford	”
TOTAL: 5 V-1s destroyed, 1 aircraft destroyed, 1 damaged.					

O'CONNOR Brian John   Flying Officer   RNZAF No. 402747
From Stoke in New Zealand, Brian O'Connor joined 486 Squadron in December 1943, remaining with the unit until May 1945. He was awarded a DFC, gazetted on 20 July 1945; he died on 3 August 1993.

1944					
16 Jun	V-1	Tempest V	JN809 SA-M	Rye-Dungeness	486 Sqn
5 Jul	V-1	”	JN803 SA-D	6-7m S Beachy Head	”
6 Jul	1/2 V-1	”	”	Marden area	”
	V-1	”	”	N Hastings	”
11 Jul	V-1	”	JN767 SA-B	nr Ewell	”
13 Jul	V-1	”	JN866 SA-U	7m S West Malling	”
27 Jul	V-1	”	JN801 SA-L	Beachy Head	”
4 Aug	V-1	”	”	6m NNW Rye	”
29 Aug	V-1	”	EJ577 SA-F	nr West Malling	”
31 Aug	V-1	”	JN802 SA-C	E Maidstone	”
1945					
15 Apr	FW 190	”	SN129 SA-M	Velzen	”
TOTAL: 9 and 1 shared V-1s destroyed, 1 aircraft destroyed.					

OSBORNE Anthony Frederick   Flight Lieutenant   RAF No. 128997
Tony Osborne was posted to the Mediterranean area at the end of 1942, joining 249 Squadron on Malta in January 1943. During April, as a Flg Off, he shared in shooting down a Ju 52/3m transport over the sea between Malta and Tunisia, with his commanding officer, the American Sqn Ldr J.J.Lynch. During 1944 he undertook a

second tour as a flight commander in 129 Squadron, now flying Mustang IIIs. He was awarded a DFC, gazetted on 11 May 1945.

1943						
28 Apr	1/2	Ju 52/3m	Spitfire VC	AB535 T-Z	6m N Cap Cafafu	249 Sqn
1944						
22 Jul	1/2	V-1	Mustang III	FX874 DV-G	S Ashford	129 Sqn
”		V-1	”	FB123	2m SE Tonbridge	”
”		V-1	”	”	N Ashford	”
23 Jul	1/2	V-1	”	FB212 DV-Q	Kingsnorth airfield	”
30 Jul		V-1	”		20m S Hastings	”
29 Aug		V-1	”	FB392 DV-N	W Le Touquet	”
TOTAL: 4 and 2 shared V-1s destroyed, 1 aircraft shared destroyed.						

PARKER-REES Alastair   Squadron Leader   RAF No. 85665
Commissioned on 21 September 1940, Parker-Rees was a night fighter pilot with 96 Squadron in 1944, flying with Flt Lt Bennett as his radar operator. During the night of 17/18 July 1944, having just shot down two V-1s, they prepared to attack a third, when their own Mosquito was hit by fire from an unidentified aircraft, and they were obliged to bale out into the sea. They were picked up six hours later by HMS *Obedient*, and returned safely to England. Parker-Rees was then posted to command 501 Squadron in October, to fly Tempests at night. He was awarded a DFC during this month, and was to remain with the unit until it was disbanded on 20 April 1945. He was then posted to HQ, 13 Group.

1944						
15/16 Jan		FW 190	Mosquito XIII		Dungeness	96 Sqn
24/25 Feb		He 177 probable	”		Sussex	”
13/14 Apr		Ju 88	”		off Dungeness	”
14/15 Apr		Me 410	”			”
16/17 Jun		V-1	”	MM497	off Dover	”
5/6 Jul	2	V-1s	”	”	over sea	”
6/7 Jul		V-1	”	”	”	”
9/10 Jul		V-1	”	MM562	Worthing	”
17/18 Jul	2	V-1s	”	MM511	N Abbeville	”
14/15 Aug		V-1	”	MM525	over sea	”
5/6 Dec		V-1	Tempest V	SD-P		501 Sqn
TOTAL: 9 V-1s destroyed, 3 aircraft destroyed, 1 probable.						

PIETRZAK Aleksander   Warrant Officer   RAF No. P783147
Pietrzak was a Polish pilot who served with 302 and 316 Squadrons, receiving the Virtuti Militari, 5th Class, and the Cross of Valour with two Bars. He should not be confused with Henryk Pietrzak, who flew with 306 and 315 Squadrons, who also gained success flying against the V-1s.

1943						
11 Sep		FW 190 Damaged	Spitfire VB	EE679	Rouen area	302 Sqn
27 Sep		FW 190	Spitfire IX	MH327	10m W Le Treport	”
1944						
4 Jul		V-1	Mustang III	161 SZ-I	3m NW Boulogne	316 Sqn
7 Jul		V-1	”		10m off Bexhill	”
12 Jul		V-1	”	378 SZ-X	2m NW Appledore	”
		V-1	”	”	N Lympne	”
???	1/4	V-1	”		”	”
14 Oct		Bf 109	”	386 SZ-L	10m NW Duisberg	”
18 Oct	1/2	Bf 109F	”	841 SZ-A	10m NE Aalborg	”
”		Bf 109F	”	”	”	”
1945						
23 Mar		Me 262 Damaged	”	SR418 SZ-D	10m S Dummer See	”
TOTAL: 4 and 1 shared V-1s destroyed, 3 and 1 shared aircraft destroyed, 2 damaged.						

PLESMAN J.L.   Flight Lieutenant   RAF No.
A Dutch pilot, who served as a flight commander in 322 Squadron during summer 1944.

1944					
22 Jun	V-1	Spitfire XIV	VL-V	Maidstone-Ashford	322 Sqn
27 Jun	V-1	”	”	20m NW Hastings	”
29 Jun	V-1	”	VL-W	S Hastings	”
10 Jul	V-1	”	”	S Beachy Head	”
14 Jul	V-1	”	”	Robertsbridge	”
”	V-1	”	”	Appledore	”
19 Jul	V-1	”	”	W Hawkshurst	”
20 Jul	V-1	”	”	WNW Ashford	”
4 Aug	V-1	”		2m N Hailsham	”

6 Aug	V-1			VL-P	over sea		,,
10 Aug	V-1		Spitfire XIVE	VL-W			,,

TOTAL: 11 V-1s destroyed.

POLLEY William F.   Flying Officer   RAF No. 155000

William Polley served with 501 Squadron, reportedly claiming six V-1s shot down whilst with this unit; details of only three of these have been discovered. In 1945, when the unit was disbanded, he was posted to 165 Squadron to fly Mustang IIIs.

1944						
5 Aug	V-1		Tempest V	EJ598 SD-H	NE Ashford	501 Sqn
18/19 Aug	V-1	-	,,	EJ591 SD-Z		,,
26/27 Aug	V-1		,,	EJ598 SD-H		,,

TOTAL: 6 V-1s destroyed (3 no details).

PORTEOUS James Kerrow   Squadron Leader   RNZAF No. 401030

Jim Porteous was sent to the UK on completion of his training, and as a Sgt was one of the original pilots forming 485 (New Zealand) Squadron in March 1941. He was posted to 93 Squadron the following year, serving with this unit in Tunisia as a Flg Off. In spring 1943 he was posted to 243 Squadron as a flight commander, and in July was awarded a DFC. Returning to the UK at the end of his tour, he attended CGS and was promoted, becoming Gunnery Leader, Portreath as a Sqn Ldr. Anxious to return to operations, he took a drop in rank to become a flight commander in 165 Squadron during summer 1944, flying Spitfire IXBs with this unit against the V-1s. On 9 September he was again promoted Sqn Ldr, taking command of 122 Squadron on Mustang IIIs, leading this unit until November, when his second tour ended.

1942						
4 Dec	$\frac{1}{2}$	Bf 109 on ground	Spitfire V			93 Sqn
1943						
18 Apr		Bf 109	Spitfire VC	EE668 SN-V	Teboursouk	243 Sqn
,,	2	Bf 109s Damaged	,,	,,		,,
1944						
8 Jul		V-1	Spitfire IX	MK854 SK-H	W Hailsham	165 Sqn
11 Jul		V-1	,,	ML418 SK-G	6m W Bexhill	,,
16 Jul		V-1	,,	ML242 SK-A	3m N Hythe	,,
18 Jul	$\frac{1}{2}$	V-1	,,	MK738 SK-L	SW Tenterden	,,
20 Jul		V-1	,,	MK425 SK-I	W Ashford	,,
4 Aug		V-1	,,	MK854 SK-H	E Marden	,,

TOTAL: 5 and 1 shared V-1s destroyed,1 aircraft destroyed, 2 damaged, 1 shared destroyed on the ground.

PORTER D.A.   Flight Lieutenant   RAF No.

He served with 257 Squadron as a Flg Off during early 1944, and was later posted to 501 Squadron as a flight commander.

1944						
29 Jan	$\frac{1}{4}$	Do 217	Typhoon IB	JP975 FM-P	Fecamp	257 Sqn
29 Apr	$\frac{1}{3}$	LeO 45	,,	MN381	nr Lisieux	,,
23/24 Oct		V-1	Tempest V			501 Sqn
3 /4 Nov		V-1	,,	SD-K		,,
8/9 Nov		V-1	,,	,,		,,
9/10 Nov	$\frac{1}{2}$	V-1	,,	,,		,,
7/8 Dec		V-1	,,	,,		,,

TOTAL: 4 and 1 shared V-1s destroyed, 2 aircraft shared destroyed.

POTTINGER R.W.   Flying Officer   RAF No. 182715

Pottinger was serving with 3 Squadron as an NCO in early 1944. On 22 March his Typhoon, R8895, QO-E, suffered engine failure and he ditched safely in Bradwell Bay. He then converted to Tempests, flying against the V-1s during the summer. Following the unit's move to Holland late in the year, on 1 January 1945 his aircraft, EJ719, JF-R, was shot down by Flak near Dulmen, and he became a POW for the rest of the war. On return to the UK after the conclusion of hostilities, he was posted to 56 OTU as an instructor.

1944						
24 Feb	$\frac{1}{2}$	LeO 451	Typhoon IB	JP744	nr Louvain	3 Sqn
16 Jun		V-1	Tempest V	JN743	nr Ashford	,,
23 Jun		V-1	,,			,,
28 Jun		V-1	,,			,,
12 Jul	$\frac{1}{2}$	V-1	,,			,,
14 Jul	$\frac{1}{2}$	V-1	,,			,,
30 Jul	$\frac{1}{2}$	V-1	,,			,,
3 Aug		V-1	,,			,,

TOTAL: 4 and 3 shared V-1s destroyed, 1 aircraft shared destroyed.

POWELL Neville Joseph   Flight Lieutenant   RNZAF No.

'Pip' Powell, from Dargaville, New Zealand, joined 486 Squadron in March 1944, becoming a flight commander in February 1945. On 8 April he broke his leg in a vehicle accident, which ended operational flying for him. A keen fisherman, he was drowned in a boating accident in New Zealand whilst on a fishing trip on 13 August 1969.

1944						
18 Jun		V-1	Tempest V	JN804 SA-R	sea, 5m S Dungeness	486 Sqn
27 Jun		V-1	„	JN866 SA-U	Hastings	„
4 Jul		V-1	„	EJ527 SA-Q	Crowborough area	„
3 Aug		V-1	„	JN808 SA-N		„
18 Aug		V-1	„	EJ523 SA-Z	N Haywards Heath	„
1945						
24 Feb		Bf 109 (a)	„	NV763 SA-N	NE Bramsche	„

TOTAL: 5 V-1s destroyed, 1 aircraft destroyed.
(a) Bf 109G-10 WNr 490221 of 14/JG 27; Uffz Rudolph Prisilie wounded.

REDHEAD E.   Warrant Officer   RAF No.

Wt Off Redhead flew Mustang IIIs with 129 Squadron during summer 1944.

1944						
12 Jul	½	V-1	Mustang III	FB292 DV-N	SE Hastings	129 Sqn
22 Jul		V-1	„	FB389 DV-J	Maidstone	„
2 Aug		V-1	„	FB364 DV-P	15m off Dungeness	„
6 Aug		V-1	„	FX942 DV-P	2m SW Ham Street	„
19 Aug		V-1	„	FB125 DV-F	15m N Dungeness	„

TOTAL: 4 and 1 shared V-1s destroyed.

ROBB Robert Landry Thomas   Flight Lieutenant   RAF No. 113877

'Jackson' Robb was commissioned on 25 November 1941, completing his training as a night fighter pilot. He subsequently served with 85 Squadron, where he gained one victory during 1943. In early summer 1944 he was posted to the special night-flying Tempest Flight of the FIU at Newchurch. When this unit formed the nucleus of a reformed 501 Squadron in July, he stayed on with this squadron as one of the more successful V-1 hunters.

1943						
17/18 Jun		FW 190 Damaged	Mosquito		Tonbridge	85 Sqn
30/31 Oct		Ju 188 (a)	„	VY-G	22m SE Rye	„
19 Jul		V-1	Tempest V			FIU
25 Jul		V-1	„			„
28 Jul	2	V-1s	„			„
3 Aug	2	V-1s	„			„
7 Aug	2	V-1s	„			„
9 Aug	2	V-1s	„			„
13/14 Aug	2	V-1s	„	EJ598 ZQ-U (b)		501 Sqn
25/16 Oct		V-1	„	SD-Y		„

TOTAL: 13 V-1s destroyed, 1 aircraft destroyed, 1 damaged.
(a) Actually a Ju 88S-1 of III/KG 6 — either WNr 140485, 3E+KS, or WNr 140585, 3E+AS; (b) This aircraft was still carrying the code letters of the FIU.

ROEDIGER Keith Alexander   Flight Lieutenant   RAAF No. 415227

Born in Balaklava, Southern Australia, on 25 May 1921, Keith Roediger worked in Northam, Western Australia, as a butcher before joining the RAAF. As a night fighter pilot in 456 Squadron, with Aus 413179 Flt Lt R.J.H.Dobson as his radar operator, he became his unit's top-scorer against the V-1s, claiming nine of the unit's tally of 24. He also claimed two bombers shot down.

1944						
21/22 Mar		Ju 88	Mosquito XVII	HK297	off Rye	456 Sqn
25/26 Apr		Ju 88	„	HK353	S Selsey	„
9/10 Jul		V-1	„	HK297	over sea	„
13/14 Jul		V-1	„	„	„	„
18/19 Jul		V-1	„	„	„	„
4/5 Aug		V-1	„	„	„	„
6/7 Aug		V-1	„	„	„	„
9/10 Aug		V-1	„	„	„	„
19/20 Aug		V-1	„	„	„	„
23/24 Aug	2	V-1s	„	„	„	„

TOTAL: 9 V-1s destroyed, 2 aircraft destroyed.

ROGOWSKI Jan   Warrant Officer   RAF No. P780965

Born on 16 August 1917, Jan Rogowski served in the Polish Air Force with 162 Eskadra at Lvov. Escaping via Rumania in September 1939, he reached England in 1940 and joined 303 Squadron on its formation in July. He was slightly wounded in combat on 6 September, and did not return to action until 23 October, by which time

Luftwaffe activity was much reduced. He was awarded the Cross of Valour on 23 December. On 2 February 1941 he joined 74 Squadron, moving in August to 308 Squadron. On 1 July 1942 he joined 1489 Flight, a target towing unit, where he remained until June 1943. He then joined 302 Squadron as a Flt Sgt, on 1 September receiving two Bars to his Cross of Valour. He was posted to 16 FTS, Newton, on 9 January 1944 on an instructor's course, and then in May to 2 AGS as a staff pilot. On 10 June he joined 306 Squadron, becoming a Wt Off on 1 July, and here he flew against the V-1s. The award of the Virtuti Militari, 5th Class, followed, and the Silver Cross of Merit with Swords. He remained with the unit for the duration of the war, then being sent on a further instructor's course at 2 SFTS in August 1945. At the end of the year he went to the Polish Air Force Depot at Blackpool, where he was released from the service in 1946.

1940						
2 Sep		Bf 109E	Hurricane I	R4217	nr Dover	303 Sqn
1941						
7 Apr		Bf 109	Spitfire II		Cap Gris Nez	74 Sqn
1944						
16 Aug		V-1	Mustang III		nr Appledore	306 Sqn
„	sh	V-1	„		7m N Tonbridge	„
28 Aug		V-1	„		NW Canterbury	„
„		V-1	„		3m S Canterbury	„

TOTAL: 3 and 2 shared V-1s destroyed (no detail of one share), 2 aircraft destroyed.

ROSE Morris James Alexander   Pilot Officer   RAF No. 189177
An RAFVR pilot who served with 3 Squadron, he was awarded a DFC, gazetted on 18 September 1945, but with effect from 9 February of that year.

1944						
16 Jun		V-1	Tempest V	JN760	S Maidstone	3 Sqn
17 Jun	½	V-1	„	JN769	N Ham Street	„
18 Jun		V-1	„	JN753	Beachy Head	„
„		V-1	„	JN745	Westerham area	„
22 Jun		V-1	„			„
23 Jun		V-1	„			„
25 Jun		V-1	„	JN817	Goudsbridge area	„
3 Jul		V-1	„	JN754	Ashford-Maidstone road	„
18 Jul		V-1	„	EJ504	3-4m S Mayfield	„
21 Jul		V-1	„	„	30m S Hastings	„
22 Jul		V-1	„	„	Newenden	„
30 Jul		V-1	„			„
17 Dec		Bf 109	„	EJ777	Scahle	„
1945						
1 Jan		Bf 109	„	EJ827	N Helmond	„
14 Jan	2	FW 190s Damaged on ground	„			„
24 Jan		E/a Damaged	„			„

TOTAL: 11 and 1 shared V-1s destroyed, 2 aircraft destroyed, 1 damaged, 2 damaged on the ground.

RUDOWSKI Stanislaw   Flight Sergeant   RAF No. P782513
A Polish pilot who flew with 317 and 306 Squadrons. He was awarded the Cross of Valour and Bar.

1943						
8 Sep		Bf 109F	Spitfire VC	AR515	10m NW Lille	317 Sqn
1944						
7 Jun		Bf 109F	Mustang III	UZ-B	10m E Argentan	306 Sqn
„		Bf 109F Damaged	„	„	„	„
10 Jul		V-1	„	UZ-E	4m S Kenley	„
19 Jul		V-1	„	UZ-F	4m SW Cranbrook	„
„		V-1	„	„	Lamberhurst	„
„		V-1	„	„	Maidstone	„
22 Jul		V-1	„	UZ-M	Hastings	„
27 Jul		V-1	„	UZ-F		„
„	½	V-1	„	„	Staplehurst-Tonbridge	„
31 Jul		V-1	„	„	W Rye	„
3 Aug		V-1	„	„	Bexhill-Hastings	„
„	½	V-1	„	„	W Hastings	„
16 Aug		V-1	„		Maidstone	„

TOTAL: 9 and 2 shared V-1s destroyed (or possibly 7 and 3 shared), 2 aircraft destroyed, 1 damaged.

SAMES Arthur Norman   Flying Officer   RNZAF No. 411453
A New Zealander from Auckland, Artie Sames joined 486 Squadron as a Sgt in March 1942, flying Hurricanes and then Typhoons with this unit; he was commissioned in 1943, leaving the squadron in December of that year. During 1944 he flew with 137 Squadron, the only Typhoon unit retained for home defence duties following the start of the Normandy invasion. He was the only pilot to shoot down five V-1s whilst flying Typhoons. He was

awarded a DFC on 28 March 1944. He died on 12 December 1980.

1942						
17 Oct	½	FW 190 (a)	Typhoon IB	R8681 SA-E	9m S Hastings	486 Sqn
19 Dec		FW 190 (b)	,,	R8660 SA-T	30m S Shoreham	,,
1943						
15 Jul		FW 190 (c)	,,	R8697 SA-Z	off Le Havre	,,
1944						
26 Jun		V-1	,,	MN134	nr Bexhill	137 Sqn
		V-1	,,	,,	coast, nr Bexhill	,,
13 Jul		V-1	,,	MN169	N Rye	,,
14 Jul		V-1	,,	MN134	S Dungeness	,,
4 Aug		V-1	,,	MN169		,,

TOTAL: 5 V-1s destroyed, 2 and 1 shared aircraft destroyed.
(a) WNr 2403 'Black 14' of 10(Jabo)/JG 26; Fw Klaus Niesel killed; (b) WNr 395 '3+' of 3(F)/122; Fw P.Gellert killed; (c) Aircraft of I/JG2.

SHORT Sydney John   Flight Sergeant   RNZAF No.

Sid Short, from Auckland, New Zealand, served with 486 Squadron from December 1943 until the end of the war. He died on 22 September 1973.

1944					
23 Jun	V-1	Tempest V	JN810 SA-P	8-10m N Beachy Head	486 Sqn
25 Jun	V-1	,,		NE Battle	,,
29 Jun	V-1	,,	EJ527 SA-Q	4m E Rye	,,
	V-1	,,	,,	2m S Rye, in sea	,,
30 Jun	V-1	,,	JN810 SA-P	Dungeness	,,
27 Dec	FW 190 (a)	,,	JN808 SA-N	Munster area	,,

TOTAL: 5 V-1s destroyed, 1 aircraft destroyed.
(a) FW 190D-9 of III/JG 54.

SIEKIERSKI Jan   Flight Lieutenant/Kapitan   RAF No. P1032

Jan Siekierski was a Polish flight commander in 306 Squadron during 1944.

1944						
7 Jun		Bf 109F	Mustang III	UZ-C	Port Audemer area	306 Sqn
		Bf 109F Damaged	,,	,,	,,	,,
11 Jul		V-1	,,	UZ-Z	5m S Hythe	,,
18 Jul		V-1	,,	,,	4m N Hastings	,,
22 Jul		V-1	,,	UZ-S	5m W Ashford	,,
		V-1	,,	,,	2m N Tenterden	,,
		V-1	,,	,,	Appledore	,,
4 Aug		V-1	,,	UZ-I	1m NE Tenterden	,,
6 Aug	2	V-1s	,,	UZ-U	Channel	,,
		V-1	,,	,,	3m SW Ashford	,,
17 Aug		V-1	,,		Kingsnorth	,,

TOTAL: 10 V-1s destroyed (or 7 and 3 shared), 1 aircraft destroyed, 1 damaged.

SIWEK Kazimierz   Flight Sergeant   RAF No. P783226

A Polish pilot with 315 Squadron, he was awarded the Virtuti Militari, 5th Class, and the Cross of Valour. He was killed in action on 13 September 1944.

1944						
22 Jul	½	V-1	Mustang III	PK-F	Appledore	315 Sqn
		V-1	,,	,,	5m E Ashford	,,
23 Jul		V-1	,,		NW Lympne	,,
		V-1	,,		S Mersham station	,,
	½	V-1	,,		airfield SE Ashford	,,
16 Aug		V-1	,,		2m N Woodchurch	,,
		V-1	,,		Ashford Junction	,,
		V-1	,,		N Headcorn-Pluckley railway	,,
18 Aug	3	FW 190s	,,	PK-B	Beauvais area	,,

TOTAL: 6 and 2 shared V-1s destroyed (but may have been downgraded to 2 and 3 shared), 3 aircraft destroyed.

SLADE-BETTS Kenneth Gordon   Pilot Officer   RAF No. 175509

He flew Tempests with 3 Squadron during 1944, receiving a DFC, gazetted on 22 September 1944; the citation recorded the destruction by him of 20 V-1s. Later in the year, operating from Volkel, Holland, as part of 2nd TAF, the unit became involved in a fight with Bf 109Gs of IV/JG 27 on 29 December; during this engagement his Tempest, JN803, was shot down north of Rheine and he was killed

1944				
31 May	⅕ of 2 Ju 188s on ground	Tempest V		3 Sqn

„	⅕ of 2 Ju 188s Damaged on ground		„			3 Sqn
18 Jun	½	V-1	„	JN755	in sea	„
„		V-1	„	JN812	N Bexhill	„
20 Jun		V-1	„	JN705	6m N Eastbourne	„
22 Jun		V-1	„			„
23 Jun		V-1	„			„
28 Jun	2	V-1s	„			„
29 Jun		V-1	„			„
30 Jun		V-1	„	JN755	4m S Maidstone	„
3 Jul		V-1	„	EJ504	15m N Hastings	„
„		V-1	„	„	6m S Hastings	„
4 Jul		V-1	„	JN817	4m S Eastbourne	„
8 Jul	2	V-1s	„			„
9 Jul		V-1	„			„
12 Jul		V-1	„			„
13 Jul		V-1	„			„
21 Jul		V-1	„	JN817	14m N Beachy Head	„
„		V-1	„	„	15m S Hastings	„
„		V-1	„	„		„

TOTAL: 19 and 1 shared V-1s destroyed, 2 aircraft shared destroyed on the ground, 2 shared damaged on the ground.

SMITH Keith Alexander   Flying Officer   RNZAF No.

From Masterton, New Zealand, Keith Smith joined 486 Squadron in April 1944, just in time to take part in the operations against the V-1s. After the move to Holland later in the year he was to claim victories over two aircraft, the second an Me 262 jet over Lübeck airfield on 25 April 1945. Next day however, his Tempest, NV967, was hit by Flak north of Uithiele and he had to make a force-landing, being captured. With the war nearing its close, he was able to escape on 4 May from the POW camp to which he had been sent, safely reaching Allied lines.

1944						
3 Jul	2	V-1s	Tempest V	JN801 SA-L	Hastings area	486 Sqn
26 Jul		V-1	„	JN803 SA-D	9-10m N Pevensey	„
4 Aug	2	V-1s	„	JN821 SA-H	Tunbridge Wells area	„
„		V-1	„	„	nr Maidstone	„
16 Aug		V-1	„	JN808 SA-N	5m NNW Tenterden	„
29 Aug		V-1	„	JN770 SA-V	N Ashford	„
27 Dec		FW 190 (a)	„	EJ711 SA-Q	Munster area	„
1945						
25 Apr		Me 262	„		Lübeck airfield	„

TOTAL: 8 V-1s destroyed, 2 aircraft destroyed.
(a) FW 190D-9 of III/JG 54.

SPENCER Terence   Squadron Leader   RAF No. 47269

Previously a Lieutenant in the Royal Engineers, Terry Spencer volunteered for aircrew and received a temporary commission in the RAF on 11 October 1941. He served as a flight commander in 165 Squadron in spring 1944, then being posted to 41 Squadron. He was promoted to command 350 (Belgian) Squadron for a brief period in April 1945. On 26 February 1945 whilst on an armed reconnaissance in the Rheine-Lingen area, his aircraft caught fire due to a technical fault and he was obliged to bale out, being captured. After two weeks in prison camp, he and another POW noted that the main gate was open, the guards distracted, and two bicycles were nearby. They reached the bikes, mounted and pedalled through the gates, and kept going. Reaching Allied lines subsequently, he was swiftly back with his unit. On 19 April, now with 350 Squadron, he strafed a Ju 88 on the ground, but as he returned over Wismar Bay, he spotted a trawler. As he went down alone to strafe this, fellow pilots saw his Spitfire disintegrate just above the sea, apparently hit by a rocket fired by a German destroyer; they returned to report that he had been killed in action. He had in fact been thrown clear at a height of about 50 feet, and his parachute had opened just before he hit the water alongside the tail of his aircraft. Looking towards the shore, he saw what he took to be a second Spitfire hit the ground 100 yards from the water's edge. He later discovered that it was the main section of SM814, his own aircraft — he had reached the sea before it ! He swam for some time, but became exhausted. Dropping his legs, he found that he was standing in only three-four feet of water! Wading ashore, he was again captured, but he was liberated by advancing British troops on 4 May, and returned to the UK.

1944						
23 Jun		V-1	Spitfire XII	MB856	10-15m NNE Hastings	41 Sqn
25 Jun		V-1	„	EN224	Hastings	„
9 Aug		V-1 (a)	„	MB875	5m N Hastings	„
19 Aug		V-1	„		2m NNW Appledore	„
23 Aug		V-1	„	MB882	N Folkestone	„
„		V-1	„	„	nr Harrietsham	„
27 Aug		V-1	„		N Rye	„

3 Sep   FW 190 (b)   „   Tirlemont   „
TOTAL: 7 V-1s destroyed, 1 aircraft destroyed.
(a) Toppled with wingtip: (b) This was almost certainly the aircraft flown by Hpt Emil "Bully" Lang (Ritterkreuz mit Eichenlaub, 173 victories) of II/JG 26, who was killed.

SWISTUN Gwido   Flying Officer   RAF No. P2478
Polish pilot with 315 Squadron in 1944.

1944						
11 Jul		V-1	Mustang III	PK-Y		315 Sqn
12 Jul	2	V-1s	„			„
29 Jul	½	V-1	„	SS (a)		„
30 Jul	½	Bf 109F	„	PK-Y	30m W Lister airfield,	„
„		Bf 109F	„	„	Norway	
3 Aug		V-1	„			„
7 Aug		V-1	„	PK-Q	12m NW Brenzett	„
16 Aug		V-1	„		3m N Maidstone	„
18 Aug		FW 190	„	PK-U	Beauvais area	„
„		FW 190 Probable	„	„	„	„

TOTAL: 6 and 1 shared V-1s destroyed (possibly downgraded to 1 and 5 shared), 2 and 1 shared aircraft destroyed, 1 probable.
(a) This was the personal aircraft of the Wing Leader, Stanislaw Skalski.

SZYMANKIEWICZ Teofil   Flight Lieutenant/Kapitan   RAF No. P0744
Teofil Szymankiewicz, a Polish pilot, served with 317 and 316 Squadrons, becoming a flight commander in the latter unit. He was awarded a Cross of Valour with two Bars.

1942						
15 Jul	½	FW 190	Spitfire VB	R7296	over sea off Boulogne	317 Sqn
1944						
8 Jul		V-1	Mustang III	391 SZ-E	2m N Beccles	316 Sqn
9 Jul		V-1	„	„	15m SE Dungeness	„
„		V-1	„	„	4m SW Dungeness	„
6 Aug		V-1	„	824 SZ-N	8m SW Newhaven	„
8 Aug		V-1	„	831 SZ-I	10m SW Beachy Head	„
9 Aug		V-1	„	396 SZ-F	20m SSE Hastings	„

TOTAL: 6 V-1s destroyed (or 5 and 1 shared), 1 aircraft shared destroyed.

SZYMANSKI Tadeusz   Sergeant   RAF No. P781044
Szymanski was a Polish NCO pilot who flew with 316 Squadron from 1942-44.

1942						
4 Apr		FW 190	Spitfire VB	AD119	St Omer area	316 Sqn
„		FW 190 Probable	„	„	„	„
12 Apr		FW 190	„	W3230	S Gravelines	„
1944						
7 Jul		V-1	Mustang III	377 SZ-R	2m NW Appledore	„
12 Jul		V-1	„	351 SZ-B	20m N Beachy Head	„
„		V-1	„	„	6m SE Crowborough	„
6 Aug	2	V-1s	„	824 SZ-N	S Hastings	„
9 Aug	2	V-1s	„	878 SZ-X	mid Channel	„

TOTAL: 7 or 8 V-1s destroyed, 2 aircraft destroyed, 1 probable.

TANNER Eric William   Flight Lieutenant   RNZAF No.
'Rick' Tanner was a New Zealander from Tauranga, who joined 486 Squadron in December 1943, remaining with the unit until February 1945. He died on 15 November 1984.

1944						
30 Jun	2	V-1s	Tempest V	JN770 SA-V	N Rye	486 Sqn
		V-1	„	„	S Cranbrook	„
12 Jul	½	V-1	„	EJ528 SA-P	6-7m N Rye	„
24 Jul	½	V-1	„	JN732 SA-I	E Ninfield	„
27 Dec		FW 190 (a)	„	EJ541 SA-T	Munster area	„
„		FW 190 Damaged (a)	„	„	„	„

TOTAL: 3 and 2 shared V-1s destroyed, 1 aircraft destroyed, 1 damaged.
(a) FW 190D-9s of III/JG 54.

THORNTON Cyril Brooking   Flight Lieutenant   RAF No. 117692
Thornton received a direct entry commission on 21 February 1942. He served in the FIU's special Tempest Flight in June 1944, and then with 501 Squadron when the flight was incorporated into that unit in July. With the former unit he was reported to have shot down six V-1s, details of only four of which have been found. He was killed in a flying accident on 21 August 1944 in bad weather, crashing in Tempest EJ602, SD-P, at Woodnesboro, Kent.

1944						
3 Aug	2	V-1s	Tempest V			FIU
6 Aug		V-1	„			„
9 Aug		V-1	„			„
11/12 Aug	3	V-1s	T „	855 SD-U		501 Sqn

TOTAL: 9 V-1s destroyed (3 no details, with FIU).

TOPHAM E.   Flying Officer   RAF No.

He served with 91 Squadron during 1944-45.

1944						
21 Jun		V-1	Spitfire XIV	NH707		91 Sqn
27 Jun		V-1	„	RB183	SE Detling	„
29 Jun	1/2	V-1	„	NH707	Dungeness	„
„		V-1	„	NH654	Sittingbourne	„
„		V-1	„	RB169	S Ashford	„
4 Jul		V-1	„	RB181	Sevenoaks	„
10 Jul		V-1	„	NH698	Wittersham	„
22 Jul		V-1	„	NH707	NE Bexhill	„
29 Jul		V-1			SE Tunbridge Wells	„
23 Aug		V-1	Spitfire IX	MK998	SW West Malling	„
5 Dec		Bf 109 Damaged	„			„

TOTAL: 9 and 1 shared V-1s destroyed, 1 aircraft damaged.

TROTT William Allan Liddell   Flying Officer   RNZAF No. 417131

From Dunedin, New Zealand, Bill Trott joined 486 Squadron in August 1943. After operating against the V-1s during the summer of 1944, he moved with the unit to Holland later in the year. Operating over Germany on 14 February 1945, he was hit by a fragment from a Flak shell, and very badly wounded, though he was able to fly back to base and land. A considerable period in hospital in the UK followed, after which he was returned to New Zealand. Making a complete recovery, he decided to remain in the RNZAF, and served with the occupation forces in Japan. On return to New Zealand, he was to be sent to the UK to attend the RAF Staff College, but on 17 February 1955 he was killed when a Devon aircraft in which he was flying crashed near Wellington.

1944						
13 Jul		V-1	Tempest V	JN866 SA-U	5-6m W Tunbridge Wells	486 Sqn
23 Jul		V-1	„	JN758 SA-Y	Hastings	„
„		V-1	„	„	Etchingham area	„
27 Jul		V-1	„	JN763 SA-F	S West Malling	„
6 Aug		V-1	„	EJ528 SA-P	Newhaven	„
28 Aug		V-1	„	JN863 SA-R	2m W Tenterden	„
1945						
1 Jan		FW 190	„	EJ606 SA-U	Venlo	„

TOTAL: 6 V-1s destroyed, 1 aircraft destroyed.

VAN ARKEL J.   Flying Officer   RAF No.

A Dutch pilot, Van Arkel served with 41 Squadron as a Sgt in 1942, and in 1943 with 167 Squadron, which was subsequently renumbered as 322 Squadron. Re-equipped with Spitfire XIVs, he saw action with the latter unit against the V-1s during the summer of 1944.

1942						
4 May	1/2	FW 190	Spitfire VB		Le Havre	41 Sqn
1943						
3 May		FW 190 Damaged	„		Ijmuiden	167 Sqn
1944						
23 Jun	1/2	V-1	Spitfire XIV	VL-V	Tonbridge area	322 Sqn
27 Jun		V-1	„	VL-T	4m S Edenbridge	„
30 Jun		V-1	„	VL-D	3m SW Ashford	„
14 Jul		V-1	„		SW Ashford	„
16 Jul		V-1	„	VL-V	NE Ashford	„
26 Jul		V-1	„	VL-W	N Tenterden	„
9 Aug		V-1	„			„

TOTAL: 6 and 1 shared V-1s destroyed, 1 aircraft shared destroyed, 1 damaged.

VAN BEERS R.L.   Flight Sergeant   RAF No.

A Dutch NCO pilot in 322 Squadron during 1944, Van Beers made two shared claims on 2 August, one with Peter Nash of 91 Squadron. Since the latter, if not shared, would be the squadron's 100th V-1, for which a sweepstake had been held, Nash voluntarily relinquished his share of the claim in order that Van Beers could formally win the sweepstake.

1944							
21 Jun		V-1	Spitfire XIV	VL-K	5m N Beachy Head	322 Sqn
27 Jun		V-1	„	VL-H	S Hastings	„
14 Jul		V-1	„	„	over sea	„
2 Aug	2	V-1s	„	VL-C	Tunbridge Wells area	„

TOTAL: 5 V-1s destroyed.

VAN EEDENBORG C.M.   Squadron Leader   RAF No.

Formerly a member of the Dutch Navy, Van Eedenborg undertook one tour of operations with 167/322 Squadron during 1942-43. In February 1944 he returned to the unit for a second tour as a flight commander, and in September became commanding officer, retaining this post until November of that year. On 9 August 1944 he claimed the unit's last V-1, bringing the total to 108.5.

1944					
20 Jun	V-1	Spitfire XIV	VL-C	NE Swanley Junction	322 Sqn
5 Jul	V-1 (a)	„	VL-B	N Appledore over sea	„
„	V-1	„	„	SE Maidstone	„
8 Jul	V-1	„	„	3m SW West Malling	„
10 Jul	V-1	„	„	over sea	„
18 Jul	V-1	„	VL-A		„
19 Jul	V-1	„	VL-B	nr Paddock Wood	„
9 Aug	V-1	„	VL-I	over sea	„

TOTAL: 7 V-1s destroyed.
(a) This claim was disallowed; (4 claims were made by two pilots, but only 1 and 1 shared were confirmed).

WALTON R.C.   Flight Lieutenant   RAF No.

A night intruder pilot with 605 Squadron, Walton flew with Sgt F.Pritchard, RNZAF, as his navigator.

1944				
24/25 Jun		V-1	Mosquito VI	605 Sqn
27/28 Jun	2	V-1s	„	„
28/29 Jun	2	V-1s	„	„
30/31 Jul		V-1	„	„

TOTAL: 6 V-1s destroyed.

WARD Donald Leslie   Flight Lieutenant   RAF No. 106851

Commissioned in the RAFVR on 13 September 1941, Donald Ward flew as a Plt Off in 68 Squadron in 1942, claiming one victory with this unit. By early 1944 he was serving with 96 Squadron as a Flt Lt, with which unit he claimed two more aircraft shot down, with 116703 Flt Lt Ernest Derek Eyles as his radar operator. During the night of 16/17 June 1944 he claimed the unit's first V-1, whilst he was subsequently also to claim the 100th. Ward was awarded a DFC, gazetted on 3 October 1944, while in December, when the unit was disbanded, he and Eyles were posted to 25 Squadron. Here on 17 April 1945 Eyles was also awarded a DFC, having taken part in victories over four aircraft with Ward and other pilots.

1942						
30/31 Jul		Do 217	Beaufighter IF		off Norfolk coast	68 Sqn
1944						
24/25 Feb		Me 410	Mosquito XIII	HK370	off Beachy Head	96 Sqn
13/14 Apr		Me 410	„		off Dungeness	„
16/17 Jun		V-1	„	HK415	Dungeness-Boulogne	„
19/20 Jun		V-1	„	„	off Beachy Head	„
27/28 Jun		V-1	„		6m S Dungeness	„
5/6 Jul		V-1	„	HK415	over sea	„
6/7 Jul		V-1	„	„	„	„
9/10 Jul	2	V-1s	„	MM579	Worthing	„
14/15 Jul		V-1	„	MM524	NNE Boulogne	„
17/18 Jul		V-1	„	„	18m N Boulogne	„
25/26 Jul		V-1	„	„	over sea	„
26/27 Jul		V-1	„	„	„	„
23/24 Aug		V-1	„	„	„	„

TOTAL: 12 V-1s destroyed, 3 aircraft destroyed.

WHITMAN G.A.   Flight Lieutenant   RAF No.

'Lefty' Whitman was a US citizen who served with 3 Squadron as a Sgt during 1943. He twice lost Typhoons during the summer, crashing EK217, QO-N, whilst landing at Tangmere on 7 July, and ditching JP594 whilst on an ASR flight on 13 September. Commissioned by early 1944, on 8 June he claimed one of the first aerial victories to be achieved by the new Tempest whilst providing cover to the Normandy landings. Subsequently he saw action against the V-1s.

1944						
8 Jun		Bf 109	Tempest V	JN743 JF-P	N Rouen	3 Sqn
16 Jun	1/2	V-1	,,	,,	W Lewes	,,
18 Jun	1/2	V-1	,,		Bexley area	,,
19 Jun	1/2	V-1	,,	JN759	8m SW Ashford	,,
,,		V-1	,,	,,	Cranbrook	,,
23 Jun		V-1	,,	,,		,,
25 Jun		V-1				,,
,,	1/2	V-1	,,	JN743	3-4m SW Ashford	,,
28 Jun		V-1	,,			,,
10 Jul	1/4	V-1	,,			,,
26 Jul		V-1	,,	EJ540	nr Tunbridge Wells	,,
TOTAL: 5 and 5 shared V-1s destroyed, 1 aircraft destroyed.						

WILLIAMS Brian   Flight Lieutenant   No. 107314

Brian Williams was commissioned on 20 September 1941, then becoming an intruder pilot with 605 Squadron. On most occasions he flew with Wt Off Stephen Hardy, an ex-418 Squadron navigator, in the second seat of his Mosquito VI. He was awarded a DFC on 20 January 1945.

1944						
5 May		Do 217 Damaged	Mosquito VI			605 Sqn
6/7 Jul	3	V-1s	,,			,,
18/19 Aug	2	V-1s	,,			,,
1945						
2 May		FW 190	,,	UP-K	Lecke, S Denmark	,,
,,		E/a Damaged	,,	,,	,,	,,
TOTAL: 5 V-1s destroyed, 1 aircraft destroyed, 2 damaged.						

WILLIAMS Stanford Seaton   Flight Lieutenant   RNZAF No.

'Bill' Williams was a New Zealander from Orini. He joined 486 Squadron in January 1944, seeing action against both V-1s over Southern England and against German aircraft over Europe later in the year. On 22 December 1944 his Tempest, EJ715, SA-B, was shot down by Flak near Verden, and he was killed. He was subsequently Mentioned in Despatches.

1944						
18 Jun		V-1	Tempest V	JN810 SA-P	2-3m off North Foreland	486 Sqn
21 Jun		V-1	,,	JN866 SA-U	18m N Dungeness	,,
25 Jun		V-1	,,	JN758 SA-Y	10m N Newchurch	,,
4 Jul	1/2	V-1	,,	JN820 SA-P	NW Ninfield	,,
12 Jul	1/2	V-1	,,	EJ523 SA-X	12m N Hastings	,,
14 Jul		V-1	,,	JN860 SA-Z	Westerham-Sevenoaks	,,
19 Jul		V-1	,,	EJ523 SA-X	Tenterden area	,,
3 Aug		V-1	,,	JN858 SA-Y	N Tonbridge	,,
,,		V-1	,,	,,	12m NE Hastings	,,
30 Sep		Bf 109	,,	EJ715 SA-B	Didam	,,
26 Nov	1/2	Ju 188	,,	EJ577 SA-F	Munster area	,,
TOTAL: 7 and 2 shared V-1s destroyed, 1 and 1 shared aircraft destroyed.						

WINGATE H.R.   Pilot Officer   RAF No. 171013

Wingate was a 3 Squadron Tempest pilot, who shot down a considerable number of V-1s.

1944						
18 Jun		V-1	Tempest V	JN739	nr Biggin Hill	3 Sqn
,,	1/2	V-1	,,	JN752	nr Appledore	,,
19 Jun		V-1	,,			,,
20 Jun		V-1	,,	JN735	SW Hastings	,,
22 Jun		V-1	,,			,,
28 Jun		V-1	,,			,,
3 Jul	3	V-1s	,,	EJ582	nr Hastings	,,
5 Jul	1/2	V-1	,,	JN793	10m NW Edenbridge	,,
6 Jul	1/2	V-1	,,	,,		,,
7 Jul		V-1	,,	JN521	4m S Bexhill	,,
9 Jul		V-1	,,			,,
11 Jul		V-1	,,			,,
19 Jul		V-1	,,	JN760	Tenterden area	,,
22 Jul		V-1	,,	JN521	3-4m W Tonbridge	,,
16 Aug		V-1	,,			,,
17 Aug	2	V-1s	,,			,,
19 Aug	2	V-1s	,,			,,
27 Aug		V-1	,,			,,
TOTAL: 19 and 3 shared V-1s destroyed.						

WORTHINGTON John Colin   Flight Lieutenant   RNZAF No. 415727

John Worthington was a New Zealander who flew as an intruder pilot with 605 Squadron with Plt Off F.A.Friar, RNZAF, as his navigator. They were reported to have shot down five V-1s, although details of only three have been found. Worthington was awarded a DFC on 14 September 1945.

1944				
7/8 Jul	V-1	Mosquito VI		605 Sqn
9/10 Jul	V-1	,,		,,
1945				
25 Mar	V-1	,,		,,

TOTAL: 3 V-1s destroyed (plus possibly 2 more).

WRIGHT G. C.   Flight Lieutenant   RAF No.

G.C.Wright flew with 605 Squadron as a Flt Lt, AFC, in summer 1944, at which time 86684 Sqn Ldr Geoffrey John Wright was still serving with the unit. Both these pilots made claims against V-1s, which presents the danger of confusion between the two. It was G.C.Wright who achieved the greater success however, claiming eight of the bombs with Flg Off J.G.Insall flying alongside as his navigator.

1944					
17/18 Jun	3	V-1s	Mosquito VI		605 Sqn
21/22 Jun		V-1	,,		,,
28/29 Jun	2	V-1s	,,		,,
29/30 Jun		V-1	,,		,,
23/24 Jul		V-1	,,		,,

TOTAL: 8 V-1s destroyed.

WYLDE G.H.   Flying Officer   RAF No. 186957

After serving with 56 Squadron as a Flt Sgt, Wylde was commissioned and posted to 501 Squadron. Here however, his Tempest EJ603, SD-M, suffered engine failure over the sea off Colchester, Essex, on 23 September 1944. He baled out and was picked up safely.

1944						
7 Jul	1/2	V-1	Tempest V	EJ559 US-L	NNW Hastings	56 Sqn
12 Jul		V-1	,,	EJ526 US-N	4-5m W Rye	,,
6 Aug		V-1	,,	,,	15m N Hastings	,,
		V-1	,,	,,	6m NNW Rye	,,
7 Aug		V-1	,,	,,	nr Biddenden	,,
,,		V-1	,,	,,	over sea	,,

TOTAL: 5 and 1 shared V-1s destroyed.

ZALENSKI Jozef   Flight Sergeant   RAF No. P

Zalenski was a Polish pilot who flew Mustang IIIs with 306 Squadron during summer 1944.

1944						
16 Jul		V-1	Mustang III	UZ-U	2m N Rye	306 Sqn
26 Jul		V-1	,,	UZ-Z	W Rye	,,
,,		V-1	,,	,,	Ham Street	,,
,,		V-1	,,	,,	15m SSE Hastings	,,
28 Jul		V-1	,,	,,	5m SE Maidstone	,,
29 Jul		V-1	,,	UZ-U	Hastings	,,
30 Jul	1/2	V-1	,,	UZ-Z	NW Appledore	,,
7 Aug		V-1	,,	UZ-U	2m SW Darlinton	,,
17 Aug		V-1	,,		E Rye	,,
19 Aug		V-1	,,		7m W Tonbridge	,,

TOTAL: 9 and 1 shared V-1s destroyed (possibly 5 and 6 shared).

NB. In *Aces High* four other pilots were listed as having claimed five or more V-1s in this section of the book. Further research has revealed the following:-

BEDKOWSKI S.Z.   Warrant Officer

This Polish pilot who flew with 315 Squadron, was credited with only two shared V-1s.

1944					
26 Jul	1/2	V-1	Mustang III	10m S Hastings	315 Sqn

TOTAL: 2 shared V-1s destroyed (1 no detail).

GIBBS R.T.H.   Wing Commander

No pilot of this name appears on the Officers' List during the period under review. However, a Plt Off N.P.Gibbs served with 41 Squadron during 1944, claiming four V-1s in June and early July.

Plt Off N.P.Gibbs claims:
1944

20 Jun	V-1	Spitfire XIV	MB875	N Eastbourne	41 Sqn
21 Jun	V-1	„	„		„
24 Jun	V-1	„	„	8m S Hastings	„
8 Jul	V-1	„			„

TOTAL: 4 V-1s destroyed.

MADDEN B.M.   Flight Lieutenant
Flt Lt Madden did indeed fly against the V-1s with 610 Squadron. Only one shared claim has been found for him however.

1944
11 Jul   ½   V-1   Spitfire XIV   610 Sqn
TOTAL: 1 shared V-1 destroyed.

PAGRAM B.   Flying Officer
This pilot was listed as a Pole. No pilot of this name, or any similar name, has been found in any of the three Polish Mustang squadrons involved in the V-1 campaign, nor indeed in any of the other units operating at this time and in this role.

These four names are therefore removed from the listing.

LISTING

Name and Rank	Nationality	Unit(s)	Aircraft	V-1s	Claims Against Aircraft	Comments
BERRY, Sqn Ldr J	British	FIU, 501	Tempest V	60(59 & 1 sh)	3	MB
VAN LIERDE, Sqn Ldr R.	Begian	3	Tempest V	44(35 & 9 sh)	6	MB
MELLERSH, Flt Lt F.R.L.	British	96	Mosquito XIII	39(or 42)	8	MB
BEAMONT, Wg Cdr R.P.	British	150 Wg	Tempest V	31(26 & 5 sh)	9 & 1 sh	MB
CLAPPERTON, Flg Off R.H.	British	3	Tempest V	24		
COLE, Flg Off R.W.	British	3	Tempest V	24(20 & 4 sh)	1 & 1 sh	
MOORE, Flt Lt A.R.	British	56	Tempest V	24(23 & 1 sh)	4	
BURGWAL, Flg Off R.F.	Dutch	322	Spitfire XIV	23(20 & 3 sh)	—	
EAGLESON, Flg Off O.D.	New Zealand	486	Tempest V	23(20 & 3 sh)	3 & 1 sh	
CAMMOCK, Flg Off R.J.	New Zealand	486	Tempest V	21(20 & 1 sh)	—	
KYNASTON, Sqn Ldr N.A.	British	91	Spitfire XIV	21	4 & 1 sh	MB
CREW, Wg Cdr E.D.	British	96	Mosquito XIII	21	12 & 1 sh	MB
WINGATE, Plt Off H.R.	British	3	Tempest V	21(19 & 2 sh)	—	
McCAW, Sqn Ldr J.H.	New Zealand	486	Tempest V	20(19 & 1 sh)		
NASH, Flt Lt R.S.	British	91	Spitfire XIV	20(17 & 3 sh)	2 & 1 sh	
SLADE-BETTS, Plt Off K.R.	British	3	Tempest V	20(19 & 1 sh)	—	
BANNOCK, Wg Cdr R.	Canadian	418	Mosquito II	19(18 & 1 sh)	9	MB
DRYLAND, Flg Off R.	British	3	Tempest V	18(14 & 4 sh)	1	
CULLEN, Sqn Ldr J.R.	New Zealand	486	Tempest V	18(14 & 4 sh)	—	
UMBERS, Sqn Ldr A.E.	New Zealand	3	Tempest V	18(14 & 4 sh)	4 & 1 sh	MB
CHUDLEIGH, Sqn Ldr R.N.	British	96	Mosquito XIII	15	2	
BAILEY, Flg Off H.G.	British	3	Tempest V	14(12 & 2 sh)	—	
JOHNSON, Flt Lt H.D.	British	91	Spitfire XIV	14(13 & 1 sh)	—	
MacKERRAS, Flt Sgt D.J.		3	Tempest V	14(11 & 3 sh)	—	
BARKLEY, Flg Off R.E.	British	3	Tempest V	13(12 & 1 sh)	—	
DANZEY, Flg Off R.J.	New Zealand	486	Tempest V	13(9 & 4 sh)	—	
DOBIE, Flt Lt I.A.	British	96,85	Mosquito XIII	13	1	
GREEN, Wg Cdr W.P.	British	96	Mosquito XIII	13	14	MB
ROBB, Flt Lt R.L.T.	British	FIU,501	Tempest V	13	1	
EDWARDS, Flt Lt M.F.	British	3	Tempest V	12(7 & 5 sh)	—	
FELDMAN, Plt Off S.B.	US	3	Tempest V	12(9 & 3 sh)	1	
HARTLEY, Flg Off J.		129	Mustang III	12	—	
MUSGRAVE, Flt Lt J.G.	British	605	Mosquito VI	12	—	
ROSE, Plt Off M.J.A.	British	3	Tempest V	12(11 & 1 sh)	2	
SWEETMAN, Sqn Ldr H.N.	New Zealand	486	Tempest V	12(11 & 1 sh)	1 & 2 sh	MB
WARD, Flt Lt D.L.	British	96	Mosquito XIII	12	3	
CRUIKSHANK, Flg Off A.R.	British	91	Spitfire XIV	11(10 & 1 sh)	—	
PLESMAN, Flt Lt J.L.	Dutch	322	Spitfire XIV	11	—	
RUDOWSKI, Flt Sgt S.	Polish	306	Mustang III	11(9 & 2 sh)	2	
SHAW, Flg Off H.	British	56	Tempest V	11(8 & 3 sh)	2 & 3 sh	MB
WILLIAMS, Flt Lt E.L.	Rhodsian	FIU,501	Tempest V	11	5 or 6	MB

Name	Nationality	Squadron	Aircraft	V-1		MB
SIEKIERSKI, Flt Lt J.	Polish	306	Mustang III	10(7 & 3 sh)	1	
BOND, Sqn Ldr P.M.	British	91	Spitfire XIV	10(7 & 3 sh)	—	
DE BORDAS, Capt H.F.	French	91	Spitfire XIV	10(9 & 1 sh)	—	
HOOPER, Flg Off G.J.M.	New Zealand	486	Tempest V	10(7 & 3 sh)	1	
JANKOWSKI, Wt Off T.	Polish	315	Mustang III	10(4 & 6 sh)	2 & 1 sh	
JONGBLOED, Flt Lt G.F.J.	Dutch	322,222	Spitfire XIV, Tempest V	10(8 & 2 sh)	1	
NEWBERY, Sqn Ldr R.A.	British	610	Spitfire XIV	10(8 & 2 sh)	4	
O'CONNOR, Flg Off B.J.	New Zealand	486	Tempest V	10(9 & 1 sh)	1	
TOPHAM, Flg Off E.		91	Spitfire XIV	10(9 & 1 sh)	—	
WHITMAN, Flt Lt G.A.	US	3	Tempest V	10(5 & 5 sh)	1	
ZALENSKI, Flt Sgt J.	Polish	306	Mustang III	10(9 & 1 sh)	—	
BREMNER, Flg Off R.D.	New Zealand	486	Tempest V	9(5 & 4 sh)	2 sh	
HALL, Flg Off B.M.	New Zealand	486	Tempest V	9(6 & 3 sh)	—	
LAWLESS, Flg Off F.B.	New Zealand	486	Tempest V	9	1	
MILLER, Flt Off B.F.	US	605,FIU, 501	Mosquito VI, Tempest V	9	1	
PARKER-REES, Sqn Ldr A.	British	96,501	Mosquito XIII, Tempest V	9	3	
ROEDIGER, Flt Lt K.A.	Australian	456	Mosquito XVII	9	2	
RUCHWALDY,Flg Off D.F.	British	129	Mustang III	9(8 & 1 sh)	7	MB
THORNTON, Flt Lt C.B.	British	FIU,501	Tempest V	9	—	
WILLIAMS, Flt Lt S.S.	New Zealand	486	Tempest V	9(7 & 2 sh)	1 & 1 sh	
BENSTEAD, Flg Off B.G.	British	605	Mosquito VI	8	—	
DELEUZE, Flg Off R.C.	French	274,501	Tempest V	8	—	
ELCOCK, Flt Lt A.R.	British	91	Spitfire XIV	8(7 & 1 sh)	—	
JANSSEN, Flt Sgt M.J.	Dutch	322	Spitfire XIV	8	—	
KALKA, Flg Off W.A.	New Zealand	486	Tempest V	8	—	
KLEINMAYER, Flt Lt R.G.	New Zealand	129	Mustang III	8(7 & 1 sh)	—	
McLARDY, Plt Off W.A.		96	Mosquito XIII	8(6 & 2 sh)	—	
McPHIE, Flg Off R.A.	Canadian	91	Spitfire XIV	8(5 & 3 sh)	—	
MOFFET, Flt Lt H.B.	Canadian	91	Spitfire XIV	8	—	
SHEDDAN, Sqn Ldr C.J.	New Zealand	486	Tempest V	8(7 & 1 sh)	4 & 3 sh	MB
SIWEK, Flt Sgt K.	Polish	315	Mustang III	8(6 & 2 sh)	3	
SMITH, Flg Off K.A.	New Zealand	486	Tempest V	8	2	
STAFFORD, Flt Lt J.H.	New Zealandbd	486	Tempest V	8	2 & 3 sh	MB
WRIGHT, Flt Lt G.C.	British	605	Mosquito VI	8	—	
HART, Flg Off W.A.	New Zealand	486	Tempest V	8(6 & 2 sh)	—	
BALASSE, Flg Off M.A.L.	Belgian	41	Spitfire XII	7(5 & 2 sh)	—	
BRYAN, Flt Sgt J.		96	Mosquito XIII	7	—	
CHISHOLM, Sqn Ldr J.H.M.		157	Mosquito XIX	7	—	
COLLIER, Flg Off K.R.	Australian	91	Spitfire XIV	7	—	
DAVY, Flt Lt D.H.	British	1	Spitfire IXB	7(6 & 1 sh)	—	
EVANS, Flt Lt C.J.	Canadian	418	Mosquito II	7	1 & 1 sh	
EVERSON, L.G.	British	3	Tempest V	7(6 & 1 sh)	—	
HEAD, Flt Lt N.S.	British	96	Mosquito XIII	7(or 8)	4	
MARIDOR, Flt Lt J-M.	French	91	Spitfire XIV	7(5 & 2 sh)	3 & 1 sh	MB
MARSHALL, Flt Lt W.C.	British	91	Spitfire XIV	7	2	
MASON, Wg Cdr H.M.	New Zealand	486	Tempest V	7(5 & 2 sh)	—	
MIELNECKI, Sgt J.A.	Polish	316	Mustang III	7(6 & 1 sh)	—	
MILLER, Flt Lt W.L.	New Zealand	486	Tempest V	7	—	
POTTINGER, Flg Off R.W.	British	3	Tempest V	7(4 & 3 sh)	1 sh	
SHEPHERD, Sqn Ldr J.B.	British	610	Spitfire XIV	7(5 & 2 sh)	8 & 5 sh	MB
SWISTUN, Flg Off G	Polish	315	Mustang III	7(6 & 1 sh)	2 & 1 sh	
SZYMANSKI, Sgt T.	Polish	316	Mustang III	7(or 8)	2	
VAN ARKEL, Flg Off J.	Dutch	322	Spitfire XIV	7(6 & 1 sh)	1 sh	
VAN EEDENBORG, Sqn Ldr C.M.	Dutch	322	Spitfire XIV	7	—	
BARLLOMIEJCZYK, Wt Off C.	Polish	316	Mustang III	6	1	
BENSON, Wg Cdr J.G.	British	157	Mosquito XIX	6	10	MB
BURTON, Flt Lt H.		501	Tempest V	6	—	
CALDWELL, Sqn Ldr G.L.		96	Mosquito XIII	6	1	
CHOLAJDA, Flt Lt A.	Polish	316	Mustang III	6(5 & 1 sh)	2	
CWYNAR, Sqn Ldr M.	Polish	315	Mustang III	6(2 & 4 sh)	5 or 6 & 1 sh	MB
DRAPER, Flt Lt J.W.P.	Canadian	91	Spitfire XIV	6	4 & 1 sh	MB
FAULKNER, Flg Off J.A.		91	Spitfire XIV	6(4 & 2 sh)	1	
FOSTER, Flt Sgt J.K.	British	3	Tempest V	6(4 & 2 sh)	—	
GOODE, Flg Off J.		96	Mosquito XIII	6(or 8 & 1 sh)	—	
GOUGH, Flt Lt W.J.	British	96	Mosquito XIII	6	2	
JONKER, Flg Off J.	Dutch	322	Spitfire XIV	6(5 & 1 sh)	—	
KLAWE, Flt Lt W.	Polish	306	Mustang III	6(4 & 2 sh)	1	

LAWSON, Flg Off C.M.	Australian	165	Spitfire IXB	6	—	
MacLAREN, Flg Off W.R.	British	56	Tempest V	6(5 & 1 sh)	3	
MAJEWSKI, Flt Lt L.	Polish	316	Mustang III	6(5 & 1 sh)	1 sh	
McCARTHY, Plt Off K.	New Zealand	486	Tempest V	6	—	
OSBORNE, Flt Lt A.F.	British	129	Mustang III	6(4 & 2 sh)	1 sh	
PARKER, Flt Lt G.R.I.	British	219	Mosquito XVII	6	9	MB
POLLEY, Flg Off W.F.	British	501	Tempest V	6(or 3)	—	
PORTEOUS, Sqn Ldr J.K.,	New Zealand	165	Spitfire IXB	6(5 & 1 sh)	1	
SPENCER, Sqn Ldr T.	British	41	Spitfire XII	6(or 7)	1	
SZYMANKIEWICZ, Flt Lt T.	Polish	316	Mustang III	6	1 sh	
TINSEY, Flt Lt T.D.	British	165	Spitfire IXB	6(5 & 1 sh)	3 or 4	MB
TROTT, Flg Off W.A.L.	New Zealand	486	Tempest V	6	1	
WALTON, Flt Lt R.C.		605	Mosquito VI	6	—	
WYLDE, Flt Sgt G.H.	British	56	Tempest V	6(5 & 1 sh)	—	
BANGERTER, Flt Lt B.M.	Belgian	610	Spitire XIV	5(3 & 2 sh)	2 & 1 sh	
BEYER, Flg Off A.	Polish	306	Mustang III	5	1 & 2 sh	
BONHAM, Flt Lt G.L.	New Zealand	FIU,501	Tempest V	5	1	
BROOKE, Flg Off P.deL.	British	264	Mosquito XIII	5	2	
CRAMM, Flt Sgt H.C.	Dutch	322	Spitfire XIV	5(or 4)	—	
DREDGE, Wg Cdr A.S.	British	3	Tempest V	5	4	
EDWARDS, Flg Off E.W.	British	129	Mustang III	5	2	
HALL, Sqn Ldr A.R.	British	56	Tempest V	5	3	
HARRIES, Wg Cdr R.H.	British	135 Wg	Spitfire IXB	5(or 1)	15 & 3 sh	MB
HASTINGS, Plt Off I.		1	Spitfire IXB	5(4 & 1 sh)	—	
HORBACZEWSKI, Sqn Ldr E.	Polish	315	Mustang III	5(1 & 4 sh)	16 & 1 sh	MB
HOWARD, Wg Cdr B.	Australian	465	Mosquito XVII	5	3	
KARNKOWSKI, Flg Off S.	Polish	316	Mustang III	5(3 & 2 sh)	1 & 1 sh	
LEGGAT, Flg Off P.S.	Canadian	418	Mosquito II	5	—	
MacFADYEN, Sqn Ldr D.A.	Canadian	418	Mosquito II	5	7	MB
MATHEWS, Sqn Ldr J.O.	British	157	Mosquito XIX	5	9	MB
MAY, Flt Lt N.S.	Canadian	418	Mosquito II	5		
McKINLEY, Flg Off G.M.	British	610	Spitfire XIV	5(4 & 1 sh)	—	
NEIL, Flg Off H.M.	British	91	Spitfire XIV	5	—	
NESS, Flg Off D..	Canadian	56	Tempest V	5(4 & 1 sh)	5 & 1 sh	MB
NOWOCZYN, Flt Sgt W.	Polish	306	Mustang III	5	1	
PIETRZAK, Wt Off A.	Polish	316	Mustang III	5(4 & 1 sh)	3 & 1 sh	
PIETRZAK, Sqn Ldr H.J.	Polish	315	Mustang III	5(4 & 1 sh)	7 & 2 sh	MB
PORTER, Flt Lt D.A.	British	501	Tempest V	5(4 & 1 sh)	2 sh	
POWELL, Flt Lt N.J.	New Zealand	486	Tempest V	5	1	
REDHEAD, Wt Off E.		129	Mustang III	5(4 & 1 sh)	—	
ROGOWSKI, Wt Off J.A.	Polish	306	Mustang III	5(3 & 2 sh)	2	
SAMES, Flg Off A.N.	New Zealand	137	Typhoon IB	5	2 & 1 sh	
SHORT, Flt Sgt S.J.	New Zealand	486	Tempest V	5	1	
TANNER, Flt Lt E.W.	New Zealand	486	Tempest V	5(3 & 2 sh)	1	
VAN BEERS, Flt Sgt R.L.	Dutch	322	Spitfire XIV	5	—	
WILLIAMS, Flt Lt B.	British	605	Mosquito VI	5	1	
WORTHINGTON, Flt Lt J.C.	New Zealand	605	Mosquito VI	5	—	

NB. MB indicates the pilot's biography will be found in the main Chapters (Chapter Five in *Aces High*, or Chapter Four in this volume), rather than in this chapter.

CHAPTER SEVEN

Subsequent Actions

Since the end of World War II, fighter pilots of the British and Commonwealth air forces have become engaged in aerial combat during three separate conflicts. During the withdrawal from Palestine and the birth of the State of Israel, RAF fighters were attacked and suffered losses to Israeli Spitfires of the IDF/AF 101 Squadron. They were also engaged on one occasion by Egyptian Spitfire LF IXs on 22 May 1948, four of these being claimed shot down by Spitfire FR XVIIIs of 208 Squadron.

A number of pilots who had flown with the RAF or RCAF during World War II flew as volunteers with the Israelis in 1948-49, four of those included in *Aces High* and/or this volume, increasing their totals here. They were J.J.Doyle, J.F.McElroy and C.D. Wilson (all Canadians) and S.B. Feldman (a US citizen). All made claims against Egyptian aircraft, but McElroy's claims included two RAF Spitfires.

During the Korean War a quite substantial number of Commonwealth fighter pilots served with 77 RAAF Squadron (Mustangs, then Meteor F.8s), 2 SAAF Squadron (Mustangs) and with various Fleet Air Arm carrier-borne fighter units (predominantly Sea Furies). Australian Meteor pilots were credited with the destruction of two MiG 15s, and a Fleet Air Arm pilot, Lt P.Carmichael, RN, with one more. More success was gained by RAF and RCAF pilots flying F-86 Sabres on attachment to USAF units, Sqn Ldr J.D.Lindsay and Sqn Ldr J.MacKay, both "aces" of the RCAF during World War II, adding further victories to their totals here, whilst Flt Lt J.A.O.Levesque, who had claimed four victories in the earlier conflict, gained his fifth success here.

Amongst the RAF pilots, the most successful was 52935 Flt Lt Graham Stanley Hulse, DFC, who flew with the 336th Fighter Interceptor Squadron, 4th Fighter Interceptor Wing, claiming one and two shared, and 58144 Flt Lt John Moreton Nicholls, who flew with the 335th Fighter Interceptor Squadron in the same Wing, claiming one MiG and being awarded a DFC on 2 June 1953. Hulse had been awarded his DFC in August 1945 for service as a flight commander in 213 Squadron during the closing stages of the earlier war. In total, 23 confirmed claims were made by British and Commonwealth pilots, all for MiG 15s.

The greatest successes to be gained by British fighter pilots subsequent to 1945 occurred during the Falklands War of April-June 1982. These were all gained by the pilots of two Hawker Sea Harrier squadrons of the Fleet Air Arm — 800 Squadron aboard HMS *Hermes* and 801 Squadron on HMS *Invincible*. During May and June 22 confirmed and three probable victories were claimed by the pilots of these units, who were predominantly officers of the FAA, but included a number of attached RAF personnel. The two squadrons had been brought up to full strength by an infusion of pilots from 899 Squadron. On conclusion of hostilities one DSO and five DSCs were awarded to pilots from these units. 15 pilots made claims; the most successful were:-

Flt Lt David Morgan (899 Squadron, attached 800 Squadron)	3 and 1 shared
Lt Cdr Nigel Ward (801 Squadron)	3
Lt Cdr David Smith (800 Squadron)	2 and 1 shared
Lt Cdr Andrew Auld (800 Squadron)	2
Flt Lt John Leeming (800 Squadron)	2
Lt Stephen Thomas (801 Squadron)	1 and 2 probables
Lt Cdr Michael Blissett (800 Squadron)	1 and 1 probable

Morgan, Ward, Auld and Thomas received DSCs.

Some details of the two most successful of these pilots follow:-

MORGAN David Henry Spencer   **Flight Lieutenant**   **RAF No.**
Although born with a hole in his heart, 'Moggy' Morgan made so complete a recovery that he was able to join the RAF for pilot training, becoming a battlefield helicopter pilot. Subsequently converting to Harriers, he was attached to the FAA, serving with 899 Squadron when the Falklands crisis arose. Attached to 800 Squadron on HMS *Hermes*, he took part in the first strafing attack on Port Stanley airfield, where his aircraft received a hit in

the tail from a 20mm AA shell. On 23 May 1982 he and his wingman, Flt Lt John Leeming, spotted three helicopters flying up a fjord towards West Island. These were two Pumas and an A109A Hirundo of Ca de Ataque 601. Morgan pursued Puma AE 503, which crashed into a hillside when the pilot lost control in trying to evade the Sea Harrier, all the crew escaping unhurt. Meanwhile Leeming attacked the other Puma, AE 337; Morgan then joined him and the aircraft was forced down, its destruction being completed on the ground by cannon fire; again the crew escaped. The Hirundo, AE 500, circled the wreck of AE 503, but this too was hit by fire from Morgan's aircraft, although no claim was made. It was, however, obliged to land as it had been damaged, and was destroyed on the ground by two of 801 Squadron's Sea Harriers 15 minutes later. On 8 June Morgan intercepted four jets which he identified as Mirages — they were in fact Douglas A-4B Skyhawks — and he shot down two of these, his wingman claiming a third. The fourth was believed to have crashed into the sea without being attacked, but in fact escaped. It is understood that after the war Morgan transferred to the Fleet Air Arm to command a Sea Harrier unit. He was awarded a DSC.

1982							
23 May		Puma (a)	Sea Harrier	ZA192	nr West Island	800 Sqn
„	½	Puma (b)	„	„	„	„
8 Jun	2	Mirages	„	ZA177		„

TOTAL: 3 and 1 shared destroyed.
(a) AE 503 of Ca de Assalto 601; crew unhurt; (b) AE 500 forced to land and destroyed on the ground — same unit as AE 503; crew unhurt; (c) A-4Bs of Grupo 5 de Caza, both shot down with A1M-9L missiles; C-226, Ten J.J. Arraras killed; C-228, Alferez J.A. Vazquez ejected, but killed.

WARD Nigel David   Lieutnant Commander

'Sharkey' Ward was born in Canada of British parentage. He was educated in England, attending Reading School, where he was awarded an RAF Flying Scholarship, gaining his private pilot's licence. He then entered the Britannia Royal Naval College, Dartmouth, in 1962 as a cadet. After naval training in the Bahamas and Hong Kong, he attended RAF Linton-on-Ouse for basic flying training, completing his advanced training as a fighter pilot on Hunters and Sea Vixens, then joining 892 Squadron in 1969. Here he flew F-4K Phantoms on HMS *Ark Royal*. He then qualified as an Air Warfare Instructor, subsequently serving at NATO HQ, AFNORTH. He rejoined 892 Squadron as Senior Pilot in 1974, but in 1976 was posted to the Ministry of Defence as Sea Harrier Desk Officer, responsible for final development and introduction to service. During 1979 he commanded the Sea Harrier Intensive Flying Trials Unit, 700A Squadron, and then 899 Squadron, the Sea Harrier Headquarters unit, continuing to develop tactics and train pilots. In 1981 he took command of 801 Squadron on board HMS *Invincible*. He flew 60 sorties during the Falklands operations, providing leadership and guidance, as well as obtaining three aerial victories. On return to the UK, he attended the Royal Naval Staff College, Greenwich, then being posted to the Ministry of Defence again in 1983, first as Air Weapons Adviser, and then as Fixed Wing Air Warfare Adviser to the Naval Staff and First Sea Lord. In 1985 he took early retirement from the service to set up and run his own company, Defence Analysts Ltd, which provided expertise in the defence of oil tankers in the Arabian Gulf during the Iran-Iraq war. He was awarded a DSC for his Falklands operations, and an AFC in 1982. He is a member of the Royal Aeronautical Society and a Freeman of the City of London. He subsequently went to live in Turkey, where he was believed still to be living at the time of writing. His autobiographical account of the Falklands war, *Sea Harrier over the Falklands; A Maverick at War*, was published by BCA/Leo Cooper(Pen & Sword Books Ltd) in 1992.

1982						
21 May		Pucara (a)	Sea Harrier	XZ451	nr Drone Hill, East Falkland	801 Sqn
„		Mirage (b)	„	ZA175	West Falkland	„
1 Jun		C-130 (c)	„	XZ451	N Pebble Island	„

TOTAL: 3 destroyed.
(a) A-511 of Grupo 3 de Ataque; Maj Carlos Tomba ejected safely; shot down by cannonfire; (b) Actually Dagger C-407 of Grupo 6 de Caza; Primer Ten J.D.Senn ejected safely; shot down with A1M-9L Sidewinder missile; (c) C-130E Hercules of Grupo 1 de Trasporte Aereo Esc 1; shot down with both A1M-9L missile and cannon fire; Vicecomodora H.C.Meisner and crew of six all killed.

CHAPTER EIGHT

Gatherings of Aces

There have been relatively few gatherings of British fighter pilots generally, although the pilots of the Battle of Britain Fighter Association have met frequently in the past, as have a number of squadron associations. An opportunity was afforded for such an event with the publication of *Aces High* in August 1994. Following Press and television publicity, 31 pilots gathered at the Royal Air Force Museum, Hendon, on the morning of Saturday, 20 August, for a Fighter Pilots' Symposium. Ten of them took their places on the stage of the Museum's theatre, with this author as Moderator, whilst the rest were seated in the first two rows of seats. Following introduction of the participants to a packed audience, a very successful question and answer session followed until lunchtime, concluding with a standing ovation for the pilots.

After lunch in the first floor art gallery, the pilots were seated behind a line of tables, the public then passing along the line to talk with them and to obtain signatures in their new copies of *Aces High*, and in other books brought for the occasion.

The consequence of this successful day was the collection of some £800 from those who had obtained signatures, for the benefit of the Royal Air Force Benevolent Fund. This sum was subsequently increased to over £2,700 by the authors and publisher, who donated half the profits from the sale of the Special Edition of the book as an appreciation of the help and support they had received in its preparation.

Pilots present included three who had made the journey from Norway — Ola Aanjesen, Svein Heglund and Ragnar Dogger — and the following British personnel:-

J.A.'Sandy' Sandeman Allen

Eric Barwell	Owen Hardy	A.J. 'Ginger' Owen
John Cunningham	Ronnie Hay	Geoffrey Page
Tom Dalton-Morgan	Peter Hearne	Ian Ponsford
Dennis David	W.J. 'Jesse' Hibbert	R.J.H. 'Robbie' Robertson
Billy Drake	Norman Jones	R.W.F. 'Sammy' Sampson
Gerry Edge	Kenneth 'Hawkeye' Lee	Allan Scott
Joe Ekbury	Geoff Lord	Joe Singleton
John Gibson	W.H. 'Andy' Miller	L.W.F. 'Pinkie' Stark
Richard Goucher	Frank 'Spud' Murphy	Jas Storrar

Two years later the visit of a number of members of the American Fighter Aces Association allowed a further event to be organised, when the US pilots indicated a desire to meet a number of their RAF counterparts whilst in England. Headcorn in Kent was the chosen venue, where the visiting party arrived on Saturday, 28 September 1996, to find 15 British pilots on hand, together with a collection of aircraft, military vehicles and an Air Training Corps band. Members of the Aircrew Association, together with an ex-Prisoners of War group and ex-WAAFs also attended. The Battle of Britain Memorial Flight laid on a demonstration by a Hurricane II, and a P-51D Mustang painted in the markings of the 354th Fighter Group, which had operated for a time from Headcorn, and in which one of the visiting US pilots, Clayton Kelly Gross, had served, also flew, as did two AT-6 Harvards. The Mustang was available for inspection after its flight, and it proved possible to organise flights in the AT-6s in formation for Kelly Gross and Grp Capt Billy Drake. Present on this occasion on behalf of the British pilots were:-

Douglas Benham	W.J. 'Jesse' Hibbert	L.W.F. 'Pinkie' Stark
Billy Drake	K.N.T. 'Hawkeye' Lee	Jack Stokoe
Neville Duke	Willie Lindsay	Johnnie Surman
John Hall	T.F. 'Ginger' Neil	Archie Winskill
Peter Hearne	Garry Nowell	John Young*

*Battle of Britain Fighter Association Historian.

CHAPTER NINE

Corrections and Additions to Stars and Bars
by Frank Olynyk

August 30, 1998

page 71, line -2, change 12.166 to 11.166 on the entry for P C DeLong (typo)

page 101, VF(N)-101 was formed on Jan 1, 1944.

page 108, Fred Ackerman died in FM-2 47309, his rank was Lt(jg); he had 788.2 h flying time

page 115, Alex Anderson died February 26, 1997 Millbrook, New York

page 115, Charles Frederick Anderson, Jr was born March 31, 1919

page 116, Richard Anderson died March 18, 1995, Albany, New York

page 118, John Andre died on July 7, 1983

page 120, David Archibald died on February 12, 1998 in Centerville, Massachusetts

page 120, William Aron was born on July 23, 1923

page 126, Donald Balch died August 1, 1995 Santa Barbara, California

page 132, Tex Barrick died September 6, 1997 Chickasaw, Alabama

page 137, Edward Beavers was born November 22, 1918, in Pennsylvania

page 138, Walt Beckham died May 31, 1996, Albuquerque, New Mexico

page 140, Don Beerbower received a (British) DFC

page 144, H Thomas Biel was born on July 28, 1916

page 145: Henry Bille died October 8, 1996 in Paradise, California.

page 150: Larry Blumer died October 23, 1997 in Springfield, Oregon, of leukemia

page 151, Hampton Boggs received a (British) DFC.

page 154, Robert Bonebrake died on March 25, 1985

page 154, Dick Bong received a (British) DFC; add biography *Memories*, by Marge Bong Drucker,
     (Drucker Publishing, 1995)

page 158, Boyington was flying 17744 on December 23, 17883 on December 27, and 17915 on December 28, 1943

page 172, Robert Buchanan died February 29, 1996, Norristown, Pennsylvania

page 174, Robert Burnett was KIFA on May 13, 1947, in Tampico, Mexico (civil)

page 178, Jim Cain died on April 27, 1998 in Long Beach California of a heart attack

page 180, Marion Carl was murdered by an intruder on June 28, 1998 in Roseburg, Oregon

page 181, Kendall Carlson died on January 28, 1977

page 182, William Carlton died June 1, 1984 (residence: Tustin, California)

page 184, Bruce Carr died on April 25, 1998 in St Cloud, Florida of prostate cancer

page 184, George Carr died on December 3, 1952

page 185, Walter Carroll was born on September 11, 1917

page 186, Jim Carter died April 6, 1996, Las Cruces, New Mexico

page 186, William Case died November 25, 1995, Portland, Oregon

page 188, Cyrus Chambers died on February 28, 1964

page 190, Van Chandler died on March 11, 1998 in Greeley, Colorado

page 190, Philip Chapman was born on January 15, 1919

page 191, Levi Chase did not received a (British) DFC in the MTO; he received an additional (British)
     DFC for service in Korea.

page 192, Art Chin died on September 3, 1997 in Portland, Oregon

page 199, Thaddeus Coleman died Septebmer 30, 1995, Ponte Vedra Beach, Florida

page 200, William M Collins died on April 8, 1979

page 204, Henry Lozier Condon, II was born on November 9, 1919; his WO serial was T-60297

page 205, Walter Cook died January 24, 1997 Dallas, Texas

page 206, Merle Coons died on December 13, 1997

page 207, Zeke Cormier had 1227.5 hours flight time at the end of Nov 1944. He flew BuNo 71433 on Nov 14 (15 in flight
     log); 71861 on Jan 3, 1944; and 70101 on Feb 16.

page 208, Ralph Cox was born on November 19, 1919 and died on September 27, 1988 (residence: Boerne, Texas)

page 211, Ray Crawford died February 1, 1996, Covina, California

page 211, Claude Crenshaw died on March 17, 1972

page 212, Don Cronin died October 29, 1996, Mays Chapel, Maryland, of cancer

page 214, Arthur Cundy was born on July 4, 1924

page 218, Edward Czarnecki died on July 27, 1955 (no further information)

page 219, Lucian Dade died on August 2, 1983

page 221, Fernley Hilmer Damstrom's date of birth was August 19, 1923

page 221, William Daniel died on May 16, 1998 Boyce, Louisiana

page 222, J S Daniell died on September 21, 1975

page 222, Robert Davenport received a (British) DFC.

page 226, Gus Daymond died December 17, 1996 in Newport Beach, California. He was born Fred Beaty, and changed his
     name on joining the RAF.

page 226, Richard Sherfey Deakins was born on March 6, 1919

page 227, Zach Dean was shot down in Korea, near Sunchon. on April 23, 1951, by ground fire, and was a PoW for the remainder of the war. He was flying F-51D 44-84899
page 228, John Dear died June 14, 1996 in Jackson, Mississippi
page 230, George Della died August 14, 1996 in Strathmore, California
page 232, Robert Dibb was killed in F6F-5 58818
page 233, Joseph Dillard died on September 16, 1983
page 234, William Dillard was born on December 7, 1921 and died on December 12, 1988
page 234, John Dobbin died July 29, 1995, Orlando, Florida
page 236, Arthur Donahue was born on January 29, 1913
page 238, Frederick Dorsch was born on May 29, 1920
page 238, Paul Douglas received a (British) DFC for service in World War 2
page 239, Irwin Dregne received a (British) DFC for service in World War 2
page 243, John Dunaway was born December 23, 1922; he was killed in P-38J-20 44-23537
page 244, Glenn Duncan received a (British) DFC for service in World War 2
page 243, George Duncan died December 15, 1995, Alexandria, Virginia, heart attack
page 250, William Eccles died on May 9, 1989
page 250, Bert Eckard died on November 2, 1985
page 253, John Elder died July 27, 1996, Washington, District of Columbia, aneurysm; he received a (British) DFC for service in World War 2
page 257, Eugene Emmons was born on February 17, 1921 and died on September 20, 1981
page 262, Robert Farnsworth died on July 24, 1966 (in service)
page 265, Sylvan Feld was born on August 20, 1918
page 265, James Fenex was born on April 14, 1920 in Douglas, Wyoming, and died on February 19, 1975 in Glenrock, Wyoming (suicide). He attended the University of Colorado for at least two years. Pronunciation: Phoenix.
page 267, William Fiedler, Jr was born on June 5, 1920
page 269, Don Fisher died October 2, 1995 Beaufort, South Carolina, after heart surgery
page 270, Jack Fisk was born on April 2, 1918 and was KIFA on November 12, 1948 4 m E of Attica, Indiana
page 274, Paul Fontana died February 26, 1997 New Bern, North Carolina
page 278, William Foulis died October 23, 1996 Menlo Park, California of lung cancer
page 280, Magnus Wilson Francis was born on October 3, 1918
page 281, John Franks died on August 1, 1996 of kidney failure
page 283, James French died January 2, 1996 Bakersfield, California, respiratory illness
page 284, Alfred Froning died February 26, 1975, in Piper PA-28 Cherokee N5389L
page 284, Robert Fry died on May 7, 1985; he received a (British) DFC for service in World War 2
page 285, Gabby Gabreski received a (British) DFC for service in World War 2
page 286, Franklin Gabriel died on May 16, 1969
page 288, Dwight Galt died March 31, 1996
page 291, William Garry died on November 14, 1964
page 292, Don Gentile received a (British) DFC
page 295, Roy Gillespie died on June 20, 1997
page 297, George Gleason died on April 5, 1969
page 300, Robert Goodnight died on August 22, 1964
page 302, Mathew Gordon was born on April 21, 1919
page 303, Gordon Graham's autobiography, *Down For Double: Anecdotes of a Fighter Pilot*, was published in 1996 by Brandylane Publishers
page 303, Lindol Graham was born on May 15, 1918
page 305, Lester Gray, flew 42534 on June 11, 41000 on June 12, and FG-1D 82317 on April 12. He had 599.5 hours flying time at the end of May 1944.
page 306, Herky Green's autobiography *Herky!* was published in 1996 by Schiffer.
page 306, Lee Gregg was born on the date given
page 307, Billy Gresham was born January 5, 1923
page 308, Robert Griffith was born on September 2, 1923
page 310, Charles Gumm was born October 29, 1920
page 312, Mayo Hadden died on December 9, 1986
page 314, Bill Halton was MIA in F-51D-25NA 44-73959 at Ib'o-ri, North Korea
page 315, John Hampshire was born on May 16, 1919
page 316, Bill Hanes died on December 29, 1996 in Cocoa Beach, Florida
page 317, Troy Hanna received a (British) DFC
page 320, biography of Bill Harris: Bill, *A Pilot's Story* (Brooklyn Harris, self-published, 1995)
page 322, Frederick Harris was born on January 9, 1918
page 323, Thomas L Harris died on February 10, 1957
page 324, Cameron Hart was born on October 8, 1919
page 324, Kenneth Hart was born on April 26, 1920 and died in Martinez, California in an automobile accident
page 326, Leonel Hatch died on November 13, 1996
page 328, Thomas Haywood died on April 28, 1979
page 332, William Joseph Hennon
page 334, Edwin Hernan was KIA in F4U-5N 124530
page 339, John Hockery died on May 19, 1967
page 340, William Hodges died on November 14, 1988
page 341, William Hoelscher died on January 7, 1984
page 342, Cullen Hoffman died on October 20, 1971; the date of birth given is correct

page 343, Roy Hogg died on February 13, 1980
page 344, James Holloway was born on March 14, 1919
page 345, Cyril Homer died on August 10, 1975
page 347, Billy Hovde died March 13, 1996, San Antonio, Texas
page 348, Robert Howard died on September 14, 1979
page 350, Mark Hubbard died on August 26, 1984
page 351, Edward Hunt was born May 5, 1919
page 353, Joe Icard was born on February 1, 1922
page 354, Clayton Isaacson died December 6, 1996, Fargo, South Dakota
page 355, James Jabara received a (British) DFC for service in Korea
page 356, line 8, change F-86E to F-86F (typo)
page 362, Evan Johnson died on December 1, 1977
page 362, Gerald R Johnson was killed in B-25H-1 43-4149
page 363, Jerry Johnson's autobiography, titled *Called to Command*, was published in 1996 by Turner.
page 364, Jimmy Johnson died on August 15, 1997
page 366, John Johnston died February 16, 1999, in Oklahoma
page 367, Frank Jones was born October 23, 1919, and crashed 20 m SW of Stavenger, Norway
page 367, Cyril Jones was born October 3, 1921
page 368, George Jones died on February 18, 1997 Vero Beach, Florida
page 370, Warren Jones died on September 30, 1953
page 372, William Houston Julian was born on June 12, 1917 and died on March 20, 1973
page 375, William Kemp died on February 6, 1965 (slight possibility that he died in 1968)
page 376, Daniel Kennedy was born in July 1919
page 377, Melvin Kimball was born on January 11, 1917
page 380, King, William Bolin should be William Benjamin (Ben, Bill). Serial number is O-832441.
page 382, Lenton Kirkland was born March 8, 1920 in West Green, Georgia
page 382, Floyd Kirkpatrick died on April 13, 1997
page 385, Carroll Knott the date of birth given is correct
page 387, Ward Kuentzel was born on April 24, 1922
page 391, John Landers received a (British) DFC for service in the ETO
page 392, Ned Langdon died November 13, 1986, in Corpus Christi, Texas
page 395, Franklin Lathrope died on December 22, 1965
page 397, Frank Lawlor died on June 21, 1973
page 397, Earl Lazear was born on July 5, 1921 and died on December 4, 1989
page 402, Lawrence Peisch Liebers was born July 1, 1920
page 405, Robert Little received a (British) DFC
page 414, Lowell Connor Lutton was born on March 13, 1918
page 414, John Joseph Lynch, Jr. was born Februaary 3, 1918
page 418, Chris Magee died December 28, 1995 in Chicago, Illinois
page 419, William James Maguire was born January 17, 1921
page 420, Grant Mahony received a (British) DFC
page 421, Bud Mahurin received a (British) DFC for service in the ETO
page 427, Joe Mason received a (British) DFC for service in World War 2
page 428, Milden Mathre died on July 30, 1972
page 431, T H McArthur was born May 25, 1920 in Albany, Texas
page 432, David McCampbell died June 30, 1996 in Riviera Beach, Florida
page 435, Edward Otis McComas
page 437, Leo McCuddin died on November 15, 1983
page 437, Scott McCuskey died on June 15, 1997
page 439, William Floyd McDonough was born January 24, 1919 in Whittier, California
page 439, Don McDowell was born on December 19, 1916 in Kansas
page 441, Selva McGinty died February 14, 1996 in Moab, Utah
page 442, Bernard McGrattan was born March 9, 1920
page 445, Murray McLaughlin died on October 12, 1972; he was born August 26, 1917
page 446, Evan McMinn was born on April 25, 1919 in Ohio. He served in the RCAF.
page 451, George Merritt was born July 20, 1914
page 451, Donald Meuten was born on February 3, 1922
page 453, Armour Miller died July 22, 1996, Albany, New York
page 457, Robert Mims died on September 19, 1966
page 458, John Mitchell died November 15, 1995, San Anselmo, California, pancreatic cancer
page 460, William Momyer received a (British) DFC for service in World War 2
page 460, Franklin Monk died on December 7, 1981
page 467, Jim Mugavero died March 15, 1996 in San Mateo, California, after a long illness
page 467, Robert Mulhollem died on August 19, 1982; the date of birth given is correct
page 469, Alva C Murphy was born January 26, 1918
page 470, Jennings Myers was born on May 4, 1917
page 473, John Newkirk received a (British) DFC
page 475, Louis Herman Norley was born in Conrad, Montana; he received a (British) DFC
page 479, Edward O'Hare biography has appeared as *Fateful Rendezvous*, by Steve Ewing and John B Lundstrom
        (Naval Institute Press, 1997)
page 481, Norman Edward Olson

page 483, John George O'Neill died on September 30, 1966
page 484, Ernie Osher died on September 26, 1980
page 484, Eddie Outlaw died March 5, 1996, Durham, North Carolina
page 485, Robert Overcash died on March 8, 1986
page 494, James Peck was born June 14, 1921
page 498, Harvey Picken died March 18, 1997. He claimed only a half share in the Dinah on Sept 10, 1944, and only
     a half share in one of the Bettys on Sept 21.
page 498, Joseph Pierce was born on October 30, 1921
page 499, Donald Pieri was in fact KIA on May 3, 1945
page 500, John Pietz died July 6, 1985
page 501, James Noble Poindexter was born April 27, 1921 in Texas
page 503, Albert Pope died September 22, 1995 Fairfax, Virginia
page 506, Joe Harry Powers, Jr was KIA 15 m E of Seoul, in F-51D 45-11647
page 506, MacArthur Powers died on February 3, 1996
page 513, C B Ray died on August 21, 1980
page 514, Ed Rector received a (British) DFC
page 515, William Reese was born on September 30, 1921
page 517, Hunter Reinburg died on June 23, 1997 in Coronado, California
page 518, Thomas Rennemo died on April 3, 1969
page 518, Joseph Reulet died May 3, 1995
page 519, Andrew Reynolds died on October 27, 1976
page 520, Elmer Richardson died January 25, 1996 Ft. Worth, Texas, cancer
page 521, Robert Riddle died on May 17, 1997
page 523, Ben Rimerman was born on October 10, 1913
page 524, Andy Ritchey died December 2, 1996, Arlington, Texas, cancer.
page 530, Robert Ross died on February 7, 1963
page 533, LeRoy Ruder was born May 22, 1921, and crashed at St Michel en Greve, France
page 534, Roy Rushing died on January 8, 1986, possibly in St Louis, Missouri
page 535, William Aloysius Rynne was born on February 11, 1915, in New York City, New York. He died of cancer on
     January 8, 1990, in La Linea, Spain. On March 28, 1944 he was in fact a POW, not KIA. He graduated from
     St Francis College (New York) in 1937 with a BS degree in Engineering. *Pronunciation*: Rinn.
Page 535, Robert Sandell received a (British) DFC
page 535, Philip Sangermano was born April 28, 1924, and was killed in 42-103410 #45
page 540, Frank Schiel received a (British) DFC
page 541, Dave Schilling received a (British) DFC
page 547, Robert See died on July 13, 1971
page 547, Manny Segal died on June 3, 1998 in Scottsdale, Arizona
page 548, Robert Seidman was born on September 24, 1919
page 548, Robert Shackford died on June 30, 1987
page 550, Robert Shaw, was born on October 6, 1918 and died on May 22, 1987
page 555, William Simmons was born in April 1921
page 556, Frank Sistrunk was KIA in AD-4L 123967; his rank was Lt.
page 557, Albert Slack did in fact die in Lufkin, Texas
oage 557, Dixie Sloan died January 30, 1999 in Xenia, Ohio
page 560, Cornelius Smith died on December 4, 1997
page 560, Daniel Smith received a Letter of Commentdation while serving with VP-31 in 1942. For his service with VF-20
     he receeived a NC, SS, 4 DFCs, 2 AMs, and a LM.
page 561, Jack Smith died on January 24, 1990
page 563, Kenneth G Smith died on October 20, 1947
page 564, Nicholas Smith died on December 20, 1997. He had 746.5 h flying time by the end of May 1944; he flew
     BuNo 58605 on July 25, 1944; 58396 on Aug 31; and 70342 on Oct 17 & 24 (thanks to Carlo Marlow)
page 565, Robert Eugene Smith
page 568, Kenneth Carl Sparks was born on July 12, 1920
page 572, Carlton Starkes died on March 17, 1978
page 574, Ev Stewart received a (British) DFC
page 575, Charlie Stimpson earned a DFC and 2 AMs at Guadalcanal, and a NC, 2 DFCs and an AM on the *Hornet*.
page 576, Robert Stone was born on October 16, 1921 and died on August 24, 1994
page 579, Johnnie Strange died on June 4, 1977
page 579, Frederick Streig died August 31, 1995 Livermore, California, tuberculosis
page 585, Stan Synar died on April 30, 1998 in Tulsa, Oklahoma
page 585, Gilbert Talbot died on April 21, 1965
page 587, Ralph Taylor died on September 18, 1997 Las Vegas, Nevada, heart attack
page 596, Philip Tovrea died January 18, 1981; he was the brother-in-law of Butch O'Hare
page 598, Myron Truax died on November 23, 1984
page 599, Grant Marion Turley was born on June 18, 1922, in Arizona
page 600, Charles Turner died on June 3, 1959
page 600, Edward Turner died on February 21, 1998 in Augusta, Georgia
page 601, William Turner died on October 12, 1966
page 603, Witold Urbanowicz died August 17, 1996 Manhattan, New York
page 606, George Vanden Heuval died on February 15, 1996, in London, England
page 607, Robert Vaught died on June 19, 1978

page 609, Arnold Vinson was born August 12, 1918; his hometown was Monticello, Mississippi

page 610, Hal Vita died on April 14, 1998 in Solano Beach, California of cancer

page 614, Lance Wade received a 2nd Bar to the DFC for service with 145 Sqn.

page 615, John Wainwright was born on January 26, 1924; his hometown was Marshall, Texas; he received a (British) DFC

page 616, Walter Walker was born in Brooklyn, New York, and did in fact die in Cooperstown

page 617, Ken Walsh died July 30, 1998 Santa Ana, California, heart attack

page 620, Jack Warren was born on December 12, 1917, in California

page 622, Sidney Weatherford was killed in F-84D 48-769A

page 625, George Welch was killed in F-100A 52-5764

page 627, Arthur Wenige was KIFA on February 4, 1956, 7 m S of Lakeland, Florida

page 628, Warren Wesson was born July 14, 1920, and died November 1, 1988

page 629, Richard West was shot down on Nov 15, 1944, and returned to his unit on Nov 28

page 629, Robert West died on December 4, 1985

page 629, Robert Westbrook was born in San Antonio, Texas and KIA in P-38J-15 44-23394

page 631, William Whalen died on May 15, 1970

page 631, Mel Wheadon died June 26, 1998

page 632, Henry White died on January 10, 1972

page 633, Thomas White's highest rank in military service was Major

page 634, Paul Wilkins died on April 12, 1985

page 635, James Willard Wilkinson was born Nov 9, 1916 in Newark, Ohio

page 636, Felix Williamson received a (British) DFC

page 637, Robert Wilson died on September 23, 1969

page 637, William Wilson was born on September 7, 1918

page 640, John Wirth was killed in FM-2 56792, 4 m W of Alpine, California, hit high-tension wires

page 640, Kenneth Wise was born on November 1, 1921 and died on March 4, 1997, residence: Bradonton, Florida

page 641, Fritz Wolf died on April 24, 1997 in Madison, Wisconsin

page 642, John Wolford was born on October 7, 1919

page 646, Malcolm Wordell died February 26, 1996 San Diego, California, heart attack

page 647, Max Wright was born on October 17, 1921 and died on October 24, 1944, KIFA Nadzab, New Guinea, P-38, while serving in the Student Detachment, 360th Service Group

page 647, Vasseure Howe Wynn died on May 8, 1987

page 650, Henry (Hank) Zary died February 11, 1946 Ste Agathe, Quebec, Canada. He graduated from New York University with a BS degree in Physical Education, in 1940

page 651, Hub Zemke received a (British) DFC

page 652, Charles Zubarik died on September 19, 1979

page 662, the unreleased name is Capt. Robert Gordon Wright, Jr.

January 30, 1999

page 123, Oscar Bailey died on July 18, 1998 on Marco Island, Florida

page 144, Carl Bickel died November 7, 1998 in Alhambra, California

page 179, Richard Campbell died December 9, 1998 in Baton Rouge, Louisiana

page 186, William Case (Bill), flew 02537, 17475, 17421, 03820, 17464, 02722, 17504, 02714 respectively for his claims. He had 437.4 h flight time at the end of June 1943

page 244, Glenn Duncan died on February 11, 1998 in Salem, Oregon

page 269, Don Fisher (Mo)

page 296, Cy Gladen died on February 11, 1998

page 304, James Gray died August 28, 1998, in Coronado, California after a long illness

page 348, Robert Lawrence Howard died on September 14, 1979 in Sebastopol, California of pneumonia. He was born in California.

Page 365, Bob Johnson died on December 27, 1998 in Tulsa, Oklahoma

Page 385, Carroll Scott Knott was born on February 16, 1916 in Texas; he died in Delano, California

page 418, Chris Magee (Mad Man) flew 17450 on Dec 23, 1943, and 17879 on Dec 28, 1943. He had 388.0 h flight time at the end of August 1943

page 426, Ken Martin died December 15, 1998 in Kansas City, Kansas

page 468, Paul Mullen flew 17646 on Dec 27, 1943 and 17879 on Jan 4, 1944

page 482, Eugene O'Neill died on August 30, 1998

page 492, Heyward Paxton died on November 16, 1998 in New Smyrna Beach, Florida

page 586, Bill Tanner died on May 11, 1998 in San Antonio, Texas

page 592, Jack Thornell died September 3, 1998 in Green Valley, Arizona

page 619, Jack Warner died on November 7, 1998 in Glacier County, Montana of pneumonia

page 643, John Wong was born ?, and spells his name John P-Y Hwong

page 649, Don Yost died on August 7, 1998 in Winter Park, Florida of respiratory problems.